RAND NATIONAL DEFENSE RESEARCH INSTITUTE

T0195458

# 2015 Department of Defense Health Related Behaviors Survey (HRBS)

Sarah O. Meadows, Charles C. Engel, Rebecca L. Collins, Robin L. Beckman,
Matthew Cefalu, Jennifer Hawes-Dawson, Molly Doyle, Amii M. Kress,
Lisa Sontag-Padilla, Rajeev Ramchand, Kayla M. Williams

Prepared for the Defense Health Agency

For more information on this publication, visit www.rand.org/t/RR1695

Library of Congress Cataloging-in-Publication Data
ISBN: 978-0-8330-9831-3

Published by the RAND Corporation, Santa Monica, Calif.
© Copyright 2018 RAND Corporation
**RAND**® is a registered trademark.

*Cover photo credits from top to bottom:*

*Photo by Cpl. Judith Harter; Photo by Sgt. Connie Jones; U.S. Air Force photo by Airman 1st Class Destinee Sweeney; U.S. Navy photo by Jacob Sippel; U.S. Coast Guard photo by Petty Officer 1st Class Shawn Egger*

*Cover design by Eileen Delson La Russo*

### Support RAND
Make a tax-deductible charitable contribution at
www.rand.org/giving/contribute

www.rand.org

# Preface

The Health Related Behaviors Survey (HRBS) is the U.S. Department of Defense's flagship survey for understanding the health, health-related behaviors, and well-being of service members. Originally implemented to assess substance use (i.e., illicit drugs, alcohol, and tobacco), the survey now includes content areas—such as mental and physical health, sexual behavior, and postdeployment problems—that may affect force readiness or the ability to meet the demands of military life. The HRBS is intended to supplement administrative data already collected by the armed forces.

In 2014, the Defense Health Agency asked the RAND Corporation to review previous iterations of the HRBS, update survey content, administer a revised version of the survey, and analyze data from the resulting 2015 HRBS of active-duty personnel. The 2015 HRBS included U.S. Air Force, Army, Marine Corps, Navy, and Coast Guard personnel, and this report details the survey methodology and results. No expertise in health, health-related behaviors, or health care is required to read this report. However, it may be of most use to individuals who provide direct care related to the health and health-related behaviors of active-duty service members or who are responsible for making related policy decisions. Additional information can be found in a series of online appendixes.

This research was sponsored by the Defense Health Agency and conducted within the Forces and Resources Policy Center of the RAND National Defense Research Institute, a federally funded research and development center sponsored by the Office of the Secretary of Defense, the Joint Staff, the Unified Combatant Commands, the Navy, the Marine Corps, the defense agencies, and the defense Intelligence Community.

For more information on the RAND Forces and Resources Policy Center, see www.rand.org/nsrd/ndri/centers/frp or contact the director (contact information is provided on the web page).

# Contents

# Figures

# Tables

# Summary

The Health Related Behaviors Survey (HRBS) is the U.S. Department of Defense (DoD)'s flagship survey for understanding the health, health-related behaviors, and well-being of service members. The survey includes content areas—such as alcohol, tobacco, and substance use, as well as mental and physical health, sexual behavior, and postdeployment problems—that may affect force readiness or the ability to meet the demands of military life. The Defense Health Agency asked the RAND Corporation to review previous iterations of the HRBS, update survey content, administer a revised version of the survey, and analyze data from the resulting 2015 HRBS of active-duty personnel in the U.S. Air Force, Army, Marine Corps, Navy, and Coast Guard.

Total Force Fitness (TFF) is a useful framework for conceptualizing how data from the HRBS can help DoD create and maintain a ready force. TFF is a holistic approach to well-being that focuses on both mind and body in the following eight domains: psychological, spiritual, social, physical, medical and dental, nutritional, environmental, and behavioral. Factors within each domain contribute to a service member's ability to meet the demands of military life. In other words, these factors set the stage for readiness. And by monitoring aggregate levels of key factors, the armed forces can assess how prepared they are to accomplish their missions.

The 2015 HRBS contains factors in all of the eight TFF domains. We highlight some of the key factors in the list below:

- psychological: depression, anxiety, posttraumatic stress disorder (PTSD), suicide and suicide ideation
- spiritual: complementary and alternative medicine (CAM)[1]
- social: marital status, social support
- physical: physical activity, functional limitations
- medical and dental: chronic conditions, medication use
- nutritional: energy drink use, supplement use
- environmental: deployment experiences
- behavioral: alcohol use, tobacco use, substance use, sexual behavior, sleep.

This report reviews survey methods, sample demographics, key findings, and policy implications. Key health outcomes and health-related behaviors in the report are organized around the following domains: health promotion and disease prevention; substance use; mental

---

[1] Note that many CAM treatments could fall under other domains, such as physical and medical. For example, yoga may be considered physical and acupuncture may be considered medical, but both may also have a spiritual component.

and emotional health; physical health and functional limitations; sexual behavior and health; sexual orientation, transgender identity, and health; and deployment experiences and health.

One key limitation of the 2015 HRBS is the low response rate (discussed later). Future versions of the survey will need to address the possible reasons for this, particularly how the sample is selected and the survey is implemented. Based on our experiences, we offer some recommendations in the final section of this summary.

## Methodology

Starting from the 2011 and 2014 versions of the HRBS, the RAND team revised and edited the survey (e.g., removed some items; improved skip patterns; aligned scales with existing, validated measures used in civilian research; and added items relevant to current and emerging health issues related to readiness) with help from the sponsor, as well as a group of subject-matter experts across DoD and the U.S. Coast Guard. The final survey was approved by RAND's Institutional Review Board (known as the Human Subjects Protection Committee), ICF International's Institutional Review Board,[2] the Office of the Under Secretary of Defense for Personnel and Readiness's Research Regulatory Oversight Office, the Office of the Assistant Secretary of Defense for Health Affairs and the Defense Health Agency's Human Research Protection Office, the Coast Guard's Institutional Review Board, and the DoD Security Office. All survey materials included the survey report control system license number: DD-HA(BE)2189 (expires February 9, 2019).

The sampling frame of the 2015 HRBS included all active component personnel who were not deployed as of August 31, 2015, and not enrolled as cadets in service academies, senior military colleges, and other Reserve Officers' Training Corps programs.[3] Personnel in an active National Guard or reserve program and full-time National Guard members and reservists were classified as members of their reserve-component branch of service and excluded from our population of interest. We used data provided by the Defense Manpower Data Center to construct the sampling frame based on three strata: service branch, pay grade, and gender.

The 2015 HRBS disproportionately sampled from strata. We determined our sample size within each stratum using power calculations based on response rates from the 2011 HRBS. We used a different sampling strategy for the Coast Guard, sampling half of the service members within each stratum defined by pay grade and gender. All stratum-specific sample sizes were capped at 75 percent of the total stratum size. After determining the primary sample strata sizes, we sampled service members within each stratum with equal probability and without replacement.

A total of 1,374,590 service members were in the eligible population, and we invited 201,990 to participate in the survey via letter; we subsequently sent postcard or email reminders. All surveys were completed on the web and were completely anonymous.

Of the service members invited to participate, 23,357 logged into the survey website. Figure S.1 depicts how we got from that number to the final analytic sample of 16,699 surveys. Of the 23,357 individuals who logged in, a little fewer than 2,700 did not proceed through the

---

[2]  ICF International was the subcontractor to RAND and implemented the web-based survey.

[3]  A *deployed* service member is defined as any service member who is called up for overseas contingency operations. Ships at sea would be considered deployed if they are in the area of responsibility of such operations.

**Figure S.1**
**Flowchart for the 2015 HRBS Final Analytic Sample**

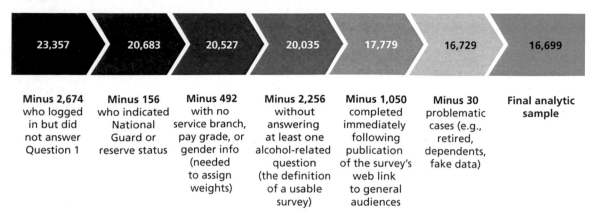

| 23,357 | 20,683 | 20,527 | 20,035 | 17,779 | 16,729 | 16,699 |

| Minus 2,674 who logged in but did not answer Question 1 | Minus 156 who indicated National Guard or reserve status | Minus 492 with no service branch, pay grade, or gender info (needed to assign weights) | Minus 2,256 without answering at least one alcohol-related question (the definition of a usable survey) | Minus 1,050 completed immediately following publication of the survey's web link to general audiences | Minus 30 problematic cases (e.g., retired, dependents, fake data) | Final analytic sample |

RAND *RR1695-S.1*

front material to the first question, and we considered these nonusable surveys. We removed from our sample the 156 respondents who indicated that they were in a reserve or National Guard component and not on active duty. Roughly 500 respondents did not provide enough information to allow a poststratification weight to be computed (e.g., they had missing self-reported data on service branch, pay grade, or gender).[4] We dropped an additional 2,256 surveys that did not meet our criterion for a usable survey (that is, a weight could not be computed or the respondent did not provide at least one response to an alcohol-related item; this is the same definition used in the 2011 HRBS). We also removed 1,050 surveys that were completed immediately following the publication of the survey's web link on af.mil, in the *Air Force Times*, and in *Military Times*, which could have contaminated our stratified random sampling frame.[5] Finally, we removed 30 respondents who said they were currently retired or a dependent or who provided obviously false data (e.g., a pay grade and job title that did not reasonably match).

The overall response rate was 8.6 percent.[6] The response rate was highest among Coast Guard (20.4 percent), followed by Air Force (14.2 percent), Navy (6.7 percent), Marine Corps (6.6 percent), and Army (4.7 percent). Senior officers (O4–O10) had the highest response rate (20.6 percent), and junior enlisted (E1–E4) had the lowest (3.1 percent). The response rate was 7.8 percent for men and 10.2 percent for women.

---

[4]   Poststratification weights were calculated to ensure the correct distribution of service members by service branch, pay grade, and gender. These weights adjust for the sampling design and nonresponse by using the product of the inverse probability of sample response based on a service member's reported service branch, pay grade, and gender (i.e., nonresponse) and the inverse probability of a service member being in a given service branch, pay grade, and gender group (i.e., the design of the survey).

[5]   In particular, we determined that the optimal strategy was to exclude any surveys that were collected between Thursday, January 21 and Tuesday, January 26, 2016, for Air Force personnel and any surveys that were collected between Sunday, January 24 and Tuesday, January 26, 2016, for personnel in all other service branches.

[6]   Response rates were calculated by removing service members whom we were unable to contact by mail or email. Specifically, *noncontacts* were defined as (1) individuals in the sample frame for whom we received a returned postcard or letter and a returned email or (2) individuals in the sample frame who did not have a valid postal address and for whom we received a returned email. The total number of service members who were unable to be contacted was 6,770, or 3.4 percent of the invited sample. The response rate was calculated as the ratio of the number of the final analytic sample (16,699) to the number of contactable service members (195,220).

We tested differences in health outcomes and health-related behaviors by domain across levels of key factors or by subgroups (service branch, pay grade, gender, age group, race/ethnicity, and education level) using a two-stage procedure. First, we used the Rao-Scott chi-square test as an overall test of the relationship between the outcome and the factor. This tests the hypothesis that there is any difference in the outcome across levels of the factor. We used a simple $t$-test to explore statistically significant relationships between the outcome and the factor, adjusting the $p$-values for multiple comparisons using the Tukey-Kramer method, which is designed to account for the multiple testing associated with all possible pairwise comparisons across factor levels. We computed confidence intervals for percentages using the Clopper-Pearson method (exact binomial confidence intervals) and confidence intervals for all other data types using a normal approximation. Only point estimates are presented in this summary; confidence intervals depicting the uncertainty around estimates are presented in the main report.

Only statistically significantly different subgroup differences ($p < 0.05$) are described in the text.

## Sample Demographics

Table S.1 presents the distribution of service branch, pay grade, and gender from the 2015 HRBS weighted respondent sample and from a September 2014 sample of the DoD population of active-duty service members, which can be used as a point of comparison.[7] The first column of data includes the Coast Guard portion of the HRBS sample. Because the 2014 DoD comparison population did not include the Coast Guard, the second column in the table uses only respondents from the four DoD services—the Air Force, Army, Marine Corps, and Navy. Finally, Table S.1 does not include confidence intervals because the respondent sample was weighted to exactly match the sampling frame on service branch, pay grade, and gender.

Based on Table S.1, the largest portion of the weighted respondent sample was in the Army (38.5 percent), and the largest pay grade group was junior enlisted ranks between E1 and E4 (44.5 percent). The overall distribution of respondents by pay grade mirrors the benchmark active-duty population.

Other demographic characteristics (for all five service branches) include the following:

- Among the weighted respondent sample, 84.4 percent were men. More than two-thirds of the sample (70.6 percent) was under age 35.
- Most of the weighted respondent sample was non-Hispanic white (58.4 percent), with Hispanics being the largest minority group (16.4 percent). The remaining sample was 11.5 percent non-Hispanic black, 5.1 percent non-Hispanic Asian, and 8.5 percent other (which included Native Hawaiian, Pacific Islander, and multiracial respondents).
- About one-fifth (20.4 percent) of the weighted respondent sample had a high school diploma, General Educational Development (GED) certification, or less; 48.5 percent had attended some college; and 31.0 percent had at least a bachelor's degree.

---

[7] The 2015 Demographics report was not available at the time of the survey; for the 2014 version of the report, see Office of the Deputy Assistant Secretary of Defense for Military Community and Family Policy, 2014. Note that the Demographics report does not include the Coast Guard in its calculations of active-duty service members (see Chapter 2). The data in that report come from the Defense Manpower Data Center master file, which is the source for the last column in Table S.1 of this report.

**Table S.1**
**Distribution of Service Branch, Pay Grade, and Gender in the 2015 HRBS Weighted Respondent Sample, with 2014 DoD Comparison**

|  | 2015 HRBS Weighted Respondent Sample with Coast Guard (%) | 2015 HRBS Weighted Respondent Sample Without Coast Guard (%) | 2014 DoD Active-Duty Population (%) |
|---|---|---|---|
| **Service branch** |  |  |  |
| Air Force | 22.3 | 23.0 | 23.6 |
| Army | 37.3 | 38.5 | 38.0 |
| Marine Corps | 14.0 | 14.4 | 14.2 |
| Navy | 23.4 | 24.1 | 24.2 |
| Coast Guard | 3.0 | Excluded[a] | NA[b] |
| **Pay grade** |  |  |  |
| E1–E4 | 44.2 | 44.5 | 43.2 |
| E5–E6 | 29.1 | 28.9 | 29.1 |
| E6–E9 | 9.4 | 9.4 | 10.0 |
| W1–W5 | 1.5 | 1.4 | 1.5 |
| O1–O3 | 9.7 | 9.7 | 9.9 |
| O4–O10 | 6.2 | 6.2 | 6.4 |
| **Gender** |  |  |  |
| Men | 84.4 | 84.4 | 84.9 |
| Women | 15.6 | 15.6 | 15.1 |

SOURCE: The information in the first two columns is from the 2015 HRBS; the third column is from Defense Manpower Data Center, 2014.

NOTE: All HRBS data are weighted.

[a] Coast Guard data were not included in this calculation.

[b] NA = not applicable. DoD does not maintain demographic information about the Coast Guard.

- Overall, 57.3 percent of the weighted respondent sample was married; 35.2 percent was single; and 7.5 percent was separated, divorced, or widowed. In addition, 40.5 percent of the weighted respondent sample had at least one dependent under age 18 in the home.
- Among the weighted respondent sample, 59.5 percent reported living off the installation or base, 23.7 percent lived in dorms or barracks on the installation or base, 15.5 percent lived on an installation or base in privatized housing, and 1.3 percent lived in some "other" housing situation (e.g., with parents or in temporary housing).

Although not included in Table S.1, we also examined the pay grade and gender distributions among only the Coast Guard sample. The Coast Guard is evenly split between the E1–E4 and E5–E6 pay grades (34.2 percent in each), with an additional 10.9 percent senior enlisted (E6–E9), 4.2 percent warrant officers (W1–W5), 9.8 percent junior officers (O1–O3), and 6.6 percent mid-grade and senior officers (O4–O10). The gender distribution of the Coast Guard is similar to that of the DoD services: 84.8 percent men and 15.2 percent women.

The following section presents results by key health outcome and health-related behavior domains. Quantitative results generally refer to point estimates from the weighted sample, and confidence intervals are available in the main report. When interpreting comparisons between the U.S. active-duty military and the general U.S. population, it is important to keep in mind the demographic differences (e.g., gender, age) between the two. These, as well as differences in unobservable characteristics (e.g., personality traits), may make direct comparisons difficult to interpret.

## Health Promotion and Disease Prevention

Within this domain, we examined physical activity, weight, routine medical care, CAM, sleep health, supplement use, and texting while driving. Key findings include the following:

- Based on 2015 survey estimates, active-duty service members met or exceeded Healthy People 2020 (HP2020) targets for physical activity.[8] Nevertheless, roughly one in four service members (24.4 percent) reported that they exercise as much as they would like, and work commitments were the most frequently cited reason for lack of exercise (38.8 percent). More than three-fourths of service members (80.5 percent) reported that they play electronic games outside of work or school for less than two hours per day; electronic game play is often a sedentary behavior that is not conducive to physical activity.

- Survey estimates from the 2015 HRBS show that about one-third (32.5 percent) of active-duty service members aged 20 or older were a healthy (normal) weight, which is slightly below the HP2020 target (33.9 percent) and the percentage reporting normal weight in the 2011 HRBS (34.7 percent).[9] In addition, 14.7 percent of service members were obese, which is well within the HP2020 goal of no more than 30.5 percent obese.

- However, when looking at individual weight categories—underweight, normal weight, overweight, and obese—the majority of active-duty service members (65.7 percent) were overweight or obese. It is important to note that body mass index, which was used to categorize individuals as overweight or obese, is an indirect measure of body fat, and muscular service members may have been misclassified into the overweight or obese categories.

- Among active-duty service members, 93.2 percent reported having a routine doctor checkup within the past two years, a practice that may help identify the early onset of chronic disease and ensure appropriate preventive care. DoD regulations require service members to have an annual physical examination.

- Nearly half (47.6 percent) of service members used CAM, such as massage therapy, relaxation techniques, exercise or movement therapy, and creative outlets (e.g., art, music, writing therapy). The best current estimates for the U.S. population suggest that 38 percent of the general population has used CAM (National Center for Complementary and

---

[8]   HP2020 is a set of goals and objectives with ten-year targets designed to guide national health promotion and disease prevention efforts to improve the health of all people in the United States (see U.S. Department of Health and Human Services, 2010a).

[9]   For complete data from the 2011 HRBS, see Barlas et al., 2013.

Integrative Health, 2007), and the 2005 HRBS estimated that 45 percent of active-duty service members used CAM.[10]

- More than half of active-duty service members got less sleep than they need (56.3 percent), and 29.9 percent were moderately or severely bothered by lack of energy due to poor sleep. In addition, 8.6 percent reported using sleep medications every day or almost every day.

- Overall, 32.0 percent of service members reported using at least one dietary supplement daily. Daily supplement use ranged from 5.9 percent for herbal supplements to 16.9 percent for protein powder. Current estimates suggest that just more than half (53 percent) of U.S. adults use at least one dietary supplement (Gahche et al., 2011). Use of joint supplements, including fish oil, increases with age; however, use of protein powder and body building supplements decreases with age.

- Among active-duty service members, 51.0 percent used caffeine-containing energy drinks (CCEDs) in the past month, 16.8 percent used them weekly, and 7.2 percent used them daily. The Centers for Disease Control and Prevention (CDC) found that 45 percent of deployed service members consumed CCEDs daily and 15 percent consumed three or more per day (CDC, 2012).

- Overall, 12.8 percent of service members frequently (6.1 percent) or regularly (6.7 percent) texted or emailed while driving.

## Substance Use

Within this domain, we examined use of alcohol; tobacco; illicit drugs; and prescription drugs, including use as prescribed, misuse (i.e., using a drug without a valid prescription), and overuse (i.e., using more of a drug than prescribed). Key findings include the following:

- According to survey estimates, nearly one in three service members (30.0 percent) were current binge drinkers. In the 2011 HRBS, the rate of binge drinking was 33.1 percent, and according to the 2014 National Survey on Drug Use and Health, the rate among U.S. adults (over age 18) was 24.7 percent (Center for Behavioral Health Statistics and Quality [CBHSQ], 2015b).

- Rates of hazardous drinking, as measured by the Alcohol Use Disorders Identification Test (AUDIT) for Consumption (AUDIT-C), were also high (35.3 percent). The 2008 HRBS, using the AUDIT, found that 33.1 percent of active-duty service members met the criteria for hazardous drinking.[11]

- One in 12 service members (8.2 percent) experienced serious consequences (e.g., "I hit my spouse/significant other after having too much to drink") from drinking in the past year.

- Among active-duty service members, 68.2 percent perceived the military culture as supportive of drinking, and 42.4 percent indicated that their supervisor does not discourage alcohol use. These perceptions were more common among younger and junior enlisted personnel, who were the most likely to binge drink. Service members were as

---

[10]  For complete data from the 2005 HRBS, see Bray, Hourani, Olmstead, et al., 2006.

[11]  For complete data from the 2008 HRBS, see Bray, Pemberton, et al., 2009.

likely to report purchasing alcohol mainly on base as they were to report purchasing it mostly off base.

- According to our survey, 13.9 percent of service members currently smoked and 7.4 percent smoked daily. Nevertheless, cigarette smoking was less common among the military than the general population (where 16.8 percent were current cigarette smokers and 12.9 percent were daily smokers) (CDC, 2015d), and it has decreased among service members by nearly half since 2011.

- Among active-duty service members, 16.9 percent reported past-week exposure to secondhand smoke at work.

- Smokeless tobacco use remains relatively high in the military compared with civilians: Among service members in our survey, 12.7 percent currently used smokeless tobacco, while 3.4 percent of the general U.S. population did in a 2015 study (CBHSQ, 2015b).

- Electronic cigarette (e-cigarette) use is increasing, as 35.7 percent of service members reported ever having tried it (a nearly eight-fold increase since 2011), and 11.1 percent reported being daily e-cigarette smokers (a three-fold increase since 2011). In 2014, 12.6 percent of the general population had ever tried e-cigarettes and 3.7 percent were current users (used some days or every day) (Schoenborn and Gindi, 2015).

- More than three-fourths of service members (80.7 percent) reported buying cigarettes on base. About one-fourth (25.6 percent) felt that tobacco use is strongly discouraged by their supervisor.

- Rates of illicit drug use were substantially lower among service members than among the general U.S. population. For example, current and past-year marijuana users made up 8.5 percent and 13.3 percent, respectively, of U.S. adults in 2014. In the same year, 10.3 percent of U.S. adults were current and 16.6 percent were past-year users of any illicit drug (CBHSQ, 2015b). In 2015, use of any illicit drug in the past year, including marijuana or synthetic cannabis, was reported by 0.7 percent of service members.

- Among service members, 21.0 percent reported use of opioid pain relievers in the past year, more than twice the percentage who used sedatives, stimulants, or anabolic steroids in the same time frame. Opioids were also more likely to be misused (2.4 percent used them without a prescription) and overused (0.7 percent used more than prescribed). However, the percentage of service members currently using opioid pain relievers was 6.2 percent in 2015, compared with 10.4 percent in 2011.

## Mental and Emotional Health

We examined mental health indicators (i.e., probable depression, anxiety, and PTSD); social and emotional factors associated with mental health (i.e., anger and aggression, high impulsivity); unwanted sexual contact and physical abuse history; self-harm, including suicide ideation and suicide attempts; and mental health service utilization and how it is affected by stigma. Key findings include the following:

- Among active-duty service members, 17.9 percent experienced at least one of three mental health problems—probable depression (9.4 percent), probable generalized anxiety disorder (GAD) (14.2 percent), or probable PTSD (8.5 percent)—and 9.7 percent suffered from two or more disorders. Although the prevalence of probable depression in service members was comparable to that in the general population (where it was 6 percent in the past year) (CBHSQ, 2015b), the prevalence of probable GAD and probable PTSD in the past year may be higher than that in the general population (where it was 3 percent and 4 percent, respectively) (Kessler, Berglund, et al., 2005).

- Among active-duty service members, 47.0 percent reported aggressive behavior in the past month, and 8.4 percent reported at least five episodes of such behavior; 12.7 percent met the criteria for high impulsivity.

- Lifetime unwanted sexual contact was reported by 16.9 percent of service members and was reported far more often by women (46.1 percent) than men (11.7 percent). The 2011 HRBS estimated that 14.3 percent of service members reported any history of unwanted sexual contact in their lifetime. The majority of 2015 HRBS respondents (72.2 percent) reported that these events occurred while not on active duty, and 38.2 percent reported an event that occurred on active duty; 10.4 percent reported an unwanted sexual contact event both when on active duty and when not on active duty.

- Lifetime physical abuse was reported by 13.0 percent of service members; this percentage was 17.1 percent in the 2011 HRBS. The data indicate that although relatively few military personnel have experienced physical abuse only while on active duty (23.2 percent), a larger percentage of personnel only experienced physical abuse while not on active duty (79.3 percent). In addition, 2.4 percent reported a physical abuse both when on active duty and when not on active duty.

- Lifetime non-suicidal self-injury was reported by 11.3 percent of service members, and 5.1 percent reported that this behavior occurred since joining the military. These figures are comparable to the 2011 HRBS.

- Almost one-fifth (18.1 percent) of service members reported thinking about trying to kill themselves at some point in their lives (12.3 percent since joining the military and 6.3 percent in the past 12 months), which is well above the roughly 4 percent reported from 2008 to 2014 in the general population (Lipari et al., 2015).

- Overall, 5.1 percent of service members reported that they attempted to kill themselves at some point in their lives (2.6 percent since joining the military and 1.4 percent in the past 12 months). The past-year rate of suicide attempts is three times higher than reported in the 2011 HRBS (0.5 percent) and again higher than observed in the general population, where the rate has been roughly 0.5 percent of adults 18 and older from 2008 to 2014 (Lipari et al., 2015).

- Among active-duty service members, 29.7 percent reported a self-perceived need for mental health services in the past 12 months, while 17.5 percent reported that others perceived that they should seek treatment. Self-assessed need for treatment in the 2011 HRBS was similar at 25.6 percent.

- About one in four service members (26.2 percent) reported using mental health services in the past year. The HRBS percentage of service members reporting that they use mental health services has increased over time (2002: 12.2 percent;[12] 2005: 14.6 percent; 2008: 19.9 percent; 2011: 24.9 percent), possibly in part because of the addition of survey items assessing self-help support group visits (starting in 2005) and visits to some "other source of counseling, therapy or treatment" (2015).

---

[12] For complete data from the 2002 HRBS, see Bray, Hourani, Rae, et al., 2003.

- Service members were more likely to report receiving mental health services from a specialist (e.g., psychiatrist, psychologist, social worker) (18.8 percent) than from a general medical doctor (9.9 percent) or from a civilian clergyperson or military chaplain (8.0 percent).
- The average active-duty service member reported 4.5 mental health visits in the past year. Of these, 0.8 were to a civilian provider (e.g., paid out of pocket, by TRICARE, or by other private insurance), 2.5 were to a military provider, and 1.1 were to a self-help group or other provider.
- Among service members who said they needed care in the past year but did not receive it (36.1 percent), the most frequently endorsed reasons for not receiving mental health treatment were a desire to handle one's own problem (61.5 percent), belief it would harm one's career (34.5 percent), belief that treatment would not help (33.5 percent), fear that the supervisor would have a negative opinion of the service member (31.5 percent), and concerns about confidentiality (30.1 percent).
- Among active-duty service members, regardless of need for or actual receipt of care, 35.0 percent indicated that seeking mental health treatment is damaging to one's military career. Although a downward trend was observed in the early 2000s, since the 2008 HRBS, the decline in perceived stigma has essentially leveled off (2002: 48.1 percent; 2005: 44.1 percent; 2008: 36.1 percent; 2011: 37.7 percent).

## Physical Health and Functional Limitations

We examined chronic conditions, physical symptoms, and health-related functional limitations. Key findings include the following:

- About two in five service members (38.6 percent) reported at least one diagnosed chronic physical health condition in their lifetime, and 6.2 percent reported three or more conditions. The most common provider-diagnosed conditions were high blood pressure (17.7 percent), high cholesterol (13.3 percent), and arthritis (12.3 percent). The prevalence of most chronic conditions (i.e., high blood pressure, high cholesterol, diabetes, arthritis) was lower among active-duty service members than the general U.S. population; however, demographic differences (i.e., distribution of age, gender, employment status) between the military and general population make direct comparisons difficult.
- The percentage of service members taking related medications for their diagnosed condition ranged from 3.9 percent among service members with skin cancer to 38.5 percent among those with physician-diagnosed ulcers.
- Among active-duty service members, 35.7 percent reported that they were bothered a lot by at least one physical symptom (including headaches) in the past 30 days. One in five service members (21.1 percent) had high physical symptom severity (based on a survey of eight common physical symptoms). About one-third of service members reported that a health problem led to at least moderate impairment at work or school (33.0 percent), in their social life (30.0 percent), or in their family life/home responsibilities (30.5 percent).
- Among active-duty service members, 3.0 percent reported missing more than 14 days of service in the past month because of physical or emotional health problems, while 13 percent reported reduced work productivity for more than 14 work days in the past month.

## Sexual Behavior and Health

Within this domain, we examined high-risk sexual behavior in the past year, including sex with more than one partner, sex with a new partner without using a condom, experience of a sexually transmitted infection (STI), inconsistent use of birth control during most-recent vaginal sex, and unintended pregnancy. Key findings include the following:

- Among active-duty service members, 19.4 percent reported more than one sexual partner in the past year.
- More than one-third (36.7 percent) had sex with a new partner in the past year without using a condom.
- STI was reported by 1.7 percent of service members, compared with 1.4 percent in 2011.
- The HRBS defines *high risk for human immunodeficiency virus (HIV) infection* as having sex with more than one partner in the past year, having a past-year STI other than HIV, or being a man who had sex with one or more men in the past year. In the 2015 HRBS, 20.9 percent of service members were at high risk for HIV infection.
- Overall, 73.5 percent of service members reported having been tested for HIV in the past year. Among service members at high risk for HIV infection, 79.4 percent were tested in the past year.
- Multiplying the 20.6 percent of untested high-risk individuals by the 20.9 percent of personnel at high risk for HIV infection means that 4.3 percent of service members overall were both at high risk for HIV infection and untested in the past year.
- Across all services, 22.2 percent of personnel used a condom the most-recent time they had vaginal sex. This percentage was significantly higher among unmarried and noncohabitating service members (34.8 percent) than among married or cohabiting service members (14.2 percent).
- Among service members not already expecting a child or trying to conceive, 19.4 percent did not use birth control the most-recent time they had vaginal sex in the past year. Significant differences were found by marital status: Among unmarried (including noncohabiting) service members, this percentage was 12.2 percent; among married and cohabiting service members, it was 24.0 percent.
- Unintended pregnancy was experienced or caused by 2.4 percent of military personnel. The percentage of unintended pregnancies reported by military women is about the same as that for women of reproductive age in the general population—4.8 percent for military women compared with 4.5 percent for civilian women (Finer and Zolna, 2016).
- Two short-acting methods of contraception—birth control pills and condoms—were by far the most commonly used methods.

## Sexual Orientation, Transgender Identity, and Health

The 2015 HRBS provides the first direct estimate of the percentage of service personnel who identify as lesbian, gay, bisexual, or transgender (LGBT), as well as of their health-related behavior and status. Key findings include the following:

- Based on the 2015 HRBS, LGBT personnel made up 6.1 percent of service members. In the U.S. general population in 2011, the percentage of LGBT adults was 3.4 (Gates and Newport, 2012). This is the most-recent estimate available.[13]
- In the 2015 HRBS, lesbian, gay, or bisexual (LGB) personnel (excluding transgender) constituted 5.8 percent of service members. With respect to LGB sexual identity, a recent national study of high school students in grades 9 through 12 found that 2.0 percent identified as gay or lesbian, 6.0 percent identified as bisexual, and 3.2 percent were not sure of their sexual identity (Kann et al., 2016). These estimates are somewhat higher than the estimates for adults reported by Ward and colleagues (2014) using the National Health Interview Survey, who found that 1.6 percent of adults between ages 18 and 64 identified as gay or lesbian, 0.7 percent identified as bisexual, and 1.1 percent identified as "something else," stated "I don't know the answer," or refused to provide an answer. Given the age profile of the HRBS sample (and the military in general), it is not surprising that our estimates of sexual identity fall somewhere between these two reports but align more closely with the younger population. Key 2015 HRBS findings related to sexual orientation and transgender identity include the following:
  - Sexual attraction: 2.2 percent of men and 7.6 percent of women reported themselves as mostly or only attracted to members of the same sex.
  - Sexual activity: 3.3 percent of men and 9.4 percent of women had had sex with one or more members of the same sex in the past 12 months.
  - Sexual identity: 5.8 percent of active-duty service members identified as LGB (with 0.3 percent not responding to the sexual identity question). If all nonresponders identified as LGB, the LGB percentage would be 6.0 percent.
  - Transgender identity: 0.6 percent of service members described themselves as transgender. This is the same as the percentage of U.S. adults who describe themselves in this manner (Flores et al., 2016). Less than 1 percent of respondents (0.4 percent) declined to answer the transgender question. If all nonresponders were in fact transgender, the overall transgender percentage would be 1.1 percent.
- More women (16.6 percent) identified as LGBT than men (4.2 percent).
- Among the service branches, the Navy had the largest percentage of self-identified LGBT service members at 9.1 percent. LGBT identity was highest among junior enlisted and younger (below age 35) service members.
- LGBT personnel received routine medical care in percentages similar to non-LGBT personnel, with 81.7 percent reporting a routine checkup in the past 12 months.
- LGBT personnel were less likely to be overweight than other service personnel.

---

[13] As this report was in the final stages of production, findings from the 2016 Workplace and Gender Relations Survey of Active Duty Members were released, indicating that 12 percent of female service members and 3 percent of male service members identify as LGBT (Davis et al., 2017).

- LGBT personnel were more likely than non-LGBT personnel to have engaged in some risk behaviors, including the following:
  - binge drinking: 37.6 percent of LGBT personnel compared with 29.3 percent of non-LGBT personnel
  - current cigarette smoking: 24.8 percent of LGBT personnel compared with 16.0 percent of non-LGBT personnel
  - unprotected sex with a new partner: 42.4 percent of LGBT personnel compared with 35.6 percent of non-LGBT personnel
  - more than one sexual partner in the past year: 40.2 percent of LGBT personnel compared with 17.7 percent of non-LGBT personnel
  - STI in the past year: 7.4 percent of LGBT personnel compared with 1.4 percent of non-LGBT personnel
  - no birth control during the most-recent vaginal sex: 31.5 percent of LGBT personnel compared with 21.6 percent of non-LGBT personnel.
- LGBT personnel were more likely to report experiencing mental health issues or a history of abuse, including the following:
  - moderate depression: 13.2 percent of LGBT personnel compared with 8.5 percent of non-LGBT personnel
  - severe depression: 13.7 percent of LGBT personnel compared with 8.8 percent of non-LGBT personnel
  - lifetime history of self-injury: 26.5 percent of LGBT personnel compared with 10.3 percent of non-LGBT personnel
  - lifetime suicide ideation: 32.7 percent of LGBT personnel compared with 17.1 percent of non-LGBT personnel
  - lifetime suicide attempt: 13.0 percent of LGBT personnel compared with 4.6 percent of non-LGBT personnel
  - suicide attempt in the past 12 months: 4.8 percent of LGBT personnel compared with 1.2 percent of non-LGBT personnel
  - lifetime history of unwanted sexual contact: 39.9 percent of LGBT personnel compared with 15.4 percent of non-LGBT personnel
  - ever physically abused: 21.4 percent of LGBT personnel compared with 12.4 percent of non-LGBT personnel.

## Deployment Experiences and Health

Within this domain, we examined deployment frequency and duration, combat exposure, deployment-related injuries or traumatic brain injuries (TBIs), deployment-related substance use, and deployment-related mental and physical health. Key findings include the following:

- Among active-duty service members, 61.3 percent reported at least one deployment since joining the military. Among those who deployed,
  - Four-fifths (80.9 percent) had experienced at least one combat deployment, and 60.1 percent had spent more than 12 months deployed in their military career.
  - More than one-third (38.4 percent) reported deployment starting in the past three years, and 64.3 percent of those deployments were to combat zones.

- Among service members reporting at least one previous deployment, 64.9 percent reported exposure to at least one combat-related event, and 45.8 percent reported at least five such exposures. The most commonly reported lifetime combat exposures included taking fire from small arms, artillery, rockets, or mortars (49.8 percent); being sent outside the wire on patrols (42.1 percent); seeing dead bodies or remains (38.6 percent); firing on the enemy (35.7 percent); and suffering unit casualties (35.6 percent).
- Of those reporting at least one previous deployment, 27.7 percent suffered a combat injury, 11.9 percent screened positive for deployment-related mild TBI (mTBI), and 8.6 percent reported postconcussive symptoms that could be related to a deployment-related injury, a concussion, or a head injury.
- Two-thirds of service members who had ever deployed (67.6 percent) reported some substance use during their most-recent deployment, and use of alcohol (36.2 percent), cigarettes (28.0 percent), cigars (23.3 percent), smokeless tobacco (18.9 percent), and prescription drugs (18.9 percent) were far more common than marijuana (0.1 percent) or opiates (0.1 percent).
- Among service members who were recently deployed (that is, deployed in the past three years), those with high levels of combat exposure were more likely than those with low to moderate exposure to report the following:
  - deployed use of smokeless tobacco (22.4 percent compared with 16.9 percent) and cigars (28.1 percent compared with 19.5 percent)
  - use of prescription drugs in the past year (36.2 percent compared with 23.7 percent)—specifically, stimulants (4.4 percent compared with 2.0 percent), sedatives (16.4 percent compared with 7.3 percent), pain relievers (25.8 percent compared with 17.1 percent), and antidepressants (14.0 percent compared with 4.9 percent)
  - alcohol use (48.6 percent compared with 28.9 percent) during their most-recent deployment
  - current binge drinking (34.6 percent compared with 28.2 percent).
- Among service members deployed in the past three years, those with deployment-related probable mTBI (compared with those with no TBI) were
  - more likely to report using cigarettes (34.4 percent compared with 26.8 percent) and smokeless tobacco (26.8 percent compared with 18.2 percent) during their most-recent deployment
  - less likely to report using alcohol (29.2 percent compared with 41.6 percent) during their most-recent deployment
  - more likely to have used prescription medication during their most-recent deployment (32.1 percent compared with 17.6 percent) and more likely to report current use of prescription sedatives (23.9 percent compared with 9.5 percent), pain relievers (32.3 percent compared with 19.2 percent), and antidepressants (18.4 percent compared with 7.5 percent).
- Among active-duty service members deployed in the past three years, 10.4 percent met the criteria for probable depression, 15.0 percent met the criteria for probable GAD, and 9.9 percent met the criteria for probable PTSD. Half of those deploying in the past three years (50.6 percent) reported aggressive behavior in the past month, and 8.4 percent reported such behavior at least five times in the past month. In addition, 12.2 percent met the criteria for high impulsivity.

- Among active-duty service members deployed in the past three years, those with high exposure to combat were more likely than those with low or moderate exposure to report probable GAD (18.8 percent compared with 12.3 percent) and probable PTSD (12.8 percent compared with 7.9 percent). In addition,
  - Recently deployed service members with probable mTBI were nearly three times more likely to screen positive for probable depression (24.5 percent) than those without TBI (8.8 percent). Similarly, those with probable mTBI were about three times more likely than those without TBI to screen positive for probable GAD (35.3 percent compared with 12.6 percent) and probable PTSD (29.5 percent compared with 7.6 percent).
  - Recently deployed service members with probable mTBI were also more likely than those deploying but without TBI to report displaying any angry behavior in the past month (71.7 percent compared with 48.2 percent) or doing so at least five times in the past month (20.1 percent compared with 7.1 percent).
- Among those deployed in the past three years, 11.7 percent reported lifetime non-suicidal self-injury.
- With respect to suicide:
  - Among those deployed in the past three years, 17.7 percent reported lifetime suicide ideation, including 5.7 percent reporting having such thoughts in the past 12 months, 12.0 percent since joining the military, and 5.0 percent during a deployment.
  - Just under 5 percent (4.6 percent) of those deploying in the past three years reported a lifetime suicide attempt, with 1.3 percent reporting an attempt in the past 12 months, 2.4 percent reporting an attempt since joining the military, 2.6 percent reporting an attempt before joining the military, and 0.6 percent reporting an attempt during a deployment.
  - Among recently deployed members, those with high exposure to combat were more likely than those with low or moderate exposure to report suicide ideation since joining the military (15.7 percent compared with 9.8 percent) and during a deployment (6.8 percent compared with 3.7 percent).
  - Suicidal thoughts at any time in the past 12 months, since joining the military, or during a deployment were reported more than twice as often among those with probable mTBI (11.6 percent in the past 12 months, 24.8 percent since joining the military, and 10.6 percent during a deployment) than among those with no TBI (4.9 percent in the past 12 months, 10.5 percent since joining the military, and 4.3 percent during a deployment).
- Among those deployed in the past three years, 22.8 percent had a high somatic symptom score, and 37.8 percent reported chronic symptoms. In addition,
  - Among recently deploying members, those with high levels of combat exposure were more likely than those with lower levels of combat exposure to have a high somatic symptom score (28.6 percent compared with 18.8 percent) and chronic symptoms (47 percent compared with 32 percent).
  - Among recently deployed service members, those with probable mTBI were more likely than those without TBI to have a high somatic symptom score (47.3 percent compared with 19.6 percent) and to report chronic symptoms (62.2 percent compared with 35.0 percent).

## Key Subgroup Differences

We tested differences in each outcome by such characteristics as service branch, pay grade, gender, age group, race/ethnicity, and education level. Below, we highlight key findings by subgroup.

### Service Branch

Differences across the services are likely tied to the very different demographics of service members in the Air Force, Army, Marine Corps, Navy, and Coast Guard. Differences are also likely tied to the types of duties and missions conducted within each branch. With this in mind, we note the following findings:

- The Army, at 29.8 percent, had the highest percentage of service members with at least 300 minutes of moderate physical activity per week (an HP2020 benchmark), while the Air Force had the lowest, at 20.0 percent.
- Both the Air Force (35.3 percent) and the Marine Corps (37.8 percent) exceeded the HP2020 target for healthy weight. The prevalence of obesity ranged from 6.4 percent in the Marine Corps to 18.0 percent in the Army.
- Service members in the Army (59.4 percent), Marine Corps (56.9 percent), and Navy (57.5 percent) were most likely to report receiving less sleep than what they need to feel refreshed and perform well. Respondents in the Army (33.2 percent), Marine Corps (32.8 percent), and Navy (32.8 percent) were also most likely to report a lack of energy due to poor sleep.
- Daily body-building supplement use ranged from 7.6 percent in the Coast Guard to 17.7 percent in the Marine Corps.
- Daily CCED consumption ranged from 3.9 percent in the Coast Guard to 11.8 percent in the Marine Corps.
- Binge, heavy, and hazardous drinking varied substantially by service. These rates were lowest in the Air Force and highest in the Marine Corps, where nearly half of Marines engaged in hazardous drinking.
- Marines were also most likely to perceive military culture as supportive of drinking and least likely to report that their supervisor strongly discourages alcohol use.
- All forms of tobacco use (cigarettes, cigars, smokeless, and e-cigarettes) were more common in the Marine Corps.
- The Army had the highest levels of prescription sedative, pain reliever, and antidepressant use, while the Coast Guard had the lowest. Prescription drug misuse was also highest in the Army and lowest in the Coast Guard.
- The Army and Marine Corps had the highest levels of probable depression, GAD, and PTSD.
- Prevalence of lifetime non-suicidal self-injury and lifetime suicide attempts was higher in the Army, Marine Corps, and Navy than in the Air Force or Coast Guard.
- Army respondents (32.1 percent) had the highest use of mental health services, while Coast Guard respondents (17.5 percent) had the lowest.
- Prevalence of at least one diagnosed chronic health condition (e.g., high blood pressure, diabetes, asthma) ranged from 31.6 percent in the Air Force to 46.0 percent in the Army.

- The prevalence of physical symptoms in the past 30 days was highest in the Army (42.5 percent) and Marine Corps (40.4 percent) and lowest in the Coast Guard (24.3 percent). The Army (25.6 percent) and Marine Corps (25.8 percent) had the highest prevalence of high physical symptom severity on a somatic symptom scale.
- The Marine Corps, followed by the Navy, had the highest percentage of members who were at high risk for HIV infection, who reported multiple sex partners in the past year, and who reported causing or experiencing an unintended pregnancy. The Marine Corps, Army, and Navy also had higher percentages than the Air Force and Coast Guard of members reporting sex with a new partner in the past year without using a condom.

**Pay Grade**

Many of the differences that we observed by pay grade stem from inherent differences in the military experiences, both positive and negative, that senior staff have had compared with their junior colleagues. Differences by pay grade are also likely highly correlated with differences across age and education level. Noteworthy differences we found include the following:

- Relative to officers, enlisted service members were more likely to report having less than four hours of sleep during the work week, more likely to report being moderately or severely bothered by lack of energy due to poor sleep, and less likely to report being satisfied with their sleep.
- The percentage of respondents reporting receiving routine medical care in the past two years was lowest among junior enlisted (92.6 percent) and highest among mid-grade and senior officers (95.9 percent).
- Junior and mid-level enlisted members (E1–E6) tended to be more problematic drinkers than others. Junior enlisted service members (E1–E4) were also most likely to experience serious drinking consequences and productivity loss and to see military culture as supportive of drinking. Nevertheless, the group with the highest percentage of hazardous, possibly disordered, drinkers was junior officers (O1–O3 officers; 39.2 percent), which also had the second-highest percentage of binge drinkers.
- One-fifth of junior enlisted service members currently used e-cigarettes, compared with 10.8 percent of mid-level enlisted personnel (E5–E6), 6.1 percent of senior enlisted personnel, 3.4 percent of warrant officers (W1–W5), 2.2 percent of junior officers, and 0.9 percent of mid-grade or senior officers (O4–O10).
- Senior enlisted and warrant officers were more likely to use prescription sedatives, pain relievers, and antidepressants than others. Senior enlisted personnel were also most likely to misuse prescription drugs.
- Officers reported lower levels of probable depression, GAD, and PTSD than their enlisted and warrant officer peers. Lifetime and past-12-month suicide ideation were lower among mid-grade and senior officers relative to all other pay grades.
- Significantly more warrant and junior officers than senior non-commissioned officers (E7–E9) and senior officers endorsed the belief that seeking mental health treatment would damage their military career.
- Enlisted service members were more likely to report being bothered "a lot" by at least one physical symptom, with 50.8 percent of senior non-commissioned officers doing so.
- Junior enlisted service members were at higher risk than other members in nearly every sexual health category.

**Gender**

Data collection for the 2015 HRBS coincided with Secretary of Defense Ashton Carter's December 2015 announcement that, as of 2016, all combat jobs would be open to women, essentially ending all gender segregation in the military. Although it is not clear whether this policy change will eliminate gender differences across health and well-being outcomes, it may reduce disparities in exposure (e.g., combat-related trauma). Nonetheless, we did observe some differences across gender in our survey data. It will be important to track these trends going forward as women have the opportunity to expand their roles in the military. We note the following findings:

- Men were more likely than women to report playing electronic games outside of work or school (e.g., iPads, laptops, handheld games) for at least two hours daily.
- Women (64.2 percent) were more likely than men (44.5 percent) to report CAM use.
- Men were more likely to report using supplements for joint health (11.2 percent compared with 9.0 percent for women), fish oil (15.9 percent compared with 13.9 percent), protein powder (17.9 percent compared with 11.2 percent), and supplements for body building (13.0 percent compared with 5.4 percent). Men were less likely to report using herbal supplements (5.5 percent compared with 8.2 percent for women) and weight-loss supplements (6.3 percent compared with 8.6 percent). Women were more likely to report never using CCEDs (66.4 percent compared with 45.8 percent for men).
- Men were more likely than women to report binge (31.2 percent compared with 23.0 percent), heavy (6.1 percent compared with 1.3 percent), and hazardous (36.0 percent compared with 31.3 percent) drinking.
- Women were more likely than men to report using prescription sedatives (16.8 percent compared with 9.7 percent), pain relievers (27.4 percent compared with 19.8 percent), and antidepressants (15.5 percent compared with 7.6 percent).
- Women reported higher levels than men of lifetime unwanted sexual contact (46.1 percent compared with 11.7 percent) and lifetime physical abuse (18.9 percent compared with 11.9 percent).
- Women were more likely than men to report being bothered a lot by headaches (19.1 percent compared with 10.5 percent); feeling tired or having low energy (31.7 percent compared with 21.7 percent); and experiencing at least one physical symptom (including headaches) (41.4 percent compared with 34.7 percent).

**Age Group**

Observed differences across age groups stem at least in part from cumulative exposure. Some differences across age groups are also due to younger individuals, whether in the military or not, engaging in riskier behaviors. Differences we found by age group among military members include the following:

- Relative to those 45 or older, service members aged 17–24 were more likely to
  - use CCEDs weekly (21.5 percent compared with 4.8 percent) or daily (7.8 percent compared with 3.4 percent)
  - text while driving (8.2 percent compared with 2.6 percent)
  - be binge, heavy, and hazardous drinkers (37.3 percent, 9.5 percent, and 42.5 percent, respectively, compared with 14.8 percent, 2.1 percent, and 22.0 percent).

Service members aged 17–24 were also more likely to see military culture as supportive of drinking and less likely to see their supervisor as strongly discouraging drinking.

- Service members aged 17–24 were more likely to meet the threshold for high impulsivity (22.0 percent compared with 10.9 percent for those aged 25–34, 6.6 percent for those aged 35–44, and 6.9 percent for those 45 or older).
- Past-year suicide ideation was higher among those aged 17–24 relative to those 35 or older. Lifetime suicide attempts were also higher among younger service members. Younger service members were less likely to receive mental health care than their older peers.
- The prevalence of any medical diagnosis for a chronic condition was 18.5 percent among service members aged 17–24 but 75.2 percent among those 45 or older.
- Younger age was also consistently related to higher rates of sexual risk behaviors and negative outcomes, with the exception of use of condoms and other contraceptives during the most-recent vaginal sex in the past year; younger service members reported higher rates than older members on those measures.

### Race/Ethnicity

Although it is not clear whether one should expect significant differences in health and health-related behaviors across racial or ethnic groups in the armed forces, such differences do exist in the civilian population. Where differences do exist, DoD can leverage this information to improve readiness among specific racial or ethnic groups and target intervention and policy to reduce such disparities. Noteworthy differences we found by race/ethnicity include the following:

- Non-Hispanic whites were more likely to be hazardous or disordered drinkers (40.6 percent compared with 19.5 percent among non-Hispanic Asian and 18.8 percent among non-Hispanic black service members).
- Non-Hispanic blacks were least likely to smoke cigarettes.
- Non-Hispanic blacks and service members of the "other" race/ethnicity group (which includes Native Hawaiian and Pacific Islander, as well as multi-racial) had higher levels of probable PTSD.
- Non-Hispanic whites and those in the "other" race/ethnicity category had higher lifetime suicide ideation rates than non-Hispanic blacks and Hispanics.
- Non-Hispanic blacks were least likely to report that seeking mental health treatment would damage their military career, while non-Hispanic whites and those of other races/ethnicities were most likely to endorse this belief.
- Hispanics were most likely to report having more than one sex partner and having sex with a new partner without a condom; this group also had the largest percentage at high risk for HIV infection. Sex without contraception was less common among non-Hispanic whites and all other races/ethnicities than among non-Hispanic Asian service members.

### Education Level

Differences across education level largely correlate with differences observed by pay grade, as officers tend to be more highly educated than their enlisted peers. Noteworthy differences by education level include the following:

- Self-reported CAM use increased with education level, ranging from 38.4 percent among service members with no more than a high school education to 53.8 percent among those with a college degree.
- Binge and heavy drinking were more common among those with no more than a high school diploma (38.1 percent and 9.9 percent, respectively) than among those with at least some college (28.9 percent and 5.2 percent, respectively) or at least a bachelor's degree (26.2 percent and 2.6 percent, respectively). Productivity loss due to drinking and serious consequences from drinking were more frequently reported by those with no more than a high school diploma (8.4 percent and 12.9 percent, respectively) than by those with a college degree (4.8 percent and 5.7 percent, respectively). Less-educated respondents were also more likely to report more use of tobacco in all forms studied.
- College-degree holders were the least likely to have probable depression, GAD, or PTSD.
- Less-educated members were more likely than their more-educated peers to have had multiple sex partners, had sex with a new partner without a condom, been at high risk for HIV infection, or had or caused an unintended pregnancy.

## Limitations

Our findings are subject to many limitations common to survey research. First, response rates were lower in 2015 than in prior HRBSs and many other recent military surveys. Potential reasons for the low response rate in the 2015 HRBS include survey fatigue (the 2014 HRBS was still in the field well into 2015), survey length (the survey took roughly 45 minutes to complete), survey content (i.e., sensitive behaviors), and information technology issues (e.g., most calls to the help desk were about problems accessing the survey website). Low response rates do not *automatically* mean that the results are biased (Groves, 2006), but they do increase the likelihood that service members who did not respond were in some way qualitatively different from those who did respond. However, we have no way to assess how the bias might have affected the results. On the one hand, one could hypothesize that service members with the worst health or the most health problems did not participate when asked. If so, the results may overestimate the health of the force. On the other hand, if some service members were unhappy about the way DoD and the Coast Guard handled some specific aspect of health or health care (e.g., quality of mental health treatment) and wanted a mechanism to provide feedback, the results could possibly underestimate the health of the force. Low response rates also imply higher variances around point estimates; however, this added variance is captured in wider confidence intervals.

Second, because we made edits to prior HRBS content, largely to shorten the survey, responses may not be strictly comparable to those of prior versions. This is not true of every survey item, as many are directly comparable to prior surveys (e.g., tobacco and alcohol use, self-harm and suicide, mental health service utilization, stigma).

Third, comparison to civilian populations may also be problematic because, in addition to demographic characteristics (e.g., gender, age, race/ethnicity, education level) for which we might control in statistical analysis, there may be other, unknown differences between civilian and military populations that may influence outcomes for health, health-related behavior, and well-being.

Fourth, as with any self-reported survey, responses may reflect social desirability. That is, respondents may feel pressure to answer survey questions that make them appear healthier or confirm that they conform to social norms. This could be especially problematic in a survey like the HRBS, which asks about many sensitive behaviors.

## Policy Implications and Recommendations

We offer two sets of policy implications. The first addresses ways in which DoD and the Coast Guard can improve the readiness, health, and well-being of the force. The second offers suggestions for future iterations of the HRBS.

### Force Readiness, Health, and Well-Being

At the time this report was written, DoD had already experienced downsizing (since roughly 2012), and it was expected to face more cuts in manpower and other resources. Thus, it is more important than ever to understand how to strategically maximize force health and readiness. The results from the 2015 HRBS can help identify areas and subgroups where readiness may be at risk now or in the future. Therefore, we offer several observations to help DoD and the Coast Guard identify immediate and future threats to the readiness, health, and well-being of the force, and we outline relevant policy implications derived from those observations. We discuss these threats in order of magnitude, as determined by the research team.

**Although DoD and the Coast Guard are doing well in several areas, a few health outcomes and health-related behaviors warrant immediate policy attention given their clinical importance**. These outcomes and behaviors include the following:

- *Binge and hazardous drinking*: Roughly one-third of service personnel met criteria indicative of hazardous drinking and possible alcohol use disorder. Nearly one-third of service members reported binge drinking in the past month. Problematic drinking could be addressed by shifting the culture and climate surrounding alcohol use (e.g., communicating disapproval of heavy drinking and changing on-base alcohol prices and sales policies).
- *Smoking and e-cigarette use*: Cigarette smoking is a major health hazard. The health consequences of e-cigarette use are not yet established, but the dramatic increase in e-cigarette use, especially among younger service members, is worth attention now and continued tracking in the future.
- *Overweight or obesity*: The large percentage of the population that continues to meet the criteria for being overweight or obese is cause for concern. Overweight or obese personnel reduce overall force fitness and readiness and pose policy issues for military recruitment, retention, and the standards used to qualify or disqualify individuals from service. In addition to directly affecting readiness, overweight or obese status is associated with morbidities (i.e., diabetes, asthma, hypertension, joint pain) that adversely affect readiness and health care utilization and costs. If the large percentage of overweight service members is indeed correlated with physical fitness (i.e., body mass index may be higher among those with more muscle mass), then this may be less of a concern. Unfortunately, the 2015 HRBS data do not allow us to determine if this is the case.
- *Inconsistent use of contraception*: Inconsistent use of contraception increases the risk for unintended pregnancy and presents a possible threat to readiness (because pregnan-

cies reduce personnel availability). Continued monitoring of use, as well as efforts to increase use of long-acting methods of contraception (e.g., oral contraceptives, intrauterine devices), are warranted.

- *High risk for HIV infection*: High risk for HIV infection was defined as having sex with more than one partner in the past year, having a past-year STI other than HIV, or being a man who had sex with one or more men in the past year. Current attention should focus on unmarried (noncohabiting) service members, of whom more than 40 percent were in the high-risk category. Revisions to policy could mandate increased HIV testing frequency for all those at high risk for HIV infection and could implement interventions to increase use of condoms with new partners. High-risk behaviors should also be monitored into the future.
- *Sleep*: More than half of service members reported getting less sleep than they need, and one-third were bothered by lack of energy due to poor sleep. Insufficient sleep is associated with adverse health outcomes and has the potential to impair military readiness.
- *Energy drinks*: More than half of service members reported using energy drinks in the past month. CCEDs are associated with emergency room visits and other adverse health-related behaviors.
- *High absenteeism and presenteeism due to health conditions*: *Absenteeism* refers to lost work days because of a health condition, and *presenteeism* refers to days present on duty but the usual level of performance is compromised because of a health condition. Overall, 13 percent of service members reported reduced productivity because of health conditions for at least two weeks in the past month. This has significant implications for productivity and suggests that there is a need to address this issue immediately through policy or programs that target the underlying health conditions (e.g., chronic disease, physical symptoms, functional impairment) that lead to reduced or limited productivity.

**DoD and the Coast Guard should consider heightened scrutiny and continued monitoring of several health outcomes and health-related behaviors, especially those related to mental health treatment and suicide**. Our findings include the following:

- In the 2015 HRBS, more than one-third of respondents who stated they had a need for mental health counseling reported not receiving counseling from any source. *Efforts should be made to characterize the population reach of existing mental health services and to identify when certain types of individuals (e.g., based on demographic or military factors) are not receiving needed care.* Programs with the greatest reach should be identified, evaluated, and monitored for quality and effectiveness. Existing mechanisms, such as the Periodic Health Assessment, may be one way to identify service members in need of treatment.
- Stigma associated with mental health treatment remains a concern. HRBS indicators suggest that modest decreases in perceived stigma occurred from 2002 to 2008. Since then, however, stigma levels have remained largely unchanged, even as DoD has experienced persistent pressure to better define, operationalize, track, and reduce it. *Efforts are needed to develop, test, and implement consistent, military-relevant surveillance indices of mental health stigma, and research is needed to understand how and why stigma remains a barrier to care for many service members, despite DoD mitigation efforts.*
- Further, the findings presented here suggest that roughly half of mental health services were delivered by nonspecialists. *Efforts should be made to better identify, improve, and*

*evaluate the sources, quality, and outcomes of those nonspecialty mental health services in the military.*

- We also found that a significant minority of service members received mental health care in a civilian setting; *future research should better determine the reasons that service members seek treatment options outside the military health system and the impact of these services on continuity of mental health care.* Insufficient access to high-quality services and lack of continuity of care across the military and civilian systems may pose a real risk to service member well-being and to force health and readiness.

- Findings from the 2015 HRBS indicate that suicide ideation, which may be a marker of distress and mental anguish, is a major concern among service members. *The military is already devoting large amounts of funding to understand suicide in the military, but more information is needed on early precursors to suicide and how different strategies may be needed for different populations, depending on their levels of risk.* Such prevention strategies also need to be evaluated to better understand their effectiveness, accessibility, and acceptability. The military continues to rely heavily on peer models (e.g., gatekeeper trainings) to prevent suicide, in which peers are instructed on how to intervene with service members in crisis. Little is known about whether service members have been witness to or concerned about such situations in the past; whether they have intervened; and if they did intervene, what they did, and if they did not intervene, why not. Understanding these nuances would allow the military to better tailor its prevention efforts and target its resources more effectively and efficiently.

Results from the 2015 HRBS suggest that, based on demographics (e.g., age group), certain groups of service members warrant targeted interventions to prevent multiple negative health outcomes and to improve current health-related behaviors. Cultural tailoring of prevention messages is a recommended public health strategy. For example, messages that resonate with service members who are 20 years old and single may not be as salient with those who are 40 years old and married. Similarly, messages that appeal to the Army or Marine Corps ethos may not work as well in the context of Air Force culture.

It is also worth noting that although targeted interventions may be designed with a specific subgroup of the population in mind, those interventions could benefit all active-duty service members. For example, health disparities between LGBT and non-LGBT service members warrant closer DoD and Coast Guard attention. Although one option is to target the LGBT population with clinical and population efforts, such an approach may stigmatize the target population. Therefore, it may be best to apply these efforts equally across the military, which could lead to broader population benefits. With regard to subgroups that might benefit from targeted interventions, our findings include the following:

- Consistently, the *Army, Navy, and Marine Corps* reported higher levels of mental health problems, suggesting a particular focus on these branches. Service members in the Army and Marine Corps also reported the highest use of CCEDs and the lowest levels of sleep quality. Rates of binge and hazardous drinking were concerning across all service branches, particularly in the Marine Corps. Understanding the reasons for inter-service variation may lead to service-specific programs that more directly address service-specific needs.

- *Women and service members with lower education levels* reported higher levels of mental health problems, including suicide ideation and attempts. Women also reported higher levels of impairment and presenteeism and lower levels of sleep quality. Binge drinking, loss of productivity related to drinking, sexual risk behaviors (e.g., multiple sex partners, sex with a new partner without a condom), and all forms of tobacco use were also greater among less-educated service members. Thus, these are high-risk groups, and efforts may need to be targeted directly to them.

- *Younger service members*, particularly those aged 17–24, were more likely than older service members to use energy drinks regularly and engage in binge, heavy, and hazardous drinking and sexual risk behaviors (except condom use during the most-recent vaginal sex). In addition, a higher percentage of younger service members reported recent suicide ideation than older service members. Furthermore, high impulsivity was also more common among this group than among older service members, which suggests that there is an opportunity for military leaders to target prevention efforts by age group.

- *LGBT service members* reported higher rates of mental health problems (e.g., depression, suicide ideation) and possible precursors to subsequent problems (e.g., history of unwanted sexual contact, history of physical abuse) than their non-LGBT peers. They also reported higher rates of some health-related risk behaviors, including smoking, binge drinking, STI, sex with more than one partner in the past year, and vaginal sex without use of birth control. These differences are not unlike those observed for LGBT people in the civilian population (Institute of Medicine, 2011). These findings suggest that policy and programmatic efforts are needed to target this population and that trends in the health and well-being of this population should continue to be monitored. This will be especially important in the Navy, which has the highest percentage of gay or bisexual men and of LGBT service members overall, and in the Marine Corps, which has the highest percentage of lesbian or bisexual women serving.

Finally, DoD and the Coast Guard should establish population benchmarks of health and health-related behaviors for the military. Some benchmarks currently exist, primarily in the form of requirements to do (or, in some cases, not to do) certain behaviors (e.g., receive an annual health exam, abstain from using illicit drugs). However, in other cases, like overweight and obese status or leader attitudes toward smoking or alcohol use, no clear benchmarks for the military exist. General population benchmarks are available for many health outcomes and health-related behaviors (e.g., HP2020), but it is not clear whether they are truly applicable to the military—a characteristically unique population. Although the ultimate goal for many behaviors may be zero incidence of them, such a goal may not be realistic or attainable, especially in the short term. Thus, it could be very useful for DoD and the Coast Guard to develop population benchmarks designed to move the population averages in the desired direction. Periodic review and updating of these benchmarks would also be needed.

## Future Iterations of the HRBS

In this section, we offer suggestions for future iterations of the HRBS, based on several issues that we encountered during implementation of the survey. To provide some background for these recommendations, we offer a brief description of the environment in which we launched the survey. First, shortly before we sent invitation emails, we were alerted to a change in DoD information technology policy that meant that any hyperlinks included in emails sent from a non-DoD account would be identified as possibly hazardous and thus blocked. Further, some email servers were blocking invitation emails despite our attempts to "whitelist" the email address from which the invitations were sent and use the appropriate email certificates. Second, the 2014 HRBS had left the field only a few months prior to the 2015 survey beginning. The near overlap of the 2014 and 2015 HRBSs increased the survey burden on an already highly surveyed population. Third, while the survey assured anonymity, it asked about very sensitive topics, including some that could result in a service member being dismissed from the military, which likely made some respondents reluctant to answer. Together, these events and conditions set the stage for an implementation of the HRBS that was less than optimal. To improve implementation, we offer the following recommendations.

*Dramatically shorten the survey and focus content.* Originally designed to assess substance use, the HRBS has expanded well beyond that. Some of the data it requests (e.g., on service utilization) can be obtained from existing administrative data sets. By focusing more strictly on content that cannot be obtained elsewhere, the survey could be dramatically shortened. The current length of the survey makes it somewhat inflexible and unable to address new and emerging areas of concern. With the help of an advisory committee, such as the one we used for the 2015 HRBS, survey content could be streamlined. DoD and the Coast Guard could also consider developing official policy about what should, and should not, be included in the survey content.

*Send survey invitations from a .mil account to address information technology issues.* Given our issues with blocked emails and blocked content within emails (e.g., the web link to the survey), future iterations of the HRBS should explore whether it is possible and advisable to send survey invitations from a .mil email address. Although this seems like an easy fix, it could have implications for how respondents view the security of their personal data. If respondents believe that a survey request for highly sensitive information coming from a military email account will lead to loss of anonymity or confidentiality, response rates and quality may deteriorate. A thoughtful analysis of the costs and benefits for using a military email address should be undertaken prior to the next iteration of the HRBS.

*Explore options to contact nonresponders (confidential versus anonymous survey).* Switching from an anonymous survey to a confidential one would allow for targeted nonresponse messages. That is, it would be possible for the survey contractor, but *not* DoD or the Coast Guard, to know who has and has not completed the survey. The 2015 HRBS used up to nine generic email and four postcard reminders. These were often viewed as annoying to participants, especially if they had already completed the survey. Survey-method research has shown that personalized invitations to web-based surveys improve response rates. A confidential survey could also offer DoD and the Coast Guard information on what types of individuals are more or less likely to complete surveys and allow for survey weights to better account for nonresponse among certain subgroups. Future iterations of the HRBS could use both an anonymous and a confidential approach in order to assess which yields the highest response rates and data quality.

*Consider offering incentives.* A final consideration for future HRBSs is to offer an incentive, either as an enticement before completion (e.g., receiving $2 with an invitation to take a survey) or as payment after completion. Assuming any regulatory issues can be addressed, offering incentives for survey completion may improve response rates. Survey-method research clearly shows that incentives improve response rates. Incentives could also be combined with a confidential survey in order to target nonresponders or demographic groups for which response rates are low.

*Investigate the feasibility of a service member panel.* Given the trend of declining response rates to surveys in general, a data collection method different from traditional survey methodology may prove to be useful to DoD and the Coast Guard. One option is a panel, where individuals agree to remain available for interview for a period of time. After that time, the sample is replenished with new members, creating a mix of old and new members. A panel design helps alleviate response burden. Further, the panel would be available for all sorts of real-time data collection, and surveys need not be limited to health and health-related behaviors. However, it is important to note that the sampling design used to create a panel and the actual composition of panel members may limit the usefulness of the panel for addressing some issues. For example, low-base-rate behaviors (e.g., illicit substance use) may be very difficult to accurately assess via a panel without the size of the panel becoming unwieldy. Thus, a service member panel may be an option for some, but not all, of the topics in the HRBS.

## Conclusion

The 2015 HRBS was designed to help DoD and the Coast Guard evaluate the current health and well-being of the force and address possible threats to readiness. This report provides an overview of health outcomes and health-related behaviors across seven domains. Going forward, this survey can be used to supplement data already collected by DoD and the Coast Guard to track key trends, as well as to inform policy initiatives and make programmatic decisions aimed at helping the force meet its mission today and into the future.

# Acknowledgments

The research team would like to thank several individuals who helped make this research possible. At ICF International, we would like to thank Bradford Booth, Patricia Vanderwolf, and Bryan Higgins. At the RAND Corporation, we would like to thank Andrew Morral, Terry Schell, and Terri Tanielian for their role in internal quality assurance, as well as Gina Frost and Donna White for administrative assistance and Cliff Grammich for clarifying the text and improving the readability of the report. Abby Schendt, Steven Davenport, and Etienne Rosas also provided help with formatting and tables. Andrew Morral and COL Paul Bliese (retired) served as reviewers on the final report, and we thank them for their excellent reviews. Their helpful comments and insights made the report stronger.

We also wish to especially thank our Program Officer, Diana Jeffery (Defense Health Agency), and Senior Advisers Donald Shell (Office of the Assistant Secretary of Defense for Health Affairs, Health Services Policy and Oversight) and Mark Mattiko (U.S. Coast Guard) for their assistance throughout every step of the process. Their support was absolutely essential to this effort.

We also thank the service liaison officers who helped us to coordinate with the services: Laura Mitvalsky (Army), LCDR Sam Stephens (Marine Corps), Millie King (Navy), and Lt Col Karen Downes (Air Force).[1] And we acknowledge the very helpful advice and input we received from our U.S. Department of Defense Advisory Committee throughout the course of the project. The committee included LTC Tom Martin (Office of the Under Secretary of Defense for Personnel and Readiness), Nate Galbreath (Sexual Assault Prevention and Response Office), Bill Crowley (Defense Suicide Prevention Office), Cara Krulewitch (Office of the Assistant Secretary of Defense), Commander Jennifer Bodart (Defense Health Agency), Paul Fitzpatrick (Defense Health Agency), Col Tom Moore (Air Force), Lt Col Donna Smith (Air Force), Theresa Jackson Santo (Army), Charles Hoge (Walter Reed National Military Medical Center), CAPT Scott L. Johnston (Navy), Bob MacDonald (Navy), and Patricia Deuster (Uniformed Services University).

And finally, we thank the many service members who took the time to complete the survey.

---

[1] Office affiliations were current as of the writing of this report.

# Abbreviations

| | |
|---|---|
| AUDIT | Alcohol Use Disorders Identification Test |
| AUDIT-C | Alcohol Use Disorders Identification Test for Consumption |
| BMI | body mass index |
| CAM | complementary and alternative medicine |
| CBHSQ | Center for Behavioral Health Statistics and Quality |
| CCED | caffeine-containing energy drink |
| CDC | Centers for Disease Control and Prevention |
| CI | confidence interval |
| CONUS | continental United States |
| DMDC | Defense Manpower Data Center |
| DoD | U.S. Department of Defense |
| DSM | *Diagnostic and Statistical Manual of Mental Disorders* |
| FAQ | frequently asked question |
| GAD | generalized anxiety disorder |
| GAD-7 | Generalized Anxiety Disorder 7-Item Scale |
| HHS | U.S. Department of Health and Human Services |
| HIV | human immunodeficiency virus |
| HP2020 | Healthy People 2020 |
| HRBS | Health Related Behaviors Survey |
| IED | improvised explosive device |
| IUD | intrauterine device |
| LGB | lesbian, gay, or bisexual |
| LGBT | lesbian, gay, bisexual, or transgender |
| MPA | moderate physical activity |
| mTBI | mild traumatic brain injury |
| MTF | military treatment facility |

| | |
|---|---|
| NCO | non-commissioned officer |
| NSDUH | National Survey of Drug Use and Health |
| NSSI | non-suicidal self-injury |
| OCONUS | outside the continental United States |
| PCL | PTSD Checklist |
| PCL-C | PTSD Checklist–Civilian |
| PHQ-9 | Patient Health Questionnaire-9 |
| PROMIS | Patient Reported Outcomes Measurement Information System |
| PTSD | posttraumatic stress disorder |
| STI | sexually transmitted infection |
| TBI | traumatic brain injury |
| TFF | Total Force Fitness |
| UCMJ | Uniform Code of Military Justice |
| VA | U.S. Department of Veterans Affairs |
| VPA | vigorous physical activity |

# Introduction

The Health Related Behaviors Survey (HRBS) is the U.S. Department of Defense (DoD)'s flagship survey for understanding the health, health-related behaviors, and well-being of service members. Originally implemented to assess substance use (i.e., illicit drugs, alcohol, and tobacco), the survey now includes content areas—such as mental and physical health, sexual behavior, and postdeployment problems—that may affect force readiness or the ability to meet the demands of military life. Using a stratified random sampling approach, the survey anonymously collects information from all four DoD branches—the U.S. Air Force, Army, Marine Corps, and Navy—and from the U.S. Coast Guard, which falls under the U.S. Department of Homeland Security. Title 14 of the United States Code refers to these five entities collectively as the *armed forces*.

The HRBS is intended to supplement administrative data already collected by the armed forces. For example, although DoD maintains a system of medical records that can provide the number of service members seen for a particular chronic condition or who utilize mental health care, the system cannot provide data on service members who may have a problem and do not seek care or who are just below the threshold of a diagnosis. Further, many of the behaviors and attitudes assessed in the HRBS are potentially predictive of future, more-serious health problems that may affect readiness. Assessing these behaviors and attitudes allows DoD and the Coast Guard to get ahead of emerging problems. Thus, data from the HRBS are a complement to existing administrative data.

Since its inception more than 30 years ago, the HRBS has influenced many policy and programmatic changes that have had a profound impact on the health and well-being of service members. Further, data from the HRBS are routinely used by researchers to advance the field of military medicine. In short, the HRBS is one of the most important ongoing studies of the health and well-being of service members.

## Context for the 2015 Health Related Behaviors Survey

After more than a decade of U.S. military conflicts in the Middle East, including in Iraq and Afghanistan, the 2015 HRBS is poised to provide DoD with a comprehensive look at how service members have coped with the stress and strain associated with deployment experiences as part of Operations Iraqi Freedom, Enduring Freedom, and New Dawn. The needs of service members may have changed now that the operational tempo of these conflicts has decreased; existing problems may have waned, with new issues taking their place. At the time this report was written, DoD had already experienced downsizing (since roughly 2012), and it was expected to face more cuts in manpower and other resources. Thus, it is more important than ever to understand how to strategically maximize force health and readiness.

Total Force Fitness (TFF) is a useful framework for thinking about how data from the HRBS can help DoD create and maintain a ready force. In 2010, with assistance from the Consortium for Health and Military Performance at the Uniformed Services University of the Health Sciences, former Chairmen of the Joint Chiefs of Staff ADM Michael Mullen outlined the TFF concept in a special issue of the journal *Military Medicine*. He noted, "A total force that has achieved total fitness is healthy, ready, and resilient; capable of meeting challenges and surviving threats" (Mullen, 2010, p. 1).

TFF is a holistic approach to well-being that focuses on both mind and body in the eight domains outlined in Figure 1.1. Factors within each domain contribute to a service member's ability to meet the demands of military life. In other words, these factors set the stage for readiness (and resilience).[1] And by monitoring aggregate levels of key factors, the armed forces can assess how prepared they are to accomplish their missions.

The 2015 HRBS contains factors in all of the eight TFF domains. We highlight some of the key factors in the list below:

- psychological: depression, anxiety, posttraumatic stress disorder (PTSD), suicide and suicidal ideation
- spiritual: complementary and alternative medicine (CAM)[2]
- social: marital status, social support
- physical: physical activity, functional limitations

**Figure 1.1**
**Eight Domains of Total Force Fitness**

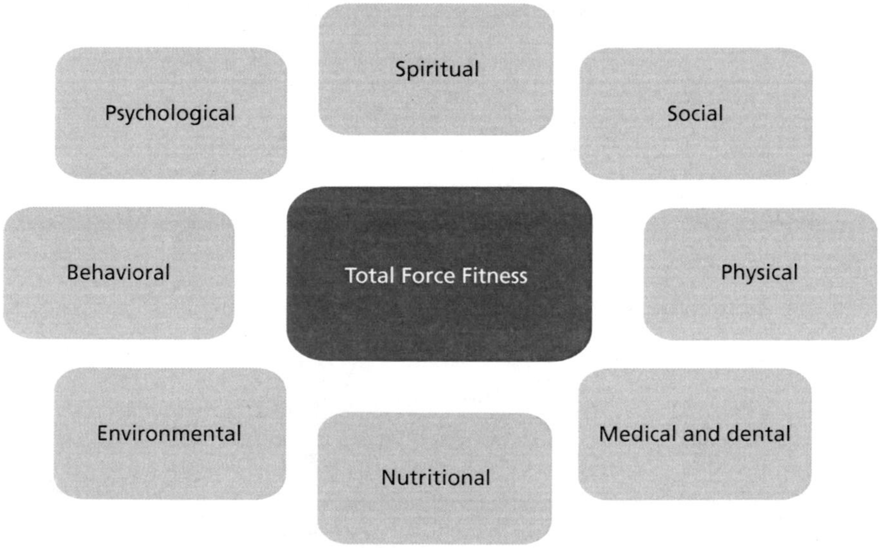

RAND RR1695-1.1

---

[1]  See Meadows, Miller, and Robson (2015) for a discussion of the relationship between TFF, readiness, and resilience.

[2]  Note that many CAM treatments could fall under other domains, such as physical and medical. For example, yoga may be considered physical and acupuncture may be considered medical, but both may also have a spiritual component.

- medical and dental: chronic conditions, medication use
- nutritional: energy drink use, supplement use
- environmental: deployment experiences
- behavioral: alcohol use, tobacco use, substance use, sexual behavior, sleep.

## Report Overview

This report provides results from the 2015 DoD HRBS of active-duty service members. The study was sponsored by the Office of the Assistant Secretary of Defense for Health Affairs on behalf of the Office of the Under Secretary of Defense for Personnel and Readiness, implemented by the Clinical Support Division of the Defense Health Agency, and completed by the RAND Corporation, with assistance from ICF International. The report presents data from all five branches of the armed forces. Where possible, results are compared with prior iterations of the HRBS to understand trends over time. In addition, results are compared with civilians when equivalent measures are utilized. The report may be used to formulate policies and programs that target the health, health-related behaviors, and well-being of current service members. In so doing, it will help the armed forces assess the current level of readiness, as well as identify areas that should be addressed in order to maintain readiness across the total force. The results may also be used by practitioners, service providers, and the general public to better understand the current needs of service members.

## Survey History and Background

The 2015 HRBS represents the twelfth iteration of the survey; the most-recent versions were in 2009 (reserve component only), 2011 (active duty only), and 2014 (both active duty and reserve components). Survey administration generally occurs every three to four years. As noted earlier, the survey was originally mandated as a way to assess substance use among personnel, particularly those returning from Vietnam. The results were used to develop appropriate intervention programs and related policies. The current HRBS is authorized in DoD Instructions 1010.4 and 1010.01. However, the HRBS is not designed to evaluate any specific program or set of programs.

Both the survey content and methodology have changed over time. Over the past 30 years, new questions have been added to address such topics as health-related behaviors; stress; nutrition and fitness; prescription drug use; and attitudes on substance use, stigma, and various conditions, such as human immunodeficiency virus (HIV). Survey items have been adapted so that they could be compared with civilian populations, including the Healthy People 2020 (HP2020) objectives established by the U.S. Department of Health and Human Services (HHS) Office of Disease Prevention and Health Promotion.[3] Furthermore, deployment-specific modules have collected information about service members' experiences in contemporary combat and noncombat deployments.

Methodologically, the survey migrated from a group-administered, paper-and-pencil approach to an entirely web-based approach starting in 2011. Once the survey content expanded

---

[3]  For more information on the HP2020 objectives, see HHS, 2010a.

from substance use to other health topics, a paper survey quickly became unwieldy. With the move to a web-based format, skip patterns allowed respondents to answer only relevant questions. Additionally, the survey sampling approach moved from a cluster approach at selected installations to a population-based, stratified-random approach based on service member characteristics (e.g., service branch, pay grade, gender).

## Overview of the 2015 Health Related Behaviors Survey

The 2015 HRBS expands and improves on the 2011 and 2014 web-based surveys (which were identical in content) in several ways. For example, the 2015 version of the survey was roughly 25-percent shorter than the prior version. Through consultation with the sponsor, as well as an advisory committee of key DoD stakeholders and subject-matter experts (discussed more in Chapter Two), several existing content areas were reduced or removed, and new, more-relevant content areas were added, including the following:

- financial distress
- housing situation
- texting while driving
- somatic symptom severity and functional impairment
- location of alcohol and cigarette purchases
- use of electronic cigarettes (e-cigarettes) and exposure to secondhand smoke
- use of nonprescription cough or cold medicine
- sexual behavior and sexual orientation, including transgender identity
- most-recent HIV test
- use of mental health services
- sleep.

In addition to adding new content areas, we used validated survey items and scales to improve measurement of some existing areas. Where possible, we used scales that have comparable versions in civilian populations, which allows for a comparison between service members and their civilian peers. Along these lines, we made significant revisions to content areas to better align HRBS measures with the following civilian measures:

- electronic game play from the National Health and Nutrition Evaluation Survey
- alcohol use items from the National Health Interview Survey and the National Survey of Drug Use and Health (NSDUH), including use of the Alcohol Use Disorders Identification Test (AUDIT) for Consumption (AUDIT-C)
- tobacco use items from the Behavioral Risk Factor Surveillance System, the NSDUH, and the National Youth Tobacco Survey
- key mental and emotional health scales from existing civilian surveys, including depressive symptoms from the Patient Health Questionnaire-9 (PHQ-9), generalized anxiety from the Generalized Anxiety Disorder 7-Item Scale (GAD-7), perceived emotional support from the Patient Reported Outcomes Measurement Information System (PROMIS) Emotional Support Form 4a, anger from the PROMIS 5 Anger Scale, suicide from the NSDUH, and PTSD from the PTSD Checklist (PCL)–Civilian (PCL-C) version

- mental health service use items from the NSDUH and Behavioral Risk Factor Surveillance System, including reasons why health services were needed but not used
- reduction and clarification of deployment-related items, including use of the Brief Traumatic Brain Injury Screen.

## Organization of the Report

The purpose of this report is to present results from the 2015 HRBS. Chapter Two briefly summarizes the methodology of the survey, including the sampling design, questionnaire development, survey administration, weights, and the general analytic plan. Chapter Three provides a summary of the weighted final sample in terms of sociodemographic and military characteristics. The remaining chapters each focus on a key substantive issue addressed in the survey, as follows:

- Chapter Four: Health Promotion and Disease Prevention
- Chapter Five: Substance Use
- Chapter Six: Mental and Emotional Health
- Chapter Seven: Physical Health and Functional Limitations
- Chapter Eight: Sexual Behavior and Health
- Chapter Nine: Sexual Orientation, Transgender Identity, and Health
- Chapter Ten: Deployment Experiences and Health.

Chapter Eleven provides a brief, high-level summary of the results and outlines policy implications for DoD, the Coast Guard, and the Defense Health Agency to consider. The results of the substantive chapters may help DoD and the Coast Guard identify established and emerging health problems among service members, develop programs and policies that target negative health-related behaviors, and ultimately help to maintain a ready force.

The report also contains four appendixes. Appendix A reproduces the web-based 2015 DoD HRBS, and Appendix B reproduces recruitment materials, including the invitation letter from RAND and ICF International, as well as the letters of support from the services. Appendix C provides the list of frequently asked questions (FAQs) and answers provided to respondents on the Defense Health Agency's website. Appendix D contains a description of key measures (organized by each substantive chapter), including how values were recoded, transformed, or combined for analysis and reporting. It also includes information on how we calculated scales and composite measures.

Finally, we remind readers that these survey results can offer only statistical *estimates* of true population characteristics. In a report of this magnitude, it is often challenging to consistently balance the dual imperative for precise language and circumspect tone with the need for simple, clear, and concise presentation. For example, we could have started the title of each results table with "Estimate of . . . ," but because all of the tables present estimates, that word is implied; we therefore opted to streamline some of the language. We hope that readers will keep this in mind and appreciate the trade-off in favor of a more straightforward and hopefully less burdensome presentation.

# CHAPTER TWO

# Methodology

This chapter reviews the methodology used to conduct the 2015 HRBS. At the onset of the study, the research team reviewed prior HRBSs, with a focus on updating the 2011 and 2014 HRBSs of active-duty military personnel. As noted in Chapter One, we removed some existing content areas while adding others in order to measure emerging areas of concern. The remainder of this chapter provides a detailed description of the process used to review and revise survey content, the administration of the survey, the population and sampling plan, the creation of survey weights, the analytic plan for the final data set, and finally, limitations of the approach described here.

## Questionnaire Development

The 2015 HRBS was largely based on the 2011 (and 2014) version of the active-duty survey. The following goals guided edits to survey content:

- Reduce respondent burden through reduction of items and through skip patterns.
- Remove items not used in prior analyses.
- Align scales with existing scales used in civilian research.
- Add items relevant to current and emerging health issues, as nominated by the sponsor (Office of the Assistant Secretary of Defense for Health Affairs) and advisory group.

This means that, in some instances, longitudinal comparison of the 2015 HRBS and prior iterations is not possible because question content was not identical. However, our goal was to develop a shorter, more direct, clearer survey using as many state-of-the art measures as possible. Thus, we did not manipulate existing scales (e.g., use a subset of scale items) to match prior versions of the HRBS. Doing so could have altered the established psychometric properties of the scale.

### Advisory Group

At the beginning of the study, the sponsor coordinated a group of key stakeholders and subject-matter experts to serve on an advisory group. The role of the group was to provide input on survey content (including the selection of questionnaire items), the sampling plan, priority areas for analysis, and dissemination of results. The group consisted of representatives from each of the DoD services, the Coast Guard, and multiple DoD offices, including the Reserve Medical Programs office (of the Office of the Assistant Secretary of Defense for Manpower and Reserve Affairs), Defense Health Agency (specifically, the Women's Health, Medical Ethics, and Patient Advocacy division; Clinical Support division; and Communications division), Drug Testing and Program Policy office (of the Office of the Under Secretary of Defense for Personnel and Readiness), Sexual Assault Prevention and Response Office, Defense Suicide Prevention Office, Walter Reed National Military Medical Center, and Uniformed Services University. The group met with the research team quarterly throughout the study.

### Cognitive Pretesting

A draft version of the survey was reviewed by military fellows at RAND in early 2015. These fellows represented the Army and Air Force active components and were all at the level of major or lieutenant colonel. During a single focus group, the fellows were asked to review specific items that had changed since the 2011 HRBS. The discussion, led by a member of the research team, focused on the clarity of the items. The fellows' feedback was then incorporated into the questionnaire.

### Approval Processes

The final survey, the sampling plan, all communication with potential respondents, and the data security plan were reviewed by RAND's Institutional Review Board (known as the Human Subjects Protection Committee), the ICF International Institutional Review Board, the Defense Manpower Data Center (DMDC)'s Institutional Review Board, the Office of the Under Secretary of Defense for Personnel and Readiness's Research Regulatory Oversight Office, the Office of the Assistant Secretary of Defense for Health Affairs and the Defense Health Agency's Human Research Protection Office, the Coast Guard's Institutional Review Board, and the DoD Security Office. All survey materials included the survey report control system license number: DD-HA(BE)2189 (expires February 9, 2019). See Appendix A for the final 2015 DoD HRBS.

## Survey Administration

This section reviews the procedures used to administer the 2015 HRBS. RAND partnered with ICF International, which implemented the web-based survey as a subcontractor. The survey opened in November 2015 and concluded in April 2016.

### Service Liaison Officers

Each of the services and components, including the Coast Guard, identified a senior officer or contact to serve as a service liaison officer whose primary function was to facilitate data-collection activities. Specifically, the service liaison officers were tasked with the following three primary functions:

- Work with each service's information technology department to whitelist the survey's web link on their respective computer systems.
- Obtain a letter of support from a flag officer within their command to encourage participation and provide confirmation that the survey is an officially sponsored DoD endeavor (see Appendix B).
- Develop a marketing strategy for the survey, including posters, flyers, and press releases to relevant media.

## Sample Recruitment

Service members received an initial invitation letter from RAND and ICF, as well as the letter of support from the appropriate service branch (see Appendix B). Subsequently, service members received follow-up notifications (via email and/or postcard) to complete the survey. Service members who had a valid email address received up to nine reminders; those who did not have a valid email address but who did have a valid mailing address received up to five postcard reminders. Emails were sent roughly weekly for 11 weeks (excluding holiday weeks), and postcards were sent roughly every two weeks. The final email or postcard reminded invitees that they had two weeks to complete the survey before it closed. DMDC provided all contact information (e.g., email and mailing addresses).

## Ensuring Anonymity

Because the survey asked about many health-related behaviors that are typically considered private and, if admitted to, could result in legal action under the Uniform Code of Military Justice (UCMJ), it was important to maintain the anonymity of the service members who completed the survey. This meant that a respondent's answers could not be traced back to him or her, nor was any identifying information (e.g., name, address, Social Security Number) collected in the survey. Log-in codes or passwords were not required to access the survey. At the start of the survey, potential respondents were provided with a series of screens that included a privacy statement and informed consent material (see Appendix A). This statement was also available to print out as a single document if the respondent chose to do so. All contact material sent to potential respondents (i.e., letters, postcards, and emails) clearly stated that the survey was anonymous. In addition, as described later, the analysis plan included provisions that no reported data be identifiable by inference; that is, given the demographic and behavioral data reported, it would not be possible to infer the identity of a given respondent. For example, instead of reporting illicit drug use by individual ages, age would be grouped into categories. To further ensure respondent anonymity, results are not reported if the calculation involved fewer than 20 individuals.[1]

## Survey Support and Help Desk

In the event of technical problems, assistance was available from ICF's Survey Operations Center help desk, which could be reached by email or toll-free telephone number. The help desk responded to email and phone calls between 8 a.m. and 6 p.m. Eastern Time; calls were automatically routed to voicemail outside of these hours. ICF responded to most messages or contacts within one to two business days. RAND also maintained an email for service members to use, but it was very infrequently used compared with ICF's support and help desk.[2]

A list of FAQs and answers was also available to potential respondents (see Appendix C). The document contained an email address to direct questions about the overall study, as well as contact information for RAND's Human Subjects Protection Committee in case respondents had questions about their rights as participants.

---

[1]  The use of 20 respondents as a cutoff was negotiated with the client and other review agencies during the human subjects protection review process. It refers to the denominator of estimates, not the numerator.

[2]  In fact, the RAND email was never used to address any issues related to problems with or concerns about the survey. The three or four emails the RAND team did receive were about access to the data once collected or a date for release of the results.

## Population and Sample

### Population

The sampling frame of the 2015 HRBS included all active-duty personnel who were not deployed as of August 31, 2015,[3] and not enrolled as cadets in service academies, senior military colleges, and other Reserve Officers' Training Corps programs.[4] Personnel in an active National Guard or reserve program and full-time National Guard members and reservists are classified as members of their reserve-component branch of service and excluded from our population of interest. We used data provided by DMDC to construct the sampling frame. Table 2.1 provides the 2015 HRBS sampling frame, broken down by service branch, pay grade, and gender. Additional details on the sampling frame can be found in Tables 2.2 through 2.8.

### Sampling Plan

To guarantee representation from all members of the sampling frame, we constructed a stratified random sample by service branch, pay grade, and gender. Because of the competing goals of the 2015 HRBS (e.g., reporting the prevalence of key health-related behaviors at various combinations of service branch, pay grade, and gender), several sampling designs were considered. There were very few differences in the expected margin of error across the designs; therefore, we chose the simplest design.

**Table 2.1**
**2015 HRBS Sampling Frame**

|  | Total | Air Force | Army | Marine Corps | Navy | Coast Guard |
|---|---|---|---|---|---|---|
| Pay grade |  |  |  |  |  |  |
| E1–E4 | 607,189 | 116,539 | 232,987 | 114,010 | 129,601 | 14,052 |
| E5–E6 | 399,891 | 100,140 | 133,030 | 43,974 | 108,667 | 14,080 |
| E7–E9 | 129,294 | 29,757 | 52,674 | 13,237 | 29,132 | 4,494 |
| W1–W5 | 20,171 | NA[a] | 14,786 | 2,067 | 1,577 | 1,741 |
| O1–O3 | 132,958 | 34,992 | 49,637 | 12,504 | 31,790 | 4,035 |
| O4–O10 | 85,087 | 25,060 | 30,071 | 6,384 | 20,844 | 2,728 |
| Gender |  |  |  |  |  |  |
| Men | 1,160,564 | 247,218 | 439,060 | 177,162 | 262,227 | 34,897 |
| Women | 214,026 | 59,270 | 74,125 | 15,014 | 59,384 | 6,233 |
| Total | 1,374,590 | 306,488 | 513,185 | 192,176 | 321,611 | 41,130 |

[a] NA = not applicable. The Air Force does not use the Warrant Officer designation.

---

[3] A *deployed* service member is defined as any service member who is called up for overseas contingency operations. Ships at sea would be considered deployed if they are in the area of responsibility of such operations.

[4] Technically, the sampling frame was restricted to only the active component, but the DMDC sampling files differentiated between active duty, reserve, and National Guard. Reserve and National Guard were removed from the file prior to sampling.

The 2015 HRBS disproportionately sampled from strata. We determined the total sample size within each stratum using two sets of power calculations:

1.  Within the stratum defined by service branch, pay grade, and gender, we calculated the total number of completed surveys needed for a 4-percentage-point margin of error with 95-percent confidence.
2.  Within the stratum defined by service branch and pay grade, we calculated the total number of completed surveys needed for a 3-percentage-point margin of error with 95-percent confidence.

These power calculations provided us with the number of completed surveys needed for a given margin of error; however, nonresponse is high in surveys of military personnel and must be accounted for in the sampling design (see Miller and Aharoni, 2015). We thus chose to use the response rates from the 2011 HRBS to convert the sample sizes from the number of completed surveys to the number of surveys in the primary sample. If the primary sample size determined by the power calculation in (1) did not meet the requirements of (2), then additional samples were added to the corresponding strata. We combined small strata for the power calculations, and we split the resulting sample proportional to size among those combined.

Table 2.2 describes the strata that were combined. Note that the Coast Guard was sampled using a different strategy; for that service branch, we sampled half of the service members within each stratum defined by gender and pay grade. All stratum-specific sample sizes were capped at 75 percent of the total stratum size. After determining the primary sample strata sizes, we sampled service members within each stratum with equal probability and without replacement.

In the event that response rates in the primary sample were lower than anticipated, we constructed a secondary sample. The number of completed surveys was monitored semi-continuously at weekly intervals. Six weeks after the primary batch of surveys was sent, we compared the observed number of completed surveys by strata with the minimum number of completed surveys based on the power calculations. At that point, we determined that the full secondary sample was needed because of low response rates.

### Unintended Convenience Sample

Given extremely low response rates and potential technological and security problems with the web survey, the service liaison officers helped with general awareness of and marketing for the 2015 HRBS. On Thursday, January 21, 2016, the Air Force posted an article on its af.mil website describing the HRBS and encouraging participation. The article used information from a suggested press release created by the RAND research team and approved by all human subjects protection committees. However, the article also included a web link to the survey

**Table 2.2**
**Sampling Strata That Were Combined During Power Calculations**

| Service Branch | Gender | Combined Pay Grades |
|---|---|---|
| Marine Corps | Women | W1–W5, O1–O10 |
| Marine Corps | Women | E5–E6, E7–E9 |
| Navy | Women | W1–W5, O1–O3 |

itself. Subsequently, on the morning of Sunday, January 24, a similar story was posted on the *Air Force Times* website and then picked up by the *Military Times* website. These stories also contained the survey web link. Because no login or password was required to access the survey, this meant that anyone clicking on the link could respond. By January 30, the survey link was removed from all marketing pages and articles.

Because the 2015 HRBS was anonymous, there was no way to determine whether service members who were not sampled as part of the 2015 HRBS completed the survey after reading the marketing materials. This convenience sample (i.e., self-selection into the survey) has the potential to bias our results. On Monday, February 8, a screener question was added to the beginning of the survey to identify service members who were not sampled and subsequently skip them out of the survey via a "thank you" screen. The question was as follows:

How did you hear about this survey? Please check all that apply.

1. Email from the study team (RAND or ICF)
2. Postcard from the study team (RAND or ICF)
3. Letter from the study team (RAND or ICF)
4. A website
5. Friend or colleague
6. Commander
7. Other

Anyone who selected one of the first three response options or skipped the question was allowed to complete the survey, while all others were skipped out of the survey via the "thank you" screen. The potential convenience sample ran from January 21 to February 8 (referred to as the *convenience window*), affecting 19 days of data collection. This accounts for 2,910 submitted surveys. To put this number into perspective, in the 19 days preceding and the 19 days following the convenience window, there were 2,881 and 2,893 submitted surveys, respectively.

During the convenience window, the responders were a mix of three groups: those who were sampled and did not see the marketing materials, those who were sampled and responded after seeing the marketing materials, and those who were not sampled. The anonymity of the HRBS makes it impossible to differentiate these three groups during the convenience window, but some information about the size of these groups is available from before and after the convenience window.

We estimated the excess number of responses during the convenience window over what was expected from the probability sample. We used data from the period before the convenience window to model the expected number of responses over time. This model included terms for service branch, pay grade, gender, day of the week, indicator of an email reminder, and holiday effects (e.g., Christmas, New Year's Day, and Martin Luther King, Jr. Day).

Specifically, let $R_{ijkt}$ be the number of respondents for gender $i$, in service branch $j$, and in pay grade $k$ at time $t$. Let $S_{ijk}$ be the number of sampled service members in the same group. Then, define

$$N_{ijkt} = S_{ijk} - \sum_{l<t} R_{ijkl}$$

as the number of sampled service members yet to respond prior to time $t$. We modeled the number of respondents using the following Poisson model:

$$\log(\mathrm{E}[R_{ijkt}]) = \log(N_{ijkt}) + \alpha_i + \beta_j + \gamma_k + f(t),$$

where $\alpha_i$, $\beta_j$, and $\gamma_k$ are gender, service branch, and pay grade effects and $f(t)$ is a function of time that includes an indicator of the day of the week, an indicator of an email reminder, an indicator of the first email reminder, an indicator for the period between the opening of the survey and the first email reminder, an indicator of a holiday (December 23, 24, 25, 26, and 27, 2015, and January 1, 2, 3, 16, 17, and 18, 2016), and an indicator for the week following the new year to account for service members returning from leave (January 4, 5, 6, 7, and 8). Training of this model was restricted to respondents *prior to* the convenience window, and predictions from this model will be denoted as $\widehat{R}_{ijkt}$.

Figure 2.1 provides the observed number of responses (black line) and the expected number of responses from the model (red line) between the release of the survey and the end of the convenience window. The convenience window is the region shaded in gray. As shown in the figure, the expected number of responses from the model closely follows the observed number of responses until the beginning of the convenience window (Thursday, January 21), at which point the observed number of responses is higher than expected. This pattern is not persistent throughout the entire convenience window, with the observed number of responses aligning with the expected number of responses starting on Wednesday, January 27. The largest difference between the observed and expected number of responses occurred on Monday,

**Figure 2.1**
**Observed and Expected Number of Survey Responses Through February 8, 2016**

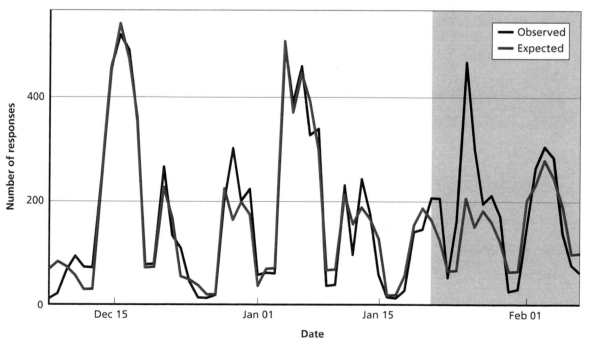

January 25, with 464 observed responses but only 204 expected responses. The differences are consistent across the service branches from Sunday, January 24 through Tuesday, January 26 (not shown); however, only the Air Force exceeded the expected number of responses from Thursday, January 21 through Saturday, January 23. This coincides with the timing of the Air Force article published on af.mil (Thursday, January 21) and the *Military Times* article (Sunday, January 24).

Based on these results, we determined that the optimal strategy for handling the convenience sample was to exclude any surveys that were collected between Thursday, January 21 and Tuesday, January 26 for Air Force personnel and any surveys that were collected between Sunday, January 24 and Tuesday, January 26 for personnel in all other service branches. This exclusion totaled 1,050 surveys, or roughly 6 percent of usable surveys.

### Final Analytic Sample

Figure 2.2 provides a flowchart showing how the research team arrived at the final analytic sample of 16,699 surveys. The chart begins with the 23,357 individuals who logged into the survey website. Just more than 2,600 did not proceed through the front material to the first question. We then removed 156 respondents who indicated that they were in the reserve or National Guard components and not on active duty. Roughly 500 respondents did not provide enough information to allow a weight to be computed (e.g., missing service branch, pay grade, or gender). An additional 2,256 cases were dropped because they were not considered a *usable survey*, which we defined as one in which a weight could be computed and the respondent provided at least one response to an alcohol-related item. This is similar to how a usable survey was defined for the 2011 HRBS. As noted, we also removed the 1,050 cases that occurred immediately following the publication of the survey web link on af.mil, *Air Force Times*, and *Military Times*. Finally, we dropped 30 respondents who indicated they were currently retired or a dependent or who provided obviously false data (e.g., a pay grade and job title that did not reasonably match). Thus, the final analytic sample was 16,699 surveys.

**Figure 2.2**
**Flowchart for the 2015 HRBS Final Analytic Sample**

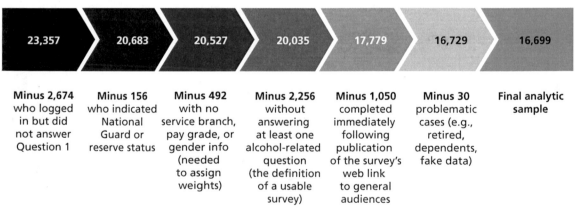

| 23,357 | 20,683 | 20,527 | 20,035 | 17,779 | 16,729 | 16,699 |
|---|---|---|---|---|---|---|
| **Minus 2,674** who logged in but did not answer Question 1 | **Minus 156** who indicated National Guard or reserve status | **Minus 492** with no service branch, pay grade, or gender info (needed to assign weights) | **Minus 2,256** without answering at least one alcohol-related question (the definition of a usable survey) | **Minus 1,050** completed immediately following publication of the survey's web link to general audiences | **Minus 30** problematic cases (e.g., retired, dependents, fake data) | **Final analytic sample** |

**Response Rates**

Response rates were calculated by removing service members whom we were unable to contact by mail or email. Specifically, these *noncontacts* were defined as (1) individuals in the sample frame for whom we received a returned postcard or letter and a returned email or (2) individuals in the sample frame who did not have a valid postal address and for whom we received a returned email. The total number of noncontacts was 6,770, or 3.4 percent of the invited sample. The overall response rate was 8.6 percent.[5] The rate was calculated as the ratio of the number of usable responses in the analytic sample (16,699) to the number of contactable service members (195,220).

Table 2.3 breaks down the sampling frame, sample size, and response rates (including noncontacts and usable surveys in the analytic sample) by service branch, pay grade, and gender. The primary sample size was 118,656, and the secondary sample size was 83,334, for a total sample size of 201,990. Of the 16,699 usable surveys in the analytic sample, the Coast Guard (4,152) and Air Force (4,150) completed the most. Usable surveys were approximately evenly distributed across pay grades, and there were more usable surveys among men than women. The response rate was highest among the Coast Guard (20.4 percent) and lowest among the Army (4.7 percent). Senior officers (O4–O10) were the most likely to respond (20.6 percent), and junior enlisted (E1–E4) were the least likely to respond (3.1 percent).

**Table 2.3**
**Sampling Frame, Sample Size, and Response Rates, Overall Sample**

| | Sampling Frame | Primary Sample Size | Secondary Sample Size | Noncontacts | Usable Surveys in Analytic Sample | Response Rate (%) |
|---|---|---|---|---|---|---|
| Service branch | | | | | | |
| Air Force | 306,488 | 15,689 | 13,674 | 171 | 4,150 | 14.2 |
| Army | 513,185 | 36,392 | 31,859 | 633 | 3,197 | 4.7 |
| Marine Corps | 192,176 | 20,621 | 15,902 | 3,359 | 2,184 | 6.6 |
| Navy | 321,611 | 25,394 | 21,899 | 2,374 | 3,016 | 6.7 |
| Coast Guard | 41,130 | 20,560 | 0 | 233 | 4,152 | 20.4 |
| Pay grade | | | | | | |
| E1–E4 | 607,189 | 49,098 | 40,682 | 5,428 | 2,595 | 3.1 |
| E5–E6 | 399,891 | 22,806 | 15,022 | 254 | 3,505 | 9.3 |
| E7–E9 | 129,294 | 11,801 | 8,210 | 134 | 2,948 | 14.8 |
| W1–W5 | 20,171 | 6,975 | 1,953 | 127 | 1,156 | 13.1 |
| O1–O3 | 132,958 | 17,685 | 11,132 | 729 | 3,092 | 11.0 |
| O4–O10 | 85,087 | 10,291 | 6,335 | 98 | 3,403 | 20.6 |
| Gender | | | | | | |
| Men | 1,160,564 | 82,474 | 56,146 | 5,230 | 10,368 | 7.8 |
| Women | 214,026 | 36,182 | 27,188 | 1,540 | 6,331 | 10.2 |
| Total | 1,374,590 | 118,656 | 83,334 | 6,770 | 16,699 | 8.6 |

---

[5]  We discuss implications of the response rate in the limitations section later in this chapter.

Tables 2.4 through 2.8 provide a summary of the sampling frame, sample size, and response rates for each service branch, broken down by pay grade and gender.

**Table 2.4**
**Sampling Frame, Sample Size, and Response Rates, Air Force**

|  | Sampling Frame | Primary Sample Size | Secondary Sample Size | Noncontacts | Usable Surveys in Analytic Sample | Response Rate (%) |
|---|---|---|---|---|---|---|
| **Men** |  |  |  |  |  |  |
| E1–E4 | 94,801 | 2,674 | 2,585 | 34 | 382 | 7.3 |
| E5–E6 | 80,669 | 1,596 | 1,543 | 12 | 359 | 11.5 |
| E7–E9 | 24,107 | 1,176 | 1,058 | 7 | 400 | 19.0 |
| O1–O3 | 26,797 | 2,266 | 1,698 | 40 | 495 | 12.6 |
| O4–O10 | 20,844 | 1,458 | 1,093 | 14 | 439 | 17.3 |
| Total | 247,218 | 9,170 | 7,977 | 107 | 2,075 | 12.2 |
| **Women** |  |  |  |  |  |  |
| E1–E4 | 21,738 | 1,698 | 1,642 | 30 | 422 | 12.8 |
| E5–E6 | 19,471 | 1,338 | 1,294 | 5 | 396 | 15.1 |
| E7–E9 | 5,650 | 1,007 | 906 | 1 | 372 | 19.5 |
| O1–O3 | 8,195 | 1,492 | 1,118 | 23 | 470 | 18.2 |
| O4–O10 | 4,216 | 984 | 737 | 5 | 415 | 24.2 |
| Total | 59,270 | 6,519 | 5,697 | 64 | 2,075 | 17.1 |
| Air Force total | 306,488 | 15,689 | 13,674 | 171 | 4,150 | 14.2 |

NOTE: The Air Force does not use warrant officers.

**Table 2.5**
**Sampling Frame, Sample Size, and Response Rates, Army**

|  | Sampling Frame | Primary Sample Size | Secondary Sample Size | Noncontacts | Usable Surveys in Analytic Sample | Response Rate (%) |
|---|---|---|---|---|---|---|
| **Men** |  |  |  |  |  |  |
| E1–E4 | 197,518 | 11,609 | 11,225 | 261 | 185 | 0.8 |
| E5–E6 | 116,355 | 3,052 | 2,951 | 21 | 227 | 3.8 |
| E7–E9 | 46,730 | 1,735 | 1,561 | 54 | 252 | 7.8 |
| W1–W5 | 13,383 | 2,499 | 1,873 | 65 | 332 | 7.7 |
| O1–O3 | 39,674 | 3,010 | 2,256 | 49 | 312 | 6.0 |
| O4–O10 | 25,400 | 1,101 | 825 | 21 | 289 | 15.2 |
| Total | 439,060 | 23,006 | 20,691 | 471 | 1,597 | 3.7 |
| **Women** |  |  |  |  |  |  |
| E1–E4 | 35,469 | 5,226 | 5,053 | 55 | 241 | 2.4 |
| E5–E6 | 16,675 | 2,491 | 2,409 | 12 | 264 | 5.4 |
| E7–E9 | 5,944 | 1,640 | 1,475 | 16 | 348 | 11.2 |
| W1–W5 | 1,403 | 1,052 | 0 | 34 | 116 | 11.4 |
| O1–O3 | 9,963 | 1,756 | 1,316 | 24 | 245 | 8.0 |
| O4–O10 | 4,671 | 1,221 | 915 | 21 | 386 | 18.3 |
| Total | 74,125 | 13,386 | 11,168 | 162 | 1,600 | 6.6 |
| Army total | 513,185 | 36,392 | 31,859 | 633 | 3,197 | 4.7 |

**Table 2.6**
**Sampling Frame, Sample Size, and Response Rates, Marine Corps**

| | Sampling Frame | Primary Sample Size | Secondary Sample Size | Noncontacts | Usable Surveys in Analytic Sample | Response Rate (%) |
|---|---|---|---|---|---|---|
| Men | | | | | | |
| E1–E4 | 104,600 | 6,808 | 6,583 | 2,371 | 202 | 1.8 |
| E5–E6 | 40,582 | 2,179 | 2,107 | 47 | 196 | 4.6 |
| E7–E9 | 12,533 | 1,463 | 1,316 | 9 | 320 | 11.6 |
| W1–W5 | 1,949 | 1,284 | 80 | 13 | 191 | 14.1 |
| O1–O3 | 11,415 | 2,326 | 1,744 | 306 | 296 | 7.9 |
| O4–O10 | 6,083 | 1,844 | 1,242 | 12 | 499 | 16.2 |
| Total | 177,162 | 15,904 | 13,072 | 2,758 | 1,704 | 6.5 |
| Women | | | | | | |
| E1–E4 | 9,410 | 2,015 | 1,949 | 514 | 125 | 3.6 |
| E5–E6 | 3,392 | 1,107 | 847 | 7 | 124 | 6.4 |
| E7–E9 | 704 | 466 | 34 | 1 | 73 | 14.6 |
| W1–W5 | 118 | 88 | 0 | 0 | 14 | 15.9 |
| O1–O3 | 1,089 | 816 | 0 | 77 | 83 | 11.2 |
| O4–O10 | 301 | 225 | 0 | 2 | 61 | 27.4 |
| Total | 15,014 | 4,717 | 2,830 | 601 | 480 | 6.9 |
| Marine Corps total | 192,176 | 20,621 | 15,902 | 3,359 | 2,184 | 6.6 |

**Table 2.7**
**Sampling Frame, Sample Size, and Response Rates, Navy**

| | Sampling Frame | Primary Sample Size | Secondary Sample Size | Noncontacts | Usable Surveys in Analytic Sample | Response Rate (%) |
|---|---|---|---|---|---|---|
| Men | | | | | | |
| E1–E4 | 99,999 | 8,350 | 8,074 | 1,418 | 155 | 1.0 |
| E5–E6 | 91,418 | 2,448 | 2,367 | 96 | 288 | 6.1 |
| E7–E9 | 26,110 | 1,256 | 1,130 | 29 | 280 | 11.9 |
| W1–W5 | 1,483 | 1,112 | 0 | 15 | 185 | 16.9 |
| O1–O3 | 25,283 | 2,553 | 1,914 | 137 | 372 | 8.6 |
| O4–O10 | 17,934 | 1,229 | 921 | 17 | 399 | 18.7 |
| Total | 262,227 | 16,948 | 14,406 | 1,712 | 1,679 | 5.7 |
| Women | | | | | | |
| E1–E4 | 29,602 | 3,693 | 3,571 | 531 | 139 | 2.1 |
| E5–E6 | 17,249 | 1,556 | 1,504 | 51 | 251 | 8.3 |
| E7–E9 | 3,022 | 812 | 730 | 8 | 237 | 15.5 |
| W1–W5 | 94 | 70 | 0 | 0 | 16 | 22.9 |
| O1–O3 | 6,507 | 1,449 | 1,086 | 66 | 307 | 12.4 |
| O4–O10 | 2,910 | 866 | 602 | 6 | 387 | 26.5 |
| Total | 59,384 | 8,446 | 7,493 | 662 | 1,337 | 8.8 |
| Navy total | 321,611 | 25,394 | 21,899 | 2,374 | 3,016 | 6.7 |

**Table 2.8**
**Sampling Frame, Sample Size, and Response Rates, Coast Guard**

|  | Sampling Frame | Primary Sample Size | Secondary Sample Size | Noncontacts | Usable Surveys in Analytic Sample | Response Rate (%) |
|---|---|---|---|---|---|---|
| **Men** |  |  |  |  |  |  |
| E1–E4 | 11,375 | 5,687 | 0 | 166 | 507 | 9.2 |
| E5–E6 | 12,421 | 6,210 | 0 | 3 | 1,163 | 18.7 |
| E7–E9 | 4,127 | 2,063 | 0 | 7 | 601 | 29.2 |
| W1–W5 | 1,620 | 810 | 0 | 0 | 272 | 33.6 |
| O1–O3 | 3,041 | 1,520 | 0 | 6 | 352 | 23.3 |
| O4–O10 | 2,313 | 1,156 | 0 | 0 | 418 | 36.2 |
| Total | 34,897 | 17,446 | 0 | 182 | 3,313 | 19.2 |
| **Women** |  |  |  |  |  |  |
| E1–E4 | 2,677 | 1,338 | 0 | 48 | 237 | 18.4 |
| E5–E6 | 1,659 | 829 | 0 | 0 | 237 | 28.6 |
| E7–E9 | 367 | 183 | 0 | 2 | 65 | 35.9 |
| W1–W5 | 121 | 60 | 0 | 0 | 30 | 50.0 |
| O1–O3 | 994 | 497 | 0 | 1 | 160 | 32.3 |
| O4–O10 | 415 | 207 | 0 | 0 | 110 | 53.1 |
| Total | 6,233 | 3,114 | 0 | 51 | 839 | 27.4 |
| Coast Guard total | 41,130 | 20,560 | 0 | 233 | 4,152 | 20.4 |

## Weights

### Poststratification Weights

The 2015 HRBS was anonymous, and responses to the survey were not linked to individual service members. This precluded the possibility of assigning sampling weights or nonresponse weights to individuals; however, we did calculate poststratification weights to ensure the correct distribution of service members by service branch, pay grade, and gender. Let $N_{bpg}$ be the number of service members in service branch $b$, pay grade $p$, and gender $g$, and let $r_{bpg}$ be the number of usable responses in service branch $b$, pay grade $p$, and gender $g$. The poststratification weight for a service member in service branch $b$, pay grade $p$, and gender $g$ is given by

$$w_{bpg} = \frac{N_{bpg}}{r_{bpg}}.$$

Note that poststratification implicitly adjusts for the sampling design and nonresponse. To see this, let $n_{bpg}$ be the number of sampled service members in service branch $b$, pay grade $p$, and gender $g$. The probability that a service member in service branch $b$, pay grade $p$, and gender $g$ was sampled is given by

$$S_{bpg} = \frac{n_{bpg}}{N_{bpg}}.$$

The design-based weight is the inverse of this probability.

Nonresponse adjustment is possible using only aggregate data because there is no way to link the completed surveys to individual service members (because the 2015 HRBS was anonymous). The probability of response among those sampled for a service member in service branch $b$, pay grade $p$, and gender $g$ is given by

$$R_{bpg} = \frac{r_{bpg}}{n_{bpg}}.$$

The nonresponse weight is the inverse of this probability. The final weight that incorporates both the survey design and nonresponse is simply the product of the two individual weights, or

$$w_{bpg} = \frac{1}{S_{bpg}} * \frac{1}{R_{bpg}} = \frac{N_{bpg}}{n_{bpg}} * \frac{n_{bpg}}{r_{bpg}} = \frac{N_{bpg}}{r_{bpg}}.$$

This illustrates that the poststratification weights are accounting for the survey design and any nonresponse that is attributable to service branch, pay grade, and gender.

After we constructed the poststratification weights, we approximated a design effect of 4.5 using Kish's effective sample size formula (Kish, 1965). A *design effect* is defined as the ratio of the variance of the actual sample design and the variance of a simple random sample of the same size, and it can be understood as the ratio of the observed sample size to that of the effective sample size. This suggests that the effective sample size of the 2015 HRBS was less than a quarter of the size of the observed sample. This loss of information was caused by the differential response patterns across the sampling strata and the poststratification weighting used to ensure that the sample reflected the population. The poststratification weights constructed for the 2015 HRBS did not account for nonresponse that was attributable to factors outside of the sampling strata, such as age, race, education level, or marital status. Failure to account for these additional factors may lead to bias in the estimates, while accounting for them increases the variance of the estimates. In large surveys where the variance is expected to be small, unbiased estimation is preferred. However, because of the lower-than-expected response rates and the large design effects, the variance of the estimates from the 2015 HRBS was of great concern. For this reason, the weighting scheme for the 2015 HRBS was chosen to provide the optimal bias-variance trade-off. We found that failing to account for the additional factors in the weights produced little to no bias across most study outcomes but resulted in substantial reductions in variance.

Specifically, the bias-variance trade-off was explored using the mean squared error, which combines bias and variance into a single metric. For illustration, consider two weighting schemes: (1) poststratification weights using only the sampling strata and (2) weights derived using age in addition to the sampling strata. We applied the two schemes to the observed data, and results from analyses using the weights that included the additional factors were assumed to be unbiased. The biases from analyses using poststratification weights that included only the sampling strata were approximated as the difference in the estimates between the two weighting schemes. We explored the bias-variance trade-off for each of the study outcomes. Estimates from analyses using the weights accounting for only the sampling strata tended to have smaller mean squared errors than estimates from analyses using the more complex weighting scheme.

In other words, the poststratification weights using only the sampling strata optimized the bias-variance trade-off across most of the study outcomes, and these weights were used for all results presented in this report.

In general, results from the two weighting schemes differ when there is heterogeneity in the outcomes across groups not accounted for in the weights. One such outcome with an extreme level of heterogeneity is the prevalence of current e-cigarette smokers: Service members aged 17–24 were almost ten times more likely to be a current e-cigarette smoker than service members aged 45 or older (see Table 5.22 later in the report). Despite this high level of heterogeneity, the overall estimates of the proportion of service members who were current e-cigarette smokers using the two weighting schemes are comparable with overlapping confidence intervals (CIs): 12.4 percent (CI: 11.2–13.7) from the poststratification weights using only the sampling strata versus 13.8 percent (CI: 12.4–15.2) from the weights derived using age in addition to the sampling strata.[6] Outcomes with considerable heterogeneity across age groups include binge drinking, prescription sedative use in the past 12 months, and more than one sexual partner in the past 12 months, among others.

## Analytic Approach

All analyses, unless otherwise noted, used the poststratification weights previously described to account for the sample design and survey response patterns. In most circumstances, differences in each outcome were tested across levels of key factors or by subgroups (service branch, pay grade, gender, age group, race/ethnicity, and education level; see Chapter Three) using a two-stage procedure. First, we used the Rao-Scott chi-square test as an overall test of the relationship between the outcome and the factor. This tests the hypothesis that there is *any* difference in the outcome across all levels of the factor. If this test concluded that there was a statistically significant relationship between the outcome and the factor, then we attempted to identify the levels of the factor in which the outcome differed by constructing all possible pairwise comparisons of the outcome across the levels of the factor. We used a simple *t*-test and adjusted the *p*-values for multiple comparisons using the Tukey-Kramer adjustment, which is designed to account for the multiple testing associated with all possible pairwise comparisons across factor levels. Confidence intervals for percentages were computed using the Clopper-Pearson method (exact binomial confidence intervals; Korn and Graubard, 1998), and confidence intervals for all other data types were computed using a normal approximation.

## Limitations

Survey research is inherently difficult for a number of reasons, many of which are relevant to the 2015 HRBS and may limit its validity or generalizabilty. First, response rates were lower than in prior HRBSs and in many other recent military surveys. This is a historical trend, not limited to surveys in the military. Current research shows that longer surveys and those using web technology generally have lower response rates than surveys that are shorter and completed by phone or mail (Dillman, Smyth, and Christian, 2009), and this is especially true for

---

[6]   All confidence intervals in parentheses in this report are at the 95-percent level. We omit this for ease of presentation.

junior enlisted service members (Miller and Aharoni, 2015). There are several potential reasons for the low response rate in the 2015 HRBS—for example, survey fatigue (the 2014 HRBS was still in the field well into 2015), survey length (the survey took roughly 45 minutes to complete), survey content (asked about sensitive behaviors), and information technology issues (e.g., most calls to the help desk were about problems accessing the survey website).

Still, low response rates do not *automatically* mean that the results are biased (Davern, 2013; Groves, 2006; Krosnick, 1999), but the low rates do increase the likelihood that service members who did not respond were in some way qualitatively different from those who did respond. However, we have no way to assess how the bias might have affected the results. On the one hand, one could hypothesize that service members with the worst health or the most health problems did not participate when asked. If so, the results may overestimate the health of the force. On the other hand, if some service members were unhappy about the way DoD and the Coast Guard handled some specific aspect of health or health care (e.g., quality of mental health treatment) and wanted a mechanism to provide feedback, the results could possibly underestimate the health of the force. Some research suggests that passive nonresponders—that is, those individuals who want to participate but simply forget to complete the survey, cannot access it because of technical problems, or miss the deadline because of competing demands—are more closely aligned with responders than those who actively ignore survey requests (Halbesleben and Whitman, 2013). Nonresponse bias is a common problem in survey research (Brick and Williams, 2013; Halbesleben and Whitman, 2013; Sax, Gilmartin, and Bryant, 2003), and as noted earlier, we took the available steps to remedy this potential problem. Nonetheless, because it is not possible to identify nonrespondents in an anonymous survey, the ability to address nonresponse bias and reasons for nonresponse are limited.

Second, because we made edits to survey content, largely in an attempt to shorten the survey, some measures were not comparable to prior HRBS versions. This precluded analysis of historical trends in these cases. However, it may be necessary to continue to revise and focus the HRBS in the future because doing so could have a large effect on the accuracy of survey results and on response rates.

Third, comparison to civilian populations may also be problematic. Even if the military and civilian populations are matched on known demographics that differ between the groups (e.g., gender, age, race/ethnicity, education level), there may be additional unknown factors that also differ and may influence outcomes for health, health-related behaviors, and well-being. Further, it is not always clear what differences between military and civilian populations should be considered acceptable. For example, body mass index (BMI) may actually be higher among service members given the emphasis on strength and physical fitness. We may also expect other behaviors, such as binge drinking or tobacco use, to be higher in the military given its demographic profile (i.e., predominantly young and male). For other health outcomes (e.g., substance use, chronic disease), we may expect lower rates than in the general population. That is, given the general health status of service members and rules and regulations surrounding health and health-related behaviors, we would expect rates of certain negative outcomes to be lower in the military than they are in the general population.

Finally, as with any self-reported survey, responses may reflect social desirability. That is, respondents may feel pressure to answer survey questions that make them appear healthier or confirm that they conform to social norms. This could be especially problematic in a survey like the HRBS, which asks about many sensitive behaviors.

# CHAPTER THREE

# Demographics

This chapter presents key demographics of the 2015 HRBS weighted respondent sample. The chapter is designed to provide context for the substantive chapters that follow.

## Service Branch, Pay Grade, and Gender

By definition of the poststratification weights, the 2015 HRBS weighted respondent sample matches the 2015 HRBS sampling frame on the three sampling strata: service branch, pay grade, and gender. Table 3.1 presents the distribution of these strata from the weighted respondent sample and from a September 2014 sample of the DoD population of active-duty service members, which can be used as a point of comparison.[1] The first column of data includes the Coast Guard portion of the HRBS sample. Because the 2014 DoD comparison population did not include the Coast Guard, the second column in the table uses only respondents from the four DoD services—the Air Force, Army, Marine Corps, and Navy. Finally, Table 3.1 does not include confidence intervals because the respondent sample was weighted to exactly match the sampling frame on service branch, pay grade, and gender.[2]

As seen in the table, the largest portion of both the 2015 HRBS weighted respondent sample and the 2014 DoD population was in the Army (just more than one-third), followed by the Navy, the Air Force, and the Marine Corps. The largest pay grade group was junior enlisted ranks between E1 and E4 (44 percent). Approximately 85 percent of both the HRBS weighted respondent sample and the 2014 DoD population were men.

Although not included in Table 3.1, we also examined the pay grade and gender distributions among only the Coast Guard sample. The Coast Guard was evenly split between the E1–E4 and E5–E6 pay grades (34.2 percent in each), with an additional 10.9 percent senior enlisted (E6–E9), 4.2 percent warrant officers (W1–W5), 9.8 percent junior officers (O1–O3), and 6.6 percent mid-grade and senior officers (O4–O10). The gender distribution of the Coast Guard was similar to that of the DoD services: 84.8 percent men and 15.2 percent women.

---

[1] The 2015 Demographics report was not available at the time of the survey; for the 2014 version of the report, see Office of the Deputy Assistant Secretary of Defense for Military Community and Family Policy, 2014. Note that the Demographics report does not include the Coast Guard in its calculations of active-duty service members (see Chapter 2). The data in that report come from the DMDC master file, which is the source for the last column in Table 3.1 of this report.

[2] For all relevant tables in this report, percentages may not sum exactly to 100 because of rounding.

**Table 3.1**
**Distribution of Service Branch, Pay Grade, and Gender in the 2015 HRBS Weighted Respondent Sample, with 2014 DoD Comparison**

|  | 2015 HRBS Weighted Respondent Sample with Coast Guard (%) | 2015 HRBS Weighted Respondent Sample Without Coast Guard (%) | 2014 DoD Active-Duty Population (%) |
|---|---|---|---|
| Service branch |  |  |  |
| Air Force | 22.3 | 23.0 | 23.6 |
| Army | 37.3 | 38.5 | 38.0 |
| Marine Corps | 14.0 | 14.4 | 14.2 |
| Navy | 23.4 | 24.1 | 24.2 |
| Coast Guard | 3.0 | Excluded[a] | NA[b] |
| Pay grade |  |  |  |
| E1–E4 | 44.2 | 44.5 | 43.2 |
| E5–E6 | 29.1 | 28.9 | 29.1 |
| E6–E9 | 9.4 | 9.4 | 10.0 |
| W1–W5 | 1.5 | 1.4 | 1.5 |
| O1–O3 | 9.7 | 9.7 | 9.9 |
| O4–O10 | 6.2 | 6.2 | 6.4 |
| Gender |  |  |  |
| Men | 84.4 | 84.4 | 84.9 |
| Women | 15.6 | 15.6 | 15.1 |

SOURCE: The information in the first two columns is from the 2015 HRBS; the third column is from Defense Manpower Data Center, 2014.

NOTE: All HRBS data are weighted.

[a] Coast Guard data were not included in this calculation.

[b] NA = not applicable. DoD does not maintain demographic information about the Coast Guard.

Tables 3.2, 3.3, and 3.4 present other cross-tabulations based on the sample strata variables that may be of interest. Note that these tables do not include confidence intervals or use significance tests because the respondent sample was weighted to exactly match the sampling frame on service branch, pay grade, and gender. Key findings include the following:

- Noticeably, the Marine Corps had a larger percentage of junior service members in the enlisted and officer ranks (Table 3.2).
- The Marine Corps had the greatest percentage of men, and the Air Force had the greatest percentage of women (Table 3.3).
- The percentage of women in the junior ranks, both enlisted (E1–E4) and officer (O1–O3) was larger than the percentage of men (Table 3.4), consistent with observed differences in retention rates by gender (Office of the Under Secretary of Defense for Personnel and Readiness, 2015).

**Table 3.2**
**Pay Grade by Service Branch, Weighted Respondent Sample**

|  | Air Force (%) | Army (%) | Marine Corps (%) | Navy (%) | Coast Guard (%) |
|---|---|---|---|---|---|
| E1–E4 | 38.0 | 45.4 | 59.3 | 40.3 | 34.2 |
| E5–E6 | 32.7 | 25.9 | 22.9 | 33.8 | 34.2 |
| E7–E9 | 9.7 | 10.3 | 6.9 | 9.1 | 10.9 |
| W1–W5 | NA[a] | 2.9 | 1.1 | 0.5 | 4.2 |
| O1–O3 | 11.4 | 9.7 | 6.5 | 9.9 | 9.8 |
| O4–O10 | 8.2 | 5.9 | 3.3 | 6.5 | 6.6 |

NOTE: All data are weighted.
[a] NA = not applicable. The Air Force does not use warrant officers.

**Table 3.3**
**Gender by Service Branch, Weighted Respondent Sample**

|  | Air Force (%) | Army (%) | Marine Corps (%) | Navy (%) | Coast Guard (%) |
|---|---|---|---|---|---|
| Men | 80.7 | 85.6 | 92.2 | 81.5 | 84.8 |
| Women | 19.3 | 14.4 | 7.8 | 18.5 | 15.2 |

NOTE: All data are weighted.

**Table 3.4**
**Gender by Pay Grade, Weighted Respondent Sample**

|  | E1–E4 (%) | E5–E6 (%) | E7–E9 (%) | W1–W5 (%) | O1–O3 (%) | O4–O10 (%) |
|---|---|---|---|---|---|---|
| Men | 43.8 | 29.4 | 9.8 | 1.6 | 9.2 | 6.3 |
| Women | 46.2 | 27.3 | 7.3 | 0.8 | 12.5 | 5.8 |

NOTE: All data are weighted.

## Age

Respondents reported age in years. Table 3.5 presents the percentage of service members in each age group in the full 2015 HRBS weighted respondent sample and by service branch, Table 3.6 presents age groups by pay grade, and Table 3.7 presents age groups by gender. Key findings include the following:

- The Marine Corps was characterized by a younger population, whereas the Army and Coast Guard had a larger percentage of members over age 35 (Table 3.5).
- Younger service members were disproportionately found among the lower pay grades, while older service members were found in the higher pay grades (Table 3.6).
- Men were disproportionately represented in the older age groups (age 35 and above) compared with women (Table 3.7).

**Table 3.5**
**Age Groups Total and by Service Branch, Weighted Respondent Sample**

|  | Total | Air Force | Army | Marine Corps | Navy | Coast Guard |
|---|---|---|---|---|---|---|
| Ages 17–24 | 28.7% | 27.7% | 20.9% | 53.6% | 29.1% | 16.1% |
|  | (27.4–30.1) | (26.0–29.3) | (18.0–23.9) | (50.5–56.7) | (26.3–31.8) | (14.8–17.4) |
| Ages 25–34 | 41.9% | 45.3% | 41.6% | 31.6% | 44.3% | 48.9% |
|  | (40.3–43.4) | (43.3–47.4) | (38.4–44.8) | (28.4–34.9) | (41.3–47.4) | (47.3–50.5) |
| Ages 35–44 | 22.5% | 22.6% | 27.4% | 12.1% | 20.2% | 28.0% |
|  | (21.5–23.5) | (21.2–23.9) | (25.1–29.8) | (10.9–13.3) | (18.5–21.8) | (26.9–29.1) |
| Ages 45+ | 6.8% | 4.4% | 10.1% | 2.6% | 6.4% | 7.0% |
|  | (6.3–7.3) | (4.0–4.9) | (8.9–11.2) | (2.3–2.9) | (5.6–7.3) | (6.4–7.5) |

NOTE: All data are weighted. 95-percent confidence intervals are presented in parentheses.

**Table 3.6**
**Age Groups by Pay Grade, Weighted Respondent Sample**

|  | E1–E4 | E5–E6 | E7–E9 | W1–W5 | O1–O3 | O4–O10 |
|---|---|---|---|---|---|---|
| Ages 17–24 | 58.0% | 7.7% | 0.0% | NA | 8.7% | NA |
|  | (55.0–61.0) | (6.4–9.0) | (0.01–0.0) |  | (7.5–10.0) |  |
| Ages 25–34 | 37.6% | 59.2% | 11.9% | 11.8% | 65.1% | 7.5% |
|  | (34.6–40.6) | (56.6–61.9) | (10.2–13.7) | (9.3–14.4) | (62.9–67.3) | (6.4–8.7) |
| Ages 35–44 | 4.0% | 28.9% | 65.7% | 53.1% | 22.8% | 51.5% |
|  | (2.6–5.4) | (26.5–31.4) | (63.0–68.4) | (49.4–56.9) | (20.9–24.8) | (49.1–53.8) |
| Ages 45+ | 0.4% | 4.1% | 22.3% | 35.0% | 3.4% | 41.0% |
|  | (0.0–0.8) | (2.9–5.3) | (19.9–24.7) | (31.5–38.6) | (2.5–4.3) | (38.7–43.4) |

NOTE: All data are weighted. 95-percent confidence intervals are presented in parentheses.

NA = not applicable (zero individuals in the cell).

**Table 3.7**
**Age Groups by Gender, Weighted Respondent Sample**

|  | Men | Women |
|---|---|---|
| Ages 17–24 | 28.6% | 29.6% |
|  | (27.0–30.2) | (27.9–31.3) |
| Ages 25–34 | 41.2% | 45.8% |
|  | (39.4–43.0) | (43.9–47.6) |
| Ages 35–44 | 23.2% | 18.9% |
|  | (22.0–24.4) | (17.8–20.0) |
| Ages 45+ | 7.0% | 5.7% |
|  | (6.5–7.6) | (5.2–6.3) |

NOTE: All data are weighted. 95-percent confidence
intervals are presented in parentheses.

## Race/Ethnicity

Two survey items asked about respondents' ethnicity (Hispanic or Latino, or Not Hispanic or Latino) and race (white, black or African American, American Indian or Alaska Native, Asian, Native Hawaiian or other Pacific Islander). These variables were combined and coded hierarchically such that if a service member responded that he or she was of Hispanic or Latino ethnicity, that identity outweighed any other racial category. Thus, in Table 3.8 (total and by service branch), Table 3.9 (by pay grade), and Table 3.10 (by gender), categories include non-Hispanic white, non-Hispanic black, Hispanic, non-Hispanic Asian, and other (which includes American Indian or Alaska Native, Native Hawaiian, Pacific Islander, and multi-racial). Key findings include the following:

- Although all of the DoD services, as well as the Coast Guard, were predominantly non-Hispanic white, the distribution of minority racial and ethnic groups differed by branch (Table 3.8). The Army and Navy had a larger percentage of non-Hispanic blacks and non-Hispanic Asians; the Marine Corps had a larger percentage of Hispanics; and the Coast Guard, Marine Corps, and Navy had the largest percentage of service members falling into the "other" race/ethnicity category.
- The racial and ethnic distribution across pay grade was different, with more diversity in the lower pay grades, especially among enlisted service members (Table 3.9). Among service members in the most senior officer positions (i.e., O4–O10), 78 percent were non-Hispanic white.
- The racial and ethnic distribution across gender also differed, with a larger percentage of women compared with men in minority racial and ethnic groups, especially non-Hispanic black and other (Table 3.10).

**Table 3.8**
**Race/Ethnicity Total and by Service Branch, Weighted Respondent Sample**

|  | Total | Air Force | Army | Marine Corps | Navy | Coast Guard |
|---|---|---|---|---|---|---|
| Non-Hispanic white | 58.4% (56.8–60.0) | 65.8% (63.7–67.9) | 53.4% (50.1–56.6) | 58.1% (54.0–62.1) | 58.1% (55.0–61.2) | 70.1% (68.5–71.7) |
| Non-Hispanic black | 11.5% (10.5–12.5) | 9.3% (8.0–10.6) | 15.1% (12.9–17.3) | 7.7% (5.6–9.7) | 11.2% (9.3–13.1) | 3.5% (2.9–4.2) |
| Hispanic | 16.4% (15.2–17.8) | 12.7% (11.2–14.3) | 18.4% (15.7–21.1) | 21.1% (17.7–24.6) | 14.6% (12.3–16.0) | 13.9% (12.7–15.2) |
| Non-Hispanic Asian | 5.1% (4.3–5.9) | 3.8% (2.9–4.6) | 5.9% (4.2–7.6) | 3.5% (1.9–5.1) | 6.4% (4.8–7.9) | 1.5% (1.1–1.9) |
| Other | 8.5% (7.7–9.4) | 8.4% (7.2–9.6) | 7.2% (5.7–8.7) | 9.7% (7.2–12.1) | 9.7% (7.7–11.6) | 10.9% (9.8–12.0) |

NOTE: All data are weighted. 95-percent confidence intervals are presented in parentheses.

**Table 3.9**
**Race/Ethnicity by Pay Grade, Weighted Respondent Sample**

|  | E1–E4 | E5–E6 | E7–E9 | W1–W5 | O1–O3 | O4–O10 |
|---|---|---|---|---|---|---|
| Non-Hispanic white | 54.2% (51.1–57.2) | 56.7% (54.0–59.3) | 54.2% (51.5–56.9) | 62.1% (58.4–65.7) | 74.3% (72.3–76.3) | 77.8% (75.8–79.8) |
| Non-Hispanic black | 11.2% (9.3–13.1) | 12.5% (10.7–14.2) | 19.7% (17.4–22.0) | 11.9% (9.5–14.4) | 5.6% (4.6–6.8) | 6.0% (4.8–7.1) |
| Hispanic | 20.2% (17.6–22.7) | 16.1% (14.1–18.1) | 15.2% (13.2–17.3) | 13.5% (10.9–16.0) | 9.4% (8.1–10.7) | 5.9% (4.8–7.0) |
| Non-Hispanic Asian | 6.3% (4.7–7.9) | 4.8% (3.6–6.0) | 2.5% (1.8–3.2) | 2.9% (1.7–4.2) | 3.8% (3.0–4.6) | 3.7% (2.8–4.5) |
| Other | 8.2% (6.7–9.7) | 10.0% (8.4–11.6) | 8.4% (6.9–9.9) | 9.6% (7.4–11.3) | 6.9% (5.8–8.0) | 6.7% (5.4–7.9) |

NOTE: All data are weighted. 95-percent confidence intervals are presented in parentheses.

**Table 3.10**
**Race/Ethnicity by Gender, Weighted Respondent Sample**

|  | Men | Women |
|---|---|---|
| Non-Hispanic white | 59.6% (57.8–61.5) | 51.8% (49.8–53.7) |
| Non-Hispanic black | 10.6% (9.4–11.8) | 16.4% (15.0–17.9) |
| Hispanic | 16.7% (15.2–18.2) | 15.4% (14.0–17.0) |
| Non-Hispanic Asian | 5.0% (4.1–5.9) | 5.4% (4.4–6.4) |
| Other | 8.1% (7.1–9.1) | 10.9% (9.7–12.1) |

NOTE: All data are weighted. 95-percent confidence intervals are presented in parentheses.

## Education Level

One survey question asked respondents about their highest level of education. Response options ranged from "I did not graduate from high school" to "graduate or professional degree." We collapsed these categories into three: high school degree or less (including a General Educational Development [GED] certification), some college (including an associate's degree), and bachelor's degree or above (including graduate and professional degrees, such as a master's, doctorate, or law degree). These distributions among these education levels are shown in Table 3.11 (total and by service branch), Table 3.12 (by pay grade), and Table 3.13 (by gender). Key findings include the following:

- The Marine Corps had more service members with a high school degree or less (Table 3.11). The Army had the largest percentage of service members with a bachelor's degree or more, followed by the Coast Guard and the Air Force. About half of service members across all branches, including the Coast Guard, had some college experience.

- Education level varied with pay grade; enlisted service members were more likely than officers to have a high school degree or less or some college experience (Table 3.12). Conversely, the overwhelming majority of officers had a bachelor's degree or more.
- More men than women had a high school degree or less, and significantly more women than men had a bachelor's degree or more (Table 3.13).

**Table 3.11**
**Education Level Total and by Service Branch, Weighted Respondent Sample**

|  | Total | Air Force | Army | Marine Corps | Navy | Coast Guard |
|---|---|---|---|---|---|---|
| High school or less | 20.4% (19.1–21.8) | 12.3% (10.7–13.9) | 15.7% (13.0–18.4) | 45.4% (41.4–49.4) | 21.2% (18.4–24.0) | 18.1% (16.7–19.5) |
| Some college | 48.5% (47.0–50.1) | 55.8% (53.8–57.7) | 45.6% (42.4–48.8) | 40.7% (36.7–44.6) | 50.8% (47.8–53.9) | 49.8% (48.2–51.4) |
| Bachelor's degree or more | 31.0% (29.8–32.3) | 31.9% (30.6–33.3) | 38.7% (35.9–41.5) | 13.9% (12.6–15.3) | 28.0% (26.0–30.0) | 32.1% (30.7–33.4) |

NOTE: All data are weighted. 95-percent confidence intervals are presented in parentheses.

**Table 3.12**
**Education Level by Pay Grade, Weighted Respondent Sample**

|  | E1–E4 | E5–E6 | E7–E9 | W1–W5 | O1–O3 | O4–O10 |
|---|---|---|---|---|---|---|
| High school or less | 34.6% (31.7–37.4) | 15.1% (13.3–17.0) | 7.4% (6.0–8.8) | 2.7% (1.9–3.6) | 0.3% (0.05–0.5) | 0.04% (0.0–0.1) |
| Some college | 50.5% (47.4–53.5) | 67.8% (65.3–70.3) | 59.4% (56.7–62.1) | 46.6% (42.9–50.4) | 2.0% (1.4–2.6) | 0.7% (0.4–1.0) |
| Bachelor's degree or more | 15.0% (12.7–17.3) | 17.1% (15.0–19.1) | 33.2% (30.6–35.8) | 50.6% (46.9–54.4) | 97.7% (97.1–98.3) | 99.3% (99.0–99.6) |

NOTE: All data are weighted. 95-percent confidence intervals are presented in parentheses.

**Table 3.13**
**Education Level by Gender, Weighted Respondent Sample**

|  | Men | Women |
|---|---|---|
| High school or less | 21.8% (20.2–23.4) | 13.0% (11.6–14.5) |
| Some college | 48.1% (46.3–49.9) | 51.0% (49.2–52.8) |
| Bachelor's degree or more | 30.1% (28.7–31.5) | 35.9% (34.5–37.3) |

NOTE: All data are weighted. 95-percent confidence intervals are presented in parentheses.

## Marital Status

A single survey item asked service members for their current marital status. Table 3.14 (total and by service branch), Table 3.15 (by pay grade), and Table 3.16 (by gender) show the percentage of service members falling into each of the following categories: married, single (including cohabitants), separated or divorced, and widowed. Key findings include the following:

- More service members in the Army and Coast Guard were married, compared with the other service branches (Table 3.14). Conversely, more service members in the Marine Corps were single (or cohabiting), and fewer were divorced or separated. A very small percentage of service members were widowed.
- Rates of marriage were highest in the higher pay grades (both enlisted and officer) and lowest among junior enlisted service members.
- More men than women were married, but more women than men were separated or divorced (Table 3.16).
- Widowhood among service members was extremely rare.

**Table 3.14**
**Marital Status Total and by Service Branch, Weighted Respondent Sample**

|  | Total | Air Force | Army | Marine Corps | Navy | Coast Guard |
|---|---|---|---|---|---|---|
| Married | 57.3% | 56.7% | 62.3% | 48.4% | 54.1% | 65.6% |
|  | (55.8–58.8) | (54.7–58.8) | (59.2–65.5) | (44.5–52.2) | (51.0–57.1) | (64.0–67.2) |
| Single | 35.2% | 35.6% | 28.7% | 48.1% | 38.3% | 27.9% |
|  | (33.7–36.7) | (33.6–37.5) | (25.7–31.7) | (44.2–51.9) | (35.3–41.3) | (26.4–29.5) |
| Separated or divorced | 7.3% | 7.5% | 8.6% | 3.5% | 7.4% | 6.4% |
|  | (6.6–8.0) | (6.5–8.6) | (7.0–10.2) | (2.5–4.6) | (6.1–8.9) | (5.6–7.2) |
| Widowed | 0.2% | 0.2% | 0.4% | 0.02% | 0.2% | 0.04% |
|  | (0.04–0.4) | (0.01–0.4) | (0.0–0.9) | (0.0–0.05) | (0.0–0.4) | (0.0–0.1) |

NOTE: All data are weighted. 95-percent confidence intervals are presented in parentheses.

**Table 3.15**
**Marital Status by Pay Grade, Weighted Respondent Sample**

|  | E1–E4 | E5–E6 | E7–E9 | W1–W5 | O1–O3 | O4–O10 |
|---|---|---|---|---|---|---|
| Married | 40.2%<br>(37.2–43.3) | 66.3%<br>(63.9–68.7) | 81.1%<br>(79.1–83.1) | 86.5%<br>(84.1–88.9) | 62.7%<br>(60.5–64.8) | 85.3%<br>(83.7–86.9) |
| Single | 55.3%<br>(52.3–58.4) | 22.0%<br>(19.9–24.1) | 7.3%<br>(6.0–8.7) | 4.1%<br>(2.7–5.5) | 31.9%<br>(29.8–33.9) | 7.6%<br>(6.5–8.8) |
| Separated or divorced | 4.2%<br>(3.0–5.4) | 11.5%<br>(9.9–13.1) | 11.1%<br>(9.6–12.8) | 9.3%<br>(7.2–11.3) | 5.5%<br>(4.4–6.5) | 6.7%<br>(5.5–7.9) |
| Widowed | 0.2%<br>(0.0–0.6) | 0.2%<br>(0.0–0.5) | 0.4%<br>(0.02–0.7) | 0.2%<br>(0.0–0.6) | NA | 0.4%<br>(0.1–0.7) |

NOTE: All data are weighted. 95-percent confidence intervals are presented in parentheses.

NA = not applicable (zero individuals in the cell).


**Table 3.16**
**Marital Status by Gender, Weighted Respondent Sample**

|  | Men | Women |
|---|---|---|
| Married | 58.8%<br>(57.0–60.6) | 49.3%<br>(47.4–51.2) |
| Single | 35.0%<br>(33.2–36.7) | 36.1%<br>(34.3–38.0) |
| Separated or divorced | 6.0%<br>(5.2–6.8) | 14.4%<br>(13.1–15.7) |
| Widowed | 0.2%<br>(0.03–0.5) | 0.2%<br>(0.1–0.4) |

NOTE: All data are weighted. 95-percent confidence intervals are presented in parentheses.

## Parental Status

Respondents were asked to indicate the number of children under age 18 living in their household for whom they were legally responsible (i.e., dependents). Table 3.17 (total and by service branch), Table 3.18 (by pay grade), and Table 3.19 (by gender) show the percentage of service members reporting at least one dependent in their household. Key findings include the following:

- More service members in the Army and Coast Guard had dependents in the household; fewer in the Marine Corps had dependents (Table 3.17).
- Service members in the higher pay grades, including both enlisted and officers, were more likely to have dependents than those in the lower pay grades (Table 3.18).
- More men than women had dependents under age 18 in the household (Table 3.19).

**Table 3.17**
**Parental Status Total and by Service Branch, Weighted Respondent Sample**

|  | Total | Air Force | Army | Marine Corps | Navy | Coast Guard |
|---|---|---|---|---|---|---|
| Dependent in household | 40.5% (39.1–41.9) | 38.6% (36.7–40.4) | 47.3% (44.2–50.4) | 29.1% (26.2–31.9) | 37.6% (35.1–40.2) | 46.5% (45.0–48.0) |

NOTE: All data are weighted. 95-percent confidence intervals are presented in parentheses.

**Table 3.18**
**Parental Status by Pay Grade, Weighted Respondent Sample**

|  | E1–E4 | E5–E6 | E7–E9 | W1–W5 | O1–O3 | O4–O10 |
|---|---|---|---|---|---|---|
| Dependent in household | 20.9% (18.3–23.5) | 54.3% (51.6–56.9) | 67.4% (64.8–70.0) | 66.6% (63.1–70.1) | 40.5% (38.3–42.7) | 68.4% (66.3–70.6) |

NOTE: All data are weighted. 95-percent confidence intervals are presented in parentheses.

**Table 3.19**
**Parental Status by Gender, Weighted Respondent Sample**

|  | Men | Women |
|---|---|---|
| Dependent in household | 41.5% (39.9–43.2) | 34.9% (33.2–36.7) |

NOTE: All data are weighted. 95-percent confidence intervals are presented in parentheses.

## Housing Status

Finally, the survey asked service members to indicate where they lived at the time of the survey, including both on and off installation options. Table 3.20 (total and by service branch), Table 3.21 (by pay grade), and Table 3.22 (by gender) show the percentage of service members living on an installation in dorms or barracks, other on an installation (including privatized military housing), outside an installation (including privatized military housing, personally mortgaged housing, and rental housing), and in some other housing situation (including with parents or in temporary housing). Key findings include the following:

- More service members in the Marine Corps lived on an installation compared with the other services; the Coast Guard had the fewest members living on an installation and the most living outside an installation, followed by the Navy and the Air Force (Table 3.20).
- Rates of living off an installation increased with pay grade: The greatest number of service members living on an installation was among junior enlisted (E1–E4), and the largest percentage of service members living off an installation was among officers (there were no statistically significant differences between junior and mid-grade or senior officers) (Table 3.21).
- More men lived on an installation, either in dorms or in privatized housing, compared with women; more women than men lived off an installation (Table 3.22).

**Table 3.20**
**Housing Status Total and by Service Branch, Weighted Respondent Sample**

|  | Total | Air Force | Army | Marine Corps | Navy | Coast Guard |
|---|---|---|---|---|---|---|
| Dorms or barracks on an installation | 23.7% (22.3–25.1) | 16.8% (15.1–18.4) | 24.8% (21.8–27.8) | 45.0% (41.2–48.7) | 18.4% (15.8–21.1) | 3.7% (2.9–4.3) |
| Other on an installation | 15.5% (14.3–16.7) | 16.5% (14.8–18.2) | 19.9% (17.3–22.6) | 14.4% (11.8–17.0) | 9.3% (7.4–11.2) | 6.1% (5.2–7.0) |
| Off an installation | 59.5% (58.0–61.0) | 66.3% (64.3–68.3) | 54.3% (51.2–57.4) | 39.3% (35.8–42.8) | 69.9% (67.0–72.7) | 89.1% (88.0–90.3) |
| Other housing situation | 1.3% (0.9–1.7) | 0.5% (0.2–0.8) | 1.0% (0.4–1.7) | 1.3% (0.6–2.1) | 2.4% (1.3–3.5) | 1.1% (0.8–1.5) |

NOTE: All data are weighted. 95-percent confidence intervals are presented in parentheses.

**Table 3.21**
**Housing Status by Pay Grade, Weighted Respondent Sample**

|  | E1–E4 | E5–E6 | E7–E9 | W1–W5 | O1–O3 | O4–O10 |
|---|---|---|---|---|---|---|
| Dorms or barracks on an installation | 46.7% (43.7–49.8) | 8.6% (7.1–10.2) | 2.4% (1.6–3.3) | 4.3% (2.7–5.9) | 2.2% (1.6–2.9) | 0.6% (0.4–0.9) |
| Other on an installation | 14.5% (12.3–16.7) | 16.3% (14.3–18.3) | 18.2% (16.0–20.4) | 20.7% (17.6–23.8) | 12.6% (11.0–14.2) | 17.7% (15.8–19.5) |
| Off an installation | 37.3% (34.4–40.2) | 73.6% (71.2–76.0) | 78.3% (76.0–80.6) | 73.9% (70.6–77.3) | 84.5% (82.8–86.2) | 81.5% (79.6–83.4) |
| Other housing situation | 1.5% (0.7–2.2) | 1.4% (0.8–2.1) | 1.1% (0.6–1.5) | 1.0% (0.3–1.8) | 0.7% (0.3–1.1) | 0.2% (0.1–0.3) |

NOTE: All data are weighted. 95-percent confidence intervals are presented in parentheses.

**Table 3.22**
**Housing Status by Gender, Weighted Respondent Sample**

|  | Men | Women |
|---|---|---|
| Dorms or barracks on an installation | 24.7%<br>(23.1–26.4) | 18.2%<br>(16.6–19.8) |
| Other on an installation | 15.9%<br>(14.5–17.3) | 13.2%<br>(11.9–14.5) |
| Off an installation | 58.1%<br>(56.4–59.9) | 67.2%<br>(65.4–69.0) |
| Other housing situation | 1.3%<br>(0.8–1.7) | 1.4%<br>(0.9–1.9) |

NOTE: All data are weighted. 95-percent confidence intervals are presented in parentheses.

## Summary

By definition of the poststratification weights, the 2015 HRBS weighted respondent sample matches the sample frame on the three sampling strata: service branch, pay grade, and gender. The largest portion of the weighted respondent sample was in the Army, followed by the Navy, Air Force, and Marine Corps. The largest group in terms of pay grade was junior enlisted personnel (E1–E4), followed by mid-grade enlisted personnel (E5–E6), junior officers (O1–O3), senior enlisted (E7–E9), mid-grade and senior officers (O4–O10), and warrant officers (W1–W5). Approximately 85 percent of the HRBS weighted respondent sample was men. The average weighted HRBS respondent was under age 35, was non-Hispanic white, was married with no child in the household, was living off an installation, and had at least some college experience. When reviewing the rest of the report, it is important to keep demographic differences across service branches and the Coast Guard in mind. For example, the Marine Corps—and, to a lesser extent, the Army and Navy—is predominantly composed of young, enlisted men with a high school degree. These characteristics are often highly correlated with health outcomes and health-related behaviors.

# CHAPTER FOUR

# Health Promotion and Disease Prevention

This chapter presents analyses of several health promotion and disease prevention activities among active-duty service members. Specific areas include physical activity, weight status, routine medical care, CAM, sleep health, and supplement use, as well as several health-related risk behaviors, including sedentary time (measured by hours of electronic game play), energy drink use, and texting or emailing while driving.

In addition, we present active-duty service members' progress toward HP2020 objectives—a set of goals designed by HHS to improve the health of the U.S. population (see HHS, 2010a)—for physical exercise, weight management, and sleep health. However, the military has notably different demographics from the general population; for example, active-duty service members are disproportionately younger and male compared with the general population, and individuals enter military service only if it is determined that they are in good general health. These differences may affect the prevalence of some outcomes (e.g., obesity, physical activity) and, therefore, the applicability of the HP2020 objectives. If anything, the HP2020 objectives represent a conservative threshold; that is, one would expect that the thresholds for weight management and physical exercise would be higher in the active-duty population than in the civilian population. Thus, it is important to consider the demographic differences when interpreting comparisons of the active-duty estimates with the general population and civilian benchmarks.

Each section of this chapter reviews the relevance of the health promotion and disease prevention topic to the military and provides estimates by service branch. Key measures used are described in the applicable section, and additional details about these measures can be found in Appendix D. Results are also presented by pay grade, gender, age group, race/ethnicity, and education level. All analyses demonstrated statistically significant omnibus tests (a Rao-Scott chi-square test for categorical variables and $F$-tests for continuous variables) unless otherwise noted in the tables. Statistically significant group differences (pairwise comparisons) are presented within each table. However, only statistically significant differences that the research team's subject-matter experts determined to be substantively meaningful (i.e., could be used to change or develop policy or contribute to inequalities in health outcomes across subgroups) are discussed in the text. Readers should use caution when interpreting comparisons between the 2015 HRBS results and other populations or prior versions of the HRBS because these comparisons are not necessarily statistically significant and could simply reflect sampling variability across the two samples being compared; however, where available, we provide confidence intervals for comparisons.

## Physical Activity

According to HP2020 data, the majority of the U.S. population (80 percent) does not meet national guidelines for physical activity, including muscle-strengthening activities; such activities are important for physical and mental health, including reducing risk of premature death, cardiovascular disease, cancer, and depression (HHS, 2010e). According to the 2008 and 2011 HRBSs (Bray, Pemberton, et al., 2009; Barlas et al., 2013), active-duty service members have met or exceeded civilian recommendations, which is likely a result of physical fitness requirements in the military and the aforementioned demographic differences between service members and the general population.

The armed forces have physical fitness and body fat standards—including for aerobic capacity, muscular strength, muscular endurance, and body fat composition—that are designed to encourage service members to maintain their physical readiness.[1] Service members who do not maintain their physical readiness may be unable to complete assigned tasks. Physical inactivity is also associated with a range of chronic conditions that can adversely affect military readiness, individual quality of life, and health care utilization and costs.

The 2015 HRBS asked respondents about the frequency and duration of moderate physical activity (MPA), vigorous physical activity (VPA), and strength training in the past 30 days. If respondents felt that they had not exercised as much as they would have liked in the past 30 days, they were asked to select the main reason from six common reasons (e.g., work commitments, no access to facilities). There are several HP2020 targets for physical activity, and we compare the HRBS results with these targets when appropriate. Note that we are unable to directly compare the HP2020 goal of two or more days of strength training per week because the HRBS measure was for one or two days per week. We did, however, use a cutoff of three or more days, and we acknowledge that we are thus underestimating the percentage of service members who met the HP2020 target.

Results are presented in Tables 4.1 through 4.6 at the end of this section. Key findings include the following:

- According to survey estimates, the majority of active-duty service members exceeded all of the HP2020 targets for physical activity (Table 4.1). Overall, 64.1 percent of service members engaged in at least 150 minutes of MPA per week, including 25.0 percent who engaged in at least 300 minutes or more. Half (50.0 percent) of service members engaged in at least 75 minutes of VPA per week, including 41.3 percent who engaged in at least 150 minutes. There was notable service-level variation in physical activity. The percentage of service members with at least 300 minutes of MPA was highest in the Army (29.8 percent) and lowest in the Air Force (20.0 percent). The Army also had the largest percentage of respondents with at least 150 minutes of VPA (46.8 percent).

- Nearly half (46.5 percent) of service members engaged in strength training for three or more days per week, on average (Table 4.1). Again, this is a higher criterion than the HP2020 target of two or more days per week. The percentage of service members report-

---

[1]  Military physical fitness tests generally include some combination of push-ups, sit-ups, pull-ups, and a two-mile run, graded by age and gender. Body composition (or body fat composition) is also used by some of the services to assess physical fitness, especially at the time of accession; assessment typically involves measuring different parts of the body (e.g., neck, waist). The 2015 HRBS did not include any of these measures.

ing strength training at least three days per week ranged from 38.5 percent in the Navy to 54.9 percent in the Marine Corps.

- About one-quarter (24.4 percent) of service members indicated that they were able to exercise as much as they would have liked in the past 30 days (Table 4.1). Work commitments were the most frequently endorsed reason for not being able to work out (38.8 percent).
- Men were more likely than women to exercise 300 or more minutes per week (MPA: 26.1 percent compared with 19.2 percent; VPA: 42.9 percent compared with 33.0 percent) and engage in strength training three or more times per week (48.4 percent compared with 36.7 percent) (Table 4.3).
- There were few notable differences in physical activity by pay grade, age group, race/ethnicity, or education level (see Tables 4.2, 4.4, 4.5, and 4.6). Service members aged 17–24 were more likely to report more than 300 minutes of MPA per week (29.0 percent) than those aged 25 and above (Table 4.4).

**Electronic Game Play**

Electronic game play is typically a sedentary activity that is inversely related to physical activity. In addition to limiting time for physical activity, electronic media use (including electronic game play) is associated with time spent sitting, which is a risk factor for many cardiometabolic diseases and mortality independent of time spent exercising (Owen et al., 2010; Stamatakis, Hamer, and Dunstan, 2011). Limited physical activity combined with increased time spent sitting and chronic conditions have numerous negative implications for service members' health and readiness.

The 2015 HRBS asked respondents to indicate, on average, how many hours per day over the past 30 days they played electronic games outside of work or school. They were instructed to include games played on a computer, laptop, phone, tablet (e.g., iPad), or other handheld device (e.g., Nintendo DS) or gaming system (e.g., PlayStation). This item is similar to what appears in the National Health and Nutrition Examination Survey. See Tables 4.1 through 4.6 for results. Key findings include the following:

- The majority of service members (80.5 percent) played electronic games outside of work or school for less than two hours per day (Table 4.1).
- Women (88.3 percent) were more likely than men (79.0 percent) to report playing electronic games for less than two hours per day (Table 4.3).
- There were few notable differences in electronic media by pay grade, age group, race/ethnicity, or education level. Service members aged 17–24 had the lowest percentage reporting playing electronic games for less than two hours per day (67.2 percent) (Table 4.4).

**Table 4.1**
**Past-Month Physical Activity, by Service Branch**

| | Total (1) | Air Force (2) | Army (3) | Marine Corps (4) | Navy (5) | Coast Guard (6) |
|---|---|---|---|---|---|---|
| **HP2020** | | | | | | |
| MPA for at least 150 mins/week or VPA for at least 75 mins/week (HP2020 target: 47.9%) | 73.7% (72.3–75.0) | 73.4%[b,d] (71.5–75.3) | 78.5%[a,d,e] (75.9–81.1) | 76.3%[d] (72.9–79.7) | 64.8%[a,b,c,e] (61.9–67.7) | 71.0%[b,d] (69.4–72.5) |
| MPA for more than 300 mins/week or VPA for at least 150 mins/week (HP2020 target: 31.3%) | 48.2% (46.6–49.8) | 46.4%[b,d] (44.2–48.7) | 53.9%[a,d,e] (50.6–57.1) | 51.5%[d,e] (47.4–55.6) | 39.2%[a,b,c,e] (36.1–42.3) | 44.8%[b,c,d] (43.1–46.5) |
| Muscle-strengthening activities on 3+ days/week[h] (HP2020 target [2+ days/week]: 24.1%) | 46.5% (44.9–48.1) | 48.2%[c,d] (46.0–50.4) | 47.6%[c,d] (44.3–50.9) | 54.9%[a,b,d,e] (50.9–59.0) | 38.5%[a,b,c,e] (35.4–41.6) | 44.6%[c,d] (42.9–46.3) |
| **MPA mins/week** | | | | | | |
| <150 mins/week | 35.9% (34.4–37.4) | 38.0%[b] (35.9–40.2) | 31.4%[a,d,e] (28.4–34.4) | 33.3%[d] (29.5–37.1) | 42.2%[b,c] (39.2–45.3) | 37.8%[b] (36.2–39.5) |
| 150–299 mins/week[f] | 39.1% (37.5–40.7) | 42.0% (39.8–44.2) | 38.8% (35.6–42.0) | 39.1% (35.1–43.1) | 36.8% (33.8–39.9) | 39.2% (37.5–40.8) |
| 300+ mins/week | 25.0% (23.5–26.5) | 20.0%[b,c] (18.1–21.8) | 29.8%[a,d,e] (26.7–32.9) | 27.6%[a,d] (23.9–31.4) | 20.9%[b,c] (18.3–23.6) | 23.0%[b] (21.5–24.4) |
| **VPA mins/week** | | | | | | |
| <75 mins/week | 49.9% (48.3–51.5) | 48.5%[d,e] (46.3–50.7) | 44.7%[d,e] (41.5–47.9) | 47.4%[d] (43.3–51.5) | 60.7%[a,b,c,e] (57.7–63.8) | 52.9%[a,b,d] (51.2–54.6) |
| 75–149 mins/week | 8.7% (7.8–9.7) | 10.5%[d] (9.2–11.9) | 8.5% (6.7–10.4) | 8.8% (6.4–11.2) | 7.3%[a] (5.7–9.0) | 9.2% (8.2–10.3) |
| 150+ mins/week | 41.3% (39.7–42.9) | 41.0%[b,d] (38.8–43.2) | 46.8%[a,d,e] (43.5–50.1) | 43.9%[d] (39.8–47.9) | 31.9%[a,b,c,e] (28.9–34.9) | 37.8%[b,d] (36.2–39.5) |
| **Strength training** | | | | | | |
| <1 day/week | 28.9% (27.5–30.3) | 26.0%[d] (24.1–27.9) | 25.9%[d] (23.1–28.7) | 26.4%[d] (22.8–30.0) | 37.8%[a,b,c,e] (34.8–40.8) | 29.1%[d] (27.6–30.7) |
| 1–2 days/week | 24.6% (23.2–25.9) | 25.8%[c] (24.0–27.7) | 26.5%[c] (23.6–29.3) | 18.7%[a,b,e] (15.7–21.7) | 23.7% (21.1–26.3) | 26.2%[c] (24.8–27.7) |
| 3+ days/week | 46.5% (44.9–48.1) | 48.2%[c,d] (46.0–50.4) | 47.6%[c,d] (44.3–50.9) | 54.9%[a,b,d,e] (50.9–59.0) | 38.5%[a,b,c,e] (35.4–41.6) | 44.6%[c,d] (42.9–46.3) |

**Table 4.1—Continued**

| | Total (1) | Air Force (2) | Army (3) | Marine Corps (4) | Navy (5) | Coast Guard (6) |
|---|---|---|---|---|---|---|
| **Reasons for not exercising9** | | | | | | |
| I have exercised as much as I would like | 24.4% (22.9–25.8) | 25.8% (23.8–27.8) | 25.1% (22.1–28.0) | 28.0% (24.1–31.8) | 19.9% (17.3–22.4) | 22.4% (20.9–23.9) |
| No access to facilities | 1.0% (0.7–1.3) | 0.7% (0.3–1.1) | 0.8% (0.3–1.3) | 1.4% (0.4–2.5) | 1.1% (0.3–1.9) | 2.5% (1.9–3.0) |
| Disabilities or injuries | 14.9% (13.7–16.0) | 12.3% (10.9–13.7) | 20.8% (18.2–23.4) | 13.6% (10.9–16.3) | 9.5% (7.8–11.2) | 8.1% (7.2–9.0) |
| Work commitments | 38.8% (37.3–40.3) | 38.4% (36.3–40.5) | 33.8% (30.7–36.8) | 39.4% (35.5–43.3) | 46.9% (43.8–50.1) | 38.0% (36.4–39.7) |
| Family commitments | 10.0% (9.1–11.0) | 10.2% (8.9–11.5) | 9.8% (7.8–11.8) | 6.3% (4.6–8.0) | 11.6% (9.6–13.6) | 17.2% (16.0–18.5) |
| Cost | 0.6% (0.3–0.9) | 0.2% (0.0–0.5) | 0.8% (0.1–1.6) | 0.7% (0.0–1.4) | 0.5% (0.1–1.0) | 0.9% (0.6–1.3) |
| Other | 10.3% (9.4–11.3) | 12.3% (10.8–13.8) | 8.9% (7.0–10.7) | 10.6% (8.0–13.3) | 10.5% (8.6–12.4) | 10.8% (9.7–11.9) |
| **Electronic game play** | | | | | | |
| Played less than 2 hours/day | 80.5%[e] (79.1–81.9) | 80.8%[e] (78.9–82.7) | 81.0% (78.2–83.8) | 75.9%[e] (72.2–79.7) | 81.4% (78.7–84.1) | 84.9%[a,c] (83.6–86.2) |

NOTE: All data are weighted. 95-percent confidence intervals are presented in parentheses.

[a] Estimate is significantly different from the estimate in column 2 (Air Force).

[b] Estimate is significantly different from the estimate in column 3 (Army).

[c] Estimate is significantly different from the estimate in column 4 (Marine Corps).

[d] Estimate is significantly different from the estimate in column 5 (Navy).

[e] Estimate is significantly different from the estimate in column 6 (Coast Guard).

[f] The omnibus chi-square test was not statistically significant (p > 0.05).

[g] No statistical tests were performed.

[h] The HP2020 goal is for two or more days per week, but the HRBS measure cannot be disaggregated this way. Instead, it represents strength training of three or more days per week, which thus underestimates the percentage of service members meeting the HP2020 goal.

**Table 4.2**
**Past-Month Physical Activity, by Pay Grade**

| | E1–E4 (1) | E5–E6 (2) | E7–E9 (3) | W1–W5 (4) | O1–O3 (5) | O4–O10 (6) |
|---|---|---|---|---|---|---|
| **MPA mins/week** | | | | | | |
| <150 mins/week | 32.1% [b,e,f] (29.3–35.0) | 37.9% [a,f] (35.3–40.4) | 37.2% [f] (34.6–39.9) | 38.4% (34.7–42.1) | 39.9% [a] (37.7–42.1) | 44.2% [a,b,c] (41.9–46.6) |
| 150–299 mins/week | 38.9% (35.9–41.9) | 38.8% (36.2–41.4) | 42.8% [f] (40.1–45.6) | 42.7% (39.0–46.4) | 38.0% (35.8–40.2) | 37.2% [c] (34.9–39.5) |
| 300+ mins/week | 28.9% [b,c,d,e,f] (26.1–31.8) | 23.4% [a,f] (21.0–25.7) | 19.9% [a] (17.6–22.2) | 18.9% [a] (16.0–21.9) | 22.1% [a] (20.1–24.0) | 18.5% [a,b] (16.7–20.4) |
| **VPA mins/week** | | | | | | |
| <75 mins/week | 47.6% [c,d] (44.6–50.7) | 51.5% [d] (48.9–54.2) | 54.7% [a,e] (52.0–57.4) | 58.3% [a,b,f] (54.6–62.0) | 48.4% [c,d] (46.2–50.6) | 51.6% [d] (49.2–54.0) |
| 75–149 mins/week[g] | 9.2% (7.4–10.9) | 8.0% (6.6–9.5) | 8.0% (6.5–9.5) | 9.5% (7.3–11.7) | 10.0% (8.6–11.3) | 8.1% (6.8–9.4) |
| 150+ mins/week | 43.2% [d] (40.1–46.3) | 40.4% [d] (37.8–43.0) | 37.3% (34.7–40.0) | 32.2% [a,b,f] (28.6–35.7) | 41.6% [d] (39.4–43.8) | 40.3% [d] (38.0–42.6) |
| **Strength training** | | | | | | |
| <1 day/week | 27.5% [c,f] (24.7–30.2) | 28.9% (26.6–31.2) | 33.0% [a,e] (30.4–35.6) | 33.8% [e] (30.3–37.4) | 27.8% [c,d,f] (25.8–29.8) | 33.2% [a,e] (31.0–35.4) |
| 1–2 days/week | 22.1% [e,f] (19.5–24.6) | 24.9% [f] (22.6–27.3) | 26.9% (24.5–29.4) | 26.2% (22.9–29.5) | 28.6% [a] (26.6–30.6) | 30.7% [a,b] (28.5–32.8) |
| 3+ days/week | 50.5% [c,d,e,f] (47.4–53.6) | 46.2% [c,f] (43.5–48.8) | 40.1% [a,b] (37.3–42.8) | 39.9% [a] (36.2–43.5) | 43.6% [a,f] (41.3–45.8) | 36.2% [a,b,e] (33.8–38.5) |
| **Reasons for not exercising[h]** | | | | | | |
| I have exercised as much as I would like | 29.6% (26.8–32.4) | 21.6% (19.3–23.8) | 21.5% (19.2–23.9) | 18.3% (15.5–21.1) | 16.9% (15.2–18.6) | 17.6% (15.7–19.5) |
| No access to facilities | 1.1% (0.5–1.7) | 1.0% (0.4–1.5) | 0.7% (0.2–1.3) | 1.0% (0.3–1.7) | 1.2% (0.7–1.6) | 0.5% (0.1–0.8) |
| Disabilities or injuries | 13.0% (10.9–15.2) | 17.4% (15.3–19.5) | 24.0% (21.5–26.4) | 23.1% (19.9–26.3) | 8.6% (7.2–9.9) | 10.1% (8.7–11.6) |
| Work commitments | 33.9% (31.0–36.9) | 39.0% (36.4–41.6) | 36.2% (33.6–38.8) | 38.3% (34.7–42.0) | 53.7% (51.5–56.0) | 53.2% (50.9–55.6) |
| Family commitments | 8.6% (6.8–10.4) | 11.6% (10.0–13.3) | 8.9% (7.5–10.3) | 10.3% (8.0–12.5) | 11.0% (9.6–12.5) | 12.8% (11.3–14.4) |

**Table 4.2—Continued**

| | E1–E4 (1) | E5–E6 (2) | E7–E9 (3) | W1–W5 (4) | O1–O3 (5) | O4–O10 (6) |
|---|---|---|---|---|---|---|
| Cost | 1.0% (0.3–1.7) | 0.2% (0.0–0.4) | 0.7% (0.2–1.3) | 0.1% (0.0–0.2) | 0.2% (0.0–0.4) | 0.1% (0.0–0.3) |
| Other | 12.7% (10.8–14.6) | 9.2% (7.7–10.7) | 8.0% (6.5–9.4) | 8.9% (6.7–11.1) | 8.4% (7.2–9.6) | 5.6% (4.5–6.7) |
| Electronic game play | | | | | | |
| Played less than 2 hours/day | 72.0%[b,c,d,e,f] (69.2–74.8) | 83.9%[a,d,e,f] (81.9–85.9) | 87.4%[a,e,f] (85.4–89.4) | 91.0%[a,b,f] (88.9–93.2) | 91.5%[a,b,c,f] (90.1–92.8) | 94.9%[a,b,c,d,e] (93.8–96.0) |

NOTE: All data are weighted. 95-percent confidence intervals are presented in parentheses.

[a] Estimate is significantly different from the estimate in column 1 (E1–E4).

[b] Estimate is significantly different from the estimate in column 2 (E5–E6).

[c] Estimate is significantly different from the estimate in column 3 (E7–E9).

[d] Estimate is significantly different from the estimate in column 4 (W1–W5).

[e] Estimate is significantly different from the estimate in column 5 (O1–O3).

[f] Estimate is significantly different from the estimate in column 6 (O4–O10).

[g] At the aggregate, the chi-square test was statistically significant; however, none of the individual pairwise comparisons was.

[h] No statistical tests were performed.

**Table 4.3**
**Past-Month Physical Activity, by Gender**

| | Men (1) | Women (2) |
|---|---|---|
| **MPA mins/week** | | |
| <150 mins/week | 35.2%[a] (33.4–36.9) | 39.7% (37.8–41.5) |
| 150–299 mins/week[b] | 38.7% (36.9–40.6) | 41.1% (39.2–43.0) |
| 300+ mins/week | 26.1%[a] (24.4–27.8) | 19.2% (17.7–20.7) |
| **VPA mins/week** | | |
| <75 mins/week | 48.4%[a] (46.5–50.2) | 58.2% (56.3–60.1) |
| 75–149 mins/week[b] | 8.7% (7.7–9.8) | 8.8% (7.7–10.0) |
| 150+ mins/week | 47.9%[a] (41.0–44.7) | 33.0% (31.2–34.8) |
| **Strength training** | | |
| <1 day/week | 27.9%[a] (26.3–29.6) | 34.1% (32.2–35.9) |
| 1–2 days/week | 23.7%[a] (22.1–25.3) | 29.2% (27.5–30.9) |
| 3+ days/week | 48.4%[a] (46.5–50.2) | 36.7% (34.9–38.6) |
| **Reasons for not exercising[c]** | | |
| I have exercised as much as I would like | 25.3% (23.6–27.0) | 19.1% (17.6–20.7) |
| No access to facilities | 1.0% (0.7–1.4) | 0.7% (0.4–1.1) |
| Disabilities or injuries | 14.4% (13.1–15.8) | 17.3% (15.9–18.8) |
| Work commitments | 39.3% (37.6–41.1) | 35.9% (34.1–37.7) |
| Family commitments | 9.9% (8.8–11.0) | 10.7% (9.6–11.9) |
| Cost | 0.6% (0.3–1.0) | 0.5% (0.2–0.8) |
| Other | 9.3% (8.2–10.4) | 15.7% (14.3–17.2) |
| **Electronic game play** | | |
| Played less than 2 hours/day | 79.0%[a] (77.4–80.7) | 88.3% (86.9–89.6) |

NOTE: All data are weighted. 95-percent confidence intervals are presented in parentheses.

[a] Estimate is significantly different from the estimate in column 2 (women).

[b] At the aggregate, the chi-square test was statistically significant; however, none of the individual pairwise comparisons was.

[c] No statistical tests were performed.

**Table 4.4**
**Past-Month Physical Activity, by Age Group**

| | Ages 17–24 (1) | Ages 25–34 (2) | Ages 35–44 (3) | Ages 45+ (4) |
|---|---|---|---|---|
| **MPA mins/week** | | | | |
| <150 mins/week | 34.2%[d] (30.8–37.5) | 35.3%[d] (33.0–37.6) | 37.3% (34.7–39.8) | 41.8%[a,b] (37.9–45.7) |
| 150–299 mins/week | 36.8% (33.5–40.2) | 39.5% (37.0–42.0) | 41.9% (39.2–44.5) | 37.2% (33.5–41.0) |
| 300+ mins/week | 29.0%[c,d] (25.6–32.3) | 25.2% (22.9–27.5) | 20.9%[a] (18.4–23.3) | 21.0%[a] (17.8–24.1) |
| **VPA mins/week** | | | | |
| <75 mins/week | 46.4%[c,d] (42.9–49.9) | 49.2%[d] (46.7–51.7) | 53.5%[a] (50.8–56.2) | 56.9%[a,b] (53.0–60.7) |
| 75–149 mins/week | 10.7%[d] (8.5–12.9) | 8.4% (7.1–9.6) | 7.6% (6.1–9.2) | 6.6%[a] (4.7–8.4) |
| 150+ mins/week[e] | 42.9% (39.3–46.4) | 42.4% (39.9–44.9) | 38.8% (36.2–41.5) | 36.5% (32.8–40.2) |
| **Strength training** | | | | |
| <1 day/week | 26.5%[d] (23.4–29.6) | 28.6%[d] (26.3–30.9) | 29.6%[d] (27.4–31.9) | 38.0%[a,b,c] (34.2–41.8) |
| 1–2 days/week | 22.3%[c] (19.4–25.2) | 23.4%[c] (21.3–25.5) | 29.1%[a,b] (26.6–31.6) | 26.9% (23.2–30.5) |
| 3+ days/week | 51.3%[c,d] (47.7–54.8) | 48.0%[c,d] (45.5–50.5) | 41.3%[a,b,d] (38.5–44.0) | 35.1%[a,b,c] (31.5–38.8) |
| **Reasons for not exercising[f]** | | | | |
| I have exercised as much as I would like | 31.3% (28.0–34.7) | 23.2% (21.0–25.4) | 18.7% (16.5–20.8) | 21.1% (18.1–24.1) |
| No access to facilities | 1.3% (0.5–2.2) | 1.0% (0.6–1.5) | 0.7% (0.3–1.1) | 0.3% (0.0–0.5) |
| Disabilities or injuries | 9.7% (7.4–11.9) | 13.9% (12.0–15.8) | 20.5% (18.2–22.8) | 24.3% (20.8–27.9) |
| Work commitments | 37.3% (33.9–40.7) | 39.2% (36.8–41.6) | 39.7% (37.1–42.4) | 39.4% (35.6–43.2) |
| Family commitments | 5.7% (4.1–7.3) | 12.3% (10.6–14.0) | 12.6% (10.8–14.3) | 6.0% (4.8–7.3) |
| Cost | 0.8% (0.0–1.6) | 0.8% (0.3–1.3) | 0.2% (0.0–0.3) | 0.2% (0.0–0.5) |
| Other | 13.9% (11.5–16.2) | 9.6% (8.2–11.0) | 7.7% (6.3–9.0) | 8.6% (6.1–11.2) |
| **Electronic game play** | | | | |
| Played less than 2 hours/day | 67.2%[b,c,d] (63.8–70.6) | 83.5%[a,c,d] (81.5–85.5) | 88.1%[a,b,d] (86.0–90.1) | 92.5%[a,b,c] (90.3–94.7) |

NOTE: All data are weighted. 95-percent confidence intervals are presented in parentheses.

[a] Estimate is significantly different from the estimate in column 1 (ages 17–24).

[b] Estimate is significantly different from the estimate in column 2 (ages 25–34).

[c] Estimate is significantly different from the estimate in column 3 (ages 35–44).

[d] Estimate is significantly different from the estimate in column 4 (ages 45+).

[e] At the aggregate, the chi-square test was statistically significant; however, none of the individual pairwise comparisons was.

[f] No statistical tests were performed.

**Table 4.5**
**Past-Month Physical Activity, by Race/Ethnicity**

| | Non-Hispanic White (1) | Non-Hispanic Black (2) | Hispanic (3) | Non-Hispanic Asian (4) | Other (5) |
|---|---|---|---|---|---|
| **MPA mins/week** | | | | | |
| <150 mins/week[f] | 36.5% (34.6–38.5) | 34.1% (29.7–38.5) | 33.5% (29.3–37.6) | 36.9% (29.3–44.6) | 37.7% (32.9–42.5) |
| 150–299 mins/week[f] | 38.5% (36.5–40.5) | 44.0% (39.2–48.7) | 38.2% (34.0–42.4) | 38.8% (30.8–46.8) | 38.5% (33.5–43.6) |
| 300+ mins/week[f] | 24.9% (23.1–26.8) | 21.9% (17.6–26.3) | 28.3% (24.3–32.4) | 24.3% (16.9–31.6) | 23.8% (19.1–28.5) |
| **VPA mins/week** | | | | | |
| <75 mins/week[f] | 49.0% (47.0–51.0) | 54.6% (49.8–59.4) | 46.2% (41.8–50.5) | 57.6% (49.5–65.7) | 52.1% (46.9–57.3) |
| 75–149 mins/week[f] | 9.7% (8.5–10.8) | 6.7% (4.2–9.3) | 8.3% (6.1–10.5) | 5.8% (2.2–9.3) | 7.9% (4.6–11.2) |
| 150+ mins/week[f] | 41.3% (39.3–43.4) | 38.6% (33.9–43.4) | 45.5% (41.1–49.9) | 36.6% (28.7–44.5) | 40% (35.0–45.0) |
| **Strength training** | | | | | |
| <1 day/week | 30.7%[c] (28.8–32.5) | 29.2% (24.8–33.5) | 23.4%[a] (19.8–27.0) | 29.3% (22.0–36.7) | 26.7% (22.4–31.0) |
| 1–2 days/week[g] | 25.0% (23.3–26.7) | 24.5% (20.5–28.5) | 21.4% (17.8–24.9) | 24.3% (17.5–31.2) | 27.9% (23.1–32.7) |
| 3+ days/week | 44.3%[c] (42.3–46.3) | 46.3% (41.5–51.1) | 55.2%[a,e] (50.9–59.6) | 46.3% (38.1–54.5) | 45.4%[c] (40.2–50.5) |
| **Reasons for not exercising[h]** | | | | | |
| I have exercised as much as I would like | 23.8% (21.9–25.6) | 28.1% (23.9–32.3) | 25.2% (21.4–29.1) | 28.9% (21.2–36.6) | 18.8% (14.9–22.7) |
| No access to facilities | 0.9% (0.6–1.3) | 0.9% (0.0–1.8) | 1.7% (0.4–3.0) | 0.8% (0.0–1.8) | 0.3% (0.1–0.5) |
| Disabilities or injuries | 15.1% (13.6–16.6) | 16.2% (12.7–19.7) | 12.4% (9.6–15.2) | 15.4% (9.0–21.9) | 15.5% (11.6–19.4) |
| Work commitments | 39.8% (37.9–41.8) | 32.4% (27.8–37.0) | 39.4% (35.1–43.7) | 36.8% (29.2–44.5) | 40.8% (35.7–45.9) |
| Family commitments | 10.5% (9.3–11.7) | 9.5% (6.6–12.4) | 8.7% (6.4–11.0) | 6.5% (2.8–10.3) | 12.2% (8.6–15.9) |

**Table 4.5—Continued**

| | Non-Hispanic White (1) | Non-Hispanic Black (2) | Hispanic (3) | Non-Hispanic Asian (4) | Other (5) |
|---|---|---|---|---|---|
| Cost | 0.5% (0.1–0.8) | 0.4% (0.0–0.7) | 1.3% (0.0–2.7) | 0.2% (0.0–0.6) | 0.7% (0.0–1.4) |
| Other | 9.3% (8.2–10.5) | 12.6% (9.2–15.9) | 11.2% (8.5–14.0) | 11.2% (6.3–16.1) | 11.7% (8.5–14.8) |
| **Electronic game play** | | | | | |
| Played less than 2 hours/day | 82.1%[c] (80.4–83.9) | 80.9% (76.8–85.0) | 74.3%[a] (70.1–78.5) | 81.2% (75.0–87.5) | 80.0% (75.6–84.3) |

NOTE: All data are weighted. 95-percent confidence intervals are presented in parentheses.

[a] Estimate is significantly different from the estimate in column 1 (non-Hispanic white).

[b] Estimate is significantly different from the estimate in column 2 (non-Hispanic black).

[c] Estimate is significantly different from the estimate in column 3 (Hispanic).

[d] Estimate is significantly different from the estimate in column 4 (non-Hispanic Asian).

[e] Estimate is significantly different from the estimate in column 5 (other).

[f] The omnibus chi-square test was not statistically significant (p > 0.05).

[g] At the aggregate, the chi-square test was statistically significant; however, none of the individual pairwise comparisons was.

[h] No statistical tests were performed.

**Table 4.6**
**Past-Month Physical Activity, by Education Level**

| | High School or Less (1) | Some College (2) | Bachelor's Degree or More (3) |
|---|---|---|---|
| **MPA mins/week** | | | |
| <150 mins/week[d] | 35.6% (31.6–39.6) | 36.1% (33.8–38.3) | 35.8% (33.7–37.9) |
| 150–299 mins/week[d] | 35.7% (31.7–39.7) | 39.5% (37.2–41.8) | 40.7% (38.3–43.1) |
| 300+ mins/week[d] | 28.7% (24.7–32.7) | 24.4% (22.3–26.6) | 23.5% (21.3–25.7) |
| **VPA mins/week** | | | |
| <75 mins/week[d] | 50.7% (46.5–54.9) | 49.2% (46.9–51.6) | 50.5% (48.1–52.8) |
| 75–149 mins/week[d] | 8.1% (5.9–10.4) | 9.2% (7.8–10.5) | 8.5% (7.2–9.8) |
| 150+ mins/week[u] | 41.1% (37.0–45.3) | 41.6% (39.3–44.0) | 41.0% (38.7–43.4) |
| **Strength training** | | | |
| <1 day/week[e] | 30.5% (26.7–34.4) | 29.5% (27.3–31.6) | 26.8% (24.9–28.7) |
| 1–2 days/week | 19.3%[c] (16.0–22.6) | 23.2%[c] (21.2–25.1) | 30.3%[a,b] (28.0–32.5) |
| 3+ days/week | 50.2%[c] (46.0–54.4) | 47.3%[c] (45.0–49.7) | 42.9%[a,b] (40.5–45.3) |
| **Reasons for not exercising[f]** | | | |
| I have exercised as much as I would like | 30.7% (26.8–34.6) | 23.3% (21.3–25.4) | 21.8% (19.6–24.0) |
| No access to facilities | 0.6% (0.0–1.2) | 1.2% (0.7–1.8) | 0.9% (0.5–1.3) |
| Disabilities or injuries | 14.2% (11.1–17.2) | 16.4% (14.7–18.1) | 13.0% (11.3–14.6) |
| Work commitments | 34.6% (30.7–38.5) | 36.3% (34.0–38.5) | 45.6% (43.2–47.9) |
| Family commitments | 6.2% (4.2–8.1) | 11.5% (10.0–13.0) | 10.3% (8.9–11.8) |
| Cost | 1.1% (0.0–2.3) | 0.5% (0.2–0.8) | 0.5% (0.0–1.0) |
| Other | 12.6% (9.8–15.4) | 10.8% (9.4–12.2) | 8.0% (6.8–9.2) |
| **Electronic game play** | | | |
| Played less than 2 hours/day | 68.2%[b,c] (64.2–72.2) | 80.2%[a,c] (78.2–82.2) | 88.9%[a,b] (87.1–90.8) |

NOTE: All data are weighted. 95-percent confidence intervals are presented in parentheses.

[a] Estimate is significantly different from the estimate in column 1 (high school or less).

[b] Estimate is significantly different from the estimate in column 2 (some college).

[c] Estimate is significantly different from the estimate in column 3 (bachelor's degree or more).

[d] The omnibus chi-square test was not statistically significant ($p > 0.05$).

[e] At the aggregate, the chi-square test was statistically significant; however, none of the individual pairwise comparisons was.

[f] No statistical tests were performed.

## Weight Status

According to HHS data, more than one-third of the U.S. adult population is obese (HHS, 2010d). Obesity is a risk factor for early mortality and many chronic diseases, including cardiovascular disease and cancer (National Institutes of Health, 1998). DoD has body fat standards—including for aerobic capacity, muscular strength, muscular endurance, and body fat composition—that are designed to encourage service members to maintain their physical readiness (DoD, 2002), and service members who do not maintain their physical readiness may be unable to complete their assigned tasks. Overweight or obese personnel reduce over-all force fitness and readiness and pose policy issues for military recruitment, retention, and the standards used to qualify or disqualify individuals from service. In addition to directly affecting readiness, overweight or obese status is associated with morbidities (e.g., diabetes, asthma, hypertension, joint pain) that adversely affect readiness and health care utilization and costs. Recent estimates suggest that the prevalence of obesity doubled among service members (from 10 to 20 percent) between 2001 and 2008 (Rush, LeardMann, and Crum-Cianflone, 2016). Service members who were obese were more likely than normal-weight individuals to have hypertension, diabetes, and sleep apnea (Rush, LeardMann, and Crum-Cianflone, 2016). Maintaining a healthy weight and reducing overweight and obesity is important for the military and is included as one of HP2020's goals for the nation.

Weight status in the 2015 HRBS was based on BMI, which was calculated from two standard items that asked respondents to report their height and weight. We then categorized BMI into weight status categories using Centers for Disease Control and Prevention (CDC) criteria. The CDC calculates BMI as a person's weight in kilograms (kg) divided by the square of height in meters ($m^2$) (CDC, 2015a). The categories for service members aged 20 or older were as follows:

- underweight (less than 18.5 $kg/m^2$)
- normal weight (18.5–24.9 $kg/m^2$)
- overweight (25.0–29.9 $kg/m^2$)
- obese (30 or more $kg/m^2$).

For service members younger than age 20, weight categories were based on age and sex-specific definitions established by the CDC (CDC, 2015b). It is important to note that BMI is an indirect measure of body fat, and muscular service members may have been misclassified as overweight or obese. Recent research on male firefighters, who may be more similar to military personnel than other occupational cohorts, found significant misclassification, both false positive and false negative, of obesity when comparing BMI-based measures with more-sensitive measures, including percent body fat and waist circumference (Jitnarin et al., 2014).

Weight status results are presented in Tables 4.7 through 4.12. Key findings include the following:

- The HP2020 target for healthy weight is at least 33.9 percent of the adult population (HHS, 2010d). Overall, 32.5 percent of active-duty service members aged 20 or older were a normal weight, which is slightly below the HP2020 target and similar to the 2011 HRBS normal-weight estimate (34.7 percent; CI: 33.9–35.5) (Barlas et al., 2013) (Table 4.7). The Air Force (35.3 percent) and Marine Corps (37.8 percent) exceeded the HP2020 target for healthy weight.

- The HP2020 target for obesity prevalence is at or below 30.5 percent of the adult population (HHS, 2010d). Many fewer active-duty service members aged 20 or older were obese (15.0 percent), easily achieving the HP2020 obesity target. The prevalence of obesity among those aged 20 or older ranged from 6.7 percent in the Marine Corps to 18.5 percent in the Army (Table 4.7).
- Among all active-duty service members aged 17 or older, 0.5 percent were underweight, 33.8 percent were normal weight, 51.0 percent were overweight, and 14.7 percent were obese (Table 4.7). The prevalence of healthy (normal) weight ranged from 30.3 percent in the Army to 38.9 percent in the Marine Corps. The prevalence of obesity among active-duty service members aged 17 or older ranged from 6.4 percent in the Marine Corps to 18.0 percent in the Army.
- The prevalence of healthy (normal) weight decreased and the prevalence of obesity increased with increasing pay grade among enlisted service members and officers (Table 4.8).
- Women were more likely to be a healthy (normal) weight (52.2 percent) than men (30.4 percent) (Table 4.9). Women were also less likely than men to be categorized as obese (8.0 percent compared with 15.9 percent).
- As expected, the prevalence of healthy weight decreased with increasing age (Table 4.10).

## Table 4.7
## Weight Status, by Service Branch

|  | Total (1) | Air Force (2) | Army (3) | Marine Corps (4) | Navy (5) | Coast Guard (6) |
|---|---|---|---|---|---|---|
| HP2020 |  |  |  |  |  |  |
| Obesity among those aged 20+ (HP2020 target: 30.5% or less) | 15.0% (13.9–16.2) | 13.6%[b,c] (12.1–15.1) | 18.5%[a,c,e] (16.0–21.0) | 6.7%[a,b,d,e] (4.8–8.7) | 16.0%[c] (13.7–18.2) | 13.2%[b,c] (12.1–14.2) |
| Healthy (normal) weight among those aged 20+ (HP2020 target: 33.9% or more) | 32.5% (31.0–34.0) | 35.3%[b,e] (33.2–37.3) | 28.5%[a,c] (25.5–31.4) | 37.8%[b,e] (33.8–41.9) | 33.4% (30.5–36.4) | 31.3%[a,c] (29.7–32.9) |
| Weight categories |  |  |  |  |  |  |
| Underweight | 0.5% (0.3–0.7) | 0.7% (0.3–1.1) | 0.2%[d] (0.1–0.4) | 0.2%[d] (0.0–0.3) | 1.0%[b,c] (0.2–1.8) | 0.3% (0.1–0.4) |
| Normal weight | 33.8% (32.3–35.3) | 36.1%[b,e] (34.1–38.2) | 30.3%[a,c] (27.3–33.3) | 38.9%[b,e] (34.9–42.9) | 34.4% (31.4–37.4) | 31.9%[a,c] (30.3–33.5) |
| Overweight | 51.0% (49.4–52.6) | 49.8%[e] (47.6–52.0) | 51.4% (48.1–54.7) | 54.5% (50.4–58.6) | 48.9%[e] (45.8–52.0) | 54.7%[a,d] (53.0–56.4) |
| Obese | 14.7% (13.5–15.8) | 13.3%[b,c] (11.9–14.8) | 18.0%[a,c,e] (15.6–20.4) | 6.4%[a,b,d,e] (4.5–8.3) | 15.7%[c] (13.5–17.9) | 13.1%[b,c] (12.1–14.1) |

NOTE: All data are weighted. 95-percent confidence intervals are presented in parentheses.

[a] Estimate is significantly different from the estimate in column 2 (Air Force).

[b] Estimate is significantly different from the estimate in column 3 (Army).

[c] Estimate is significantly different from the estimate in column 4 (Marine Corps).

[d] Estimate is significantly different from the estimate in column 5 (Navy).

[e] Estimate is significantly different from the estimate in column 6 (Coast Guard).

**Table 4.8**
**Weight Status, by Pay Grade**

|  | E1–E4 (1) | E5–E6 (2) | E7–E9 (3) | W1–W5 (4) | O1–O3 (5) | O4–O10 (6) |
|---|---|---|---|---|---|---|
| Underweight[g] | 0.8% (0.3–1.2) | 0.3% (0.1–0.5) | 0.5% (0.1–0.8) | 0.6% (0.0–1.2) | 0.3% (0.1–0.5) | 0.3% (0.1–0.4) |
| Normal weight | 42.7%[b,c,d,f] (39.7–45.7) | 25.7%[a,c,d,e] (23.4–27.9) | 17.6%[a,b,e,f] (15.6–19.6) | 19.3%[a,b,e,f] (16.4–22.2) | 38.1%[b,c,d,f] (36.0–40.2) | 29.8%[a,c,d,e] (27.8–31.8) |
| Overweight | 47.1%[c,d,e,f] (44.1–50.2) | 52.1%[c] (49.4–54.8) | 58.6%[a,b,e] (55.9–61.3) | 57.0%[a] (53.3–60.8) | 53.4%[a,c] (51.1–55.6) | 56.7%[a] (54.4–59.1) |
| Obese | 9.4%[b,c,d] (7.5–11.3) | 21.9%[a,e,f] (19.6–24.3) | 23.3%[a,e,f] (20.9–25.8) | 23.0%[a,e,f] (19.8–26.3) | 8.2%[b,c,d,f] (6.9–9.6) | 13.2%[b,c,d,e] (11.5–14.9) |

NOTE: All data are weighted. 95-percent confidence intervals are presented in parentheses.

[a] Estimate is significantly different from the estimate in column 1 (E1–E4).

[b] Estimate is significantly different from the estimate in column 2 (E5–E6).

[c] Estimate is significantly different from the estimate in column 3 (E7–E9).

[d] Estimate is significantly different from the estimate in column 4 (W1–W5).

[e] Estimate is significantly different from the estimate in column 5 (O1–O3).

[f] Estimate is significantly different from the estimate in column 6 (O4–O10).

[g] At the aggregate, the chi-square test was statistically significant; however, none of the individual pairwise comparisons was.

**Table 4.9**
**Weight Status, by Gender**

|  | Men (1) | Women (2) |
|---|---|---|
| Underweight | 0.4%[a] (0.2–0.7) | 1.0% (0.7–1.4) |
| Normal weight | 30.4%[a] (28.7–32.2) | 52.2% (50.3–54.1) |
| Overweight | 53.3%[a] (51.4–55.1) | 38.8% (36.9–40.6) |
| Obese | 15.9%[a] (14.6–17.2) | 8.0% (7.0–8.9) |

NOTE: All data are weighted. 95-percent confidence intervals are presented in parentheses.

[a] Estimate is significantly different from the estimate in column 2 (women).

**Table 4.10**
**Weight Status, by Age Group**

|  | Ages 17–24 (1) | Ages 25–34 (2) | Ages 35–44 (3) | Ages 45+ (4) |
|---|---|---|---|---|
| Underweight[e] | 0.7% (0.2–1.3) | 0.4% (0.1–0.8) | 0.3% (0.1–0.5) | 0.6% (0.2–1.1) |
| Normal weight | 48.0%[b,c,d] (44.4–51.5) | 33.6%[a,c,d] (31.3–35.9) | 20.1%[a,b] (18.0–22.1) | 21.0%[a,b] (18.1–23.9) |
| Overweight | 43.3%[b,c,d] (39.7–46.8) | 52.5%[a] (50.0–55.0) | 56.3%[a] (53.6–59.0) | 57.0%[a] (53.1–60.9) |
| Obese | 8.0%[b,c,d] (5.9–10.1) | 13.5%[a,c,d] (11.7–15.3) | 23.3%[a,b] (21.0–25.7) | 21.4%[a,b] (17.9–24.8) |

NOTE: All data are weighted. 95-percent confidence intervals are presented in parentheses.

[a] Estimate is significantly different from the estimate in column 1 (ages 17–24).

[b] Estimate is significantly different from the estimate in column 2 (ages 25–34).

[c] Estimate is significantly different from the estimate in column 3 (ages 35–44).

[d] Estimate is significantly different from the estimate in column 4 (ages 45+).

[e] At the aggregate, the chi-square test was statistically significant; however, none of the individual pairwise comparisons was.

**Table 4.11**
**Weight Status, by Race/Ethnicity**

|  | Non-Hispanic White (1) | Non-Hispanic Black (2) | Hispanic (3) | Non-Hispanic Asian (4) | Other (5) |
|---|---|---|---|---|---|
| Underweight[f] | 0.5% (0.2–0.8) | 0.9% (0.0–1.8) | 0.4% (0.1–0.8) | 0.2% (0.0–0.4) | 0.2% (0.1–0.4) |
| Normal weight | 34.3% (32.4–36.2) | 34.3% (29.6–38.9) | 31.2%[d] (27.0–35.3) | 43.6%[c,e] (35.6–51.6) | 28.8%[d] (24.3–33.4) |
| Overweight | 52.1%[b] (50.1–54.1) | 43.3%[a,c] (38.6–48.0) | 52.6%[b] (48.2–57.0) | 49.0% (40.8–57.1) | 52.1% (47.0–57.3) |
| Obese | 13.0%[b,e] (11.6–14.5) | 21.6%[a,d] (17.6–25.6) | 15.8%[d] (12.7–18.9) | 7.2%[b,c,e] (3.9–10.5) | 18.8%[a,d] (14.9–22.7) |

NOTE: All data are weighted. 95-percent confidence intervals are presented in parentheses.

[a] Estimate is significantly different from the estimate in column 1 (non-Hispanic white).

[b] Estimate is significantly different from the estimate in column 2 (non-Hispanic black).

[c] Estimate is significantly different from the estimate in column 3 (Hispanic).

[d] Estimate is significantly different from the estimate in column 4 (non-Hispanic Asian).

[e] Estimate is significantly different from the estimate in column 5 (other).

[f] At the aggregate, the chi-square test was statistically significant; however, none of the individual pairwise comparisons was.

**Table 4.12**
**Weight Status, by Education Level**

|  | High School or Less (1) | Some College (2) | Bachelor's Degree Or More (3) |
|---|---|---|---|
| Underweight | 1.1%[c] (0.3–2.0) | 0.4% (0.1–0.6) | 0.3%[a] (0.2–0.5) |
| Normal weight | 42.6%[b,c] (38.5–46.8) | 30.5%[a] (28.3–32.7) | 33.2%[a] (31.0–35.4) |
| Overweight | 46.5%[c] (42.3–50.7) | 51.2% (48.8–53.5) | 53.8%[a] (51.4–56.1) |
| Obese | 9.8%[b] (7.4–12.1) | 18.0%[a,c] (16.1–19.8) | 12.7%[b] (11.1–14.4) |

NOTE: All data are weighted. 95-percent confidence intervals are presented in parentheses.

[a] Estimate is significantly different from the estimate in column 1 (high school or less).

[b] Estimate is significantly different from the estimate in column 2 (some college).

[c] Estimate is significantly different from the estimate in column 3 (bachelor's degree or more).

## Routine Medical Care

Routine medical care is important for ensuring the receipt of age-appropriate screening to identify health problems early. DoD established annual Periodic Health Assessments to evaluate the medical readiness of active-duty service members (DoD, 2014). In addition to assessing readiness overall, these exams are important for identifying early onset of chronic diseases, including cardiovascular conditions, weight problems, and behavioral health issues.

The 2015 HRBS asked respondents when they last visited a doctor for a routine checkup (e.g., a general physical exam, not an exam for a specific injury, illness, or condition). Response options included within the past 12 months, more than 12 months ago but within the past two years, more than two years ago, and never. We estimated that failure to obtain a routine checkup within the previous two years suggests the need for a current medical reassessment, as current military policy requires service members across all services to receive annually a face-to-face, clinical health assessment (Assistant Secretary of Defense for Health Affairs, 2006; DoD, 2014; Headquarters, Department of the Army, 2007; U.S. Air Force, 2014; Department of the Navy, 2007).

Results are presented in Table 4.13. Key findings include the following:

- Overall, 93.2 percent of active-duty service members had a routine checkup with a doctor within the past two years. Receipt of routine medical care in the past two years ranged from 90.8 percent in the Marine Corps to 96.5 percent in the Coast Guard.
- There were no significant differences in routine medical care by gender, age group, or race/ethnicity.
- The percentage of service members reporting receiving a routine medical checkup in the past two years was lowest among junior enlisted personnel (92.6 percent) and highest among mid-grade and senior officers (95.9 percent).
- Self-reported receipt of routine medical care was highest among service members with a bachelor's degree or more (94.9 percent).

**Table 4.13**
**Receipt of a Routine Medical Checkup in the Past Two Years, by Subgroup**

|  | Received a Routine Medical Checkup in the Past Two Years |
|---|---|
| Total | 93.2% (92.4–94.1) |
| **Service branch** | |
| Air Force | 93.5%[e] (92.4–94.6) |
| Army | 94.9%[c,d] (93.4–96.3) |
| Marine Corps | 90.8%[b,e] (88.4–93.2) |
| Navy | 91.4%[b,e] (89.6–93.3) |
| Coast Guard | 96.5%[a,c,d] (95.9–97.1) |
| **Pay grade** | |
| E1–E4 | 92.6%[i] (91.1–94.2) |
| E5–E6 | 93.1%[i] (91.7–94.5) |
| E7–E9 | 93.9% (92.6–95.1) |
| W1–W5 | 95.3% (93.9–96.8) |
| O1–O3 | 93.8%[i] (92.8–94.9) |
| O4–O10 | 95.9%[f,g,h] (95.1–96.7) |
| **Gender[l]** | |
| Men | 93.1% (92.2–94.1) |
| Women | 93.7% (92.7–94.7) |
| **Age group[l]** | |
| Ages 17–24 | 92.2% (90.3–94.1) |
| Ages 25–34 | 93.5% (92.3–94.8) |
| Ages 35–44 | 94.0% (92.8–95.2) |
| Ages 45+ | 93.7% (91.5–95.9) |
| **Race/ethnicity[l]** | |
| Non-Hispanic white | 94.0% (93.1–94.9) |
| Non-Hispanic black | 91.4% (88.5–94.4) |
| Hispanic | 92.4% (90.0–94.8) |
| Non-Hispanic Asian | 92.8% (88.7–96.9) |
| Other | 92.4% (89.9–94.8) |

**Table 4.13—Continued**

| | Received a Routine Medical Checkup in the Past Two Years |
|---|---|
| Education level | |
| High school or less | 92.7%<br>(90.6–94.8) |
| Some college | 92.4%[k]<br>(91.1–93.7) |
| Bachelor's degree or more | 94.9%[j]<br>(93.9–95.9) |

NOTE: All data are weighted. 95-percent confidence intervals are presented in parentheses.

[a] Estimate is significantly different from Air Force.

[b] Estimate is significantly different from Army.

[c] Estimate is significantly different from Marine Corps.

[d] Estimate is significantly different from Navy.

[e] Estimate is significantly different from Coast Guard.

[f] Estimate is significantly different from E1–E4.

[g] Estimate is significantly different from E5–E6.

[h] Estimate is significantly different from O1–O3.

[i] Estimate is significantly different from O4–O10.

[j] Estimate is significantly different from some college.

[k] Estimate is significantly different from bachelor's degree or more.

[l] The omnibus chi-square test was not statistically significant ($p > 0.05$).

## Complementary and Alternative Medicine

CAM consists of diverse practices (e.g., chiropractic, biofeedback, meditation) that are not part of conventional medicine. Best estimates suggest that approximately 38 percent of adults in the United States use CAM, although these data are ten years old (National Center for Complementary and Integrative Health, 2007). Little is known about CAM use and attitudes toward CAM in the military. One study, using data from the 2005 HRBS, found that 46 percent (CI: 44–48) of active-duty survey respondents used at least one alternative practice and that use in the military was higher than civilian estimates of CAM therapy (Goertz et al., 2013). Another study of active-duty and reserve-component personnel found that approximately 41 percent used CAM, and users were more likely to have health conditions or symptoms (Jacobson, White, et al., 2009).

One item in the 2015 HRBS asked respondents whether, in the past 12 months, they had used each of the following 11 types of CAM: acupuncture, relaxation techniques, massage therapy, energy healing (such as reiki, polarity therapy), exercise/movement therapy (such as Tai Chi, yoga), hypnosis or hypnotherapy (self-led or led by practitioner), guided imagery therapy (such as mediation or aromatherapy), creative outlets (such as art, music, or writing therapy), chiropractic, biofeedback, and other health approach.

Results are presented in Tables 4.14 through 4.19. Key findings include the following:

- Approximately half (47.6 percent) of active-duty service members used some type of CAM in the past year (Table 4.14). The most-common types of CAM were massage therapy (20.4 percent), relaxation techniques (18.2 percent), exercise/movement therapy (17.8 percent), and creative outlets (17.3 percent).

- The percentage of service members reporting any CAM use increased with pay grade, from 43.1 percent among junior enlisted personnel (E1–E4) to 54.4 percent among mid-grade and senior officers (O4–O10) (Table 4.15).
- Women were more likely to report any CAM use (64.2 percent) compared with men (44.5 percent) (Table 4.16).
- The percentage of service members reporting any CAM use increased with age, from 41.2 percent among those aged 17–24 to 52.8 percent among those aged 45 or older (Table 4.17). Similarly, self-reported CAM use increased with education level, from 38.4 percent among those with a high school education or less to 53.8 percent among those with a bachelor's degree or more (Table 4.19).

**Table 4.14**
**Past-Year Use of Complementary and Alternative Medicine, by Service Branch**

| | Total (1) | Air Force (2) | Army (3) | Marine Corps (4) | Navy (5) | Coast Guard (6) |
|---|---|---|---|---|---|---|
| Any CAM | 47.6% (46.0–49.2) | 47.8% (45.6–50.0) | 47.5% (44.2–50.7) | 43.4% (39.4–47.4) | 50.3%[e] (47.1–53.4) | 45.2%[d] (43.5–46.8) |
| Acupuncture | 5.1% (4.5–5.8) | 4.9%[e] (4.0–5.7) | 6.7%[c,e] (5.2–8.1) | 3.5%[b] (2.4–4.7) | 4.1% (3.0–5.3) | 2.8%[a,b] (2.3–3.3) |
| Relaxation techniques[f] | 18.2% (17.0–19.3) | 18.3% (16.6–19.9) | 17.7% (15.5–19.9) | 17.4% (14.3–20.4) | 19.6% (17.2–22.0) | 15.9% (14.7–17.2) |
| Massage therapy | 20.4% (19.2–21.6) | 20.5%[d] (18.9–22.1) | 18.1%[d,e] (15.8–20.4) | 18.7%[d] (15.7–21.6) | 24.7%[a,b,c] (22.1–27.3) | 22.3%[b] (21.0–23.7) |
| Energy healing (such as reiki, polarity therapy)[f] | 1.6% (1.2–2.0) | 1.8% (1.2–2.4) | 1.5% (0.8–2.2) | 1.8% (0.7–2.9) | 1.5% (0.7–2.2) | 1.4% (1.0–1.7) |
| Exercise/movement therapy (such as Tai Chi, yoga) | 17.8% (16.7–18.9) | 18.7%[c] (17.1–20.3) | 17.0%[e] (14.7–19.2) | 14.0%[a,d,e] (11.5–16.6) | 20.1%[c] (17.6–22.5) | 21.6%[b,c] (20.3–23.0) |
| Hypnosis or hypnotherapy (self-led or led by practitioner)[f] | 0.9% (0.6–1.2) | 0.6% (0.2–0.9) | 0.9% (0.4–1.3) | 1.2% (0.2–2.2) | 1.2% (0.5–2.0) | 0.8% (0.5–1.1) |
| Guided imagery therapy (such as meditation or aromatherapy) | 5.1% (4.5–5.7) | 4.7% (3.8–5.5) | 4.4%[d] (3.3–5.4) | 4.7% (3.0–6.4) | 7.1%[b,e] (5.4–8.7) | 4.0%[d] (3.4–4.7) |
| Creative outlets (such as art, music, or writing therapy) | 17.3% (16.1–18.5) | 17.7% (16.0–19.3) | 15.3%[d] (13.1–17.5) | 15.2%[d] (12.3–18.1) | 21.2%[b,c] (18.6–23.9) | 17.7% (16.4–19.0) |
| Chiropractic[f] | 11.4% (10.5–12.3) | 11.6% (10.3–12.9) | 12.3% (10.4–14.2) | 10.3% (8.1–12.6) | 10.6% (8.9–12.3) | 9.5% (8.6–10.4) |
| Biofeedback | 1.8% (1.4–2.3) | 1.0%[b,e] (0.6–1.5) | 3.4%[a,c,d,e] (2.3–4.6) | 1.0%[b] (0.3–1.8) | 0.8%[b] (0.3–1.3) | 0.3%[a,b] (0.1–0.6) |
| Other health approach | 10.7% (9.7–11.7) | 8.9%[c] (7.7–10.2) | 10.1% (8.1–12.0) | 13.4%[a,e] (10.7–16.0) | 12.2%[e] (10.0–14.4) | 8.8%[c,d] (7.8–9.8) |

NOTE: All data are weighted. 95-percent confidence intervals are presented in parentheses.
[a] Estimate is significantly different from the estimate in column 2 (Air Force).
[b] Estimate is significantly different from the estimate in column 3 (Army).
[c] Estimate is significantly different from the estimate in column 4 (Marine Corps).
[d] Estimate is significantly different from the estimate in column 5 (Navy).
[e] Estimate is significantly different from the estimate in column 6 (Coast Guard).
[f] The omnibus chi-square test was not statistically significant ($p > 0.05$).

**Table 4.15**
**Past-Year Use of Complementary and Alternative Medicine, by Pay Grade**

| | E1–E4 (1) | E5–E6 (2) | E7–E9 (3) | W1–W5 (4) | O1–O3 (5) | O4–O10 (6) |
|---|---|---|---|---|---|---|
| Any CAM | 43.1% [b,d,e,f] (40.0–46.1) | 49.9% [a] (47.3–52.6) | 48.3% [e,f] (45.6–51.1) | 53.5% [a] (49.8–57.3) | 54.9% [a,c] (52.6–57.1) | 54.4% [a,c] (52.1–56.8) |
| Acupuncture | 3.5% [c,d,f] (2.4–4.7) | 6.0% [c] (4.7–7.2) | 8.9% [a,b,e] (7.3–10.5) | 8.1% [a,e] (6.1–10.0) | 4.6% [c,d,f] (3.7–5.5) | 7.0% [a,e] (5.8–8.1) |
| Relaxation techniques | 14.8% [b,d,e,f] (12.8–16.9) | 21.0% [a] (18.9–23.1) | 19.2% (17.0–21.3) | 21.4% [a] (18.3–24.5) | 22.1% [a] (20.2–23.9) | 20.2% [a] (18.3–22.0) |
| Massage therapy | 15.4% [b,c,d,e,f] (13.2–17.5) | 22.2% [a,e,f] (20.0–24.3) | 21.5% [a,e,f] (19.3–23.6) | 24.5% [a,f] (21.4–27.7) | 29.4% [a,b,c] (27.4–31.3) | 30.8% [a,b,c,d] (28.7–33.0) |
| Energy healing (such as reiki, polarity therapy) | 1.4% (0.8–2.0) | 2.2% [e] (1.4–3.0) | 1.5% (0.8–2.2) | 1.6% (0.8–2.3) | 1.0% [b] (0.6–1.4) | 1.4% (0.9–2.0) |
| Exercise/movement therapy (such as Tai Chi, yoga) | 15.3% [e,f] (13.2–17.4) | 18.5% [e] (16.5–20.5) | 16.6% [e,f] (14.6–18.6) | 19.1% [e] (16.1–22.0) | 25.4% [a,b,c,d] (23.5–27.2) | 21.9% [a,c] (20.0–23.7) |
| Hypnosis or hypnotherapy (self-led or led by practitioner)[g] | 0.8% (0.3–1.2) | 1.2% (0.6–1.8) | 0.9% (0.4–1.5) | 0.9% (0.2–1.6) | 0.8% (0.4–1.3) | 1.0% (0.5–1.5) |
| Guided imagery therapy (such as meditation or aromatherapy)[g] | 4.7% (3.5–5.8) | 5.7% (4.6–6.9) | 4.7% (3.5–5.8) | 3.4% (2.2–4.6) | 5.7% (4.7–6.7) | 5.5% (4.4–6.5) |
| Creative outlets (such as art, music, or writing therapy) | 18.5% [c,d,f] (16.3–20.8) | 18.0% [c,d,f] (16.0–19.9) | 11.3% [a,b,e] (9.6–13.0) | 11.2% [a,b,e] (8.9–13.5) | 18.1% [c,d,f] (16.5–19.8) | 14.3% [a,b,e] (12.7–15.9) |
| Chiropractic | 7.4% [b,c,d,e,f] (5.8–9.1) | 12.7% [a,c,d] (11.0–14.5) | 17.3% [a,b] (15.2–19.4) | 21.9% [a,b,e,f] (18.8–25.1) | 14.9% [a,d] (13.3–16.5) | 16.2% [a,d] (14.4–18.0) |
| Biofeedback[g] | 1.5% (0.6–2.3) | 2.4% (1.4–3.3) | 1.9% (1.1–2.7) | 1.9% (0.9–3.0) | 1.9% (1.2–2.6) | 2.1% (1.3–2.9) |
| Other health approach[g] | 11.6% (9.6–13.6) | 10.2% (8.7–11.7) | 10.6% (9.0–12.3) | 10.2% (8.0–12.4) | 8.9% (7.6–10.2) | 10.0% (8.5–11.4) |

NOTE: All data are weighted. 95-percent confidence intervals are presented in parentheses.

[a] Estimate is significantly different from the estimate in column 1 (E1–E4).

[b] Estimate is significantly different from the estimate in column 2 (E5–E6).

[c] Estimate is significantly different from the estimate in column 3 (E7–E9).

[d] Estimate is significantly different from the estimate in column 4 (W1–W5).

[e] Estimate is significantly different from the estimate in column 5 (O1–O3).

[f] Estimate is significantly different from the estimate in column 6 (O4–O10).

[g] The omnibus chi-square test was not statistically significant ($p > 0.05$).

**Table 4.16**
**Past-Year Use of Complementary and Alternative Medicine, by Gender**

| | Men (1) | Women (2) |
|---|---|---|
| Any CAM | 44.5%[a] (42.6–46.3) | 64.2% (62.4–66.1) |
| Acupuncture | 4.5%[a] (3.8–5.3) | 8.2% (7.2–9.2) |
| Relaxation techniques | 16.3%[a] (15.0–17.6) | 28.4% (26.7–30.1) |
| Massage therapy | 18.2%[a] (16.8–19.5) | 32.3% (30.6–34.0) |
| Energy healing (such as reiki, polarity therapy)[b] | 1.5% (1.1–1.9) | 2.2% (1.6–2.7) |
| Exercise/movement therapy (such as Tai Chi, yoga) | 15.3%[a] (14.0–16.6) | 31.2% (29.5–33.0) |
| Hypnosis or hypnotherapy (self-led or led by practitioner)[b] | 0.9% (0.6–1.2) | 1.1% (0.7–1.4) |
| Guided imagery therapy (such as meditation or aromatherapy) | 4.1%[a] (3.4–4.8) | 10.5% (9.3–11.6) |
| Creative outlets (such as art, music, or writing therapy) | 15.0%[a] (13.6–16.3) | 29.7% (27.9–31.4) |
| Chiropractic | 10.7%[a] (9.6–11.8) | 15.1% (13.8–16.5) |
| Biofeedback[b] | 1.9% (1.3–2.4) | 1.7% (1.2–2.2) |
| Other health approach | 10.1%[a] (9.0–11.3) | 13.9% (12.6–15.3) |

NOTE: All data are weighted. 95-percent confidence intervals are presented in parentheses.

[a] Estimate is significantly different from the estimate in column 2 (women).

[b] The omnibus chi-square test was not statistically significant ($p > 0.05$).

**Table 4.17**
**Past-Year Use of Complementary and Alternative Medicine, by Age Group**

| | Ages 17–24 (1) | Ages 25–34 (2) | Ages 35–44 (3) | Ages 45+ (4) |
|---|---|---|---|---|
| Any CAM | 41.2%[b,c,d] (37.8–44.7) | 49.3%[a] (46.8–51.8) | 50.7%[a] (48.0–53.4) | 52.8%[a] (48.9–56.8) |
| Acupuncture | 1.4%[b,c,d] (0.7–2.2) | 5.6%[a,d] (4.4–6.8) | 7.2%[a,d] (5.8–8.6) | 11.1%[a,b,c] (8.6–13.7) |
| Relaxation techniques | 13.8%[b,c,d] (11.6–16.0) | 19.0%[a] (17.1–20.9) | 21.3%[a] (19.1–23.4) | 21.3%[a] (17.8–24.7) |
| Massage therapy | 14.3%[b,c,d] (11.9–16.6) | 22.3%[a] (20.4–24.3) | 23.5%[a] (21.4–25.6) | 23.7%[a] (20.2–27.3) |
| Energy healing (such as reiki, polarity therapy)[e] | 1.6% (0.8–2.4) | 1.3% (0.9–1.8) | 1.9% (1.0–2.9) | 2.0% (1.0–2.9) |
| Exercise/movement therapy (such as Tai Chi, yoga)[f] | 15.5% (13.0–18.0) | 19.4% (17.6–21.2) | 17.9% (16.0–19.9) | 16.7% (14.0–19.4) |
| Hypnosis or hypnotherapy (self-led or led by practitioner)[e] | 0.7% (0.1–1.3) | 0.9% (0.5–1.4) | 1.1% (0.6–1.7) | 1.3% (0.6–2.0) |
| Guided imagery therapy (such as meditation or aromatherapy)[f] | 4.0% (2.9–5.0) | 5.9% (4.7–7.0) | 4.9% (3.8–6.1) | 6.0% (4.2–7.7) |
| Creative outlets (such as art, music, or writing therapy) | 19.3%[c] (16.7–21.9) | 17.5% (15.7–19.4) | 15.0%[a] (13.1–17.0) | 14.6% (11.5–17.8) |
| Chiropractic | 6.4%[b,c,d] (4.7–8.1) | 11.1%[a,c,d] (9.6–12.6) | 15.9%[a,b] (14.0–17.8) | 19.3%[a,b] (16.1–22.4) |
| Biofeedback | 0.9%[d] (0.3–1.6) | 2.0% (1.2–2.8) | 2.0% (1.1–3.0) | 4.1%[a] (2.3–5.9) |
| Other health approach[e] | 11.3% (9.0–13.6) | 10.6% (9.1–12.2) | 9.8% (8.1–11.4) | 11.8% (9.7–13.9) |

NOTE: All data are weighted. 95-percent confidence intervals are presented in parentheses.

[a] Estimate is significantly different from the estimate in column 1 (ages 17–24).

[b] Estimate is significantly different from the estimate in column 2 (ages 25–34).

[c] Estimate is significantly different from the estimate in column 3 (ages 35–44).

[d] Estimate is significantly different from the estimate in column 4 (ages 45+).

[e] The omnibus chi-square test was not statistically significant ($p > 0.05$).

[f] The omnibus chi-square test was statistically significant ($p > 0.05$), but the power was too low to identify group differences.

**Table 4.18**
**Past-Year Use of Complementary and Alternative Medicine, by Race/Ethnicity**

| | Non-Hispanic White (1) | Non-Hispanic Black (2) | Hispanic (3) | Non-Hispanic Asian (4) | Other (5) |
|---|---|---|---|---|---|
| Any CAM | 46.5%[e] (44.5–48.5) | 47.3% (42.5–52.1) | 45.9%[e] (41.5–50.2) | 50.6% (42.5–58.8) | 56.5%[a,c] (51.3–61.6) |
| Acupuncture[f] | 5.7% (4.8–6.7) | 2.9% (1.9–4.0) | 4.9% (3.1–6.6) | 5.2% (2.4–8.1) | 4.3% (2.5–6.1) |
| Relaxation techniques | 17.9%[e] (16.5–19.3) | 16.8%[e] (13.7–19.9) | 17.0%[e] (13.9–20.0) | 17.3% (11.2–23.4) | 24.8%[a,b,c] (20.3–29.3) |
| Massage therapy | 20.5%[e] (19.0–22.1) | 19.3%[e] (15.9–22.7) | 16.8%[e] (13.9–19.6) | 16.5%[e] (11.5–21.5) | 29.8%[a,b,c,d] (25.0–34.7) |
| Energy healing (such as reiki, polarity therapy)[f] | 1.4% (1.0–1.8) | 2.1% (0.4–3.8) | 2.0% (1.0–3.1) | 0.2% (0.0–0.3) | 2.1% (0.9–3.4) |
| Exercise/movement therapy (such as Tai Chi, yoga)[f] | 18.1% (16.7–19.5) | 16.2% (12.8–19.5) | 16.8% (13.5–20.1) | 15.6% (10.4–20.7) | 20.8% (16.8–24.7) |
| Hypnosis or hypnotherapy (self-led or led by practitioner)[f] | 0.9% (0.5–1.3) | 0.4% (0.0–0.8) | 1.1% (0.4–1.9) | 1.5% (0.0–3.6) | 1.1% (0.1–2.0) |
| Guided imagery therapy (such as meditation or aromatherapy)[f] | 4.9% (4.2–5.7) | 3.6% (2.0–5.3) | 5.5% (3.8–7.1) | 8.0% (3.4–12.6) | 5.9% (3.9–8.0) |
| Creative outlets (such as art, music, or writing therapy)[f] | 16.8% (15.4–18.2) | 15.5% (12.3–18.7) | 18.4% (15.0–21.9) | 20.5% (13.8–27.2) | 18.9% (15.2–22.5) |
| Chiropractic[f] | 11.8% (10.6–13.0) | 9.5% (6.5–12.4) | 10.7% (8.3–13.1) | 8.3% (4.9–11.8) | 14.5% (11.1–17.9) |
| Biofeedback[f] | 1.7% (1.2–2.3) | 1.9% (0.3–3.4) | 2.2% (0.9–3.5) | 1.8% (0.0–4.9) | 2.0% (0.9–3.2) |
| Other health approach | 9.4%[e] (8.3–10.6) | 10.4% (7.3–13.4) | 12.2% (9.2–15.2) | 11.0% (6.9–15.0) | 16.9%[a] (12.6–21.1) |

NOTE: All data are weighted. 95-percent confidence intervals are presented in parentheses.

[a] Estimate is significantly different from the estimate in column 1 (non-Hispanic white).

[b] Estimate is significantly different from the estimate in column 2 (non-Hispanic black).

[c] Estimate is significantly different from the estimate in column 3 (Hispanic).

[d] Estimate is significantly different from the estimate in column 4 (non-Hispanic Asian).

[e] Estimate is significantly different from the estimate in column 5 (other).

[f] The omnibus chi-square test was not statistically significant ($p > 0.05$).

**Table 4.19**
**Past-Year Use of Complementary and Alternative Medicine, by Education Level**

| | High School or Less (1) | Some College (2) | Bachelor's Degree or More (3) |
|---|---|---|---|
| Any CAM | 38.4%[b,c] (34.3–42.4) | 47.4%[a,c] (45.1–49.8) | 53.8%[a,b] (51.4–56.2) |
| Acupuncture | 3.0%[c] (1.5–4.5) | 5.5% (4.4–6.5) | 6.0%[a] (5.1–6.9) |
| Relaxation techniques | 12.1%[b,c] (9.5–14.6) | 19.3%[a] (17.5–21.1) | 20.4%[a] (18.7–22.0) |
| Massage therapy | 13.7%[b,c] (11.0–16.4) | 18.5%[a,c] (16.8–20.3) | 27.7%[a,b] (25.7–29.7) |
| Energy healing (such as reiki, polarity therapy)[d] | 1.5% (0.6–2.4) | 1.9% (1.2–2.5) | 1.3% (0.9–1.6) |
| Exercise/movement therapy (such as Tai Chi, yoga) | 11.6%[b,c] (9.1–14.2) | 17.8%[a,c] (16.1–19.6) | 21.8%[a,b] (20.1–23.5) |
| Hypnosis or hypnotherapy (self-led or led by practitioner)[d] | 0.8% (0.1–1.6) | 0.9% (0.5–1.4) | 1.0% (0.6–1.3) |
| Guided imagery therapy (such as meditation or aromatherapy) | 3.0%[b,c] (1.9–4.1) | 5.8%[a] (4.7–6.8) | 5.4%[a] (4.5–6.4) |
| Creative outlets (such as art, music, or writing therapy) | 14.6%[b] (11.9–17.4) | 19.1%[a,c] (17.3–21.0) | 16.1%[b] (14.5–17.7) |
| Chiropractic | 6.5%[b,c] (4.6–8.5) | 11.3%[a,c] (9.9–12.7) | 14.8%[a,b] (13.3–16.3) |
| Biofeedback[d] | 0.9% (0.1–1.8) | 1.9% (1.2–2.7) | 2.3% (1.6–3.1) |
| Other health approach[d] | 10.9% (8.2–13.6) | 10.9% (9.5–12.4) | 10.4% (8.9–11.8) |

NOTE: All data are weighted. 95-percent confidence intervals are presented in parentheses.

[a] Estimate is significantly different from the estimate in column 1 (high school or less).

[b] Estimate is significantly different from the estimate in column 2 (some college).

[c] Estimate is significantly different from the estimate in column 3 (bachelor's degree or more).

[d] The omnibus chi-square test was not statistically significant ($p > 0.05$).

## Sleep Health

Sleep disorders—including insufficient sleep duration, poor sleep quality, daytime sleepiness, fatigue, nightmares, insomnia, and obstructive sleep apnea—are commonly diagnosed among military personnel (McLay, Klam, and Volkert, 2010; Capaldi, Guerrero, and Kilgore, 2011; Mysliwiec, Gill, et al., 2013; Mysliwiec, McGraw, et al., 2013). There is a high prevalence of insufficient sleep duration, poor sleep quality, daytime sleepiness, fatigue, and nightmares in the military (Troxel et al., 2015). Sleep disturbances are a common reaction to stress and are also symptoms of PTSD, depression, anxiety, and traumatic brain injury (TBI) (Bramoweth and Germain, 2013; Hoge, Castro, et al., 2004). Insufficient sleep is associated with adverse mental and physical/cognitive functioning, including depression, suicide, PTSD, accidents/injuries, cardiovascular events, and mortality, all of which may affect readiness (Bramoweth and Germain, 2013; Wesensten and Balkin, 2013). The side effects of sleep medications used by service members may further limit military readiness. One study found that 18 percent of service members used sleep medications (Troxel et al., 2015). Further, sleep disturbances may continue to affect quality of life after military service (Pietrzak, Morgan, and Southwick, 2010; Seelig et al., 2010; Swinkels et al., 2013; Plumb, Peachey, and Zelman, 2014).

Respondents were asked to report, on average, how many hours of sleep they get in a 24-hour period. They were instructed to enter different response options for "during the work/duty week" and "during the weekends/days off." Respondents were next asked how many hours of sleep per night they need to feel fully refreshed and perform well. Two items then assessed (1) how bothered they had been in the past week by lack of energy because of poor sleep and (2) general satisfaction with their sleep in the past week. A final item asked how often they used prescription or over-the-counter medications to help with sleep.

Results are presented in Tables 4.20 through 4.25. Key findings include the following:

- Among service members, 35.3 percent reported sleeping for seven or more hours per night during the work week, and 79.4 percent reported sleeping for seven hours or more per night during the weekend (Table 4.20). The HP2020 target is to increase the proportion of adults who get sufficient sleep (defined as eight or more hours for those aged 18 to 21 and seven or more hours for those aged 22 or older) to 70.8 percent (HHS, 2010f). According to this definition, 34.9 percent of active-duty service members get sufficient sleep.
- More than half (56.3 percent) of active-duty service members reported getting less sleep than they need (Table 4.20). Service members in the Army (59.4 percent), Marine Corps (56.9 percent), and Navy (57.5 percent) were most likely to report receiving less sleep than they need to feel refreshed and perform well.
- Nearly one-third (29.9 percent) of service members were moderately or severely bothered by lack of energy due to poor sleep, and 8.6 percent took over-the-counter medications to help them sleep (Table 4.20).
- Service members in the Army (33.2 percent), Marine Corps (32.8 percent), and Navy (32.8 percent) were most likely to report being bothered by lack of energy due to poor sleep (Table 4.20).
- Less than half (44.4 percent) of service members rated their sleep satisfaction as excellent or good. Sleep satisfaction ranged from 38.6 percent in the Marine Corps to 53.1 percent in the Air Force (Table 4.20).

- There were few statistically significant differences in self-reported sleep by pay grade; however, compared with officers, enlisted service members were more likely to report having less than four hours of sleep during the work week, more likely to report being moderately or severely bothered by lack of energy due to poor sleep, and less likely to report being satisfied with their sleep on average (Table 4.21).
- Overall, there were no significant gender differences in self-reported hours of sleep; however, women were less likely than men to report getting enough sleep (26.8 percent compared with 29.7 percent), more likely to report getting less sleep than needed (64.3 percent compared with 54.8 percent), and less likely to report getting more sleep than needed (8.9 percent compared with 15.5 percent) (Table 4.22). Women were also more likely than men to report being moderately or severely bothered by lack of energy due to poor sleep (36.7 percent compared with 28.6 percent), less likely to report being satisfied with their sleep (40.6 percent compared with 45.1 percent), and more likely to report taking sleep medications almost every day (12.4 percent compared with 7.9 percent).
- There were few statistically significant differences in sleep by age group (Table 4.23).
- Sleep varied by race, with 8.6 percent of non-Hispanic whites and 17.7 percent of non-Hispanic blacks reporting less than four hours of sleep per night (Table 4.24).
- On average, sleep satisfaction increased with increasing education level (Table 4.25).

**Table 4.20**
**Sleep Health, by Service Branch**

| | Total (1) | Air Force (2) | Army (3) | Marine Corps (4) | Navy (5) | Coast Guard (6) |
|---|---|---|---|---|---|---|
| **Average hours of sleep per 24 hours during the work/duty week** | | | | | | |
| 4 hours or less | 10.6% (9.4–11.7) | 5.6% [b,c,d] (4.4–6.7) | 14.1% [a,e] (11.7–16.5) | 10.0% [a,e] (7.2–1?.8) | 10.7% [a,e] (8.6–12.9) | 4.4% [b,c,d] (3.7–5.2) |
| 5–6 hours | 54.2% (52.4–55.9) | 49.5% [b,d] (47.0–51.9) | 55.6% [a] (52.1–59.2) | 55.0% (50.5–59.6) | 56.3% [a,e] (52.9–59.7) | 50.2% [d] (48.4–52.0) |
| 7–8 hours | 34.0% (32.4–35.6) | 43.6% [b,c,d] (41.2–46.0) | 29.0% [a,e] (25.8–32.3) | 33.7% [a,e] (29.4–38.0) | 31.8% [a,e] (28.6–35.0) | 44.2% [b,c,d] (42.4–46.0) |
| 9+ hours | 1.3% (0.9–1.7) | 1.4% (0.8–2.0) | 1.2% (0.4–2.0) | 1.3% (0.3–?.3) | 1.2% (0.4–2.0) | 1.2% (0.8–1.5) |
| **Average hours of sleep per 24 hours during the weekend/days off** | | | | | | |
| 4 hours or less | 2.8% (2.2–3.3) | 1.3% [b] (0.8–1.9) | 3.9% [a,e] (2.7–5.1) | 2.9% [e] (1.4–4.5) | 2.4% [e] (1.4–3.4) | 1.2% [b,c,d] (0.8–1.5) |
| 5–6 hours | 17.8% (16.5–19.2) | 14.9% [b] (13.2–16.7) | 19.5% [a] (16.8–22.3) | 15.8% (12.8–18.9) | 19.2% (16.5–21.8) | 16.7% (15.3–18.0) |
| 7–8 hours | 55.3% (53.5–57.1) | 56.9% [c] (54.5–59.3) | 55.2% (51.6–58.7) | 49.3% [a,e] (44.8–53.8) | 56.8% (53.4–60.2) | 60.6% [c] (58.8–62.4) |
| 9+ hours | 24.1% (22.6–25.6) | 26.8% [b,d,e] (24.7–28.9) | 21.4% [a,c] (18.4–24.5) | 31.9% [b,d,e] (27.6–36.3) | 21.6% [a,c] (18.6–24.5) | 21.6% [a,c] (20.0–23.1) |
| **Average hours of sleep per 24 hours compared with average number of hours needed to feel fully refreshed and perform well** | | | | | | |
| Enough sleep | 29.2% (27.6–30.8) | 32.8% [d] (30.5–35.1) | 27.9% [e] (24.7–31.1) | 29.0% (24.9–33.1) | 27.5% [a,e] (24.5–30.5) | 33.3% [b,d] (31.6–35.0) |
| Less sleep than needed | 56.3% (54.5–58.0) | 50.1% [b,d] (47.7–52.5) | 59.4% [a,e] (55.9–63.0) | 56.3% [e] (52.4–61.4) | 57.5% [a,e] (54.1–60.9) | 49.5% [b,c,d] (47.7–51.4) |
| More sleep than needed | 14.5% (13.2–15.8) | 17.1% (15.2–19.0) | 12.7% [e] (10.2–15.1) | 14.1% (10.8–17.3) | 15.0% (12.4–17.6) | 17.2% [b] (15.7–18.6) |

Table 4.20—Continued

| | Total (1) | Air Force (2) | Army (3) | Marine Corps (4) | Navy (5) | Coast Guard (6) |
|---|---|---|---|---|---|---|
| Moderately or severely bothered by lack of energy due to poor sleep | 29.9% (28.2–31.5) | 20.3%[b,c,d] (18.3–22.2) | 33.2%[a,e] (29.9–36.5) | 32.8%[a,e] (28.6–37.1) | 32.8%[a,e] (29.5–36.1) | 22.2%[b,c,d] (20.7–23.7) |
| Satisfied with sleep (excellent or good) | 44.4% (42.7–46.2) | 53.1%[b,c,d] (50.6–55.5) | 40.6%[a,e] (37.1–44.1) | 38.6%[a,e] (34.2–43.0) | 45.2%[a] (41.8–48.6) | 50.1%[b,c] (48.3–51.9) |
| Take sleep meds every day or almost every day | 8.6% (7.6–9.5) | 7.5%[b,e] (6.3–8.7) | 10.6%[a,d,e] (8.7–12.6) | 9.9%[e] (7.1–12.7) | 6.0%[b] (4.5–7.4) | 4.6%[a,b,c] (3.9–5.3) |

NOTE: All data are weighted. 95-percent confidence intervals are presented in parentheses.

[a] Estimate is significantly different from the estimate in column 2 (Air Force).

[b] Estimate is significantly different from the estimate in column 3 (Army).

[c] Estimate is significantly different from the estimate in column 4 (Marine Corps).

[d] Estimate is significantly different from the estimate in column 5 (Navy).

[e] Estimate is significantly different from the estimate in column 6 (Coast Guard).

**Table 4.21**
**Sleep Health, by Pay Grade**

| | E1–E4 (1) | E5–E6 (2) | E7–E9 (3) | W1–W5 (4) | O1–O3 (5) | O4–O10 (6) |
|---|---|---|---|---|---|---|
| **Average hours of sleep per 24 hours during the work/duty week** | | | | | | |
| 4 hours or less | 9.8% b,e,f (7.7–11.9) | 14.4% a,e,f (12.2–16.6) | 14.0% e,f (11.8–16.3) | 11.6% e,f (8.9–1.2) | 4.2% a,b,c,d (3.2–5.2) | 3.8% a,b,c,d (2.8–4.8) |
| 5–6 hours | 52.9% (49.4–56.3) | 56.4% e (53.5–59.4) | 59.1% e,f (56.1–62.0) | 58.0% e (54.0–2.0) | 49.2% b,c,d (46.8–51.6) | 52.4% c (49.9–54.9) |
| 7–8 hours | 35.5% b,c,e,f (32.2–38.7) | 28.1% a,e,f (25.5–30.7) | 26.4% a,e,f (23.8–29.0) | 29.6% e,f (25.9–3.3) | 45.8% a,b,c,d (43.4–48.1) | 43.5% a,b,c,d (41.0–46.0) |
| 9+ hours | 1.9% c,f (1.0–2.7) | 1.0% (0.4–1.6) | 0.5% a (0.1–0.8) | 0.8% (0.1–.5) | 0.9% (0.5–1.2) | 0.3% a (0.1–0.5) |
| **Average hours of sleep per 24 hours during the weekend/days off** | | | | | | |
| 4 hours or less | 1.8% b,c,d (0.9–2.7) | 4.3% a,e,f (3.0–5.6) | 5.0% a,e,f (3.6–6.4) | 4.6% a,e,f (2.8–6.4) | 1.3% b,c,d (0.7–1.9) | 1.1% b,c,d (0.6–1.7) |
| 5–6 hours | 15.0% b,c,d (12.5–17.5) | 21.0% a,c,d,e,f (18.5–23.4) | 28.5% a,b,e,f (25.7–31.3) | 28.4% a,b,e,f (24.8–32.1) | 11.2% b,c,d,f (9.6–12.8) | 14.7% b,c,d,e (12.9–16.5) |
| 7–8 hours | 49.4% b,e,f (46.0–52.9) | 57.1% a,e,f (54.2–60.1) | 54.5% e,f (51.5–57.5) | 55.5% e,f (51.5–59.6) | 64.9% a,b,c,d,f (62.6–67.1) | 71.0% a,b,c,d,e (68.7–73.2) |
| 9+ hours | 33.8% b,c,d,e,f (30.5–37.0) | 17.6% a,c,d,e,f (15.4–19.8) | 12.0% a,b,e (10.2–13.9) | 11.5% a,b,e (8.8–14.1) | 22.7% a,b,c,d,f (20.7–24.6) | 13.2% a,b,e (11.6–14.8) |
| **Average hours of sleep per 24 hours compared with average number of hours needed to feel fully refreshed and perform well** | | | | | | |
| Enough sleep | 27.4% f (24.3–30.5) | 29.1% (26.4–31.8) | 30.5% (27.7–33.3) | 30.9% (27.1–34.7) | 32.5% (30.3–34.7) | 34.0% a (31.6–36.4) |
| Less sleep than needed | 55.7% (52.2–59.1) | 58.2% (55.3–61.1) | 56.2% (53.2–59.2) | 56.6% (52.–60.6) | 54.5% (52.1–56.9) | 54.6% (52.1–57.1) |
| More sleep than needed | 17.0% f (14.4–19.5) | 12.7% (10.7–14.6) | 13.3% (11.2–15.4) | 11.6% (9.–15.2) | 13.0% (11.4–14.6) | 11.4% a (9.8–13.0) |

**Table 4.21—Continued**

| | E1–E4 (1) | E5–E6 (2) | E7–E9 (3) | W1–W5 (4) | O1–O3 (5) | O4–O10 (6) |
|---|---|---|---|---|---|---|
| Moderately or severely bothered by lack of energy due to poor sleep | 31.1%[e,f] (27.9–34.3) | 33.2%[e,f] (30.4–36.0) | 30.1%[e,f] (27.3–32.9) | 30.9%[e,f] (27.1–34.7) | 22.2%[a,b,c,d] (20.2–24.3) | 19.1%[a,b,c,d] (17.1–21.0) |
| Satisfied with sleep (excellent or good) | 43.8%[e,f] (40.4–47.2) | 40.2%[e,f] (37.3–43.1) | 39.8%[e,f] (36.8–42.7) | 42.5%[e,f] (38.5–46.5) | 55.7%[a,b,c,d] (53.3–58.1) | 56.3%[a,b,c,d] (53.8–58.8) |
| Take sleep meds everyday or almost every day | 7.2%[c,d] (5.5–8.9) | 10.1%[e,f] (8.3–11.9) | 12.5%[a,e,f] (10.4–14.6) | 12.0%[a,e,f] (9.4–14.6) | 6.9%[b,c,d] (5.6–8.2) | 6.7%[c,d] (5.4–8.0) |

NOTE: All data are weighted. 95-percent confidence intervals are presented in parentheses.

[a] Estimate is significantly different from the estimate in column 1 (E1–E4).

[b] Estimate is significantly different from the estimate in column 2 (E5–E6).

[c] Estimate is significantly different from the estimate in column 3 (E7–E9).

[d] Estimate is significantly different from the estimate in column 4 (W1–W5).

[e] Estimate is significantly different from the estimate in column 5 (O1–O3).

[f] Estimate is significantly different from the estimate in column 6 (O4–O10).

**Table 4.22**
**Sleep Health, by Gender**

| | Men (1) | Women (2) |
|---|---|---|
| **Average hours of sleep per 24 hours during the work/duty week** | | |
| 4 hours or less[b] | 10.4% (9.1–11.7) | 11.5% (10.1–13.0) |
| 5–6 hours[b] | 54.6% (52.5–56.6) | 51.9% (49.8–54.0) |
| 7–8 hours[b] | 34.0% (32.1–35.9) | 34.2% (32.3–36.1) |
| 9+ hours | 1.1%[a] (0.6–1.5) | 2.4% (1.7–3.1) |
| **Average hours of sleep per 24 hours during the weekend/days off** | | |
| 4 hours or less[b] | 2.7% (2.1–3.4) | 3.0% (2.3–3.8) |
| 5–6 hours | 19.3%[a] (16.7–19.8) | 15.7% (14.2–17.3) |
| 7–8 hours | 56.4%[a] (54.4–58.4) | 49.2% (47.1–51.3) |
| 9+ hours | 22.7%[a] (20.9–24.5) | 32.0% (30.0–34.0) |
| **Average hours of sleep per 24 hours compared with average number of hours needed to feel fully refreshed and perform well** | | |
| Enough sleep | 29.7%[a] (27.8–31.5) | 26.8% (24.9–28.6) |
| Less sleep than needed | 54.8%[a] (52.8–56.8) | 64.3% (62.3–66.3) |
| More sleep than needed | 15.5%[a] (14.0–17.0) | 8.9% (7.8–10.1) |
| Moderately or severely bothered by lack of energy due to poor sleep | 28.6%[a] (26.7–30.5) | 36.7% (34.7–38.8) |
| Satisfied with sleep (excellent or good) | 45.1%[a] (43.1–47.1) | 40.6% (38.6–42.7) |
| Take sleep meds every day or almost every day | 7.9%[a] (6.8–8.9) | 12.4% (11.1–13.8) |

NOTE: All data are weighted. 95-percent confidence intervals are presented in parentheses.

[a] Estimate is significantly different from the estimate in column 2 (women).

[b] At the aggregate, the chi-square test was statistically significant; however, none of the individual pairwise comparisons was.

**Table 4.23**
**Sleep Health, by Age Group**

| | Ages 17–24 (1) | Ages 25–34 (2) | Ages 35–44 (3) | Ages 45+ (4) |
|---|---|---|---|---|
| Average hours of sleep per 24 hours during the work/duty week | | | | |
| 4 hours or less[f] | 9.7% (7.3–12.2) | 9.7% (7.9–11.5) | 11.9% (10.0–13.8) | 14.6% (10.7–18.5) |
| 5–6 hours | 50.9%[c] (46.9–54.9) | 53.9% (51.1–56.6) | 59.0%[a] (56.2–61.8) | 52.5% (48.3–56.6) |
| 7–8 hours | 37.4%[c] (33.6–41.2) | 35.2%[c] (32.6–37.8) | 28.7%[a,b] (26.2–31.1) | 31.7% (28.0–35.3) |
| 9+ hours | 2.0%[c] (1.0–3.0) | 1.2% (0.6–1.9) | 0.4%[a] (0.1–0.7) | 1.3% (0.0–2.6) |
| Average hours of sleep per 24 hours during the weekend/days off | | | | |
| 4 hours or less | 1.4%[c,d] (0.6–2.1) | 2.6%[d] (1.6–3.6) | 3.7%[a] (2.6–4.9) | 5.8%[a,b] (3.4–8.2) |
| 5–6 hours | 12.4%[c,d] (9.7–15.1) | 16.4%[c,d] (14.3–18.5) | 24.1%[a,b] (21.6–26.7) | 26.4%[a,b] (22.3–30.6) |
| 7–8 hours | 46.6%[b,c,d] (42.6–50.6) | 58.6%[a] (55.9–61.4) | 59.0%[a] (56.1–61.8) | 57.9%[a] (53.7–62.2) |
| 9+ hours | 39.7%[b,c,d] (35.8–43.5) | 22.4%[a,c,d] (20.1–24.7) | 13.2%[a,b] (11.3–15.0) | 9.8%[a,b] (7.5–12.1) |
| Average hours of sleep per 24 hours compared with average number of hours needed to feel fully refreshed and perform well | | | | |
| Enough sleep[f] | 25.5% (22.1–29.0) | 31.2% (28.6–33.8) | 29.8% (27.2–32.3) | 30.5% (26.8–34.2) |
| Less sleep than needed[f] | 55.7% (51.7–59.6) | 54.6% (51.8–57.4) | 59.3% (56.5–62.1) | 58.3% (54.2–62.3) |
| More sleep than needed | 18.8%[c,d] (15.7–21.9) | 14.2% (12.2–16.2) | 10.9%[a] (9.1–12.8) | 11.3%[a] (8.7–13.8) |
| Moderately or severely bothered by lack of energy due to poor sleep[e] | 31.9% (28.1–35.6) | 27.5% (25.0–30.0) | 30.8% (27.9–33.6) | 33.0% (28.6–37.4) |
| Satisfied with sleep (excellent or good) | 43.1% (39.2–47.0) | 47.1%[c] (44.3–49.8) | 41.3%[b] (38.5–44.1) | 44.1% (40.1–48.1) |
| Take sleep meds every day or almost every day | 6.9%[d] (4.9–9.0) | 8.1% (6.7–9.5) | 10.5% (8.7–12.2) | 11.4%[a] (8.7–14.0) |

NOTE: All data are weighted. 95-percent confidence intervals are presented in parentheses.

[a] Estimate is significantly different from the estimate in column 1 (ages 17–24).

[b] Estimate is significantly different from the estimate in column 2 (ages 25–34).

[c] Estimate is significantly different from the estimate in column 3 (ages 35–44).

[d] Estimate is significantly different from the estimate in column 4 (ages 45+).

[e] The omnibus chi-square test was not statistically significant ($p > 0.05$).

[f] At the aggregate, the chi-square test was statistically significant; however, none of the individual pairwise comparisons was.

**Table 4.24**
**Sleep Health, by Race/Ethnicity**

| | Non-Hispanic White (1) | Non-Hispanic Black (2) | Hispanic (3) | Non-Hispanic Asian (4) | Other (5) |
|---|---|---|---|---|---|
| **Average hours of sleep per 24 hours during the work/duty week** | | | | | |
| 4 hours or less | 8.6%[b] (7.3–9.9) | 17.7%[a] (13.2–22.1) | 11.4% (8.3–14.6) | 12.1% (5.8–18.4) | 13.0% (9.0–17.0) |
| 5–6 hours[f] | 53.7% (51.6–55.9) | 54.5% (49.0–60.0) | 52.7% (47.7–57.6) | 56.1% (47.0–65.1) | 58.7% (53.1–64.4) |
| 7–8 hours | 36.8%[b,e] (34.8–38.9) | 24.5%[a,c] (19.8–29.1) | 34.2%[b] (29.5–39.0) | 31.2% (22.8–39.6) | 27.2%[a] (22.2–32.2) |
| 9+ hours | 0.8%[b] (0.4–1.3) | 3.4%[a] (1.6–5.2) | 1.7% (0.3–3.1) | 0.6% (0.0–1.5) | 1.1% (0.3–1.8) |
| **Average hours of sleep per 24 hours during the weekend/days off** | | | | | |
| 4 hours or less | 2.3%[b] (1.6–3.0) | 5.6%[a] (3.4–7.8) | 3.3% (1.7–4.8) | 1.1% (0.0–2.9) | 2.4% (0.8–4.1) |
| 5–6 hours | 15.6%[b] (14.0–17.2) | 27.5%[a,c] (22.5–32.4) | 17.4%[b] (13.8–21.0) | 17.8% (11.0–24.6) | 21.4% (17.0–25.7) |
| 7–8 hours | 58.3%[b] (56.1–60.5) | 45.4%[a] (39.9–50.8) | 52.1% (47.1–57.0) | 58.6% (49.9–67.4) | 50.8% (45.0–56.6) |
| 9+ hours[f] | 23.7% (21.9–25.6) | 21.6% (17.0–26.1) | 27.3% (22.6–31.9) | 22.5% (15.5–29.5) | 25.4% (19.9–30.9) |
| **Average hours of sleep per 24 hours compared with average number of hours needed to feel fully refreshed and perform well** | | | | | |
| Enough sleep[f] | 30.6% (28.5–32.6) | 27.6% (22.8–32.4) | 28.1% (23.7–32.6) | 26.1% (18.8–33.4) | 25.6% (21.0–30.3) |
| Less sleep than needed | 54.4%[e] (52.3–56.6) | 55.8% (50.4–61.2) | 57.6% (52.7–62.5) | 62.2% (53.6–70.8) | 63.9%[a] (58.6–69.2) |
| More sleep than needed[f] | 15.0% (13.4–16.6) | 16.6% (12.7–20.5) | 14.3% (10.6–17.9) | 11.7% (5.6–17.8) | 10.5% (7.3–13.6) |
| Moderately or severely bothered by lack of energy due to poor sleep | 28.1%[e] (26.1–30.1) | 28.3% (23.4–33.2) | 34.4% (29.7–39.2) | 29.6% (21.2–38.1) | 36.2%[a] (30.5–41.8) |
| Satisfied with sleep (excellent or good)[f] | 46.9% (44.7–49.1) | 39.2% (34.0–44.4) | 41.5% (36.6–46.3) | 44.4% (35.5–53.3) | 39.1% (33.5–44.7) |
| Take sleep meds every day or almost every day[f] | 8.6% (7.4–9.8) | 10.9% (7.9–14.0) | 6.2% (4.1–8.4) | 12.6% (6.4–18.8) | 7.4% (4.8–10.0) |

NOTE: All data are weighted. 95-percent confidence intervals are presented in parentheses.

[a] Estimate is significantly different from the estimate in column 1 (non-Hispanic white).

[b] Estimate is significantly different from the estimate in column 2 (non-Hispanic black).

[c] Estimate is significantly different from the estimate in column 3 (Hispanic).

[d] Estimate is significantly different from the estimate in column 4 (non-Hispanic Asian).

[e] Estimate is significantly different from the estimate in column 5 (other).

[f] At the aggregate, the chi-square test was statistically significant; however, none of the individual pairwise comparisons was.

**Table 4.25**
**Sleep Health, by Education Level**

| | High School or Less (1) | Some College (2) | Bachelor's Degree or More (3) |
|---|---|---|---|
| Average hours of sleep per 24 hours during the work/duty week | | | |
| 4 hours or less | 10.8%[c] (8.0–13.7) | 12.9%[c] (11.1–14.7) | 7.0%[a,b] (5.5–8.5) |
| 5–6 hours[e] | 54.5% (49.9–59.2) | 55.8% (53.2–58.4) | 51.5% (49.0–54.1) |
| 7–8 hours | 32.0%[c] (27.6–36.3) | 30.4%[c] (28.0–32.8) | 40.5%[a,b] (38.1–43.0) |
| 9+ hours | 2.6%[b,c] (1.0–4.3) | 0.9%[a] (0.5–1.4) | 0.9%[a] (0.5–1.3) |
| Average hours of sleep per 24 hours during the weekend/days off | | | |
| 4 hours or less[e] | 3.0% (1.6–4.4) | 3.2% (2.2–4.1) | 2.1% (1.4–2.7) |
| 5–6 hours | 17.0% (13.6–20.4) | 19.7%[c] (17.7–21.8) | 15.5%[b] (13.7–17.4) |
| 7–8 hours | 45.8%[b,c] (41.2–50.5) | 53.4%[a,c] (50.7–56.0) | 63.8%[a,b] (61.4–66.2) |
| 9+ hours | 34.2%[b,c] (29.7–38.8) | 23.7%[a,c] (21.5–26.0) | 18.6%[a,b] (16.8–20.5) |
| Average hours of sleep per 24 hours compared with average number of hours needed to feel fully refreshed and perform well | | | |
| Enough sleep[e] | 27.9% (23.7–32.1) | 28.6% (26.2–31.0) | 30.9% (28.6–33.2) |
| Less sleep than needed[e] | 53.7% (49.0–58.4) | 57.9% (55.4–60.5) | 55.3% (52.8–57.8) |
| More sleep than needed | 18.4%[b] (14.6–22.2) | 13.5%[a] (11.7–15.2) | 13.8% (11.8–15.7) |
| Moderately or severely bothered by lack of energy due to poor sleep | 30.9%[c] (26.6–35.2) | 33.6%[c] (31.1–36.1) | 23.8%[a,b] (21.6–25.9) |
| Satisfied with sleep (excellent or good) | 40.0%[c] (35.4–44.6) | 41.5%[c] (38.9–44.1) | 51.4%[a,b] (48.9–54.0) |
| Take sleep meds every day or almost every day[d] | 7.8% (5.3–10.2) | 9.3% (7.8–10.7) | 8.0% (6.8–9.3) |

NOTE: All data are weighted. 95-percent confidence intervals are presented in parentheses.

[a] Estimate is significantly different from the estimate in column 1 (high school or less).

[b] Estimate is significantly different from the estimate in column 2 (some college).

[c] Estimate is significantly different from the estimate in column 3 (bachelor's degree or more).

[d] The omnibus chi-square test was not statistically significant ($p > 0.05$).

[e] At the aggregate, the chi-square test was statistically significant; however, none of the individual pairwise comparisons was.

## Supplements and Energy Drinks

### Dietary Supplements

Dietary supplements are commonly used in the United States (Gahche et al., 2011). The percentage of adults who report using dietary supplements is increasing, and more than half (53 percent) of adults use at least one dietary supplement (Gahche et al., 2011). There is considerable debate in medical and scientific communities about the risks and benefits of such supplements (Coulter, Newberry, and Hilton, 2011; Institute of Medicine, 2008). DoD also has concerns about the safety and effectiveness of supplements and their use by service members (Coulter, Newberry, and Hilton, 2011; Institute of Medicine, 2008). Specific health concerns include lack of scientific evidence, tainted supplements, and excessive nutrient and protein intake, among others. In 2008, the Institute of Medicine recommended that DoD monitor supplement use, report adverse events, ask service members about their supplement use, and provide information on supplements (Institute of Medicine, 2008). DoD has institutionalized the DoD Nutrition Committee to coordinate and address department-wide efforts to educate service members regarding supplement use and related matters (DoD, 2013b).

Despite the generally unclear evidence regarding use, safety, and effectiveness, as noted, more than half of U.S. adults report some use of dietary supplements (Rock, 2007). A systematic review of use by military personnel found that it ranges from 55 percent among men in the Army to 61 percent among men in the Marine Corps. Among women, the prevalence ranged from 65 percent in the Army to 76 percent in the Air Force (Knapik et al., 2014).

The 2015 HRBS asked respondents how often, in the past 12 months, they took any of the following six types of supplements: supplements for joint health, fish oil, protein powder, other legal body-building supplements, herbal supplements, and weight-loss products. Results are presented in Tables 4.26 through 4.31. Overall, 32.0 percent (CI: 30.6–33.5) of active-duty service members reported using at least one supplement daily. Other key findings include the following:

- Daily supplement use ranged from 5.9 percent for herbal supplements to 16.9 percent for protein powder (Table 4.26). Another 11.8 percent of active-duty service members used body-building supplements. There was notable service variation, with daily body-building supplement use ranging from 7.6 percent in the Coast Guard to 17.7 percent in the Marine Corps.
- Men were more likely than women to report using supplements for joint health (11.2 percent compared with 9.0 percent), fish oil (15.9 percent compared with 13.9 percent), protein powder (17.9 percent compared with 11.2 percent), and body-building supplements (13.0 percent compared with 5.4 percent). Men were also less likely than women to report using herbal supplements (5.5 percent compared with 8.2 percent) and weight-loss supplements (6.3 percent compared with 8.6 percent) (Table 4.28).
- On average, the percentage of service members reporting supplement use increased with increasing rank (Table 4.27) and education level (Table 4.31).
- Use of joint supplements, including fish oil, increased with age; however, use of protein powder and body-building supplements decreased with age (Table 4.29).
- There were few statistically significant differences in supplement use by race/ethnicity (Table 4.30).

**Energy Drinks**

Energy drinks contain large amounts of caffeine, which has demonstrated efficacy in operational situations and augments physical and cognitive performance. Caffeine-containing energy drinks (CCEDs) have become very popular; however, data on use of CCEDs are very limited. The health concerns regarding CCEDs primarily result from the high amount and concentration of caffeine in these drinks. From 2007 to 2011, there was a two-fold increase nationally in emergency department visits attributed to CCEDs, and CCEDs have been associated with alcohol use among college students (Substance Abuse and Mental Health Services Administration, 2013; Miller, 2008; Thombs et al., 2010).

While data on CCED use are lacking in the military, military members may be at increased risk for misuse. The CDC found that 45 percent of service members deployed to Afghanistan consumed at least one CCED daily, and 15 percent consumed three or more per day in 2010 (CDC, 2012). CCED consumption was associated with sleep disruptions and sleeping less than four hours per night (CDC, 2012).

The 2015 HRBS asked respondents how often they drank energy drinks or shots (e.g., Red Bull, Monster, 5-Hour Energy, Power Shots) in the past 30 days. Results are also shown in Tables 4.26 through 4.31. Key findings include the following:

- More than half (51.0 percent) of service members reported using energy drinks in the past month, and 7.2 percent reported daily energy drink use (Table 4.26). Daily energy drink consumption ranged from 3.9 percent in the Coast Guard to 11.8 percent in the Marine Corps.
- Women were more likely than men to report never using energy drinks (66.4 percent compared with 45.8 percent) and less likely to report infrequent, weekly, or daily energy drink consumption (Table 4.28).
- The percentage of service members reporting never using energy drinks increased with increasing pay grade (Table 4.27), age group (Table 4.29), and education level (Table 4.31). On average, self-reported infrequent, weekly, and daily energy drink consumption decreased with increasing pay grade, age group, and education level.
- There were few statistically significant differences in energy drink consumption by race/ethnicity (Table 4.30).

**Table 4.26**
**Past-Year Use of Dietary Supplements and Past-Month Use of Energy Drinks, by Service Branch**

| | Total (1) | Air Force (2) | Army (3) | Marine Corps (4) | Navy (5) | Coast Guard (6) |
|---|---|---|---|---|---|---|
| **Daily use of supplements in the past year** | | | | | | |
| Supplements for joint health[f] | 10.9% (9.9–11.9) | 10.5% (9.1–11.9) | 11.4% (9.4–13.4) | 12.3% (9.9–14.7) | 10.1% (8.1–12.0) | 7.5% (6.6–8.4) |
| Fish oil[f] | 15.6% (14.5–16.7) | 16.5% (14.8–18.1) | 15.5% (13.2–17.7) | 15.2% (12.5–18.0) | 15.4% (13.1–17.6) | 14.3% (13.1–15.4) |
| Protein powder | 16.9% (15.7–18.1) | 18.3%[b,c,e] (16.5–20.1) | 14.0%[a,c] (11.7–16.3) | 25.1%[a,b,d,e] (21.4–28.7) | 15.5%[c] (13.0–17.9) | 14.6%[a,c] (13.3–15.9) |
| Body-building supplements | 11.8% (10.7–12.9) | 11.5%[c,e] (9.9–13.0) | 10.1%[c] (8.0–12.2) | 17.7%[a,b,d,e] (14.4–21.0) | 12.0%[c,e] (9.7–14.3) | 7.6%[a,c,d] (6.7–8.6) |
| Herbal supplements[f] | 5.9% (5.2–6.6) | 6.6% (5.5–7.7) | 5.3% (3.9–6.7) | 5.3% (3.7–6.9) | 6.8% (5.2–8.3) | 5.7% (4.9–6.5) |
| Weight-loss supplements | 6.6% (5.9–7.4) | 6.2%[c,e] (5.1–7.2) | 5.9%[c] (4.5–7.3) | 10.5%[a,b,d,e] (8.0–12.9) | 6.2%[c] (4.7–7.8) | 4.2%[a,c] (3.5–4.9) |
| **Use of energy drinks in the past 30 days** | | | | | | |
| Never | 49.0% (47.4–50.6) | 52.7%[c,e] (50.5–54.9) | 50.1%[c,e] (46.9–53.3) | 33.4%[a,b,d,e] (29.8–37.0) | 51.9%[c,e] (48.8–54.9) | 58.4%[a,b,c,d] (56.8–60.1) |
| Infrequent | 27.0% (25.5–28.5) | 24.5%[c] (22.5–26.4) | 28.1% (25.0–31.1) | 31.5%[a,e] (27.6–35.4) | 25.4% (22.6–28.3) | 24.1%[c] (22.6–25.6) |
| Weekly | 16.8% (15.5–18.1) | 16.3%[c] (14.6–18.1) | 15.8%[c] (13.2–18.4) | 23.4%[a,b,d,e] (19.8–27.0) | 15.3%[c] (12.9–17.8) | 13.5%[c] (12.3–14.8) |
| Daily | 7.2% (6.3–8.0) | 6.5%[c,e] (5.3–7.7) | 6.0%[c] (4.5–7.5) | 11.8%[a,b,d,e] (9.1–14.5) | 7.4%[c,e] (5.6–9.2) | 3.9%[a,c,d] (3.2–4.6) |

NOTE: All data are weighted. 95-percent confidence intervals are presented in parentheses.

[a] Estimate is significantly different from the estimate in column 2 (Air Force).

[b] Estimate is significantly different from the estimate in column 3 (Army).

[c] Estimate is significantly different from the estimate in column 4 (Marine Corps).

[d] Estimate is significantly different from the estimate in column 5 (Navy).

[e] Estimate is significantly different from the estimate in column 6 (Coast Guard).

[f] The omnibus chi-square test was not statistically significant ($p > 0.05$).

**Table 4.27**
**Past-Year Use of Dietary Supplements and Past-Month Use of Energy Drinks, by Pay Grade**

| | E1–E4 (1) | E5–E6 (2) | E7–E9 (3) | W1–W5 (4) | O1–O3 (5) | O4–O10 (6) |
|---|---|---|---|---|---|---|
| **Daily use of supplements in the past year** | | | | | | |
| Supplements for joint health | 9.3%[d] (7.4–11.1) | 12.7% (10.9–14.5) | 12.4% (10.6–14.2) | 16.3%[a,e] (13.5–19.0) | 10.0%[d] (8.6–11.4) | 12.0% (10.4–13.5) |
| Fish oil | 13.0%[b,c,d,f] (10.9–15.0) | 17.3%[a] (15.3–19.4) | 18.8%[a] (16.7–21.0) | 20.3%[a] (17.2–23.3) | 15.7%[f] (14.1–17.4) | 20.4%[a,e] (18.4–22.3) |
| Protein powder | 17.8%[c,d,f] (15.5–20.1) | 18.7%[c,d,f] (16.6–20.7) | 12.4%[a,b,e] (10.6–14.1) | 12.1%[a,b] (9.6–14.6) | 16.4%[c,f] (14.7–18.1) | 10.8%[a,b,e] (9.2–12.3) |
| Body-building supplements | 13.8%[c,d,e,f] (11.6–15.9) | 13.1%[c,d,e,f] (11.3–14.9) | 9.0%[a,b,f] (7.3–10.6) | 6.8%[a,b,f] (4.9–8.7) | 8.3%[a,b,f] (7.0–9.6) | 3.4%[a,b,c,d,e] (2.5–4.3) |
| Herbal supplements[g] | 5.1% (3.8–6.4) | 7.4% (6.1–8.7) | 6.5% (5.2–7.8) | 5.8% (4.1–7.5) | 5.2% (4.3–6.2) | 5.3% (4.2–6.3) |
| Weight-loss supplements | 5.9%[c] (4.6–7.3) | 8.4%[e,f] (6.9–9.9) | 9.0%[a,e,f] (7.5–10.5) | 5.6% (3.9–7.3) | 4.2%[b,c] (3.3–5.1) | 3.8%[b,c] (2.9–4.7) |
| **Use of energy drinks in the past 30 days** | | | | | | |
| Never | 39.7%[b,c,d,e,f] (36.8–42.7) | 47.4%[a,c,d,e,f] (44.8–50.1) | 59.4%[a,b,d,f] (56.6–62.1) | 68.2%[a,b,c,f] (64.7–71.8) | 63.1%[a,b,f] (61.0–65.3) | 80.4%[a,b,c,d,e] (78.4–82.3) |
| Infrequent | 32.8%[b,c,d,e,f] (29.9–35.8) | 25.5%[a,d,e,f] (23.1–27.9) | 23.3%[a,d,f] (20.9–25.7) | 16.1%[a,b,c,f] (13.3–18.8) | 20.2%[a,b,f] (18.4–22.0) | 11.2%[a,b,c,d,e] (9.6–12.7) |
| Weekly | 20.1%[c,d,e,f] (17.5–22.6) | 17.6%[c,d,e,f] (15.6–19.6) | 11.3%[a,b,f] (9.6–13.1) | 10.7%[a,b,f] (8.3–13.1) | 12.5%[a,b,f] (11.0–14.1) | 6.2%[a,b,c,d,e] (5.0–7.4) |
| Daily | 7.4%[e,f] (5.8–8.9) | 9.5%[c,d,e,f] (7.9–11.0) | 6.0%[b,f] (4.7–7.3) | 5.0%[b,f] (3.3–6.6) | 4.1%[a,b,f] (3.2–5.1) | 2.3%[a,b,c,d,e] (1.6–3.1) |

NOTE: All data are weighted. 95-percent confidence intervals are presented in parentheses.

[a] Estimate is significantly different from the estimate in column 1 (E1–E4).

[b] Estimate is significantly different from the estimate in column 2 (E5–E6).

[c] Estimate is significantly different from the estimate in column 3 (E7–E9).

[d] Estimate is significantly different from the estimate in column 4 (W1–W5).

[e] Estimate is significantly different from the estimate in column 5 (O1–O3).

[f] Estimate is significantly different from the estimate in column 6 (O4–O10).

[g] The omnibus chi-square test was not statistically significant ($p > 0.05$).

Table 4.28
**Past-Year Use of Dietary Supplements and Past-Month Use of Energy Drinks, by Gender**

|  | Men (1) | Women (2) |
|---|---|---|
| Daily use of supplements in the past year |  |  |
| Supplements for joint health | 11.2%[a] (10.1–12.4) | 9.0% (8.0–10.1) |
| Fish oil | 15.9%[a] (14.6–17.3) | 13.9% (12.6–15.1) |
| Protein powder | 17.9%[a] (16.5–19.3) | 11.2% (10.0–12.4) |
| Body-building supplements | 13.0%[a] (11.7–14.3) | 5.4% (4.5–6.3) |
| Herbal supplements | 5.5%[a] (4.7–6.3) | 8.2% (7.1–9.3) |
| Weight-loss supplements | 6.3%[a] (5.4–7.1) | 8.6% (7.5–9.6) |
| Use of energy drinks in the past 30 days |  |  |
| Never | 45.8%[a] (44.0–47.6) | 66.4% (64.5–68.2) |
| Infrequent | 28.6%[a] (26.8–30.3) | 18.5% (16.9–20.0) |
| Weekly | 18.1%[a] (16.6–19.6) | 9.8% (8.6–11.0) |
| Daily | 7.5%[a] (6.5–8.5) | 5.4% (4.4–6.3) |

NOTE: All data are weighted. 95-percent confidence intervals are presented in parentheses.

[a] Estimate is significantly different from the estimate in column 2 (women).

**Table 4.29**
**Past-Year Use of Dietary Supplements and Past-Month Use of Energy Drinks, by Age Group**

| | Ages 17–24 (1) | Ages 25–34 (2) | Ages 35–44 (3) | Ages 45+ (4) |
|---|---|---|---|---|
| Daily use of supplements in the past year | | | | |
| Supplements for joint health | 8.5%[d] (6.6–10.5) | 11.5% (9.8–13.2) | 11.7% (10.0–13.4) | 14.4%[a] (11.8–16.9) |
| Fish oil | 13.1%[d] (10.8–15.5) | 15.5%[d] (13.7–17.2) | 17.2% (15.2–19.2) | 21.6%[a,b] (18.5–24.6) |
| Protein powder | 20.3%[c,d] (17.5–23.1) | 17.7%[c,d] (15.9–19.6) | 13.1%[a,b] (11.2–15.0) | 9.8%[a,b] (7.5–12.0) |
| Body-building supplements | 17.0%[b,c,d] (14.2–19.7) | 11.4%[a,d] (9.8–13.0) | 8.4%[a,d] (6.8–10.1) | 4.3%[a,b,c] (2.6–6.0) |
| Herbal supplements[e] | 5.3% (3.8–6.8) | 5.9% (4.9–7.0) | 6.7% (5.4–8.0) | 5.9% (4.2–7.6) |
| Weight-loss supplements[e] | 6.8% (5.1–8.5) | 6.5% (5.4–7.6) | 7.0% (5.7–8.2) | 5.2% (3.7–6.8) |
| Use of energy drinks in past 30 days | | | | |
| Never | 36.9%[b,c,d] (33.5–40.2) | 47.9%[a,c,d] (45.4–50.4) | 57.4%[a,b,d] (54.7–60.2) | 78.9%[a,b,c] (75.5–82.4) |
| Infrequent | 33.9%[b,c,d] (30.5–37.3) | 26.4%[a,d] (24.0–28.7) | 23.7%[a,d] (21.2–26.2) | 12.9%[a,b,c] (10.3–15.4) |
| Weekly | 21.5%[c,d] (18.5–24.4) | 17.6%[c,d] (15.6–19.6) | 13.0%[a,b,d] (11.0–15.0) | 4.8%[a,b,c] (2.9–6.8) |
| Daily | 7.8%[d] (5.9–9.7) | 8.1%[d] (6.8–9.5) | 5.8% (4.6–7.1) | 3.4%[a,b] (1.4–5.3) |

NOTE: All data are weighted. 95-percent confidence intervals are presented in parentheses.

[a] Estimate is significantly different from the estimate in column 1 (ages 17–24).

[b] Estimate is significantly different from the estimate in column 2 (ages 25–34).

[c] Estimate is significantly different from the estimate in column 3 (ages 35–44).

[d] Estimate is significantly different from the estimate in column 4 (ages 45+).

[e] The omnibus chi-square test was not statistically significant ($p > 0.05$).

**Table 4.30**
**Past-Year Use of Dietary Supplements and Past-Month Use of Energy Drinks, by Race/Ethnicity**

| | Non-Hispanic White (1) | Non-Hispanic Black (2) | Hispanic (3) | Non-Hispanic Asian (4) | Other (5) |
|---|---|---|---|---|---|
| Daily use of supplements in the past year | | | | | |
| Supplements for joint health | 10.0%[e] (8.9–11.2) | 9.2% (6.3–12.0) | 13.4% (10.3–16.4) | 8.7% (3.7–13.7) | 15.7%[a] (11.8–19.6) |
| Fish oil[f] | 15.7% (14.3–17.2) | 12.8% (9.6–16.0) | 16.1% (13.1–19.0) | 11.8% (7.0–16.5) | 20.2% (15.9–24.5) |
| Protein powder | 16.5%[c] (15.0–18.0) | 12.7%[c] (9.8–15.7) | 22.5%[a,b,d] (18.6–26.3) | 10.7%[c] (5.8–15.5) | 17.5% (13.7–21.3) |
| Body-building supplements | 11.2%[c] (9.8–12.5) | 10.2% (7.2–13.2) | 16.0%[a] (12.5–19.5) | 7.8% (3.0–12.6) | 12.9% (9.3–16.5) |
| Herbal supplements[f] | 5.5% (4.6–6.4) | 6.1% (3.8–8.3) | 7.1% (5.0–9.2) | 3.2% (1.5–4.8) | 7.8% (5.5–10.0) |
| Weight loss supplements | 6.0%[e] (5.1–6.9) | 6.4% (4.2–8.6) | 8.1% (6.0–10.3) | 3.7%[?] (1.3–6.0) | 9.5%[?,d] (6.8–12.9) |
| Use of energy drinks in the past 30 days | | | | | |
| Never | 48.1%[b] (46.2–50.1) | 58.1%[a,c] (53.3–63.0) | 44.6%[b] (40.3–48.9) | 51.8% (43.6–60.0) | 48.9% (43.8–54.0) |
| Infrequent[g] | 25.6% (23.7–27.4) | 25.4% (20.9–29.9) | 30.0% (25.8–34.1) | 33.8% (25.6–42.1) | 29.4% (24.4–34.4) |
| Weekly[g] | 18.3% (16.6–20.0) | 13.3% (9.7–17.0) | 17.1% (13.5–20.6) | 11.8% (6.9–16.6) | 14.0% (10.0–18.0) |
| Daily | 8.0%[b] (6.8–9.1) | 3.2%[a,c,e] (1.7–4.6) | 8.4%[b] (5.9–10.8) | 2.6% (0.5–4.7) | 7.7%[b] (4.8–10.7) |

NOTE: All data are weighted. 95-percent confidence intervals are presented in parentheses.

[a] Estimate is significantly different from the estimate in column 1 (non-Hispanic white).

[b] Estimate is significantly different from the estimate in column 2 (non-Hispanic black).

[c] Estimate is significantly different from the estimate in column 3 (Hispanic).

[d] Estimate is significantly different from the estimate in column 4 (non-Hispanic Asian).

[e] Estimate is significantly different from the estimate in column 5 (other).

[f] The omnibus chi-square test was not statistically significant ($p > 0.05$).

[g] At the aggregate, the chi-square test was statistically significant; however, none of the individual pairwise comparisons was.

Table 4.31

**Past-Year Use of Dietary Supplements and Past-Month Use of Energy Drinks, by Education Level**

| | High School or Less (1) | Some College (2) | Bachelor's Degree or More (3) |
|---|---|---|---|
| **Daily use of supplements in the past year** | | | |
| Supplements for joint health | 7.8%[b,c] (5.7–9.9) | 11.4%[a] (9.9–12.9) | 12.2%[a] (10.5–13.8) |
| Fish oil | 11.9%[b,c] (9.4–14.3) | 16.1%[a] (14.4–17.9) | 17.3%[a] (15.5–19.0) |
| Protein powder[d] | 18.6% (15.5–21.8) | 17.2% (15.4–19.0) | 15.2% (13.5–17.0) |
| Body-building supplements | 14.5%[c] (11.7–17.4) | 12.7%[c] (11.1–14.4) | 8.7%[a,b] (7.1–10.3) |
| Herbal supplements | 4.2%[b] (2.6–5.8) | 6.9%[a] (5.8–8.1) | 5.5% (4.6–6.4) |
| Weight-loss supplements | 5.6% (3.9–7.4) | 7.8%[c] (6.6–9.0) | 5.4%[b] (4.4–6.5) |
| **Use of energy drinks in the past 30 days** | | | |
| Never | 33.6%[b,c] (29.7–37.5) | 46.1%[a,c] (43.8–48.5) | 63.6%[a,b] (61.2–66.1) |
| Infrequent | 34.3%[b,c] (30.3–38.4) | 28.3%[a,c] (26.1–30.5) | 20.1%[a,b] (18.0–22.3) |
| Weekly | 22.0%[c] (18.4–25.6) | 18.0%[c] (16.2–19.9) | 11.5%[a,b] (9.7–13.2) |
| Daily | 10.1%[c] (7.7–12.5) | 7.5%[c] (6.3–8.7) | 4.8%[a,b] (3.6–5.9) |

NOTE: All data are weighted. 95-percent confidence intervals are presented in parentheses.

[a] Estimate is significantly different from the estimate in column 1 (high school or less).

[b] Estimate is significantly different from the estimate in column 2 (some college).

[c] Estimate is significantly different from the estimate in column 3 (bachelor's degree or more).

[d] The omnibus chi-square test was not statistically significant ($p > 0.05$).

## Texting or Emailing While Driving

Because typing and reading text while driving has adverse effects on stimulus detection, reaction time, and other components required for safe driving, texting while driving has been shown to be dangerous and associated with injuries and mortality from motor vehicle accidents (Caird et al., 2014). Injuries and accidents associated with texting while driving, both on and off duty, have a direct influence on personnel health—and, therefore, readiness. Using an existing item from the National Youth Risk Behavior Survey, respondents were asked on how many of the past 30 days they texted or emailed while driving a car or other vehicle. We considered between zero and five days to be occasional, between six and 19 days to be frequent, and 20 or more days to be regular. Results are presented in Tables 4.32 through 4.37. Key findings include the following:

- Overall, self-reported texting or emailing while driving was not common. Among service members, 12.8 percent reported frequently or regularly texting or emailing while driving (Table 4.32).
- On average, regular texting or emailing while driving decreased with increasing pay grade (Table 4.33).
- There were few statistically significant differences in self-reported texting or emailing while driving by gender (Table 4.34).
- Regular texting or emailing while driving decreased with age, from 8.2 percent among service members aged 17–24 to 2.6 percent among service members aged 45 or older (Table 4.35).
- There were no statistically significant differences in texting or emailing while driving by race/ethnicity (Table 4.36) and few significant differences by education level (Table 4.37).

**Table 4.32**
**Past-Month Texting or Emailing While Driving, by Service Branch**

|  | Total (1) | Air Force (2) | Army (3) | Marine Corps (4) | Navy (5) | Coast Guard (6) |
|---|---|---|---|---|---|---|
| Occasionally (0–5 days) | 87.2% (86.1–88.3) | 89.9%[c,d] (88.6–91.2) | 87.9%[c,e] (85.8–90.0) | 80.8%[a,b,e] (77.2–84.3) | 86.3%[a,e] (84.1–88.4) | 91.1%[b,c,d] (90.1–92.1) |
| Frequently (6–19 days) | 6.1% (5.4–6.8) | 4.9%[c] (4.0–5.9) | 5.4% (4.1–6.6) | 8.7%[a] (6.2–11.1) | 7.0% (5.5–8.5) | 5.7% (4.9–6.6) |
| Regularly (20+ days) | 6.7% (5.8–7.6) | 5.2%[c,e] (4.1–6.2) | 6.7%[e] (5.0–8.5) | 10.6%[a,e] (7.8–13.4) | 6.7%[e] (5.0–8.4) | 3.2%[a,b,c,d] (2.6–3.8) |

NOTE: All data are weighted. 95-percent confidence intervals are presented in parentheses.

[a] Estimate is significantly different from the estimate in column 2 (Air Force).

[b] Estimate is significantly different from the estimate in column 3 (Army).

[c] Estimate is significantly different from the estimate in column 4 (Marine Corps).

[d] Estimate is significantly different from the estimate in column 5 (Navy).

[e] Estimate is significantly different from the estimate in column 6 (Coast Guard).

**Table 4.33**
**Past-Month Texting or Emailing While Driving, by Pay Grade**

|  | E1–E4 (1) | E5–E6 (2) | E7–E9 (3) | W1–W5 (4) | O1–O3 (5) | O4–O10 (6) |
|---|---|---|---|---|---|---|
| Occasionally (0–5 days) | 87.7%[e] (85.6–89.8) | 87.9%[e] (86.0–89.7) | 89.3%[e] (87.5–91.1) | 90.3%[e] (88.0–92.6) | 79.7%[a,b,c,d,f] (77.9–81.5) | 89.1%[e] (87.6–90.6) |
| Frequently (6–19 days) | 4.6%[e] (3.4–5.9) | 5.8%[e] (4.5–7.2) | 6.6%[e] (5.1–8.1) | 5.7%[e] (4.0–7.5) | 11.4%[a,b,c,d,f] (10.0–12.8) | 6.9%[e] (5.7–8.0) |
| Regularly (20+ days) | 7.6%[c,f] (5.8–9.5) | 6.3% (4.9–7.7) | 4.1%[a,e] (3.1–5.2) | 4.0%[e] (2.4–5.5) | 8.8%[b,c,f] (7.5–10.2) | 4.0%[a,e] (3.1–5.0) |

NOTE: All data are weighted. 95-percent confidence intervals are presented in parentheses.

[a] Estimate is significantly different from the estimate in column 1 (E1–E4).

[b] Estimate is significantly different from the estimate in column 2 (E5–E6).

[c] Estimate is significantly different from the estimate in column 3 (E7–E9).

[d] Estimate is significantly different from the estimate in column 4 (W1–W5).

[e] Estimate is significantly different from the estimate in column 5 (O1–O3).

[f] Estimate is significantly different from the estimate in column 6 (O4–O10).

**Table 4.34**
**Past-Month Texting or Emailing While Driving, by Gender**

|  | Men (1) | Women (2) |
|---|---|---|
| Occasionally (0–5 days) | 87.6%[a] (86.4–88.9) | 85.0% (83.6–86.4) |
| Frequently (6–19 days) | 5.7%[a] (4.9–6.5) | 8.1% (7.0–9.1) |
| Regularly (20+ days)[b] | 6.7% (5.7–7.7) | 6.9% (5.9–7.9) |

NOTE: All data are weighted. 95-percent confidence intervals are presented in parentheses.

[a] Estimate is significantly different from the estimate in column 2 (women).

[b] At the aggregate, the chi-square test was statistically significant; however, none of the individual pairwise comparisons was.

**Table 4.35**
**Past-Month Texting or Emailing While Driving, by Age Group**

|  | Ages 17–24 (1) | Ages 25–34 (2) | Ages 35–44 (3) | Ages 45+ (4) |
|---|---|---|---|---|
| Occasionally (0–5 days) | 85.7%[d] (83.2–88.3) | 86.2%[d] (84.5–87.9) | 88.5%[d] (86.7–90.3) | 94.1%[a,b,c] (92.4–95.8) |
| Frequently (6–19 days) | 6.1%[d] (4.5–7.7) | 6.6%[d] (5.5–7.6) | 6.0%[d] (4.7–7.3) | 3.3%[a,b,c] (2.2–4.3) |
| Regularly (20+ days) | 8.2%[d] (6.1–10.2) | 7.3%[d] (5.8–8.7) | 5.5% (4.2–6.8) | 2.6%[a,b] (1.2–4.1) |

NOTE: All data are weighted. 95-percent confidence intervals are presented in parentheses.

[a] Estimate is significantly different from the estimate in column 1 (ages 17–24).

[b] Estimate is significantly different from the estimate in column 2 (ages 25–34).

[c] Estimate is significantly different from the estimate in column 3 (ages 35–44).

[d] Estimate is significantly different from the estimate in column 4 (ages 45+).

**Table 4.36**
**Past-Month Texting or Emailing While Driving, by Race/Ethnicity**

|  | Non-Hispanic White (1) | Non-Hispanic Black (2) | Hispanic (3) | Non-Hispanic Asian (4) | Other (5) |
|---|---|---|---|---|---|
| Occasionally (0–5 days)[a] | 86.4% (85.0–87.8) | 88.8% (85.9–91.7) | 89.7% (87.4–92.1) | 87.1% (81.1–93.2) | 86.3% (82.5–90.2) |
| Frequently (6–19 days)[a] | 6.8% (5.9–7.8) | 4.2% (2.7–5.8) | 5.5% (3.7–7.4) | 4.4% (2.0–6.9) | 4.9% (2.9–7.0) |
| Regularly (20+ days)[a] | 6.8% (5.6–7.9) | 6.9% (4.4–9.5) | 4.7% (3.2–6.2) | 8.4% (2.7–14.1) | 8.7% (5.3–12.1) |

NOTE: All data are weighted. 95-percent confidence intervals are presented in parentheses.

[a] The omnibus chi-square test was not statistically significant ($p > 0.05$).

**Table 4.37**
**Past-Month Texting or Emailing While Driving, by Education Level**

|  | High School or Less (1) | Some College (2) | Bachelor's Degree or More (3) |
|---|---|---|---|
| Occasionally (0–5 days) | 86.4% (83.4–89.3) | 88.7%[c] (87.2–90.2) | 85.5%[b] (83.7–87.2) |
| Frequently (6–19 days) | 5.6% (3.8–7.4) | 5.4%[c] (4.4–6.4) | 7.4%[b] (6.3–8.5) |
| Regularly (20+ days)[d] | 8.0% (5.6–10.5) | 5.9% (4.8–7.1) | 7.2% (5.7–8.6) |

NOTE: All data are weighted. 95-percent confidence intervals are presented in parentheses.

[a] Estimate is significantly different from the estimate in column 1 (high school or less).

[b] Estimate is significantly different from the estimate in column 2 (some college).

[c] Estimate is significantly different from the estimate in column 3 (bachelor's degree or more).

[d] At the aggregate, the chi-square test was statistically significant; however, none of the individual pairwise comparisons was.

## Summary

This chapter presented analyses of several health promotion and disease prevention activities among active-duty service members. Overall, service members are doing well in this domain. Based on 2015 HRBS estimates, active-duty service members met or exceeded HP2020 targets for physical activity, and the majority (80.5 percent) reported playing electronic games outside of work or school for less than two hours per day.

Overall, 32.5 percent of active-duty service members aged 20 or older were a healthy (normal) weight, which is slightly below the HP2020 target and lower than the 2011 HRBS normal-weight estimate (34.7 percent). Even so, the proportion of obese service members aged 20 or older (15.0 percent) was considerably lower than the HP2020 target of 30.5 percent. In addition, active-duty service members were close to or exceeded national standards for BMI, and the majority (65.7 percent) of service members were deemed overweight or obese, which may be cause for concern. Overweight or obese service members reduce overall force fitness and readiness. However, because we categorized weight status by BMI, which is an indirect measure of body fat, the percentage of service members deemed overweight or obese was likely inflated because muscular body types may have been misclassified.

More than half (56.3 percent) of active-duty service members reported getting less sleep than they need, and one-third (29.9 percent) were moderately or severely bothered by lack of energy due to poor sleep. According to HP2020's definition of sufficient sleep, active-duty service members (34.9 percent) were not meeting the HP2020 target (70.8 percent). Insufficient sleep is associated with numerous adverse health outcomes that may limit quality of life and military readiness.

A majority of respondents (93.2 percent) reported having a routine checkup with a doctor in the past two years, which may help identify the early onset of chronic disease and ensure appropriate preventive care. Furthermore, use of CAM was common among respondents (47.6 percent); however, daily supplement use was not prevalent, with estimates ranging from 5.9 percent for herbal supplements to 16.9 percent for protein powder. Self-reported texting or emailing while driving was also not commonly reported. Approximately 12.8 percent of service members reported frequently or regularly texting or emailing while driving.

More than half (51.0 percent) of respondents reported using energy drinks in the past month, and 7.2 percent reported daily energy drink use. These data suggest that the military may be at increased risk for CCED misuse, which is associated with several adverse health outcomes, including poor sleep, emergency department visits, and alcohol use.

# CHAPTER FIVE

# Substance Use

This chapter details self-reported substance use across the armed forces. We provide some background information and then present percentages of service members consuming alcohol in various patterns, using tobacco in a variety of forms, and using illicit and prescription drugs (including use as prescribed, misuse, and overuse). We examine differences across key subgroups and offer some key contextual information on where these substances are obtained and the culture surrounding alcohol and tobacco use.

Each section highlights the importance or relevance of the substance use topic to the general population and to the military and then provides an analysis of each topic by service branch. When relevant, we present an analysis of each topic by pay grade, gender, age group, race/ethnicity, and education level. Key measures used are described in the applicable sections, and additional details about these measures can be found in Appendix D. All analyses demonstrated statistically significant omnibus tests (a Rao-Scott chi-square test for categorical variables and $F$-tests for continuous variables) unless otherwise noted in the tables. Statistically significant group differences (pairwise comparisons) are presented within each table. However, only those statistically significant differences that the research team's subject-matter experts determined to be substantively meaningful (i.e., could be used to change or develop policy or contribute to inequalities in health outcomes across subgroups) are discussed in the text. Readers should use caution when interpreting comparisons between the 2015 HRBS results and other populations or prior versions of the HRBS because these comparisons are not necessarily statistically significant and could simply reflect sampling variability across the two samples being compared; however, where available, we provide confidence intervals for comparisons.

## Alcohol

Excessive alcohol consumption, including binge and heavy drinking, is one of the leading preventable causes of death in the United States. It can lead to risky sexual activity, accidents, violence, and other serious consequences. Alcohol misuse is linked to a variety of adverse outcomes in the military and is a costly problem for DoD (Dall et al., 2007; Harwood et al., 2009).

This section describes alcohol use among service members, including the percentages of personnel who are binge drinkers, heavy drinkers, and hazardous or possibly disordered drinkers. It also reports on consequences of drinking, including serious negative consequences from drinking, alcohol-related risk behaviors, and alcohol-related productivity loss. Perceptions of the military drinking culture are described using assessments of perceived drinking norms in the military, as well as perceived supervisor attitudes toward drinking. Finally, we provide service members' reports of where they typically purchase alcohol. This measure is new to the 2015 HRBS. Health promotion efforts increasingly include limiting access to products that can adversely affect health, including alcohol (Cohen, Scribner, and Farley, 2000). Policies on alcohol sales have been shown to have a substantial effect on alcohol consumption and negative consequences from alcohol (Babor, 2010). For each alcohol measure, we report prevalence overall and by service branch, pay grade, gender, age group, race/ethnicity, and education level. Where available, we report on comparable percentages from prior HRBSs and estimates of the U.S. general population to assist with interpretation.

*Binge drinking* was defined as consuming five or more drinks on one occasion for men and four or more drinks for women at least once in the past month. *Heavy drinking* was defined as consuming five or more drinks on one occasion (i.e., binge drinking) on five or more days in the past month. This definition differs from prior HRBSs but is consistent with the NSDUH, facilitating civilian comparisons.[1] The 2008 HRBS defined heavy drinking as five or more drinks on four days in the past month (Bray, Pemberton, et al., 2009), and the 2011 HRBS defined heavy drinking as 14 drinks per week among men and seven drinks per week among women (Barlas et al., 2013).

*Hazardous or disordered drinking* (that is, drinking that meets criteria for a possible alcohol use disorder) was measured using the AUDIT-C. For this classification, we used scores on the AUDIT-C of four or more for men and three or more for women because those scores indicate probable hazardous drinking or a probable alcohol use disorder (Bradley et al., 2007; Bush et al., 1998). We included three measures of negative drinking outcomes: serious consequences from drinking, productivity loss from drinking, and risk behavior from drinking. Each of the drinking outcome items has been included in previous HRBSs, but the specific derivation of estimates for serious consequences and productivity loss varied from the 2015 version. For this reason, we do not report comparisons with prior years for these measures.

### Binge Drinking, Heavy Drinking, and Hazardous or Disordered Drinking

Tables 5.1 through 5.6 present percentages of service members who meet criteria for binge drinking, heavy drinking, and hazardous or disordered drinking overall and by service branch and demographic group—pay grade, gender, age group, race/ethnicity, and education level. Key findings include the following:

- In the 2015 HRBS, 30.0 percent of service members were binge drinkers, compared with 33.1 percent (CI: 32.3–33.9) in 2011 (Table 5.1) (Barlas et al., 2013). In the most recent comparable U.S. general population estimate, 24.7 percent (CI: 24.1–25.3) among those 18 and older were binge drinkers (Center for Behavioral Health Statistics and Quality [CBHSQ], 2015b, Table 2.46B). Some of the disparity between the military and general populations is likely due to the high percentage of men and young adults in the armed forces; both groups are more likely to binge drink within the U.S. general population (CBHSQ, 2015b, Table 2.46B). The HP2020 target for the general population is for no more than 24.4 percent of adults to engage in binge drinking (HHS, 2010a).
- Across all services, 5.4 percent of personnel were heavy drinkers (Table 5.1). In the U.S. general population in 2014, 6.7 percent (CI: 6.4–7.0) were heavy drinkers (CBHSQ, 2015b).

---

[1]  See Substance Abuse and Mental Health Services Administration, 2016.

- More than one in three service personnel (35.3 percent) met criteria indicative of hazardous drinking or possible alcohol use disorder (Table 5.1). Although the 2011 HRBS did not report overall percentages for this measure, the 2008 report did (using the AUDIT, a measure roughly comparable to the AUDIT-C). At that time, the percentage of hazardous drinkers was 33.1 percent (CI: 31.1–35.3) (Bray, Pemberton, et al., 2009).
- Binge, heavy, and hazardous drinking all varied substantially by service. The percentage of all three behaviors was highest in the Marine Corps, where hazardous drinking occurred in nearly half of service members. The Air Force had the lowest percentages of these drinking patterns among the services (Table 5.1).
- In general, higher percentages of problematic drinkers (all three categories) were found among junior and mid-grade enlisted members (E1–E6). However, the percentage of hazardous or possibly disordered drinkers was highest among junior officers (O1–O3), at 39.2 percent. This group also had the second-highest percentage of binge drinkers (Table 5.2).
- Binge, heavy, and hazardous drinking were all more common among men than among women (Table 5.3).
- Progressively higher percentages of binge, heavy, and hazardous drinking were present with decreasing age. Percentages of binge and hazardous drinkers were about twice as high among those aged 17–24 as among those aged 45 or older, and the percentage of heavy drinkers was more than four times as high (9.5 percent compared with 2.1 percent) (Table 5.4).
- Greater percentages of non-Hispanic whites and Hispanic service members were binge drinkers, relative to non-Hispanic blacks and non-Hispanic Asians. Whites were also the group with the greatest percentage of hazardous or disordered drinkers (40.6 percent compared with 32.9 percent among Hispanic service members, 19.5 percent among non-Hispanic Asians, and 18.8 percent among non-Hispanic blacks) (Table 5.5).
- Those with a high school education or less were more likely to be binge, heavy, or hazardous drinkers (Table 5.6).

**Table 5.1**
**Alcohol Use, by Service Branch**

| | Total (1) | Air Force (2) | Army (3) | Marine Corps (4) | Navy (5) | Coast Guard (6) |
|---|---|---|---|---|---|---|
| Binge drinking | 30.0% (28.4–31.5) | 20.5%[b,c,d,e] (18.6–22.3) | 28.2%[a,c,d] (25.1–31.2) | 42.6%[a,b,d,e] (38.5–46.8) | 34.2%[a,b,c] (31.1–37.3) | 31.5%[a,c] (29.9–33.1) |
| Heavy drinking | 5.4% (4.6–6.1) | 2.7%[c,d] (1.8–3.5) | 4.1%[c] (2.8–5.5) | 12.4%[a,b,d,e] (9.3–15.4) | 6.0%[a,c,e] (4.3–7.7) | 3.5%[c,d] (2.8–4.1) |
| Hazardous or disordered drinking | 35.3% (33.7–36.9) | 26.1%[b,c,d,e] (24.1–28.1) | 33.1%[a,c,d] (30.0–36.2) | 48.6%[a,b,d,e] (44.4–52.7) | 39.8%[a,b,c,e] (36.7–43.0) | 34.0%[a,c,d] (32.4–35.6) |

NOTE: All data are weighted. 95-percent confidence intervals are presented in parentheses.
[a] Estimate is significantly different from the estimate in column 2 (Air Force).
[b] Estimate is significantly different from the estimate in column 3 (Army).
[c] Estimate is significantly different from the estimate in column 4 (Marine Corps).
[d] Estimate is significantly different from the estimate in column 5 (Navy).
[e] Estimate is significantly different from the estimate in column 6 (Coast Guard).

**Table 5.2**
**Alcohol Use, by Pay Grade**

| | E1–E4 (1) | E5–E6 (2) | E7–E9 (3) | W1–W5 (4) | O1–O3 (5) | O4–O10 (6) |
|---|---|---|---|---|---|---|
| Binge drinking | 33.0%[c,d,f] (30.1–36.0) | 28.8%[f] (26.3–31.2) | 24.0%[a,e] (21.6–26.4) | 24.9%[a,e] (21.6–28.2) | 31.4%[c,d,f] (29.3–33.6) | 21.8%[a,b,e] (19.8–23.8) |
| Heavy drinking | 6.9%[d,e,f] (5.3–8.4) | 5.1%[e,f] (3.8–6.4) | 4.3%[f] (3.1–5.6) | 3.2%[a] (1.9–4.6) | 2.5%[a,b] (1.8–3.3) | 2.2%[a,b,c] (1.4–2.9) |
| Hazardous or disordered drinking | 37.2%[c] (34.1–40.2) | 33.1%[e] (30.6–35.6) | 30.5%[a,e] (28.0–33.1) | 30.7%[e] (27.2–34.2) | 39.2%[b,c,d] (37.0–41.4) | 34.7% (32.4–37.0) |

NOTE: All data are weighted. 95-percent confidence intervals are presented in parentheses.

[a] Estimate is significantly different from the estimate in column 1 (E1–E4).

[b] Estimate is significantly different from the estimate in column 2 (E5–E6).

[c] Estimate is significantly different from the estimate in column 3 (E7–E9).

[d] Estimate is significantly different from the estimate in column 4 (W1–W5).

[e] Estimate is significantly different from the estimate in column 5 (O1–O3).

[f] Estimate is significantly different from the estimate in column 6 (O4–O10).

**Table 5.3**
**Alcohol Use, by Gender**

| | Men (1) | Women (2) |
|---|---|---|
| Binge drinking | 31.2%[a] (29.5–33.0) | 23.0% (21.4–24.7) |
| Heavy drinking | 6.1%[a] (5.2–7.0) | 1.3% (0.8–1.8) |
| Hazardous or disordered drinking | 36.0%[a] (34.2–37.9) | 31.3% (29.5–33.1) |

NOTE: All data are weighted. 95-percent confidence intervals are presented in parentheses.

[a] Estimate is significantly different from the estimate in column 2 (women).

**Table 5.4**
**Alcohol Use, by Age Group**

| | Ages 17–24 (1) | Ages 25–34 (2) | Ages 35–44 (3) | Ages 45+ (4) |
|---|---|---|---|---|
| Binge drinking | 37.3%[b,c,d] (33.8–40.8) | 31.8%[a,c,d] (29.3–34.2) | 22.1%[a,b,d] (19.9–24.3) | 14.8%[a,b,c] (12.3–17.3) |
| Heavy drinking | 9.5%[b,c,d] (7.3–11.6) | 4.1%[a] (3.0–5.1) | 3.6%[a] (2.5–4.6) | 2.1%[a] (1.2–3.0) |
| Hazardous or disordered drinking | 42.5%[c,d] (39.0–46.1) | 36.9%[c,d] (34.5–39.4) | 27.2%[a,b,d] (24.9–29.5) | 22.0%[a,b,c] (19.2–24.9) |

NOTE: All data are weighted. 95-percent confidence intervals are presented in parentheses.

[a] Estimate is significantly different from the estimate in column 1 (ages 17–24).

[b] Estimate is significantly different from the estimate in column 2 (ages 25–34).

[c] Estimate is significantly different from the estimate in column 3 (ages 35–44).

[d] Estimate is significantly different from the estimate in column 4 (ages 45+).

**Table 5.5**
**Alcohol Use, by Race/Ethnicity**

| | Non-Hispanic White (1) | Non-Hispanic Black (2) | Hispanic (3) | Non-Hispanic Asian (4) | Other (5) |
|---|---|---|---|---|---|
| Binge drinking | 32.7%[b,d] (30.7–34.6) | 18.4%[a,c,e] (14.6–22.2) | 31.0%[b] (26.9–35.0) | 21.5%[a] (14.8–28.3) | 30.3%[b] (25.4–35.2) |
| Heavy drinking[f] | 5.8% (4.7–6.9) | 2.6% (1.0–4.2) | 6.1% (4.1–8.2) | 2.8% (0.3–5.3) | 5.8% (3.1–8.4) |
| Hazardous or disordered drinking | 40.6%[b,c,d] (38.6–42.7) | 18.8%[a,c,e] (15.2–22.4) | 32.9%[a,b,d] (28.7–37.1) | 19.5%[a,c,e] (13.1–25.9) | 35.2%[b,d] (30.2–40.2) |

NOTE: All data are weighted. 95-percent confidence intervals are presented in parentheses.

[a] Estimate is significantly different from the estimate in column 1 (non-Hispanic white).

[b] Estimate is significantly different from the estimate in column 2 (non-Hispanic black).

[c] Estimate is significantly different from the estimate in column 3 (Hispanic).

[d] Estimate is significantly different from the estimate in column 4 (non-Hispanic Asian).

[e] Estimate is significantly different from the estimate in column 5 (other).

[f] The omnibus chi-square test was not statistically significant ($p > 0.05$).

**Table 5.6**
**Alcohol Use, by Education Level**

| | High School or Less (1) | Some College (2) | Bachelor's Degree or More (3) |
|---|---|---|---|
| Binge drinking | 38.1%[b,c] (34.0–42.3) | 28.9%[a] (26.7–31.1) | 26.2%[a] (24.1–28.4) |
| Heavy drinking | 9.9%[b,c] (7.4–12.3) | 5.2%[a,c] (4.1–6.4) | 2.6%[a,b] (1.8–3.4) |
| Hazardous or disordered drinking | 40.2%[c] (36.0–44.3) | 35.1% (32.8–37.4) | 32.4%[a] (30.1–34.6) |

NOTE: All data are weighted. 95-percent confidence intervals are presented in parentheses.

[a] Estimate is significantly different from the estimate in column 1 (high school or less).

[b] Estimate is significantly different from the estimate in column 2 (some college).

[c] Estimate is significantly different from the estimate in column 3 (bachelor's degree or more).

**Negative Drinking Outcomes: Serious Consequences, Risk Behaviors, and Productivity Loss from Drinking**

Tables 5.7 through 5.12 display the percentages of personnel overall and in various subgroups who reported any serious consequences from drinking (e.g., "I hit my spouse/significant other after having too much to drink"), any risk behaviors from drinking (e.g., "I drove a car or other vehicle when I had too much to drink"), and any alcohol-related job productivity loss. Key findings from all active-duty respondents include the following:

- In the 2015 HRBS, 8.2 percent of service members experienced one or more serious consequences of drinking (Table 5.7).
- The percentage of personnel reporting any drinking-related risk behaviors was 6.9 percent (Table 5.7). In the 2011 HRBS, the overall percentage reporting risk behaviors from drinking was 9.7 percent.
- Across the services, 6.1 percent of personnel reported work-related productivity loss from alcohol use (Table 5.7).

For all three of these negative outcomes associated with drinking, significant differences emerged among demographic groups. Key findings include the following:

- Among the services, Coast Guard personnel were the least likely to report serious consequences from drinking, and Air Force personnel were the least likely to report productivity loss. Marines were the most likely to report serious consequences. The percentages of Navy and Marine Corps personnel who reported productivity loss from drinking were roughly equal (Table 5.7).
- Junior enlisted (E1–E4) service members were the most likely to experience serious drinking consequences and productivity loss (Table 5.8).
- No statistically significant differences by gender emerged for any of the three outcomes (Table 5.9).
- Younger service members were more likely than older personnel to experience each of the three negative consequences from drinking (Table 5.10). In particular, serious consequences (1.8 percent) and productivity loss (2.1 percent) were uncommon among those aged 45 or older.
- There was no evidence of statistically significant differences in serious consequences or risk behavior by race/ethnicity (Table 5.11). Non-Hispanic blacks were significantly less likely than other racial or ethnic groups to report productivity loss from drinking.
- Service members with a high school degree or less were more likely to report both serious drinking consequences and productivity loss; the percentages among those with a high school education or less were nearly twice as high as those with a college degree or more (Table 5.12). There were no statistically significant differences by education level in alcohol-related risk behaviors.

**Table 5.7**
**Serious Consequences, Risk Behaviors, and Productivity Loss from Drinking, by Service Branch**

| | Total (1) | Air Force (2) | Army (3) | Marine Corps (4) | Navy (5) | Coast Guard (6) |
|---|---|---|---|---|---|---|
| Any serious consequences | 8.2% (7.2–9.1) | 4.7%[b,c,d] (3.7–5.6) | 7.4%[a,c,e] (5.5–9.3) | 15.0%[a,b,d,e] (11.8–18.1) | 9.1%[a,c,e] (7.0–11.1) | 4.6%[b,c,d] (3.8–5.3) |
| Any alcohol-related risk behaviors | 6.9% (5.9–7.8) | 4.6%[b,c] (3.5–5.7) | 7.9%[a] (5.9–9.9) | 9.1%[a,e] (6.3–11.8) | 6.3% (4.7–7.9) | 5.4%[a] (4.6–6.2) |
| Any productivity loss | 6.1% (5.3–6.9) | 3.1%[c,d] (2.3–3.9) | 5.2%[d] (3.8–6.6) | 8.8%[a,e] (6.3–11.3) | 9.1%[a,b,e] (7.1–11.1) | 4.4%[c,d] (3.7–5.1) |

NOTE: All data are weighted. 95-percent confidence intervals are presented in parentheses.

[a] Estimate is significantly different from the estimate in column 2 (Air Force).

[b] Estimate is significantly different from the estimate in column 3 (Army).

[c] Estimate is significantly different from the estimate in column 4 (Marine Corps).

[d] Estimate is significantly different from the estimate in column 5 (Navy).

[e] Estimate is significantly different from the estimate in column 6 (Coast Guard).

**Table 5.8**
**Serious Consequences, Risk Behaviors, and Productivity Loss from Drinking, by Pay Grade**

| | E1–E4 (1) | E5–E6 (2) | E7–E9 (3) | W1–W5 (4) | O1–O3 (5) | O4–O10 (6) |
|---|---|---|---|---|---|---|
| Any serious consequences | 11.7%[b,c,d,e,f] (9.7–13.8) | 6.4%[a,d,f] (5.1–7.7) | 4.0%[a] (2.9–5.1) | 3.1%[a,b] (1.8–4.4) | 5.4%[a,f] (4.4–6.4) | 2.6%[a,b,e] (1.9–3.4) |
| Any alcohol-related risk behaviors[g] | 7.7% (5.8–9.6) | 6.7% (5.2–8.3) | 5.6% (4.0–7.1) | 5.3% (3.4–7.2) | 7.0% (5.8–8.3) | 4.1% (3.1–5.1) |
| Any productivity loss | 7.1%[c] (5.6–8.7) | 5.8% (4.5–7.2) | 4.1%[a] (3.0–5.2) | 4.2% (2.7–5.7) | 5.6% (4.6–6.7) | 4.7% (3.6–5.7) |

NOTE: All data are weighted. 95-percent confidence intervals are presented in parentheses.

[a] Estimate is significantly different from the estimate in column 1 (E1–E4).

[b] Estimate is significantly different from the estimate in column 2 (E5–E6).

[c] Estimate is significantly different from the estimate in column 3 (E7–E9).

[d] Estimate is significantly different from the estimate in column 4 (W1–W5).

[e] Estimate is significantly different from the estimate in column 5 (O1–O3).

[f] Estimate is significantly different from the estimate in column 6 (O4–O10).

[g] The omnibus chi-square test was not statistically significant ($p > 0.05$).

**Table 5.9**
**Serious Consequences, Risk Behaviors, and Productivity Loss from Drinking, by Gender**

| | Men (1) | Women (2) |
|---|---|---|
| Any serious consequences[a] | 8.2% (7.0–9.3) | 8.1% (7.0–9.3) |
| Any alcohol-related risk behaviors[a] | 7.1% (6.0–8.2) | 5.7% (4.7–6.7) |
| Any productivity loss[a] | 6.3% (5.3–7.2) | 5.3% (4.3–6.3) |

NOTE: All data are weighted. 95-percent confidence intervals are presented in parentheses.

[a] The omnibus chi-square test was not statistically significant ($p > 0.05$).

Table 5.10
**Serious Consequences, Risk Behaviors, and Productivity Loss from Drinking, by Age Group**

|  | Ages 17–24 (1) | Ages 25–34 (2) | Ages 35–44 (3) | Ages 45+ (4) |
|---|---|---|---|---|
| Any serious consequences | 13.2%[b,c,d] (10.8–15.6) | 7.8%[a,c,d] (6.3–9.3) | 4.2%[a,b,d] (3.0–5.3) | 1.8%[a,b,c] (1.1–2.6) |
| Any alcohol-related risk behaviors | 7.9%[c,d] (5.8–10.1) | 8.1%[c,d] (6.5–9.8) | 3.9%[a,b] (3.0–4.9) | 4.0%[a,b] (2.6–5.4) |
| Any productivity loss | 9.1%[b,c,d] (7.0–11.2) | 5.6%[a,d] (4.5–6.7) | 4.5%[a,d] (3.5–5.6) | 2.1%[a,b,c] (1.3–3.0) |

NOTE: All data are weighted. 95-percent confidence intervals are presented in parentheses.

[a] Estimate is significantly different from the estimate in column 1 (ages 17–24).

[b] Estimate is significantly different from the estimate in column 2 (ages 25–34).

[c] Estimate is significantly different from the estimate in column 3 (ages 35–44).

[d] Estimate is significantly different from the estimate in column 4 (ages 45+).

Table 5.11
**Serious Consequences, Risk Behaviors, and Productivity Loss from Drinking, by Race/Ethnicity**

|  | Non-Hispanic White (1) | Non-Hispanic Black (2) | Hispanic (3) | Non-Hispanic Asian (4) | Other (5) |
|---|---|---|---|---|---|
| Any serious consequences[f] | 8.3% (7.0–9.6) | 5.9% (3.4–8.3) | 8.0% (5.5–10.5) | 7.0% (2.0–12.1) | 11.0% (7.6–14.5) |
| Any alcohol-related risk behaviors[f] | 7.5% (6.2–8.8) | 5.1% (2.8–7.4) | 6.0% (3.6–8.4) | 5.1% (0.9–9.4) | 6.8% (3.9–9.7) |
| Any productivity loss | 6.5%[b] (5.5–7.6) | 2.9%[a,c] (1.5–4.2) | 7.4%[b] (4.9–9.8) | 6.3% (2.0–10.7) | 5.2% (2.9–7.5) |

NOTE: All data are weighted. 95-percent confidence intervals are presented in parentheses.

[a] Estimate is significantly different from the estimate in column 1 (non-Hispanic white)

[b] Estimate is significantly different from the estimate in column 2 (non-Hispanic black)

[c] Estimate is significantly different from the estimate in column 3 (Hispanic)

[d] Estimate is significantly different from the estimate in column 4 (non-Hispanic Asian)

[e] Estimate is significantly different from the estimate in column 5 (other).

[f] The omnibus chi-square test was not statistically significant ($p > 0.05$).

Table 5.12
**Serious Consequences, Risk Behaviors, and Productivity Loss from Drinking, by Education Level**

|  | High School or Less (1) | Some College (2) | Bachelor's Degree or More (3) |
|---|---|---|---|
| Any serious consequences | 12.9%[b,c] (10.1–15.7) | 7.7%[a] (6.3–9.0) | 5.7%[a] (4.3–7.2) |
| Any alcohol-related risk behaviors[d] | 8.4% (5.7–11.0) | 6.6% (5.3–7.9) | 6.4% (5.0–7.9) |
| Any productivity loss | 8.4%[c] (6.0–10.8) | 6.0% (4.9–7.2) | 4.8%[a] (3.8–5.8) |

NOTE: All data are weighted. 95-percent confidence intervals are presented in parentheses.

[a] Estimate is significantly different from the estimate in column 1 (high school or less).

[b] Estimate is significantly different from the estimate in column 2 (some college).

[c] Estimate is significantly different from the estimate in column 3 (bachelor's degree or more).

[d] The omnibus chi-square test was not statistically significant ($p > 0.05$).

**Military Drinking Culture, On-Base Alcohol Purchases, and Perceived Supervisor Attitudes Toward Alcohol Use**

Service members' perceptions of military alcohol culture, their place of purchase for alcohol, and their perceptions of their supervisor's attitude toward drinking are presented in Tables 5.13 through 5.18. Key findings include the following:

- More than two-thirds (68.2 percent) of service members endorsed one or more items indicating that they perceive military culture to be supportive of drinking (Table 5.13).
- Alcohol purchases were about equally distributed on and off base. More than one-third (37.6 percent) of service members most often purchased alcohol on base, a nearly equal percentage (38.3 percent) purchased alcohol mostly off base, and the remainder (24.1 percent) purchased alcohol equally often on and off base (Table 5.13).
- Fewer than one in five service members (18.9 percent) felt that their supervisor strongly discourages alcohol use (Table 5.13).
- These patterns varied by service branch (Table 5.13). Perceptions of the military culture as supportive of drinking were most common among Marines. Marines were also the least likely to report that their supervisor strongly discourages alcohol use. Although members of the other services purchased alcohol on and off base about equally often, Navy and Coast Guard personnel were more likely to purchase alcohol off base than on.
- Junior enlisted service members were the most likely to see military culture as supportive of drinking (Table 5.14). Officers were less likely than others to buy their alcohol on base and less likely to see their supervisors as discouraging alcohol use.
- Women were slightly less likely than men to see military culture as supportive of drinking, more likely to say their supervisors strongly discourage drinking, and slightly more likely to buy their alcohol off base (Table 5.15).
- Younger service members (aged 17–24) were substantially more likely to see the military culture as supportive of drinking and, along with those aged 25–34, were less likely to see their supervisor as strongly discouraging drinking (Table 5.16).
- Non-Hispanic blacks and Non-Hispanic Asians were more likely than personnel from other racial or ethnic backgrounds to see their supervisors as strongly discouraging alcohol use (Table 5.17). Non-Hispanic blacks also saw the military culture as somewhat less supportive of drinking. There were no statistically significant racial or ethnic differences in the place of alcohol purchase.
- Personnel with a high school education or less were more likely to see the military as supportive of drinking, although those with some college or a college degree were more likely to report that their supervisors do not discourage drinking (Table 5.18). Those with a college degree or more were more likely to purchase alcohol off base.

**Table 5.13**
**Military Drinking Culture, On-Base Alcohol Purchases, and Perceived Supervisor Attitudes Toward Alcohol Use, by Service Branch**

| | Total (1) | Air Force (2) | Army (3) | Marine Corps (4) | Navy (5) | Coast Guard (6) |
|---|---|---|---|---|---|---|
| Military culture supportive of drinking | 68.2% (66.8–69.7) | 65.3%[c,e] (63.2–67.4) | 69.2%[e] (66.3–72.1) | 74.1%[a,d,e] (70.6–77.6) | 67.0%[c,e] (64.2–69.9) | 60.1%[a,b,c,d] (58.5–61.8) |
| Mainly purchased alcohol on base | 37.6% (35.8–39.4) | 40.2%[d,e] (37.8–42.7) | 43.3%[d,e] (39.6–47.1) | 41.0%[d,e] (36.5–45.5) | 27.5%[a,b,c,e] (24.4–30.6) | 14.7%[a,b,c,d] (13.4–16.0) |
| Mainly purchased alcohol off base | 38.3% (36.5–40.0) | 34.6%[d,e] (32.3–36.9) | 35.4%[d,e] (31.9–39.0) | 33.6%[d,e] (29.5–37.7) | 44.9%[a,b,c,e] (41.4–48.4) | 66.3%[a,b,c,d] (64.5–68.0) |
| Purchased alcohol equally on and off base | 24.1% (22.6–25.7) | 25.2%[e] (23.1–27.3) | 21.2%[d] (18.2–24.3) | 25.4%[e] (21.4–29.4) | 27.5%[b,e] (24.3–30.7) | 19.1%[a,c,d] (17.6–20.5) |
| Supervisor does not discourage alcohol use | 42.4% (40.9–44.0) | 48.8%[c,d,e] (46.6–51.0) | 43.8%[d,e] (40.5–47.0) | 38.6%[a] (34.7–42.6) | 37.2%[a,b] (34.2–40.3) | 37.1%[a,b] (35.5–38.8) |
| Supervisor somewhat discourages alcohol use | 38.7% (37.1–40.2) | 34.5%[c,d,e] (32.3–36.6) | 35.0%[c,d,e] (31.9–38.2) | 44.8%[a,b] (40.7–48.9) | 44.3%[a,b] (41.1–47.4) | 42.8%[a,b] (41.1–44.5) |
| Supervisor strongly discourages alcohol use | 18.9% (17.6–20.2) | 16.7%[b,e] (15.1–18.3) | 21.2%[a] (18.5–23.9) | 16.5% (13.5–19.6) | 18.5% (16.1–21.0) | 20.1%[a] (18.7–21.5) |

NOTE: All data are weighted. 95-percent confidence intervals are presented in parentheses.

[a] Estimate is significantly different from the estimate in column 2 (Air Force).

[b] Estimate is significantly different from the estimate in column 3 (Army).

[c] Estimate is significantly different from the estimate in column 4 (Marine Corps).

[d] Estimate is significantly different from the estimate in column 5 (Navy).

[e] Estimate is significantly different from the estimate in column 6 (Coast Guard).

**Table 5.14**
**Military Drinking Culture, On-Base Alcohol Purchases, and Perceived Supervisor Attitudes Toward Alcohol Use, by Pay Grade**

| | E1–E4 (1) | E5–E6 (2) | E7–E9 (3) | W1–W5 (4) | O1–O3 (5) | O4–O10 (6) |
|---|---|---|---|---|---|---|
| Military culture supportive of drinking | 75.0%[b,c,d,e,f] (72.3–77.7) | 68.1%[a,c,d,f] (65.6–70.6) | 56.3%[a,b,e,f] (53.5–59.1) | 55.6%[a,b,e,f] (51.8–59.4) | 64.8%[a,c,d,f] (62.7–67.0) | 47.9%[a,b,c,d,e] (45.5–50.3) |
| Mainly purchased alcohol on base | 41.2%[e,f] (37.6–44.8) | 37.3%[e] (34.4–40.2) | 39.0%[e,f] (36.0–42.0) | 41.0%[e,f] (36.8–45.2) | 25.8%[a,b,c,d,f] (23.6–28.0) | 33.1%[a,c,d,e] (30.7–35.6) |
| Mainly purchased alcohol off base | 33.9%[e,f] (30.5–37.4) | 40.3%[e] (37.4–43.2) | 36.2%[e] (33.3–39.1) | 35.4%[e] (31.4–39.4) | 49.4%[a,b,c,d,f] (46.9–51.8) | 41.3%[a,e] (38.8–43.9) |
| Purchased alcohol equally on and off base[g] | 24.9% (21.7–28.1) | 22.4% (20.0–24.8) | 24.8% (22.2–27.4) | 23.6% (20.1–27.2) | 24.8% (22.7–26.9) | 25.5% (23.3–27.8) |
| Supervisor does not discourage alcohol use | 40.1%[e,f] (37.0–43.1) | 43.5% (40.9–46.2) | 43.1% (40.3–45.8) | 47.0% (43.2–50.7) | 45.7%[a] (43.5–48.0) | 47.1%[a] (44.7–49.4) |
| Supervisor somewhat discourages alcohol use[g] | 39.9% (36.9–42.9) | 38.4% (35.9–41.0) | 36.1% (33.5–38.7) | 33.1% (29.7–36.6) | 38.9% (36.7–41.1) | 35.7% (33.5–38.0) |
| Supervisor strongly discourages alcohol use | 20.0%[e] (17.6–22.5) | 18.0% (15.9–20.1) | 20.8%[e] (18.6–23.1) | 19.9% (16.9–22.9) | 15.4%[a,c] (13.8–17.1) | 17.2% (15.4–19.0) |

NOTE: All data are weighted. 95-percent confidence intervals are presented in parentheses.

[a] Estimate is significantly different from the estimate in column 1 (E1–E4).

[b] Estimate is significantly different from the estimate in column 2 (E5–E6).

[c] Estimate is significantly different from the estimate in column 3 (E7–E9).

[d] Estimate is significantly different from the estimate in column 4 (W1–W5).

[e] Estimate is significantly different from the estimate in column 5 (O1–O3).

[f] Estimate is significantly different from the estimate in column 6 (O4–O10).

[g] At the aggregate, the chi-square test was statistically significant; however, none of the individual pairwise comparisons was.

**Table 5.15**
**Military Drinking Culture, On-Base Alcohol Purchases, and Perceived Supervisor Attitudes Toward Alcohol Use, by Gender**

|  | Men (1) | Women (2) |
|---|---|---|
| Military culture supportive of drinking | 69.1%[a] (67.4–70.8) | 63.3% (61.5–65.1) |
| Mainly purchased alcohol on base | 38.6%[a] (36.6–40.6) | 32.1% (30.1–34.2) |
| Mainly purchased alcohol off base | 37.3%[a] (35.4–39.3) | 43.3% (41.2–45.4) |
| Purchased alcohol equally on and off base[b] | 24.1% (22.3–25.8) | 24.6% (22.7–26.5) |
| Supervisor does not discourage alcohol use | 42.9%[a] (41.1–44.8) | 39.8% (38.0–41.7) |
| Supervisor somewhat discourages alcohol use[b] | 39.0% (37.2–40.9) | 36.7% (34.8–38.5) |
| Supervisor strongly discourages alcohol use | 18.0%[a] (16.6–19.5) | 23.5% (21.9–25.1) |

NOTE: All data are weighted. 95-percent confidence intervals are presented in parentheses.

[a] Estimate is significantly different from the estimate in column 2 (women).

[b] At the aggregate, the chi-square test was statistically significant; however, none of the individual pairwise comparisons was.

**Table 5.16**
**Military Drinking Culture, On-Base Alcohol Purchases, and Perceived Supervisor Attitudes Toward Alcohol Use, by Age Group**

|  | Ages 17–24 (1) | Ages 25–34 (2) | Ages 35–44 (3) | Ages 45+ (4) |
|---|---|---|---|---|
| Military culture supportive of drinking | 77.7%[b,c,d] (74.7–80.7) | 69.7%[a,c,d] (67.4–72.0) | 59.2%[a,b,d] (56.5–61.9) | 49.7%[a,b,c] (45.7–53.6) |
| Mainly purchased alcohol on base | 41.3% (37.1–45.5) | 34.8%[d] (32.1–37.5) | 37.5% (34.6–40.4) | 42.0%[b] (37.7–46.3) |
| Mainly purchased alcohol off base | 31.7%[b,c] (27.9–35.6) | 42.1%[a,d] (39.4–44.8) | 39.6%[a,d] (36.7–42.5) | 33.0%[b,c] (29.2–36.9) |
| Purchased alcohol equally on and off base[e] | 27.0% (23.2–30.8) | 23.1% (20.8–25.4) | 22.9% (20.6–25.1) | 25.0% (20.9–29.1) |
| Supervisor does not discourage alcohol use | 37.3%[b,c] (33.8–40.7) | 44.7%[a] (42.2–47.3) | 45.1%[a] (42.4–47.8) | 41.5% (37.7–45.4) |
| Supervisor somewhat discourages alcohol use | 43.6%[c,d] (40.1–47.2) | 38.3% (35.9–40.8) | 34.6%[a] (32.1–37.2) | 33.0%[a] (29.4–36.6) |
| Supervisor strongly discourages alcohol use | 19.1%[d] (16.2–22.0) | 16.9%[d] (15.0–18.9) | 20.3% (18.0–22.5) | 25.5%[a,b] (22.0–28.9) |

NOTE: All data are weighted. 95-percent confidence intervals are presented in parentheses.

[a] Estimate is significantly different from the estimate in column 1 (ages 17–24).

[b] Estimate is significantly different from the estimate in column 2 (ages 25–34).

[c] Estimate is significantly different from the estimate in column 3 (ages 35–44).

[d] Estimate is significantly different from the estimate in column 4 (ages 45+).

[e] At the aggregate, the chi-square test was statistically significant; however, none of the individual pairwise comparisons was.

Table 5.17
Military Drinking Culture, On-Base Alcohol Purchases, and Perceived Supervisor Attitudes Toward Alcohol Use, by Race/Ethnicity

| | Non-Hispanic White (1) | Non-Hispanic Black (2) | Hispanic (3) | Non-Hispanic Asian (4) | Other (5) |
|---|---|---|---|---|---|
| Military culture supportive of drinking | 68.1% (66.3–69.9) | 63.8%[e] (59.2–68.4) | 70.1% (66.1–74.1) | 65.4% (57.6–73.2) | 73.5%[b] (69.1–78.0) |
| Mainly purchased alcohol on base[f] | 36.7% (34.5–38.9) | 44.0% (38.4–49.6) | 37.5% (32.6–42.3) | 33.8% (24.8–42.8) | 38.6% (32.8–44.4) |
| Mainly purchased alcohol off base[f] | 40.3% (38.1–42.4) | 35.0% (29.4–40.6) | 35.6% (30.8–40.4) | 34.4% (25.1–43.7) | 34.8% (29.6–40.0) |
| Purchased alcohol equally on and off base[f] | 23.1% (21.2–24.9) | 20.9% (16.6–25.3) | 26.9% (22.5–31.3) | 31.9% (22.7–41.0) | 26.6% (21.4–31.9) |
| Supervisor does not discourage alcohol use[g] | 43.9% (41.9–46.0) | 37.9% (33.3–42.4) | 41.0% (36.7–45.3) | 38.6% (30.6–46.6) | 43.4% (38.2–48.5) |
| Supervisor somewhat discourages alcohol use | 41.2%[b] (39.1–43.2) | 33.2%[a] (28.6–37.9) | 35.9% (31.7–40.1) | 31.7% (24.4–39.0) | 38.6% (33.5–43.7) |
| Supervisor strongly discourages alcohol use | 14.9%[b,c,d] (13.5–16.4) | 28.9%[a,e] (24.6–33.3) | 23.1%[a] (19.4–26.9) | 29.7%[a,e] (22.1–37.4) | 18.0%[b,d] (14.3–21.7) |

NOTE: All data are weighted. 95-percent confidence intervals are presented in parentheses.

[a] Estimate is significantly different from the estimate in column 1 (non-Hispanic white).

[b] Estimate is significantly different from the estimate in column 2 (non-Hispanic black).

[c] Estimate is significantly different from the estimate in column 3 (Hispanic).

[d] Estimate is significantly different from the estimate in column 4 (non-Hispanic Asian).

[e] Estimate is significantly different from the estimate in column 5 (other).

[f] The omnibus chi-square test was not statistically significant ($p > 0.05$).

[g] At the aggregate, the chi-square test was statistically significant; however, none of the individual pairwise comparisons was.

**Table 5.18**
**Military Drinking Culture, On-Base Alcohol Purchases, and Perceived Supervisor Attitudes Toward Alcohol Use, by Education Level**

| | High School or Less (1) | Some College (2) | Bachelor's Degree or More (3) |
|---|---|---|---|
| Military culture supportive of drinking | 75.2%[b,c] (71.6–78.8) | 68.3%[a,c] (66.1–70.5) | 63.5%[a,b] (61.4–65.7) |
| Mainly purchased alcohol on base | 40.7%[c] (35.7–45.7) | 40.1%[c] (37.5–42.8) | 32.0%[a,b] (29.6–34.4) |
| Mainly purchased alcohol off base | 32.2%[c] (27.8–36.7) | 36.7%[c] (34.1–39.2) | 44.1%[a,b] (41.5–46.7) |
| Purchased alcohol equally on and off base[d] | 27.1% (22.5–31.7) | 23.2% (21.0–25.4) | 23.9% (21.7–26.2) |
| Supervisor does not discourage alcohol use | 35.6%[b,c] (31.5–39.6) | 43.4%[a] (41.1–45.8) | 45.4%[a] (43.0–47.8) |
| Supervisor somewhat discourages alcohol use | 46.1%[b,c] (41.8–50.3) | 37.3%[a] (35.0–39.6) | 36.0%[a] (33.7–38.2) |
| Supervisor strongly discourages alcohol use[d] | 18.4% (15.2–21.5) | 19.3% (17.4–21.2) | 18.7% (16.7–20.6) |

NOTE: All data are weighted. 95-percent confidence intervals are presented in parentheses.

[a] Estimate is significantly different from the estimate in column 1 (high school or less).

[b] Estimate is significantly different from the estimate in column 2 (some college).

[c] Estimate is significantly different from the estimate in column 3 (bachelor's degree or more).

[d] At the aggregate, the chi-square test was statistically significant; however, none of the individual pairwise comparisons was.

## Tobacco

Tobacco use is the single-most preventable cause of disease and death in the United States and causes a wide variety of health problems (HHS, 2014). Exposure to secondhand smoke also poses grave risks, including lung cancer. Cigarette smoking is the most common form of tobacco use. The percentage of current adult smokers in the nation has been declining over the past decade, as has the percentage of daily smokers and the number of cigarettes typically consumed by them (CDC, 2015d). However, smoking rates remain particularly high among men and younger adults—demographic groups that make up much of the U.S. military.

Other forms of tobacco use are also of concern. Smokeless tobacco (e.g., chewing tobacco, snuff) is a particular issue in the military (Peterson et al., 2007). And although the health effects of e-cigarettes are not yet known, they contain chemicals that may cause harm to users and those with secondhand exposure (Callahan-Lyon, 2014).

This section presents data on current (past month) and daily cigarette smoking and average cigarettes smoked by daily users. We also describe current cigar smoking; lifetime and current use of smokeless tobacco; and lifetime, past-year, and current use of e-cigarettes. For most of these measures (daily smoking is an exception), we provide information on differences in prevalence by service branch and other demographic groups. We present data on smoking cessation attempts and secondhand smoke exposure, as well as the percentage of service members who purchase cigarettes on base and the percentages that see their supervisor as discouraging tobacco use (cigarettes or smokeless tobacco).

As noted in the section on alcohol use, health promotion efforts increasingly include limiting access to products that can adversely affect health (Cohen, Scribner, and Farley, 2000). Consistent with this, the CDC recommends tobacco sale restrictions and price increases as effective methods of reducing smoking and related disease and death (CDC, 2014). A new item was added to the 2015 HRBS to examine the percentage of service members who purchase cigarettes on versus off base.

### Cigarette, E-Cigarette, Cigar, and Smokeless Tobacco Use

Tables 5.19 through 5.24 show the percentages of service members who currently smoke cigarettes, e-cigarettes, and cigars and who use smokeless tobacco, presented by service branch and demographic characteristics. Key findings from all active-duty respondents include the following:

- Across all services and demographics, 13.9 percent of service members were current cigarette smokers; 7.4 percent smoked cigarettes daily (Table 5.19). The percentages among U.S. adults in 2014 were 16.8 percent (CI: 16.1–17.4) current smokers and 12.9 percent daily smokers (CDC, 2015d). The 2011 HRBS found that 24.0 percent (CI: 23.4–24.6) of service personnel reported that they were current cigarette smokers. The HP2020 target is to reduce the percentage of adult current cigarette smokers in the general population to 12 percent or less.
- Among daily smokers, 10.8 cigarettes were consumed each day, on average. In 2014, daily adult smokers in the United States smoked an average of 13.8 cigarettes each day (CDC, 2015d).
- More than one-third of service members had ever tried e-cigarettes (35.7 percent; CI: 34.1–37.3), 12.4 percent (CI: 11.2–13.7) were current (past-month) users, and 11.1 percent

(CI: 9.0–13.2) were daily e-cigarette smokers (Table 5.19). The 2011 HRBS measured past-year e-cigarette use; at that time, 4.6 percent (CI: 4.2–5.0) of service members had smoked e-cigarettes in the past year. In 2014, 12.6 percent of the general population had ever tried e-cigarettes, and 3.7 percent were current users (used some days or every day) (Schoenborn and Gindi, 2015).

- In the 2015 HRBS, 8.7 percent of service personnel were current (past-month) cigar smokers (Table 5.19). In the general population of adults, 4.8 percent (CI: 4.6–5.0) were current cigar smokers (CBHSQ, 2015b). The 2011 HRBS did not report past-month cigar smoking (Barlas et al., 2013).
- The percentage of service members who had ever used smokeless tobacco was 32.7 percent (CI: 31.1–34.3). The percentage who used currently (in the past month) was 12.7 percent (Table 5.19). Among U.S. adults in the general population, current use was 3.4 percent (CI: 3.2–3.6) in 2014 (CBHSQ, 2015b). No comparable figure was provided for current (past-month) use in the 2011 HRBS.

Several important differences by service branch and demographic group emerged. Key findings include the following:

- All forms of tobacco use were more common among personnel in the Marine Corps than in any other service branch (Table 5.19). All four forms of use were least common in the Air Force and Coast Guard, for the most part, although the percentage of Army personnel smoking cigars was the lowest among all services.
- Junior enlisted service members were much more likely than more-senior enlisted personnel to engage in all forms of tobacco use, apart from cigars; warrant officers were less likely to smoke cigarettes than enlisted personnel but more likely to do so than officers; and senior officers had the lowest rates of e-cigarette use (Table 5.20).
- More men than women engaged in all four forms of tobacco use, but the difference was highly pronounced for smokeless tobacco, where the prevalence of use among men was more than seven times higher than among women (Table 5.21).
- Younger personnel (Table 5.22) and those with less education (Table 5.24) were also more likely than their peers to engage in all forms of tobacco use. The percentage using tobacco in each form rapidly decreased with increases in age and education level.
- Non-Hispanic blacks had the lowest percentage of cigarette smokers, and non-Hispanic Asians were least likely to be users of smokeless tobacco (Table 5.23).

These patterns are mostly consistent with the U.S. general population, where men are more often users of tobacco than women, non-Hispanic whites tend to be tobacco users more so than other racial or ethnic groups, and those who are younger and less educated are more likely to use tobacco (CDC, 2015d; CBHSQ, 2015b; Schoenborn and Gindi, 2015).

Table 5.19
Current Tobacco Use, by Service Branch

| | Total (1) | Air Force (2) | Army (3) | Marine Corps (4) | Navy (5) | Coast Guard (6) |
|---|---|---|---|---|---|---|
| Current cigarette smoker | 13.9% (12.7–15.2) | 9.0%[b,c,d] (7.6–10.4) | 15.0%[a,e] (12.4–17.6) | 20.7%[a,d,e] (17.0–24.4) | 13.5%[a,c,e] (11.2–15.8) | 9.2%[b,c,d] (8.2–10.2) |
| Current e-cigarette smoker | 12.4% (11.2–13.7) | 10.5%[c] (9.0–12.1) | 11.2% (8.7–13.6) | 16.1%[a,e] (12.7–19.5) | 14.5%[e] (11.9–17.0) | 9.3%[c,d] (8.2–10.3) |
| Current cigar smoker | 8.7% (7.7–9.6) | 7.1%[c] (5.8–8.3) | 6.7%[c] (5.0–8.3) | 14.7%[a,b,e] (11.6–17.7) | 9.9%[e] (7.8–12.0) | 9.1%[c] (8.1–10.2) |
| Current smokeless tobacco user | 12.7% (11.5–14.0) | 8.5%[b,c] (7.1–9.9) | 12.7%[a,c] (10.3–15.1) | 23.4%[a,b,d,e] (19.6–27.1) | 11.0%[c] (8.7–13.3) | 9.5%[c] (8.4–10.6) |

NOTE: All data are weighted. 95-percent confidence intervals are presented in parentheses.

[a] Estimate is significantly different from the estimate in column 2 (Air Force).

[b] Estimate is significantly different from the estimate in column 3 (Army).

[c] Estimate is significantly different from the estimate in column 4 (Marine Corps).

[d] Estimate is significantly different from the estimate in column 5 (Navy).

[e] Estimate is significantly different from the estimate in column 6 (Coast Guard).

Table 5.20
Current Tobacco Use, by Pay Grade

| | E1–E4 (1) | E5–E6 (2) | E7–E9 (3) | W1–W5 (4) | O1–O3 (5) | O4–O10 (6) |
|---|---|---|---|---|---|---|
| Current cigarette smoker | 17.9%[c,d,e,f] (15.3–20.4) | 15.1%[d,e,f] (13.1–17.1) | 12.4%[a,d,e,f] (10.5–14.3) | 6.9%[a,b,c,e,f] (4.9–8.8) | 3.4%[a,b,c,d] (2.5–4.3) | 1.8%[a,b,c,d] (1.1–2.5) |
| Current e-cigarette smoker | 19.2%[b,c,d,e,f] (16.6–21.8) | 10.8%[a,c,d,e,f] (9.1–12.5) | 6.1%[a,b,e,f] (4.7–7.5) | 3.4%[a,b,f] (2.1–4.6) | 2.2%[a,b,c,f] (1.5–2.8) | 0.9%[a,b,c,d,e] (0.4–1.4) |
| Current cigar smoker[g] | 9.9% (8.0–11.8) | 7.6% (6.2–9.0) | 7.1% (5.6–8.5) | 7.0% (5.0–8.9) | 9.6% (8.2–10.9) | 7.2% (5.9–8.5) |
| Current smokeless tobacco user | 15.2%[c,e,f] (12.8–17.6) | 13.6%[c,e,f] (11.6–15.6) | 9.2%[a,b] (7.5–10.9) | 10.6%[f] (8.2–13.0) | 7.2%[a,b] (5.9–8.4) | 6.6%[a,b,d] (5.3–7.9) |

NOTE: All data are weighted. 95-percent confidence intervals are presented in parentheses.

[a] Estimate is significantly different from the estimate in column 1 (E1–E4).

[b] Estimate is significantly different from the estimate in column 2 (E5–E6).

[c] Estimate is significantly different from the estimate in column 3 (E7–E9).

[d] Estimate is significantly different from the estimate in column 4 (W1–W5).

[e] Estimate is significantly different from the estimate in column 5 (O1–O3).

[f] Estimate is significantly different from the estimate in column 6 (O4–O10).

[g] The omnibus chi-square test was statistically significant ($p > 0.05$), but the power was too low to identify group differences.

**Table 5.21**
**Current Tobacco Use, by Gender**

|  | Men (1) | Women (2) |
|---|---|---|
| Current cigarette smoker | 14.4%[a] (12.9–15.9) | 11.4% (10.1–12.8) |
| Current e-cigarette smoker | 13.0%[a] (11.6–14.4) | 9.2% (7.9–10.5) |
| Current cigar smoker | 9.6%[a] (8.5–10.8) | 3.5% (2.8–4.2) |
| Current smokeless tobacco user | 14.7%[a] (13.3–16.1) | 2.0% (1.4–2.6) |

NOTE: All data are weighted. 95-percent confidence intervals are presented in parentheses.

[a] Estimate is significantly different from the estimate in column 2 (women).

**Table 5.22**
**Current Tobacco Use, by Age Group**

|  | Ages 17–24 (1) | Ages 25–34 (2) | Ages 35–44 (3) | Ages 45+ (4) |
|---|---|---|---|---|
| Current cigarette smoker | 19.5%[b,c,d] (16.4–22.6) | 12.5%[a,d] (10.6–14.3) | 12.5%[a,d] (10.5–14.6) | 4.3%[a,b,c] (2.9–5.8) |
| Current e-cigarette smoker | 22.8%[b,c,d] (19.5–26.1) | 10.8%[a,c,d] (9.1–12.6) | 5.4%[a,b,d] (4.2–6.6) | 2.5%[a,b,c] (1.6–3.5) |
| Current cigar smoker | 12.1%[b,c,d] (9.7–14.5) | 8.1%[a] (6.7–9.5) | 6.6%[a] (5.3–7.8) | 5.4%[a] (3.6–7.3) |
| Current smokeless tobacco user | 18.4%[b,c,d] (15.4–21.4) | 11.4%[a,d] (9.7–13.2) | 10.1%[a] (8.2–11.9) | 6.3%[a,b] (4.1–8.5) |

NOTE: All data are weighted. 95-percent confidence intervals are presented in parentheses.

[a] Estimate is significantly different from the estimate in column 1 (ages 17–24).

[b] Estimate is significantly different from the estimate in column 2 (ages 25–34).

[c] Estimate is significantly different from the estimate in column 3 (ages 35–44).

[d] Estimate is significantly different from the estimate in column 4 (ages 45+).

Table 5.23
Current Tobacco Use, by Race/Ethnicity

| | Non-Hispanic White (1) | Non-Hispanic Black (2) | Hispanic (3) | Non-Hispanic Asian (4) | Other (5) |
|---|---|---|---|---|---|
| Current cigarette smoker | 14.6%[b] (12.9–16.3) | 8.5%[a,e] (5.9–11.2) | 14.6% (11.0–18.2) | 13.2% (7.5–18.9) | 16.1%[b] (11.9–20.2) |
| Current e-cigarette smoker[g] | 12.4% (10.8–14.0) | 9.7% (6.4–13.0) | 15.8% (12.0–19.5) | 7.8% (3.7–11.9) | 12.8% (8.9–16.8) |
| Current cigar smoker[f] | 9.3% (8.0–10.6) | 6.4% (4.1–8.7) | 8.4% (6.0–10.8) | 4.6% (1.7–7.5) | 10.5% (7.0–14.0) |
| Current smokeless tobacco user | 16.4%[b,c,d] (14.7–18.1) | 4.2%[a,e] (1.8–6.7) | 9.7%[a,d] (6.8–12.6) | 1.3%[a,c,e] (0.0–2.9) | 11.9%[b,d] (7.8–16.0) |

NOTE: All data are weighted. 95-percent confidence intervals are presented in parentheses.

[a] Estimate is significantly different from the estimate in column 1 (non-Hispanic white).

[b] Estimate is significantly different from the estimate in column 2 (non-Hispanic black).

[c] Estimate is significantly different from the estimate in column 3 (Hispanic).

[d] Estimate is significantly different from the estimate in column 4 (non-Hispanic Asian).

[e] Estimate is significantly different from the estimate in column 5 (other).

[f] The omnibus chi-square test was not statistically significant ($p > 0.05$).

[g] The omnibus chi-square test was statistically significant ($p > 0.05$), but the power was too low to identify group differences.

Table 5.24
Current Tobacco Use, by Education Level

| | High School or Less (1) | Some College (2) | Bachelor's Degree or More (3) |
|---|---|---|---|
| Current cigarette smoker | 25.1%[b,c] (21.3–29.0) | 14.3%[a,c] (12.5–16.1) | 6.1%[a,b] (4.5–7.7) |
| Current e-cigarette smoker | 23.0%[b,c] (19.1–26.9) | 14.3%[a,c] (12.4–16.1) | 2.8%[a,b] (2.1–3.5) |
| Current cigar smoker | 12.9%[b,c] (9.8–16.0) | 7.7%[a] (6.4–8.9) | 7.6%[a] (6.4–8.8) |
| Current smokeless tobacco user | 21.5%[b,c] (17.8–25.2) | 12.4%[a,c] (10.7–14.1) | 7.6%[a,b] (6.1–9.1) |

NOTE: All data are weighted. 95-percent confidence intervals are presented in parentheses.

[a] Estimate is significantly different from the estimate in column 1 (high school or less).

[b] Estimate is significantly different from the estimate in column 2 (some college).

[c] Estimate is significantly different from the estimate in column 3 (bachelor's degree or more).

## Smoking Cessation

In the 2015 HRBS, 53.4 percent of service members who were daily cigarette smokers attempted to quit smoking. In the general population in 2012, 42.7 percent (CI: 40.9–44.5) of adults who smoked daily attempted to quit (HHS, 2014). The 2011 HRBS did not report a comparable measure of cessation attempts (Barlas et al., 2013). HP2020 sets a target for quit attempts among current, rather than daily, cigarette smokers. It estimates that in 2008, 48.3 percent (CI: 46.5–50.1) of the general population of current smokers made a past-year quit attempt, and it set a goal of 80 percent or more by 2020 (HHS, 2010a). Among active-duty service members, 52.9 percent (CI: 47.9–58.0) of current cigarette smokers made an attempt to quit.

**Secondhand Smoke Exposure**

Among nonsmoking service members, 16.9 percent (CI: 15.5–18.3) reported past-week exposure to secondhand smoke at work. In the general population, 20.4 percent (CI: 19.6–21.2) of employed nonsmokers reported past-week exposure to secondhand smoke in their workplace. The general population percentage was lower—16.4 percent (CI: 15.7–17.2)—among individuals with an indoor nonsmoking workplace policy (King et al., 2014).

**On-Base Cigarette Purchases and Perceived Supervisor Attitudes Toward Tobacco**

Tables 5.25 through 5.30 report the percentage of service members who purchased cigarettes on and off base or post. Key findings include the following:

- Most cigarette purchases by service members were completed on base (Table 5.25). Just more than half (56.0 percent) of service members who bought cigarettes in the past year bought them mainly on base, 24.8 percent bought cigarettes on and off base equally often, and only 19.2 percent bought them mainly off base.
- About one in four service personnel perceived their supervisor as strongly discouraging cigarette smoking (25.6 percent) or use of smokeless tobacco (26.1 percent) (Table 5.25).
- The Marine Corps, the service with the largest percentage of current cigarette smokers, had the largest percentage of smokers who bought cigarettes mostly on base, although the percentage of on-base purchasers among Army personnel approached that for Marines (Table 5.25). Likewise, members of the Marine Corps were the least likely to report that their supervisor strongly discourages cigarette smoking or use of smokeless tobacco.
- Air Force, Navy, and Coast Guard members were less likely than members of other service branches to purchase cigarettes on base (Table 5.25). Army and Marine Corps personnel generally saw their supervisors as less discouraging of cigarette smoking and smokeless tobacco use.
- Junior enlisted personnel were the least likely to purchase their cigarettes off base compared with all other pay grades (Table 5.26). They were also somewhat less likely to see their supervisors as discouraging use of cigarettes and smokeless tobacco.
- Men were less likely than women to see their supervisors as discouraging either cigarette or smokeless tobacco use (Table 5.27). There were no statistically significant differences in purchasing patterns by gender.
- Personnel aged 17–24 were far less likely to purchase cigarettes off base (Table 5.28). Those aged 45 or older were more likely than younger service members to see their supervisors as discouraging use of cigarettes and smokeless tobacco (and for strongly doing so).
- Non-Hispanic blacks were more likely, and non-Hispanic whites less likely, than other racial groups to perceive their supervisors as strongly discouraging use of cigarettes and smokeless tobacco (Table 5.29).
- Personnel with a bachelor's degree or more were more likely to see their supervisors as discouraging use of cigarettes and smokeless tobacco (Table 5.30).

Table 5.25
**Cigarette Purchases and Perceived Supervisor Attitudes Toward Tobacco Use, by Service Branch**

| | Total (1) | Air Force (2) | Army (3) | Marine Corps (4) | Navy (5) | Coast Guard (6) |
|---|---|---|---|---|---|---|
| Mainly purchased cigarettes on base | 56.0% (51.8–60.1) | 49.9%[c,e] (42.9–57.0) | 61.7%[d,e] (53.9–69.5) | 66.6%[a,d,e] (58.5–74.8) | 44.4%[b,c,e] (36.4–52.4) | 21.6%[a,b,c,d] (17.6–25.6) |
| Mainly purchased cigarettes off base | 19.2% (16.3–22.2) | 24.3%[c,e] (18.2–30.4) | 15.4%[e] (10.2–20.6) | 10.4%[a,d,e] (6.3–14.6) | 26.4%[c,e] (19.4–33.4) | 55.7%[a,b,c,d] (50.7–60.7) |
| Purchased cigarettes equally on and off base[f] | 24.8% (21.1–28.5) | 25.8% (19.6–31.9) | 22.9% (15.9–29.9) | 22.9% (15.3–30.6) | 29.2% (21.8–36.5) | 22.7% (18.5–27.0) |
| Supervisor does not discourage cigarette use | 44.2% (42.6–45.8) | 40.5%[b,e] (38.3–42.7) | 48.1%[a,e] (44.8–51.3) | 45.1%[e] (41.0–49.2) | 42.4%[e] (39.3–45.6) | 33.7%[a,b,c,d] (32.1–35.3) |
| Supervisor somewhat discourages cigarette use | 30.2% (28.7–31.7) | 31.1% (29.0–33.2) | 26.5%[c,e] (23.6–29.4) | 34.8%[b] (30.9–38.7) | 32.2% (29.3–35.2) | 33.0%[b] (31.4–34.6) |
| Supervisor strongly discourages cigarette use | 25.6% (24.2–26.9) | 28.4%[c,e] (26.5–30.3) | 25.4%[e] (22.7–28.2) | 20.1%[a,e] (16.9–23.3) | 25.3%[e] (22.7–28.0) | 33.3%[a,b,c,d] (31.7–34.9) |
| Supervisor does not discourage smokeless tobacco use | 46.1% (44.5–47.7) | 39.9%[b,c,e] (37.7–42.1) | 50.9%[a,d,e] (47.6–54.2) | 49.5%[a,e] (45.4–53.6) | 43.7%[b,e] (40.6–46.8) | 35.6%[a,b,c,d] (34.0–37.3) |
| Supervisor somewhat discourages smokeless tobacco use | 27.8% (26.4–29.2) | 30.0%[b] (28.0–32.1) | 23.5%[a,c,d,e] (20.7–26.3) | 32.3%[b] (28.5–36.1) | 29.3%[b] (26.5–32.2) | 32.1%[b] (30.5–33.7) |
| Supervisor strongly discourages smokeless tobacco use | 26.1% (24.7–27.4) | 30.1%[c] (28.1–32.0) | 25.6%[c,e] (22.8–28.3) | 18.2%[a,b,d,e] (15.2–21.3) | 26.9%[c,e] (24.2–29.6) | 32.2%[b,c,d] (30.6–33.8) |

NOTE: All data are weighted. 95-percent confidence intervals are presented in parentheses.

[a] Estimate is significantly different from the estimate in column 2 (Air Force).

[b] Estimate is significantly different from the estimate in column 3 (Army).

[c] Estimate is significantly different from the estimate in column 4 (Marine Corps).

[d] Estimate is significantly different from the estimate in column 5 (Navy).

[e] Estimate is significantly different from the estimate in column 6 (Coast Guard).

[f] At the aggregate, the chi-square test was statistically significant; however, none of the individual pairwise comparisons was.

**Table 5.26**
**Cigarette Purchases and Perceived Supervisor Attitudes Toward Tobacco Use, by Pay Grade**

| | E1–E4 (1) | E5–E6 (2) | E7–E9 (3) | W1–W5 (4) | O1–O3 (5) | O4–O10 (6) |
|---|---|---|---|---|---|---|
| Mainly purchased cigarettes on base | 60.8%[e] (54.3–67.3) | 51.0% (44.9–57.0) | 53.3%[e] (45.9–60.7) | 59.5%[e] (47.4–71.6) | 32.9%[a,c,d] (22.1–43.7) | 39.1% (25.8–52.5) |
| Mainly purchased cigarettes off base | 13.2%[b,e,f] (9.0–17.4) | 25.7%[a,f] (20.5–30.9) | 23.2%[f] (16.8–29.6) | 21.7% (11.6–31.8) | 39.3%[a] (28.3–50.3) | 46.4%[a,b,c] (32.6–60.3) |
| Purchased cigarettes equally on and off base[g] | 26.0% (20.0–32.0) | 23.3% (18.2–28.5) | 23.5% (17.1–29.9) | 18.8% (9.3–28.2) | 27.8% (17.4–38.1) | 14.4% (4.4–24.5) |
| Supervisor does not discourage cigarette use | 45.1%[e,f] (42.0–48.1) | 47.3%[e,f] (44.6–49.9) | 42.6%[f] (39.8–45.3) | 47.2%[e,f] (43.4–50.9) | 38.9%[a,b,d,f] (36.7–41.1) | 33.9%[a,b,c,d,e] (31.7–36.2) |
| Supervisor somewhat discourages cigarette use | 31.6% (28.7–34.4) | 29.5% (27.1–31.9) | 27.9% (25.5–30.3) | 27.3% (24.0–30.6) | 31.3%[f] (29.3–33.4) | 26.6%[e] (24.6–28.7) |
| Supervisor strongly discourages cigarette use | 23.4%[c,e,f] (20.8–26.0) | 23.2%[c,e,f] (21.0–25.4) | 29.5%[a,b,f] (27.0–32.0) | 25.5%[f] (22.2–28.8) | 29.8%[a,b,f] (27.8–31.8) | 39.4%[a,b,c,d,e] (37.1–41.8) |
| Supervisor does not discourage smokeless tobacco use | 48.3%[e,f] (45.2–51.4) | 47.4%[e,f] (44.8–50.1) | 42.6%[f] (39.8–45.3) | 48.5%[e,f] (44.8–52.3) | 41.9%[a,b,f] (39.7–44.1) | 35.9%[a,b,c,d,e] (33.6–38.1) |
| Supervisor somewhat discourages smokeless tobacco use | 27.7% (25.0–30.4) | 27.9% (25.5–30.3) | 27.7% (25.3–30.1) | 25.8% (22.5–29.0) | 30.2%[f] (28.2–32.2) | 25.5%[e] (23.4–27.5) |
| Supervisor strongly discourages smokeless tobacco use | 24.0%[c,f] (21.5–26.6) | 24.7%[c,f] (22.4–26.9) | 29.7%[a,b,f] (27.2–32.2) | 25.7%[f] (22.4–29.0) | 27.9%[f] (26.0–29.9) | 38.7%[a,b,c,d,e] (36.3–41.0) |

NOTE: All data are weighted. 95-percent confidence intervals are presented in parentheses.

[a] Estimate is significantly different from the estimate in column 1 (E1–E4).

[b] Estimate is significantly different from the estimate in column 2 (E5–E6).

[c] Estimate is significantly different from the estimate in column 3 (E7–E9).

[d] Estimate is significantly different from the estimate in column 4 (W1–W5).

[e] Estimate is significantly different from the estimate in column 5 (O1–O3).

[f] Estimate is significantly different from the estimate in column 6 (O4–O10).

[g] At the aggregate, the chi-square test was statistically significant; however, none of the individual pairwise comparisons was.

**Table 5.27**
**Cigarette Purchases and Perceived Supervisor Attitudes Toward Tobacco Use, by Gender**

|  | Men (1) | Women (2) |
|---|---|---|
| Mainly purchased cigarettes on base[b] | 56.8% (52.2–61.5) | 50.2% (44.7–55.6) |
| Mainly purchased cigarettes off base[b] | 18.8% (15.5–22.1) | 22.1% (17.5–26.6) |
| Purchased cigarettes equally on and off base[b] | 24.4% (20.2–28.6) | 27.8% (22.8–32.7) |
| Supervisor does not discourage cigarette use | 45.0%[a] (43.1–46.9) | 39.9% (38.0–41.8) |
| Supervisor somewhat discourages cigarette use | 30.8%[a] (29.1–32.5) | 27.1% (25.3–28.8) |
| Supervisor strongly discourages cigarette use | 24.2%[a] (22.6–25.8) | 33.0% (31.2–34.7) |
| Supervisor does not discourage smokeless tobacco use | 47.3%[a] (45.5–49.2) | 39.5% (37.6–41.3) |
| Supervisor somewhat discourages smokeless tobacco use | 28.4%[a] (26.7–30.0) | 24.8% (23.1–26.6) |
| Supervisor strongly discourages smokeless tobacco use | 24.3%[a] (22.7–25.9) | 35.7% (33.9–37.5) |

NOTE: All data are weighted. 95-percent confidence intervals are presented in parentheses.

[a] Estimate is significantly different from the estimate in column 2 (women).

[b] The omnibus chi-square test was not statistically significant ($p > 0.05$).

**Table 5.28**
**Cigarette Purchases and Perceived Supervisor Attitudes Toward Tobacco Use, by Age Group**

|  | Ages 17–24 (1) | Ages 25–34 (2) | Ages 35–44 (3) | Ages 45+ (4) |
|---|---|---|---|---|
| Mainly purchased cigarettes on base[e] | 63.1% (55.7–70.4) | 52.3% (45.7–59.0) | 51.1% (43.5–58.7) | 42.3% (27.1–57.4) |
| Mainly purchased cigarettes off base | 9.6%[b,c,d] (6.0–13.2) | 25.0%[a] (19.5–30.5) | 25.2%[a] (18.9–31.5) | 27.6%[a] (11.5–43.7) |
| Purchased cigarettes equally on and off base[e] | 27.4% (20.4–34.3) | 22.7% (17.1–28.3) | 23.7% (16.9–30.4) | 30.2% (15.0–45.3) |
| Supervisor does not discourage cigarette use | 43.7% (40.1–47.2) | 45.5%[d] (43.0–48.0) | 44.4%[d] (41.7–47.2) | 38.0%[b,c] (34.1–41.9) |
| Supervisor somewhat discourages cigarette use | 32.9%[d] (29.6–36.3) | 30.6%[d] (28.2–32.9) | 28.4% (26.0–30.8) | 23.0%[a,b] (19.8–26.2) |
| Supervisor strongly discourages cigarette use | 23.4%[d] (20.4–26.4) | 23.9%[d] (21.8–26.1) | 27.2%[d] (25.0–29.4) | 39.0%[a,b,c] (35.2–42.8) |
| Supervisor does not discourage smokeless tobacco use | 46.0%[d] (43.4–50.5) | 46.9%[d] (44.4–49.4) | 45.9%[d] (43.2–48.7) | 38.6%[a,b,c] (34.7–42.5) |
| Supervisor somewhat discourages smokeless tobacco use | 30.4%[d] (27.2–33.6) | 27.9% (25.7–30.1) | 25.8% (23.6–28.1) | 23.2%[a] (19.9–26.5) |
| Supervisor strongly discourages smokeless tobacco use | 22.7%[c,d] (19.8–25.5) | 25.2%[d] (23.0–27.4) | 28.2%[a,d] (25.9–30.5) | 38.2%[a,b,c] (34.5–42.0) |

NOTE: All data are weighted. 95-percent confidence intervals are presented in parentheses.

[a] Estimate is significantly different from the estimate in column 1 (ages 17–24).

[b] Estimate is significantly different from the estimate in column 2 (ages 25–34).

[c] Estimate is significantly different from the estimate in column 3 (ages 35–44).

[d] Estimate is significantly different from the estimate in column 4 (ages 45+).

[e] At the aggregate, the chi-square test was statistically significant; however, none of the individual pairwise comparisons was.

**Table 5.29**
**Cigarette Purchases and Perceived Supervisor Attitudes Toward Tobacco Use, by Race/Ethnicity**

| | Non-Hispanic White (1) | Non-Hispanic Black (2) | Hispanic (3) | Non-Hispanic Asian (4) | Other (5) |
|---|---|---|---|---|---|
| Mainly purchased cigarettes on base[f] | 57.1% (51.9–62.3) | 48.2% (33.7–62.6) | 55.4% (44.1–66.7) | 64.0% (45.6–82.5) | 52.3% (40.1–64.6) |
| Mainly purchased cigarettes off base[f] | 20.4% (16.6–24.2) | 14.8% (5.1–24.5) | 18.3% (10.2–26.4) | 16.6% (3.4–29.9) | 18.1% (10.6–25.6) |
| Purchased cigarettes equally on and off base[f] | 22.5% (18.0–26.9) | 37.1% (22.6–51.5) | 26.3% (15.9–36.7) | 19.3% (4.8–33.8) | 29.5% (18.4–40.7) |
| Supervisor does not discourage cigarette use[g] | 43.8% (41.8–45.8) | 43.1% (38.3–47.8) | 44.8% (40.4–49.2) | 45.7% (37.5–53.8) | 46.5% (41.3–51.7) |
| Supervisor somewhat discourages cigarette use | 32.4%[b] (30.5–34.3) | 22.5%[a] (18.5–26.5) | 30.3% (26.2–34.3) | 23.7% (16.9–30.4) | 29.8% (24.9–34.6) |
| Supervisor strongly discourages cigarette use | 23.8%[b] (22.1–25.4) | 34.4%[a,c,e] (29.9–39.0) | 25.0%[b] (21.4–28.5) | 30.6% (23.1–38.2) | 23.8%[b] (19.7–27.8) |
| Supervisor does not discourage smokeless tobacco use[g] | 46.2% (44.2–48.3) | 42.1% (37.4–46.8) | 47.0% (42.6–51.4) | 46.4% (38.2–54.7) | 49.0% (43.8–54.1) |
| Supervisor somewhat discourages smokeless tobacco use | 30.8%[b,d] (28.9–32.6) | 19.7%[a] (16.0–23.4) | 26.8%[d] (22.9–30.7) | 16.3%[a,c,e] (11.4–21.1) | 27.4%[d] (22.8–32.0) |
| Supervisor strongly discourages smokeless tobacco use | 23.0%[b,d] (21.4–24.6) | 38.2%[a,c] (33.4–42.9) | 26.2%[b] (22.6–29.8) | 37.3%[a,e] (29.3–45.3) | 23.6%[d] (19.7–27.6) |

NOTE: All data are weighted. 95-percent confidence intervals are presented in parentheses.

[a] Estimate is significantly different from the estimate in column 1 (non-Hispanic white).

[b] Estimate is significantly different from the estimate in column 2 (non-Hispanic black).

[c] Estimate is significantly different from the estimate in column 3 (Hispanic).

[d] Estimate is significantly different from the estimate in column 4 (non-Hispanic Asian).

[e] Estimate is significantly different from the estimate in column 5 (other).

[f] The omnibus chi-square test was not statistically significant ($p > 0.05$).

[g] At the aggregate, the chi-square test was statistically significant; however, none of the individual pairwise comparisons was.

**Table 5.30**
**Cigarette Purchases and Perceived Supervisor Attitudes Toward Tobacco Use, by Education Level**

| | High School or Less (1) | Some College (2) | Bachelor's Degree or More (3) |
|---|---|---|---|
| Mainly purchased cigarettes on base[d] | 56.1% (48.3–63.9) | 55.4% (49.9–60.9) | 57.9% (47.6–68.2) |
| Mainly purchased cigarettes off base[d] | 15.2% (10.0–20.4) | 21.6% (17.4–25.8) | 21.2% (13.8–28.5) |
| Purchased cigarettes equally on and off base[d] | 28.7% (21.5–36.0) | 23.0% (18.3–27.7) | 20.9% (12.5–29.4) |
| Supervisor does not discourage cigarette use | 45.2% (41.0–49.5) | 45.9%[c] (43.5–48.3) | 40.9%[b] (38.5–43.3) |
| Supervisor somewhat discourages cigarette use | 34.1%[c] (30.1–38.0) | 29.7% (27.6–31.9) | 28.5%[a] (26.3–30.6) |
| Supervisor strongly discourages cigarette use | 20.7%[c] (17.4–24.0) | 24.4%[c] (22.4–26.4) | 30.6%[a,b] (28.6–32.7) |
| Supervisor does not discourage smokeless tobacco use | 48.5%[c] (44.3–52.8) | 47.5%[c] (45.1–49.8) | 42.4%[a,b] (40.0–44.7) |
| Supervisor somewhat discourages smokeless tobacco use[e] | 31.0% (27.2–34.8) | 27.6% (25.5–29.7) | 26.1% (24.0–28.1) |
| Supervisor strongly discourages smokeless tobacco use | 20.4%[c] (17.2–23.7) | 24.9%[c] (22.9–26.9) | 31.6%[a,b] (29.4–33.7) |

NOTE: All data are weighted. 95-percent confidence intervals are presented in parentheses.

[a] Estimate is significantly different from the estimate in column 1 (high school or less).

[b] Estimate is significantly different from the estimate in column 2 (some college).

[c] Estimate is significantly different from the estimate in column 3 (bachelor's degree or more).

[d] The omnibus chi-square test was not statistically significant ($p > 0.05$).

[e] At the aggregate, the chi-square test was statistically significant; however, none of the individual pairwise comparisons was.

## Illicit Drug Use and Prescription Drug Use, Misuse, and Overuse

This section describes illicit drug use, prescription drug use, prescription drug misuse (i.e., using without a prescription), and prescription drug overuse (i.e., using more of a medication than prescribed). The 2015 HRBS measured use of the following 12 illicit substances: marijuana or hashish, synthetic cannabis, cocaine (including crack), lysergic acid diethylamide (LSD), phencyclidine (PCP), 3,4-methylenedioxy-methamphetamine (MDMA, commonly called ecstasy), other hallucinogens, methamphetamine, heroin, gamma hydroxybutyrate (GHB) and gamma-butyrolactone (GBL), inhalants, and synthetic stimulants (bath salts). Use of prescription drugs was assessed for the following five types of substances:

- stimulants or attention enhancers (e.g., Adderall, amphetamines, Ritalin, prescription diet pills)
- sedatives, tranquilizers, muscle relaxers, or barbiturates (e.g., Ambien, Quaalude, Valium, Xanax, Rohypnol, Phenobarbital, Ketamine)
- pain relievers (e.g., Oxycontin/Oxycodone, Percocet, cough syrups with codeine, Methadone, hydrocodone, Vicodin)
- anabolic steroids (e.g., Deca Durbolin, Testosterone)
- antidepressants (e.g., Cymbalta, Strattera, Prozac, Paxil, Zoloft).

Because levels of use for most substances are low, breakdowns by service branch and other demographics are presented only for select drugs or groups of drugs—and, in some cases, only for larger demographic groups. For example, marijuana was combined with use of synthetic cannabis (i.e., the variable indicates any use of either), and all of the remaining drugs were combined to reflect use of any other illicit drug. In the case of prescription drugs, we created a single variable reflecting any misuse or overuse.

### Illicit Drug Use

Key findings for illicit drug use among service members include the following:

- Use of either marijuana or synthetic cannabis in the past year was reported by 0.6 percent of personnel; any *other* illicit drugs were used by 0.3 percent of personnel in the past year (Table 5.31).
- A smaller percentage (0.3 percent) of service members were current (past 30 days) users of marijuana or cannabis; an even smaller percentage (0.1 percent) used any *other* illegal drug in the past 30 days (Table 5.31).
- Among active-duty service members, use of *any* illicit drug during the past year was reported by 0.7 percent, and 0.3 percent used *any* illicit drug in the past month (Table 5.31).

In contrast to military percentages, current and past-year marijuana users made up 8.5 percent (CI: 8.2–8.8) and 13.3 percent (CI: 12.9–13.7), respectively, of U.S. adults in 2014. In the same year, 10.3 percent (CI: 9.9–10.7) of U.S. adults were current and 16.6 percent (CI: 16.1–17.1) were past-year users of any illicit drug (CBHSQ, 2015b). The percentages reported in the 2015 HRBS were also lower than those reported in the 2011 HRBS. In 2011, 0.9 percent (CI: 0.7–1.1) of personnel used marijuana, and 1.1 percent (CI: 0.9–1.3) used synthetic cannabis; 1.4 percent (CI: 1.2–1.6) used any illicit drug (Barlas et al., 2013).

Tables 5.32 through 5.37 display past-year use of marijuana or synthetic cannabis, use of other illicit drugs, and use of *any* illicit drug, by service branch and demographic group. Because the absolute numbers of users for individual drugs are small (as shown in Table 5.31), we do not show percentages by subgroup. Note also that we collapsed pay grade into all enlisted and all officers (including warrant officers), and we collapsed race/ethnicity into non-Hispanic white and all minority categories (including other) to accommodate the small numbers involved.

**Table 5.31**
**Illicit Drug Use, Overall Sample**

| | Past 30 Days (1) | Past Year (2) |
|---|---|---|
| Used marijuana[a] | 0.3% (0.0–0.5) | 0.6% (0.3–1.0) |
| Used any *other* illicit drug[b] | 0.1% (0.02–0.1) | 0.3% (0.1–0.4) |
| Used *any* illicit drug | 0.3% (0.1–0.6) | 0.7% (0.4–1.1) |

NOTE: All data are weighted. 95-percent confidence intervals are presented in parentheses.

[a] Includes hashish and synthetic cannabis.

[b] Excludes marijuana, hashish, and synthetic cannabis.

### Marijuana

Key findings for marijuana use among service members include the following:

- A difference in use of marijuana or synthetic cannabis across the services could not be detected (Table 5.32).
- The highest percentage of marijuana or synthetic cannabis users was among enlisted service members, particularly junior enlisted personnel (E1–E4) (Table 5.33). Correspondingly, service members aged 17–24 and 25–34 were the most likely to report past-year cannabis use (Table 5.35).
- Men and women were equally likely to use marijuana or synthetic cannabis (Table 5.34), and there were no statistically significant differences in use by race/ethnicity (Table 5.36) or education level (Table 5.37).

### Illicit Drugs Other Than Marijuana or Synthetic Cannabis

No statistically significant differences by service branch or other demographics were observed for illicit drugs other than cannabis (Tables 5.32 through 5.37). Note, however, that *the very small percentage of users limited our ability to test for such differences.*

In the U.S. general population, 2014 estimates indicate that men were more likely than women to use marijuana, and those with less than a college degree were more likely to use marijuana than those with such a degree. Non-Hispanic blacks were more likely to use marijuana than non-Hispanic whites, and Hispanics were less likely to use than whites. The same patterns held true for use of any illicit drug (CBHSQ, 2015b).

**Table 5.32**
**Past-Year Illicit Drug Use, by Service Branch**

|  | Total (1) | Air Force (2) | Army (3) | Marine Corps (4) | Navy (5) | Coast Guard (6) |
|---|---|---|---|---|---|---|
| Used marijuana[a] | 0.6% (0.3–1.0) | 0.4% (0.1–0.8) | 0.9% (0.2–1.6) | 0.2% (0.0–0.4) | 0.8% (0.0–1.5) | 0.2% (0.0–0.3) |
| Used any *other* illicit drug[a] | 0.3% (0.1–0.4) | 0.4% (0.1–0.7) | 0.2% (0.0–0.3) | 0.2% (0.0–0.4) | 0.4% (0.0–0.9) | 0.2% (0.0–0.3) |
| Used *any* illicit drug[a] | 0.7% (0.4–1.1) | 0.6% (0.2–1.0) | 0.9% (0.3–1.6) | 0.2% (0.0–0.5) | 0.9% (0.1–1.7) | 0.2% (0.1–0.4) |

NOTE: All data are weighted. 95-percent confidence intervals are presented in parentheses.

[a] The omnibus chi-square test was not statistically significant (*p* > 0.05).

**Table 5.33**
**Past-Year Illicit Drug Use, by Pay Grade**

|  | Enlisted (1) | Officers (2) |
|---|---|---|
| Used marijuana | 0.7% (0.3–1.1) | 0.2%[a] (0.0–0.3) |
| Used any *other* illicit drug[b] | 0.3% (0.1–0.5) | 0.2% (0.1–0.4) |
| Used *any* illicit drug | 0.8% (0.4–1.2) | 0.4%[a] (0.2–0.6) |

NOTE: All data are weighted. 95-percent confidence intervals are presented in parentheses. Column 2 includes warrant officers.

[a] Estimate is significantly different from the estimate in column 1 (enlisted).

[b] The omnibus chi-square test was not statistically significant (*p* > 0.05).

**Table 5.34**
**Past-Year Illicit Drug Use, by Gender**

|  | Men (1) | Women (2) |
|---|---|---|
| Used marijuana[a] | 0.6% (0.2–0.9) | 0.9% (0.5–1.4) |
| Used any *other* illicit drug[a] | 0.3% (0.1–0.4) | 0.4% (0.1–0.7) |
| Used *any* illicit drug[a] | 0.7% (0.3–1.1) | 1.1% (0.6–1.6) |

NOTE: All data are weighted. 95-percent confidence intervals are presented in parentheses.

[a] The omnibus chi-square test was not statistically significant ($p > 0.05$).

**Table 5.35**
**Past-Year Illicit Drug Use, by Age Group**

|  | Ages 17–24 (1) | Ages 25–34 (2) | Ages 35–44 (3) | Ages 45+ (4) |
|---|---|---|---|---|
| Used marijuana[e] | 1.0% (0.3–1.6) | 0.8% (0.1–1.4) | 0.1% (0.0–0.3) | 0.3% (0.0–0.7) |
| Used any *other* illicit drug[e] | 0.5% (0.1–0.9) | 0.2% (0.0–0.4) | 0.2% (0.0–0.3) | 0.3% (0.0–0.7) |
| Used *any* illicit drug | 1.1%[c] (0.4–1.8) | 0.9%[c] (0.3–1.5) | 0.2%[a,b] (0.0–0.4) | 0.3% (0.0–0.7) |

NOTE: All data are weighted. 95-percent confidence intervals are presented in parentheses.

[a] Estimate is significantly different from the estimate in column 1 (ages 17–24).

[b] Estimate is significantly different from the estimate in column 2 (ages 25–34).

[c] Estimate is significantly different from the estimate in column 3 (ages 35–44).

[d] Estimate is significantly different from the estimate in column 4 (ages 45+).

[e] The omnibus chi-square test was not statistically significant ($p > 0.05$).

**Table 5.36**
**Past-Year Illicit Drug Use, by Race/Ethnicity**

|  | Non-Hispanic White (1) | All Minority (Includes Other) (2) |
|---|---|---|
| Used marijuana[a] | 0.5% (0.1–0.8) | 0.9% (0.3–1.5) |
| Used any *other* illicit drug[a] | 0.2% (0.1–0.3) | 0.4% (0.1–0.8) |
| Used *any* illicit drug[a] | 0.6% (0.3–1.0) | 0.9% (0.3–1.5) |

NOTE: All data are weighted. 95-percent confidence intervals are presented in parentheses.

[a] The omnibus chi-square test was not statistically significant ($p > 0.05$).

**Table 5.37**
**Past-Year Illicit Drug Use, by Education Level**

|  | High School or Less (1) | Some College (2) | Bachelor's Degree or More (3) |
|---|---|---|---|
| Used marijuana[a] | 0.8% (0.0–1.5) | 0.7% (0.3–1.2) | 0.4% (0.0–0.9) |
| Used any *other* illicit drug[a] | 0.5% (0.0–1.1) | 0.2% (0.1–0.4) | 0.2% (0.1–0.3) |
| Used *any* illicit drug[a] | 0.9% (0.1–1.6) | 0.8% (0.3–1.3) | 0.5% (0.0–1.1) |

NOTE: All data are weighted. 95-percent confidence intervals are presented in parentheses.

[a] The omnibus chi-square test was not statistically significant ($p > 0.05$).

## Prescription Drug Use

Use of specific types of prescription drugs is displayed in Table 5.38. Note that use in this table includes *any* use and does not take prescription status into account (i.e., whether the service member had a valid prescription to use a specific drug).

Key findings include the following:

- About one in seven (14.3 percent) service members reported past-month use of one or more of the types of prescription drugs examined in the survey (Table 5.38).
- The prescription drug type used most commonly in the past year and ever was pain relievers, used by more than twice as many service members as any of the other four drugs studied for these periods (Table 5.38).

Compared with the 2011 HRBS, the overall percentage of current (past 30 days) prescription drug users was lower in 2015. The 2011 HRBS reported that 15.2 percent of service members used a prescription drug in the past month (CI: 14.6–15.8; see Barlas et al., 2013), but that estimate did not include use of antidepressants. When we recalculate the 2015 estimate of current prescription drug use to also exclude this group of drugs, 10.3 percent of service members (CI: 9.3–11.3) currently used a prescription drug.

The percentage of service members currently using prescription sedatives (4.4 percent) has decreased by nearly half (was 8.0 percent in 2011 [CI: 7.6–8.4]); current use of prescription pain relievers (6.2 percent) has also declined (was 10.4 percent in 2011 [CI: 10.0–10.8]). The percentages using prescription stimulants and anabolic steroids has remained fairly stable (stimulant use in 2011 was 1.8 percent [CI: 1.6–2.0]; anabolic steroid use in 2011 was 0.7 percent [CI: 0.5–0.9]).

Because of the small percentages of service members reporting on prescription stimulants and anabolic steroids, we focus Tables 5.39 through 5.44 on use of prescription sedatives, pain relievers, and antidepressants in the past year. Again, use in these tables includes *any* use and does not take prescription status into account (i.e., whether the service member had a valid prescription to use a specific drug). Key findings include the following:

- Prescription sedatives were more likely to be used by women and members of the Air Force and Army and less likely to be used by men and members of the Coast Guard and Marine Corps (Tables 5.39 and 5.41). They were used by greater percentages of senior enlisted and warrant officers (Table 5.40).

- Use of sedatives increased with service member age (Table 5.42), and sedatives were used most by those with some college experience but no degree (Table 5.44). There were no statistically significant differences in use of this drug type by race/ethnicity (Table 5.43).
- Demographic predictors of use of prescription pain relievers largely mirrored those for sedatives.
- Antidepressant use followed the same demographic patterns as use of sedatives and pain relievers but a somewhat different pattern by service branch and pay grade. Antidepressant use was particularly elevated within the Army and particularly low within the Coast Guard. Use was greatest among senior enlisted personnel and not as elevated among warrant officers when compared with the other drug types.

## Table 5.38
## Prescription Drug Use, Overall Sample

|  | Past 30 Days (1) | Past Year (2) | Ever Used (3) | Ever Prescribed (4) |
|---|---|---|---|---|
| Prescription stimulants | 2.1% (1.6–2.6) | 2.8% (2.3–3.4) | 10.3% (9.2–11.3) | 6.8% (6.0–7.6) |
| Prescription sedatives | 4.4% (3.8–5.0) | 10.8% (9.9–11.7) | 27.8% (26.5–29.2) | 26.9% (25.6–28.2) |
| Prescription pain relievers | 6.2% (5.4–7.0) | 21.0% (19.7–22.3) | 59.6% (57.9–61.2) | 66.9% (65.3–68.6) |
| Prescription anabolic steroids | 0.6% (0.4–0.9) | 1.3% (0.9–1.6) | 4.1% (3.5–4.7) | 3.8% (3.2–4.4) |
| Prescription antidepressants | 7.0% (6.2–7.8) | 8.8% (7.9–9.7) | 16.2% (15.0–17.3) | 16.2% (15.0–17.3) |
| Any prescription drug use | 14.3% (13.2–15.4) | 28.9% (24.7–30.4) | 64.4% (62.8–66.0) | 71.0% (69.4–72.5) |

NOTE: All data are weighted. 95-percent confidence intervals are presented in parentheses.

## Table 5.39
## Past-Year Prescription Drug Use, by Service Branch

|  | Total (1) | Air Force (2) | Army (3) | Marine Corps (4) | Navy (5) | Coast Guard (6) |
|---|---|---|---|---|---|---|
| Prescription sedatives | 10.8% (9.9–11.7) | 11.7%[c,e] (10.3–13.0) | 12.3%[c,e] (10.4–14.2) | 7.2%[a,b] (5.5–9.0) | 10.2%[e] (8.4–12.0) | 6.4%[a,b,d] (5.6–7.2) |
| Prescription pain relievers | 21.0% (19.7–22.3) | 20.8%[e] (18.9–22.6) | 24.5%[d,e] (21.7–27.2) | 18.7%[e] (15.5–21.9) | 17.8%[b,e] (15.4–20.3) | 13.8%[a,b,c,d] (12.7–14.9) |
| Prescription antidepressants | 8.8% (7.9–9.7) | 7.3%[b,e] (6.1–8.4) | 11.5%[a,d,e] (9.6–13.3) | 7.8%[e] (5.6–9.9) | 6.9%[b] (5.4–8.5) | 4.9%[a,b,c] (4.2–5.7) |

NOTE: All data are weighted. 95-percent confidence intervals are presented in parentheses.

[a] Estimate is significantly different from the estimate in column 2 (Air Force).

[b] Estimate is significantly different from the estimate in column 3 (Army).

[c] Estimate is significantly different from the estimate in column 4 (Marine Corps).

[d] Estimate is significantly different from the estimate in column 5 (Navy).

[e] Estimate is significantly different from the estimate in column 6 (Coast Guard).

**Table 5.40**
**Past-Year Prescription Drug Use, by Pay Grade**

| | E1–E4 (1) | E5–E6 (2) | E7–E9 (3) | W1–W5 (4) | O1–O3 (5) | O4–O10 (6) |
|---|---|---|---|---|---|---|
| Prescription sedatives | 7.6%[b,c,d,f] (5.9–9.2) | 13.0%[a] (11.1–14.9) | 17.1%[a,e] (14.9–19.2) | 16.2%[a,e] (13.4–19.0) | 9.8%[c,f] (8.5–11.2) | 13.6%[a,e] (11.9–15.2) |
| Prescription pain relievers | 19.8%[c,d] (17.3–22.3) | 22.3%[c,e] (20.0–24.6) | 28.1%[a,b,e,f] (25.5–30.7) | 26.0%[a,e,f] (22.6–29.4) | 16.3%[b,c,d] (14.5–18.0) | 18.5%[c,d] (16.6–20.4) |
| Prescription antidepressants | 7.5%[c] (5.9–9.1) | 10.7%[e,f] (9.0–12.4) | 13.0%[a,e,f] (11.0–14.9) | 10.9%[e,f] (8.5–13.4) | 5.6%[b,c,d] (4.5–6.7) | 6.9%[b,c,d] (5.6–8.2) |

NOTE: All data are weighted. 95-percent confidence intervals are presented in parentheses.

[a] Estimate is significantly different from the estimate in column 1 (E1–E4).

[b] Estimate is significantly different from the estimate in column 2 (E5–E6).

[c] Estimate is significantly different from the estimate in column 3 (E7–E9).

[d] Estimate is significantly different from the estimate in column 4 (W1–W5).

[e] Estimate is significantly different from the estimate in column 5 (O1–O3).

[f] Estimate is significantly different from the estimate in column 6 (O4–O10).

**Table 5.41**
**Past-Year Prescription Drug Use, by Gender**

| | Men (1) | Women (2) |
|---|---|---|
| Prescription sedatives | 9.7%[a] (8.6–10.8) | 16.8% (15.3–18.3) |
| Prescription pain relievers | 19.8%[a] (18.3–21.4) | 27.4% (25.6–29.2) |
| Prescription antidepressants | 7.6%[a] (6.5–8.6) | 15.5% (14.1–17.0) |

NOTE: All data are weighted. 95-percent confidence intervals are presented in parentheses.

[a] Estimate is significantly different from the estimate in column 2 (women).

**Table 5.42**
**Past-Year Prescription Drug Use, by Age Group**

| | Ages 17–24 (1) | Ages 25–34 (2) | Ages 35–44 (3) | Ages 45+ (4) |
|---|---|---|---|---|
| Prescription sedatives | 5.7%[b,c,d] (4.1–7.3) | 10.7%[a,c,d] (9.1–12.3) | 15.6%[a,b] (13.6–17.5) | 16.5%[a,b] (14.0–18.9) |
| Prescription pain relievers | 17.9%[c,d] (15.1–20.8) | 19.3%[c,d] (17.2–21.3) | 26.1%[a,b] (23.7–28.6) | 27.0%[a,b] (23.7–30.4) |
| Prescription antidepressants | 6.6%[c,d] (4.8–8.4) | 8.1%[c,d] (6.7–9.5) | 11.2%[a,b] (9.5–12.9) | 14.0%[a,b] (11.0–17.0) |

NOTE: All data are weighted. 95-percent confidence intervals are presented in parentheses.

[a] Estimate is significantly different from the estimate in column 1 (ages 17–24).

[b] Estimate is significantly different from the estimate in column 2 (ages 25–34).

[c] Estimate is significantly different from the estimate in column 3 (ages 35–44).

[d] Estimate is significantly different from the estimate in column 4 (ages 45+).

Table 5.43
Past-Year Prescription Drug Use, by Race/Ethnicity

|  | Non-Hispanic White (1) | Non-Hispanic Black (2) | Hispanic (3) | Non-Hispanic Asian (4) | Other (5) |
|---|---|---|---|---|---|
| Prescription sedatives[a] | 11.6% (10.4–12.9) | 10.0% (7.5–12.6) | 9.9% (7.2–12.6) | 7.0% (3.7–10.4) | 9.9% (7.4–12.4) |
| Prescription pain relievers[a] | 21.4% (19.7–23.2) | 21.3% (17.5–25.0) | 18.1% (14.7–21.5) | 25.3% (18.2–32.5) | 20.4% (16.3–24.6) |
| Prescription antidepressants[a] | 9.5% (8.3–10.6) | 7.9% (5.6–10.3) | 8.9% (6.4–11.3) | 6.1% (2.5–9.6) | 6.7% (4.0–9.5) |

NOTE: All data are weighted. 95-percent confidence intervals are presented in parentheses.

[a] The omnibus chi-square test was not statistically significant ($p > 0.05$).

Table 5.44
Past-Year Prescription Drug Use, by Education Level

|  | High School or Less (1) | Some College (2) | Bachelor's Degree or More (3) |
|---|---|---|---|
| Prescription sedatives | 6.7%[b,c] (4.7–8.8) | 12.5%[a] (10.9–14.0) | 10.9%[a] (9.7–12.0) |
| Prescription pain relievers | 18.3%[b] (15.0–21.6) | 23.5%[a,c] (21.5–25.6) | 18.8%[b] (17.1–20.6) |
| Prescription antidepressants | 6.6%[b] (4.6–8.6) | 10.6%[a,c] (9.2–12.1) | 7.4%[b] (6.3–8.5) |

NOTE: All data are weighted. 95-percent confidence intervals are presented in parentheses.

[a] Estimate is significantly different from the estimate in column 1 (high school or less).

[b] Estimate is significantly different from the estimate in column 2 (some college).

[c] Estimate is significantly different from the estimate in column 3 (bachelor's degree or more).

**Prescription Drug Misuse and Overuse**

Table 5.45 shows percentages of service members misusing and overusing each of the five prescription drug categories assessed in the 2015 HRBS. *Misuse* was defined as using a drug without a valid prescription, and *overuse* was defined as using more of a drug than prescribed. Key findings include the following:

- Among active-duty service members, 4.1 percent misused one or more of the prescription drug types in the past year (Table 5.45).
- In addition, 0.9 percent of service personnel overused one or more prescription drugs in the past year (Table 5.45).

In the general population in 2014, nonmedical use of prescription drugs occurred in 5.6 percent of adults (CBHSQ, 2015b). This national estimate is measured somewhat differently, so it is not directly comparable but provides a context that suggests that overall rates in the services are in line with those in the general population. The 2011 HRBS did not report overall rates of overuse and misuse.

Key findings regarding specific prescription drugs include the following:

- Among the prescription drugs studied in the 2015 HRBS, pain relievers were the most likely to be misused and the most likely to be overused; 2.4 percent of service members misused prescription pain relievers, and 0.7 percent overused them.
- Sedatives were also misused more often than other drugs (by 1.6 percent of service members), but less so than pain relievers. Sedatives were overused by 0.1 percent of personnel.

Because the denominator for calculating misuse and overuse of specific drugs in 2011 was different from that used in 2015, we cannot directly compare the 2015 and 2011 percentages. However, the *relative* percentages misusing each drug in 2011 were similar to those observed in 2015: In both years, pain relievers and sedatives were more commonly misused and overused relative to steroids and stimulants (Barlas et al, 2013).

Table 5.45
Past-Year Prescription Drug Misuse and Overuse, Overall Sample

|  | Misuse (1) | Overuse (2) |
| --- | --- | --- |
| Prescription stimulants | 0.3% (0.2–0.5) | 0.1% (0.0–0.2) |
| Prescription sedatives | 1.6% (1.2–2.0) | 0.1% (0.0–0.2) |
| Prescription pain relievers | 2.4% (1.8–2.9) | 0.7% (0.4–1.1) |
| Prescription anabolic steroids | 0.3% (0.2–0.5) | 0.0% (0.0–0.1) |
| Prescription antidepressants | 0.3% (0.1–0.5) | 0.2% (0.1–0.3) |
| Any prescription drug | 4.1% (3.5–4.8) | 0.9% (0.6–1.2) |

NOTE: All data are weighted. 95-percent confidence intervals are presented in parentheses.

Tables 5.46 through 5.51 show overall rates of prescription drug misuse and overuse by service branch and other demographics. Key findings include the following:

- Misuse was highest in the Army and lowest in the Coast Guard. There were no statistically significant differences by service branch in prescription drug overuse (Table 5.46).
- Prescription drug misuse was highest among senior enlisted personnel (Table 5.47).
- There were no statistically significant differences by gender in prescription drug misuse or overuse (Table 5.48).
- Prescription drug misuse increased with age, but there was no evidence that overuse of these drugs also did (Table 5.49).
- Non-Hispanic white service members were less likely to misuse prescription drugs than were those from other racial/ethnic backgrounds (Table 5.50). There were no statistically significant differences in prescription drug overuse by race/ethnicity.
- There was no evidence of differences in the percentages of service members that misused prescription drugs by level of education, but prescription drug overuse was lower among those with a bachelor's degree or more (Table 5.51).

**Table 5.46**
**Prescription Drug Misuse and Overuse, by Service Branch**

|  | Total (1) | Air Force (2) | Army (3) | Marine Corps (4) | Navy (5) | Coast Guard (6) |
|---|---|---|---|---|---|---|
| Misuse | 4.1% (3.5–4.8) | 3.3% (2.5–4.1) | 5.3%[e] (3.8–6.8) | 3.2% (1.9–4.6) | 3.8% (2.6–5.0) | 2.7%[b] (2.1–3.2) |
| Overuse[f] | 0.9% (0.6–1.2) | 0.5% (0.2–0.9) | 1.2% (0.5–1.9) | 1.3% (0.2–2.3) | 0.6% (0.1–1.1) | 0.4% (0.1–0.6) |

NOTE: All data are weighted. 95-percent confidence intervals are presented in parentheses.

[a] Estimate is significantly different from the estimate in column 2 (Air Force).

[b] Estimate is significantly different from the estimate in column 3 (Army).

[c] Estimate is significantly different from the estimate in column 4 (Marine Corps).

[d] Estimate is significantly different from the estimate in column 5 (Navy).

[e] Estimate is significantly different from the estimate in column 6 (Coast Guard).

[f] The omnibus chi-square test was not statistically significant ($p > 0.05$).

**Table 5.47**
**Prescription Drug Misuse and Overuse, by Pay Grade**

|  | E1–E4 (1) | E5–E6 (2) | E7–E9 (3) | W1–W5 (4) | O1–O3 (5) | O4–O10 (6) |
|---|---|---|---|---|---|---|
| Misuse | 3.7% (2.4–5.0) | 4.5%[e] (3.4–5.7) | 6.7%[e,f] (5.2–8.3) | 5.3%[e] (3.5–7.2) | 2.4%[b,c,d] (1.7–3.2) | 4.0%[c,d] (3.0–5.0) |
| Overuse[g] | 1.0% (0.4–1.6) | 1.2% (0.5–1.9) | 0.7% (0.2–1.2) | 0.8% (0.0–1.5) | 0.2% (0.0–0.5) | 0.4% (0.1–0.7) |

NOTE: All data are weighted. 95-percent confidence intervals are presented in parentheses.

[a] Estimate is significantly different from the estimate in column 1 (E1–E4).

[b] Estimate is significantly different from the estimate in column 2 (E5–E6).

[c] Estimate is significantly different from the estimate in column 3 (E7–E9).

[d] Estimate is significantly different from the estimate in column 4 (W1–W5).

[e] Estimate is significantly different from the estimate in column 5 (O1–O3).

[f] Estimate is significantly different from the estimate in column 6 (O4–O10).

[g] The omnibus chi-square test was not statistically significant ($p > 0.05$).

**Table 5.48**
**Prescription Drug Misuse and Overuse, by Gender**

|  | Men (1) | Women (2) |
|---|---|---|
| Misuse[a] | 4.0% (3.3–4.8) | 4.7% (3.8–5.6) |
| Overuse[a] | 0.9% (0.5–1.2) | 1.1% (0.7–1.6) |

NOTE: All data are weighted. 95-percent confidence intervals are presented in parentheses.

[a] The omnibus chi-square test was not statistically significant ($p > 0.05$).

**Table 5.49**
**Prescription Drug Misuse and Overuse, by Age Group**

|  | Ages 17–24 (1) | Ages 25–34 (2) | Ages 35–44 (3) | Ages 45+ (4) |
|---|---|---|---|---|
| Misuse | 3.3% (1.8–4.8) | 3.8%[d] (2.7–4.9) | 5.1% (4.1–6.2) | 6.4%[b] (4.7–8.1) |
| Overuse[e] | 1.0% (0.2–1.8) | 0.7% (0.3–1.1) | 1.1% (0.4–1.7) | 1.1% (0.0–2.4) |

NOTE: All data are weighted. 95-percent confidence intervals are presented in parentheses.

[a] Estimate is significantly different from the estimate in column 1 (ages 17–24).

[b] Estimate is significantly different from the estimate in column 2 (ages 25–34).

[c] Estimate is significantly different from the estimate in column 3 (ages 35–44).

[d] Estimate is significantly different from the estimate in column 4 (ages 45+).

[e] The omnibus chi-square test was not statistically significant ($p > 0.05$).

**Table 5.50**
**Prescription Drug Misuse and Overuse, by Race/Ethnicity**

|  | Non-Hispanic White (1) | Non-Hispanic Black (2) | Hispanic (3) | Non-Hispanic Asian (4) | Other (5) |
|---|---|---|---|---|---|
| Misuse | 3.1%[b] (2.3–3.8) | 6.2%[a] (4.0–8.4) | 5.8% (3.6–8.0) | 5.3% (1.3–9.3) | 4.8% (2.8–6.9) |
| Overuse[f] | 0.6% (0.3–1.0) | 1.1% (0.0–2.6) | 1.4% (0.4–2.4) | 1.0% (0.0–2.9) | 1.3% (0.2–2.5) |

NOTE: All data are weighted. 95-percent confidence intervals are presented in parentheses.

[a] Estimate is significantly different from the estimate in column 1 (non-Hispanic white).

[b] Estimate is significantly different from the estimate in column 2 (non-Hispanic black).

[c] Estimate is significantly different from the estimate in column 3 (Hispanic).

[d] Estimate is significantly different from the estimate in column 4 (non-Hispanic Asian).

[e] Estimate is significantly different from the estimate in column 5 (other).

[f] The omnibus chi-square test was not statistically significant ($p > 0.05$).

**Table 5.51**
**Prescription Drug Misuse and Overuse, by Education Level**

|  | High School or Less (1) | Some College (2) | Bachelor's Degree or More (3) |
|---|---|---|---|
| Misuse[d] | 3.9% | 4.8% | 3.3% |
|  | (2.0–5.8) | (3.7–5.9) | (2.6–4.0) |
| Overuse | 0.9% | 1.2%[c] | 0.4%[b] |
|  | (0.0–1.9) | (0.7–1.8) | (0.1–0.6) |

NOTE: All data are weighted. 95-percent confidence intervals are presented in parentheses.

[a] Estimate is significantly different from the estimate in column 1 (high school or less).

[b] Estimate is significantly different from the estimate in column 2 (some college).

[c] Estimate is significantly different from the estimate in column 3 (bachelor's degree or more).

[d] The omnibus chi-square test was not statistically significant ($p > 0.05$).

## Source of Prescription Drugs

Table 5.52 displays the sources (e.g., emergency room, family member, or U.S. Department of Veterans Affairs [VA] medical facility) of the prescription drugs used by service members. We do not present results by subgroup because of the small numbers in some of the source categories. Key findings include the following:

- Most service members obtained prescription drugs at a military treatment facility (MTF).
- Small percentages of service members obtained prescription drugs on the street or from family members. Among the drugs studied, stimulants were the most likely to be obtained from these sources; 2.5 percent of service personnel procured them on the street and 1.8 percent procured them from family members.
- Among the various drugs assessed, prescription antidepressants were the most likely to come from an MTF; 91.5 percent of service members who used antidepressants obtained them at an MTF.
- Anabolic steroids were the most likely among the drugs examined to be obtained from a nonmilitary health care provider (20.6 percent of steroid users procured them in this manner) and the least likely to come from an MTF (71.4 percent of users obtained them there).

Table 5.52
Source of Prescription Drugs, Overall Sample

| | Health Care Provider at MTF | Health Care Provider at VA Medical Facility | Nonmilitary Doctor or Health Care Worker | Emergency Room | Internet or Mail Order | Family Member or Friend | Dealer or Street Pharmacist | Other |
|---|---|---|---|---|---|---|---|---|
| Prescription stimulants | 81.5% (75.8–87.3) | 5.0% (0.7–9.3) | 9.2% (5.8–12.7) | 1.7% (0.0–3.3) | 0.3% (0.0–0.8) | 1.8% (0.1–3.4) | 2.5% (0.0–6.3) | 2.1% (0.1–4.0) |
| Prescription sedatives | 87.5% (84.2–90.8) | 3.1% (1.1–5.1) | 6.7% (5.2–8.2) | 7.6% (4.8–10.5) | 0.4% (0.0–0.8) | 0.3% (0.0–0.7) | 0.2% (0.0–0.6) | 0.7% (0.1–1.3) |
| Prescription pain relievers | 83.5% (81.0–86.1) | 4.7% (2.9–6.6) | 11.7% (9.8–13.6) | 9.5% (7.7–11.4) | 0.2% (0.0–0.4) | 0.5% (0.2–0.9) | 0.7% (0.0–1.7) | 0.6% (0.2–1.0) |
| Prescription anabolic steroids | 71.4% (61.1–81.7) | 1.6% (0.0–4.3) | 20.6% (10.8–30.5) | 1.5% (0.3–2.7) | 0.9% (0.0–2.7) | 1.1% (0.0–3.3) | 1.5% (0.0–4.4) | 5.5% (0.5–10.5) |
| Prescription antidepressants | 91.5% (88.3–94.7) | 4.6% (1.8–7.5) | 5.6% (3.6–7.5) | 1.4% (0.1–2.8) | 0.5% (0.0–1.0) | 0.0% (0.0–0.0) | 0.2% (0.0–0.7) | 0.5% (0.0–1.1) |

NOTE: All data are weighted. 95-percent confidence intervals are presented in parentheses. The table reflects the source of drugs among those using a given prescription drug in the past year. Respondents could select more than one source for each drug, so row percentages can sum to more than 100.

## Summary

Based on data from the 2015 HRBS, we found that rates of binge drinking in the services remained nearly as high as in 2011 and were at a level high enough to cause concern; indeed, nearly one in three service members was a current binge drinker. Percentages of service members who reported hazardous drinking were also substantial, particularly among service members in the Marine Corps. Consistent with this, one in 12 service members experienced one or more serious consequences from drinking in the past year, and among Marines, the comparable figure was nearly one in six. Responses indicate that 68.2 percent of service members perceived the military culture as supportive of drinking, and 42.4 percent said that their supervisors do not discourage alcohol use—perceptions that were even more common among younger and junior enlisted personnel, who were the most likely to binge drink. This suggests that a change in culture clearly communicated from the higher ranks could substantially reduce drinking. Given that alcohol is often purchased on base, raising prices or otherwise limiting sales may also be effective and would communicate a shift in culture.

Results indicate that cigarette smoking in the military declined substantially since 2011—by nearly 50 percent—and those who smoked were smoking less. Cigarette smoking was less common in the military than in the general population and was particularly low given the gender and age composition of the force. However, any smoking puts the immediate and long-term health of service members at risk, and one in seven service members reported that they smoke. In contrast to cigarette smoking, smokeless tobacco use was relatively high in the military compared with use among civilians. E-cigarette use was also a growing problem: The percentage of service personnel who used e-cigarettes has increased dramatically since 2011. The percentage of service members reporting secondhand smoke exposure during work was about equal to that among civilians, but there is room for improvement, especially considering that fewer service members than civilians smoke. One policy lever that appears promising is a shift in perceived military climate. Few service personnel felt that cigarette and smokeless tobacco use are discouraged by their supervisor. In addition, more than 80 percent of service members bought cigarettes on base—and that number was even higher among junior enlisted personnel and younger service members, who were also more likely to smoke. This suggests that changes to reduce on-base sales of cigarettes, or to increase their price, could reduce the level of smoking among service members.

Rates of illicit drug use have decreased in recent years. Rates among service members were low in absolute terms and were substantially lower than in the general U.S. population. Use of pain relievers and sedatives among service members have decreased by almost 50 percent since 2011. Nonetheless, both prescription drug types were misused more often than other drugs studied, and pain relievers were substantially more likely to be overused than any other drug type. Prescription drug use and misuse were elevated among senior enlisted non-commissioned officers (NCOs) (E7–E9).

# CHAPTER SIX

# Mental and Emotional Health

This chapter presents the results of a detailed analysis on the social, emotional, and mental health of active-duty service members, including mental health indicators (e.g., depression, anxiety, and PTSD), social and emotional factors associated with mental health (e.g., high risk taking and impulsivity, anger or aggression, and physical or sexual abuse history), self-inflicted injury, and suicide ideation and suicide attempts. Additionally, the chapter presents an analysis of the receipt of mental health services and stigma associated with seeking and receiving mental health treatment.

Each section highlights the importance or relevance of the mental health topic to the general population and to the military and then provides an analysis of each topic by service branch. When relevant, we present analyses by pay grade, gender, age group, race/ethnicity, and education level. Key measures used are described in the applicable section, and additional details about these measures may be found in Appendix D. All analyses in this chapter demonstrated statistically significant omnibus tests (a Rao-Scott chi-square test for categorical variables and $F$-tests for continuous variables) unless otherwise noted in the tables. Statistically significant group differences (pairwise comparisons) are presented within each table. However, only statistically significant differences that the research team's subject-matter experts determined to be substantively meaningful (i.e., could be used to change or develop policy or contribute to inequalities in health outcomes across subgroups) are discussed in the text. Readers should use caution when interpreting comparisons between the 2015 HRBS results and other populations or prior versions of the HRBS because these comparisons are not necessarily statistically significant and could simply reflect sampling variability across the two samples being compared; however, where available, we provide confidence intervals for comparisons.

When interpreting the findings of this chapter, note that social, emotional, and mental health findings are based on self-reported symptoms and behaviors. These are assessed using previously validated screening instruments, but they do not represent clinical diagnoses per se.

## Mental Health Indicators

We begin with a discussion of three mental health conditions: depression, generalized anxiety disorder (GAD), and PTSD. Overall, 17.9 percent (CI: 16.5–19.2) of service members had at least one of the three assessed mental health indicators, and 9.7 percent (CI: 8.6–10.8) met symptom criteria for two or more disorders. Detailed findings of each mental health indicator are available in the following sections. Results can be found in Tables 6.1 through 6.6 at the end of this section.

### Depression

Depression is one of the most common mental health disorders among U.S. adults, affecting approximately 6 percent of adults in the past year (CBHSQ, 2015a) and between 16 and 17 percent (CI: 15.5–17.5) in their lifetime (Kessler, Berglund, et al., 2005). Yet depression is also one of the more preventable and treatable mental disorders if it is identified early and connections are made to high-quality mental health services (Thota et al., 2012). Left untreated, depression has major financial and social costs. These costs include diminished work productivity, absenteeism, lost wages, increased use of social security insurance at younger ages, increased risk for comorbid mental (e.g., substance use, anxiety) and physical (e.g., cardiovascular disease) health issues, and, ultimately, increased societal costs (Kessler, 2012). In turn, unidentified and untreated depression and the associated costs have major implications for readiness. A recent meta-analysis of 25 epidemiological studies estimated that the prevalence of current major depression among U.S. military personnel was 12.0 percent (CI: 9.7–14.4) among those currently deployed, 13.1 percent (CI: 9.6–16.6) among those previously deployed, and 5.7 percent (CI: 3.4–8.1) among those never deployed (Gadermann et al., 2012). Lifetime prevalence of major depression among military personnel was an estimated 16.2 percent (CI: 10.1–22.3), and 5.5 percent (CI: 2.2–8.8) of military personnel had onset of depression after entering the military. Being enlisted, a woman, young (aged 17–25), and unmarried and having less than a college education were associated with higher rates of depression.

Depression was measured using the PHQ-9. Scores of 15 in primary care samples correspond to probable depression and moderate to severe depression symptom severity (Kroenke, Spitzer, and Williams, 2001). Key findings across all services include the following:

- Based on data from the 2015 HRBS, 9.4 percent of service members reported probable depression, which was higher than the target of 5.8 percent for HP2020 (HHS, 2010c).

The distribution of probable depression was statistically significantly different across service branches and demographic groups. Key findings include the following:

- The highest prevalence of probable depression was among members of the Marine Corps (13.5 percent), Army (11.0 percent), and Navy (10.1 percent) compared with the Coast Guard (4.4 percent) and Air Force (4.1 percent) (Table 6.1).
- Enlisted service members had a higher prevalence of probable depression compared with officers (Table 6.2).
- A higher prevalence of probable depression was also seen among women (Table 6.3), those whose race/ethnicity was categorized as other (Table 6.5), and those with less than a bachelor's degree (Table 6.6) when compared with their peers in other demographic groups.

### Anxiety

GAD is one of the most common anxiety disorders seen in general medical practice (Spitzer et al., 2006), affecting nearly 6 percent (CI: 5.4–6.6) of all U.S. adults in their lifetime (Kessler, Berglund, et al., 2005) and approximately 3 percent (CI: 2.6–3.4) of U.S. adults in the past year (Kessler, Chiu, et al., 2005). GAD is a disorder characterized by frequent and excessive worry. Similar to depression, anxiety disorders have important associated social and economic costs (e.g., loss of work productivity, wage loss, increased absenteeism, comorbid mental and physical health issues) that negatively affect readiness for military duty (Hoffman, Dukes, and Wittchen, 2008), particularly when left untreated.

We measured GAD in the two weeks prior to survey response using the GAD-7 scale, in which scores of 10 or more indicated probable GAD (Löwe et al., 2008; Spitzer et al., 2006). Contractor and colleagues (2015) assessed a National Guard population using a modified GAD-7 to assess lifetime symptoms. They found that, across all services, 17.1 percent of National Guard members reported one or more two-week periods with probable GAD in their lifetime. In the 2015 HRBS, prevalence of probable GAD in the two weeks prior to the survey was quite high compared with previously published general population figures using the same cut point (Löwe et al., 2008). Among service members, 14.2 percent indicated probable GAD in the past two weeks compared with 4.3 percent in a general population sample (Löwe et al., 2008). This figure is similar to the 16.7-percent (CI: 16.1–17.3) prevalence in the 2011 HRBS (Barlas et al., 2013), but that earlier figure was determined using a subset of four of the GAD-7 items used to assess symptoms in the past 30 days.

The distribution of probable GAD was statistically significantly different across service branches and demographic groups. Key findings include the following:

- Prevalence rates were highest in the Marine Corps (19.2 percent), Navy (16.4 percent), and Army (15.9 percent) compared with the Coast Guard (8.4 percent) and Air Force (6.8 percent) (Table 6.1).
- Enlisted service members and warrant officers had higher rates of probable GAD compared with junior, mid-grade, and senior officers (Table 6.2).
- Consistent with gender differences in anxiety in the general population (Kessler, Berglund, et al., 2005), significantly more women than men met the criteria for probable GAD (Table 6.3).
- Additionally, service members with lower levels of education had higher rates of probable GAD (Table 6.6).

## Posttraumatic Stress Disorder

Studies suggest that during an American's lifetime, a majority experience one or more psychological traumas of a severity sufficient to trigger PTSD. However, the majority of persons who experience these traumas do not develop symptoms of PTSD, which must persist for 30 days after the traumatic event. Approximately 7 percent (CI: 6.2–7.8) of the general U.S. population met criteria for PTSD at some point in their lives, and 3.5 percent (CI: 2.9–4.1) met criteria in the past year (Kessler, Berglund, et al., 2005).

The experience of psychological trauma is a well-known hazard associated with military service. Estimates of PTSD prevalence in current military samples vary widely and are contingent on the sample's exposure to combat (Ramchand, Rudavsky, et al., 2015; Ramchand, Schell, Karney, et al., 2010; Sundin et al., 2010). Problems from PTSD cause suffering and impairment and contribute to military attrition, absenteeism, misconduct, and sick call visits (Hoge, Terhakopian, et al., 2007; Hoge, Grossman, et al., 2014). PTSD is consistently associated with increased health care utilization, medical morbidity, and health-compromising behaviors, such as tobacco and alcohol abuse (Hoge, Terhakopian, et al., 2007; Schnurr, 2015). The high prevalence and negative health effects of PTSD have led to increased mental health screening for this disorder in VA and DoD clinics (Belsher et al., 2014; Tsan et al., 2012).

In the 2015 HRBS, we measured PTSD using the PCL-C. The PCL is widely used in military PTSD studies, and we used the civilian version because it assesses PTSD symptoms related to all psychological traumas, not just those directly related to military service. A cut point of 50 was used to indicate probable PTSD (Weathers et al., 1993; see Appendix D for details). A significant debate has surrounded the issue of PCL cut points in various settings and for various purposes. We chose a cut point of 50 because it is the cut point most often used in research performed in military population surveillance studies (e.g., Hoge, Castro, et al., 2004), maximizing specificity and positive predictive value in this context (Bliese et al., 2008; Terhakopian et al., 2008). Key findings from the 2015 HRBS include the following:

- Across all services, 8.5 percent of service members reported probable PTSD (Table 6.1), a figure slightly lower than the estimated 13 to 18 percent following recent combat deployments (Hoge, Castro, et al., 2004; Tanielian and Jaycox, 2008). The 2015 HRBS PTSD prevalence was consistent with or slightly higher than the 5.9 percent of personnel (CI: 5.3–6.5) with high PTSD symptoms reported in the 2011 HRBS report (Barlas et al., 2013), although the 2011 report used only a subset of four items from the 17-item PCL scale.
- The 2015 HRBS distribution of probable PTSD was statistically significantly different across service branches (Table 6.1). Similar to rates of depression and anxiety, rates of PTSD were highest in the Army (10.5 percent), Navy (9.7 percent), and Marine Corps (9.1 percent) compared with the Coast Guard (4.1 percent) and Air Force (3.9 percent) (Table 6.1).
- Enlisted service members and warrant officers had higher rates of probable PTSD compared with junior, mid-grade, and senior officers (Table 6.2).
- Women had a significantly higher prevalence of probable PTSD than men; however, the size of the actual difference was small (Table 6.3).
- Additionally, service members who identified as non-Hispanic black and whose race/ethnicity was categorized as other had higher rates of probable PTSD (Table 6.5), as did those with lower levels of education (Table 6.6).

**Table 6.1**
**Mental Health Indicators, by Service Branch**

| | Total (1) | Air Force (2) | Army (3) | Marine Corps (4) | Navy (5) | Coast Guard (6) |
|---|---|---|---|---|---|---|
| Probable depression | 9.4% (8.4–10.5) | 4.1%[b,c,d] (3.1–5.1) | 11.0%[a,e] (8.9–13.1) | 13.5%[a,e] (10.4–16.6) | 10.1%[a,e] (8.0–12.3) | 4.4%[b,c,d] (3.7–5.2) |
| Probable GAD | 14.2% (13.0–15.5) | 6.8%[b,c,d] (5.6–8.0) | 15.9%[a,e] (13.4–18.4) | 19.2%[a,e] (15.7–22.7) | 16.4%[a,e] (13.8–19.0) | 8.4%[b,c,d] (7.4–9.4) |
| Probable PTSD | 8.5% (7.4–9.5) | 3.9%[b,c,d] (2.9–4.8) | 10.5%[a,e] (8.4–12.6) | 9.1%[a,e] (6.7–11.5) | 9.7%[a,e] (7.5–11.9) | 4.1%[b,c,d] (3.4–4.8) |

NOTE: All data are weighted. 95-percent confidence intervals are presented in parentheses.
[a] Estimate is significantly different from the estimate in column 2 (Air Force).
[b] Estimate is significantly different from the estimate in column 3 (Army).
[c] Estimate is significantly different from the estimate in column 4 (Marine Corps).
[d] Estimate is significantly different from the estimate in column 5 (Navy).
[e] Estimate is significantly different from the estimate in column 6 (Coast Guard).

Table 6.2
**Mental Health Indicators, by Pay Grade**

|  | E1–E4 (1) | E5–E6 (2) | E7–E9 (3) | W1–W5 (4) | O1–O3 (5) | O4–O10 (6) |
|---|---|---|---|---|---|---|
| Probable depression | 10.8%[d,e,f] (8.7–12.8) | 11.2%[d,e,f] (9.3–13.1) | 8.2%[e,f] (6.5–9.9) | 6.4%[a,b,f] (4.5–8.4) | 4.7%[a,b,c,f] (3.6–5.8) | 2.5%[a,b,c,d,e] (1.8–3.3) |
| Probable GAD | 16.7%[e,f] (14.3–19.2) | 15.6%[e,f] (13.5–17.8) | 13.3%[e,f] (11.2–15.4) | 12.5%[e,f] (9.8–15.3) | 7.1%[a,b,c,d,f] (5.8–8.4) | 4.6%[a,b,c,d,e] (3.6–5.6) |
| Probable PTSD | 8.9%[e,f] (7.0–10.9) | 9.7%[e,f] (7.9–11.5) | 10.3%[e,f] (8.4–12.2) | 9.3%[e,f] (6.9–11.7) | 4.6%[a,b,c,d,] (3.5–5.7) | 3.0%[a,b,c,d] (2.1–3.9) |

NOTE: All data are weighted. 95-percent confidence intervals are presented in parentheses.

[a] Estimate is significantly different from the estimate in column 1 (E1–E4).

[b] Estimate is significantly different from the estimate in column 2 (E5–E6).

[c] Estimate is significantly different from the estimate in column 3 (E7–E9).

[d] Estimate is significantly different from the estimate in column 4 (W1–W5).

[e] Estimate is significantly different from the estimate in column 5 (O1–O3).

[f] Estimate is significantly different from the estimate in column 6 (O4–O10).

Table 6.3
**Mental Health Indicators, by Gender**

|  | Men (1) | Women (2) |
|---|---|---|
| Probable depression | 9.1%[a] (7.9–10.4) | 11.0% (9.6–12.5) |
| Probable GAD | 13.6%[a] (12.1–15.1) | 17.8% (16.1–19.5) |
| Probable PTSD[b] | 8.2% (7.1–9.4) | 9.6% (8.3–10.9) |

NOTE: All data are weighted. 95-percent confidence intervals are presented in parentheses.

[a] Estimate is significantly different from the estimate in column 2 (women).

[b] The omnibus chi-square test was not statistically significant ($p > 0.05$).

Table 6.4
**Mental Health Indicators, by Age Group**

|  | Ages 17–24 (1) | Ages 25–34 (2) | Ages 35–44 (3) | Ages 45+ (4) |
|---|---|---|---|---|
| Probable depression[a] | 10.9% (8.5–13.2) | 8.9% (7.3–10.6) | 8.5% (6.7–10.3) | 9.8% (6.5–13.1) |
| Probable GAD[a] | 16.2% (13.4–18.9) | 13.8% (11.9–15.8) | 13.3% (11.2–15.4) | 12.2% (8.5–15.9) |
| Probable PTSD[a] | 7.4% (5.5–9.3) | 8.4% (6.7–10.1) | 9.4% (7.5–11.2) | 10.3% (7.2–13.4) |

NOTE: All data are weighted. 95-percent confidence intervals are presented in parentheses.

[a] The omnibus chi-square test was not statistically significant ($p > 0.05$).

**Table 6.5**
**Mental Health Indicators, by Race/Ethnicity**

| | Non-Hispanic White (1) | Non-Hispanic Black (2) | Hispanic (3) | Non-Hispanic Asian (4) | Other (5) |
|---|---|---|---|---|---|
| Probable depression[f] | 9.0% (7.7–10.4) | 8.2% (5.6–10.9) | 9.8% (7.1–12.5) | 8.0% (2.6–13.4) | 14.2% (10.1–18.2) |
| Probable GAD[f] | 13.8% (12.2–15.4) | 11.4% (8.3–14.5) | 15.6% (12.2–19.1) | 16.2% (9.3–23.1) | 17.5% (13.2–21.8) |
| Probable PTSD | 7.7%[e] (6.4–9.0) | 10.0% (7.1–12.9) | 8.5% (5.9–11.0) | 5.5% (1.2–9.8) | 12.9%[a] (9.0–16.9) |

NOTE: All data are weighted. 95-percent confidence intervals are presented in parentheses.

[a] Estimate is significantly different from the estimate in column 1 (non-Hispanic white).

[b] Estimate is significantly different from the estimate in column 2 (non-Hispanic black).

[c] Estimate is significantly different from the estimate in column 3 (Hispanic).

[d] Estimate is significantly different from the estimate in column 4 (non-Hispanic Asian).

[e] Estimate is significantly different from the estimate in column 5 (other).

[f] The omnibus chi-square test was not statistically significant ($p > 0.05$).

**Table 6.6**
**Mental Health Indicators, by Education Level**

| | High School or Less (1) | Some College (2) | Bachelor's Degree or More (3) |
|---|---|---|---|
| Probable depression | 10.8%[c] (8.0–13.5) | 11.7%[c] (10.0–13.4) | 5.3%[a,b] (4.1–6.4) |
| Probable GAD | 16.7%[c] (13.5–19.9) | 16.6%[c] (14.7–18.6) | 9.2%[a,b] (7.5–10.9) |
| Probable PTSD | 9.0% (6.6–11.4) | 10.0%[c] (8.3–11.6) | 5.8%[b] (4.5–7.2) |

NOTE: All data are weighted. 95-percent confidence intervals are presented in parentheses.

[a] Estimate is significantly different from the estimate in column 1 (high school or less).

[b] Estimate is significantly different from the estimate in column 2 (some college).

[c] Estimate is significantly different from the estimate in column 3 (bachelor's degree or more).

## Social and Emotional Factors Associated with Mental Health

We turn now to social and emotional factors that are associated with mental health, including anger and impulsivity. Detailed descriptions of each measure can be found in Appendix D. Results are shown in Tables 6.7 through 6.12.

### Anger and Aggression

Because anger and aggression are frequently reported among combat veterans (Jakupcak et al., 2007; Killgore et al., 2008), items assessing recent angry or aggressive behaviors were included in the 2015 HRBS. Aggressive behavior may result in military personnel physically harming themselves or others, lead to domestic violence and other illegal acts, and potentially affect military readiness (Killgore et al., 2008; Thomas et al., 2010). Identifying baseline levels of aggressive behavior among the military population may suggest the need for policy or programmatic responses.

To assess levels of aggressive behavior, respondents were asked to report how often in the past 30 days they had expressed anger in explosive or aggressive ways, as illustrated in four scenarios (get angry at someone and yell or shout; get angry with someone and kick, slam, or punch something; make a violent threat; fight/hit someone) (Thomas et al., 2010). Nearly half (47.0 percent) of active-duty service members reported at least one of the four aggressive behaviors in the past 30 days (Table 6.7), although less than 2 percent engaged in physical fighting at least one time in the past month. Key findings include the following:

- Among service members, 8.4 percent reported a recent pattern of aggressive behaviors (one or more of the four behaviors occurring five or more times in the past 30 days) (Table 6.7).
- The percentage of service members reporting frequent aggressive behavior was higher in the Army, Marine Corps, and Navy than in the Coast Guard and Air Force (Table 6.7).
- Service members in all enlisted pay grades (Table 6.8) and those with less than a bachelor's degree (Table 6.12) demonstrated higher rates of frequent aggressive behaviors relative to their peers.
- Non-Hispanic Asian service members were the least likely to engage in frequent aggressive behavior compared with other racial or ethnic groups (Table 6.11).

### Impulsivity

A risk-taking disposition includes a series of associated characteristics, one of which is being impulsive. *Impulsivity* involves the tendency to act on a whim, without considering the possible risks or consequences of the action (Eysenck and Eysenck, 1978). In the general population, impulsivity is particularly characteristic of adolescent youth; recent research links the impulsivity of youth to a stage of brain development during adolescence (see Steinberg, 2008, for a review). Impulsivity has been linked to accidental injury (Cherpitel, 1993; 1999), pathological gambling (Wolkowitz, Roy, and Doran, 1985), risky sexual activity (Kahn et al., 2002), and alcohol use (Bray, Pemberton, et al., 2009). The 2008 HRBS demonstrated that these relationships hold true for service members (Bray, Pemberton, et al., 2009). Specifically, results showed that impulsivity and sensation-seeking among military personnel were related to less-frequent seat belt use, increased drinking (any consumption of alcohol in the past 30 days whether driving or not), heavy drinking, driving after drinking too much, and other substance use.

Differences on the drinking and driving item were pronounced: Of those classified as high in impulsivity, 13.6 percent reported driving after drinking too much; 3 percent of those scoring low on the impulsivity measure reported doing so.

The impulsivity items in the 2015 HRBS were adapted from the 2011 HRBS (Barlas et al., 2013). This measure was specific to impulsivity; the 2008 measure had also included items on risk-taking behaviors (Bray, Pemberton, et al., 2009). Mean scores across all items of between 3 ("somewhat") and 5 ("a great deal") were categorized as high impulsivity (Barlas et al., 2013). Key findings from the 2015 HRBS include the following:

- Overall, 12.7 percent of service members were categorized as high in impulsivity, slightly higher than the 10.3 percent (CI: 9.7–10.9) reported in the 2011 HRBS report (Barlas et al., 2013) (Table 6.7).
- Rates of impulsivity were highest in the Marine Corps (21.3 percent), much higher than in the next-closest service, the Navy (13.6 percent) (Table 6.7).
- Rates were also comparable across other demographics, although junior and mid-level enlisted personnel (E1–E4 and E5–E6) (Table 6.8), younger service members (Table 6.10), and those with lower education levels (Table 6.12) showed slightly larger percentages of high impulsivity.

**Table 6.7**
**Social and Emotional Factors Associated with Mental Health, by Service Branch**

|  | Total (1) | Air Force (2) | Army (3) | Marine Corps (4) | Navy (5) | Coast Guard (6) |
|---|---|---|---|---|---|---|
| Any aggressive behavior in the past month | 47.0% (45.3–48.6) | 31.5%[b,c,d,e] (29.4–33.6) | 48.9%[a,c,e] (45.5–52.3) | 58.1%[a,b,e] (53.8–62.4) | 52.7%[a,e] (49.4–56.0) | 40.1%[a,b,c,d] (38.4–41.8) |
| Aggressive behavior 5+ times in the past month | 8.4% (7.4–9.4) | 3.1%[b,c,d] (2.3–3.9) | 10.2%[a,e] (8.2–12.2) | 10.6%[a,e] (8.0–13.1) | 9.8%[a,e] (7.7–11.9) | 3.8%[b,c,d] (3.1–4.4) |
| High impulsivity | 12.7% (11.4–14.0) | 8.4%[c,d] (6.9–9.9) | 11.9%[c,e] (9.4–14.4) | 21.3%[a,b,d,e] (17.4–25.2) | 13.6%[a,c,e] (11.0–16.1) | 8.3%[b,c,d] (7.2–9.3) |

NOTE: All data are weighted. 95-percent confidence intervals are presented in parentheses.

[a] Estimate is significantly different from the estimate in column 2 (Air Force).

[b] Estimate is significantly different from the estimate in column 3 (Army).

[c] Estimate is significantly different from the estimate in column 4 (Marine Corps).

[d] Estimate is significantly different from the estimate in column 5 (Navy).

[e] Estimate is significantly different from the estimate in column 6 (Coast Guard).

**Table 6.8**
**Social and Emotional Factors Associated with Mental Health, by Pay Grade**

| | E1–E4 (1) | E5–E6 (2) | E7–E9 (3) | W1–W5 (4) | O1–O3 (5) | O4–O10 (6) |
|---|---|---|---|---|---|---|
| Any aggressive behavior in the past month | 44.8%[b,c,e] (41.5–48.1) | 52.6%[a,e,f] (49.7–55.4) | 52.8%[a,e,f] (49.9–55.7) | 49.2%[e,f] (45.2–53.1) | 36.9%[a,b,c,d,f] (34.6–39.1) | 43.1%[b,c,d,e] (40.6–45.5) |
| Aggressive behavior 5+ times in the past month | 7.7% (5.9–9.6) | 11.5%[d,e,f] (9.6–13.5) | 9.4%[e,f] (7.6–11.2) | 6.1%[b] (4.1–8.0) | 3.9%[a,b,c,d] (2.9–4.9) | 5.1%[b,c] (4.0–6.2) |
| High impulsivity | 18.2%[b,c,d,e,f] (15.5–20.8) | 11.6%[a,c,d,e,f] (9.7–13.5) | 7.2%[a,b,f] (5.6–8.8) | 4.2%[a,b] (2.6–5.7) | 5.8%[a,b,f] (4.6–6.9) | 2.9%[a,b,c,e] (2.0–3.8) |

NOTE: All data are weighted. 95-percent confidence intervals are presented in parentheses.
[a] Estimate is significantly different from the estimate in column 1 (E1–E4).
[b] Estimate is significantly different from the estimate in column 2 (E5–E6).
[c] Estimate is significantly different from the estimate in column 3 (E7–E9).
[d] Estimate is significantly different from the estimate in column 4 (W1–W5).
[e] Estimate is significantly different from the estimate in column 5 (O1–O3).
[f] Estimate is significantly different from the estimate in column 6 (O4–O10).

**Table 6.9**
**Social and Emotional Factors Associated with Mental Health, by Gender**

| | Men (1) | Women (2) |
|---|---|---|
| Any aggressive behavior in the past month | 46.2%[a] (44.3–48.2) | 51.0% (49.0–53.0) |
| Aggressive behavior 5+ times in the past month[b] | 8.6% (7.4–9.7) | 7.4% (6.2–8.6) |
| High impulsivity | 13.5%[a] (12.0–15.0) | 8.2% (6.9–9.4) |

NOTE: All data are weighted. 95-percent confidence intervals are presented in parentheses.
[a] Estimate is significantly different from the estimate in column 2 (women).
[b] The omnibus chi-square test was not statistically significant ($p > 0.05$).

**Table 6.10**
**Social and Emotional Factors Associated with Mental Health, by Age Group**

| | Ages 17–24 (1) | Ages 25–34 (2) | Ages 35–44 (3) | Ages 45+ (4) |
|---|---|---|---|---|
| Any aggressive behavior in the past month | 45.7%[c] (41.9–49.4) | 45.3%[c] (42.7–48.0) | 52.1%[a,b,d] (49.3–54.9) | 45.3%[c] (41.3–49.4) |
| Aggressive behavior 5+ times in the past month[e] | 8.5% (6.4–10.7) | 7.9% (6.4–9.4) | 9.0% (7.3–10.8) | 8.8% (5.7–11.9) |
| High impulsivity | 22.0%[b,c,d] (18.7–25.3) | 10.9%[a,c] (9.0–12.7) | 6.6%[a,b] (4.9–8.2) | 6.9%[a] (4.3–9.6) |

NOTE: All data are weighted. 95-percent confidence intervals are presented in parentheses.
[a] Estimate is significantly different from the estimate in column 1 (ages 17–24).
[b] Estimate is significantly different from the estimate in column 2 (ages 25–34).
[c] Estimate is significantly different from the estimate in column 3 (ages 35–44).
[d] Estimate is significantly different from the estimate in column 4 (ages 45+).
[e] The omnibus chi-square test was not statistically significant ($p > 0.05$).

**Table 6.11**
**Social and Emotional Factors Associated with Mental Health, by Race/Ethnicity**

| | Non-Hispanic White (1) | Non-Hispanic Black (2) | Hispanic (3) | Non-Hispanic Asian (4) | Other (5) |
|---|---|---|---|---|---|
| Any aggressive behavior in the past month | 49.0%[d] (46.8–51.1) | 42.4% (37.2–47.5) | 43.6% (39.0–48.3) | 36.9%[a,e] (28.9–44.8) | 52.0%[d] (46.5–57.4) |
| Aggressive behavior 5+ times in the past month | 8.9% (7.6–10.3) | 6.7% (4.2–9.3) | 7.3% (5.1–9.5) | 3.0%[e] (0.5–5.5) | 12.3%[d] (8.4–16.3) |
| High impulsivity | 12.8%[b] (11.1–14.5) | 6.5%[a,c,e] (3.7–9.3) | 16.1%[b] (12.3–19.9) | 8.4% (3.8–13.0) | 16.7%[b] (11.8–21.6) |

NOTE: All data are weighted. 95-percent confidence intervals are presented in parentheses.

[a] Estimate is significantly different from the estimate in column 1 (non-Hispanic white).

[b] Estimate is significantly different from the estimate in column 2 (non-Hispanic black).

[c] Estimate is significantly different from the estimate in column 3 (Hispanic).

[d] Estimate is significantly different from the estimate in column 4 (non-Hispanic Asian).

[e] Estimate is significantly different from the estimate in column 5 (other).

**Table 6.12**
**Social and Emotional Factors Associated with Mental Health, by Education Level**

| | High School or Less (1) | Some College (2) | Bachelor's Degree or More (3) |
|---|---|---|---|
| Any aggressive behavior in the past month | 49.8%[c] (45.3–54.3) | 49.2%[c] (46.7–51.7) | 41.9%[a,b] (39.4–44.3) |
| Aggressive behavior 5+ times in the past month | 11.3%[c] (8.6–14.0) | 8.9%[c] (7.4–10.4) | 5.9%[a,b] (4.6–7.2) |
| High impulsivity | 24.3%[b,c] (20.2–28.5) | 12.0%[a,c] (10.2–13.7) | 6.6%[a,b] (5.1–8.2) |

NOTE: All data are weighted. 95-percent confidence intervals are presented in parentheses.

[a] Estimate is significantly different from the estimate in column 1 (high school or less).

[b] Estimate is significantly different from the estimate in column 2 (some college).

[c] Estimate is significantly different from the estimate in column 3 (bachelor's degree or more).

## Assault and Abuse History

### Unwanted Sexual Contact

The experience of a sexual assault has consequences for the victim, as well as costs for society. Consequences for the victim may include immediate physical harm (from the assault itself) and increased risks of sexually transmitted illnesses, pregnancy, mental health problems (such as PTSD), and chronic health problems (Ciccone et al., 2005; Fanslow and Robinson, 2004; Frayne et al., 1999; Golding, 1994; Kilpatrick, Edmunds, and Seymour, 1992; Kilpatrick et al., 1997; Resnick et al., 2007). Koss found that in the year after sexual assault, outpatient medical visits increased by 56 percent in a sample of women enrolled in a health maintenance organization, and this increased utilization persisted for at least three years (Koss, 1994). The empirical literature on the consequences of sexual assault among service members is not as advanced as among civilians. However, there is evidence that assaulted service members suffer a range of significant problems (for reviews, see Turchik and Wilson, 2010; Weaver and Clum, 1995). Unwanted sexual contact is important to assess because it represents a breakdown in good order and discipline, and it may have negative effects on retention, recruitment, and readiness.

RAND's recent assessment of sexual assault and sexual harassment in the U.S. military estimates that 4.9 percent (CI: 4.7–5.1) of service members have experienced a sexual assault in their lifetime; that includes 2.6 percent (CI: 2.3–2.8) of men and 17.9 percent (CI: 17.5–18.3) of women (National Defense Research Institute, 2014). The 2011 HRBS estimates that 14.3 percent (CI: 13.7–14.9) of service members reported any history of unwanted sexual contact in their lifetime (Barlas et al., 2013). The percentage of service members reporting unwanted sexual contact is likely higher in the 2011 HRBS report than in the RAND report because the RAND Military Workplace Study defined sexual assault more narrowly—that is, as a sex crime under UCMJ Article 120. The 2015 HRBS used a much broader definition of unwanted sexual contact. For this reason, the HRBS measures and the 2014 RAND report are not directly comparable.

The 2015 HRBS found that, among all active-duty service members, 16.9 percent reported having any unwanted sexual contact in their lifetime (Table 6.13).

Of those who reported any unwanted sexual contact in their lifetime, key findings include the following:

- More than one-third (38.2 percent) experienced unwanted sexual contact only when on active duty (Table 6.13). The 2015 HRBS did not differentiate between unwanted sexual contact experienced before or after joining the military.[1]
- Almost three-quarters (72.2 percent) experienced unwanted sexual contact only when not on active duty (Table 6.13).
- One in ten (10.4 percent) experienced unwanted sexual contact both when on and when not on active duty (Table 6.13).
- Women reported higher levels of unwanted sexual contact in their lifetime than men (46.1 percent compared with 11.7 percent) (Table 6.15); however, the frequency at which this unwanted sexual contact occurred when not on active duty did not differ substantially by gender.

There were few notable statistically significant differences in reports of unwanted sexual contact across service branch (Table 6.13), pay grade (Table 6.14), age group (Table 6.16), race/ethnicity (Table 6.17), or education level (Table 6.18).

---

[1]   The response option "not on active duty" could include time spent in a reserve status prior to becoming active duty.

**Table 6.13**
**Unwanted Sexual Contact, by Service Branch**

|  | Total (1) | Air Force (2) | Army (3) | Marine Corps (4) | Navy (5) | Coast Guard (6) |
|---|---|---|---|---|---|---|
| Lifetime | 16.9% (15.8–18.1) | 14.5%[b,d] (13.1–15.9) | 18.3%[a,e] (15.9–20.8) | 14.1%[d] (11.3–16.8) | 19.2%[a,c,e] (16.8–21.5) | 13.8%[b,d] (12.8–14.9) |
| When on active duty[f] | 38.2% (34.7–41.8) | 38.3% (33.6–42.9) | 38.5% (31.7–45.2) | 32.8% (23.6–42.0) | 39.6% (32.9–46.2) | 43.9% (39.7–48.1) |
| When not on active duty[f] | 72.2% (69.0–75.4) | 72.0% (67.7–76.3) | 72.7% (66.6–78.8) | 76.0% (67.7–84.3) | 70.6% (64.6–76.5) | 64.4% (60.3–68.5) |
| Both when on and when not on active duty[f] | 10.4% (8.2–12.6) | 10.3% (7.5–13.0) | 11.2% (7.0–15.4) | 8.8% (3.6–14.0) | 10.2% (5.9–14.4) | 8.3% (6.1–10.5) |

NOTE: All data are weighted. 95-percent confidence intervals are presented in parentheses.

[a] Estimate is significantly different from the estimate in column 2 (Air Force).

[b] Estimate is significantly different from the estimate in column 3 (Army).

[c] Estimate is significantly different from the estimate in column 4 (Marine Corps).

[d] Estimate is significantly different from the estimate in column 5 (Navy).

[e] Estimate is significantly different from the estimate in column 6 (Coast Guard).

[f] The omnibus chi-square test was not statistically significant ($p > 0.05$).

**Table 6.14**
**Unwanted Sexual Contact, by Pay Grade**

|  | E1–E4 (1) | E5–E6 (2) | E7–E9 (3) | W1–W5 (4) | O1–O3 (5) | O4–O10 (6) |
|---|---|---|---|---|---|---|
| Lifetime[g] | 17.1% (14.8–19.4) | 18.1% (16.1–20.1) | 14.2% (12.5–16.0) | 15.1% (12.5–17.8) | 17.1% (15.6–18.7) | 15.0% (13.5–16.5) |
| When on active duty | 30.7%[b] (24.0–37.4) | 49.5%[a,e,f] (43.4–55.6) | 41.5% (35.8–47.3) | 35.2% (26.8–43.6) | 34.8%[b] (30.2–39.4) | 35.9%[b] (30.7–41.2) |
| When not on active duty | 79.2%[b] (73.3–85.0) | 63.2%[a] (57.3–69.1) | 68.6% (63.5–73.7) | 70.6% (62.1–79.0) | 72.4% (68.0–76.8) | 72.8% (68.0–77.7) |
| Both when on and when not on active duty[g] | 9.9% (5.5–14.3) | 12.7% (9.5–16.0) | 10.1% (6.6–13.6) | 5.7% (3.1–8.4) | 7.2% (4.9–9.5) | 8.8% (5.9–11.6) |

NOTE: All data are weighted. 95-percent confidence intervals are presented in parentheses.

[a] Estimate is significantly different from the estimate in column 1 (E1–E4).

[b] Estimate is significantly different from the estimate in column 2 (E5–E6).

[c] Estimate is significantly different from the estimate in column 3 (E7–E9).

[d] Estimate is significantly different from the estimate in column 4 (W1–W5).

[e] Estimate is significantly different from the estimate in column 5 (O1–O3).

[f] Estimate is significantly different from the estimate in column 6 (O4–O10).

[g] The omnibus chi-square test was not statistically significant ($p > 0.05$).

**Table 6.15**
**Unwanted Sexual Contact, by Gender**

|  | Men (1) | Women (2) |
|---|---|---|
| Lifetime | 11.7%[a] (10.3–13.0) | 46.1% (44.0–48.1) |
| When on active duty | 32.1%[a] (26.4–37.9) | 46.7% (43.7–49.6) |
| When not on active duty[b] | 74.7% (69.5–79.8) | 68.7% (66.0–71.5) |
| Both when on and when not on active duty | 6.8%[a] (3.3–10.3) | 15.4% (13.3–17.5) |

NOTE: All data are weighted. 95-percent confidence intervals are presented in parentheses.

[a] Estimate is significantly different from the estimate in column 2 (women).

[b] The omnibus chi-square test was not statistically significant ($p > 0.05$).

**Table 6.16**
**Unwanted Sexual Contact, by Age Group**

|  | Ages 17–24 (1) | Ages 25–34 (2) | Ages 35–44 (3) | Ages 45+ (4) |
|---|---|---|---|---|
| Lifetime[a] | 15.8% (13.3–18.4) | 17.4% (15.5–19.3) | 17.9% (15.8–20.0) | 15.5% (12.9–18.0) |
| When on active duty[a] | 31.6% (23.6–39.6) | 42.0% (36.4–47.5) | 40.1% (33.7–46.5) | 32.3% (24.9–39.6) |
| When not on active duty[a] | 77.2% (69.8–84.6) | 68.3% (63.3–73.4) | 72.3% (66.9–77.7) | 78.1% (71.5–84.7) |
| Both when on and when not on active duty[a] | 8.8% (4.8–12.7) | 10.3% (6.8–13.8) | 12.4% (7.6–17.2) | 10.3% (6.4–14.2) |

NOTE: All data are weighted. 95-percent confidence intervals are presented in parentheses.

[a] The omnibus chi-square test was not statistically significant ($p > 0.05$).

**Table 6.17**
**Unwanted Sexual Contact, by Race/Ethnicity**

| | Non-Hispanic White (1) | Non-Hispanic Black (2) | Hispanic (3) | Non-Hispanic Asian (4) | Other (5) |
|---|---|---|---|---|---|
| Lifetime[a] | 16.7% (15.1–18.2) | 17.2% (13.4–21.1) | 16.5% (13.6–19.4) | 13.5% (7.5–19.4) | 21.6% (17.6–25.5) |
| When on active duty[a] | 38.7% (34.0–43.4) | 35.5% (24.5–46.5) | 40.3% (31.3–49.4) | 30.3% (10.7–49.9) | 38.6% (28.9–48.3) |
| When not on active duty[a] | 72.2% (68.1–76.3) | 72.3% (61.7–83.0) | 67.7% (58.7–76.6) | 73.9% (55.0–92.9) | 77.7% (70.6–84.7) |
| Both when on and when not on active duty[a] | 10.9% (7.8–14.0) | 7.8% (4.8–10.9) | 8.0% (4.5–11.5) | 4.2% (0.3–8.1) | 16.3% (7.5–25.0) |

NOTE: All data are weighted. 95-percent confidence intervals are presented in parentheses.

[a] The omnibus chi-square test was not statistically significant ($p > 0.05$)

**Table 6.18**
**Unwanted Sexual Contact, by Education Level**

| | High School or Less (1) | Some College (2) | Bachelor's Degree or More (3) |
|---|---|---|---|
| Lifetime | 13.8%[b] (10.9–16.8) | 19.0%[a] (17.1–20.8) | 15.8% (14.3–17.4) |
| When on active duty[d] | 32.7% (22.8–42.5) | 41.8% (36.5–47.2) | 34.8% (30.1–39.6) |
| When not on active duty[d] | 71.8% (62.3–81.4) | 71.7% (67.0–76.4) | 73.3% (68.7–77.8) |
| Both when on and when not on active duty | 4.5%[b] (1.5–7.5) | 13.5%[a] (9.7–17.3) | 8.1% (6.4–9.8) |

NOTE: All data are weighted. 95-percent confidence intervals are presented in parentheses.

[a] Estimate is significantly different from the estimate in column 1 (high school or less).

[b] Estimate is significantly different from the estimate in column 2 (some college).

[c] Estimate is significantly different from the estimate in column 3 (bachelor's degree or more).

[d] The omnibus chi-square test was not statistically significant ($p > 0.05$).

**Physical Abuse**

History of physical abuse has been assessed in the 2005 (Bray, Hourani, Olmstead, et al., 2006), 2008 (Bray, Pemberton, et al., 2009), and 2011 (Barlas et al., 2013) versions of the HRBS because of the strong relationship between trauma and poor health-related behaviors. The 2008 report found that 26.9 percent (CI: 26.1–27.7) of service members indicated experiencing some form of physical punishment (i.e., ever being physically punished or beaten by a parent, caretaker, or teacher so that you were very frightened; thought you would be injured; or received bruises, cuts, welts, lumps, or other injuries) in their lifetime. A large majority of service members' physical abuse occurred before the age of 18 and thus before they entered the military. In the 2011 HRBS, 17.1 percent (CI: 16.5–17.7) of service members reported any history of physical abuse (this measure is in line with the 2015 HRBS measure).

Slightly lower than levels reported in the 2011 HRBS, the 2015 HRBS found that 13.0 percent of service members reported having experienced any physical abuse in their lifetime (Table 6.19). Although the 2011 HRBS had a slightly different set of questions assessing the timing of physical abuse (it assessed physical abuse since joining the military separately for "contact from anyone in the military" and "contact from any civilian"), the lifetime estimates are comparable.

Of those who reported any lifetime physical abuse, key findings include the following:

- Almost one-quarter (23.2 percent) experienced physical abuse only when on active duty (Table 6.19). The 2015 HRBS does not differentiate between physical abuse experienced before or after joining the military.[2]
- More than three-fourths (79.3 percent) experienced physical abuse only when not on active duty (Table 6.19).
- A small portion (2.4 percent) experienced physical abuse both when on and when not on active duty (Table 6.19).
- More women than men reported lifetime physical abuse (18.9 percent compared with 11.9 percent) (Table 6.21); however, the rate at which physical abuse occurred when on active duty and when not on active duty did not differ substantially by gender.

There were few statistically significant differences in percentages of service members who reported physical abuse across service branch (Table 6.19), pay grade (Table 6.20), age group (Table 6.22), race/ethnicity (Table 6.23), or education level (Table 6.24). Overall, the data indicate that although relatively few military personnel have experienced physical abuse while in the military, a large number of personnel have experienced physical abuse in their lifetime.

---

[2]  The response option "not on active duty" could include time spent in a reserve status prior to becoming active duty.

**Table 6.19**
**Physical Abuse, by Service Branch**

| | Total (1) | Air Force (2) | Army (3) | Marine Corps (4) | Navy (5) | Coast Guard (6) |
|---|---|---|---|---|---|---|
| Lifetime | 13.0% (11.8–14.1) | 9.1%[b,c,d] (7.8–10.4) | 14.6%[a,e] (12.4–16.9) | 13.4%[a,e] (10.5–16.3) | 14.3%[a,e] (11.9–16.7) | 8.3%[b,c,d] (7.4–9.3) |
| When on active duty | 23.2% (19.3–27.0) | 13.9%[c] (9.0–18.8) | 25.7% (18.7–32.7) | 38.2%[a,d,e] (26.4–50.0) | 16.1%[c] (9.7–22.4) | 19.2%[c] (14.4–24.0) |
| When not on active duty | 79.3% (75.5–83.1) | 88.0%[c] (83.5–92.5) | 77.3% (70.5–84.2) | 66.4%[a,d] (54.9–78.0) | 84.6%[c] (78.3–90.9) | 81.9% (77.2–86.7) |
| Both when on and when not on active duty[f] | 2.4% (1.3–3.6) | 1.9% (0.0–4.1) | 3.0% (1.3–4.8) | 4.6% (0.0–9.7) | 0.6% (0.0–1.2) | 1.1% (0.1–2.1) |

NOTE: All data are weighted. 95-percent confidence intervals are presented in parentheses.

[a] Estimate is significantly different from the estimate in column 2 (Air Force).

[b] Estimate is significantly different from the estimate in column 3 (Army).

[c] Estimate is significantly different from the estimate in column 4 (Marine Corps).

[d] Estimate is significantly different from the estimate in column 5 (Navy).

[e] Estimate is significantly different from the estimate in column 6 (Coast Guard).

[f] The omnibus chi-square test was not statistically significant ($p > 0.05$).

**Table 6.20**
**Physical Abuse, by Pay Grade**

| | E1–E4 (1) | E5–E6 (2) | E7–E9 (3) | W1–W5 (4) | O1–O3 (5) | O4–O10 (6) |
|---|---|---|---|---|---|---|
| Lifetime | 11.9%[e] (9.8–14.0) | 16.2%[e,f] (14.0–18.3) | 14.9%[e,f] (12.9–16.9) | 15.3%[e,f] (12.5–18.1) | 8.0%[a,b,c,d] (6.7–9.3) | 10.1%[b,c,d] (8.6–11.6) |
| When on active duty | 22.4%[d] (14.9–30.0) | 27.6%[d] (21.1–34.1) | 19.3% (14.3–24.4) | 9.4%[a,b,e] (5.3–13.4) | 21.5%[d] (14.4–28.6) | 12.5%[b] (7.5–17.4) |
| When not on active duty[g] | 79.2% (71.7–86.7) | 75.8% (69.5–82.1) | 83.2% (78.5–87.9) | 91.8% (87.9–95.8) | 82.1% (75.3–88.9) | 88.3% (83.4–93.3) |
| Both when on and when not on active duty[g] | 1.6% (0.0–3.5) | 3.4% (1.3–5.6) | 2.5% (0.3–4.7) | 1.2% (0.0–2.5) | 3.6% (0.5–6.7) | 0.8% (0.2–1.4) |

NOTE: All data are weighted. 95-percent confidence intervals are presented in parentheses.

[a] Estimate is significantly different from the estimate in column 1 (E1–E4).

[b] Estimate is significantly different from the estimate in column 2 (E5–E6).

[c] Estimate is significantly different from the estimate in column 3 (E7–E9).

[d] Estimate is significantly different from the estimate in column 4 (W1–W5).

[e] Estimate is significantly different from the estimate in column 5 (O1–O3).

[f] Estimate is significantly different from the estimate in column 6 (O4–O10).

[g] The omnibus chi-square test was not statistically significant ($p > 0.05$).

**Table 6.21**
**Physical Abuse, by Gender**

|  | Men (1) | Women (2) |
|---|---|---|
| Lifetime | 11.9%[a] (10.6–13.2) | 18.9% (17.3–20.6) |
| When on active duty | 21.4%[a] (16.5–26.2) | 29.3% (25.2–33.4) |
| When not on active duty[b] | 80.3% (75.5–85.1) | 75.8% (71.8–79.8) |
| Both when on and when not on active duty | 1.7%[a] (0.3–3.1) | 5.1% (3.4–6.8) |

NOTE: All data are weighted. 95-percent confidence intervals are presented in parentheses.

[a] Estimate is significantly different from the estimate in column 2 (women).

[b] The omnibus chi-square test was not statistically significant ($p > 0.05$).

**Table 6.22**
**Physical Abuse, by Age Group**

|  | Ages 17–24 (1) | Ages 25–34 (2) | Ages 35–44 (3) | Ages 45+ (4) |
|---|---|---|---|---|
| Lifetime | 12.4% (9.9–14.9) | 11.0%[c] (9.4–12.7) | 16.5%[b] (14.4–18.6) | 15.4% (11.8–19.0) |
| When on active duty[e] | 22.0% (14.4–29.6) | 24.4% (17.1–31.7) | 21.9% (16.1–27.7) | 26.0% (14.5–37.5) |
| When not on active duty[e] | 80.7% (73.4–88.1) | 76.6% (69.3–83.9) | 81.6% (76.2–87.0) | 77.9% (66.5–89.2) |
| Both when on and when not on active duty[e] | 2.7% (0.0–5.6) | 1.0% (0.4–1.6) | 3.6% (0.9–6.2) | 3.9% (1.0–6.8) |

NOTE: All data are weighted. 95-percent confidence intervals are presented in parentheses.

[a] Estimate is significantly different from the estimate in column 1 (ages 17–24).

[b] Estimate is significantly different from the estimate in column 2 (ages 25–34).

[c] Estimate is significantly different from the estimate in column 3 (ages 35–44).

[d] Estimate is significantly different from the estimate in column 4 (ages 45+).

[e] The omnibus chi-square test was not statistically significant ($p > 0.05$).

**Table 6.23**
**Physical Abuse, by Race/Ethnicity**

| | Non-Hispanic White (1) | Non-Hispanic Black (2) | Hispanic (3) | Non-Hispanic Asian (4) | Other (5) |
|---|---|---|---|---|---|
| Lifetime[f] | 13.1% (11.6–14.5) | 12.9% (9.3–16.4) | 10.4% (8.0–12.7) | 13.7% (7.6–19.8) | 16.9% (13.2–20.7) |
| When on active duty | 26.7%[b] (21.1–32.4) | 12.1%[a] (7.1–17.1) | 23.9% (14.3–33.5) | 13.9% (2.6–25.3) | 19.5% (10.6–28.4) |
| When not on active duty | 75.9%[b] (70.2–81.5) | 90.2%[a] (85.8–94.7) | 80.2% (71.2–89.3) | 86.2% (74.9–97.5) | 81.6% (72.8–90.4) |
| Both when on and when not on active duty[f] | 2.6% (0.9–4.3) | 2.3% (0.6–4.0) | 4.1% (0.3–7.9) | 0.2% (0.0–0.5) | 1.1% (0.0–2.1) |

NOTE: All data are weighted. 95-percent confidence intervals are presented in parentheses.

[a] Estimate is significantly different from the estimate in column 1 (non-Hispanic white).

[b] Estimate is significantly different from the estimate in column 2 (non-Hispanic black).

[c] Estimate is significantly different from the estimate in column 3 (Hispanic),

[d] Estimate is significantly different from the estimate in column 4 (non-Hispanic Asian).

[e] Estimate is significantly different from the estimate in column 5 (other)

[f] The omnibus chi-square test was not statistically significant ($p > 0.05$).

**Table 6.24**
**Physical Abuse, by Education Level**

| | High School or Less (1) | Some College (2) | Bachelor's Degree or More (3) |
|---|---|---|---|
| Lifetime | 14.8%[c] (11.6–17.9) | 14.3%[c] (12.6–15.9) | 9.9%[a,b] (8.4–11.5) |
| When on active duty[e] | 33.4% (22.2–44.5) | 20.2% (15.8–24.7) | 20.1% (13.4–26.8) |
| When not on active duty | 68.1%[b] (57.0–79.2) | 82.6%[a] (78.3–86.8) | 82.5% (75.9–89.2) |
| Both when on and when not on active duty[d] | 1.5% (0.0–4.3) | 2.8% (1.2–4.4) | 2.6% (1.2–4.0) |

NOTE: All data are weighted. 95-percent confidence intervals are presented in parentheses.

[a] Estimate is significantly different from the estimate in column 1 (high school or less).

[b] Estimate is significantly different from the estimate in column 2 (some college).

[c] Estimate is significantly different from the estimate in column 3 (bachelor's degree or more).

[d] The omnibus chi-square test was not statistically significant ($p > 0.05$).

[e] The omnibus chi-square test was statistically significant ($p > 0.05$), but the power was too low to identify group differences.

## Non-Suicidal Self-Injury

Non-suicidal self-injury (NSSI) refers to "behavior that is self-directed and deliberately results in injury or the potential for injury to oneself. There is no evidence, whether implicit or explicit, of suicidal intent" (Crosby, Ortega, and Melanson, 2011, p. 21). Some studies indicate that NSSI predicts subsequent suicide attempts in both military and veteran samples (Kimbrel et al., 2015; Bryan and Bryan, 2014; Bryan, Bryan, et al., 2015; Bryan, Rudd, et al., 2015).

### Lifetime

The 2015 HRBS asked service members if they had *ever* intentionally hurt themselves—"for example, by scratching, cutting, or burning—even though you were not trying to kill yourself." In total, 11.3 percent reported NSSI in their lifetime, a percentage comparable to what was reported in the 2011 HRBS (10.8 percent [CI: 10.2–11.4]; Barlas et al., 2013). In the 2015 HRBS, prevalence of lifetime NSSI was lower in the Air Force and the Coast Guard relative to the Army, Marine Corps, and Navy (Table 6.25).

Lifetime prevalence of NSSI was also statistically significantly different among various subgroups. Key findings include the following:

- Prevalence was lower among mid-grade and senior officers (O4–O10) relative to all lower pay grades; lower among senior NCOs (E7–E9) relative to mid-level enlisted personnel (E5–E6); and higher among junior enlisted personnel (E1–E4) relative to senior enlisted and junior officers (O1–O3) (Table 6.26).
- Prevalence was higher among women than men (Table 6.27).
- Prevalence was higher among those aged 17–24 and those aged 25–34 relative to those aged 35 and older (Table 6.28).
- Prevalence was higher among non-Hispanic whites relative to non-Hispanic blacks, but the difference was not statistically significant (Table 6.29).
- Prevalence was higher among those with a high school degree or less relative to those with more education; it was also higher among those with some college relative to those with a bachelor's degree or more (Table 6.30).

### Since Joining the Military

For those who reported ever having engaged in NSSI, the HRBS also asked how often those service members engaged in NSSI behaviors since joining the military. Overall, 5.1 percent of active-duty service members reported engaging in NSSI behavior since joining the military (Table 6.25). This is again comparable to prevalence of NSSI reported in the 2011 HRBS (5.2 percent [CI: 4.8–5.6]; Barlas et al., 2013). Among active-duty service members, prevalence was statistically significantly lower in the Air Force and Coast Guard relative to the Marine Corps and Navy, and also significantly lower in the Coast Guard relative to the Army.

NSSI since joining the military was also statistically significantly different among various subgroups. Key findings include the following:

- Prevalence since joining the military was lower among mid-grade and senior officers relative to all lower pay grades and was lower among junior officers relative to junior enlisted and mid-level enlisted personnel (Table 6.26).
- Prevalence was higher among women than men (Table 6.27).
- Prevalence was higher among those with a high school degree or less relative to those with more education; it was also higher among those with some college relative to those with a bachelor's degree or more (Table 6.30).

**Table 6.25**
**Non-Suicidal Self-Injury, by Service Branch**

|  | Total (1) | Air Force (2) | Army (3) | Marine Corps (4) | Navy (5) | Coast Guard (6) |
|---|---|---|---|---|---|---|
| Lifetime | 11.3% | 7.8%[b,c,d] | 11.2%[a,e] | 13.4%[a,e] | 14.1%[a,e] | 7.1%[b,c,d] |
|  | (10.2–12.4) | (6.5–9.1) | (9.1–13.4) | (10.4–16.5) | (11.6–16.5) | (6.2–8.0) |
| Since joining the military | 5.1% | 3.1%[c,d] | 4.8%[e] | 6.9%[a,e] | 6.7%[a,e] | 2.9%[b,c,d] |
|  | (4.3–5.9) | (2.3–4.0) | (3.5–6.2) | (4.6–9.1) | (4.8–8.6) | (2.3–3.4) |

NOTE: All data are weighted. 95-percent confidence intervals are presented in parentheses.

[a] Estimate is significantly different from the estimate in column 2 (Air Force).

[b] Estimate is significantly different from the estimate in column 3 (Army).

[c] Estimate is significantly different from the estimate in column 4 (Marine Corps).

[d] Estimate is significantly different from the estimate in column 5 (Navy).

[e] Estimate is significantly different from the estimate in column 6 (Coast Guard).

**Table 6.26**
**Non-Suicidal Self-Injury, by Pay Grade**

|  | E1–E4 (1) | E5–E6 (2) | E7–E9 (3) | W1–W5 (4) | O1–O3 (5) | O4–O10 (6) |
|---|---|---|---|---|---|---|
| Lifetime | 13.8%[c,e,f] | 12.0%[c,f] | 6.6%[a,b,f] | 9.3%[f] | 8.9%[a,f] | 3.3%[a,b,c,d,e] |
|  | (11.6–16.0) | (10.1–13.8) | (5.1–8.1) | (6.9–11.7) | (7.6–10.2) | (2.5–4.2) |
| Since joining the military | 6.0%[e,f] | 5.9%[e,f] | 3.6%[f] | 4.9%[f] | 3.1%[a,b,f] | 1.5%[a,b,c,d,e] |
|  | (4.5–7.5) | (4.5–7.3) | (2.4–4.7) | (3.1–6.7) | (2.3–3.9) | (1.0–2.1) |

NOTE: All data are weighted. 95-percent confidence intervals are presented in parentheses.

[a] Estimate is significantly different from the estimate in column 1 (E1–E4).

[b] Estimate is significantly different from the estimate in column 2 (E5–E6).

[c] Estimate is significantly different from the estimate in column 3 (E7–E9).

[d] Estimate is significantly different from the estimate in column 4 (W1–W5).

[e] Estimate is significantly different from the estimate in column 5 (O1–O3).

[f] Estimate is significantly different from the estimate in column 6 (O4–O10).

Table 6.27
**Non-Suicidal Self-Injury, by Gender**

|  | Men (1) | Women (2) |
|---|---|---|
| Lifetime | 10.0%[a] (8.7–11.3) | 18.5% (16.8–20.3) |
| Since joining the military | 4.6%[a] (3.7–5.5) | 7.8% (6.6–9.0) |

NOTE: All data are weighted. 95-percent confidence intervals are presented in parentheses.

[a] Estimate is significantly different from the estimate in column 2 (women).

Table 6.28
**Non-Suicidal Self-Injury, by Age Group**

|  | Ages 17–24 (1) | Ages 25–34 (2) | Ages 35–44 (3) | Ages 45+ (4) |
|---|---|---|---|---|
| Lifetime | 15.0%[c,d] (12.3–17.7) | 11.6%[c,d] (9.9–13.3) | 8.1%[a,b] (6.5–9.8) | 5.5%[a,b] (3.2–7.8) |
| Since joining the military[e] | 6.6% (4.8–8.4) | 4.9% (3.7–6.1) | 4.2% (3.1–5.4) | 3.2% (1.1–5.3) |

NOTE: All data are weighted. 95-percent confidence intervals are presented in parentheses.

[a] Estimate is significantly different from the estimate in column 1 (ages 17–24).

[b] Estimate is significantly different from the estimate in column 2 (ages 25–34).

[c] Estimate is significantly different from the estimate in column 3 (ages 35–44).

[d] Estimate is significantly different from the estimate in column 4 (ages 45+).

[e] At the aggregate, the chi-square test was statistically significant; however, none of the individual pairwise comparisons was.

Table 6.29
**Non-Suicidal Self-Injury, by Race/Ethnicity**

|  | Non-Hispanic White (1) | Non-Hispanic Black (2) | Hispanic (3) | Non-Hispanic Asian (4) | Other (5) |
|---|---|---|---|---|---|
| Lifetime[a] | 12.1% (10.6–13.7) | 7.3% (4.8–9.8) | 10.2% (7.4–12.9) | 13.6% (7.7–19.5) | 11.6% (8.2–15.0) |
| Since joining the military[a] | 4.8% (3.8–5.7) | 3.9% (1.8–6.1) | 5.2% (3.2–7.3) | 6.7% (2.6–10.8) | 8.0% (5.0–11.1) |

NOTE: All data are weighted. 95-percent confidence intervals are presented in parentheses.

[a] The omnibus chi-square test was not statistically significant ($p > 0.05$).

Table 6.30
**Non-Suicidal Self-Injury, by Education Level**

|  | High School or Less (1) | Some College (2) | Bachelor's Degree or More (3) |
|---|---|---|---|
| Lifetime | 16.9%[b,c] (13.5–20.3) | 11.6%[a,c] (10.0–13.3) | 7.3%[a,b] (6.0–8.7) |
| Since joining the military | 8.6%[c] (6.1–11.1) | 5.1%[c] (4.0–6.2) | 3.0%[a,b] (2.2–3.7) |

NOTE: All data are weighted. 95-percent confidence intervals are presented in parentheses.

[a] Estimate is significantly different from the estimate in column 1 (high school or less).

[b] Estimate is significantly different from the estimate in column 2 (some college).

[c] Estimate is significantly different from the estimate in column 3 (bachelor's degree or more).

## Suicidality

There has been significant attention devoted to the increased rates of suicide among active-duty personnel (e.g., Ramchand, Acosta, et al., 2011), as well as investments by DoD, the VA, and external organizations into research and strategies for prevention (Ramchand, Eberhart, et al., 2014). Surveillance into suicides and suicidal thoughts and behaviors can inform such investments and direct resources to where attention is most needed. Consistent with past HRBS surveys and with the NSDUH,[3] the 2015 HRBS asked all respondents about two aspects of suicide: a history of thoughts of taking one's own life (suicide ideation) and past suicide attempts.

### Suicide Ideation

There is some evidence to suggest that thoughts of suicide may be a precursor to dying by suicide (Bryan, Bryan, et al., 2015), although empirically derived correlations between ideation and eventual death by suicide are not strong (e.g., Nock, Borges, et al., 2008). However, given the ubiquitous nature of this construct in suicide research and the availability of national comparisons from the NSDUH, it provides an important construct to measure distress or anguish among active-duty personnel compared with civilians.

The 2015 HRBS asked service members if they had ever had such thoughts and, if so, whether they had those thoughts in the past year, since joining the military, before joining the military (which is important to identify those at risk for future suicidality before even joining the military) (see Nock, Ursano, et al., 2015), and during a deployment.

### *Lifetime*

Overall, 18.1 percent of service members reported thinking about trying to kill themselves at some point in their lifetime (Table 6.31).[4] Among the service branches, there was no evidence of a difference in the prevalence of lifetime suicide ideation between the Air Force and the Coast Guard, but the prevalence was significantly lower in these service branches than it was in the Army, Marine Corps, and Navy (Table 6.31).

Lifetime ideation was also statistically significantly different across subgroups. Key findings include the following:

- Prevalence was lower among mid-grade and senior officers relative to all other pay grades (Table 6.32).
- Prevalence was higher among women than men (Table 6.33).
- Prevalence was lower among those aged 45 or older compared with those aged 17–24 and aged 35–44 (Table 6.34).
- Prevalence was higher among non-Hispanic whites and those of other races or ethnicities relative to non-Hispanic blacks and Hispanics (Table 6.35).
- Prevalence was lower among those with a bachelor's degree or more relative to those with some college, but the difference was not statistically significant (Table 6.36).

---

[3]  See Substance Abuse and Mental Health Services Administration, 2016.

[4]  Lifetime prevalence of suicide ideation and attempts was not presented in the 2011 HRBS report.

## By Time of Occurrence

Overall, 6.3 percent of active-duty service members reported some suicide ideation in the past year (Table 6.31). This is higher than in the 2011 HRBS, in which 3.9 percent (CI: 3.5–4.3) of all service members reported having had such thoughts in the past year (Barlas et al., 2013). It is also higher than what is observed in the general population, where the prevalence has been roughly 4 percent from 2008 to 2014 (Lipari et al., 2015). The prevalence of past-year suicide ideation was lower among those in the Air Force and Coast Guard relative to those in the Army, Marine Corps, and Navy (Table 6.31).

Past-year suicide ideation was also statistically significantly different among certain subgroups. Key findings include the following:

- Prevalence was higher among junior enlisted personnel relative to senior enlisted personnel, warrant officers, junior officers, and mid-grade and senior officers. It was also higher among mid-level enlisted personnel relative to mid-grade and senior officers (Table 6.32).
- Prevalence was higher among those aged 17–24 relative to those aged 35–44 and those 45 or older; it was also higher among those aged 25–34 relative to those 45 or older (Table 6.34).

In addition, among active-duty service members, 12.3 percent had these thoughts since joining the military, 10.4 percent had them before joining the military, and 3.2 percent had them during a deployment (Table 6.31).[5]

**Table 6.31**
**Suicide Ideation, by Service Branch**

| | Total (1) | Air Force (2) | Army (3) | Marine Corps (4) | Navy (5) | Coast Guard (6) |
|---|---|---|---|---|---|---|
| Lifetime | 18.1% (16.7–19.4) | 12.1%[b,c,d] (10.5–13.6) | 20.2%[a,e] (17.5–22.8) | 19.8%[a,e] (16.2–23.4) | 20.3%[a,e] (17.5–23.1) | 11.7%[b,c,d] (10.6–12.8) |
| Past 12 months | 6.3% (5.3–7.2) | 3.2%[b,c,d] (2.3–4.1) | 7.0%[a,e] (5.1–8.9) | 7.7%[a,e] (5.2–10.2) | 7.6%[a,e] (5.6–9.7) | 3.0%[b,c,d] (2.4–3.6) |
| Since joining the military | 12.3% (11.2–13.5) | 7.3%[b,c,d] (6.2–8.5) | 15.0%[a,e] (12.6–17.4) | 13.1%[a,e] (10.1–16.1) | 13.0%[a,e] (10.6–15.4) | 7.5%[b,c,d] (6.6–8.4) |
| Before joining the military | 10.4% (9.3–11.5) | 7.3%[b,c,d] (6.1–8.6) | 11.0%[a,e] (8.9–13.0) | 12.0%[a,e] (9.0–15.1) | 12.0%[a,e] (9.7–14.3) | 6.4%[b,c,d] (5.5–7.2) |
| During deployment | 3.2% (2.6–3.8) | 1.2%[b,c,d] (0.6–1.7) | 4.2%[a,e] (3.0–5.3) | 3.6%[a,e] (1.9–5.3) | 3.4%[a,e] (2.1–4.8) | 1.6%[b,c,d] (1.2–2.1) |

NOTE: All data are weighted. 95-percent confidence intervals are presented in parentheses.

[a] Estimate is significantly different from the estimate in column 2 (Air Force).

[b] Estimate is significantly different from the estimate in column 3 (Army).

[c] Estimate is significantly different from the estimate in column 4 (Marine Corps).

[d] Estimate is significantly different from the estimate in column 5 (Navy).

[e] Estimate is significantly different from the estimate in column 6 (Coast Guard).

---

[5] We cannot compare these estimates to the 2011 HRBS; in that survey, estimates were presented for suicide ideation since joining the military or before joining the military but exclude those who had such thoughts in the past year.

**Table 6.32**
**Suicide Ideation, by Pay Grade**

| | E1–E4 (1) | E5–E6 (2) | E7–E9 (3) | W1–W5 (4) | O1–O3 (5) | O4–O10 (6) |
|---|---|---|---|---|---|---|
| Lifetime | 18.1%[f] (15.6–20.7) | 19.9%[f] (17.5–22.3) | 17.1%[f] (14.9–19.4) | 19.5%[f] (16.3–22.8) | 17.4%[f] (15.5–19.2) | 12.0%[a,b,c,d,e] (10.4–13.6) |
| Past 12 months | 8.5%[c,d,e,f] (6.6–10.5) | 5.6%[f] (4.2–7.0) | 3.7%[a] (2.5–4.9) | 3.8%[a] (2.2–5.5) | 4.1%[a] (3.1–5.1) | 2.3%[a,b] (1.6–3.1) |
| Since joining the military | 11.5% (9.3–13.7) | 14.8%[f] (12.6–16.9) | 13.1%[f] (11.1–15.2) | 12.9%[f] (10.2–15.7) | 11.0% (9.4–12.6) | 8.1%[b,c,d] (6.7–9.4) |
| Before joining the military | 11.6%[c,f] (9.5–13.7) | 10.7%[f] (8.9–12.5) | 7.3%[a] (5.7–8.9) | 10.0%[f] (7.6–12.4) | 10.4%[f] (8.8–11.9) | 6.1%[a,b,d,e] (4.9–7.3) |
| During deployment | 1.7%[b,d] (0.9–2.6) | 5.6%[a,e,f] (4.1–7.0) | 3.9%[f] (2.6–5.3) | 5.8%[a,e,f] (3.8–7.7) | 2.3%[b,c,d] (1.5–3.2) | 1.6%[b,c,d] (1.0–2.3) |

NOTE: All data are weighted. 95-percent confidence intervals are presented in parentheses.

[a] Estimate is significantly different from the estimate in column 1 (E1–E4).

[b] Estimate is significantly different from the estimate in column 2 (E5–E6).

[c] Estimate is significantly different from the estimate in column 3 (E7–E9).

[d] Estimate is significantly different from the estimate in column 4 (W1–W5).

[e] Estimate is significantly different from the estimate in column 5 (O1–O3).

[f] Estimate is significantly different from the estimate in column 6 (O4–O10).

**Table 6.33**
**Suicide Ideation, by Gender**

| | Men (1) | Women (2) |
|---|---|---|
| Lifetime | 17.2%[a] (15.6–18.7) | 23.1% (21.3–24.9) |
| Past 12 months[b] | 6.2% (5.1–7.3) | 6.9% (5.7–8.0) |
| Since joining the military | 11.9%[a] (10.6–13.3) | 14.5% (13.0–16.0) |
| Before joining the military | 9.6%[a] (8.4–10.8) | 14.9% (13.3–16.5) |
| During deployment | 3.4%[a] (2.7–4.1) | 2.1% (1.6–2.6) |

NOTE: All data are weighted. 95-percent confidence intervals are presented in parentheses.

[a] Estimate is significantly different from the estimate in column 2 (women).

[b] The omnibus chi-square test was not statistically significant ($p > 0.05$).

Table 6.34
Suicide Ideation, by Age Group

| | Ages 17–24 (1) | Ages 25–34 (2) | Ages 35–44 (3) | Ages 45+ (4) |
|---|---|---|---|---|
| Lifetime | 20.3%[d] (17.1–23.4) | 16.8% (14.8–18.8) | 19.0%[d] (16.8–21.3) | 13.9%[a,c] (11.1–16.8) |
| Past 12 months | 9.1%[c,d] (6.8–11.4) | 6.0%[d] (4.6–7.5) | 4.5%[a] (3.1–5.8) | 2.9%[a,b] (1.4–4.3) |
| Since joining the military[e] | 12.6% (9.9–15.2) | 11.5% (9.7–13.2) | 14.4% (12.3–16.6) | 9.6% (7.2–11.9) |
| Before joining the military | 12.6%[d] (10.1–15.1) | 10.2%[d] (8.5–11.9) | 9.6%[d] (7.9–11.3) | 5.7%[a,b,c] (4.1–7.4) |
| During deployment | 2.8% (1.4–4.1) | 2.5%[c] (1.7–3.2) | 4.9%[b] (3.5–6.2) | 3.1% (1.2–5.0) |

NOTE: All data are weighted. 95-percent confidence intervals are presented in parentheses.

[a] Estimate is significantly different from the estimate in column 1 (ages 17–24).

[b] Estimate is significantly different from the estimate in column 2 (ages 25–34).

[c] Estimate is significantly different from the estimate in column 3 (ages 35–44).

[d] Estimate is significantly different from the estimate in column 4 (ages 45+).

[e] The omnibus chi-square test was not statistically significant ($p > 0.05$).

Table 6.35
Suicide Ideation, by Race/Ethnicity

| | Non-Hispanic White (1) | Non-Hispanic Black (2) | Hispanic (3) | Non-Hispanic Asian (4) | Other (5) |
|---|---|---|---|---|---|
| Lifetime | 19.9%[b,c] (18.1–21.7) | 13.2%[a,e] (10.0–16.4) | 13.1%[a,e] (10.2–16.1) | 18.1% (11.2–25.0) | 21.2%[b,c] (16.7–25.7) |
| Past 12 months[f] | 6.9% (5.7–8.2) | 4.0% (1.9–6.1) | 3.9% (2.1–5.6) | 7.3% (1.7–13.0) | 8.7% (5.2–12.3) |
| Since joining the military | 13.8%[c] (12.2–15.4) | 8.9% (6.1–11.7) | 8.2%[a,e] (5.9–10.6) | 12.0% (5.7–18.3) | 14.7%[c] (10.9–18.6) |
| Before joining the military | 12.1%[b,c] (10.6–13.7) | 5.9%[a] (4.1–7.6) | 7.3%[a] (5.0–9.6) | 10.3% (5.4–15.2) | 10.6% (7.4–13.8) |
| During deployment[f] | 3.6% (2.7–4.4) | 2.9% (1.2–4.7) | 2.5% (1.2–3.7) | 2.3% (0.1–4.6) | 2.6% (0.9–4.3) |

NOTE: All data are weighted. 95-percent confidence intervals are presented in parentheses.

[a] Estimate is significantly different from the estimate in column 1 (non-Hispanic white).

[b] Estimate is significantly different from the estimate in column 2 (non-Hispanic black).

[c] Estimate is significantly different from the estimate in column 3 (Hispanic).

[d] Estimate is significantly different from the estimate in column 4 (non-Hispanic Asian).

[e] Estimate is significantly different from the estimate in column 5 (other).

[f] The omnibus chi-square test was not statistically significant ($p > 0.05$).

**Table 6.36**
**Suicide Ideation, by Education Level**

|  | High School or Less (1) | Some College (2) | Bachelor's Degree or More (3) |
|---|---|---|---|
| Lifetime[a] | 19.5% (15.8–23.1) | 19.0% (17.0–21.0) | 15.8% (13.9–17.7) |
| Past 12 months[a] | 8.2% (5.6–10.9) | 6.3% (5.0–7.7) | 5.0% (3.6–6.5) |
| Since joining the military[a] | 12.9% (9.8–16.0) | 12.9% (11.2–14.6) | 11.2% (9.4–12.9) |
| Before joining the military[a] | 11.6% (8.8–14.5) | 11.0% (9.4–12.6) | 8.9% (7.3–10.4) |
| During deployment[a] | 3.9% (2.2–5.7) | 3.3% (2.5–4.2) | 2.5% (1.8–3.1) |

NOTE: All data are weighted. 95-percent confidence intervals are presented in parentheses.
[a] The omnibus chi-square test was not statistically significant ($p > 0.05$).

## Suicide Attempts

Regardless of whether respondents reported having thought about killing themselves, the 2015 HRBS asked if service members had ever attempted to kill themselves. Self-reports of past suicide attempts may capture more attempts than brought to the attention of medical personnel, and attempts are important to measure because they are the strongest predictor of suicide death (Harris and Barraclough, 1997). Moreover, existing treatments for attempters of suicide have reduced rates of subsequent attempts (Brown et al., 2005).

For those who endorsed a past suicide attempt, we asked the same questions as we did about ideation—that is, whether the attempt(s) happened in the past year, since joining the military, before joining the military, and during a deployment.

### Lifetime

Overall, 5.1 percent of service members reported attempting to kill themselves at some point in their lifetime (Table 6.37).[6] Among the service branches, there was no evidence of a difference in the prevalence of lifetime suicide attempts between the Air Force and the Coast Guard, but the prevalence was statistically significantly lower in both of these service branches than it was in the Army, Navy, and Marine Corps (Table 6.37).

Lifetime attempts were also statistically significantly different among certain subgroups. Key findings include the following:

- Prevalence was lower among mid-grade and senior officers relative to all other pay grades and was lower among junior officers relative to mid-level enlisted (E5–E6) and junior enlisted personnel (E1–E4) (Table 6.38).
- Prevalence was higher among women than men (Table 6.39).
- Prevalence was higher among those aged 17–24 relative to those 45 or older (Table 6.40).
- Prevalence was lower among Hispanics relative to non-Hispanic Asians, the race group with the highest prevalence of lifetime attempts (Table 6.41).

---

[6]   Lifetime prevalence of suicide ideation and attempts was not presented in the 2011 HRBS report.

### By Time of Occurrence

Overall, 1.4 percent of active-duty service members had attempted suicide in the past year (Table 6.37). This was three times higher than reported in the 2011 HRBS (0.5 percent; CI: 0.3–0.7) (Barlas et al., 2013) and higher than observed in the general population, where it has been roughly 0.5 percent of adults aged 18 or older from 2008 to 2014 (Lipari et al., 2015). There were no statistically significant differences between service branches.

Past-year attempts were statistically significantly different among some subgroups. Key findings include the following:

- There were no past-year suicide attempts among senior officers, making it lower in that pay grade relative to all other pay grades. Mid-grade officers also had lower rates relative to junior enlisted personnel (Table 6.38).
- Prevalence was higher among those aged 17–24 relative to those aged 25–34 and those 45 or older (Table 6.40).

In addition, among those who had attempted suicide, 2.6 percent had done so since joining the military, 3.1 percent had done so before joining the military, and 0.5 percent had done so during a deployment (Table 6.37).

**Table 6.37**
**Suicide Attempts, by Service Branch**

| | Total (1) | Air Force (2) | Army (3) | Marine Corps (4) | Navy (5) | Coast Guard (6) |
|---|---|---|---|---|---|---|
| Lifetime suicide attempt | 5.1% (4.3–5.9) | 2.8%[b,c,d] (2.0–3.7) | 5.8%[a,e] (4.2–7.4) | 6.3%[a,e] (4.0–8.5) | 5.8%[a,e] (4.1–7.5) | 2.0%[b,c,d] (1.5–2.4) |
| **Past 12 months** | | | | | | |
| Suicide attempt[f] | 1.4% (0.9–1.9) | 0.6% (0.2–1.1) | 1.5% (0.6–2.5) | 2.2% (0.7–3.6) | 1.6% (0.5–2.6) | 0.2% (0.1–0.3) |
| Medical attention for attempt[g] | 55.0% (40.5–69.5) | † | 69.8% (52.2–87.3) | † | † | † |
| **Since joining the military** | | | | | | |
| Suicide attempt | 2.6% (2.0–3.2) | 1.2%[b,c] (0.6–1.7) | 2.9%[a,e] (1.8–4.0) | 4.1%[a,e] (2.2–5.9) | 2.8%[e] (1.5–4.0) | 0.8%[b,c,d] (0.5–1.1) |
| Medical attention for attempt[f] | 52.0% (42.6–61.5) | 53.0% (27.0–79.1) | 65.8% (52.9–78.8) | 39.3% (17.3–61.4) | 38.4% (16.5–60.2) | 68.1% (53.3–82.8) |
| **Before joining the military** | | | | | | |
| Suicide attempt[f] | 3.1% (2.5–3.8) | 2.0% (1.2–2.7) | 3.5% (2.2–4.8) | 3.9% (2.1–5.7) | 3.4% (2.1–4.6) | 1.4% (1.0–1.8) |
| Medical attention for attempt | 30.8% (20.7–40.9) | 19.3% (5.9–32.7) | 40.8%[c] (20.9–60.7) | 5.7%[b,d,e] (1.8–9.6) | 37.5%[c] (17.1–57.9) | 35.1%[c] (20.4–49.8) |
| **During deployment** | | | | | | |
| Suicide attempt | 0.5% (0.2–0.7) | 0.0%[b,d] (0.0–0.1) | 0.5%[a] (0.2–0.9) | 0.2% (0.0–0.4) | 1.0%[a] (0.1–1.9) | 0.2% (0.0–0.4) |
| Medical attention for attempt[g] | 27.7% (2.4–53.1) | † | † | † | † | † |

NOTE: All data are weighted. 95-percent confidence intervals are presented in parentheses.

[a] Estimate is significantly different from the estimate in column 2 (Air Force).

[b] Estimate is significantly different from the estimate in column 3 (Army).

[c] Estimate is significantly different from the estimate in column 4 (Marine Corps).

[d] Estimate is significantly different from the estimate in column 5 (Navy).

[e] Estimate is significantly different from the estimate in column 6 (Coast Guard).

[f] The omnibus chi-square test was not statistically significant ($p > 0.05$).

[g] Because there were too few respondents for at least one category, we do not report an omnibus chi-square test.

† = Too few respondents to report (denominator < 20).

**Table 6.38**
**Suicide Attempts, by Pay Grade**

| | E1–E4 (1) | E5–E6 (2) | E7–E9 (3) | W1–W5 (4) | O1–O3 (5) | O4–O10 (6) |
|---|---|---|---|---|---|---|
| Lifetime suicide attempt | 6.3%[e,f] (4.7–7.9) | 5.7%[e,f] (4.4–7.1) | 3.7%[f] (2.5–4.9) | 3.5%[f] (2.0–4.9) | 2.5%[a,b,f] (1.7–3.3) | 1.1%[a,b,c,d,e] (0.7–1.6) |
| **Past 12 months** | | | | | | |
|     Suicide attempt | 2.2%[e,f] (1.2–3.2) | 1.0%[f] (0.4–1.6) | 0.9%[f] (0.1–1.6) | 0.4%[f] (0.0–0.8) | 0.4%[a,f] (0.1–0.8) | 0.0%[a,b,c,d,e] (0.0–0.0) |
|     Medical attention for attempt[h] | 57.8% (39.9–75.6) | 55.5% (22.5–88.5) | † | † | † | † |
| **Since joining the military** | | | | | | |
|     Suicide attempt | 3.0%[e,f] (1.9–4.1) | 3.2%[e,f] (2.1–4.2) | 2.2%[f] (1.2–3.1) | 1.9%[f] (0.8–3.0) | 1.1%[a,b] (0.6–1.7) | 0.4%[a,b,c,d] (0.1–0.7) |
|     Medical attention for attempt[h] | 60.0% (45.3–74.8) | 46.1% (30.3–61.9) | 41.5% (18.8–64.2) | † | 35.2% (15.7–54.8) | † |
| **Before joining the military** | | | | | | |
|     Suicide attempt | 4.0%[c,e,f] (2.8–5.3) | 3.6%[e,f] (2.5–4.6) | 1.7%[a] (0.9–2.5) | 1.9%[f] (0.8–3.0) | 1.3%[a,b] (0.7–1.8) | 0.6%[a,b,d] (0.3–0.9) |
|     Medical attention for attempt[h] | 30.8% (15.4–46.2) | 30.3% (14.9–45.8) | 26.7% (4.8–48.6) | † | 34.7% (12.6–56.8) | 47.0% (36.3–57.8) |
| **During deployment** | | | | | | |
|     Suicide attempt[g] | 0.4% (0.0–0.9) | 0.7% (0.2–1.2) | 0.4% (0.0–0.8) | 0.6% (0.0–1.2) | 0.3% (0.0–0.6) | 0.1% (0.0–0.2) |
|     Medical attention for attempt[h] | † | † | † | † | † | † |

NOTE: All data are weighted. 95-percent confidence intervals are presented in parentheses.

[a] Estimate is significantly different from the estimate in column 1 (E1–E4).

[b] Estimate is significantly different from the estimate in column 2 (E5–E6).

[c] Estimate is significantly different from the estimate in column 3 (E7–E9).

[d] Estimate is significantly different from the estimate in column 4 (W1–W5).

[e] Estimate is significantly different from the estimate in column 5 (O1–O3).

[f] Estimate is significantly different from the estimate in column 6 (O4–O10).

[g] The omnibus chi-square test was not statistically significant ($p > 0.05$).

[h] Because there were too few respondents for at least one category, we do not report an omnibus chi-square test.

† = Too few respondents to report (denominator < 20).

**Table 6.39**
**Suicide Attempts, by Gender**

| | Men (1) | Women (2) |
|---|---|---|
| Lifetime suicide attempt | 4.6%[a] (3.6–5.5) | 8.1% (6.9–9.4) |
| Past 12 months | | |
| Suicide attempt[b] | 1.4% (0.8–1.9) | 1.5% (0.9–2.1) |
| Medical attention for attempt[b] | 54.0% (37.3–70.7) | 60.0% (37.3–82.8) |
| Since joining military | | |
| Suicide attempt | 2.4%[a] (1.8–3.1) | 3.5% (2.7–4.3) |
| Medical attention for attempt[b] | 49.9% (38.4–61.5) | 60.0% (48.9–71.1) |
| Before joining military | | |
| Suicide attempt | 2.7%[a] (1.9–3.4) | 5.7% (4.6–6.8) |
| Medical attention for attempt[b] | 26.9% (13.5–40.3) | 40.9% (30.7–51.0) |
| During deployment | | |
| Suicide attempt[b] | 0.5% (0.2–0.8) | 0.4% (0.2–0.7) |
| Medical attention for attempt[c] | 23.6% (0.0–52.9) | † |

NOTE: All data are weighted. 95-percent confidence intervals are presented in parentheses.

[a] Estimate is significantly different from the estimate in column 2 (women).

[b] The omnibus chi-square test was not statistically significant ($p > 0.05$).

[c] Because there were too few respondents for at least one category, we do not report an omnibus chi-square test.

† = Too few respondents to report (denominator < 20).

**Table 6.40**
**Suicide Attempts, by Age Group**

| | Ages 17–24 (1) | Ages 25–34 (2) | Ages 35–44 (3) | Ages 45+ (4) |
|---|---|---|---|---|
| Lifetime suicide attempt | 6.7%[d] (4.8–8.6) | 4.7% (3.4–5.9) | 4.6% (3.3–5.9) | 3.0%[a] (1.5–4.6) |
| Past 12 months | | | | |
|   Suicide attempt | 2.6%[b,d] (1.3–3.9) | 0.8%[a] (0.3–1.3) | 1.4% (0.4–2.3) | 0.3%[a] (0.0–0.6) |
|   Medical attention for attempt[f] | 47.0% (20.0–74.0) | 59.5% (27.2–91.8) | 66.7% (38.4–95.0) | † |
| Since joining military | | | | |
|   Suicide attempt | 4.0%[b] (2.5–5.5) | 1.7%[a] (1.0–2.3) | 2.7% (1.6–3.8) | 2.1% (0.7–3.5) |
|   Medical attention for attempt[e] | 43.4% (23.8–63.0) | 63.6% (44.8–82.5) | 55.2% (35.1–75.4) | 49.7% (16.2–83.2) |
| Before joining military | | | | |
|   Suicide attempt | 4.1%[d] (2.6–5.5) | 3.3%[d] (2.2–4.4) | 2.4% (1.5–3.2) | 1.0%[a,b] (0.4–1.6) |
|   Medical attention for attempt[e] | 33.9% (18.1–49.8) | 25.7% (13.1–38.3) | 35.3% (16.1–54.4) | 45.1% (16.6–73.5) |
| During deployment | | | | |
|   Suicide attempt | 0.8%[b] (0.1–1.5) | 0.1%[a,c] (0.0–0.2) | 0.7%[b] (0.2–1.2) | 0.8% (0.0–2.0) |
|   Medical attention for attempt[f] | † | † | † | † |

NOTE: All data are weighted. 95-percent confidence intervals are presented in parentheses.

[a] Estimate is significantly different from the estimate in column 1 (ages 17–24).

[b] Estimate is significantly different from the estimate in column 2 (ages 25–34).

[c] Estimate is significantly different from the estimate in column 3 (ages 35–44).

[d] Estimate is significantly different from the estimate in column 4 (ages 45+).

[e] The omnibus chi-square test was not statistically significant ($p > 0.05$).

[f] Because there were too few respondents for at least one category, we do not report an omnibus chi-square test.

† = Too few respondents to report (denominator < 20).

**Table 6.41**
**Suicide Attempts, by Race/Ethnicity**

| | Non-Hispanic White (1) | Non-Hispanic Black (2) | Hispanic (3) | Non-Hispanic Asian (4) | Other (5) |
|---|---|---|---|---|---|
| Lifetime suicide attempt | 4.8% (3.8–5.9) | 6.4% (3.9–8.9) | 4.0%[d] (2.4–5.5) | 10.6%[c] (4.6–16.6) | 4.3% (2.1–6.5) |
| **Past 12 months** | | | | | |
| Suicide attempt[f] | 1.1% (0.6–1.6) | 1.9% (0.1–3.7) | 1.4% (0.3–2.4) | 3.9% (0.0–8.8) | 1.1% (0.0–2.3) |
| Medical attention for attempt[g] | 34.5% (13.7–55.2) | † | † | † | † |
| **Since joining military** | | | | | |
| Suicide attempt | 2.0%[d] (1.4–2.5) | 4.3% (2.0–6.7) | 2.4% (1.0–3.7) | 7.0%[a] (1.6–12.3) | 2.4% (0.6–4.2) |
| Medical attention for attempt[g] | 46.4% (31.6–61.2) | 59.1% (32.7–85.5) | 43.9% (13.6–74.3) | † | 79.8% (58.7–100.0) |
| **Before joining military** | | | | | |
| Suicide attempt[f] | 3.5% (2.6–4.5) | 3.1% (1.6–4.6) | 2.2% (1.2–3.3) | 2.7% (0.1–5.3) | 2.3% (1.0–3.6) |
| Medical attention for attempt[g] | 34.6% (20.8–48.4) | 25.0% (7.4–42.6) | 28.9% (4.5–53.2) | † | 23.9% (5.9–41.8) |
| **During deployment** | | | | | |
| Suicide attempt[f] | 0.3% (0.1–0.6) | 1.0% (0.0–2.1) | 0.7% (0.0–1.4) | 0.5% (0.0–1.6) | 0.2% (0.0–0.4) |
| Medical attention for attempt[g] | † | † | † | † | † |

NOTE: All data are weighted. 95-percent confidence intervals are presented in parentheses.

[a] Estimate is significantly different from the estimate in column 1 (non-Hispanic white).

[b] Estimate is significantly different from the estimate in column 2 (non-Hispanic black).

[c] Estimate is significantly different from the estimate in column 3 (Hispanic).

[d] Estimate is significantly different from the estimate in column 4 (non-Hispanic Asian).

[e] Estimate is significantly different from the estimate in column 5 (other).

[f] The omnibus chi-square test was not statistically significant ($p > 0.05$).

[g] Because there were too few respondents for at least one category, we do not report an omnibus chi-square test.

† = Too few respondents to report (denominator < 20).

Table 6.42
Suicide Attempts, by Education Level

| | High School or Less (1) | Some College (2) | Bachelor's Degree or More (3) |
|---|---|---|---|
| Lifetime suicide attempt[a] | 6.0% (3.8–8.2) | 5.7% (4.5–6.8) | 3.7% (2.5–5.0) |
| Past 12 months | | | |
|    Suicide attempt[a] | 2.3% (1.0–3.7) | 1.3% (0.7–1.9) | 1.0% (0.2–1.8) |
|    Medical attention for attempt[b] | † | 71.5% (48.7–94.3) | 73.7% (53.8–92.6) |
| Since joining military | | | |
|    Suicide attempt[a] | 3.8% (2.2–5.5) | 2.6% (1.8–3.4) | 1.8% (0.9–2.7) |
|    Medical attention for attempt[a] | 34.3% (13.0–55.6) | 62.3% (48.8–75.8) | 53.2% (34.8–71.5) |
| Before joining military | | | |
|    Suicide attempt[a] | 3.9% (2.1–5.7) | 3.5% (2.6–4.4) | 2.1% (1.1–3.1) |
|    Medical attention for attempt[a] | 20.4% (0.0–41.7) | 36.1% (22.7–49.4) | 29.7% (10.0–49.4) |
| During deployment | | | |
|    Suicide attempt[a] | 1.0% (0.0–2.0) | 0.3% (0.1–0.6) | 0.3% (0.0–0.6) |
|    Medical attention for attempt[b] | † | 46.7% (5.0–88.3) | † |

NOTE: All data are weighted. 95-percent confidence intervals are presented in parentheses.

[a] The omnibus chi-square test was not statistically significant ($p > 0.05$).

[b] Because there were too few respondents for at least one category, we do not report an omnibus chi-square test.

† = Too few respondents to report (denominator < 20).

### *Severity of Attempts*

Anyone who endorsed a suicide attempt during any of the time periods reported was also asked, as a marker of severity, whether subsequent medical attention was received from a doctor or other health professional during the specified time period. Between 27.7 percent and 55.0 percent of nonfatal suicide attempts resulted in the receipt of medical care, as shown in Table 6.37 and Figure 6.1.

**Figure 6.1**
**Suicide Attempts Resulting in Receipt of Medical Attention, by Time Frame, Overall Sample**

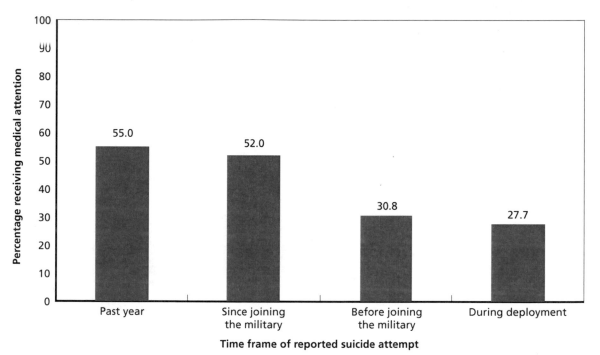

RAND *RR1695-6.1*

## Mental Health Services

Utilization of mental health services is one indication of a population's need for mental health care, and measuring such use is important for estimating adequate clinical staffing and the configuration of health resources. Such measurements are also a necessary component for determining how well service members' perceived needs for mental health care actually match the care that they seek and for understanding the reasons affecting any potential mismatch. Therefore, the 2015 HRBS asked a series of questions designed to investigate the following:

- whether mental health services were needed (perceived by self or others)
- whether and how much mental health services were used (counseling, therapy, or other mental health treatment)
- what types of providers delivered the services (mental health specialist, general medical doctor, civilian clergyperson or military chaplain, support group, other)
- where services were obtained (military health system or civilian sector)
- common reasons service members who perceived a need to receive services did not actually receive them (e.g., lack of transportation, concerns about what others will think, potential to harm military career)
- whether service members believed that obtaining mental health services would damage their military career (an aspect of mental health stigma that is highly salient in the military).

We assessed whether service members accessed mental health care and, if so, how many visits were used. These two service utilization means are presented in two ways: the mean number of mental health visits used per service member overall and the mean number of visits per service member accessing services. Survey items used to determine mental health service use relied on self-reports of utilization within the 12 months prior to completing the survey. The questions on mental health service use were as similar as possible to those used in previous versions of the HRBS to facilitate analyses of secular trends. However, wording across surveys has often undergone at least minor modification over the survey iterations, and these wording differences may sometimes yield somewhat divergent estimates (see, for example, Novins et al., 2008). When trends are assessed, we provide information on differences in question wording.

### Perceived Need for Mental Health Services

Results for perceived need for mental health services (self-perceived, other-perceived, and either self- or other-perceived) are shown in Tables 6.43 through 6.48. Key findings include the following:

- Perceived need for mental health services was relatively widespread. Roughly one-third (32.9 percent) of service members across the services reported either a self-perceived or other-perceived need for mental health services in the past year (Table 6.43).
- In general, the percentage of service members with a self-assessed need for services (29.7 percent [CI: 28.1–31.3]) was higher than the percentage told by others that they needed services (17.4 percent [CI: 16.1–18.7]) (Table 6.43). Only the self-assessed need for services was measured in previous iterations of the HRBS, and this figure has risen progressively over the past decade—2002: 18.7 percent (Bray, Hourani, Rae, et al., 2003); 2005: 17.8 percent (Bray, Hourani, Olmstead, et al., 2006); 2008: 19.8 percent

(CI: 18.6–21.0) (Bray, Pemberton, et al., 2009); and 2011: 25.6 percent (CI: 24.8–26.4) (Barlas et al., 2013).

- Among the service branches, the Army had the highest percentage of service members reporting any perceived need for mental health services (38.1 percent), and the Air Force (24.0 percent) and Coast Guard (23.8 percent) had the lowest. The Air Force and Coast Guard percentages were significantly lower than the Army, Navy, and Marine Corps percentages.
- The percentage of enlisted personnel and warrant officers who reported any perceived need was significantly higher than commissioned officers (Table 6.44).
- The percentage of women who perceived a need for services was significantly higher than men (Table 6.45). This finding is consistent with studies of the civil health sector (Regier et al., 1993; Kessler, Zhao, et al., 1999; Wang et al., 2005), although results in the military have been more mixed (Crum-Cianflone and Jacobson, 2014).
- The perceived need for mental health services (self-perceived, other-perceived, and combined) did not differ significantly across age groups or race/ethnicity.

### Table 6.43
**Perceived Need for Mental Health Services, by Service Branch**

|  | Total (1) | Air Force (2) | Army (3) | Marine Corps (4) | Navy (5) | Coast Guard (6) |
|---|---|---|---|---|---|---|
| Self-perceived need in the past 12 months | 29.7% (28.1–31.3) | 21.7%[b,c,d] (19.8–23.6) | 34.8%[a,e] (31.6–38.0) | 29.3%[a,e] (25.3–33.3) | 30.3%[a,e] (27.2–33.4) | 21.5%[b,c,d] (20.1–22.9) |
| Other-perceived need in the past 12 months | 17.4% (16.1–18.7) | 10.2%[b,c,d] (8.8–11.7) | 20.6%[a,e] (18.0–23.2) | 19.8%[a,e] (16.2–23.3) | 18.4%[a,e] (15.7–21.1) | 10.6%[b,c,d] (9.5–11.6) |
| Any perceived need in the past 12 months | 32.9% (31.3–34.6) | 24.0%[b,c,d] (22.0–26.0) | 38.1%[a,e] (34.8–41.4) | 34.0%[a,e] (29.8–38.2) | 33.7%[a,e] (30.5–36.9) | 23.8%[b,c,d] (22.3–25.3) |

NOTE: All data are weighted. 95-percent confidence intervals are presented in parentheses.

[a] Estimate is significantly different from the estimate in column 2 (Air Force).

[b] Estimate is significantly different from the estimate in column 3 (Army).

[c] Estimate is significantly different from the estimate in column 4 (Marine Corps).

[d] Estimate is significantly different from the estimate in column 5 (Navy).

[e] Estimate is significantly different from the estimate in column 6 (Coast Guard).

### Table 6.44
**Perceived Need for Mental Health Services, by Pay Grade**

|  | E1–E4 (1) | E5–E6 (2) | E7–E9 (3) | W1–W5 (4) | O1–O3 (5) | O4–O10 (6) |
|---|---|---|---|---|---|---|
| Self-perceived need in the past 12 months | 29.4%[f] (26.4–32.5) | 31.8%[e,f] (29.1–34.5) | 33.7%[e,f] (30.9–36.5) | 34.6%[e,f] (30.7–38.4) | 25.5%[b,c,d] (23.4–27.6) | 21.8%[a,b,c,d] (19.8–23.9) |
| Other-perceived need in the past 12 months | 17.7%[e,f] (15.2–20.2) | 19.6%[e,f] (17.3–22.0) | 20.5%[e,f] (18.0–23.0) | 18.6%[e,f] (15.4–21.7) | 12.4%[a,b,c,d,f] (10.8–14.0) | 8.7%[a,b,c,d,e] (7.3–10.0) |
| Any perceived need in the past 12 months | 33.0%[f] (29.9–36.2) | 35.4%[e,f] (32.6–38.1) | 36.7%[e,f] (33.9–39.6) | 36.9%[e,f] (33.0–40.8) | 27.7%[b,c,d] (25.5–29.8) | 23.6%[a,b,c,d] (21.5–25.7) |

NOTE: All data are weighted. 95-percent confidence intervals are presented in parentheses.

[a] Estimate is significantly different from the estimate in column 1 (E1–E4).

[b] Estimate is significantly different from the estimate in column 2 (E5–E6).

[c] Estimate is significantly different from the estimate in column 3 (E7–E9).

[d] Estimate is significantly different from the estimate in column 4 (W1–W5).

[e] Estimate is significantly different from the estimate in column 5 (O1–O3).

[f] Estimate is significantly different from the estimate in column 6 (O4–O10).

**Table 6.45**
**Perceived Need for Mental Health Services, by Gender**

|  | Men (1) | Women (2) |
|---|---|---|
| Self-perceived need in the past 12 months | 27.3%[a] (25.5–29.1) | 43.0% (40.9–45.0) |
| Other-perceived need in the past 12 months | 16.4%[a] (14.9–17.9) | 23.0% (21.2–24.8) |
| Any perceived need in the past 12 months | 30.5%[a] (28.6–32.4) | 46.4% (44.3–48.4) |

NOTE: All data are weighted. 95-percent confidence intervals are presented in parentheses.

[a] Estimate is significantly different from the estimate in column 2 (women).

**Table 6.46**
**Perceived Need for Mental Health Services, by Age Group**

|  | Ages 17–24 (1) | Ages 25–34 (2) | Ages 35–44 (3) | Ages 45+ (4) |
|---|---|---|---|---|
| Self-perceived need in the past 12 months[a] | 27.0% (23.6–30.4) | 29.7% (27.2–32.2) | 32.3% (29.7–35.0) | 31.8% (27.7–35.9) |
| Other-perceived need in the past 12 months[a] | 18.8% (15.7–21.8) | 16.3% (14.3–18.3) | 18.2% (16.0–20.3) | 16.0% (12.5–19.6) |
| Any perceived need in the past 12 months[a] | 31.0% (27.5–34.6) | 33.0% (30.4–35.6) | 34.9% (32.2–37.6) | 33.9% (29.8–38.0) |

NOTE: All data are weighted. 95-percent confidence intervals are presented in parentheses.

[a] The omnibus chi-square test was not statistically significant ($p > 0.05$).

**Table 6.47**
**Perceived Need for Mental Health Services, by Race/Ethnicity**

|  | Non-Hispanic White (1) | Non-Hispanic Black (2) | Hispanic (3) | Non-Hispanic Asian (4) | Other (5) |
|---|---|---|---|---|---|
| Self-perceived need in the past 12 months[a] | 30.4% (28.4–32.4) | 26.9% (22.6–31.3) | 29.1% (24.8–33.4) | 26.8% (18.5–35.0) | 31.3% (26.2–36.4) |
| Other-perceived need in the past 12 months[a] | 16.9% (15.2–18.5) | 17.3% (13.7–20.9) | 17.3% (13.7–20.8) | 17.2% (9.9–24.6) | 21.4% (16.8–26.0) |
| Any perceived need in the past 12 months[a] | 33.2% (31.1–35.3) | 30.3% (25.8–34.8) | 34.1% (29.6–38.7) | 28.2% (19.9–36.5) | 35.3% (30.1–40.6) |

NOTE: All data are weighted. 95-percent confidence intervals are presented in parentheses.

[a] The omnibus chi-square test was not statistically significant ($p > 0.05$).

**Table 6.48**
**Perceived Need for Mental Health Services, by Education Level**

|  | High School or Less (1) | Some College (2) | Bachelor's Degree or More (3) |
|---|---|---|---|
| Self-perceived need in the past 12 months | 26.4%[b] (22.4–30.4) | 33.1%[a,c] (30.6–35.5) | 26.7%[b] (24.5–28.9) |
| Other-perceived need in the past 12 months | 18.6%[c] (15.1–22.1) | 19.7%[c] (17.7–21.7) | 13.3%[a,b] (11.5–15.1) |
| Any perceived need in the past 12 months | 30.5%[b] (26.3–34.6) | 36.9%[a,c] (34.5–39.4) | 28.5%[b] (26.3–30.8) |

NOTE: All data are weighted. 95-percent confidence intervals are presented in parentheses.

[a] Estimate is significantly different from the estimate in column 1 (high school or less).

[b] Estimate is significantly different from the estimate in column 2 (some college).

[c] Estimate is significantly different from the estimate in column 3 (bachelor's degree or more).

## Mental Health Service Utilization

Tables 6.49 through 6.54 show results for the percentage of service members using mental health services (irrespective of need) from various sources (in both military and civilian health systems) in the past 12 months. Service members reporting any mental health service use in the past year showed patterns similar to those for perceived need for treatment (Tables 6.43–6.48). We defined *mental health services* broadly to include all individual or group services aimed at addressing mental health concerns (e.g., ranging from seeing a psychologist to attending a self-help group). Key findings include the following:

- Overall, 26.2 percent (CI: 24.7–27.7) of service members reported using mental health services (Table 6.49). The percentage of HRBS respondents that reported using mental health services has climbed steadily over at least the past decade—2002: 12.2 percent (Bray, Hourani, Rae, et al., 2003); 2005: 14.6 percent (Bray, Hourani, Olmstead, et al., 2006); 2008: 19.9 percent (CI: 18.5–21.3) (Bray, Pemberton, et al., 2009); and 2011: 24.9 percent (CI: 24.1–25.7) (Barlas et al., 2013). This is partly but not completely due to the addition of items assessing visits to a self-help support group (starting in 2005) and visits to some "other source of counseling, therapy, or treatment" (2015).
- The service branch with the highest percentage of service members with mental health utilization was the Army (32.1 percent), and the lowest was the Coast Guard (17.5 percent) (Table 6.49).
- The percentage of service members using civilian mental health services was highest in the Coast Guard (11.0 percent) (Table 6.49). The differences between the Coast Guard and the Air Force, Navy, and Marine Corps were each statistically significant.
- In general, the percentage reporting receipt of mental health services from a specialist (e.g., psychiatrist, psychologist, social worker) (18.8 percent) was about twice as high as the percentage reporting receipt of mental health services from a general medical doctor (9.9 percent) or from a civilian clergyperson or military chaplain (8.0 percent) (Table 6.49).
- As with survey estimates of perceived need, the percentage of service members who reported seeking services was significantly higher for enlisted personnel compared with officers (Table 6.50) and for women compared with men (Table 6.51). It was also higher for older compared with younger age groups (Table 6.52).

**Table 6.49**
**Past Year Mental Health Service Utilization, by Service Branch**

| | Total (1) | Air Force (2) | Army (3) | Marine Corps (4) | Navy (5) | Coast Guard (6) |
|---|---|---|---|---|---|---|
| Any mental health visit | 26.2% (24.7–27.7) | 21.8%[b,e] (19.9–23.8) | 32.1%[a,c,d,e] (29.0–35.2) | 22.3%[b] (18.8–25.8) | 24.3%[b,e] (21.4–27.1) | 17.5%[a,b,d] (16.2–18.9) |
| Specialist | 18.8% (17.5–20.2) | 14.9%[b,e] (13.2–16.6) | 25.4%[a,c,d,e] (22.6–28.3) | 14.2%[b] (11.3–17.2) | 15.6%[b,e] (13.2–18.0) | 10.4%[a,b,d] (9.3–11.5) |
| General medical doctor | 9.9% (8.9–10.9) | 7.7%[b] (6.4–9.0) | 12.7%[a,e] (10.5–14.9) | 8.2% (5.9–10.6) | 8.9% (7.0–10.7) | 6.4%[b] (5.5–7.3) |
| Clergyperson or chaplain | 8.0% (7.0–8.9) | 6.1%[b] (5.0–7.2) | 9.2%[a,e] (7.3–11.1) | 8.0% (5.7–10.4) | 8.1% (6.2–10.0) | 5.8%[b] (5.0–6.7) |
| Self-help group[f] | 1.6% (1.2–2.1) | 1.1% (0.6–1.5) | 1.8% (0.9–2.8) | 2.3% (1.0–3.5) | 1.5% (0.8–2.3) | 1.4% (0.9–1.8) |
| Other provider[f] | 5.7% (4.9–6.5) | 4.1% (3.2–5.0) | 6.2% (4.6–7.8) | 6.4% (4.5–8.2) | 6.2% (4.6–7.8) | 5.0% (4.2–5.8) |
| Any civilian provider visit | 7.1% (6.3–7.9) | 5.2%[b,e] (4.2–6.2) | 8.7%[a] (7.0–10.4) | 6.2%[e] (4.2–8.2) | 6.3%[e] (4.6–8.0) | 11.0%[a,c,d] (9.9–12.1) |
| Mental health professional | 4.2% (3.5–4.8) | 2.5%[b,e] (1.8–3.2) | 5.5%[a,e] (4.1–6.9) | 3.8%[e] (2.1–5.6) | 3.2%[e] (2.1–4.4) | 7.9%[a,b,c,d] (7.0–8.8) |
| General medical doctor | 2.3% (1.8–2.9) | 1.7%[e] (1.1–2.2) | 3.2% (2.0–4.5) | 1.6% (0.5–2.7) | 1.8% (0.9–2.8) | 3.0%[a] (2.4–3.6) |
| Clergyperson[f] | 2.6% (2.1–3.1) | 1.9% (1.3–2.5) | 3.2% (2.1–4.3) | 2.1% (1.0–3.2) | 2.6% (1.5–3.7) | 2.4% (1.9–3.0) |
| Any military provider visits | 22.4% (21.0–23.8) | 18.9%[b,e] (17.0–20.8) | 28.8%[a,c,d,e] (25.8–31.9) | 17.4%[b,e] (14.2–20.6) | 19.8%[b,e] (17.1–22.5) | 10.4%[a,b,c,d] (9.3–11.5) |
| Mental health professional | 16.9% (15.6–18.2) | 13.7%[b,e] (12.0–15.3) | 23.2%[a,c,d,e] (20.4–26.0) | 12.2%[b,e] (9.4–14.9) | 14.1%[b,e] (11.8–16.5) | 4.3%[a,b,c,d] (3.6–5.1) |
| General medical doctor | 9.2% (8.2–10.2) | 7.5%[b] (6.2–8.7) | 12.0%[a,c,e] (9.9–14.1) | 7.0%[b] (4.9–9.1) | 8.3%[e] (6.5–10.1) | 5.4%[b,d] (4.6–6.2) |
| Chaplain[f] | 6.5% (5.7–7.4) | 4.9% (3.9–6.0) | 7.7% (5.8–9.5) | 6.9% (4.7–9.2) | 6.2% (4.6–7.9) | 4.6% (3.8–5.3) |

NOTE: All data are weighted. 95-percent confidence intervals are presented in parentheses.

[a] Estimate is significantly different from the estimate in column 2 (Air Force).

[b] Estimate is significantly different from the estimate in column 3 (Army).

[c] Estimate is significantly different from the estimate in column 4 (Marine Corps).

[d] Estimate is significantly different from the estimate in column 5 (Navy).

[e] Estimate is significantly different from the estimate in column 6 (Coast Guard).

[f] The omnibus chi-square test was not statistically significant ($p > 0.05$).

**Table 6.50**
**Past-Year Mental Health Service Utilization, by Pay Grade**

| | E1–E4 (1) | E5–E6 (2) | E7–E9 (3) | W1–W5 (4) | O1–O3 (5) | O4–O10 (6) |
|---|---|---|---|---|---|---|
| Any mental health visit | 24.9% (22.0–27.8) | 29.0%[e,f] (26.4–31.7) | 30.5%[e,f] (27.7–33.2) | 27.9%[f] (24.3–31.6) | 23.2%[b,c] (21.2–25.3) | 20.5%[b,c,d] (18.4–22.5) |
| Specialist | 17.8% (15.2–20.4) | 21.6%[e,f] (19.1–24.0) | 22.6%[e,f] (20.1–25.2) | 21.2%[e,f] (17.9–24.6) | 14.6%[b,c,d] (12.9–16.4) | 13.8%[b,c,d] (12.0–15.6) |
| General medical doctor | 8.6%[b,c,e] (6.7–10.4) | 12.8%[a,e,f] (10.8–14.8) | 14.4%[a,e,f] (12.2–16.6) | 12.7%[e,f] (9.9–15.5) | 5.2%[a,b,c,d] (4.2–6.2) | 6.0%[b,c,d] (4.8–7.2) |
| Clergyperson or chaplain[g] | 8.3% (6.5–10.1) | 8.7% (7.0–10.4) | 6.4% (4.9–7.8) | 5.2% (3.4–7.0) | 8.1% (6.7–9.4) | 5.8% (4.6–6.9) |
| Self-help group[g] | 1.5% (0.7–2.4) | 2.1% (1.3–3.0) | 1.5% (0.8–2.2) | 1.4% (0.5–2.2) | 1.1% (0.6–1.6) | 1.3% (0.7–1.8) |
| Other provider | 5.3% (3.8–6.8) | 7.1%[e,f] (5.7–8.6) | 6.3%[f] (4.9–7.8) | 3.9% (2.5–5.4) | 4.5%[b] (3.6–5.5) | 3.6%[b,c] (2.7–4.5) |
| Any civilian provider visit | 5.5%[c,d] (4.0–7.0) | 8.3% (6.7–10.0) | 9.7%[a] (7.9–11.5) | 10.2%[a] (7.7–12.8) | 7.1% (5.9–8.4) | 7.2% (5.9–8.5) |
| Mental health professional[g] | 3.4% (2.2–4.6) | 4.8% (3.6–6.1) | 5.3% (3.9–6.8) | 6.5% (4.5–8.6) | 4.1% (3.1–5.1) | 4.2% (3.1–5.3) |
| General medical doctor[g] | 2.2% (1.1–3.2) | 2.7% (1.7–3.6) | 3.6% (2.4–4.8) | 3.0% (1.5–4.5) | 1.4% (0.8–2.0) | 1.3% (0.7–1.8) |
| Clergyperson[g] | 2.1% (1.1–3.0) | 3.0% (2.0–4.0) | 2.8% (1.9–3.8) | 2.2% (0.9–3.4) | 2.9% (2.1–3.8) | 3.4% (2.4–4.3) |
| Any military provider visit | 21.4%[c,f] (18.7–24.2) | 25.4%[e,f] (22.8–28.0) | 27.0%[a,e,f] (24.3–29.7) | 24.1%[e,f] (20.6–27.7) | 17.7%[b,c,d] (15.8–19.6) | 15.7%[a,b,c,d] (13.8–17.5) |
| Mental health professional | 16.4%[e,f] (13.9–18.9) | 19.3%[e,f] (17.0–21.6) | 20.6%[e,f] (18.1–23.1) | 18.5%[e,f] (15.3–21.7) | 12.0%[a,b,c,d] (10.3–13.6) | 10.9%[a,b,c,d] (9.2–12.5) |
| General medical doctor | 7.9%[b,c,e] (6.1–9.7) | 12.0%[a,e,f] (10.0–13.9) | 13.7%[a,e,f] (11.6–15.9) | 12.1%[e,f] (9.4–14.9) | 4.8%[a,b,c,d] (3.9–5.8) | 5.8%[b,c,d] (4.6–7.0) |
| Chaplain | 7.3%[d,f] (5.6–9.0) | 7.0%[f] (5.5–8.6) | 4.7% (3.4–6.0) | 3.7%[a] (2.2–5.2) | 6.1%[f] (4.9–7.3) | 3.7%[a,b,e] (2.8–4.6) |

NOTE: All data are weighted. 95-percent confidence intervals are presented in parentheses.

[a] Estimate is significantly different from the estimate in column 1 (E1–E4).

[b] Estimate is significantly different from the estimate in column 2 (E5–E6).

[c] Estimate is significantly different from the estimate in column 3 (E7–E9).

[d] Estimate is significantly different from the estimate in column 4 (W1–W5).

[e] Estimate is significantly different from the estimate in column 5 (O1–O3).

[f] Estimate is significantly different from the estimate in column 6 (O4–O10).

[g] The omnibus chi-square test was not statistically significant (p > 0.05).

Table 6.51
**Past-Year Mental Health Service Utilization, by Gender**

|  | Men (1) | Women (2) |
|---|---|---|
| Any mental health visit | 24.0%[a] (22.3–25.8) | 38.3% (36.3–40.3) |
|    Specialist | 17.2%[a] (15.7–18.8) | 27.6% (25.7–29.5) |
|    General medical doctor | 9.3%[a] (8.1–10.4) | 13.5% (12.0–15.0) |
|    Clergyperson or chaplain | 7.3%[a] (6.2–8.4) | 11.6% (10.2–13.1) |
|    Self-help group[b] | 1.6% (1.1–2.1) | 1.9% (1.3–2.5) |
|    Other provider | 5.0%[a] (4.1–5.9) | 9.5% (8.3–10.8) |
| Any civilian provider visit | 6.5%[a] (5.5–7.4) | 10.6% (9.3–11.8) |
|    Mental health professional | 3.8%[a] (3.1–4.6) | 6.1% (5.1–7.0) |
|    General medical doctor[b] | 2.2% (1.6–2.9) | 2.9% (2.2–3.5) |
|    Clergyperson | 2.3%[a] (1.7–2.9) | 4.1% (3.3–4.9) |
| Any military provider visit | 20.6%[a] (18.9–22.2) | 32.5% (30.5–34.5) |
|    Mental health professional | 15.4%[a] (13.9–16.9) | 25.0% (23.2–26.9) |
|    General medical doctor | 8.6%[a] (7.4–9.7) | 12.9% (11.5–14.4) |
|    Chaplain | 6.0%[a] (5.0–7.0) | 9.5% (8.1–10.8) |

NOTE: All data are weighted. 95-percent confidence intervals are presented in parentheses.

[a] Estimate is significantly different from the estimate in column 2 (women).

[b] The omnibus chi-square test was not statistically significant ($p > 0.05$).

**Table 6.52**
**Past-Year Mental Health Service Utilization, by Age Group**

| | Ages 17–24 (1) | Ages 25–34 (2) | Ages 35–44 (3) | Ages 45+ (4) |
|---|---|---|---|---|
| Any mental health visit | 22.9%[c,d] (19.7–26.1) | 25.3%[c] (22.9–27.7) | 30.5%[a,b] (27.8–33.1) | 30.7%[a] (26.7–34.7) |
| Specialist | 14.5%[c,d] (11.8–17.1) | 18.7% (16.5–20.8) | 22.7%[a] (20.1–25.3) | 24.4%[a] (20.5–28.4) |
| General medical doctor | 7.4%[c,d] (5.4–9.4) | 9.1%[c,d] (7.4–10.7) | 13.1%[a,b] (11.0–15.2) | 14.2%[a,b] (11.2–17.2) |
| Clergyperson or chaplain[e] | 9.2% (7.0–11.4) | 7.1% (5.7–8.5) | 8.3% (6.6–10.0) | 7.5% (5.2–9.9) |
| Self-help group[e] | 1.3% (0.4–2.3) | 1.7% (1.0–2.3) | 2.0% (1.0–3.0) | 1.5% (0.6–2.5) |
| Other provider | 4.3%[c] (2.9–5.7) | 5.6% (4.4–6.9) | 7.8%[a] (6.0–9.6) | 5.3% (3.4–7.1) |
| Any civilian provider visit | 3.8%[b,c,d] (2.4–5.2) | 7.6%[a] (6.2–9.0) | 9.8%[a] (8.0–11.6) | 8.5%[a] (6.6–10.5) |
| Mental health professional | 2.3%[c] (1.1–3.4) | 4.3% (3.3–5.3) | 6.3%[a] (4.7–7.8) | 3.8% (2.6–5.0) |
| General medical doctor | 0.8%[b,c,d] (0.1–1.5) | 2.8%[a] (1.7–3.8) | 3.0%[a] (1.9–4.1) | 3.6%[a] (2.1–5.0) |
| Clergyperson[e] | 1.7% (0.8–2.6) | 2.7% (1.8–3.6) | 3.4% (2.3–4.5) | 3.0% (1.9–4.2) |
| Any military provider visit | 19.8%[c,d] (16.8–22.9) | 20.9%[c,d] (18.6–23.1) | 26.5%[a,b] (23.8–29.1) | 28.1%[a,b] (24.1–32.1) |
| Mental health professional | 13.7%[c,d] (11.1–16.4) | 16.3%[d] (14.3–18.4) | 19.9%[a] (17.4–22.4) | 22.4%[a,b] (18.5–26.3) |
| General medical doctor | 7.3%[c,d] (5.3–9.2) | 8.0%[c,d] (6.5–9.5) | 12.5%[a,b] (10.4–14.5) | 13.8%[a,b] (10.9–16.8) |
| Chaplain[e] | 8.3% (6.2–10.4) | 5.6% (4.4–6.8) | 6.5% (4.8–8.1) | 5.6% (3.4–7.7) |

NOTE: All data are weighted. 95-percent confidence intervals are presented in parentheses.

[a] Estimate is significantly different from the estimate in column 1 (ages 17–24).

[b] Estimate is significantly different from the estimate in column 2 (ages 25–34).

[c] Estimate is significantly different from the estimate in column 3 (ages 35–44).

[d] Estimate is significantly different from the estimate in column 4 (ages 45+).

[e] The omnibus chi-square test was not statistically significant ($p > 0.05$).

**Table 6.53**
**Past Year Mental Health Service Utilization, by Race/Ethnicity**

| | Non-Hispanic White (1) | Non-Hispanic Black (2) | Hispanic (3) | Non-Hispanic Asian (4) | Other (5) |
|---|---|---|---|---|---|
| Any mental health visit[f] | 26.3% (24.4–28.2) | 26.7% (22.4–31.0) | 24.7% (20.6–28.8) | 25.3% (17.6–33.1) | 27.9% (22.9–33.0) |
| Specialist[f] | 19.4% (17.6–21.1) | 19.6% (15.7–23.6) | 17.3% (13.7–20.9) | 18.1% (10.7–25.5) | 16.9% (12.9–20.9) |
| General medical doctor[f] | 10.0% (8.6–11.3) | 11.6% (8.4–14.8) | 8.4% (6.1–10.7) | 8.9% (3.5–14.4) | 10.2% (6.7–13.8) |
| Clergyperson or chaplain[f] | 7.9% (6.6–9.2) | 8.7% (5.9–11.4) | 6.6% (4.7–8.5) | 9.1% (4.1–14.1) | 9.9% (6.7–13.2) |
| Self-help group[f] | 1.5% (0.9–2.1) | 1.9% (0.1–3.7) | 1.9% (0.7–3.0) | 1.8% (0.3–3.2) | 1.6% (0.3–2.9) |
| Other provider | 4.9%[e] (4.0–5.8) | 7.1% (4.5–9.7) | 5.1% (3.2–7.0) | 8.6% (3.0–14.2) | 9.0%[a] (5.6–12.3) |
| Any civilian provider visit | 7.1%[d] (6.0–8.2) | 9.1%[d] (6.3–11.9) | 5.3%[e] (3.8–6.9) | 2.6%[a,b,e] (1.0–4.2) | 10.3%[c,d] (6.6–14.0) |
| Mental health professional[f] | 4.2% (3.4–5.1) | 4.9% (2.6–7.2) | 3.3% (2.0–4.5) | 2.1% (0.6–3.7) | 5.8% (2.9–8.6) |
| General medical doctor[f] | 2.4% (1.7–3.2) | 3.4% (1.2–5.6) | 1.7% (0.9–2.5) | 0.8% (0.0–1.7) | 2.3% (0.8–3.8) |
| Clergyperson | 2.5% (1.9–3.2) | 4.2%[d] (2.1–6.3) | 1.9% (0.9–2.9) | 0.8%[b] (0.0–1.6) | 3.2% (1.1–5.3) |
| Any military provider visit[f] | 22.2% (20.3–24.0) | 24.0% (19.7–28.2) | 20.9% (17.0–24.9) | 24.8% (17.0–32.6) | 23.2% (18.4–28.0) |
| Mental health professional[f] | 17.1% (15.4–18.7) | 18.2% (14.4–22.0) | 15.9% (12.3–19.4) | 17.3% (10.0–24.7) | 15.2% (11.4–19.1) |
| General medical doctor[f] | 9.3% (8.0–10.5) | 11.0% (8.0–14.1) | 8.0% (5.7–10.2) | 8.9% (3.5–14.2) | 9.0% (5.7–12.3) |
| Chaplain[f] | 6.4% (5.2–7.6) | 6.9% (4.2–9.5) | 5.2% (3.5–7.0) | 8.9% (3.9–13.9) | 8.3% (5.4–11.1) |

NOTE: All data are weighted. 95-percent confidence intervals are presented in parentheses.

[a] Estimate is significantly different from the estimate in column 1 (non-Hispanic white).

[b] Estimate is significantly different from the estimate in column 2 (non-Hispanic black).

[c] Estimate is significantly different from the estimate in column 3 (Hispanic).

[d] Estimate is significantly different from the estimate in column 4 (non-Hispanic Asian).

[e] Estimate is significantly different from the estimate in column 5 (other).

[f] The omnibus chi-square test was not statistically significant ($p > 0.05$).

**Table 6.54**
**Past-Year Mental Health Service Utilization, by Education Level**

| | High School or Less (1) | Some College (2) | Bachelor's Degree or More (3) |
|---|---|---|---|
| Any mental health visit | 24.1% (20.1–28.0) | 28.5%[c] (26.2–30.8) | 24.1%[b] (22.0–26.2) |
| Specialist | 14.8%[b] (11.5–18.2) | 22.0%[a,c] (19.9–24.1) | 16.6%[b] (14.7–18.5) |
| General medical doctor[d] | 10.6% (7.6–13.5) | 10.3% (8.9–11.7) | 8.9% (7.3–10.5) |
| Clergyperson or chaplain[d] | 9.4% (6.6–12.2) | 8.0% (6.6–9.4) | 7.1% (5.9–8.3) |
| Self-help group[d] | 2.2% (0.8–3.7) | 1.6% (1.0–2.2) | 1.4% (0.7–2.0) |
| Other provider[d] | 4.9% (3.0–6.9) | 6.4% (5.3–7.6) | 5.1% (3.9–6.4) |
| Any civilian provider visit[d] | 5.1% (3.0–7.3) | 7.6% (6.3–8.8) | 7.6% (6.4–8.8) |
| Mental health professional[d] | 2.9% (1.2–4.5) | 4.8% (3.8–5.8) | 4.0% (3.0–4.9) |
| General medical doctor[d] | 2.4% (0.6–4.1) | 2.0% (1.4–2.6) | 2.8% (1.8–3.8) |
| Clergyperson[d] | 2.0% (0.6–3.4) | 2.6% (1.8–3.4) | 2.9% (2.2–3.7) |
| Any military provider visit | 21.7% (17.8–25.5) | 24.4%[c] (22.2–26.6) | 19.9%[b] (17.9–21.9) |
| Mental health professional | 13.6%[b] (10.4–16.8) | 19.9%[a,c] (17.9–22.0) | 14.3%[b] (12.5–16.1) |
| General medical doctor[d] | 10.1% (7.2–13.1) | 9.4% (8.1–10.8) | 8.4% (6.9–9.8) |
| Chaplain | 8.9%[c] (6.1–11.6) | 6.3% (5.1–7.5) | 5.5%[a] (4.4–6.6) |

NOTE: All data are weighted. 95-percent confidence intervals are presented in parentheses.

[a] Estimate is significantly different from the estimate in column 1 (high school or less)

[b] Estimate is significantly different from the estimate in column 2 (some college).

[c] Estimate is significantly different from the estimate in column 3 (bachelor's degree or more).

[d] The omnibus chi-square test was not statistically significant ($p > 0.05$).

Table 6.55 presents estimates of the average self reported number of mental health visits per service member in the past year for the entire active-duty population, including individuals who did and did not use mental health services. The figures for all active-duty service members are helpful for determining where the greatest volume of mental health service delivery occurs. For example, across the service branches, the average active-duty service member reported using 4.5 mental health visits in the past year. Of these 4.5 visits, 0.8 visits (18 percent) were to a civilian provider (e.g., paid out of pocket, by TRICARE, or by other private insurance), 2.5 visits (57 percent) were to a military provider, and 1.1 visits (25 percent) were to a self-help group or other provider (Figure 6.2). Similarly, of the 4.5 average annual visits, half were to a mental health specialist (e.g., psychologist, social worker, and psychiatrist), while 0.7 visits (16 percent) were to a general medical doctor, 0.4 visits (9 percent) were to a civilian clergyperson or military chaplain, and 1.1 visits (25 percent) were to a self-help group or other provider (Figure 6.3).[7] These observations are important because (1) very little is known about the content, quality, or outcomes of nonmedical sources of mental health care, and (2) civilian sources of mental health care are usually minimally visible to the military health system and the chain of command, which is a potential military readiness issue.

In addition, we looked at the average number of yearly mental health visits among those who used mental health services, which may offer insights into the relative level of clinical engagement occurring in various settings. As shown in Table 6.56, the average number of visits among those using mental health care from a specialist was greater than among those receiving mental health care from a generalist or from a clergyperson or chaplain. However, it is likely that there were important differences in the populations using these different care settings, and these differences may help explain differences in the number of visits. For example, studies of civilians that included beneficiaries of the VA health system suggest that, on average, patients seeking specialty mental health treatment have more-severe symptoms or problems than those receiving care from a generalist (Kessler, Zhao, et al., 1999; Vojvoda, Stefanovics, and Rosenheck, 2014).

---

[7]   In the civilian sector, visits to a generalist significantly outnumber visits to mental health specialists (Wang et al., 2005).

**Table 6.55**
**Average Number of Past-Year Mental Health Visits per Service Member, Overall Sample, by Service Branch**

| | Total (1) | Air Force (2) | Army (3) | Marine Corps (4) | Navy (5) | Coast Guard (6) |
|---|---|---|---|---|---|---|
| Total mental health visits | 4.5 (3.9–5.0) | 3.1[b] (2.5–3.8) | 5.4[a,e] (4.4–6.4) | 5.6 (3.4–7.8) | 3.9 (2.8–4.9) | 2.8[b] (2.3–3.4) |
| Specialist | 2.2 (2.0–2.5) | 1.6[b] (1.3–1.9) | 3.2[a,d,e] (2.6–3.8) | 2.0 (1.3–2.7) | 1.6[b] (1.2–1.9) | 1.2[b] (1.0–1.5) |
| General medical doctor | 0.7 (0.5–0.8) | 0.4[b] (0.3–0.6) | 0.9[a,e] (0.6–1.2) | 0.9 (0.3–1.4) | 0.5 (0.3–0.8) | 0.4[b] (0.3–0.6) |
| Clergyperson or chaplain | 0.4 (0.3–0.5) | 0.3 (0.2–0.5) | 0.5[e] (0.3–0.7) | 0.5 (0.2–0.7) | 0.4 (0.2–0.5) | 0.2[b] (0.1–0.2) |
| Self-help group[f] | 0.5 (0.3–0.7) | 0.4 (0.1–0.7) | 0.3 (0.1–0.5) | 1.2 (0.1–2.3) | 0.6 (0.2–0.9) | 0.5 (0.3–0.8) |
| Other provider[f] | 0.6 (0.4–0.8) | 0.4 (0.2–0.5) | 0.5 (0.3–0.7) | 1.0 (0.3–1.8) | 0.8 (0.3–1.3) | 0.5 (0.2–0.8) |
| Total civilian provider visits | 0.8 (0.6–1.0) | 0.6[e] (0.3–0.8) | 1.2 (0.7–1.8) | 0.5[e] (0.3–0.8) | 0.5[e] (0.3–0.7) | 1.1[a,c,d] (0.9–1.3) |
| Mental health professional | 0.5 (0.4–0.7) | 0.3[e] (0.2–0.5) | 0.9[c,d] (0.5–1.3) | 0.3[b,e] (0.1–0.4) | 0.3[b,e] (0.1–0.4) | 0.9[a,c,d] (0.7–1.0) |
| General medical doctor[f] | 0.1 (0.1–0.2) | 0.1 (0.0–0.2) | 0.2 (0.0–0.3) | 0.1 (0.0–0.2) | 0.1 (0.0–0.2) | 0.1 (0.1–0.2) |
| Clergyperson[f] | 0.2 (0.1–0.2) | 0.1 (0.1–0.2) | 0.2 (0.1–0.4) | 0.2 (0.0–0.3) | 0.1 (0.1–0.2) | 0.1 (0.06–0.13) |
| Total military provider visits | 2.5 (2.2–2.9) | 1.8[b,e] (1.5–2.2) | 3.4[a,d,e] (2.8–4.0) | 2.8[e] (1.6–4.0) | 2.0[b,e] (1.5–2.4) | 0.7[a,b,c,d] (0.5–0.9) |
| Mental health professional | 1.7 (1.5–1.9) | 1.2[b,e] (1.0–1.5) | 2.3[a,d,e] (1.9–2.7) | 1.7[e] (1.1–2.4) | 1.3[b,e] (1.0–1.6) | 0.4[a,b,c,d] (0.2–0.5) |
| General medical doctor | 0.5 (0.4–0.7) | 0.3[b] (0.2–0.4) | 0.7[a,e] (0.5–0.9) | 0.8 (0.2–1.3) | 0.4 (0.2–0.6) | 0.3[b] (0.2–0.4) |
| Chaplain | 0.3 (0.2–0.3) | 0.2 (0.1–0.3) | 0.3[e] (0.2–0.5) | 0.3 (0.1–0.5) | 0.2 (0.1–0.3) | 0.1[b] (0.06–0.13) |

NOTE: All data are weighted. 95-percent confidence intervals are presented in parentheses.

[a] Estimate is significantly different from the estimate in column 2 (Air Force).

[b] Estimate is significantly different from the estimate in column 3 (Army).

[c] Estimate is significantly different from the estimate in column 4 (Marine Corps).

[d] Estimate is significantly different from the estimate in column 5 (Navy).

[e] Estimate is significantly different from the estimate in column 6 (Coast Guard).

[f] The omnibus chi-square test was not statistically significant ($p > 0.05$).

**Figure 6.2**
**Past-Year Mental Health Visits, by Provider Location, Overall Sample**

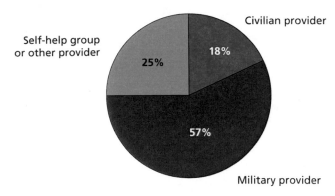

RAND RR1695-6.2

**Figure 6.3**
**Past-Year Mental Health Visits, by Provider Type, Overall Sample**

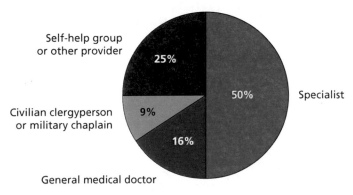

RAND RR1695-6.3

**Table 6.56**
**Average Number of Past-Year Mental Health Visits per Service Member, Mental Health Service Users Only, by Service Branch**

| | Total (1) | Air Force (2) | Army (3) | Marine Corps (4) | Navy (5) | Coast Guard (6) |
|---|---|---|---|---|---|---|
| Total mental health visits[f] | 18.1 (16.2–20.1) | 15.3 (12.5–18.2) | 17.9 (15.2–20.6) | 26.0 (16.5–35.6) | 16.7 (12.7–20.6) | 16.9 (13.8–20.0) |
| Specialist[f] | 12.8 (11.5–14.0) | 11.9 (9.9–13.9) | 13.1 (11.1–15.2) | 16.0 (11.5–20.5) | 10.9 (9.1–12.8) | 12.8 (10.7–14.8) |
| General medical doctor[f] | 7.7 (6.1–9.2) | 6.4 (4.7–8.1) | 7.7 (5.4–10.0) | 11.9 (4.7–19.1) | 6.4 (3.7–9.2) | 7.2 (4.9–9.5) |
| Clergyperson or chaplain | 5.9 (4.7–7.0) | 5.9 (3.6–8.1) | 6.5[e] (4.3–8.7) | 6.4 (3.5–9.3) | 4.8 (3.4–6.2) | 3.1[b] (2.4–3.8) |
| Self-help group | 33.2 (21.4–45.1) | 42.3[b] (21.5–63.1) | 16.9[a,c,d,e] (7.7–26.0) | 55.6[b] (10.6–100.5) | 38.1[b] (17.4–58.8) | 39.9[b] (23.8–56.0) |
| Other provider | 11.0 (8.8–14.9) | 10.2[c] (7.0–13.5) | 8.5[c,d] (5.8–11.2) | 17.6[a,b,d] (7.3–27.9) | 14.6[b,c] (8.4–22.0) | 11.0 (8.6–16.5) |
| Total civilian provider visits[f] | 12.3 (9.4–15.1) | 11.6 (7.5–15.7) | 14.9 (9.4–20.3) | 9.6 (5.9–13.4) | 8.7 (5.9–11.6) | 11.0 (9.3–12.6) |
| Mental health professional[f] | 13.7 (10.6–16.8) | 14.9 (10.0–19.9) | 16.3 (10.8–21.7) | 8.5 (5.6–11.4) | 8.9 (6.5–11.4) | 12.0 (10.2–13.8) |
| General medical doctor | 5.8 (3.4–8.2) | 7.2[b] (1.3–13.2) | 5.1[a,c,d] (1.5–8.7) | 6.7[b] (0.3–13.0) | 6.6[b] (1.7–11.4) | 5.6 (3.1–8.1) |
| Clergyperson | 6.6 (4.6–8.7) | 6.6[e] (3.6–9.5) | 7.0 (3.3–10.7) | 8.5[d,e] (1.0–15.9) | 5.3[c,e] (3.3–7.3) | 4.0[a,c,d] (2.6–5.4) |
| Total military provider visits | 12.2 (10.9–13.5) | 10.5 (8.7–12.3) | 12.6[e] (10.7–14.5) | 16.8[e] (10.5–23.2) | 10.5 (8.3–12.6) | 7.3[b,c] (5.5–9.2) |
| Mental health professional[f] | 10.9 (9.8–12.0) | 10.1 (8.6–11.6) | 10.6 (8.9–12.2) | 16.1 (11.1–21.1) | 10.1 (8.3–11.8) | 8.9 (5.5–12.4) |
| General medical doctor | 6.7 (5.4–8.1) | 5.1[c] (3.9–6.3) | 6.7[c] (4.9–8.5) | 12.3[a,b,d,e] (4.6–19.9) | 5.4[c] (3.3–7.5) | 5.4[c] (3.9–7.0) |
| Chaplain | 4.6 (3.5–5.7) | 4.9 (2.3–7.5) | 4.7[e] (2.8–6.6) | 4.9 (2.4–7.4) | 4.2 (2.6–5.9) | 1.9[b] (1.5–2.2) |

NOTE: All data are weighted. 95-percent confidence intervals are presented in parentheses.

[a] Estimate is significantly different from the estimate in column 2 (Air Force).

[b] Estimate is significantly different from the estimate in column 3 (Army).

[c] Estimate is significantly different from the estimate in column 4 (Marine Corps).

[d] Estimate is significantly different from the estimate in column 5 (Navy).

[e] Estimate is significantly different from the estimate in column 6 (Coast Guard).

[f] The omnibus chi-square test was not statistically significant ($p > 0.05$).

### Reasons for Not Receiving Needed Services for Mental Health Problems

Service members who reported a perceived need for mental health treatment and reported no mental health service use in the past year (36.1 percent [CI: 33.1–39.1] of all respondents) were asked to report the reasons they did not seek treatment. A single survey item (based on work by Adler et al., 2015; Hoge, Grossman, et al., 2014; Kim et al., 2011; and Wright et al., 2009) asked respondents about 13 perceived barriers to care, with an additional option to mark "other." Table 6.57 displays the results, ordered by the most-popular reasons. Key findings include the following:

- The most common reason for not seeking needed mental health services was that service members wanted to handle the problem on their own. Women reported this reason more often than men, and this finding is similar to what has been found in the general U.S. population for PTSD (Kessler, 2000).
- Two of the next three most common reasons were related to the military: "It would have harmed my career" and "I was afraid my supervisor/unit leadership would have a negative opinion of me."

**Table 6.57**
**Reasons for Not Receiving Needed Treatment for Mental Health Problems in the Past Year**

| Reason | Percentage of Respondents Marking That Reason |
|---|---|
| I wanted to handle the problem on my own. | 61.5% (56.3–66.8) |
| It would have harmed my career. | 34.5% (29.3–39.8) |
| I did not think treatment would help. | 33.5% (28.4–38.7) |
| I was afraid my supervisor/unit leadership would have a negative opinion of me. | 31.5% (26.4–36.5) |
| I was concerned that the information I gave the counselor might not be kept confidential. | 30.1% (25.0–35.2) |
| Other | 25.8% (20.9–30.6) |
| My coworkers would have had less confidence in me if they found out. | 24.7% (20.0–29.4) |
| It was too difficult to get time off work for treatment. | 24.2% (19.7–28.6) |
| I could have been denied security clearance in the future. | 23.7% (19.1–28.3) |
| It was too difficult to schedule an appointment. | 15.9% (12.0–19.8) |
| I could not afford the cost. | 3.8% (1.6–5.9) |
| It was too difficult to arrange transportation. | 2.1% (0.6–3.7) |
| It was too difficult to get childcare. | 1.6% (0.8–2.5) |
| My commander or supervisor asked me/us not to get treatment. | 1.1% (0.0–2.2) |

NOTE: All data are weighted. 95-percent confidence intervals are presented in parentheses. Respondents could mark more than one reason.

**Stigma Associated with Mental Health Treatment by Military Providers**

Stigma is a complex social and cultural construct that is challenging to define and measure (Link and Phelan, 2001). Even so, stigma is a modest but well-known deterrent to seeking mental health treatment (Clement et al., 2015). There is a growing literature investigating the relationship of stigma and seeking mental health treatment in the military (Acosta et al., 2014), although existing studies find mixed results (Sharp et al., 2015).

A single item in the 2015 HRBS asked respondents to indicate whether they thought it would damage a person's military career if the person was to seek counseling or mental health treatment through the military, regardless of the reason for seeking such services. Response options were yes or no. The aim of the question was to characterize an important aspect of mental health stigma in the military. The question is important for at least two reasons. First, beliefs are an important determinant of behavior, and if one believes that seeking mental health treatment will be detrimental, then they will be less likely to seek assistance. And second, if the perception is pervasive, then policy approaches may be sought to address the perception and any associated reality. The question for 2015 was the same as in previous versions of the HRBS In 2015, however, we dichotomized the response category (yes or no) for brevity. In 2002, 2005, 2008, and 2011, the question used four ordinal response options: (1) It definitely would damage a person's career; (2) It probably would damage a person's career; (3) It probably would *not* damage a person's career; (4) It definitely would *not* damage a person's career. Although a downward trend was observed in the early 2000s, since 2008, the decline in perceived stigma (those who indicated that it definitely or probably would damage a person's career) has stalled (2002: 48.1 percent [Bray, Hourani, Rae, et al., 2003]; 2005: 44.1 percent [Bray, Hourani, Olmstead, et al., 2006]; 2008: 36.1 percent; 2011: 37.7 percent [Bray, Pemberton, et al., 2009). In the 2015 HRBS, 35.0 percent of respondents indicated that seeking mental health treatment would damage a person's military career.

Table 6.58 shows the percentages of individuals who positively reported stigma associated with seeking mental health care treatment from a military provider. Key findings include the following:

- The Army had the highest percentage of individuals reporting that seeking mental health treatment would damage a person's military career, the Air Force had the lowest, and the difference was statistically significant.
- There were no statistically significant differences in percentages by gender, age group, and education level.
- There was significant variation by pay grade. Warrant (W1–W5) and junior officers (O1–O3) registered the highest percentages endorsing the belief, and senior NCOs (E7–E9) and mid-grade and senior officers (O4–O10) registered the lowest.
- Non-Hispanic black service members were the least likely to report this belief, and non-Hispanic whites and service members in the other race/ethnicity category were the most likely.

**Table 6.58**
**Belief That Seeking Mental Health Treatment Would Damage a Person's Military Career, by Subgroup**

| | Believed That Seeking Mental Health Treatment In the Military Would Damage a Person's Career |
|---|---|
| Total | 35.0% (33.3–36.7) |
| Service branch | |
| Air Force | 30.9%[b] (28.7–33.1) |
| Army | 37.0%[a] (33.7–40.4) |
| Marine Corps | 36.0% (31.7–40.3) |
| Navy | 35.2% (32.0–38.5) |
| Coast Guard | 32.9% (31.2–34.6) |
| Pay grade | |
| E1–E4 | 35.4% (32.1–38.7) |
| E5–E6 | 35.6% (32.8–38.4) |
| E7–E9 | 30.4%[d,e] (27.6–33.2) |
| W1–W5 | 40.1%[c,f] (36.2–44.1) |
| O1–O3 | 37.0%[c,f] (34.7–39.4) |
| O4–O10 | 32.1%[d,e] (29.8–34.4) |
| Gender[k] | |
| Men | 35.2% (33.2–37.1) |
| Women | 33.9% (31.9–35.9) |
| Age group[k] | |
| Ages 17–24 | 34.8% (31.0–38.6) |
| Ages 25–34 | 35.9% (33.3–38.6) |
| Ages 35–44 | 34.2% (31.5–36.9) |
| Ages 45+ | 32.5% (28.4–36.6) |
| Race/ethnicity | |
| Non-Hispanic white | 37.7%[h] (35.6–39.8) |
| Non-Hispanic black | 22.4%[g,i,j] (18.3–26.5) |
| Hispanic | 33.2%[h] (28.8–37.7) |

**Table 6.58—Continued**

|  | Believed That Seeking Mental Health Treatment In the Military Would Damage a Person's Career |
|---|---|
| Non-Hispanic Asian | 30.8% (22.3–39.4) |
| Other | 38.6%[h] (33.1–44.0) |
| Education level[k] |  |
| High school or less | 34.5% (30.1–38.9) |
| Some college | 34.7% (32.2–37.2) |
| Bachelor's degree or more | 35.8% (33.3–38.2) |

NOTE: All data are weighted. 95-percent confidence intervals are presented in parentheses.

[a] Estimate is significantly different from the estimate for Air Force.

[b] Estimate is significantly different from the estimate for Army.

[c] Estimate is significantly different from the estimate for E7–E9.

[d] Estimate is significantly different from the estimate for W1–W5.

[e] Estimate is significantly different from the estimate for O1–O3.

[f] Estimate is significantly different from the estimate for O4–O10.

[g] Estimate is significantly different from the estimate for non-Hispanic white.

[h] Estimate is significantly different from the estimate for non-Hispanic black.

[i] Estimate is significantly different from the estimate for Hispanic.

[j] Estimate is significantly different from the estimate for other.

[k] The omnibus chi-square test was not statistically significant ($p > 0.05$).

## Summary

Mental health problems remain a common concern among service members, and mental disorders (depression, GAD, and PTSD) and associated social and emotional problems occur across all branches of the military (particularly the Army, Marine Corps, and Navy), as well as all pay grades and ages. Women and service members with lower levels of education are particularly at risk for experiencing these types of problems. Although comparisons to civilian norms or past iterations of the survey are difficult because of differences in methodologies, measures, and populations, our findings highlight the need to pay particular attention to the role of mental health in the lives and readiness of service members, as well as to the possible impacts that deployment, combat, and exposure to trauma have on their long-term mental well-being.

Overall, nearly one in five service members (17.9 percent) screened positive for at least one of three common, treatable mental disorders (depression, GAD, or PTSD), and 9.7 percent screened positive for two or more disorders. Although the prevalence of depression, anxiety, and PTSD are higher in the HRBS population than in the general population, demographic and other differences between the military and the general populations make it challenging to interpret these contrasts. The Army, Marine Corps, and Navy had consistently higher levels of mental health problems compared with the Air Force and Coast Guard.

Looking across suicide and suicide ideation, results suggest that most behaviors were higher than in past years and compared with civilians. Approximately 11 percent of service members reported a lifetime history of NSSI, and 5.1 percent reported the behavior since joining the military. Alarmingly, 18.1 percent of service members reported thinking about trying to kill themselves at some point in their lives (12.3 percent since joining military), which is well above the roughly 4 percent reported from 2008 to 2014 in the general population (Lipari et al., 2015). Overall, 5.1 percent of service members attempted to kill themselves at some point in their lives (2.6 percent since joining the military, 1.4 percent in the past year).

Aggressive behaviors and impulsivity were highest in the Marine Corps and lowest in the Air Force and Coast Guard. Lifetime experiences of unwanted sexual contact were most commonly reported in the Navy and least commonly reported in the Coast Guard, and they appeared most common when off duty (versus on). We also found that unwanted sexual contact was much more common among women than men, but even among men, a sizable number reported such events. With respect to history of physical abuse, lifetime history was highest in the Army, Navy, and Marine Corps. Overall, the data indicate that although relatively few military personnel have experienced physical abuse while on active duty, a large number of personnel have experienced physical or sexual abuse in their lifetime. Prevention efforts in DoD and the civilian sector could be greatly assisted by recognizing the role that trauma plays in initiating and maintaining poor health habits.

The percentage of service members using mental health services—around one-third of service members in the past year—was significant, perhaps higher than has been previously thought when considering all potential sources of mental health care. Mental health specialists provide about half of mental health services. However, general medical doctors, pastoral counselors (including clergypeople and chaplains), and other providers contribute substantially to mental health services for service members. Unfortunately, there is limited research available from which to assess the equity, quality, consistency, adequacy, and effectiveness of these services. Similarly, a modest majority of mental health services (57 percent) are delivered in military settings; thus, a substantial minority are provided by nonmilitary providers (generalists, specialists, pastoral counselors, or others), and little or nothing is known about the equity, quality, consistency, adequacy, and effectiveness in comparison with care delivered in military settings. Future research is needed in these areas; without such research, it is difficult to assess the adequacy of the complex military mental health service system, which includes military and civilian, as well as clinical and nonclinical, mental health support services.

# CHAPTER SEVEN

# Physical Health and Functional Limitations

This chapter presents analyses of potentially important chronic conditions, physical symptoms, and health-related functional limitations. Military accession, training, and deployment, as well as health-related policies, practices, and exposures, may affect the prevalence of chronic conditions among military service members. These factors may sometimes reduce the prevalence of chronic conditions (e.g., those with serious health problems are often barred from entering military service, and administrative or medical reasons can lead to early attrition) and sometimes increase health risks (e.g., high-impact activities can cause lower-extremity or other joint problems). Chronic health conditions may adversely affect individual, unit, and population readiness, rendering some individuals or units nondeployable or marginally functional in potentially demanding situations, missions, or environments. Within the physical health and functional limitations domain, we examined chronic conditions (diagnosed by a medical provider), physical symptoms (somatic symptoms and pain), and health-related functional limitations (including assessments of absenteeism and presenteeism related to health symptoms).

Each section reviews the relevance of the topic to the military and provides estimates by service branch. We also present results by pay grade, gender, age group, race/ethnicity, and education level. Key measures used are described in the applicable section, and additional details about the measures may be found in Appendix D. All analyses demonstrated statistically significant omnibus tests (a Rao-Scott chi-square test for categorical variables and $F$-tests for continuous variables) unless otherwise noted in the tables. Statistically significant group differences (pairwise comparisons) are presented within each table. However, only statistically significant differences that the research team's subject-matter experts determined to be substantively meaningful (i.e., could be used to change or develop policy or contribute to inequalities in health outcomes across subgroups) are discussed in the text. Readers should use caution when interpreting comparisons between the 2015 HRBS results and other populations or prior versions of the HRBS because these comparisons are not necessarily statistically significant and could simply reflect sampling variability across the two samples being compared; however, where available, we provide confidence intervals for comparisons.

## Chronic Conditions

According to the CDC, 70 percent of U.S. deaths each year are attributed to chronic diseases (CDC, 2016a), and chronic diseases account for the majority of health care costs in the United States (Gerteis et al., 2014). One 2015 HRBS item asked whether respondents had ever been told by a doctor or health professional that they were diagnosed with high blood pressure, high blood sugar or diabetes, high cholesterol, respiratory problems (including asthma, sinusitis, or chronic bronchitis), arthritis, heart disease or other heart condition, ulcer (digestive system), skin cancer, or some other cancer. Response options included within the past two years, more than two years ago, and no. For those conditions marked positively, the survey asked whether the respondent was currently taking a medication for the problem. Results for any lifetime diagnosis of chronic conditions by subgroup (i.e., service branch, pay grade, gender, age group, race/ethnicity, and education level) are shown in Tables 7.1 through 7.6. Key findings include the following:

- Overall, 38.6 percent of service members reported being told by a health care provider that they had at least one of the nine chronic conditions (Table 7.1).
- The prevalence of at least one diagnosis ranged from 31.6 percent in the Air Force to 46.0 percent in the Army. This prevalence suggests the presence of a potentially large group of medically vulnerable service members—a group with implications for force readiness and general health resilience, as well as downstream health care costs and service utilization.
- The most common provider-diagnosed conditions were high blood pressure (17.7 percent), high cholesterol (13.3 percent), and arthritis (12.3 percent). The prevalence of most chronic conditions was lower among active-duty service members than among the general U.S. population, but demographic differences (i.e., distribution of age, gender) between the military and general population make direct comparisons difficult (CDC, 2015c, 2015e, 2016b, 2016d).
- HP2020 set targets for the nation to reduce the prevalence of (1) adults aged 18 or older, excluding pregnant women, with hypertension/high blood pressure to 26.9 percent and (2) adults aged 20 or older with high total blood cholesterol levels to 13.5 percent (HHS, 2010b). Overall, active-duty service members do well against these recommendations. Among service members aged 18 or older, 5.5 percent reported currently taking high blood pressure medication, and among those 20 or older, 3.4 percent reported currently taking medication for high cholesterol. Demographic differences (i.e., distribution of age, gender) between the military and general population limit direct comparisons with these benchmarks. HP2020's high cholesterol goal is based on the proportion of adults with total blood cholesterol of 240 or more milligrams per deciliter and is not equivalent to our measure of self-reported taking of medication for high cholesterol. These measurement and demographic differences should be noted when comparing the prevalence of these two conditions to the HP2020 targets.
- One-third (32.4 percent) of service members reported only one or two chronic conditions, and 6.2 percent reported three or more. The prevalence of one or two diagnoses ranged from 28.1 percent in the Air Force to 37.0 percent in the Army. The prevalence of three or more diagnoses was also lowest in the Air Force (3.5 percent) and highest in the Army (9.0 percent) (Table 7.1).
- As expected, the prevalence of chronic conditions increased with age (Table 7.4). The prevalence of any medical diagnosis increased from 18.5 percent among service members aged 17–24 to 75.2 percent among service members aged 45 or older.
- We also observed increasing prevalence of chronic conditions with increasing pay grade (Table 7.2) and education level (Table 7.6); however, we attribute this trend mainly to the increase in chronic conditions with age.
- The proportion of service members reporting any chronic condition varied by race/ethnicity, from 30.8 percent among Hispanics to 43.6 percent among non-Hispanic blacks (Table 7.5).

**Table 7.1**
**Lifetime Physician-Diagnosed Chronic Conditions and Related Medication Use, by Service Branch**

| | Total (1) | Air Force (2) | Army (3) | Marine Corps (4) | Navy (5) | Coast Guard (6) |
|---|---|---|---|---|---|---|
| Any diagnosis of a chronic condition | 38.6% (37.1–40.0) | 31.6%[b,d] (29.7–33.4) | 46.0%[a,c,d,e] (43.0–49.0) | 33.5%[b] (29.8–37.2) | 36.9%[a,b] (34.2–39.7) | 34.5%[b] (33.1–36.0) |
| High blood pressure | 17.7% (16.5–18.9) | 13.8%[b] (12.3–15.2) | 20.8%[a,e] (18.2–23.3) | 17.4% (14.4–20.4) | 17.2% (15.0–19.4) | 14.2%[b] (13.1–15.3) |
| Currently taking medication | 30.8% (27.6–33.9) | 24.2%[b] (19.7–28.7) | 37.3%[a,c] (31.2–43.4) | 16.8%[b,d,e] (11.2–22.4) | 31.5%[c] (25.5–37.5) | 31.3%[c] (27.8–34.8) |
| Diabetes | 2.6% (2.2–3.0) | 1.4%[b,d,e] (1.0–1.8) | 3.1%[a] (2.3–3.9) | 1.9% (0.9–2.9) | 3.4%[a] (2.4–4.4) | 2.2%[a] (1.8–2.7) |
| Currently taking medication[f] | 26.1% (19.2–33.1) | 23.8% (11.1–36.5) | 28.9% (16.2–41.6) | 17.1% (4.8–29.4) | 26.7% (15.3–38.1) | 19.3% (11.8–26.7) |
| High cholesterol | 13.3% (12.4–14.3) | 9.6%[b,d,e] (8.5–10.7) | 16.7%[a,c] (14.7–18.7) | 7.3%[b,d,e] (5.6–9.0) | 15.0%[a,c] (13.1–16.8) | 15.5%[a,c] (14.5–16.6) |
| Currently taking medication | 24.7% (21.6–27.8) | 18.6%[b] (14.3–23.0) | 28.7%[a] (23.2–34.2) | 17.7% (9.0–26.3) | 23.8% (18.5–29.2) | 22.0% (19.2–24.7) |
| Respiratory problems | 9.5% (8.7–10.3) | 7.1%[b] (6.1–8.1) | 11.2%[a,e] (9.5–12.8) | 10.1%[e] (7.8–12.5) | 9.0%[e] (7.4–10.7) | 6.5%[b,c,d] (5.7–7.2) |
| Currently taking medication | 34.7% (30.6–38.9) | 37.8%[c,e] (30.8–44.8) | 42.8%[c,e] (35.2–50.4) | 16.8%[a,b] (9.9–23.6) | 29.6% (21.0–38.3) | 23.3%[a,b] (18.7–27.8) |
| Arthritis | 12.3% (11.4–13.3) | 9.2%[b] (8.0–10.3) | 17.9%[a,c,d,e] (15.7–20.0) | 10.3%[b] (8.2–12.3) | 8.3%[b] (6.9–9.7) | 8.5%[b] (7.6–9.3) |
| Currently taking medication | 36.8% (32.8–40.7) | 34.6%[e] (28.4–40.9) | 43.4%[c,d,e] (36.9–49.9) | 27.3%[b] (19.1–35.6) | 24.8%[b] (17.7–32.0) | 24.3%[a,b] (20.0–28.6) |
| Heart disease[f] | 3.3% (2.8–3.9) | 2.8% (2.2–3.5) | 3.9% (2.7–5.0) | 3.6% (1.9–5.2) | 3.1% (2.0–4.1) | 1.8% (1.4–2.2) |
| Currently taking medication | 18.2% (12.7–23.7) | 23.5%[c] (12.6–34.3) | 18.4%[c] (9.9–26.9) | 2.7%[a,b,d,e] (0.7–4.7) | 24.4%[c] (8.2–40.6) | 11.2%[c] (5.2–17.2) |
| Ulcer | 3.2% (2.6–3.7) | 2.4%[b] (1.8–3.1) | 4.3%[a,d,e] (3.1–5.6) | 3.1% (1.8–4.3) | 2.2%[b] (1.4–2.9) | 2.2%[b] (1.8–2.7) |
| Currently taking medication[f] | 38.5% (30.1–46.9) | 48.0% (34.8–61.2) | 40.9% (26.1–55.7) | 18.7% (8.9–28.5) | 39.0% (24.4–53.5) | 25.9% (17.8–34.1) |
| Skin cancer[f] | 1.2% (0.9–1.5) | 1.0% (0.7–1.4) | 1.4% (0.8–1.9) | 1.1% (0.3–1.9) | 1.1% (0.7–1.5) | 1.8% (1.5–2.2) |
| Currently taking medication[f] | 3.9% (0.8–7.0) | 9.4% (0.0–23.7) | 3.0% (0.0–6.4) | 3.7% (0.0–7.5) | 0.2% (0.0–0.6) | 3.9% (2.1–11.7) |
| Other cancer[f] | 1.1% (0.9–1.4) | 1.2% (0.8–1.7) | 1.1% (0.6–1.6) | 1.0% (0.1–1.8) | 1.3% (0.7–1.9) | 0.9% (0.6–1.2) |
| Currently taking medication[f] | 13.4% (6.7–20.1) | 19.8% (4.7–34.9) | 10.5% (2.2–18.7) | 13.1% (0.0–35.3) | 11.8% (0.0–26.9) | 11.4% (2.7–20.2) |
| **Number of conditions** | | | | | | |
| No conditions | 61.4% (60.0–62.9) | 68.4%[b,d] (66.6–70.3) | 54.0%[a,c,d,e] (51.0–57.0) | 66.5%[b] (62.8–70.2) | 63.1%[a,b] (60.3–65.8) | 65.5%[b] (64.0–66.9) |
| 1–2 conditions | 32.4% (30.9–33.8) | 28.1%[b] (26.2–29.9) | 37.0%[a,c,d,e] (34.0–40.0) | 29.0%[b] (25.4–32.5) | 31.3%[b] (28.6–33.9) | 30.6%[b] (29.1–32.0) |
| 3+ conditions | 6.2% (5.5–6.9) | 3.5%[b,d] (2.8–4.1) | 9.0%[a,c,d,e] (7.5–10.5) | 4.6%[b] (3.1–6.1) | 5.6%[a,b] (4.4–6.9) | 4.0%[b] (3.4–4.5) |

NOTE: All data are weighted. 95-percent confidence intervals are presented in parentheses.
[a] Estimate is significantly different from the estimate in column 2 (Air Force).
[b] Estimate is significantly different from the estimate in column 3 (Army).
[c] Estimate is significantly different from the estimate in column 4 (Marine Corps).
[d] Estimate is significantly different from the estimate in column 5 (Navy).
[e] Estimate is significantly different from the estimate in column 6 (Coast Guard).
[f] The omnibus chi-square test was not statistically significant ($p > 0.05$).

**Table 7.2**
**Lifetime Physician-Diagnosed Chronic Conditions and Related Medication Use, by Pay Grade**

| | E1–E4 (1) | E5–E6 (2) | E7–E9 (3) | W1–W5 (4) | O1–O3 (5) | O4–O10 (6) |
|---|---|---|---|---|---|---|
| Any diagnosis of a chronic condition | 24.3% b,c,d,e,f (21.6–27.0) | 46.7% a,c,d,e,f (44.1–49.4) | 66.9% a,b,e,f (64.4–69.4) | 67.9% a,b,e (64.4–71.4) | 34.5% a,b,c,d,f (32.3–36.6) | 58.4% a,b,c,d,e (56.1–60.7) |
| High blood pressure | 12.3% b,c,d,f (10.1–14.4) | 21.8% a,c,d,e (19.5–24.1) | 29.6% a,b,e,f (27.0–32.1) | 31.2% a,b,e (27.7–34.7) | 14.5% b,c,d,f (12.8–16.2) | 21.1% a,c,d,e (19.1–23.1) |
| Currently taking medication[9] | 16.1% b,c,d,f (8.9–23.2) | 33.7% a,f (27.9–39.5) | 43.2% a,e (38.0–48.5) | 46.4% a,e (39.5–53.3) | 24.8% c,d,f (19.1–30.5) | 51.8% a,b,e (46.5–57.1) |
| Diabetes | 0.9% b,c,d,f (0.4–1.4) | 3.8% a,e (2.6–4.9) | 6.4% a,e (5.0–7.8) | 4.7% a,e (3.1–6.2) | 1.6% b,c,d,f (1.0–2.2) | 4.2% a,e (3.2–5.1) |
| Currently taking medication[9] | 8.9% (2.3–15.5) | 30.9% (16.2–45.6) | 28.6% (18.0–39.2) | 33.2% (16.6–49.9) | 32.6% (12.5–52.7) | 22.4% (11.8–33.1) |
| High cholesterol | 4.8% b,c,d,e,f (3.3–6.2) | 16.3% a,c,d,e,f (14.2–18.4) | 30.7% a,b,e (28.0–33.3) | 35.4% a,b (31.7–39.0) | 12.2% a,b,c,d,f (10.6–13.7) | 31.1% a,b,e (28.9–33.4) |
| Currently taking medication | 11.9% (0.6–23.2) | 19.2% c,d,f (13.4–25.1) | 34.7% b,e (29.6–39.8) | 38.2% b,e (31.8–44.5) | 18.4% c,d,f (12.8–24.1) | 37.4% b,e (33.0–41.8) |
| Respiratory problems | 6.2% b,c,d,e,f (4.9–7.6) | 11.2% a,c,d (9.5–12.9) | 16.5% a,b,e (14.4–18.6) | 16.2% a,b (13.5–19.0) | 9.3% a,c,d,f (8.0–10.7) | 12.8% a,e (11.2–14.4) |
| Currently taking medication | 22.2% b,c,d (12.7–31.8) | 43.1% a,e (35.0–51.1) | 43.2% a,e (36.4–50.0) | 46.4% a,e (37.1–55.7) | 24.4% b,c,d (18.0–30.9) | 35.7% (29.1–42.3) |
| Arthritis | 5.7% b,c,d,f (4.1–7.2) | 15.6% a,c,d,e,f (13.6–17.6) | 28.9% a,b,e,f (26.3–31.4) | 32.4% a,b,e,f (28.9–35.9) | 7.9% b,c,d,f (6.6–9.3) | 21.7% a,b,c,d,e (19.7–23.6) |
| Currently taking medication | 33.1% c,f (19.9–46.4) | 38.9% c (31.8–45.9) | 39.4% a,b,e (34.1–44.6) | 40.4% e (33.9–46.6) | 23.9% c,d,f (16.6–31.2) | 37.2% a,e (32.0–42.4) |
| Heart disease | 2.5% c,f (1.5–3.5) | 3.5% c (2.5–4.6) | 6.2% a,b,e (4.8–7.5) | 5.1% e (3.4–6.8) | 2.3% c,d,f (1.6–3.0) | 5.1% a,e (4.0–6.1) |
| Currently taking medication[9] | 10.1% (0.5–19.7) | 19.9% (7.6–32.2) | 26.9% (16.1–37.7) | 21.0% (6.6–35.4) | 24.8% (10.3–39.3) | 20.0% (10.6–29.4) |
| Ulcer | 2.6% c,d (1.5–3.5) | 2.5% c,d,f (1.8–3.2) | 6.5% a,b,e (5.1–7.9) | 6.5% a,b (4.6–8.4) | 2.9% c,d,f (2.1–3.7) | 4.9% b,e (3.8–6.0) |
| Currently taking medication[9] | 31.7% (11.4–52.0) | 40.8% (27.9–53.6) | 43.9% (32.4–55.4) | 49.8% (34.3–64.) | 35.2% (22.1–48.4) | 47.0% (35.3–58.7) |

**Table 7.2—Continued**

|  | E1–E4 (1) | E5–E6 (2) | E7–E9 (3) | W1–W5 (4) | O1–O3 (5) | O4–O10 (6) |
|---|---|---|---|---|---|---|
| Skin cancer | 0.5%c,d,f (0.1–1.0) | 0.8%c,d,f (0.3–1.3) | 2.4%a,b,e,f (1.6–3.3) | 3.0%a,b,e,f (1.8–4.1) | 0.7%c,d,f (0.4–1.1) | 6.4%a,b,c,d,e (5.2–7.6) |
| Currently taking medication[h] | † | 8.3% (0.0–21.8) | 2.5% (0.0–5.2) | 3.0% (1.1–4.9) | NA | 4.9% (0.1–9.7) |
| Other cancer | 0.7%c (0.2–1.2) | 1.2%c (0.7–1.6) | 2.6%a,b,e (1.7–3.5) | 2.2% (1.1–3.2) | 0.9%c,f (0.5–1.3) | 2.0%e (1.4–2.6) |
| Currently taking medication[h] | † | 25.1% (4.7–45.4) | 11.6% (0.0–23.4) | 9.7% (1.1–18.3) | 6.9% (1.6–12.1) | 25.5% (10.8–40.2) |
| **Number of conditions** |  |  |  |  |  |  |
| No conditions | 75.7%b,c,d,e,f (73.0–78.4) | 53.3%a,c,d,e,f (50.6–55.9) | 33.1%a,b,e,f (30.6–35.6) | 32.1%a,b,e,f (28.6–35.6) | 65.5%a,b,c,d,f (63.4–67.7) | 41.6%a,b,c,d,e (39.3–43.9) |
| 1–2 conditions | 21.7%b,c,d,e,f (19.1–24.3) | 39.6%a,c,d,e,f (37.0–42.2) | 50.6%a,b,e,f (47.8–53.4) | 49.1%a,b,e (45.3–52.8) | 30.9%a,b,c,d,f (28.8–33.0) | 45.0%a,b,c,e (42.6–47.3) |
| 3+ conditions | 2.5%b,c,d,f (1.5–3.6) | 7.2%a,c,d,e,f (5.7–8.6) | 16.3%a,b,e (14.2–18.5) | 18.9%a,b,e,f (15.9–21.8) | 3.6%b,c,d,f (2.7–4.5) | 13.4%a,b,d,e (11.7–15.1) |

NOTE: All data are weighted. 95-percent confidence intervals are presented in parentheses.

[a] Estimate is significantly different from the estimate in column 1 (E1–E4).

[b] Estimate is significantly different from the estimate in column 2 (E5–E6).

[c] Estimate is significantly different from the estimate in column 3 (E7–E9).

[d] Estimate is significantly different from the estimate in column 4 (W1–W5).

[e] Estimate is significantly different from the estimate in column 5 (O1–O3).

[f] Estimate is significantly different from the estimate in column 6 (O4–O10).

[g] The omnibus chi-square test was not statistically significant ($p > 0.05$).

[h] Because there were too few respondents for at least one category, we do not report an omnibus chi-square test.

† = Too few respondents to report (denominator < 20).

NA = not applicable (zero individuals in the cell).

Table 7.3
**Lifetime Physician-Diagnosed Chronic Conditions and Related Medication Use, by Gender**

| | Men (1) | Women (2) |
|---|---|---|
| Any diagnosis of a chronic condition[b] | 38.9% (37.2–40.6) | 37.0% (35.2–38.8) |
| High blood pressure | 18.9%[a] (17.5–20.3) | 11.0% (9.8–12.2) |
| Currently taking medication[b] | 30.7% (27.2–34.2) | 31.4% (26.2–36.6) |
| Diabetes[b] | 2.6% (2.1–3.1) | 2.5% (1.9–3.0) |
| Currently taking medication[b] | 27.3% (19.3–35.4) | 19.4% (10.9–27.9) |
| High cholesterol | 14.3%[a] (13.2–15.4) | 8.3% (7.4–9.2) |
| Currently taking medication | 26.0%[a] (22.6–29.4) | 12.6% (9.5–15.6) |
| Respiratory problems | 8.6%[a] (7.7–9.5) | 14.3% (13.0–15.6) |
| Currently taking medication[b] | 33.3% (28.1–38.5) | 39.4% (34.6–44.2) |
| Arthritis[b] | 12.2% (11.1–13.3) | 13.2% (12.1–14.3) |
| Currently taking medication[b] | 37.0% (32.3–41.7) | 35.6% (31.2–40.0) |
| Heart disease[b] | 3.4% (2.8–4.1) | 2.9% (2.3–3.5) |
| Currently taking medication[b] | 17.4% (11.3–23.5) | 23.4% (12.7–34.0) |
| Ulcer[b] | 3.0% (2.4–3.7) | 3.9% (3.2–4.6) |
| Currently taking medication[b] | 39.7% (29.6–49.9) | 33.2% (25.0–41.4) |
| Skin cancer[b] | 1.2% (0.9–1.5) | 1.2% (0.8–1.5) |
| Currently taking medication[b] | 3.8% (0.1–7.4) | 4.7% (2.5–6.8) |
| Other cancer | 1.0%[a] (0.7–1.3) | 1.9% (1.4–2.3) |
| Currently taking medication[b] | 13.4% (4.5–22.3) | 13.5% (8.1–18.8) |
| **Number of conditions** | | |
| No conditions[b] | 61.1% (59.4–62.8) | 63.0% (61.2–64.8) |
| 1–2 conditions[b] | 32.5% (30.8–34.1) | 31.7% (30.0–33.5) |
| 3+ conditions[b] | 6.4% (5.6–7.2) | 5.3% (4.6–6.0) |

NOTE: All data are weighted. 95-percent confidence intervals are presented in parentheses.

[a] Estimate is significantly different from the estimate in column 2 (women).

[b] The omnibus chi-square test was not statistically significant ($p > 0.05$).

**Table 7.4**
**Lifetime Physician-Diagnosed Chronic Conditions and Related Medication Use, by Age Group**

|  | Ages 17–24 (1) | Ages 25–34 (2) | Ages 35–44 (3) | Ages 45+ (4) |
|---|---|---|---|---|
| Any diagnosis of a chronic condition | 18.5%[b,c,d] (15.8–21.2) | 34.7%[a,c,d] (32.3–37.2) | 60.1%[a,b,d] (57.4–62.7) | 75.2%[a,b,c] (71.8–78.5) |
| High blood pressure | 10.0%[b,c,d] (7.8–12.1) | 17.0%[a,c,d] (15.0–19.0) | 24.3%[a,b,d] (22.0–26.5) | 32.8%[a,b,c] (29.1–36.5) |
| Currently taking medication | 8.6%[c,d] (1.9–15.2) | 19.5%[c,d] (14.0–25.0) | 42.8%[a,b,d] (37.4–48.2) | 65.3%[a,b,c] (59.0–71.7) |
| Diabetes | 0.9%[c,d] (0.3–1.5) | 1.7%[c,d] (1.1–2.3) | 4.6%[a,b,d] (3.5–5.7) | 8.4%[a,b,c] (6.0–10.7) |
| Currently taking medication[f] | † | 22.0% (8.6–35.5) | 31.6% (19.7–43.5) | 31.1% (17.1–45.1) |
| High cholesterol | 2.3%[b,c,d] (1.2–3.3) | 8.8%[a,c,d] (7.3–10.2) | 26.5%[a,b,d] (24.1–28.9) | 44.2%[a,b,c] (40.3–48.2) |
| Currently taking medication | 5.8% (0.0–17.1) | 7.2%[c,d] (3.2–11.2) | 26.2%[b,d] (21.3–31.0) | 47.5%[b,c] (41.1–53.8) |
| Respiratory problems | 5.9%[c,d] (4.4–7.4) | 8.2%[c,d] (6.9–9.5) | 13.6%[a,b,d] (11.8–15.3) | 19.1%[a,b,c] (16.1–22.2) |
| Currently taking medication | 12.9%[b,c,d] (5.0–20.7) | 36.4%[a] (28.6–44.2) | 40.5%[a] (33.4–47.6) | 45.2%[a] (36.3–54.1) |
| Arthritis | 3.5%[b,c,d] (2.1–4.9) | 8.1%[a,c,d] (6.7–9.5) | 23.6%[a,b,d] (21.2–25.9) | 38.2%[a,b,c] (34.5–41.9) |
| Currently taking medication[e] | 30.9% (10.8–50.9) | 33.3% (24.3–42.3) | 37.7% (32.0–43.4) | 41.6% (35.8–47.4) |
| Heart disease | 2.1%[d] (1.1–3.1) | 2.6%[d] (1.7–3.5) | 4.2%[d] (3.1–5.2) | 10.3%[a,b,c] (7.9–12.8) |
| Currently taking medication | 13.9% (0.0–29.4) | 7.7%[d] (1.9–13.5) | 23.2% (12.3–34.0) | 31.6%[b] (19.4–43.8) |
| Ulcer | 2.1%[d] (1.0–3.3) | 2.6%[c,d] (1.7–3.4) | 4.4%[b] (3.4–5.4) | 6.8%[a,b] (5.2–8.5) |
| Currently taking medication[e] | 21.2% (0.0–44.5) | 38.8% (21.2–56.4) | 36.8% (26.4–47.2) | 63.3% (52.1–74.4) |
| Skin cancer | 0.5%[c,d] (0.1–0.9) | 0.6%[c,d] (0.1–1.0) | 1.8%[a,b,d] (1.3–2.3) | 6.0%[a,b,c] (4.6–7.3) |
| Currently taking medication[f] | † | 1.8% (0.8–2.8) | 1.0% (0.0–2.5) | 9.5% (0.8–18.1) |
| Other cancer | 0.5%[c,d] (0.1–0.9) | 1.0%[d] (0.5–1.5) | 1.6%[a,d] (1.1–2.1) | 3.4%[a,b,c] (2.2–4.7) |
| Currently taking medication[f] | † | 8.6% (0.0–19.5) | 11.7% (2.5–21.0) | 25.9% (8.5–43.4) |

**Table 7.4—Continued**

| | Ages 17–24 (1) | Ages 25–34 (2) | Ages 35–44 (3) | Ages 45+ (4) |
|---|---|---|---|---|
| **Number of conditions** | | | | |
| No conditions | 81.5%[b,c,d] (78.8–84.2) | 65.3%[a,c,d] (62.8–67.7) | 39.9%[a,b,d] (37.3–42.6) | 24.8%[a,b,c] (21.5–28.2) |
| 1–2 conditions | 16.9%[b,c,d] (14.2–19.5) | 31.3%[a,c,d] (29.0–33.7) | 48.7%[a,b] (46.0–51.4) | 49.8%[a,b] (45.9–53.7) |
| 3+ conditions | 1.6%[c,d] (0.7–2.6) | 3.4%[c,d] (2.4–4.4) | 11.4%[a,b,d] (9.7–13.2) | 25.3%[a,b,c] (22.1–28.6) |

NOTE: All data are weighted. 95-percent confidence intervals are presented in parentheses.

[a] Estimate is significantly different from the estimate in column 1 (ages 17–24).

[b] Estimate is significantly different from the estimate in column 2 (ages 25–34).

[c] Estimate is significantly different from the estimate in column 3 (ages 35–44).

[d] Estimate is significantly different from the estimate in column 4 (ages 45+).

[e] The omnibus chi-square test was not statistically significant ($p > 0.05$).

[f] Because there were too few respondents for at least one category, we do not report an omnibus chi-square test.

† = Too few respondents to report (denominator < 20).

**Table 7.5**
**Lifetime Physician-Diagnosed Chronic Conditions and Related Medication Use, by Race/Ethnicity**

| | Non-Hispanic White (1) | Non-Hispanic Black (2) | Hispanic (3) | Non-Hispanic Asian (4) | Other (5) |
|---|---|---|---|---|---|
| Any diagnosis of a chronic condition | 38.8%[c] (36.9–40.7) | 43.6%[c] (38.9–48.2) | 30.8%[a,b,e] (27.1–34.6) | 41.6% (33.7–49.5) | 43.4%[c] (38.3–48.4) |
| High blood pressure | 17.6%[b,c] (16.0–19.2) | 23.4%[a,c] (19.4–27.4) | 11.7%[a,b,e] (9.1–14.2) | 18.7% (12.7–24.7) | 21.7%[c] (17.6–25.9) |
| Currently taking medication | 24.1%[b] (20.3–27.8) | 53.4%[a,c,e] (43.8–62.9) | 32.5%[b] (22.6–42.4) | 30.9% (16.9–45.0) | 33.2%[b] (23.6–42.9) |
| Diabetes | 2.1%[d] (1.6–2.6) | 3.3% (1.9–4.8) | 2.5% (1.4–3.6) | 5.6%[a] (2.6–8.6) | 3.4% (1.8–4.9) |
| Currently taking medication[f] | 19.6% (9.8–29.4) | 33.2% (12.7–53.7) | 21.9% (8.1–35.6) | 49.2% (21.7–76.6) | 28.5% (9.5–47.4) |
| High cholesterol | 12.6%[d] (11.5–13.8) | 15.6% (12.2–19.0) | 10.7%[d] (8.5–12.8) | 23.9%[a,c,e] (17.2–30.7) | 14.3%[d] (11.1–17.4) |
| Currently taking medication[g] | 23.7% (19.9–27.5) | 17.3% (11.4–23.1) | 32.1% (22.4–41.8) | 35.6% (20.1–51.1) | 20.0% (12.2–27.7) |
| Respiratory problems | 9.9%[c] (8.7–11.0) | 10.6% (8.1–13.0) | 6.8%[a,e] (5.2–8.4) | 5.7%[e] (2.7–8.7) | 12.7%[c,d] (9.7–15.8) |
| Currently taking medication | 31.8%[c] (26.4–37.2) | 43.9% (32.0–55.8) | 50.3%[a,e] (38.5–62.2) | 21.4% (3.4–39.4) | 27.4%[c] (17.2–37.6) |
| Arthritis | 12.8%[d] (11.5–14.1) | 15.2%[c,d] (12.3–18.1) | 9.2%[b,e] (7.1–11.4) | 5.9%[a,b,e] (3.6–8.3) | 14.9%[c,d] (11.2–18.6) |
| Currently taking medication[f] | 36.3% (31.1–41.5) | 47.4% (37.3–57.5) | 32.8% (20.9–44.7) | 28.3% (10.8–45.9) | 30.3% (19.3–41.4) |
| Heart disease[f] | 2.9% (2.2–3.5) | 5.1% (2.8–7.3) | 3.4% (1.8–5.0) | 2.8% (0.4–5.2) | 4.4% (2.4–6.4) |
| Currently taking medication[h] | 18.0% (9.8–26.1) | 9.9% (2.1–17.6) | 23.6% (7.0–40.2) | † | 19.1% (5.6–32.6) |
| Ulcer[f] | 3.0% (2.3–3.7) | 3.5% (1.8–5.3) | 2.8% (1.3–4.4) | 2.9% (1.4–4.5) | 4.3% (2.6–6.0) |
| Currently taking medication[f] | 35.1% (24.5–45.7) | 41.9% (17.1–66.7) | 42.1% (13.7–70.4) | 45.1% (19.2–71.1) | 42.3% (27.8–56.7) |

**Table 7.5—Continued**

| | Non-Hispanic White (1) | Non-Hispanic Black (2) | Hispanic (3) | Non-Hispanic Asian (4) | Other (5) |
|---|---|---|---|---|---|
| Skin cancer[f] | 1.6% (1.2–2.0) | 0.4% (0.0–0.8) | 0.7% (0.1–1.3) | 0.5% (0.0–1.4) | 1.0% (0.3–1.6) |
|   Currently taking medication[h] | 1.8% (0.2–3.3) | † | 17.6% (0.0–43.7) | † | 9.9% (0.0–24.8) |
| Other cancer[f] | 1.1% (0.7–1.5) | 1.2% (0.5–1.9) | 0.9% (0.3–1.5) | 0.9% (0.0–1.8) | 1.7% (0.7–2.7) |
|   Currently taking medication[h] | 17.1% (7.4–26.8) | 2.6% (0.0–5.7) | 13.3% (0.0–34.5) | † | 7.9% (0.0–17.9) |
| **Number of conditions** | | | | | |
| No conditions | 61.2%[c] (59.3–63.1) | 56.4%[c] (51.8–61.1) | 69.2%[a,b,e] (65.4–72.9) | 58.4% (50.5–66.3) | 56.6%[c] (51.6–61.6) |
| 1–2 conditions[g] | 33.0% (31.2–34.9) | 34.3% (29.9–38.7) | 27.2% (23.6–30.8) | 36.5% (28.7–44.3) | 32.7% (28.1–37.3) |
| 3+ conditions | 5.7%[b,e] (4.9–6.6) | 9.3%[a,c] (6.6–12.0) | 3.6%[b,e] (2.4–4.8) | 5.0% (2.7–7.4) | 10.7%[a,c] (7.5–13.9) |

NOTE: All data are weighted. 95-percent confidence intervals are presented in parentheses.

[a] Estimate is significantly different from the estimate in column 1 (non-Hispanic white).

[b] Estimate is significantly different from the estimate in column 2 (non-Hispanic black).

[c] Estimate is significantly different from the estimate in column 3 (Hispanic).

[d] Estimate is significantly different from the estimate in column 4 (non-Hispanic Asian).

[e] Estimate is significantly different from the estimate in column 5 (other).

[f] The omnibus chi-square test was not statistically significant ($p > 0.05$).

[g] At the aggregate, the chi-square test was statistically significant; however, none of the individual pairwise comparisons was.

[h] Because there were too few respondents for at least one category, we do not report an omnibus chi-square test.

† = Too few respondents to report (denominator < 20).

**Table 7.6**
**Lifetime Physician-Diagnosed Chronic Conditions and Related Medication Use, by Education Level**

| | High School or Less (1) | Some College (2) | Bachelor's Degree or More (3) |
|---|---|---|---|
| Any diagnosis of a chronic condition | 26.5%[b,c] (22.9–30.1) | 40.1%[a,c] (37.9–42.4) | 44.1%[a,b] (41.8–46.4) |
| High blood pressure | 13.9%[b] (11.1–16.7) | 19.4%[a] (17.5–21.2) | 17.6% (15.8–19.4) |
|   Currently taking medication | 18.8%[b,c] (10.9–26.6) | 32.7%[a] (27.7–37.6) | 33.7%[a] (29.2–38.1) |
| Diabetes | 1.4%[b] (0.7–2.2) | 3.0%[a] (2.3–3.7) | 2.8% (2.1–3.4) |
|   Currently taking medication[d] | 17.3% (3.6–31.1) | 24.3% (15.0–33.5) | 32.3% (19.9–44.7) |
| High cholesterol | 6.6%[b,c] (4.7–8.5) | 12.6%[a,c] (11.1–14.0) | 19.0%[a,b] (17.3–20.7) |
|   Currently taking medication[d] | 17.1% (7.8–26.4) | 24.1% (19.1–29.1) | 27.1% (23.0–31.2) |
| Respiratory problems | 7.1%[b] (5.2–9.0) | 10.2%[a] (8.9–11.5) | 9.9% (8.7–11.1) |
|   Currently taking medication | 19.7%[b,c] (10.8–28.6) | 37.3%[a] (30.8–43.8) | 37.6%[a] (31.3–43.9) |

**Table 7.6—Continued**

| | High School or Less (1) | Some College (2) | Bachelor's Degree or More (3) |
|---|---|---|---|
| Arthritis | 7.8%[b,c] (5.5–10.1) | 13.4%[a] (11.9–15.0) | 13.6%[a] (12.4–14.8) |
|    Currently taking medication[d] | 38.5% (24.2–52.7) | 36.8% (30.7–43.0) | 36.0% (31.6–40.5) |
| Heart disease[d] | 2.7% (1.4–4.0) | 3.0% (2.2–3.8) | 4.2% (3.3–5.2) |
|    Currently taking medication[d] | 4.5% (0.0–10.7) | 19.9% (11.2–28.6) | 22.1% (12.2–31.9) |
| Ulcer[d] | 2.4% (1.2–3.7) | 3.0% (2.2–3.8) | 3.9% (3.1–4.8) |
|    Currently taking medication[d] | 27.2% (9.6–44.8) | 34.3% (22.1–46.6) | 48.0% (37.2–58.9) |
| Skin cancer | 0.9% (0.0–1.7) | 0.9%[c] (0.5–1.2) | 1.9%[b] (1.6–2.3) |
|    Currently taking medication[e] | † | 1.1% (0.4–1.7) | 3.8% (0.6–7.0) |
| Other cancer[d] | 0.9% (0.0–1.8) | 1.1% (0.8–1.5) | 1.3% (1.0–1.6) |
|    Currently taking medication[e] | † | 10.8% (0.7–20.9) | 15.2% (6.9–23.6) |
| **Number of conditions** | | | |
| No conditions | 73.5%[b,c] (69.9–77.1) | 59.9%[a,c] (57.6–62.1) | 55.9%[a,b] (53.6–58.2) |
| 1–2 conditions | 22.5%[b,c] (19.1–25.9) | 33.6%[a] (31.5–35.8) | 36.9%[a] (34.6–39.1) |
| 3+ conditions | 4.0%[c] (2.3–5.6) | 6.5% (5.4–7.6) | 7.2%[a] (6.3–8.1) |

NOTE: All data are weighted. 95-percent confidence intervals are presented in parentheses.

[a] Estimate is significantly different from the estimate in column 1 (high school or less).

[b] Estimate is significantly different from the estimate in column 2 (some college).

[c] Estimate is significantly different from the estimate in column 3 (bachelor's degree or more).

[d] The omnibus chi-square test was not statistically significant ($p > 0.05$).

[e] Because there were too few respondents for at least one category, we do not report an omnibus chi-square test.

† = Too few respondents to report (denominator < 20).

## Physical Symptoms

Physical symptoms, usually presenting as multiple physical symptoms, account for more than half of outpatient visits in the general population and are associated with expensive tests and procedures (Kroenke, 2014). One-third of somatic symptoms do not have a disease-based explanation and are considered to be medically unexplained (Kroenke, 2003). Physical symptoms are also associated with increased comorbidities, including depression and anxiety, and with functional impairment (Kroenke et al., 1994; Kroenke, Jackson, and Chamberlin, 1997; Escobar et al., 1987; Kroenke, 2003; Hoedeman et al., 2010; Creed et al., 2012). Physical symptoms are common in the military, and multiple physical symptoms have been reported following deployment; in particular, chronic multisymptom illness was reported following Gulf War deployment (Hyams, Wignall, and Roswell, 1996; Fukuda et al., 1998).

HRBS respondents completed a symptom checklist comprising eight common physical symptoms (stomach or bowel problems; back pain; pain in the arms, legs, or joints; headaches; chest pain or shortness of breath; dizziness; feeling tired or having low energy; trouble sleeping[1]) using the Somatic Symptom Scale-8 (Gierk et al., 2014). Response options referenced the past 30 days and included not bothered at all, bothered a little bit, and bothered a lot. In addition to reporting the proportion of respondents who indicated being bothered a lot by *each* symptom, we present a summary measure of the proportion bothered a lot by *any* of the symptoms. We also developed a summary score by assigning each symptom a score of 0 (not bothered at all), 1 (bothered a little bit), or 2 (bothered a lot); adding the values across all eight measures (score range = 0–16); and creating a measure of *high physical symptom severity*, defined as a score of eight or higher.

Results can be found in Tables 7.7 through 7.12. Key findings include the following:

- The most-common somatic symptoms that service members reported being bothered a lot by in the past month were trouble sleeping (25.0 percent); feeling tired or having low energy (23.2 percent); back pain (22.5 percent); and pain in the arms, legs, or joints (22.0 percent) (Table 7.7).
- Overall, 35.7 percent of service members reported being bothered a lot by at least one physical symptom (including headaches) in the past 30 days. The prevalence of any symptom was lowest in the Coast Guard (24.3 percent) and highest in the Army (42.5 percent) and Marine Corps (40.4 percent) (Table 7.7).
- Among service members, 21.1 percent had a high physical symptom severity score (≥ 8). The Marine Corps and Army had the highest prevalence of high physical symptom severity (25.8 percent and 25.6 percent, respectively) (Table 7.7).
- Reports of being bothered by any physical symptom appeared to be more common among enlisted service members: More than half of senior NCOs (E7–E9) reported being bothered a lot by at least one physical symptom (including headaches) (50.8 percent) (Table 7.8).
- On average, women reported being bothered a lot by somatic symptoms more than men (Table 7.9). For example, women were more likely than men to report being bothered a lot by headaches (19.1 percent compared with 10.5 percent), feeling tired or having low

---

[1] Note that trouble sleeping could also be considered symptomatic of either a mental or physical health problem (see, for example, Swinkels et al., 2013).

188 2015 Department of Defense Health Related Behaviors Survey of Active-Duty Service Members: Final Report

energy (31.7 percent compared with 21.7 percent), and at least one symptom (including headaches) (41.4 percent compared with 34.7 percent). This is consistent with the well-characterized epidemiology of physical symptoms in other populations (e.g., Kroenke and Spitzer, 1998; Barsky, Peekna, and Borus, 2001).

- As expected, somatic symptoms increased with age (Table 7.10). The prevalence of service members being bothered a lot by at least one symptom (including headaches) increased from 30.4 percent among service members aged 17–24 to 53.6 percent among service members 45 or older.
- There was little evidence that somatic symptoms varied by race/ethnicity; however, the prevalence of high physical symptom severity ranged from 18.8 percent among non-Hispanic whites to 25.6 percent among non-Hispanic blacks (Table 7.11).
- There was not notable variation in somatic symptoms by level of education, but the prevalence appeared to be lowest, on average, among those with a bachelor's degree or more (Table 7.12).

We also examined the relationship between being bothered a lot by at least one physical symptom (in the past 30 days) and prescription drug misuse, defined as use of stimulant, sedative, or opioid prescriptions in the past year without a prescription (see Chapter Five for more details on prescription drug use and misuse). Overall, among service members who reported being bothered a lot by at least one physical symptom in the past 30 days, 0.5 percent reported stimulant misuse, 2.6 percent reported sedative misuse, and 3.4 percent reported opioid misuse (Table 7.13). Among individuals being bothered by physical symptoms, self-reported sedative misuse ranged from 1.5 percent in the Marine Corps to 3.6 percent in the Air Force (not a statistically significant difference), and self-reported opioid misuse ranged from 2.3 percent in the Coast Guard to 4.1 percent in the Army (not a statistically significant difference).

Table 7.7
Bothered a Lot by Physical Symptoms in the Past 30 Days, by Service Branch

| | Total (1) | Air Force (2) | Army (3) | Marine Corps (4) | Navy (5) | Coast Guard (6) |
|---|---|---|---|---|---|---|
| Stomach or bowel problems | 8.7% (7.8–9.5) | 6.9% b,c (5.9–8.0) | 9.8% a,e (8.1–11.6) | 10.5% a,e (8.0–13.1) | 7.7% (6.2–9.3) | 5.5% b,c (4.8–6.3) |
| Back pain | 22.5% (21.2–23.9) | 16.2% b,c (14.7–17.8) | 27.9% a,d,e (25.0–30.7) | 26.1% a,d,e (22.6–29.7) | 18.9% b,c,e (16.5–21.2) | 15.0% b,c,d (13.9–16.2) |
| Pain in the arms, legs, or joints | 22.0% (20.6–23.4) | 15.1% b,c (13.5–16.7) | 27.6% a,d,e (24.7–30.5) | 26.4% a,d,e (22.9–30.0) | 18.2% b,c,e (15.9–20.6) | 12.5% b,c,d (11.5–13.6) |
| Headaches | 11.8% (10.8–12.8) | 8.3% b,c,d (7.2–9.5) | 13.6% a,e (11.6–15.7) | 13.8% a,e (11.0–16.7) | 11.8% a,e (9.8–13.7) | 6.8% b,c,d (6.0–7.7) |
| Chest pain or shortness of breath | 4.7% (4.0–5.3) | 3.5% c (2.7–4.3) | 5.2% e (3.9–6.6) | 6.9% a,e (4.7–9.2) | 3.8% (2.6–5.0) | 2.5% b,c (1.9–3.0) |
| Dizziness | 4.4% (3.8–5.1) | 3.4% (2.7–4.3) | 5.5% e (4.1–6.8) | 5.6% e (3.6–7.7) | 3.2% (2.2–4.2) | 2.7% b,c (2.1–3.3) |
| Feeling tired or having low energy | 23.2% (21.9–24.6) | 16.8% b,c,d (15.2–18.5) | 25.0% a,e (22.2–27.7) | 26.7% a,e (23.1–30.4) | 25.4% a,e (22.7–28.2) | 16.3% b,c,d (15.0–17.5) |
| Trouble sleeping | 25.0% (23.6–26.4) | 17.0% b,c,d (15.3–18.6) | 28.6% a,e (25.8–31.5) | 31.6% a,d,e (27.7–35.4) | 23.9% a,c,e (21.2–26.7) | 16.8% b,c,d (15.6–18.1) |
| At least one symptom (excluding headaches) | 32.1% (30.6–33.6) | 24.3% b,c (22.5–26.2) | 38.7% a,d,e (35.6–41.8) | 36.5% a,d,e (32.6–40.4) | 27.6% b,c,e (24.9–30.3) | 21.6% b,c,d (20.3–22.9) |
| At least one symptom (including headaches) | 35.7% (34.2–37.3) | 27.5% b,c (25.6–29.4) | 42.5% a,d,e (39.4–45.7) | 40.4% a,d,e (36.4–44.4) | 31.4% b,c,e (28.6–34.3) | 24.3% b,c,d (23.0–25.7) |
| High physical symptom severity | 21.1% (19.8–22.4) | 13.6% b,c,d,e (12.1–15.1) | 25.6% a,c,d,e (22.9–28.3) | 25.8% a,b,d,e (22.2–29.4) | 19.7% a,b,c,e (17.2–22.1) | 11.2% a,b,c,d (10.1–12.2) |

NOTE: All data are weighted. 95-percent confidence intervals are presented in parentheses.

a Estimate is significantly different from the estimate in column 2 (Air Force).

b Estimate is significantly different from the estimate in column 3 (Army).

c Estimate is significantly different from the estimate in column 4 (Marine Corps).

d Estimate is significantly different from the estimate in column 5 (Navy).

e Estimate is significantly different from the estimate in column 6 (Coast Guard).

**Table 7.8**
**Bothered a Lot by Physical Symptoms in the Past 30 Days, by Pay Grade**

| | E1–E4 (1) | E5–E6 (2) | E7–E9 (3) | W1–W5 (4) | O1–O3 (5) | O4–O10 (6) |
|---|---|---|---|---|---|---|
| Stomach or bowel problems | 7.5%[c,d] (5.9–9.1) | 9.6% (8.1–11.2) | 12.8%[a,e,f] (10.9–14.7) | 12.1%[a,e,f] (9.6–14.5) | 7.5%[c,d] (6.3–8.7) | 7.0%[c,d] (5.8–8.3) |
| Back pain | 20.2%[c,d] (17.7–22.8) | 24.3%[c,d,e] (22.0–26.7) | 34.0%[a,b,e,f] (31.3–36.6) | 32.5%[a,b,e,f] (28.9–36.0) | 16.4%[b,c,d,f] (14.7–18.2) | 20.5%[c,d,e] (18.5–22.4) |
| Pain in the arms, legs, or joints | 20.0%[c,d,e] (17.4–22.5) | 24.9%[c,d,e,f] (22.6–27.3) | 32.6%[a,b,e,f] (30.0–35.3) | 31.3%[a,b,e,f] (27.8–34.8) | 12.8%[a,b,c,d,f] (11.2–14.4) | 18.5%[b,c,d,e] (16.6–20.3) |
| Headaches | 11.4%[c,e,f] (9.5–13.2) | 13.5%[e,f] (11.7–15.3) | 17.0%[a,e,f] (14.8–19.1) | 13.0%[e,f] (10.5–15.6) | 6.8%[a,b,c,d] (5.6–7.9) | 7.1%[a,b,c,d] (5.8–8.4) |
| Chest pain or shortness of breath[g] | 4.8% (3.5–6.1) | 4.8% (3.6–6.0) | 5.0% (3.7–6.3) | 4.6% (3.0–6.2) | 3.8% (2.9–4.7) | 3.5% (2.6–4.5) |
| Dizziness[g] | 4.1% (2.9–5.3) | 5.3% (4.0–6.5) | 4.4% (3.2–5.6) | 4.5% (2.9–6.1) | 3.7% (2.8–4.7) | 4.1% (3.1–5.2) |
| Feeling tired or having low energy | 23.2%[e,f] (20.7–25.8) | 26.6%[e,f] (24.3–29.0) | 26.1%[e,f] (23.7–28.6) | 22.6%[e,f] (19.4–25.7) | 16.5%[a,b,c,d] (14.8–18.2) | 13.7%[a,b,c,d] (12.1–15.3) |
| Trouble sleeping | 24.8%[c,e,f] (22.1–27.4) | 28.4%[e,f] (26.0–30.8) | 30.4%[a,e,f] (27.9–33.0) | 28.2%[e,f] (24.8–31.6) | 15.1%[a,b,c,d] (13.4–16.7) | 16.8%[a,b,c,d] (15.0–18.6) |
| At least one symptom (excluding headaches) | 28.6%[b,c,d,e] (25.8–31.4) | 36.0%[a,c,d,e,f] (33.4–38.5) | 46.6%[a,b,e,f] (43.8–49.3) | 44.4%[a,b,e,f] (40.7–48.2) | 22.4%[a,b,c,d,f] (20.5–24.3) | 28.9%[b,c,d,e] (26.7–31.1) |
| At least one symptom (including headaches) | 32.4%[b,c,d,e] (29.5–35.3) | 40.0%[a,c,d,e,f] (37.4–42.6) | 50.8%[a,b,e,f] (48.0–53.5) | 48.2%[a,b,e,f] (44.4–52.0) | 24.8%[a,b,c,d,f] (22.9–26.8) | 31.1%[b,c,d,e] (28.9–33.3) |
| High physical symptom severity | 19.3%[b,c,d,e,f] (16.9–21.7) | 25.1%[a,c,e,f] (22.8–27.5) | 30.9%[a,b,e,f] (28.3–33.5) | 28.3%[a,e,f] (24.9–31.7) | 12.1%[a,b,c,d] (10.6–13.6) | 12.6%[a,b,c,d] (11.1–14.2) |

NOTE: All data are weighted. 95-percent confidence intervals are presented in parentheses.

[a] Estimate is significantly different from the estimate in column 1 (E1–E4).

[b] Estimate is significantly different from the estimate in column 2 (E5–E6).

[c] Estimate is significantly different from the estimate in column 3 (E7–E9).

[d] Estimate is significantly different from the estimate in column 4 (W1–W5).

[e] Estimate is significantly different from the estimate in column 5 (O1–O3).

[f] Estimate is significantly different from the estimate in column 6 (O4–O10).

[g] The omnibus chi-square test was not statistically significant ($p > 0.05$).

**Table 7.9**
**Bothered a Lot by Physical Symptoms in the Past 30 Days, by Gender**

|  | Men (1) | Women (2) |
|---|---|---|
| Stomach or bowel problems | 8.1%[a] (7.1–9.1) | 11.6% (10.3–12.8) |
| Back pain[b] | 22.2% (20.7–23.8) | 24.3% (22.6–26.0) |
| Pain in the arms, legs, or joints[b] | 22.1% (20.5–23.6) | 21.7% (20.1–23.3) |
| Headaches | 10.5%[a] (9.3–11.6) | 19.1% (17.6–20.7) |
| Chest pain or shortness of breath[b] | 4.6% (3.8–5.4) | 4.7% (3.9–5.6) |
| Dizziness[b] | 4.3% (3.5–5.1) | 5.2% (4.3–6.1) |
| Feeling tired or having low energy | 21.7%[a] (20.1–23.3) | 31.7% (29.9–33.5) |
| Trouble sleeping | 24.4%[a] (22.8–26.0) | 28.2% (26.5–30.0) |
| At least one symptom (excluding headaches)[b] | 31.7% (30.0–33.5) | 33.9% (32.1–35.7) |
| At least one symptom (including headaches) | 34.7%[a] (32.9–36.5) | 41.4% (39.5–43.3) |
| High physical symptom severity | 20.0%[a] (18.5–21.5) | 27.2% (25.4–28.9) |

NOTE: All data are weighted. 95-percent confidence intervals are presented in parentheses.

[a] Estimate is significantly different from the estimate in column 2 (women).

[b] The omnibus chi-square test was not statistically significant ($p > 0.05$).

**Table 7.10**
**Bothered a Lot by Physical Symptoms in the Past 30 Days, by Age Group**

| | Ages 17–24 (1) | Ages 25–34 (2) | Ages 35–44 (3) | Ages 45+ (4) |
|---|---|---|---|---|
| Stomach or bowel problems | 6.9%[c,d] (5.3–8.5) | 8.0%[d] (6.6–9.4) | 10.8%[a] (9.1–12.5) | 13.2%[a,b] (10.3–16.2) |
| Back pain | 18.6%[c,d] (15.8–21.4) | 19.7%[c,d] (17.6–21.7) | 28.7%[a,b,d] (26.1–31.2) | 36.6%[a,b,c] (32.6–40.6) |
| Pain in the arms, legs, or joints | 18.9%[c,d] (16.0–21.8) | 19.8%[c,d] (17.7–21.9) | 25.4%[a,b,d] (23.1–27.7) | 37.5%[a,b,c] (33.6–41.5) |
| Headaches[e] | 11.3% (9.2–13.4) | 10.9% (9.3–12.5) | 13.5% (11.6–15.3) | 14.4% (11.6–17.1) |
| Chest pain or shortness of breath[e] | 5.1% (3.6–6.7) | 4.1% (3.1–5.1) | 4.3% (3.2–5.5) | 7.2% (4.5–9.9) |
| Dizziness | 3.9%[d] (2.7–5.2) | 3.9%[d] (3.0–4.9) | 5.0% (3.6–6.4) | 8.0%[a,b] (5.2–10.9) |
| Feeling tired or having low energy[e] | 23.2% (20.3–26.2) | 22.8% (20.6–24.9) | 23.1% (20.8–25.4) | 26.5% (22.6–30.5) |
| Trouble sleeping | 23.6%[d] (20.5–26.6) | 22.5%[c,d] (20.4–24.7) | 28.5%[b] (25.9–31.0) | 34.5%[a,b] (30.4–38.5) |
| At least one symptom (excluding headaches) | 26.4%[c,d] (23.2–29.6) | 29.0%[c,d] (26.7–31.4) | 39.1%[a,b,d] (36.5–41.8) | 51.2%[a,b,c] (47.4–55.0) |
| At least one symptom (including headaches) | 30.4%[c,d] (27.1–33.7) | 32.5%[c,d] (30.1–34.9) | 43.1%[a,b,d] (40.5–45.8) | 53.6%[a,b,c] (49.9–57.4) |
| High physical symptom severity | 18.0%[c,d] (15.3–20.7) | 19.7%[c,d] (17.6–21.8) | 24.3%[a,b,d] (21.9–26.7) | 32.6%[a,b,c] (28.4–36.7) |

NOTE: All data are weighted. 95-percent confidence intervals are presented in parentheses.

[a] Estimate is significantly different from the estimate in column 1 (ages 17–24).

[b] Estimate is significantly different from the estimate in column 2 (ages 25–34).

[c] Estimate is significantly different from the estimate in column 3 (ages 35–44).

[d] Estimate is significantly different from the estimate in column 4 (ages 45+).

[e] The omnibus chi-square test was not statistically significant ($p > 0.05$).

Table 7.11
Bothered a Lot by Physical Symptoms in the Past 30 Days, by Race/Ethnicity

| | Non-Hispanic White (1) | Non-Hispanic Black (2) | Hispanic (3) | Non-Hispanic Asian (4) | Other (5) |
|---|---|---|---|---|---|
| Stomach or bowel problems[f] | 8.3% (7.1–9.5) | 11.2% (8.3–14.0) | 9.1% (7.0–11.3) | 5.1% (2.2–8.0) | 9.0% (6.4–11.7) |
| Back pain[f] | 21.3% (19.6–23.0) | 25.8% (21.5–30.1) | 22.2% (18.8–25.7) | 24.8% (17.5–32.2) | 25.5% (21.0–30.1) |
| Pain in the arms, legs, or joints[f] | 20.6% (18.8–22.3) | 26.2% (22.0–30.3) | 23.5% (19.9–27.2) | 21.5% (14.9–28.1) | 23.4% (19.1–27.7) |
| Headaches | 10.6%[b] (9.3–11.8) | 16.7%[a] (13.3–20.1) | 13.9% (11.1–16.8) | 8.6% (4.8–12.4) | 11.7% (8.5–14.9) |
| Chest pain or shortness of breath | 4.0%[b] (3.2–4.9) | 7.5%[a] (4.9–10.1) | 4.6% (2.9–6.3) | 3.3% (0.9–5.7) | 6.2% (3.7–8.7) |
| Dizziness | 3.6%[b] (2.9–4.4) | 6.9%[a] (4.5–9.3) | 5.5% (3.6–7.5) | 3.2% (0.8–5.6) | 5.1% (3.0–7.3) |
| Feeling tired or having low energy[f] | 22.6% (20.9–24.3) | 21.9% (18.1–25.8) | 25.2% (21.4–28.9) | 20.2% (13.5–26.8) | 27.7% (23.1–32.2) |
| Trouble sleeping | 22.4%[b,c,e] (20.7–24.2) | 29.8%[a] (25.3–34.3) | 28.9%[a] (25.0–32.8) | 19.4% (12.8–26.1) | 31.8%[a] (26.9–36.7) |
| At least one symptom (excluding headaches)[f] | 30.9% (29.0–32.8) | 37.4% (32.7–42.0) | 31.2% (27.3–35.2) | 32.4% (24.8–40.0) | 34.5% (29.6–39.3) |
| At least one symptom (including headaches) | 34.0%[b] (32.1–36.0) | 43.3%[a] (38.6–48.1) | 35.4% (31.3–39.4) | 33.8% (26.1–41.4) | 38.9% (33.9–43.9) |
| High physical symptom severity | 18.8%[b,e] (17.2–20.5) | 25.6%[a] (21.5–29.8) | 23.4% (19.9–26.9) | 22.1% (15.1–29.2) | 25.7%[a] (21.3–30.2) |

NOTE: All data are weighted. 95-percent confidence intervals are presented in parentheses.

[a] Estimate is significantly different from the estimate in column 1 (non-Hispanic white).

[b] Estimate is significantly different from the estimate in column 2 (non-Hispanic black).

[c] Estimate is significantly different from the estimate in column 3 (Hispanic).

[d] Estimate is significantly different from the estimate in column 4 (non-Hispanic Asian).

[e] Estimate is significantly different from the estimate in column 5 (other).

[f] The omnibus chi-square test was not statistically significant ($p > 0.05$).

**Table 7.12**
**Bothered a Lot by Physical Symptoms in the Past 30 Days, by Education Level**

| | High School or Less (1) | Some College (2) | Bachelor's Degree or More (3) |
|---|---|---|---|
| Stomach or bowel problems[d] | 8.7% (6.3–11.0) | 9.1% (7.8–10.4) | 8.0% (6.8–9.2) |
| Back pain[d] | 22.0% (18.5–25.5) | 23.8% (21.8–25.8) | 20.9% (19.0–22.8) |
| Pain in the arms, legs, or joints | 23.0% (19.4–26.7) | 23.3%[c] (21.3–25.3) | 19.2%[b] (17.3–21.2) |
| Headaches | 11.7% (9.3–14.2) | 13.9%[c] (12.3–15.5) | 8.7%[b] (7.4–10.0) |
| Chest pain or shortness of breath[d] | 5.0% (3.2–6.8) | 5.1% (4.0–6.2) | 3.7% (2.9–4.5) |
| Dizziness[d] | 4.4% (2.7–6.0) | 4.8% (3.8–5.8) | 3.9% (3.1–4.8) |
| Feeling tired or having low energy | 25.3%[c] (21.7–28.9) | 26.5%[c] (24.4–28.5) | 16.9%[a,b] (15.1–18.6) |
| Trouble sleeping | 27.2%[c] (23.5–30.9) | 27.9%[c] (25.8–30.0) | 19.0%[a,b] (17.1–20.9) |
| At least one symptom (excluding headaches) | 31.6% (27.7–35.5) | 34.0%[c] (31.7–36.2) | 29.4%[b] (27.3–31.6) |
| At least one symptom (including headaches) | 34.2% (30.2–38.2) | 38.8%[c] (36.5–41.1) | 32.0%[b] (29.8–34.2) |
| High physical symptom severity | 22.5%[c] (19.1–26.0) | 23.1%[c] (21.2–25.1) | 17.0%[a,b] (15.2–18.9) |

NOTE: All data are weighted. 95-percent confidence intervals are presented in parentheses.

[a] Estimate is significantly different from the estimate in column 1 (high school or less).

[b] Estimate is significantly different from the estimate in column 2 (some college).

[c] Estimate is significantly different from the estimate in column 3 (bachelor's degree or more).

[d] The omnibus chi-square test was not statistically significant ($p > 0.05$).

Table 7.13
**Prescription Drug Misuse Among Those With and Without Physical Symptoms (Including Headaches) in the Past 30 Days, by Service Branch**

|  | Total (1) | Air Force (2) | Army (3) | Marine Corps (4) | Navy (5) | Coast Guard (6) |
|---|---|---|---|---|---|---|
| Prescription drug misuse among those with physical symptoms (including headaches) | | | | | | |
| Stimulant misuse[b] | 0.5% (0.2–0.9) | 0.5% (0.0–1.2) | 0.6% (0.0–1.1) | † | 0.9% (0.0–2.3) | 0.6% (0.0–1.2) |
| Sedative misuse[a] | 2.6% (1.9–3.4) | 3.6% (1.9–5.3) | 2.8% (1.4–4.2) | 1.5% (0.5–2.6) | 2.3% (0.9–3.7) | 1.7% (0.9–2.5) |
| Opioid misuse[a] | 3.4% (2.3–4.6) | 2.6% (1.2–3.9) | 4.1% (1.9–6.2) | 2.9% (0.4–5.4) | 3.3% (1.2–5.4) | 2.3% (1.4–3.3) |
| Prescription drug misuse among those without physical symptoms (including headaches) | | | | | | |
| Stimulant misuse[a] | 0.2% (0.1–0.3) | 0.2% (0.0–0.5) | 0.2% (0.0–0.3) | 0.4% (0.0–0.8) | 0.0% (0.0–0.0) | 0.3% (0.0–0.4) |
| Sedative misuse[a] | 1.0% (0.6–1.4) | 0.9% (0.4–1.4) | 1.4% (0.4–2.4) | 0.2% (0.1–0.3) | 1.1% (0.3–1.9) | 0.8% (0.4–1.1) |
| Opioid misuse[a] | 1.8% (1.2–2.4) | 1.3% (0.6–1.9) | 2.4% (1.0–3.9) | 1.8% (0.5–3.1) | 1.5% (0.5–2.4) | 1.1% (0.6–1.5) |

NOTE: All data are weighted. 95-percent confidence intervals are presented in parentheses.

[a] The omnibus chi-square test was not statistically significant ($p > 0.05$).

[b] Because there were too few respondents for at least one category, we do not report an omnibus chi-square test.

† = Too few respondents to report (denominator < 20).

## Health-Related Functional Limitations

Chronic conditions and physical symptoms may impair functioning in several domains, including work or school, social life, and family life. In addition, mental and physical symptoms may negatively affect work performance by increasing *absenteeism* (lost work days because of a health condition) and *presenteeism* (days present at work but with performance compromised because of a health condition).

Functional limitations were assessed using a modified version of the widely used Sheehan Disability Scale (Sheehan, Harnett-Sheehan, and Raj, 1996; Leon et al., 1997). Respondents completed five items assessing the extent that health problems impair functioning at work or school, in social life, and in family life or home responsibilities. Respondents were also asked how many days in the past 30 days their mental or physical symptoms caused them to miss work or school (absenteeism) or to feel so impaired that even though they went to work or school, their productivity was reduced (presenteeism). We defined *absenteeism* as a service member reporting being out for at least 14 days in the past 30 days, and we defined *presenteeism* as a service member being present but impaired for the same period. We defined *functional impairment* as being moderately, markedly, or extremely impaired as opposed to being mildly impaired or not impaired at all.

Results are presented in Tables 7.14 through 7.19. Key findings include the following:

- Approximately one-third of service members reported functional impairment in each of the three domains: 33.0 percent at work or school, 30.0 percent in social life, and 30.5 percent in family life (Table 7.14). Functional impairment was most prevalent in the Army, with prevalence ranging from 34.6 percent in social life to 39.5 percent at work.

- Among all service members, 3.0 percent reported missing 14 or more days of work in the past 30 days because of their mental or physical symptoms (Table 7.14). Absenteeism was lowest in the Coast Guard (1.4 percent) and highest in the Army (4.9 percent).
- More than one in ten service members (13.4 percent) reported that their work performance was compromised because of a health condition for 14 or more days in the past 30 days, making presenteeism more than four times more prevalent than absenteeism (3.0 percent) (Table 7.14). As with absenteeism, presenteeism was lowest in the Coast Guard (7.7 percent) and highest in the Army (16.8 percent).
- On average, functional limitations, absenteeism, and presenteeism were lower among officers compared with enlisted service members (Table 7.15).
- Women were more likely than men to report functional impairment at work or school (39.2 percent compared with 31.8 percent), in their social life (37.2 percent compared with 28.7 percent), and in their family life or home responsibilities (36.6 percent compared with 29.3 percent); women were also more likely to report presenteeism (16.3 percent compared with 12.9 percent) (Table 7.16).
- Overall, functional limitations, absenteeism, and presenteeism increased with age; however, the associations were generally not statically significant (Table 7.17).
- Functional limitations, absenteeism, and presenteeism did not vary notably by race/ethnicity (Table 7.18).
- On average, service members with some college had the highest reported functional impairment at work or school, in social life, and in family life or home responsibilities (Table 7.19). Service members with a bachelor's degree or more had the lowest self-reported functional impairment in all three domains. Absenteeism did not vary significantly by education level, but presenteeism decreased with increasing education level, from 15.7 percent among service members with a high school education or less to 9.7 percent among service members with a bachelor's degree or more.

**Table 7.14**
**Health-Related Functional Limitations, Absenteeism, and Presenteeism, by Service Branch**

| | Total (1) | Air Force (2) | Army (3) | Marine Corps (4) | Navy (5) | Coast Guard (6) |
|---|---|---|---|---|---|---|
| **Functional impairment** | | | | | | |
| Work or school | 33.0% (31.5–34.5) | 23.6%[b,c,d] (21.8–25.5) | 39.5%[a,d,e] (36.3–42.8) | 33.2%[a,e] (29.5–36.9) | 32.4%[a,b,e] (29.5–35.3) | 24.3%[b,c,d] (22.8–25.7) |
| Social life | 30.0% (28.5–31.5) | 22.3%[b,c,d] (20.4–24.1) | 34.6%[a,e] (31.5–37.7) | 30.6%[a,e] (27.0–34.3) | 30.7%[a,e] (27.8–33.6) | 22.5%[b,c,d] (21.1–23.9) |
| Family life or home responsibilities | 30.5% (29.0–31.9) | 22.8%[b,c,d] (21.0–24.6) | 34.7%[a,e] (31.6–37.7) | 31.9%[a,e] (28.3–35.5) | 31.0%[a,e] (28.1–33.8) | 25.0%[b,c,d] (23.6–26.4) |
| Absenteeism | 3.0% (2.4–3.7) | 2.1%[b] (1.4–2.7) | 4.9%[a,d,e] (3.4–6.4) | 2.4% (1.2–3.5) | 1.6%[b] (0.8–2.4) | 1.4%[b] (1.0–1.8) |
| Presenteeeism | 13.4% (12.3–14.6) | 8.8%[b,c,d] (7.6–10.1) | 16.8%[a,d,e] (14.4–19.3) | 15.3%[a,e] (12.3–18.2) | 12.1%[a,b,e] (10.1–14.1) | 7.7%[b,c,d] (6.8–8.6) |

NOTE: All data are weighted. 95-percent confidence intervals are presented in parentheses.

[a] Estimate is significantly different from the estimate in column 2 (Air Force).

[b] Estimate is significantly different from the estimate in column 3 (Army).

[c] Estimate is significantly different from the estimate in column 4 (Marine Corps).

[d] Estimate is significantly different from the estimate in column 5 (Navy).

[e] Estimate is significantly different from the estimate in column 6 (Coast Guard).

**Table 7.15**
**Health-Related Functional Limitations, Absenteeism, and Presenteeism, by Pay Grade**

| | E1–E4 (1) | E5–E6 (2) | E7–E9 (3) | W1–W5 (4) | O1–O3 (5) | O4–O10 (6) |
|---|---|---|---|---|---|---|
| **Functional impairment** | | | | | | |
| Work or school | 33.6%[e,f] (30.7–36.5) | 36.5%[e,f] (33.9–39.1) | 37.1%[e,f] (34.5–39.8) | 36.1%[e,f] (32.4–39.7) | 23.3%[a,b,c,d] (21.3–25.2) | 20.3%[a,b,c,d] (18.4–22.2) |
| Social life | 29.8%[c,e,f] (27.0–32.7) | 33.0%[e,f] (30.5–35.6) | 37.6%[a,e,f] (34.9–40.2) | 33.4%[e,f] (29.9–37.0) | 20.8%[a,b,c,d] (18.9–22.6) | 19.4%[a,b,c,d] (17.6–21.3) |
| Family life or home responsibilities | 27.8%[b,c,d,e] (25.0–30.5) | 35.6%[a,e,f] (33.1–38.2) | 39.6%[a,e,f] (36.8–42.3) | 36.9%[a,e,f] (33.3–40.5) | 22.0%[a,b,c,d] (20.1–23.9) | 23.5%[b,c,d] (21.4–25.5) |
| Absenteeism | 3.2%[f] (2.0–4.4) | 3.8%[e,f] (2.7–4.9) | 2.9%[f] (1.9–3.8) | 2.7%[f] (1.5–4.0) | 1.6%[b] (1.0–2.2) | 0.9%[a,b,c,d] (0.5–1.3) |
| Presenteeism | 13.4%[e,f] (11.3–15.5) | 16.3%[e,f] (14.3–18.3) | 14.5%[e,f] (12.5–16.5) | 13.5%[e,f] (10.9–16.1) | 8.2%[a,b,c,d] (6.9–9.5) | 7.1%[a,b,c,d] (5.8–8.3) |

NOTE: All data are weighted. 95-percent confidence intervals are presented in parentheses.

[a] Estimate is significantly different from the estimate in column 1 (E1–E4).

[b] Estimate is significantly different from the estimate in column 2 (E5–E6).

[c] Estimate is significantly different from the estimate in column 3 (E7–E9).

[d] Estimate is significantly different from the estimate in column 4 (W1–W5).

[e] Estimate is significantly different from the estimate in column 5 (O1–O3).

[f] Estimate is significantly different from the estimate in column 6 (O4–O10).

**Table 7.16**
**Health-Related Functional Limitations, Absenteeism, and Presenteeism, by Gender**

| | Men (1) | Women (2) |
|---|---|---|
| **Functional impairment** | | |
| Work or school | 31.8%[a] (30.1–33.6) | 39.2% (37.3–41.1) |
| Social life | 28.7%[a] (27.0–30.4) | 37.2% (35.3–39.1) |
| Family life or home responsibilities | 29.3%[a] (27.6–31.1) | 36.6% (34.7–38.5) |
| Absenteeism[b] | 3.0% (2.2–3.7) | 3.5% (2.7–4.3) |
| Presenteeism | 12.9%[a] (11.6–14.2) | 16.3% (14.7–17.8) |

NOTE: All data are weighted. 95-percent confidence intervals are presented in parentheses.

[a] Estimate is significantly different from the estimate in column 2 (women).

[b] The omnibus chi-square test was not statistically significant ($p > 0.05$).

**Table 7.17**
**Health-Related Functional Limitations, Absenteeism, and Presenteeism, by Age Group**

| | Ages 17–24 (1) | Ages 25–34 (2) | Ages 35–44 (3) | Ages 45+ (4) |
|---|---|---|---|---|
| **Functional impairment** | | | | |
| Work or school | 29.3%[c] (26.0–32.6) | 33.2% (30.8–35.7) | 36.7%[a] (34.0–39.4) | 34.8% (30.8–38.9) |
| Social life | 27.3%[c] (24.1–30.4) | 29.6% (27.2–32.0) | 33.6%[a] (31.0–36.2) | 32.3% (28.5–36.1) |
| Family life or home responsibilities | 24.2%[b,c,d] (21.2–27.3) | 30.3%[a,c,d] (27.9–32.6) | 36.8%[a,b] (34.2–39.5) | 36.9%[a,b] (33.0–40.9) |
| Absenteeism[e] | 2.2% (1.1–3.4) | 3.0% (2.0–4.1) | 3.7% (2.5–4.9) | 4.4% (2.1–6.6) |
| Presenteeism[e] | 11.5% (9.2–13.9) | 13.5% (11.6–15.3) | 15.2% (13.1–17.2) | 15.6% (11.8–19.3) |

NOTE: All data are weighted. 95-percent confidence intervals are presented in parentheses.

[a] Estimate is significantly different from the estimate in column 1 (ages 17–24).

[b] Estimate is significantly different from the estimate in column 2 (ages 25–34).

[c] Estimate is significantly different from the estimate in column 3 (ages 35–44).

[d] Estimate is significantly different from the estimate in column 4 (ages 45+).

[e] The omnibus chi-square test was not statistically significant ($p > 0.05$).

**Table 7.18**
**Health-Related Functional Limitations, Absenteeism, and Presenteeism, by Race/Ethnicity**

| | Non-Hispanic White (1) | Non-Hispanic Black (2) | Hispanic (3) | Non-Hispanic Asian (4) | Other (5) |
|---|---|---|---|---|---|
| **Functional impairment** | | | | | |
| Work or school[f] | 32.8% (30.8–34.8) | 32.6% (27.9–37.2) | 31.7% (27.7–35.7) | 35.3% (27.3–43.2) | 36.4% (31.3–41.4) |
| Social life[f] | 29.8% (27.9–31.7) | 29.8% (25.5–34.0) | 29.8% (25.8–33.8) | 28.6% (21.3–35.9) | 33.5% (28.6–38.4) |
| Family life or home responsibilities[f] | 30.9% (29.0–32.8) | 27.6% (23.3–31.9) | 28.6% (24.9–32.4) | 30.3% (22.8–37.8) | 34.7% (29.7–39.6) |
| Absenteeism[f] | 3.2% (2.3–4.0) | 2.7% (1.1–4.4) | 2.7% (1.5–3.9) | 1.6% (0.0–3.6) | 4.3% (1.4–7.2) |
| Presenteeism | 13.5%[b] (12.0–15.0) | 8.6%[a,e] (6.3–10.8) | 13.3% (10.3–16.3) | 14.7% (8.4–20.9) | 19.2%[b] (14.8–23.7) |

NOTE: All data are weighted. 95-percent confidence intervals are presented in parentheses.

[a] Estimate is significantly different from the estimate in column 1 (non-Hispanic white).

[b] Estimate is significantly different from the estimate in column 2 (non-Hispanic black).

[c] Estimate is significantly different from the estimate in column 3 (Hispanic).

[d] Estimate is significantly different from the estimate in column 4 (non-Hispanic Asian).

[e] Estimate is significantly different from the estimate in column 5 (other).

[f] The omnibus chi-square test was not statistically significant ($p > 0.05$).

Table 7.19
**Health-Related Functional Limitations, Absenteeism, and Presenteeism, by Education Level**

| | High School or Less (1) | Some College (2) | Bachelor's Degree or More (3) |
|---|---|---|---|
| Functional impairment | | | |
| Work or school | 32.5% (28.6–36.5) | 36.0%[c] (33.7–38.3) | 28.6%[b] (26.2–30.9) |
| Social life | 29.2% (25.4–33.0) | 33.3%[c] (31.1–35.5) | 25.4%[b] (23.2–27.6) |
| Family life or home responsibilities | 28.7% (25.0–32.5) | 33.6%[c] (31.4–35.8) | 26.7%[b] (24.5–28.9) |
| Absenteeism[d] | 4.2% (2.2–6.2) | 2.9% (2.2–3.7) | 2.5% (1.5–3.5) |
| Presenteeism | 15.7%[c] (12.5–18.8) | 14.9%[c] (13.2–16.5) | 9.7%[a,b] (8.2–11.3) |

NOTE: All data are weighted. 95-percent confidence intervals are presented in parentheses.

[a] Estimate is significantly different from the estimate in column 1 (high school or less).

[b] Estimate is significantly different from the estimate in column 2 (some college).

[c] Estimate is significantly different from the estimate in column 3 (bachelor's degree or more).

[d] The omnibus chi-square test was not statistically significant ($p > 0.05$).

## Summary

This chapter presented analyses of potentially important chronic conditions, physical symptoms, and health-related functional limitations. The prevalence of specific chronic conditions among active-duty service members was relatively low compared with the general U.S. population; however, demographic differences between the military and general population make direct comparisons difficult. Furthermore, each chronic condition may negatively affect military readiness and effectiveness, especially if the condition is not diagnosed early, monitored regularly, and treated appropriately.

Overall, 38.6 percent of service members reported at least one diagnosed chronic condition in their lifetime, and 6.2 percent reported three or more conditions. These data suggest that a substantial proportion of active-duty service members suffer from one or more medical vulnerabilities. Among service members with a diagnosed chronic condition, approximately one-third were taking medications for their condition overall. The proportion ranged from 3.9 percent among service members with skin cancer to 38.5 percent among those with ulcers.

Physical symptoms were common among active-duty service members, consistent with previous research on multiple physical symptoms in the military and in general and clinical populations (Kroenke, 2014). More than one-third (35.7 percent) of service members reported being bothered a lot by at least one physical symptom (including headaches) in the past 30 days. About one in five service members (21.1 percent) reported a high physical symptom burden based on a survey of eight common physical symptoms.

The impact of these medical vulnerabilities (diagnosed chronic conditions and physical symptoms) on overall force readiness, deployability, and organizational efficiency and cost is not well understood, but our survey findings suggest that health-related functional impairment is very common. One in three service members reported moderate to marked health limitations affecting their capacity to function at work or school, in their social life, or in their family life or home responsibilities. In addition, service members reported that they had missed (3.0 percent) or had reduced productivity (13.4 percent) for 14 or more work days in the past month because of physical or emotional health problems. These figures suggest overall productivity loss due to health problems within the ranks.

# CHAPTER EIGHT

# Sexual Behavior and Health

Sexual health is a key aspect of mental and physical well-being, and this domain includes behaviors and outcomes related to HIV, sexually transmitted infection (STI), healthy pregnancy, prevention of unintended pregnancy, and cancer prevention, among others (Douglas and Fenton, 2013). Each of these can be a factor in force readiness, especially if the behavior or outcome leads to a medical status that prevents a service member from being deployed (e.g., pregnancy). Further, DoD and the Coast Guard assume some cost in the treatment of STIs among service members.

This chapter reports on the percentages of personnel who, in the past year, had more than one sex partner, had sex with a new partner without using a condom, had an STI, were at *high risk for HIV infection* (defined as men who had sex with one or more men in the past year, service members who had vaginal or anal sex with more than one partner in the past year, and service members who had a past-year STI [CDC, 2011; CDC, 2016c]), and used a condom during their most-recent vaginal sex. We also report the percentage of service members who did not use birth control the most-recent time they had vaginal sex in the past year (excluding those who were already pregnant or trying to get pregnant) and the percentage using various methods of birth control. In addition, we report past-year unintended pregnancy (either caused, for male respondents, or personally experienced, for female respondents). Differences in these behaviors and outcomes by service branch and demographic characteristics are presented. Given the importance of marital status to interpreting many sexual behaviors, we include this as an additional demographic variable in this chapter. Note that cohabiting and married service members are included in the same category.

Comparable U.S. population data for most indicators are not available for a recent period and are reported only where available. The 2011 HRBS contained a more limited set of questions concerning sexual and reproductive health, and we compare those results with the 2015 results where possible. Readers should use caution when interpreting comparisons between the 2015 HRBS results and other populations or prior versions of the HRBS because these comparisons are not necessarily statistically significant and could simply reflect sampling variability across the two samples being compared; however, where available, we provide confidence intervals for comparisons.

Each section highlights the importance or relevance of the topic to the general population and to the military and then provides an analysis of each topic by service branch. When relevant, we present analyses by pay grade, gender, age group, race/ethnicity, and education level. Key measures used are described in the applicable section, and additional details about these measures may be found in Appendix D. All analyses demonstrated statistically significant omnibus tests (Rao-Scott chi-square test for categorical variables and $F$-tests for continuous variables) unless otherwise noted in the tables. Statistically significant group differences (pairwise comparisons) are presented within each table. However, only statistically significant differences that the research team subject-matter experts determined to be substantively meaningful (i.e., could be used to change or develop policy or contribute to inequalities is health outcomes across subgroups) are discussed in the text.

## Sexual Risk Behaviors and Outcomes

Findings related to sexual risk behaviors and outcomes across all service branches are presented in Table 8.1. Key overall findings include the following:

- In the 2015 HRBS, 19.4 percent of service members had more than one sex partner in the past year.
- More than one in three service members (36.7 percent) had past-year sex with a new partner without using a condom. In 2011, 20.8 percent of personnel reported this behavior (32.1 percent had one or more new partners and, of these, 64.8 percent did not "always" use condoms with them) (Barlas et al., 2013).
- STI was reported by 1.7 percent of service members. In 2011, this percentage was 1.4 percent (CI: 1.2–1.6) (Barlas et al., 2013).
- About one in five service members (20.9 percent) were at high risk for HIV infection.
- Across all services, 22.2 percent of personnel used a condom the most-recent time they had vaginal sex.
- About one in five service members (19.4 percent) did not use birth control the most-recent time they had vaginal sex (and were not already expecting a child or trying to conceive) in the past year.
- Unintended pregnancy was experienced or caused by 2.4 percent of personnel.

Tables 8.1 through 8.7 display the percentages of personnel engaging in sexual risk behaviors, as well as related outcomes, by service branch, pay grade, gender, age group, race/ethnicity, education level, and marital or cohabiting. Key findings include the following:

- The Marine Corps, followed by the Navy, had the highest percentage of members for most categories of risk: more than one sex partner in the past year, high risk for HIV infection, and causing or experiencing an unintended pregnancy (Table 8.1). The Army had the highest percentage of members who had sex without birth control. Percentages of service members with an STI were similar across services, as were the percentages who used a condom during their most-recent vaginal sex.
- Junior enlisted service members (E1–E4) had the highest rate in nearly every category (Table 8.2). The exception was no birth control during the most-recent vaginal sex in the past year. The percentages of personnel who did not use birth control were highest, and the percentages who did use condoms were lowest, among senior NCOs and warrant officers. This is probably related to differences in marital status across these pay grades.
- There were no differences in the percentages of women and men who had multiple sex partners, had unprotected sex with a new partner, had an STI, were at high risk for HIV infection, or did not use birth control during the most-recent vaginal sex (Table 8.3).

- The percentage of service women who did not use a form of birth control the most-recent time they had vaginal sex (17.7 percent) was similar to the 16.7 percent (CI: 15.2–18.4) in the general population (HHS, 2010a). HP2020 set a target of 8.4 percent or fewer (published as 91.6 percent of women *using* a method of contraception at most-recent sexual encounter) (HHS, 2010a).
- Women were much more likely to report experiencing an unintended pregnancy (4.8 percent) compared with men's reports of causing such a pregnancy (2.0 percent) (Table 8.3). This difference is probably a result of men having incomplete information about the occurrence of such events. The percentage of unintended pregnancies reported by military women was about the same as that for women of reproductive age in the general population (4.5 percent [CI: 4.1–4.9]) (Finer and Zolna, 2016).
- Younger age was also consistently related to sexual risk behaviors and negative outcomes; however, younger age was also associated with condom and other birth control use during the most-recent vaginal sex (Table 8.4).
- Hispanic service members were the most likely to report having more than one sex partner and having sex with a new partner without a condom; this group also had the largest percentage at high risk for HIV infection (Table 8.5). Unintended pregnancy was least common, and sex without birth control was most common, among non-Hispanic Asian service members. There were no differences by race/ethnicity in STIs or condom use.
- Education level was negatively associated with risk: Service members with a high school degree or less were more likely to have more than one sex partner, sex with a new partner without a condom, high risk for HIV infection, and an unintended pregnancy (Table 8.6). However, there were no statistically significant differences by education level for the other three indicators.
- As might be expected, substantial differences in risk were observed for married and unmarried service members; specifically, married personnel were at lower risk (Table 8.7). Just two sexual risk indicators were not statistically significantly different for married compared with unmarried personnel. The two groups were equally likely to experience an unintended pregnancy and equally likely to have sex with a new partner without using a condom. Nonetheless, married service members were not without risk. Among married personnel, 7.5 percent were at high risk for HIV infection, 6.1 percent had more than one sex partner in the past year, 1.1 percent had a past-year STI, and 24.0 percent had sex without birth control when they were not already pregnant or trying to conceive. The last statistic is consistent with the equivalent rates of unintended pregnancy in married (2.2 percent) and unmarried (2.6 percent) service members.

**Table 8.1**
**Past-Year Sexual Risk Behaviors and Outcomes, by Service Branch**

| | Total (1) | Air Force (2) | Army (3) | Marine Corps (4) | Navy (5) | Coast Guard (6) |
|---|---|---|---|---|---|---|
| More than one sex partner | 19.4% (18.0–20.8) | 18.8%[e] (16.9–20.7) | 16.6%[c] (13.9–19.3) | 24.3%[b,e] (20.4–28.1) | 22.1%[e] (19.2–25.1) | 15.5%[a,c,d] (14.2–16.9) |
| Sex with a new partner without a condom | 36.7% (35.0–38.3) | 29.1%[b,c,d] (26.9–31.2) | 39.2%[a,e] (35.8–42.5) | 40.2%[a,e] (36.0–44.4) | 38.3%[a,e] (35.0–41.5) | 32.0%[b,c,d] (30.3–33.7) |
| STI[f] | 1.7% (1.2–2.2) | 1.3% (0.8–1.9) | 1.9% (0.8–2.9) | 1.4% (0.4–2.4) | 2.1% (1.0–3.1) | 0.9% (0.5–1.2) |
| High risk for HIV infection | 20.9% (19.5–22.4) | 20.3%[e] (18.3–22.3) | 18.3%[c,d] (15.5–21.1) | 24.9%[b,e] (21.0–28.8) | 24.2%[b,e] (21.1–27.2) | 16.4%[a,c,d] (15.0–17.8) |
| Condom use during most-recent vaginal sex[f] | 22.2% (20.7–23.7) | 22.1% (20.1–24.1) | 21.4% (18.4–24.3) | 25.2% (21.3–29.1) | 22.0% (19.1–24.9) | 20.7% (19.2–22.2) |
| No birth control during most-recent vaginal sex | 19.4% (18.1–20.7) | 15.7%[b,e] (14.0–17.3) | 22.0%[a] (19.3–24.8) | 17.8% (14.7–20.9) | 19.6% (17.1–22.2) | 19.7%[a] (18.3–21.1) |
| Unintended pregnancy | 2.4% (1.9–2.9) | 2.1% (1.4–2.8) | 1.9% (0.9–2.8) | 4.1%[e] (2.3–5.9) | 2.9%[e] (1.9–3.9) | 1.5%[c,d] (1.1–2.0) |

NOTE: All data are weighted. 95-percent confidence intervals are presented in parentheses.
[a] Estimate is significantly different from the estimate in column 2 (Air Force).
[b] Estimate is significantly different from the estimate in column 3 (Army).
[c] Estimate is significantly different from the estimate in column 4 (Marine Corps).
[d] Estimate is significantly different from the estimate in column 5 (Navy).
[e] Estimate is significantly different from the estimate in column 6 (Coast Guard).
[f] The omnibus chi-square test was not statistically significant ($p > 0.05$).

**Table 8.2**
**Past-Year Sexual Risk Behaviors and Outcomes, by Pay Grade**

| | E1–E4 (1) | E5–E6 (2) | E7–E9 (3) | W1–W5 (4) | O1–O3 (5) | O4–O10 (6) |
|---|---|---|---|---|---|---|
| More than one sex partner | 26.2%[b,c,d,e,f] (23.4–29.0) | 17.1%[a,c,d,f] (15.0–19.2) | 10.7%[a,b,e,f] (8.9–12.6) | 9.9%[a,b,e,f] (7.6–12.2) | 15.0%[a,c,d,f] (13.3–16.6) | 6.0%[a,b,c,d,e] (4.9–7.2) |
| Sex with a new partner without a condom | 38.9%[e,f] (35.6–42.1) | 38.3%[e,f] (35.6–41.1) | 36.7%[e,f] (33.8–39.5) | 35.4%[f] (31.6–39.2) | 30.3%[a,b,c,f] (28.1–32.5) | 24.5%[a,b,c,d,e] (22.4–26.6) |
| STI | 2.7%[c,d,e,f] (1.6–3.7) | 1.3%[f] (0.6–1.9) | 0.5%[a] (0.1–0.9) | 0.5%[a] (0.0–1.0) | 1.0%[a,f] (0.5–1.5) | 0.2%[a,b,e] (0.0–0.3) |
| High risk for HIV infection | 28.0%[b,c,d,e,f] (25.1–30.9) | 18.6%[a,c,d,f] (16.4–20.8) | 12.0%[a,b,e,f] (10.0–13.9) | 10.5%[a,b,e] (8.1–12.9) | 16.3%[a,c,d,f] (14.5–18.0) | 6.9%[a,b,c,e] (5.6–8.1) |
| Condom use during most-recent vaginal sex | 27.7%[b,c,d,f] (24.7–30.6) | 19.7%[a,c,d,e,f] (17.4–22.0) | 10.9%[a,b,e] (9.1–12.6) | 12.1%[a,b,e] (9.4–14.7) | 25.0%[b,c,d,f] (23.0–27.1) | 11.5%[a,b,e] (10.0–13.0) |
| No birth control during most-recent vaginal sex | 16.4%[c,d,f] (13.9–18.8) | 21.1%[c,d,e] (18.7–23.4) | 30.6%[a,b,e,f] (27.8–33.3) | 31.1%[a,b,e,f] (27.4–34.7) | 13.6%[b,c,d,f] (11.9–15.3) | 22.3%[a,c,d,e] (20.2–24.3) |
| Unintended pregnancy | 3.3%[c,f] (2.3–4.4) | 2.3%[f] (1.5–3.1) | 0.9%[a] (0.5–1.4) | 1.1% (0.3–1.8) | 1.8%[f] (1.2–2.4) | 0.6%[a,b,e] (0.3–1.0) |

NOTE: All data are weighted. 95-percent confidence intervals are presented in parentheses.
[a] Estimate is significantly different from the estimate in column 1 (E1–E4).
[b] Estimate is significantly different from the estimate in column 2 (E5–E6).
[c] Estimate is significantly different from the estimate in column 3 (E7–E9).
[d] Estimate is significantly different from the estimate in column 4 (W1–W5).
[e] Estimate is significantly different from the estimate in column 5 (O1–O3).
[f] Estimate is significantly different from the estimate in column 6 (O4–O10).

**Table 8.3**
**Past-Year Sexual Risk Behaviors and Outcomes, by Gender**

|  | Men (1) | Women (2) |
|---|---|---|
| More than one sex partner[b] | 19.2% (17.5–20.8) | 20.6% (18.9–22.4) |
| Sex with a new partner without a condom[b] | 36.5% (34.6–38.4) | 37.6% (35.6–39.6) |
| STI[b] | 1.6% (1.0–2.2) | 2.4% (1.6–3.2) |
| High risk for HIV infection[b] | 20.8% (19.1–22.4) | 21.9% (20.1–23.7) |
| Condom use during most-recent vaginal sex | 23.0%[a] (21.2–24.7) | 17.9% (16.4–19.5) |
| No birth control during most-recent vaginal sex[b] | 19.7% (18.2–21.3) | 17.7% (16.1–19.3) |
| Unintended pregnancy | 2.0%[a] (1.4–2.6) | 4.8% (3.8–5.8) |

NOTE: All data are weighted. 95-percent confidence intervals are presented in parentheses.

[a] Estimate is significantly different from the estimate in column 2 (women).

[b] The omnibus chi-square test was not statistically significant ($p > 0.05$).

**Table 8.4**
**Past-Year Sexual Risk Behaviors and Outcomes, by Age Group**

|  | Ages 17–24 (1) | Ages 25–34 (2) | Ages 35–44 (3) | Ages 45+ (4) |
|---|---|---|---|---|
| More than one sex partner | 31.8%[b,c,d] (28.2–35.3) | 17.7%[a,c,d] (15.8–19.7) | 10.8%[a,b] (8.9–12.7) | 7.7%[a,b] (5.6–9.8) |
| Sex with a new partner without a condom | 40.6%[c] (36.9–44.3) | 35.6% (33.0–38.2) | 34.6%[a] (31.9–37.3) | 34.0% (30.1–37.9) |
| STI | 2.4%[c] (1.2–3.5) | 2.2%[c] (1.3–3.1) | 0.4%[a,b] (0.1–0.6) | 0.4% (0.0–0.9) |
| High risk for HIV infection | 33.8%[b,c,d] (30.2–37.4) | 19.4%[a,c,d] (17.3–21.5) | 11.7%[a,b] (9.8–13.7) | 8.7%[a,b] (6.5–11.0) |
| Condom use during most-recent vaginal sex | 31.5%[b,c,d] (27.9–35.1) | 23.1%[a,c,d] (20.8–25.3) | 13.4%[a,b,d] (11.4–15.4) | 8.5%[a,b,c] (6.3–10.7) |
| No birth control during most-recent vaginal sex | 14.6%[c,d] (12.0–17.2) | 16.9%[c,d] (14.8–19.0) | 24.8%[a,b,d] (22.3–27.3) | 35.8%[a,b,c] (31.8–39.9) |
| Unintended pregnancy | 4.7%[b,c,d] (3.1–6.2) | 1.8%[a,d] (1.3–2.3) | 1.6%[a,d] (1.0–2.2) | 0.1%[a,b,c] (0.0–0.2) |

NOTE: All data are weighted. 95-percent confidence intervals are presented in parentheses.

[a] Estimate is significantly different from the estimate in column 1 (ages 17–24).

[b] Estimate is significantly different from the estimate in column 2 (ages 25–34).

[c] Estimate is significantly different from the estimate in column 3 (ages 35–44).

[d] Estimate is significantly different from the estimate in column 4 (ages 45+).

**Table 8.5**
**Past-Year Sexual Risk Behaviors and Outcomes, by Race/Ethnicity**

| | Non-Hispanic White (1) | Non-Hispanic Black (2) | Hispanic (3) | Non-Hispanic Asian (4) | Other (5) |
|---|---|---|---|---|---|
| More than one sex partner | 18.1%[c] (16.3–19.8) | 20.2% (16.1–24.4) | 24.0%[a] (19.8–28.2) | 14.0% (8.2–19.7) | 22.2% (17.5–26.9) |
| Sex with a new partner without a condom | 35.3%[c] (33.2–37.3) | 36.8% (31.8–41.7) | 42.2%[a] (37.6–46.8) | 29.6% (21.9–37.3) | 40.3% (34.9–45.7) |
| STI[f] | 1.5% (0.9–2.2) | 2.9% (1.0–4.8) | 1.8% (0.6–3.1) | 0.1% (0.0–0.2) | 1.9% (0.4–3.4) |
| High risk for HIV infection | 19.4%[c] (17.6–21.1) | 21.8% (17.6–26.1) | 25.9%[a] (21.6–30.2) | 17.8% (11.1–24.5) | 23.4% (18.6–28.2) |
| Condom use during most-recent vaginal sex[f] | 22.4% (20.6–24.3) | 23.4% (18.9–27.9) | 23.5% (19.2–27.8) | 16.3% (9.5–23.0) | 20.1% (15.7–24.5) |
| No birth control during most-recent vaginal sex | 16.6%[b,c,d,e] (15.0–18.1) | 23.9%[a] (19.7–28.0) | 21.8%[a] (18.2–25.5) | 27.9%[a] (19.9–35.8) | 23.4%[a] (18.7–28.2) |
| Unintended pregnancy | 2.1%[d] (1.5–2.8) | 3.4%[d] (1.9–4.9) | 3.0%[d] (1.4–4.6) | 0.4%ᵃ˒ᵇ˒ᶜ (0.0–0.9) | 3.1%[d] (1.8–5.0) |

NOTE: All data are weighted. 95-percent confidence intervals are presented in parentheses.

[a] Estimate is significantly different from the estimate in column 1 (non-Hispanic white).

[b] Estimate is significantly different from the estimate in column 2 (non-Hispanic black).

[c] Estimate is significantly different from the estimate in column 3 (Hispanic).

[d] Estimate is significantly different from the estimate in column 4 (non-Hispanic Asian).

[e] Estimate is significantly different from the estimate in column 5 (other).

[f] The omnibus chi-square test was not statistically significant ($p > 0.05$).

**Table 8.6**
**Past-Year Sexual Risk Behaviors and Outcomes, by Education Level**

| | High School or Less (1) | Some College (2) | Bachelor's Degree or More (3) |
|---|---|---|---|
| More than one sex partner | 29.9%[b,c] (25.7–34.1) | 19.6%[a,c] (17.6–21.5) | 12.5%[a,b] (10.7–14.2) |
| Sex with a new partner without a condom | 43.9%[b,c] (39.5–48.4) | 36.9%[a,c] (34.5–39.3) | 31.6%[a,b] (29.3–33.9) |
| STI[d] | 1.9% (0.7–3.1) | 2.0% (1.2–2.7) | 1.2% (0.4–2.0) |
| High risk for HIV infection | 31.9%[b,c] (27.6–36.2) | 21.2%[a,c] (19.2–23.2) | 13.7%[a,b] (11.9–15.5) |
| Condom use during most-recent vaginal sex | 28.6%[b,c] (24.4–32.9) | 20.9%[a] (18.8–23.0) | 20.1%[a] (17.9–22.2) |
| No birth control during most-recent vaginal sex[d] | 19.8% (16.3–23.2) | 19.6% (17.6–21.6) | 19.0% (17.0–20.9) |
| Unintended pregnancy | 4.4%[b,c] (2.7–6.0) | 2.4%[a] (1.7–3.1) | 1.3%[a] (0.7–2.0) |

NOTE: All data are weighted. 95-percent confidence intervals are presented in parentheses.

[a] Estimate is significantly different from the estimate in column 1 (high school or less).

[b] Estimate is significantly different from the estimate in column 2 (some college).

[c] Estimate is significantly different from the estimate in column 3 (bachelor's degree or more).

[d] The omnibus chi-square test was not statistically significant ($p > 0.05$).

**Table 8.7**
**Past-Year Sexual Risk Behaviors and Outcomes, by Marital or Cohabiting Status**

|  | Married or Cohabiting (1) | Not Married or Cohabiting (2) |
| --- | --- | --- |
| More than one sex partner | 6.1%[a] (5.2–7.1) | 40.3% (37.4–43.2) |
| Sex with a new partner without a condom[b] | 35.4% (33.4–37.4) | 38.6% (35.7–41.5) |
| STI | 1.1%[a] (0.6–1.7) | 2.6% (1.6–3.6) |
| High risk for HIV infection | 7.5%[a] (6.3–8.6) | 42.2% (39.2–45.2) |
| Condom use during most-recent vaginal sex | 14.2%[a] (12.7–15.7) | 34.8% (31.9–37.7) |
| No birth control during most-recent vaginal sex | 24.0%[a] (22.3–25.7) | 12.2% (10.2–14.1) |
| Unintended pregnancy[b] | 2.2% (1.4–3.1) | 2.6% (1.9–3.2) |

NOTE: All data are weighted. 95-percent confidence intervals are presented in parentheses.

[a] Estimate is significantly different from the estimate in column 2 (not married or cohabiting).

[b] The omnibus chi-square test was not statistically significant ($p > 0.05$).

## Contraceptive Use and Unintended Pregnancy

Additional analyses examined service members' experience of unintended pregnancy in relation to use and method of birth control. Long-acting contraception, such as an intrauterine device (IUD), has been associated with substantially lower unintended pregnancy rates, even among women who, at least initially, showed a preference for short-acting contraceptives (Hubacher et al., 2016), as well as in a convenience sample of low-income women (Winner et al., 2012). To explore how contraceptive choices may affect unintended pregnancies in the military, we categorized service members into three groups according to whether they used (1) sterilization or long-acting methods, (2) short-acting methods, or (3) no contraception during their most-recent vaginal sex, and we examined associations between contraceptive method and unintended pregnancy. Readers should use caution when interpreting this analysis because it examines the contraceptive method used during the most-recent vaginal sex rather than when a pregnancy occurred.

Table 8.8 shows the percentage of service members using each of a variety of contraceptive methods during the most-recent vaginal sex. Key findings include the following:

- Two short-acting methods of contraception—condoms and birth control pills—were, by far, the most commonly used.
- We did not detect a statistically significant association between unintended pregnancy and contraceptive choice. The rate of unintended pregnancy was least common in the long-acting contraception group (1.4 percent [CI: 0.7–2.1]), most common in the no contraception group (2.9 percent [CI: 1.8–4.1]), and in between for those using short-acting methods (2.2 percent [CI: 1.3–3.1]).

**Table 8.8**
**Method of Contraception Used During Most-Recent Vaginal Sex in the Past Year**

| Method of Contraception | Percentage Reporting Use During Most-Recent Vaginal Sex |
| --- | --- |
| Birth control pill | 20.4% (19.0–21.8) |
| Condom | 22.2% (20.7–23.7) |
| Did not use any form of birth control | 19.4% (18.1–20.7) |
| Male sterilization (vasectomy) | 7.5% (6.9–8.1) |
| IUD | 7.2% (6.4–7.9) |
| Birth control shot, birth control patch, contraceptive ring, or a diaphragm | 5.4% (4.6–6.2) |
| Female sterilization (e.g., tubal ligation, hysterectomy) | 5.3% (4.7–6.0) |
| Contraceptive implant (e.g., Implanon, Nexplanon) | 4.9% (4.1–5.6) |
| Some other method | 3.7% (3.0–4.4) |
| No vaginal sex in the past 12 months | 12.9% (11.7–14.2) |
| I/my partner was already pregnant | 3.3% (2.7–3.9) |
| I/my partner was trying to get pregnant | 5.3% (4.5–6.1) |

NOTE: More than one contraceptive method could be endorsed. If respondents indicated that they had not had vaginal sex in the past year or were already pregnant or trying to get pregnant, they could not endorse a contraceptive method.

HP2020 set a goal for increasing use of the "most effective or moderately effective" contraceptive methods among women aged 20–44 who are not already pregnant or trying to become pregnant. The only contraceptive methods in Table 8.8 that do not fall into this category are condoms and "some other method." HP2020 reports that from 2011 through 2013, 63.1 percent of women aged 20–44 who were not already pregnant or trying to become pregnant used a most effective or moderately effective method; HP2020 set a target of 69.3 percent or higher. In the 2015 HRBS, 66.0 percent (CI: 63.7–68.3) of women aged 20–44 who were not already pregnant or trying to become pregnant used such a method.

## HIV Testing

Finally, we examined the timing of service members' last HIV test overall and in relation to risk for HIV infection. The CDC recommends annual testing for HIV among those at high risk (CDC, 2016c). DoD Instruction 6485.01 requires screening at least every two years (DoD, 2013a), and an HIV test result on file (within the past 24 months) is required to deploy (DoD, 2006, 2014). As noted earlier, the 2015 HRBS defined those at high risk for HIV infection as men who had sex with one or more men in the past year, service members who had vaginal or anal sex with more than one partner in the past year, and service members who had a past-year STI (see CDC, 2011, 2016d). Key findings include the following:

- Among active-duty service members, 73.5 percent (CI: 72.0–75.0) reported having been tested for HIV in the past year.
- Among service members at high risk for HIV infection, 79.4 percent (CI: 76.0–82.7) were tested in the past year. This leaves 20.6 percent of high-risk individuals untested. If we multiply this by the 20.9 percent of personnel at high risk for HIV (from Table 8.1), this is equivalent to 4.3 percent (CI: 3.5–5.0) of service members overall who were both at high risk for HIV infection and untested in the past year.

Across service branches, we found no statistically significant differences for any of the three indicators: tested in the past year, tested among those at high risk for HIV infection, and untested but at high risk. HP2020 does not have a target for testing high-risk individuals but does set a goal for men who had sex with one or more men. The target is for 68.4 percent of these men to have had an HIV test in the past year, and HP2020 reported a baseline level of 62.2 percent with a past-year HIV test in 2008. In the 2015 HRBS, 83.6 percent (CI: 74.7–92.5) of men who had sex with one or more men in the past year had a past-year HIV test.

## Summary

Unintended pregnancy rates were slightly higher among female service members than among civilian women (although the difference does not reach statistical significance) and are of particular concern given the potential impact of pregnancy on readiness. Vaginal sex without use of any birth control was not uncommon. Nearly one in four married or cohabiting service members who were not trying to conceive failed to use contraception the most-recent time they had sex. And although most service members were tested for HIV in the past year, about one-fifth of those at high risk for HIV infection went untested in that period, counter to CDC recommendations (CDC, 2016c).

# CHAPTER NINE

# Sexual Orientation, Transgender Identity, and Health

Current data suggest that the health issues and needs of lesbian, gay, bisexual, and transgender (LGBT) individuals differ somewhat from those of their peers (Institute of Medicine, 2011). Smoking, alcohol, and other drug use are greater in this group than the rest of the population, as are mental health problems, some sexual and reproductive health issues, and overweight and obesity. LGBT individuals may also be less likely to access routine health care (Institute of Medicine, 2011). All of these disparities can affect readiness among LGBT service members. The 2015 HRBS provides the first direct estimate of the percentage of service personnel who identify as LGBT.[1] Two previously published estimates specific to the lesbian, gay, or bisexual (LGB) portion of this group were derived indirectly, using data from surveys of nonmilitary personnel combined with information about military service.[2] Those studies put the percentage of LGB service members between 0.9 and 3.7 percent (Gates, 2010; National Defense Research Institute, 2010). We know of no prior examination of the health-related behavior or health status of LGBT service members, a fact made even more important by recent DoD policy changes allowing for open LGBT service in the U.S. military.[3] This chapter provides key information about these issues.

Sexual orientation can be measured as (1) relative attraction to the same compared with opposite sex, (2) sexual activity with the same compared with opposite sex, and (3) sexual identity (i.e., gay, lesbian, or bisexual) (Savin-Williams, 2009). The 2015 HRBS assessed the sexual orientation of service members in all of these ways. It also measured transgender identity, which is often considered in conjunction with sexual orientation. In the first section of this chapter, we report the percentages of service members who identified as LGBT based on all of these measures. We also provide these percentages by service branch, pay grade, gender, age group, race/ethnicity, and education level. Key measures used are described in applicable sections, and additional details about these measures may be found in Appendix D.

For the remainder of the chapter, we focus on the health status and behavior of the combined LGBT population, defining this group based on the sexual identity measure and the

---

[1]  As this report was in the final stages of production, findings from the 2016 Workplace and Gender Relations Survey of Active Duty Members were released, indicating that 12 percent of female service members and 3 percent of male service members identify as LGBT (Davis et al., 2017).

[2]  As with the other substantive chapters in this report, readers should use caution when interpreting comparisons between the 2015 HRBS results and other populations because these comparisons are not necessarily statistically significant and could simply reflect sampling variability across the two samples being compared; however, where available, we provide confidence intervals for comparisons.

[3]  On July 26, 2017, as this report was in the final stages of production, President Donald Trump announced intentions to prohibit transgender individuals from serving in the military (Diamond, 2017).

transgender identity measure. Although it is likely that there are differences in health-related behavior and outcomes by subgroup (e.g., lesbians may differ from gay men), we have an insufficient number of individuals in each subgroup to reliably estimate those differences.

## Sexual Orientation and Transgender Identity

Table 9.1 provides estimates based on the three measures of sexual orientation: attraction, activity, and identity. It also presents estimates of transgender identity and an overall estimate of LGBT identity.

### Sexual Attraction

Key findings related to sexual attraction include the following:

- In the 2015 HRBS, 2.2 percent of men described themselves as mostly or only attracted to men, 1.2 percent as equally attracted to men and women, 4.3 percent as mostly attracted to women, and 90.1 percent as only attracted to women.
- Among women, 7.6 percent described themselves as mostly or only attracted to women, 5.2 percent as equally attracted to women and men, 16.1 percent as mostly attracted to men, and 68.2 percent as only attracted to men.

### Sexual Activity

Key findings related to sexual activity include the following:

- Among men, 3.3 percent had sex with one or more men in the past 12 months.
- Among women, 9.4 percent had sex with one or more women in the past 12 months.

### Sexual Identity

Key findings related to sexual identity include the following:

- In the 2015 HRBS, 5.8 percent of service members identified as LGB. Item nonresponse may have affected this estimate. A small percentage (0.3 percent) of HRBS respondents declined to answer the sexual identity question. If all of these persons were LGB, the overall percentage would be 6.0 percent.
- Among men, 1.9 percent identified as gay and 2.0 percent identified as bisexual.
- Among women, 7.0 percent identified as lesbian and 9.1 percent identified as bisexual.

A recent national study of high school students in grades 9 through 12 found that 2.0 percent (CI: 1.7–2.5) identified as gay or lesbian, 6.0 percent (CI: 5.2–6.9) identified as bisexual, and 3.2 percent (CI: 2.7–3.7) were not sure of their sexual identity (Kann et al., 2016). These estimates are somewhat higher than the estimates for adults reported by Ward and colleagues (2014) using the National Health Interview Survey, who found that 1.6 percent (CI: 1.4–1.8) of adults aged 18–64 identified as gay or lesbian, 0.7 percent (CI: 0.6–0.8) identified as bisexual, and 1.1 percent identified as "something else," stated "I don't know the answer," or refused to provide an answer (the remainder identified as heterosexual). Given the age profile of the HRBS sample (and the military in general), it is not surprising that our estimates of sexual identity fall somewhere between these two reports but align more closely to the younger population.

**Table 9.1**
**Sexual Orientation and Transgender Identity, by Gender**

| | Men[a] | Women[a] | Overall |
|---|---|---|---|
| **Sexual attraction** | | | |
| Only attracted to men | 1.7%<br>(1.1–2.3) | 68.2%<br>(66.2–70.2) | |
| Mostly attracted to men | 0.5%<br>(0.2–0.8) | 16.1%<br>(14.6–17.7) | |
| Equally attracted to men and women | 1.2%<br>(0.7–1.8) | 5.2%<br>(4.2–6.3) | |
| Mostly attracted to women | 4.3%<br>(3.4–5.1) | 3.2%<br>(2.4–4.0) | |
| Only attracted to women | 90.1%<br>(88.8–91.4) | 4.4%<br>(3.5–5.3) | |
| Not attracted to either men or women | 0.7%<br>(0.3–1.0) | 1.3%<br>(0.7–1.9) | |
| Not sure | 1.5%<br>(0.9–2.1) | 1.7%<br>(1.1–2.3) | |
| **Sexual activity** | | | |
| Sex with one or more same-sex partners in the past 12 months | 3.3%<br>(2.6–4.1) | 9.4%<br>(8.1–10.6) | |
| **Sexual identity** | | | |
| Gay or lesbian | 1.9%<br>(1.3–2.5) | 7.0%<br>(5.8–8.1) | |
| Bisexual | 2.0%<br>(1.4–2.6) | 9.1%<br>(7.8–10.4) | |
| Total LGB[b] | | | 5.8%<br>(5.0–6.6) |
| **Transgender identity** | | | |
| Transgender | 0.5%<br>(0.2–0.8) | 1.2%<br>(0.6–1.7) | |
| Total transgender[c] | | | 0.6%<br>(0.3–0.9) |
| Total LGBT identity[d] | | | 6.1%<br>(5.3–6.9) |

NOTE: Percentages are reported for the sample overall, not among only LGBT respondents.

[a] As with all 2015 HRBS data in this report, service members are categorized by gender as self-reported in the survey.

[b] If all respondents who declined to answer this item (0.3 percent) were LGB, the overall percentage would be 6.0 percent.

[c] If all respondents who declined to answer this item (0.4 percent) were transgender, the overall percentage would be 1.0 percent. If weights were calculated based on reported gender instead of the gender in DMDC records, the overall percentage would be 1.1 percent.

[d] The total LGBT percentage does not equal a simple sum of the LGB and the transgender percentages because of overlap in the two groups (n = 40) and some differences in item-level nonresponse across the two items.

Table 9.2 shows the percentages of gay and bisexual men and of lesbian and bisexual women, by service branch. Key findings include the following:

- A larger percentage of men who identified as gay served in the Navy than in any other service branch. There were no differences observed in the percentage of bisexual men in the various services.
- Of women who identified as lesbian, fewer served in the Air Force than in all other services, apart from the Navy (that is, although the estimated percentage of serving lesbians was higher in the Navy than in the Air Force, the estimates were not statistically distinguishable from one another).
- The percentage of Marine Corps women who identified as bisexual was 18.5 percent, substantially higher than in any of the other service branches.

### Transgender Identity

Key findings related to transgender identity include the following.

- In the 2015 HRBS, 0.6 percent of military service members described themselves as transgender.[4] This is identical to the most recent estimate of the percentage of U.S. adults describing themselves as transgender, 0.6 percent (credible interval: 0.4–1.0[5]) (Flores et al., 2016).

**Table 9.2**
**Lesbian, Gay, and Bisexual Identity, by Service Branch**

| | Air Force (1) | Army (2) | Marine Corps (3) | Navy (4) | Coast Guard (5) |
|---|---|---|---|---|---|
| **Men** | | | | | |
| Gay | 1.6%[d] (0.8–2.4) | 1.3%[d] (0.4–2.2) | 0.3%[d] (0.0–0.7) | 4.5%[a,b,c,e] (2.5–6.4) | 1.3%[d] (0.8–1.8) |
| Bisexual[f] | 1.6% (0.8–2.3) | 2.1% (0.8–3.3) | 2.0% (0.7–3.4) | 2.4% (1.1–3.7) | 1.6% (1.0–2.1) |
| **Women** | | | | | |
| Lesbian | 4.7%[b,c,e] (3.5–5.9) | 8.1%[a] (5.8–10.3) | 9.8%[a] (5.9–13.7) | 6.8% (4.2–9.5) | 10.3%[a] (7.9–12.7) |
| Bisexual | 8.2%[c] (6.5–9.8) | 7.8%[c] (5.6–10.1) | 18.5%[a,b,d,e] (13.0–23.9) | 9.6%[c] (6.4–12.9) | 6.8%[c] (4.8–8.8) |

NOTE: All data are weighted. 95-percent confidence intervals are presented in parentheses.
[a] Estimate is significantly different from the estimate in column 1 (Air Force).
[b] Estimate is significantly different from the estimate in column 2 (Army).
[c] Estimate is significantly different from the estimate in column 3 (Marine Corps).
[d] Estimate is significantly different from the estimate in column 4 (Navy).
[e] Estimate is significantly different from the estimate in column 5 (Coast Guard).
[f] The omnibus chi-square test was not statistically significant ($p > 0.05$).

---

[4]  This point estimate is the same when analyses are limited to the DoD branches of the HRBS sample (i.e., if the Coast Guard is excluded).

[5]  The interpretation of a credible interval differs from that of a confidence interval. In this context, the credible interval indicates that there is a 95-percent probability that the true percentage of service members who were transgender lies between 0.4 and 1.0.

- Overall, 0.4 percent of respondents declined to answer the transgender question. If all of these persons were in fact transgender, the overall percentage would be 1.0 percent.[6]

Estimates of the percentage of service members who identified as transgender are based on weights that assume that the gender service members reported in response to the HRBS item matches the gender in their DMDC record. If we instead assume that service members responded to this question with a gender that does *not* match their DMDC record (e.g., DMDC has their gender at birth on record and the person responded to the survey with their gender identity), then the estimate becomes 1.1 percent of service members who described themselves as transgender. Key findings include the following:

- Of service members who self-reported their gender as female, 1.2 percent also reported transgender identity; 0.5 percent of those who self-reported their gender as male did so (Table 9.1).
- Said another way, among those reporting transgender status, 30.2 percent reported being female and 69.9 percent reported being male. For context, 84.4 percent of HRBS respondents reported being male.

## LGBT Identity

Combining the sexual orientation and transgender categories, 6.1 percent of service members identified as LGBT. In the U.S. general population in 2011, the most recent estimate available, the percentage of LGBT adults was estimated to be 3.4 percent (margin of sampling error less than ±1.0) (Gates and Newport, 2012).

Table 9.3 presents the percentage of service members who self-identified as LGBT by subgroup, including service branch, pay grade, gender, age group, race/ethnicity, and education level. Key findings include the following:

- The Navy, at 9.1 percent, had a significantly larger percentage of service members who identified as LGBT than the other service branches.
- Significantly more junior enlisted service members (8.4 percent) self-identified as LGBT than any other pay grade.
- Almost four times as many service members who reported being female (16.6 percent) identified as LGBT than service members who reported being male (4.2 percent).
- Significantly more service members under age 35 (9.3 percent among those aged 17–24 and 6.4 percent among those aged 25–34) self-identified as LGBT compared with those aged 35 or older (2.6 percent among those aged 35–44 and 2.8 percent among those 45 or older).
- No statistically significant differences in self-identified LGBT status were observed across race/ethnicity.
- The percentage of self-identified LGBT service members was lower among those with a bachelor's degree or more (4.0 percent) compared with those with less education (6.6 percent among those with a high school degree or less and 7.3 percent among those with some college).

---

[6]   This point estimate is the same when analyses are limited to the DoD branches of the HRBS sample (i.e., if the Coast Guard is excluded).

**Table 9.3**
**LGBT Identity, by Subgroup**

| | Identified as LGBT |
|---|---|
| Total | 6.1%<br>(5.3–6.9) |
| Service branch | |
|   Air Force | 5.3%[d]<br>(4.3–6.3) |
|   Army | 5.5%[d]<br>(4.0–6.9) |
|   Marine Corps | 4.4%[d]<br>(3.0–5.8) |
|   Navy | 9.1%[a,b,c,e]<br>(7.0–11.2) |
|   Coast Guard | 5.2%[d]<br>(4.4–6.0) |
| Pay grade | |
|   E1–E4 | 8.4%[g,h,i,j,k]<br>(6.8–10.0) |
|   E5–E6 | 5.2%[f,h,k]<br>(4.0–6.3) |
|   E7–E9 | 3.0%[f,g]<br>(2.1–3.9) |
|   W1–W5 | 2.4%[f]<br>(1.2–3.6) |
|   O1–O3 | 4.6%[f,k]<br>(3.6–5.6) |
|   O4–O10 | 2.7%[f,g,j]<br>(1.9–3.5) |
| Gender | |
|   Male | 4.2%[l]<br>(3.3–5.1) |
|   Female | 16.6%<br>(14.9–18.3) |
| Age group | |
|   Ages 17–24 | 9.3%[o,p]<br>(7.3–11.4) |
|   Ages 25–34 | 6.4%[o,p]<br>(5.2–7.7) |
|   Ages 35–44 | 2.6%[m,n]<br>(1.9–3.3) |
|   Ages 45+ | 2.8%[m,n]<br>(1.8–3.9) |
| Race/ethnicity[t] | |
|   Non-Hispanic white | 5.4%<br>(4.5–6.3) |
|   Non-Hispanic black | 7.8%<br>(4.7–10.9) |
|   Hispanic | 7.2%<br>(4.8–9.6) |
|   Non-Hispanic Asian | 6.3%<br>(2.5–10.1) |
|   Other | 6.9%<br>(4.4–9.4) |

**Table 9.3—Continued**

|  | Identified as LGBT |
|---|---|
| Education level |  |
| High school or less | 6.6%[s] (4.4–8.8) |
| Some college | 7.3%[s] (6.1–8.6) |
| Bachelor's degree or more | 4.0%[q,r] (3.0–4.9) |

NOTE: All data are weighted. 95-percent confidence intervals are presented in parentheses.

[a] Estimate is significantly different from the estimate for Air Force.

[b] Estimate is significantly different from the estimate for Army.

[c] Estimate is significantly different from the estimate for Marine Corps.

[d] Estimate is significantly different from the estimate for Navy.

[e] Estimate is significantly different from the estimate for Coast Guard.

[f] Estimate is significantly different from the estimate for E1–E4.

[g] Estimate is significantly different from the estimate for E5–E6.

[h] Estimate is significantly different from the estimate for E7–E9.

[i] Estimate is significantly different from the estimate for W1–W5.

[j] Estimate is significantly different from the estimate for O1–O3.

[k] Estimate is significantly different from the estimate for O4–O10.

[l] Estimate is significantly different from the estimate for female.

[m] Estimate is significantly different from the estimate for ages 17–24.

[n] Estimate is significantly different from the estimate for ages 25–34.

[o] Estimate is significantly different from the estimate for ages 35–44.

[p] Estimate is significantly different from the estimate for ages 45+.

[q] Estimate is significantly different from the estimate for high school or less.

[r] Estimate is significantly different from the estimate for some college.

[s] Estimate is significantly different from the estimate for bachelor's degree or more.

[t] The omnibus chi-square test was not statistically significant ($p > 0.05$).

## LGBT Health

Table 9.4 indicates the percentages of LGBT service members who reported each of a variety of key health-related behaviors and outcomes, as well as percentages among non-LGBT personnel. Note that the "total" column may not exactly match the totals reported in earlier chapters because the sample size for this analysis was different; that is, we excluded respondents who did not indicate whether they were LGBT.

**Table 9.4**
**Health-Related Behaviors and Outcomes, Overall and by LGBT Status**

| | Total<br>(1) | LGBT<br>(2) | Non-LGBT<br>(3) |
|---|---|---|---|
| Routine medical checkup in the past year[c] | 81.5%<br>(80.0–82.9) | 81.7%<br>(76.4–87.0) | 81.4%<br>(80.0–82.9) |
| Overweight or obese | 66.3%<br>(64.6–67.9) | 54.2%[a]<br>(47.5–61.0) | 67.0%<br>(65.4–68.7) |
| Binge drinking in the past month | 29.8%<br>(28.2–31.5) | 37.6%[a]<br>(31.2–44.1) | 29.3%<br>(27.6–31.0) |
| Heavy drinking in the past month[c] | 5.2%<br>(4.4–6.1) | 5.6%<br>(2.9–8.4) | 5.2%<br>(4.3–6.1) |
| Current cigarette smoker | 16.5%<br>(15.1–18.0) | 24.8%[a]<br>(18.3–31.2) | 16.0%<br>(14.5–17.5) |
| Mild depression[b] | 82.2%<br>(80.8–83.6) | 73.1%[a]<br>(67.4–78.9) | 82.8%<br>(81.3–84.2) |
| Moderate depression[b] | 8.8%<br>(7.7–9.8) | 13.2%[d]<br>(9.0–17.4) | 8.5%<br>(7.4–9.5) |
| Severe depression[b] | 9.1%<br>(8.0–10.1) | 13.7%[a]<br>(9.0–18.3) | 8.8%<br>(7.7–9.9) |
| Lifetime NSSI | 11.3%<br>(10.2–12.4) | 26.5%[a]<br>(20.7–32.3) | 10.3%<br>(9.2–11.5) |
| Lifetime suicide ideation | 18.1%<br>(16.7–19.5) | 32.7%[a]<br>(26.6–38.9) | 17.1%<br>(15.7–18.5) |
| Suicide ideation in the past year | 6.4%<br>(5.4–7.3) | 15.3%[a]<br>(10.0–20.5) | 5.8%<br>(4.8–6.8) |
| Lifetime suicide attempt | 5.1%<br>(4.3–6.0) | 13.0%[a]<br>(8.6–17.3) | 4.6%<br>(3.8–5.5) |
| Suicide attempt in the past year | 1.4%<br>(0.9–1.9) | 4.8%[a]<br>(1.6–8.0) | 1.2%<br>(0.7–1.7) |
| Lifetime unwanted sexual contact | 16.9%<br>(15.7–18.1) | 39.9%[a]<br>(33.6–46.3) | 15.4%<br>(14.2–16.6) |
| Lifetime physical abuse | 12.9%<br>(11.8–14.1) | 21.4%[a]<br>(16.1–26.7) | 12.4%<br>(11.2–13.6) |
| More than one sex partner in the past year | 19.1%<br>(17.6–20.5) | 40.2%[a]<br>(33.4–47.1) | 17.7%<br>(16.2–19.1) |
| Sex with a new partner without a condom in the past year | 36.0%<br>(34.3–37.8) | 42.4%[a]<br>(35.9–48.9) | 35.6%<br>(33.9–37.4) |
| STI in the past year | 1.8%<br>(1.2–2.3) | 7.4%[a]<br>(3.1–11.8) | 1.4%<br>(0.9–1.9) |
| HIV test in the past year[c] | 73.4%<br>(71.8–74.9) | 75.7%<br>(69.8–81.5) | 73.2%<br>(71.6–74.9) |
| No birth control during the most-recent vaginal sex (within the past year) | 22.0%<br>(20.5–23.6) | 31.5%[a]<br>(25.1–37.9) | 21.6%<br>(20.0–23.2) |
| Unintended pregnancy in the past year[c] | 2.4%<br>(1.9–3.0) | 1.6%<br>(0.6–2.6) | 2.5%<br>(1.9–3.1) |

NOTE: All data are weighted. 95-percent confidence intervals are presented in parentheses. Column 1 (total) may not exactly match the totals reported in earlier chapters because the sample size for this analysis was different (we excluded respondents who did not indicate whether they were LGBT).

[a] Estimate is significantly different from the estimate in column 3 (non-LGBT).

[b] We defined *mild depression* as a score between 0 and 9 on the PHQ-9, *moderate depression* as a score between 10 and 14 on the PHQ-9, and *severe depression* as a score of 15 or more on the PHQ-9.

[c] The omnibus chi-square test was not statistically significant (*p* > 0.05).

## Health Promotion and Disease Prevention

Key findings related to health promotion and disease prevention include the following:

- Among LGBT personnel, 81.7 percent had a routine checkup in the past 12 months, which is similar to the percentage among other service members.
- Also, 54.2 percent of LGBT service members have BMI scores that classify them as overweight or obese. The percentage is higher among non-LGBT service members (67.0 percent).

## Substance Use

Key findings related to substance use include the following:

- Across all services, 37.6 percent of LGBT personnel reported binge drinking in the past month, and 5.6 percent reported heavy drinking. Percentages among other personnel were lower for binge drinking (29.3 percent), but the percentages that reported heavy drinking were equivalent.
- In the 2015 HRBS, 24.8 percent of LGBT service members were current cigarette smokers. A smaller group of non-LGBT personnel (16.0 percent) were current cigarette smokers.

## Mental and Emotional Health

Key findings related to mental and emotional health include the following:

- Among LGBT service members, 13.2 percent had symptoms indicative of moderate depression. An additional 13.7 percent had symptoms of severe depression.
- Lifetime history of NSSI (i.e., self-inflicted injury) was reported by 26.5 percent of LGBT personnel.
- Lifetime suicide ideation (i.e., seriously considered suicide) was reported by 32.7 percent of LGBT personnel, and 15.3 percent reported having such thoughts during the past year.
- Lifetime history of suicide attempt was reported by 13.0 percent of LGBT personnel, and 4.8 percent made a suicide attempt during the past year.

The percentages of non-LGBT service members reporting all of these outcomes were substantially lower. Percentages with moderate and severe depression among other service members were about two-thirds of the LGBT percentages. The percentages of non-LGBT personnel reporting suicide and self-harm were generally less than half of those among LGBT personnel.

## Unwanted Sexual Contact and Physical Abuse

Key findings related to unwanted sexual contact and physical abuse include the following:

- During their lifetime, 39.9 percent of LGBT service members have experienced unwanted sexual contact, and 21.4 percent have experienced physical abuse.
- Among non-LGBT personnel, percentages were approximately half of these: 15.4 percent reported any lifetime experience of unwanted sexual contact, and 12.4 percent reported any lifetime physical abuse.

**Sexual and Reproductive Health**

Key findings related to sexual and reproductive health include the following:

- Across all services, 40.2 percent of LGBT service members had more than one sexual partner in the past year, and 42.4 percent had unprotected vaginal or anal sex with a new sex partner in the past year. The percentages were lower among non-LGBT personnel (17.7 percent and 35.6 percent, respectively).
- Consistent with these risk behaviors, 7.4 percent of LGBT personnel had an STI in the past year, which is much higher than the 1.4 percent among the rest of the service.
- Among LGBT service members, 75.7 percent had an HIV test in the past year. The percentage was comparable among non-LGBT personnel.
- Among LGBT service personnel who had vaginal sex in the past year, 31.5 percent did not use any form of birth control during their most-recent vaginal sex encounter (and were not trying to conceive), while the rate was 21.6 percent among other service members.
- Among LGBT service members, 1.6 percent caused or experienced an unintended pregnancy in the past year, which is comparable to the percentage among other service members.

## Summary

Results indicate that LGBT personnel make up 6.1 percent of service members. LGBT personnel get routine medical care in percentages similar to non-LGBT personnel. However, compared with non-LGBT personnel, they report more smoking, binge drinking, sexual behavior risky to their health, and adverse sexual health outcomes. The percentages of LGBT personnel reporting mental health issues, a history of unwanted sexual contact, and a history of physical abuse are particularly high. Although these individuals are a small portion of the force, the disparities in their experiences, behaviors, and outcomes warrant close attention and tracking by DoD so that their specific needs can be addressed.

# CHAPTER TEN

# Deployment Experiences and Health

This chapter presents the results of detailed analyses of active-duty service members' deployments and combat exposures and their relationships with health and health-related behaviors. Specifically, this chapter presents the frequency and duration of deployments (both most recent and lifetime), levels of exposure to combat-related experiences, the prevalence of deployment-related injuries (including TBI), the prevalence of deployment-related substance use, and deployment-related mental and physical health.

Each section highlights the importance of a deployment-related topic and the importance of the related analyses for the military community. Key measures used are described in the applicable section, and additional details about these measures may be found in Appendix D. Analyses are presented by service branch, pay grade, gender, age group, race/ethnicity, and education level. Additional analyses stratify the sample by recency of deployment, deployment-related trauma exposure, and mild TBI (mTBI) status. All analyses demonstrated statistically significant omnibus tests (Rao-Scott chi-square test for categorical variables and $F$-tests for continuous variables) unless otherwise noted in the tables. Statistically significant group differences (pairwise comparisons) are also presented. However, only statistically significant differences that the research team's subject-matter experts determined to be substantively meaningful (i.e., could be used to change or develop policy or contribute to inequalities in health outcomes across subgroups) are discussed in the text.

## Frequency and Duration of Combat and Noncombat Deployments

Extensive policy interest has surrounded the tempo of combat and deployment operations and its impact on the health and readiness of military forces (Rona et al., 2007, MacGregor et al., 2014; Armed Forces Health Surveillance Center, 2011). However, data on this question have yielded mixed findings, perhaps partly because of varied definitions and indicators of operational tempo, including deployment frequency, deployment duration, nature of deployments (e.g., noncombat, combat, intensity of combat), and the length of time between deployments (also called *dwell time*).

Six survey items in the 2015 HRBS assessed respondents' deployment history. Questions ascertained the start date, end date, type of most-recent deployment (i.e., combat zone or noncombat zone), and total time spent deployed in the past 12 months and since joining the military. Responses to the start and end date of the most-recent deployment provided a chronological context for the most-recent deployment, established a baseline of active-duty members with at least one deployment in their lifetime (hereafter referred to as *previously deployed* personnel, for simplicity), and determined which military personnel have experienced a recent deployment and which have not. The survey item asking the start date of most-recent deployment was created for the 2015 iteration of the HRBS. Items about the end date of most-recent deployment and time away for deployment in the past 12 months are standard items that were drawn from DMDC's Status of Forces Survey. In addition, items about the cumulative number of deployments and duration of all deployments provided estimates of lifetime deployment exposure.

Tables 10.1 through 10.3 present the recency, number, type (combat or noncombat), and duration (lifetime and in the past 12 months) of deployments among active-duty members across all services. Most analyses pertain only to service members with at least one previous deployment. Only service members who were not deployed at the time of survey administration were eligible to complete the survey. Key findings include the following:

- Across all services, 61.3 percent of service members had at least one previous deployment (deployed to either a combat or noncombat zone during their service in the military); 38.7 percent reported having never deployed (Table 10.1).
- Among previously deployed personnel, nearly half (49.0 percent) reported three or more deployments since joining the military (Table 10.1).
- Members of the Coast Guard were more likely than members of the other services to report three or more previous deployments; in addition, Coast Guard deployments were least likely to be to a combat zone (Table 10.1).
- Among all previously deployed service members, 64.3 percent reported that their most-recent deployment was to a combat zone. This figure was highest for the Army (79.4 percent) and lowest for the Coast Guard (12.1 percent) (Table 10.1).
- Previously deployed service members most commonly started their most-recent deployment between one and three years ago (27.2 percent) (Table 10.1).
- Among previously deployed service members, total lifetime duration of deployments varied widely: 14.5 percent deployed for a total of one to six months and 12.1 percent deployed for 49 months or more, with relatively even distribution in between. Members of the Coast Guard reported the highest total deployed duration in their lifetime (Table 10.2).
- Two-thirds of previously deployed active-duty personnel reported they had not deployed in the past 12 months. Among personnel who had deployed in the past 12 months, the highest percentage (11.5 percent) reported deploying for four to six months while the lowest percentage (2.3 percent) reported deploying for less than one month (Table 10.3).

**Table 10.1**
**Recency, Number, and Most-Recent Type of Deployment, by Service Branch**

| | Total (1) | Air Force (2) | Army (3) | Marine Corps (4) | Navy (5) | Coast Guard (6) |
|---|---|---|---|---|---|---|
| **Most-recent deployment started** | | | | | | |
| Never been deployed | 38.7% (37.2–40.2) | 43.5%[b,d] (41.5–45.5) | 37.3%[a,e] (34.3–40.3) | 43.0%[d] (39.0–47.1) | 33.2%[a,c,e] (30.3–36.1) | 43.8%[b,d] (42.0–45.5) |
| Less than 1 year ago | 11.2% (10.1–12.3) | 8.5%[c,d,e] (7.1–9.9) | 8.5%[c,d,e] (6.5–10.6) | 16.6%[a,b] (13.1–20.1) | 13.8%[a,b,e] (11.4–16.1) | 20.1%[a,b,d] (18.6–21.6) |
| 1–3 years ago | 27.2% (25.7–28.6) | 24.7%[d,e] (22.7–26.7) | 28.9%[e] (26.0–31.8) | 24.3%[e] (21.0–27.6) | 30.2%[a,e] (27.2–33.1) | 14.5%[a,b,c,d] (13.2–15.7) |
| 4–5 years ago | 11.9% (11.0–12.8) | 10.0%[b,e] (8.7–11.3) | 14.0%[a,c,e] (12.0–15.9) | 8.8%[b,d] (7.4–10.2) | 12.7%[c,e] (10.9–14.4) | 7.2%[a,b,d] (6.4–8.0) |
| More than 5 years ago | 11.0% (10.3–11.8) | 13.3%[c,d] (12.0–14.7) | 11.3%[c,e] (9.8–12.8) | 7.3%[a,b,d,e] (5.9–8.7) | 10.2%[a,c,e] (8.7–11.7) | 14.5%[b,c,d] (13.4–15.5) |
| **Total number of deployments, lifetime[f]** | | | | | | |
| 1 deployment | 31.1% (29.4–32.8) | 33.1%[d,e] (30.5–35.7) | 33.1%[d,e] (29.9–36.4) | 38.2%[d,e] (33.8–42.7) | 24.3%[a,b,c,e] (21.0–27.5) | 17.7%[a,b,c,d] (15.9–19.5) |
| 2 deployments | 19.9% (18.3–21.5) | 21.5%[e] (19.0–24.1) | 20.9%[e] (17.7–24.0) | 18.6%[e] (14.8–22.4) | 18.8%[e] (15.8–21.9) | 9.1%[a,b,c,d] (7.7–10.5) |
| 3 or more deployments | 49.0% (47.5–50.6) | 45.4%[d,e] (42.7–48.1) | 46.0%[d,e] (43.1–48.9) | 43.1%[d,e] (39.1–47.1) | 56.9%[a,b,c,e] (53.8–60.0) | 73.2%[a,b,c,d] (71.1–75.2) |
| **Most-recent deployment type[f]** | | | | | | |
| Combat zone | 64.3% (62.5–66.1) | 66.9%[b,c,d,e] (63.9–69.8) | 79.4%[a,c,d,e] (76.1–82.7) | 51.8%[a,b,e] (47.2–56.5) | 51.2%[a,b,e] (47.5–54.9) | 12.1%[a,b,c,d] (10.6–13.5) |

NOTE: All data are weighted. 95-percent confidence intervals are presented in parentheses.

[a] Estimate is significantly different from the estimate in column 2 (Air Force).

[b] Estimate is significantly different from the estimate in column 3 (Army).

[c] Estimate is significantly different from the estimate in column 4 (Marine Corps).

[d] Estimate is significantly different from the estimate in column 5 (Navy).

[e] Estimate is significantly different from the estimate in column 6 (Coast Guard).

[f] Includes only respondents who reported one or more previous combat or noncombat deployments.

**Table 10.2**
**Total Duration of All Previous Deployments, by Service Branch**

| | Total (1) | Air Force (2) | Army (3) | Marine Corps (4) | Navy (5) | Coast Guard (6) |
|---|---|---|---|---|---|---|
| 1–6 months | 14.5% (13.1–15.9) | 25.8%[b,d,e] (23.3–28.4) | 8.3%[a,c,e] (5.8–10.7) | 18.9%[b] (14.4–23.4) | 12.5%[a] (9.7–15.4) | 17.6%[a,b] (15.7–19.4) |
| 7–12 months | 25.3% (23.6–27.1) | 26.6%[e] (23.9–29.3) | 24.9%[e] (21.5–28.3) | 29.5%[e] (24.5–34.5) | 23.5% (20.2–26.8) | 19.4%[a,b,c] (17.5–21.3) |
| 13–24 months[f] | 24.1% (22.5–25.8) | 24.6% (22.1–27.1) | 23.6% (20.3–26.9) | 22.0% (18.3–25.8) | 25.4% (22.2–28.7) | 25.9% (23.9–28.0) |
| 25–48 months | 23.9% (22.5–25.3) | 16.2%[b,d,e] (14.2–18.3) | 30.2%[a,c,d,e] (27.3–33.1) | 18.7%[b] (15.9–21.5) | 23.4%[a,b] (20.7–26.0) | 20.6%[a,b] (18.9–22.3) |
| 49+ months | 12.1% (11.1–13.0) | 6.7%[b,c,d,e] (5.2–8.2) | 13.0%[a,e] (11.2–14.9) | 10.9%[a,d,e] (9.0–12.8) | 15.1%[a,c] (13.3–17.0) | 16.5%[a,b,c] (15.0–17.9) |

NOTE: All data are weighted. 95-percent confidence intervals are presented in parentheses. Table includes only respondents who reported one or more previous combat or noncombat deployments.

[a] Estimate is significantly different from the estimate in column 2 (Air Force).

[b] Estimate is significantly different from the estimate in column 3 (Army).

[c] Estimate is significantly different from the estimate in column 4 (Marine Corps).

[d] Estimate is significantly different from the estimate in column 5 (Navy).

[e] Estimate is significantly different from the estimate in column 6 (Coast Guard).

[f] The omnibus chi-square test was not statistically significant ($p > 0.05$).

**Table 10.3**
**Total Duration of Deployments in the Past 12 Months, by Service Branch**

| | Total (1) | Air Force (2) | Army (3) | Marine Corps (4) | Navy (5) | Coast Guard (6) |
|---|---|---|---|---|---|---|
| Did not deploy in the past 12 months | 66.4% (64.6–68.3) | 72.4%[c,d,e] (69.7–75.2) | 70.1%[c,e] (66.5–73.7) | 53.1%[a,b,d] (48.7–57.6) | 63.9%[a,c,e] (60.3–67.5) | 55.2%[a,b,d] (52.9–57.5) |
| Less than 1 month | 2.3% (1.8–2.9) | 2.7%[e] (1.6–3.9) | 1.7%[e] (0.7–2.6) | 1.3%[e] (0.5–2.0) | 2.9%[e] (1.6–4.2) | 7.7%[a,b,c,d] (6.5–9.0) |
| 1–3 months | 8.7% (7.5–9.9) | 6.6%[c,e] (5.1–8.2) | 7.3%[e] (5.0–9.5) | 13.2%[a] (9.2–17.2) | 9.4%[e] (7.0–11.8) | 15.7%[a,b,d] (13.9–17.4) |
| 4–6 months | 11.5% (10.2–12.8) | 13.7%[b] (11.5–16.0) | 7.7%[a,c,e] (5.4–10.1) | 17.8%[b] (13.3–22.2) | 12.1% (9.5–14.8) | 13.2%[b] (11.6–14.9) |
| 7–9 months | 7.1% (5.9–8.3) | 2.5%[b,c,d,e] (1.6–3.4) | 6.7%[a] (4.5–8.9) | 11.3%[a,e] (7.5–15.1) | 9.4%[a,e] (7.0–11.7) | 5.8%[a,c,d] (4.6–7.0) |
| 10–12 months | 4.0% (3.0–5.0) | 1.9%[b] (1.1–2.8) | 6.5%[a,d,e] (4.3–8.8) | 3.3% (1.6–5.0) | 2.3%[b] (1.1–3.6) | 2.4%[b] (1.6–3.1) |

NOTE: All data are weighted. 95-percent confidence intervals are presented in parentheses. Table includes only respondents who reported one or more previous combat or noncombat deployments.

[a] Estimate is significantly different from the estimate in column 2 (Air Force).

[b] Estimate is significantly different from the estimate in column 3 (Army).

[c] Estimate is significantly different from the estimate in column 4 (Marine Corps).

[d] Estimate is significantly different from the estimate in column 5 (Navy).

[e] Estimate is significantly different from the estimate in column 6 (Coast Guard).

## Combat Experiences During Deployment

Assessing the impact of combat exposure on health can provide insight into the long-term physical, psychological, and cognitive effects of these experiences. Many studies and reviews have shown that higher combat exposure is significantly associated with postdeployment mental health issues (Hoge, Auchterlonie, and Milliken, 2006; Sareen et al., 2007; Skipper et al., 2014; Ramchand, Schell, Karney, et al., 2010; Ramchand, Rudavsky, et al., 2015), and significant percentages of recently deployed service members report mental and physical health problems—including PTSD, TBI, generalized anxiety, and major depression—that may stem from their combat exposures (Tanielian and Jaycox, 2008; Hoge, McGurk, et al., 2008). Other studies have associated combat exposure with chronic pain (Sheffler et al., 2016) and increased dependence on substances, particularly alcohol (Ramchand, Rudavsky, et al., 2015; Wilk, Bliese, Kim, et al., 2010) and prescription drugs (e.g., opioids) (Seal et al., 2012; Toblin et al., 2014). Several studies suggest that the mental health of deployed forces is related to exposure to combat experiences rather than deployment in general (Pietrzak, Pullman, et al., 2012; Ramchand, Schell, Tanielian, et al., 2016).

In the 2015 HRBS, deployments were categorized as combat zone or noncombat zone; *combat-zone deployments* were defined as a deployment in which a service member typically receives imminent danger pay, hazardous duty pay, and/or combat zone tax exclusion benefits. Two items on the survey asked specifically about combat-zone deployments. First, respondents were asked how many of all their deployments were to combat zones, and a second item asked whether their most-recent deployment was to a combat zone.

Not all combat-zone deployments involve combat experiences, and not all combat experiences occur during combat-zone deployments. Therefore, the 2015 HRBS assessed service member reports of combat-related traumatic experiences. Eighteen subitems asked about exposure to various combat situations during deployment—for example, "I encountered mines, booby traps, or improvised explosive devices (IEDs)"; "I saw dead bodies or human remains"; and "I interacted with enemy prisoners of war." This combat exposure index is a composite of several existing combat exposure scales, including a seven-item scale used by the VA (National Center for PTSD, 2016a; Hoge, Castro, et al., 2004; Keane et al., 1989) and the 17-item Deployment Risk and Resilience Inventory (National Center for PTSD, 2016b; Vogt et al., 2013). Response options were provided on a 5-point scale (0–4), ranging from "never (0)" to "more than 50 times (4)," and a sum score was created for each item (possible range of 0 to 72) (see Appendix D for further detail). We then examined the distribution of these responses in our data and determined that a score of 5 or more would serve as a cutoff.[1] *High combat exposure* was defined as a sum score of 5 or more. No standard or common cut point has been used for these items. Our cut point was the highest quartile of combat exposure scores among all respondents, including those who had never deployed (who were assigned a combat exposure score of zero). Respondents with a score of less than 5 were categorized as having *low to moderate combat exposure*. Of note, the combat exposure inventory was administered only to respondents reporting at least one previous deployment (combat or noncombat zone). Thus, the HRBS measure of combat exposures assesses cumulative, lifetime combat experiences, including type of exposure and the number of instances of each exposure.

---

[1] A score of 5 or more correlates to roughly the 60th percentile. The median score was 3, and the 75th-percentile score was 9.

Tables 10.4 through 10.10 present the overall number of combat-zone deployments and estimates of combat exposure while deployed among all active-duty members with at least one previous deployment (including both combat or noncombat deployments).

## Overall Exposure to Combat-Zone Deployments

Key findings related to overall exposure to combat-zone deployments include the following:

- Across all services, 19.1 percent of previously deployed personnel reported no combat-zone deployments (Table 10.4). Nearly one-third (29.6 percent) reported three or more combat-zone deployments during their military career, 20.1 percent reported two such deployments, and 31.2 percent reported deploying once to a combat zone.
- Consistent with the 2011 HRBS results, significantly more Army (34.7 percent) and Air Force (30.7 percent) personnel reported three or more combat deployments than the other services, and members of the Coast Guard were the most likely to report no combat-zone deployments (73.1 percent) (Table 10.4).

## Overall Combat Experiences Among Previously Deployed Personnel

Key findings related to combat experiences among previously deployed personnel include the following:

- Overall, a significant portion (64.9 percent) of previously deployed service members reported any combat exposure, and nearly half (45.8 percent) reported having high combat exposure (Table 10.5).
- The most common combat experience, endorsed by nearly half (49.8 percent) of all previously deployed personnel, was having received incoming fire from small arms, artillery, rockets, or mortars (Table 10.5).
- Previously deployed Army personnel were the most likely to report having experienced a combat event (82.6 percent), and nearly three-fourths (70.7 percent) of Army personnel reported high combat exposure. Marine Corps and Air Force personnel followed Army personnel in percentage having experienced a combat event (63.0 percent and 60.1 percent, respectively) and high combat exposure (44.4 percent and 34.4 percent, respectively) (Table 10.5).
- Among previously deployed personnel, warrant officers and officers reported more combat experiences than did enlisted service members (Table 10.6).
- Gender differences in combat experiences were statistically significant, with more men than women reporting exposure and high exposure (Table 10.7).
- Service members in the oldest age bracket (age 45 or older) most frequently reported experiencing combat events and high exposure (Table 10.8). This rise with age is not surprising because older service members have generally had more time to be at risk for combat exposures and combat deployments.
- Few statistically significant differences emerged across race/ethnicity groups and did not yield any discernable pattern (Table 10.9).
- Individual combat trauma exposure was more frequently reported among those with some college education or a bachelor's degree or more than among those with a high school degree or less (Table 10.10).

Table 10.4
Total Number of Combat-Zone Deployments, by Service Branch

| | Total (1) | Air Force (2) | Army (3) | Marine Corps (4) | Navy (5) | Coast Guard (6) |
|---|---|---|---|---|---|---|
| 0 | 19.1% (17.6–20.7) | 16.4%[b,c,d,e] (14.0–18.7) | 8.8%[a,c,d,e] (6.1–11.5) | 28.3%[a,b,e] (23.8–32.7) | 26.6%[a,b,e] (23.2–30.0) | 73.1%[a,b,c,d] (71.2–74.9) |
| 1 | 31.2% (29.4–33.1) | 35.4%[d,e] (32.4–38.3) | 33.4%[e] (29.8–37.0) | 29.6%[e] (24.7–34.4) | 27.1%[a,e] (23.7–30.5) | 17.4%[a,b,c,d] (15.8–19.0) |
| 2 | 20.1% (18.6–21.5) | 17.6%[b,e] (15.4–19.8) | 23.1%[a,e] (20.2–26.0) | 18.4%[e] (15.7–21.1) | 19.9%[e] (17.0–22.7) | 5.4%[a,b,c,d] (4.5–6.3) |
| 3+ | 29.6% (28.2–31.0) | 30.7%[c,e] (28.1–33.2) | 34.7%[c,d,e] (32.0–37.5) | 23.7%[a,b,e] (21.1–26.4) | 26.5%[b,e] (24.0–29.1) | 4.2%[a,b,c,d] (3.3–5.0) |

NOTE: All data are weighted. 95-percent confidence intervals are presented in parentheses. Table includes only respondents who reported one or more previous combat or noncombat deployments.

[a] Estimate is significantly different from the estimate in column 2 (Air Force).

[b] Estimate is significantly different from the estimate in column 3 (Army).

[c] Estimate is significantly different from the estimate in column 4 (Marine Corps).

[d] Estimate is significantly different from the estimate in column 5 (Navy).

[e] Estimate is significantly different from the estimate in column 6 (Coast Guard).

**Table 10.5**
**Combat Experiences During Deployment, by Service Branch**

| | Total (1) | Air Force (2) | Army (3) | Marine Corps (4) | Navy (5) | Coast Guard (6) |
|---|---|---|---|---|---|---|
| Any combat exposure | 64.9% (63.2–66.9) | 60.1% b,d,e (57.2–63.0) | 82.6% a,c,d,e (79.5–85.7) | 63.0% b,d,e (58.4–67.6) | 45.6% a,b,c,e (41.9–49.2) | 37.8% a,b,c,d (35.7–39.9) |
| High combat exposure (5+ experiences) | 45.8% (44.1–47.5) | 34.4% b,c,d,e (31.6–37.1) | 70.7% a,c,d,e (67.2–74.2) | 44.4% a,b,d,e (40.3–48.5) | 21.4% a,b,c,e (18.5–24.4) | 9.3% a,b,c,d (8.1–10.5) |
| **Combat experiences** | | | | | | |
| I was sent outside the wire on combat patrols, convoys, or sorties. | 42.1% (40.4–43.7) | 27.0% b,c,d,e (24.4–29.5) | 69.5% a,c,d,e (66.0–72.9) | 42.2% a,b,d,e (38.2–46.2) | 16.0% a,b,c,e (13.4–18.5) | 5.7% a,b,c,d (4.7–6.8) |
| I, or members of my unit, received incoming fire from small arms, artillery, rockets, or mortars. | 49.8% (48.1–51.6) | 45.9% b,d,e (43.0–48.9) | 73.8% a,c,d,e (70.4–77.2) | 49.0% b,d,e (44.9–53.2) | 21.5% a,b,c,e (18.5–24.4) | 5.9% a,b,c,d (4.9–7.0) |
| I, or members of my unit, encountered mines, booby traps, or IEDs. | 32.0% (30.3–33.7) | 14.4% b,c,e (12.3–16.6) | 55.8% a,c,d,e (52.2–59.4) | 33.8% a,b,d,e (30.0–37.6) | 12.0% b,c,e (9.5–14.5) | 2.7% a,b,c,d (1.9–3.4) |
| I worked with landmines or other unexploded ordnance. | 11.5% (10.1–12.8) | 4.5% b,c,e (3.1–5.8) | 19.6% a,c,d,e (16.6–22.5) | 12.7% a,b,d,e (9.6–15.8) | 5.2% b,c,e (3.4–7.0) | 1.5% a,b,c,d (1.0–2.0) |
| My unit fired on the enemy. | 35.6% (33.8–37.3) | 17.5% b,c,e (15.3–19.8) | 56.9% a,c,d,e (53.2–60.5) | 38.9% a,b,d,e (34.9–42.8) | 18.7% b,c,e (16.0–21.5) | 7.6% a,b,c,d (6.5–8.8) |
| I personally fired my weapon at the enemy. | 16.1% (14.7–17.5) | 5.4% b,c,e (4.0–6.8) | 29.6% a,c,d,e (26.4–32.8) | 17.5% a,b,d,e (14.4–20.5) | 4.7% a,b,c,e (3.2–6.2) | 2.5% a,b,c,d (1.8–3.2) |
| I was engaged in hand-to-hand combat. | 1.8% (1.3–2.3) | 0.2% b,c,d,e (0.0–0.4) | 3.0% a (1.8–4.2) | 1.3% a (0.5–2.2) | 1.4% a (0.7–2.1) | 1.9% a (1.3–2.5) |
| I was responsible for the death or serious injury of an enemy. | 14.0% (12.8–15.3) | 9.1% b,c,d,e (7.4–10.9) | 22.0% a,d,e (19.0–24.9) | 17.1% a,d,e (14.1–20.0) | 5.6% a,b,c,e (4.0–7.1) | 1.7% a,b,c,d (1.1–2.3) |
| I witnessed members of my unit or an ally unit being wounded or killed. | 22.2% (20.6–23.7) | 10.3% b,c,e (8.5–12.1) | 37.0% a,c,d,e (33.6–40.4) | 24.9% a,b,d,e (21.3–28.5) | 9.7% b,c,e (7.5–11.8) | 3.7% a,b,c,d (2.8–4.5) |
| My unit suffered casualties. | 35.6% (33.9–37.3) | 16.0% b,c,e (13.8–18.1) | 59.4% a,c,d,e (55.9–62.9) | 38.6% a,b,d,e (34.5–42.7) | 16.7% b,c,e (14.1–19.4) | 5.2% a,b,c,d (4.2–6.2) |
| I saw dead bodies or human remains. | 38.6% (36.8–40.3) | 27.7% b,c (25.1–30.4) | 54.9% a,c,d,e (51.3–58.4) | 40.0% a,b,d,e (35.9–44.1) | 22.9% b,c (19.9–26.0) | 26.1% b,c (24.3–27.9) |
| I handled, uncovered, or removed dead bodies or human remains. | 18.7% (17.3–20.1) | 9.7% b,c,e (8.0–11.4) | 29.6% a,c,d,e (26.5–32.7) | 18.5% a,b,d (15.6–21.4) | 9.7% b,c,e (7.7–11.7) | 15.5% a,b,d (14.0–17.0) |
| Someone I knew well was killed in combat. | 31.0% (29.4–32.6) | 15.6% b,c,e (13.5–17.7) | 51.3% a,c,d,e (47.9–54.8) | 32.9% a,b,d,e (29.6–36.3) | 13.9% b,c,e (11.5–16.4) | 4.8% a,b,c,d (3.9–5.8) |

**Table 10.5—Continued**

| | Total (1) | Air Force (2) | Army (3) | Marine Corps (4) | Navy (5) | Coast Guard (6) |
|---|---|---|---|---|---|---|
| I took care of injured or dying people. | 23.7% (22.1–25.3) | 15.8%[b] (13.5–17.7) | 35.8%[a,c,d,e] (32.4–39.3) | 20.1%[b,d] (16.6–23.6) | 13.8%[b,c] (11.2–16.4) | 16.5%[b] (15.0–18.1) |
| I interacted with enemy prisoners of war. | 21.4% (20.0–22.9) | 12.0%[b,c,e] (10.2–13.9) | 34.8%[a,c,d,e] (31.7–37.9) | 22.3%[a,b,d,e] (19.2–25.5) | 9.9%[b,c,e] (7.7–12.2) | 4.2%[a,b,c,d] (3.3–5.0) |
| I witnessed or engaged in acts of cruelty, excessive force, or acts violating rules of engagement. | 5.1% (4.3–6.0) | 1.9%[b] (1.0–2.7) | 8.8%[a,c,d,e] (7.0–10.6) | 4.0%[b,e] (2.6–5.4) | 3.1%[b,e] (1.7–4.6) | 1.2%[b,c,d] (0.8–1.7) |
| I was wounded in combat. | 3.8% (3.0–4.7) | 0.7%[b,c] (0.2–1.2) | 7.7%[a,c,d,e] (5.7–9.7) | 3.8%[a,b,d,e] (2.3–5.3) | 0.8%[b,c] (0.3–1.4) | 0.4%[b,c] (0.1–0.7) |
| I witnessed civilians being wounded or killed. | 22.2% (20.7–23.7) | 12.0%[b,c,e] (10.0–14.0) | 36.4%[a,c,d,e] (33.0–39.8) | 22.4%[a,b,d,e] (19.0–25.8) | 10.3%[b,c,e] (8.0–12.5) | 6.0%[a,b,c,d] (5.0–6.9) |

NOTE: All data are weighted. 95-percent confidence intervals are presented in parentheses. Table includes only respondents who reported one or more previous combat or noncombat deployments.

[a] Estimate is significantly different from the estimate in column 2 (Air Force).

[b] Estimate is significantly different from the estimate in column 3 (Army).

[c] Estimate is significantly different from the estimate in column 4 (Marine Corps).

[d] Estimate is significantly different from the estimate in column 5 (Navy).

[e] Estimate is significantly different from the estimate in column 6 (Coast Guard).

**Table 10.6**
**Combat Experiences During Deployment, by Pay Grade**

| | E1–E4 (1) | E5–E6 (2) | E7–E9 (3) | W1–W5 (4) | O1–O3 (5) | O4–O10 (6) |
|---|---|---|---|---|---|---|
| Any combat exposure | 36.0% b,c,d,e,f (29.7–42.3) | 68.8% a,c,d,f (66.2–71.3) | 78.0% a,b,d,e,f (76.1–80.0) | 88.7% a,b,c,e,f (86.4–90.9) | 67.0% a,c,d,f (64.4–69.5) | 82.7% a,b,c,d,e (81.1–84.3) |
| High combat exposure (5+ experiences) | 22.1% b,c,d,e,f (16.5–27.8) | 48.3% a,c,d,f (45.5–51.1) | 57.4% a,b,d,e (55.1–59.7) | 71.3% a,b,c,d,f (67.9–74.7) | 46.1% a,c,d,f (43.4–48.8) | 61.5% a,b,d,e (59.4–63.6) |
| **Combat experiences** | | | | | | |
| I was sent outside the wire on combat patrols, convoys, or sorties. | 19.9% b,c,d,e,f (14.4–25.4) | 44.1% a,c,d,f (41.5–46.7) | 53.0% a,b,d,e,f (50.5–55.4) | 65.8% a,b,c,e,f (62.1–69.5) | 43.2% a,c,d,f (40.5–45.8) | 57.1% a,b,d,e (55.0–59.3) |
| I, or members of my unit, received incoming fire from small arms, artillery, rockets, or mortars. | 25.5% b,c,d,e,f (19.7–31.2) | 53.2% a,c,d,f (50.5–56.0) | 62.8% a,b,d,e (60.7–64.9) | 73.7% a,b,c,e,f (70.5–77.0) | 48.1% a,c,d,f (45.4–50.8) | 64.3% a,b,d,e (62.3–66.4) |
| I, or members of my unit, encountered mines, booby traps, or IEDs. | 16.5% b,c,d,e,f (11.2–21.7) | 35.5% a,c,d,e (32.7–38.3) | 43.4% a,b,e,f (40.9–46.0) | 45.4% a,b,e,f (41.2–49.5) | 28.3% a,b,c,d,f (25.7–31.0) | 34.5% a,c,d,e (32.2–36.7) |
| I worked with landmines or other unexploded ordnance. | 7.9% c (4.0–11.8) | 12.7% e (10.3–15.0) | 17.1% a,d,e,f (14.6–19.7) | 11.1% c (8.5–13.8) | 7.4% b,c (5.6–9.2) | 10.3% c (8.5–12.0) |
| My unit fired on the enemy. | 17.3% b,c,d,e,f (11.9–22.6) | 37.5% a,c,d,e,f (34.6–40.4) | 49.6% a,b,d,e (47.0–52.2) | 57.2% a,b,c,e,f (53.2–61.3) | 31.4% a,b,c,d,f (28.6–34.3) | 44.5% a,b,d,e (42.2–46.9) |
| I personally fired my weapon at the enemy. | 5.0% b,c,d,f (1.7–8.3) | 20.0% a,e,f (17.3–22.7) | 25.3% a,e,f (22.6–28.0) | 24.5% a,e,f (20.8–28.3) | 9.7% b,c,d,f (7.7–11.7) | 15.1% a,b,c,d,e (13.1–17.0) |
| I was engaged in hand-to-hand combat. | 0.7% (0.0–2.2) | 1.6% c (0.7–2.5) | 4.3% b,e,f (2.9–5.8) | 2.9% (1.4–4.3) | 1.1% c (0.4–1.7) | 1.5% c (0.7–2.2) |
| I was responsible for the death or serious injury of an enemy. | 4.2% b,c,d,e,f (1.4–7.0) | 15.6% a,d (13.1–18.1) | 19.6% a,e (17.0–22.2) | 24.8% a,b,e (21.0–28.6) | 12.5% a,c,d,f (10.4–14.6) | 19.3% a,e (17.2–21.5) |
| I witnessed members of my unit or an ally unit being wounded or killed. | 10.0% b,c,d,e,f (5.7–14.2) | 23.6% a,c,d (20.8–26.4) | 34.5% a,b,e,f (31.7–37.2) | 33.8% a,b,e,f (29.7–37.8) | 18.9% a,c,d,f (16.3–21.4) | 24.6% a,c,d,e (22.4–26.9) |
| My unit suffered casualties. | 15.6% b,c,d,e,f (10.5–20.7) | 36.9% a,c,d,f (34.1–39.8) | 49.5% a,b,d,e (47.1–51.9) | 63.2% a,b,c,e,f (59.3–67.0) | 35.5% a,c,d,f (32.7–38.2) | 45.2% a,b,d,e (42.9–47.4) |
| I saw dead bodies or human remains. | 17.3% b,c,d,e,f (12.1–22.5) | 41.8% a,c,d,f (38.7–44.8) | 52.0% a,b,d,e (49.4–54.7) | 60.6% a,b,c,e,f (56.6–64.6) | 36.0% a,c,d,f (33.1–39.0) | 47.9% a,b,d,e (45.5–50.3) |
| I handled, uncovered, or removed dead bodies or human remains. | 5.0% b,c,d,e,f (2.0–8.0) | 21.9% a,c,e (19.2–24.7) | 28.0% a,b,e (25.2–30.8) | 27.2% a,e (23.4–31.1) | 14.7% a,b,c,d,f (12.4–17.0) | 23.3% a,e (21.1–25.6) |
| Someone I knew well was killed in combat. | 10.8% b,c,d,e,f (6.4–15.2) | 32.3% a,c,d,f (29.4–35.1) | 45.7% a,b,d,e (43.1–48.3) | 56.3% a,b,c,e,f (52.2–60.3) | 29.5% a,c,d,f (26.7–32.3) | 41.6% a,b,d,e (39.3–44.0) |

**Table 10.6—Continued**

|  | E1–E4 (1) | E5–E6 (2) | E7–E9 (3) | W1–W5 (4) | O1–O3 (5) | O4–O10 (6) |
|---|---|---|---|---|---|---|
| I took care of injured or dying people. | 12.2%[b,c,d,f] (7.7–16.7) | 26.4%[a,e] (23.5–29.3) | 31.3%[a,d,e] (28.4–34.1) | 22.6%[a,c,f] (19.0–26.1) | 19.8%[b,c,f] (17.3–22.3) | 29.8%[a,d,e] (29.4–34.1) |
| I interacted with enemy prisoners of war. | 6.0%[b,c,d,e,f] (2.6–9.4) | 23.3%[a,c,d,f] (20.5–26.1) | 31.9%[a,b,e] (29.0–34.7) | 31.2%[a,b,e] (27.2–35.1) | 18.6%[a,c,d,f] (16.1–21.1) | 31.7%[a,b,e] (29.4–34.1) |
| I witnessed or engaged in acts of cruelty, excessive force, or acts violating rules of engagement. | 1.5%[b,c,d] (0.2–2.9) | 6.1%[a] (4.4–7.9) | 7.2%[a] (5.3–9.0) | 7.3%[a] (5.0–9.6) | 5.5% (3.9–7.2) | 4.8% (3.5–6.0) |
| I was wounded in combat. | 0.7% (0.0–2.1) | 5.9%[e,f] (4.2–7.7) | 5.5%[e] (3.8–7.1) | 2.7% (1.3–4.1) | 1.3%[b,c] (0.6–2.0) | 2.8%[b] (1.8–3.8) |
| I witnessed civilians being wounded or killed. | 9.5%[b,c,d,f] (5.3–13.6) | 25.7%[a,e] (22.8–28.5) | 30.7%[a,e,f] (27.9–33.5) | 29.5%[a,e] (25.6–33.5) | 17.9%[b,c,d,f] (15.4–20.4) | 25.4%[a,c,e] (23.2–27.7) |

NOTE: All data are weighted. 95-percent confidence intervals are presented in parentheses. Table includes only respondents who reported one or more previous combat or noncombat deployments.

[a] Estimate is significantly different from the estimate in column 1 (E1–E4).

[b] Estimate is significantly different from the estimate in column 2 (E5–E6).

[c] Estimate is significantly different from the estimate in column 3 (E7–E9).

[d] Estimate is significantly different from the estimate in column 4 (W1–W5).

[e] Estimate is significantly different from the estimate in column 5 (O1–O3).

[f] Estimate is significantly different from the estimate in column 6 (O4–O10).

Table 10.7
**Combat Experiences During Deployment, by Gender**

| | Men (1) | Women (2) |
|---|---|---|
| Any combat exposure | 65.8%[a] (63.8–67.8) | 58.8% (56.5–61.0) |
| High combat exposure (5+ experiences) | 47.5%[a] (45.5–49.4) | 34.0% (32.0–36.0) |
| **Combat experiences** | | |
| I was sent outside the wire on combat patrols, convoys, or sorties. | 44.3%[a] (42.4–46.2) | 26.5% (24.8–28.2) |
| I, or members of my unit, received incoming fire from small arms, artillery, rockets, or mortars. | 51.4%[a] (49.5–53.4) | 38.9% (36.9–40.9) |
| I, or members of my unit, encountered mines, booby traps, or IEDs. | 33.9%[a] (32.0–35.8) | 18.9% (17.3–20.6) |
| I worked with landmines or other unexploded ordnance. | 12.6%[a] (11.0–14.1) | 3.9% (2.9–4.9) |
| My unit fired on the enemy. | 37.8%[a] (35.8–39.8) | 19.9% (18.1–21.6) |
| I personally fired my weapon at the enemy. | 17.8%[a] (16.2–19.4) | 4.1% (3.2–5.0) |
| I was engaged in hand-to-hand combat. | 1.9%[a] (1.3–2.5) | 1.0% (0.6–1.5) |
| I was responsible for the death or serious injury of an enemy. | 15.5%[a] (14.1–17.0) | 3.7% (2.9–4.6) |
| I witnessed members of my unit or an ally unit being wounded or killed. | 23.7%[a] (22.0–25.5) | 11.2% (9.7–12.5) |
| My unit suffered casualties. | 37.1%[a] (35.2–39.0) | 25.0% (23.3–26.8) |
| I saw dead bodies or human remains. | 40.5%[a] (38.5–42.4) | 25.5% (23.5–27.4) |
| I handled, uncovered, or removed dead bodies or human remains. | 19.8%[a] (18.2–21.4) | 11.1% (9.7–12.5) |
| Someone I knew well was killed in combat. | 32.2%[a] (30.4–34.0) | 22.6% (20.8–24.4) |
| I took care of injured or dying people. | 24.4%[a] (22.6–26.2) | 18.5% (16.7–20.3) |
| I interacted with enemy prisoners of war. | 22.6%[a] (21.0–24.3) | 13.3% (11.9–14.7) |
| I witnessed or engaged in acts of cruelty, excessive force, or acts violating rules of engagement. | 5.4%[a] (4.5–6.3) | 3.3% (2.3–4.3) |
| I was wounded in combat. | 4.2%[a] (3.2–5.1) | 1.6% (1.0–2.1) |
| I witnessed civilians being wounded or killed. | 23.6%[a] (21.9–25.4) | 12.3% (10.7–13.9) |

NOTE: All data are weighted. 95-percent confidence intervals are presented in parentheses. Table includes only respondents who reported one or more previous combat or noncombat deployments.

[a] Estimate is significantly different from the estimate in column 2 (women).

## Table 10.8
## Combat Experiences During Deployment, by Age Group

| | Ages 17–24 (1) | Ages 25–34 (2) | Ages 35–44 (3) | Ages 45+ (4) |
|---|---|---|---|---|
| Any combat exposure | 30.9%[b,c,d] (24.0–37.8) | 60.1%[a,c,d] (57.0–63.1) | 78.5%[a,b,d] (76.3–80.7) | 83.7%[a,b,c] (80.8–86.6) |
| High combat exposure (5+ experiences) | 14.8%[b,c,d] (9.1–20.5) | 41.2%[a,c,d] (38.1–44.3) | 58.2%[a,b] (55.5–60.9) | 63.3%[a,b] (59.5–67.1) |
| **Combat experiences** | | | | |
| I was sent outside the wire on combat patrols, convoys, or sorties. | 13.2%[b,c,d] (7.6–18.8) | 37.9%[a,c,d] (34.4–41.0) | 53.2%[a,b] (50.5–55.9) | 59.1%[a,b] (55.2–63.0) |
| I, or members of my unit, received incoming fire from small arms, artillery, rockets, or mortars. | 17.5%[b,c,d] (11.7–23.4) | 45.7%[a,c,d] (42.6–48.8) | 62.5%[a,b] (60.0–65.1) | 66.6%[a,b] (62.9–70.2) |
| I, or members of my unit, encountered mines, booby traps, or IEDs. | 11.1%[b,c,d] (5.9–16.3) | 30.0%[a,c,d] (27.0–33.0) | 38.9%[a,b] (36.1–41.7) | 43.9%[a,b] (39.6–48.3) |
| I worked with landmines or other unexploded ordnance.[e] | 8.2% (3.6–12.8) | 11.8% (9.6–14.1) | 12.0% (10.1–13.9) | 12.3% (8.7–15.8) |
| My unit fired on the enemy. | 11.8%[b,c,d] (6.7–17.0) | 31.8%[a,c,d] (28.8–34.8) | 44.7%[a,b] (41.9–47.5) | 51.2%[a,b] (47.0–55.3) |
| I personally fired my weapon at the enemy. | 4.6%[b,c,d] (0.9–8.2) | 15.3%[a,d] (12.9–17.7) | 19.8%[a] (17.5–22.2) | 21.6%[a,b] (17.5–25.6) |
| I was engaged in hand-to-hand combat.[e] | 1.2% (0.0–3.5) | 1.2% (0.6–1.8) | 2.4% (1.6–3.2) | 2.7% (1.1–4.4) |
| I was responsible for the death or serious injury of an enemy. | 4.1%[b,c,d] (1.0–7.2) | 14.4%[a] (12.1–16.6) | 17.1%[a] (14.9–19.3) | 15.4%[a] (12.4–18.4) |
| I witnessed members of my unit or an ally unit being wounded or killed. | 4.7%[b,c,d] (2.0–7.4) | 20.1%[a,c,d] (17.3–22.9) | 28.6%[a,b] (26.1–31.2) | 31.6%[a,b] (27.3–35.9) |
| My unit suffered casualties. | 10.3%[b,c,d] (5.6–14.9) | 31.6%[a,c,d] (28.6–34.6) | 45.6%[a,b] (42.8–48.4) | 51.3%[a,b] (47.1–55.5) |
| I saw dead bodies or human remains. | 13.1%[b,c,d] (7.9–18.3) | 35.1%[a,c,d] (32.0–38.2) | 47.5%[a,b,d] (44.7–50.3) | 55.7%[a,b,c] (51.6–59.8) |
| I handled, uncovered, or removed dead bodies or human remains. | 4.4%[b,c,d] (1.2–7.6) | 17.6%[a,c,d] (15.1–20.1) | 23.2%[a,b] (20.8–25.6) | 26.8%[a,b] (22.9–30.7) |
| Someone I knew well was killed in combat. | 7.8%[b,c,d] (3.5–12.0) | 24.3%[a,c,d] (21.6–27.1) | 43.1%[a,b] (40.3–45.9) | 47.7%[a,b] (43.5–52.0) |
| I took care of injured or dying people. | 7.7%[b,c,d] (3.7–11.7) | 22.5%[a,c,d] (19.8–25.3) | 28.3%[a,b] (25.6–30.9) | 33.2%[a,b] (28.9–37.4) |
| I interacted with enemy prisoners of war. | 6.7%[b,c,d] (2.4–11.0) | 19.1%[a,c,d] (16.5–21.5) | 27.7%[a,b] (25.2–30.3) | 29.2%[a,b] (25.3–33.0) |
| I witnessed or engaged in acts of cruelty, excessive force, or acts violating rules of engagement. | 1.6%[d] (0.0–3.3) | 4.8% (3.4–6.1) | 6.1% (4.6–7.5) | 8.0%[a] (5.2–10.8) |
| I was wounded in combat. | NA | 3.8% (2.4–5.2) | 5.4% (3.8–7.0) | 3.8% (2.0–5.7) |
| I witnessed civilians being wounded or killed. | 5.8%[b,c,d] (2.2–9.3) | 20.7%[a,c,d] (18.1–23.4) | 28.3%[a,b] (25.7–31.0) | 29.0%[a,b] (24.8–33.3) |

NOTE: All data are weighted. 95-percent confidence intervals are presented in parentheses. Table includes only respondents who reported one or more previous combat or noncombat deployments.

[a] Estimate is significantly different from the estimate in column 1 (ages 17–24).

[b] Estimate is significantly different from the estimate in column 2 (ages 25–34).

[c] Estimate is significantly different from the estimate in column 3 (ages 35–44).

[d] Estimate is significantly different from the estimate in column 4 (ages 45+).

[e] The omnibus chi-square test was not statistically significant ($p > 0.05$).

NA = not applicable (zero individuals in the cell).

**Table 10.9**
**Combat Experiences During Deployment, by Race/Ethnicity**

| | Non-Hispanic White (1) | Non-Hispanic Black (2) | Hispanic (3) | Non-Hispanic Asian (4) | Other (5) |
|---|---|---|---|---|---|
| Any combat exposure[f] | 66.9% (64.7–69.2) | 60.7% (54.6–66.9) | 61.4% (55.7–67.1) | 58.0% (47.4–68.6) | 65.2% (58.6–71.8) |
| High combat exposure (5+ experiences)[f] | 47.1% (44.8–49.4) | 45.7% (39.7–51.6) | 44.6% (39.1–50.2) | 31.5% (21.1–42.0) | 44.2% (37.6–50.8) |
| **Combat experiences** | | | | | |
| I was sent outside the wire on combat patrols, convoys, or sorties.[f] | 43.6% (41.4–45.9) | 39.4% (33.6–45.2) | 42.0% (36.5–47.5) | 33.6% (23.3–44.0) | 38.3% (31.8–44.8) |
| I, or members of my unit, received incoming fire from small arms, artillery, rockets, or mortars.[f] | 51.0% (48.7–53.3) | 50.0% (44.0–56.1) | 47.7% (42.1–53.3) | 45.0% (34.3–55.7) | 46.9% (40.2–53.5) |
| I, or members of my unit, encountered mines, booby traps, or IEDs.[f] | 31.6% (29.4–33.8) | 32.2% (26.6–37.8) | 34.8% (29.4–40.2) | 26.3% (15.8–36.9) | 32.3% (25.9–38.6) |
| I worked with landmines or other unexploded ordnance. | 12.8%[b] (11.0–14.6) | 6.1%[a,c] (3.3–8.8) | 13.3%[b] (9.3–17.3) | 8.6% (0.0–17.2) | 7.7% (4.4–11.1) |
| My unit fired on the enemy.[f] | 35.9% (33.6–38.1) | 36.8% (30.9–42.7) | 35.0% (29.8–40.3) | 26.3% (16.0–36.6) | 36.7% (30.1–43.3) |
| I personally fired my weapon at the enemy.[f] | 16.3% (14.5–18.2) | 14.6% (10.2–19.1) | 19.4% (14.8–24.0) | 8.5% (2.5–14.5) | 14.5% (9.9–19.1) |
| I was engaged in hand-to-hand combat.[f] | 1.4% (1.0–1.9) | 2.7% (0.1–5.3) | 2.4% (0.9–3.9) | 3.5% (0.0–8.0) | 1.3% (0.4–2.2) |
| I was responsible for the death or serious injury of an enemy. | 16.6%[d] (14.9–18.4) | 9.4%[d] (5.5–13.3) | 11.0%[d] (7.9–14.2) | 2.1%[a,b,c,e] (0.1–4.0) | 12.1%[d] (7.9–16.3) |
| I witnessed members of my unit or an ally unit being wounded or killed.[f] | 22.0% (20.0–24.0) | 23.4% (18.4–28.4) | 23.3% (18.7–27.9) | 16.9% (7.5–26.3) | 21.9% (16.7–27.2) |
| My unit suffered casualties. | 35.3% (33.1–37.6) | 36.6% (31.0–42.2) | 36.7%[d,e] (31.5–41.9) | 21.1%[c] (12.8–29.5) | 40.5%[c] (33.8–47.2) |
| I saw dead bodies or human remains.[f] | 39.9% (37.6–42.2) | 35.9% (30.3–41.5) | 38.2% (32.9–43.6) | 28.1% (17.8–38.3) | 38.1% (31.7–44.4) |
| I handled, uncovered, or removed dead bodies or human remains. | 19.4%[d] (17.6–21.3) | 15.4% (11.5–19.3) | 22.5%[d] (17.9–27.1) | 8.1%[a,c] (3.7–12.5) | 17.3% (12.7–21.9) |
| Someone I knew well was killed in combat.[f] | 30.1% (28.0–32.1) | 35.2% (29.6–40.8) | 32.8% (27.6–38.0) | 22.2% (13.7–30.8) | 32.5% (26.3–38.7) |

**Table 10.9—Continued**

| | Non-Hispanic White (1) | Non-Hispanic Black (2) | Hispanic (3) | Non-Hispanic Asian (4) | Other (5) |
|---|---|---|---|---|---|
| I took care of injured or dying people.[f] | 24.2% (22.1–26.3) | 19.4% (14.9–23.8) | 28.2% (23.2–33.3) | 16.7% (8.2–25.2) | 21.8% (16.3–27.3) |
| I interacted with enemy prisoners of war.[f] | 22.6% (20.7–24.4) | 20.2% (15.2–25.2) | 23.0% (18.2–27.7) | 12.6% (6.2–19.0) | 16.9% (12.5–21.3) |
| I witnessed or engaged in acts of cruelty, excessive force, or acts violating rules of engagement.[f] | 5.3% (4.2–6.3) | 4.9% (2.3–7.5) | 5.8% (3.5–8.2) | 2.8% (0.1–5.5) | 4.5% (1.7–7.4) |
| I was wounded in combat.[f] | 4.0% (2.9–5.1) | 2.7% (0.8–4.6) | 5.2% (2.9–7.5) | 1.6% (0.0–4.1) | 3.3% (1.1–5.5) |
| I witnessed civilians being wounded or killed.[f] | 23.5% (21.4–25.6) | 19.5% (14.7–24.3) | 21.0% (16.8–25.2) | 21.1% (11.2–31.0) | 19.3% (14.3–24.3) |

NOTE: All data are weighted. 95-percent confidence intervals are presented in parentheses. Table includes only respondents who reported one or more previous combat or noncombat deployments.

[a] Estimate is significantly different from the estimate in column 1 (Non-Hispanic white).

[b] Estimate is significantly different from the estimate in column 2 (Non-Hispanic black).

[c] Estimate is significantly different from the estimate in column 3 (Hispanic).

[d] Estimate is significantly different from the estimate in column 4 (Non-Hispanic Asian).

[e] Estimate is significantly different from the estimate in column 5 (other).

[f] The omnibus chi-square test was not statistically significant ($p > 0.05$).

**Table 10.10**
**Combat Experiences During Deployment, by Education Level**

| | High School or Less (1) | Some College (2) | Bachelor's Degree or More (3) |
|---|---|---|---|
| Any combat exposure | 47.6%[b,c] (41.5–53.8) | 65.6%[a,c] (62.9–68.3) | 71.3%[a,b] (68.8–73.7) |
| High combat exposure (5+ experiences) | 30.2%[b,c] (24.7–35.7) | 46.8%[a] (44.0–49.6) | 51.0%[a] (48.5–53.5) |
| **Combat experiences** | | | |
| I was sent outside the wire on combat patrols, convoys, or sorties. | 27.2%[b,c] (21.7–32.8) | 42.0%[a,c] (39.3–44.7) | 48.4%[a,b] (46.0–50.9) |
| I, or members of my unit, received incoming fire from small arms, artillery, rockets, or mortars. | 32.2%[b,c] (26.7–37.7) | 52.1%[a] (49.3–54.9) | 54.3%[a] (51.8–56.8) |
| I, or members of my unit, encountered mines, booby traps, or IEDs. | 23.5%[b,c] (18.6–28.4) | 34.5%[a] (31.7–37.2) | 32.3%[a] (29.9–34.8) |
| I worked with landmines or other unexploded ordnance.[d] | 11.3% (7.3–15.3) | 12.5% (10.4–14.6) | 10.1% (8.3–11.9) |
| My unit fired on the enemy. | 25.5%[b,c] (20.3–30.6) | 36.9%[a] (34.1–39.7) | 38.0%[a] (35.6–40.5) |
| I personally fired my weapon at the enemy.[d] | 13.7% (9.6–17.7) | 18.0% (15.7–20.3) | 14.6% (12.7–16.5) |
| I was engaged in hand-to-hand combat. | 0.3%[b,c] (0.1–0.5) | 2.3%[a] (1.4–3.3) | 1.7%[a] (1.0–2.4) |
| I was responsible for the death or serious injury of an enemy.[d] | 10.2% (6.6–13.9) | 14.1% (12.1–16.1) | 15.6% (13.7–17.6) |
| I witnessed members of my unit or an ally unit being wounded or killed. | 16.5%[b] (12.3–20.6) | 23.9%[a] (21.3–26.4) | 22.4% (20.2–24.5) |
| My unit suffered casualties. | 26.9%[b,c] (21.6–32.3) | 35.7%[a] (32.9–38.4) | 39.2%[a] (36.8–41.6) |
| I saw dead bodies or human remains. | 28.0%[b,c] (22.9–33.1) | 40.5%[a] (37.7–43.3) | 40.5%[a] (38.0–43.0) |
| I handled, uncovered, or removed dead bodies or human remains. | 13.8%[b] (9.8–17.8) | 20.1%[a] (17.8–22.4) | 19.0% (17.1–21.0) |
| Someone I knew well was killed in combat. | 22.7%[b,c] (17.8–27.6) | 30.6%[a] (28.0–33.2) | 34.9%[a] (32.5–37.3) |
| I took care of injured or dying people. | 15.3%[b,c] (11.0–19.7) | 25.8%[a] (23.1–28.4) | 24.4%[a] (22.2–26.6) |
| I interacted with enemy prisoners of war. | 14.3%[b,c] (10.4–18.2) | 22.3%[a] (19.9–24.8) | 23.3%[a] (21.3–25.3) |
| I witnessed or engaged in acts of cruelty, excessive force, or acts violating rules of engagement.[d] | 3.3% (1.1–5.5) | 5.4% (4.1–6.8) | 5.5% (4.3–6.7) |
| I was wounded in combat.[d] | 3.8% (1.7–5.9) | 4.7% (3.2–6.1) | 2.8% (1.9–3.7) |
| I witnessed civilians being wounded or killed.[d] | 17.8% (13.2–22.4) | 23.0% (20.5–25.5) | 23.0% (20.8–25.3) |

NOTE: All data are weighted. 95-percent confidence intervals are presented in parentheses. Table includes only respondents who reported one or more previous combat or noncombat deployments.

[a] Estimate is significantly different from the estimate in column 1 (high school or less).

[b] Estimate is significantly different from the estimate in column 2 (some college).

[c] Estimate is significantly different from the estimate in column 3 (bachelor's degree or more).

[d] The omnibus chi-square test was not statistically significant ($p > 0.05$).

## Deployment-Related Injury

Deployments and exposure to combat and traumatic events place military personnel at increased risk of injury. Identifying injurious events that result in postconcussive symptoms or that can lead to concussion, mTBI, or moderate to severe TBI is critical to protecting the mental health and cognitive functioning of military personnel and to preventing future deployment-related injuries. Studies reported in Tanielian and Jaycox (2008) found that among veterans of Operation Enduring Freedom and Operation Iraqi Freedom, approximately 12.2 percent screened positively for TBI, and an additional 7.3 percent were diagnosed with TBI in conjunction with a mental health condition (PTSD or depression). Carlson and colleagues examined psychiatric diagnoses among U.S. veterans who were screened for TBI, and they found that more than 80 percent of those with positive TBI screens had psychiatric diagnoses and were up to three times more likely to have PTSD (Carlson et al., 2010). Among soldiers involved in combat deployment who indicate sustaining mTBI, many report multiple incidences of mTBI during a previous deployment, increasing their risk for depression and chronic pain (Wilk, Herrell, et al., 2012). Understanding the current prevalence of mTBI, TBI, and postconcussive symptoms will allow the military to strengthen postdeployment screening processes and identify those who are at greater risk of experiencing persistent symptoms or long-term cognitive impairment.

HRBS assessment of TBI is composed of three sets of items based on the Brief Traumatic Brain Injury Screen, which was developed by an interdisciplinary VA task force and used by the Defense and Veterans Brain Injury Center for previously deployed military veterans (Schwab et al., 2006). The assessment has been used extensively to screen troops returning from deployment and in VA clinical settings. HRBS respondents were first asked about injuries during any deployment (combat or noncombat) from each of the following sources: fragment, bullet, vehicular accident or crash, fall, blast or explosion, and other event. This item was designed to measure lifetime exposure to injuries potentially related to TBI, and we used it as our measure of "any combat injury." Next, to assess whether TBI may have occurred and to estimate its severity, respondents were asked about the outcome of any of the injuries incurred during any deployment, such as whether and for how long the injury resulted in loss of consciousness, confusion, memory loss, concussive symptoms, or head injury. Last, respondents were asked to report whether they were still experiencing any common postconcussive symptoms—such as headaches, dizziness, memory lapses, and balance problems—that they thought could be related to a head injury endured while deployed.

A positive screen for mTBI occurred when a respondent (1) reported one or more injuries during any deployment and (2) recalled having temporally related concussion or postconcussive symptoms; feeling dazed, confused, or "seeing stars"; having any associated loss of consciousness for up to 20 minutes; or being amnestic for the event. A positive screen for moderate to severe TBI occurred when a respondent reported that loss of consciousness lasted longer than 20 minutes.

Tables 10.11 through 10.17 present overall levels of deployment-related injuries (i.e., injury from fragment, bullet, vehicular accident or crash, fall, blast or explosion, or other event), estimates of individuals with possible deployment-related TBI, and deployment-related postconcussive symptoms. The sample for these analyses is also limited to service members who reported at least one previous combat or noncombat deployment.

**Overall Levels of Deployment-Related Injury, TBI, and Postconcussive Symptoms**

Key findings related to overall levels of deployment-related injury, TBI, and postconcussive symptoms among previously deployed personnel include the following:

- Of previously deployed personnel, 11.9 percent screened positive for mTBI, and 0.2 percent screened positive for a moderate to severe TBI (Table 10.11). Of all individuals who experienced a deployment-related injury, 42.9 percent also reported probable mTBI, and 0.9 percent reported a moderate to severe TBI. These figures do not change dramatically when considering only those service members who recently deployed (i.e., in the past three years) and those who deployed to a combat zone in the past three years.
- More than one-fourth of all previously deployed personnel reported sustaining a deployment-related injury (27.7 percent), with significantly more Army personnel reporting deployment-related injuries (40.4 percent) than any other service branch (Table 10.12).
- Deployment-related mTBI affected about one-fifth (18.7 percent) of previously deployed Army personnel, which was significantly more than any other service branch (Table 10.12).
- Of previously deployed personnel, 8.6 percent indicated that they had experienced postconcussive symptoms following a deployment-related injury (Table 10.12). Deployment-related postconcussive symptoms affected 15.4 percent of previously deployed Army personnel, a figure nearly twice as high as the next-closest service (Marine Corps, 8.4 percent).
- Fewer junior enlisted compared with senior enlisted personnel reported a deployment-related injury, and the same was true for junior officers compared with mid-grade and senior officers, perhaps reflecting differential exposure to deployment (i.e., on average, more-senior members have been deployed more times) (Table 10.13). A similar pattern was observed for probable mTBI among enlisted personnel and for postconcussive symptoms among enlisted personnel (but not officers). Generally, deployment-related injuries, mTBI, and postconcussive symptoms were all more frequently reported among senior enlisted personnel than among mid-grade and senior officers, again possibly because of differential cumulative exposure to combat experiences (especially high combat exposure).
- Just more than one-fifth (22.9 percent) of women reported deployment-related injuries, but men reported significantly more (28.4 percent) (Table 10.14). Both mTBI and postconcussive symptoms were more common among men than women.
- Age and deployment-related injuries were positively associated such that a larger percentage of active-duty personnel aged 35 or older reported deployment-related injuries, mTBI, and postconcussive symptoms than did younger service members (Table 10.15). Older and generally more-experienced service members with longer time in service have had more opportunities for injuries, especially musculoskeletal or repeated strain injuries.
- No significant differences across race/ethnicity (Table 10.16) or education level (Table 10.17) were observed for any combat injury, mTBI, or postconcussive symptoms.

Table 10.11
Deployment-Related Injury and TBI, by Recency and Type of Deployment

| | Among Those with a Previous Deployment | | Among Those with a Deployment in the Past 3 Years | | Among Those with a Deployment to a Combat Zone in the Past 3 Years | |
|---|---|---|---|---|---|---|
| | N | Percentage | N | Percentage | N | Percentage |
| Any deployment-related injury | 2,435 | 27.7% (26.0–29.4) | 1,422 | 26.7% (24.5–28.9) | 863 | 31.5% (28.5–34.5) |
| Positive screen for mTBI | 957 | 11.9% (10.6–13.1) | 560 | 10.8% (9.4–12.2) | 358 | 13.6% (11.6–15.7) |
| Among deployment-injured | | 42.9% (39.1–46.6) | | 40.7% (36.0–45.4) | | 43.3% (37.5–49.0) |
| Positive screen for moderate to severe TBI | 21 | 0.2% (0.1–0.4) | 13 | 0.1% (0.0–0.2) | 8 | 0.2% (0.0–0.4) |
| Among deployment-injured | | 0.9% (0.2–1.5) | | 0.5% (0.1–0.8) | | 0.6% (0.0–1.1) |

NOTE: All data are weighted. 95-percent confidence intervals are presented in parentheses. Table includes only respondents who reported one or more previous combat or noncombat deployments. By the definition used in the HRBS, any service member with a TBI must have experienced a combat injury.

Table 10.12
Deployment-Related Injury, mTBI, and Postconcussive Symptoms, by Service Branch

| | Total (1) | Air Force (2) | Army (3) | Marine Corps (4) | Navy (5) | Coast Guard (6) |
|---|---|---|---|---|---|---|
| Any deployment-related injury | 27.7% (26.0–29.4) | 18.3%[b,c] (16.0–20.7) | 40.4%[a,c,d,e] (36.8–44.0) | 27.4%[a,b,d,e] (23.2–31.6) | 17.2%[b,c] (14.5–19.8) | 15.8%[b,c] (14.1–17.4) |
| Positive screen for mTBI | 11.9% (10.6–13.1) | 5.4%[b,c] (4.0–6.8) | 18.7%[a,c,d,e] (16.0–21.3) | 12.4%[a,b,d,e] (9.6–15.2) | 6.9%[b,c] (5.0–8.8) | 6.0%[b,c] (4.9–7.1) |
| Postconcussive symptoms | 8.6% (7.5–9.7) | 2.7%[b,c] (1.7–3.7) | 15.4%[a,c,d,e] (12.9–18.0) | 8.4%[a,b,d,e] (6.0–10.8) | 3.4%[b,c] (2.3–4.5) | 2.9%[b,c] (2.1–3.6) |

NOTE: All data are weighted. 95-percent confidence intervals are presented in parentheses. Table includes only respondents who reported one or more previous combat or noncombat deployments.

[a] Estimate is significantly different from the estimate in column 2 (Air Force).

[b] Estimate is significantly different from the estimate in column 3 (Army).

[c] Estimate is significantly different from the estimate in column 4 (Marine Corps).

[d] Estimate is significantly different from the estimate in column 5 (Navy).

[e] Estimate is significantly different from the estimate in column 6 (Coast Guard).

**Table 10.13**
**Deployment-Related Injury, mTBI, and Postconcussive Symptoms, by Pay Grade**

| | E1–E4 (1) | E5–E6 (2) | E7–E9 (3) | W1–W5 (4) | O1–O3 (5) | O4–O10 (6) |
|---|---|---|---|---|---|---|
| Any deployment-related injury | 16.9%[b,c,d] (11.9–21.9) | 31.0%[a,c,e,f] (28.0–34.0) | 40.5%[a,b,e,f] (37.6–43.5) | 37.1%[a,e,f] (33.0–41.1) | 19.2%[b,c,d,f] (16.7–21.7) | 25.4%[b,c,d,e] (23.2–27.7) |
| Positive screen for mTBI | 4.6%[b,c,d] (1.7–7.5) | 14.0%[a,c,e,f] (11.6–16.3) | 21.2%[a,b,e,f] (18.5–23.8) | 15.5%[a,e,f] (12.4–18.5) | 7.1%[b,c,d] (5.3–8.9) | 9.2%[b,c,d] (7.6–10.9) |
| Postconcussive symptoms | 3.2%[c,d] (0.6–5.8) | 9.3%[c] (7.2–11.3) | 17.7%[a,b,d,e,f] (15.1–20.2) | 11.5%[a,c,e,f] (8.8–14.2) | 5.6%[c,d] (4.0–7.2) | 6.1%[c,d] (4.7–7.5) |

NOTE: All data are weighted. 95-percent confidence intervals are presented in parentheses. Table includes only respondents who reported one or more previous combat or noncombat deployments.

[a] Estimate is significantly different from the estimate in column 1 (E1–E4).

[b] Estimate is significantly different from the estimate in column 2 (E5–E6).

[c] Estimate is significantly different from the estimate in column 3 (E7–E9).

[d] Estimate is significantly different from the estimate in column 4 (W1–W5).

[e] Estimate is significantly different from the estimate in column 5 (O1–O3).

[f] Estimate is significantly different from the estimate in column 6 (O4–O10).

**Table 10.14**
**Deployment-Related Injury, mTBI, and Postconcussive Symptoms, by Gender**

| | Men (1) | Women (2) |
|---|---|---|
| Any deployment-related injury | 28.4%[a] (26.5–30.4) | 22.9% (20.9–25.0) |
| Positive screen for mTBI | 12.5%[a] (11.1–13.9) | 7.3% (6.0–8.6) |
| Postconcussive symptoms | 9.1%[a] (7.8–10.3) | 5.3% (4.3–6.3) |

NOTE: All data are weighted. 95-percent confidence intervals are presented in parentheses. Table includes only respondents who reported one or more previous combat or noncombat deployments.

[a] Estimate is significantly different from the estimate in column 2 (women).

**Table 10.15**
**Deployment-Related Injury, mTBI, and Postconcussive Symptoms, by Age Group**

| | Ages 17–24 (1) | Ages 25–34 (2) | Ages 35–44 (3) | Ages 45+ (4) |
|---|---|---|---|---|
| Any deployment-related injury | 13.1%[b,c,d] (8.2–18.1) | 23.9%[a,c,d] (21.0–26.7) | 35.2%[a,b] (32.4–38.0) | 37.8%[a,b] (33.6–41.9) |
| Positive screen for mTBI | 4.0%[b,c,d] (1.5–6.6) | 10.1%[a,c,d] (8.1–12.2) | 16.1%[a,b] (13.8–18.3) | 15.3%[a,b] (12.3–18.2) |
| Postconcussive symptoms | 1.4%[b,c,d] (0.0–3.0) | 6.7%[a,c,d] (4.9–8.5) | 12.3%[a,b] (10.3–14.4) | 13.1%[a,b] (10.0–16.2) |

NOTE: All data are weighted. 95-percent confidence intervals are presented in parentheses. Table includes only respondents who reported one or more previous combat or noncombat deployments.

[a] Estimate is significantly different from the estimate in column 1 (ages 17–24).

[b] Estimate is significantly different from the estimate in column 2 (ages 25–34).

[c] Estimate is significantly different from the estimate in column 3 (ages 35–44).

[d] Estimate is significantly different from the estimate in column 4 (ages 45+).

**Table 10.16**
**Deployment-Related Injury, mTBI, and Postconcussive Symptoms, by Race/Ethnicity**

| | Non-Hispanic White (1) | Non-Hispanic Black (2) | Hispanic (3) | Non-Hispanic Asian (4) | Other (5) |
|---|---|---|---|---|---|
| Any deployment-related injury[a] | 27.1% (24.8–29.3) | 27.7% (22.7–32.8) | 27.7% (22.9–32.5) | 29.7% (19.3–40.0) | 31.6% (25.7–37.5) |
| Positive screen for mTBI[a] | 12.1% (10.4–13.7) | 9.6% (6.6–12.7) | 11.7% (8.5–14.9) | 9.0% (3.4–14.6) | 14.9% (10.2–19.5) |
| Postconcussive symptoms[a] | 8.4% (7.0–9.9) | 9.1% (5.9–12.2) | 8.7% (6.0–11.4) | 4.0% (0.0–8.1) | 10.4% (6.7–14.2) |

NOTE: All data are weighted. 95-percent confidence intervals are presented in parentheses. Table includes only respondents who reported one or more previous combat or noncombat deployments.

[a] The omnibus chi-square test was not statistically significant ($p > 0.05$).

**Table 10.17**
**Deployment-Related Injury, mTBI, and Postconcussive Symptoms, by Education Level**

| | High School or Less (1) | Some College (2) | Bachelor's Degree or More (3) |
|---|---|---|---|
| Any deployment-related injury[a] | 27.3% (21.7–32.9) | 29.9% (27.2–32.6) | 25.0% (22.8–27.1) |
| Positive screen for mTBI[a] | 14.2% (10.1–18.4) | 12.2% (10.3–14.1) | 10.4% (8.8–12.1) |
| Postconcussive symptoms[a] | 10.1% (6.5–13.7) | 8.4% (6.8–10.0) | 8.2% (6.7–9.8) |

NOTE: All data are weighted. 95-percent confidence intervals are presented in parentheses. Table includes only respondents who reported one or more previous combat or noncombat deployments.

[a] The omnibus chi-square test was not statistically significant ($p > 0.05$).

## Deployment and Substance Use

Several studies have explored the relationship between combat exposure and substance use and misuse (Jeffery and Mattiko, 2016; Jacobson, Ryan, et al., 2008; Santiago et al., 2010; Skipper et al., 2014). Jacobson, Ryan, and colleagues (2008) found that service members who deployed and reported combat exposure were at increased risk of alcohol misuse (i.e., new onset of drinking, binge drinking, and alcohol dependency). Substance abuse has also been linked with PTSD and other mental disorders that are often associated with experiencing traumatic events, such as those associated with combat (Jacobson, Ryan, et al., 2008). Larson and colleagues (2016) found that, among enlisted Army personnel who had a recent deployment to Operation Enduring Freedom or Operation Iraqi Freedom, those with a combat specialist occupation were more likely than those in other occupation types to test positive for illicit drugs. In 2011, HRBS data indicated that personnel exposed to high levels of combat were heavy cigarette smokers more often than personnel exposed to little or no combat and were heavy drinkers more often than personnel exposed to lower levels of combat (Barlas et al., 2013). The 2011 HRBS also found that, across all services, personnel who experienced high levels of combat exposure reported prescription drug use, including proper use and misuse, more often than those with lower levels of combat exposure.

Although the military has made progress toward reducing cigarette smoking and illicit drug use among active-duty service members, alcohol and prescription drug use continue to be pervasive throughout the military (see Chapter Five and Williams et al., 2015). Understanding the trends in tobacco, alcohol, and substance use during and after deployment are vital to informing defense policies to maintain the health and readiness of the armed forces.

To capture the self-reported prevalence of substance use while on a deployment to a combat or noncombat zone, we used a question modified from the NSDUH (see Substance Abuse and Mental Health Services Administration, 2016). This item measures the frequency of use of alcohol, tobacco, smokeless tobacco, cigars, prescription drugs, marijuana, and opiates (opium, heroin, morphine, and related medications) during a service member's most-recent deployment. When interpreting these figures, it is important to note that DoD policies regarding alcohol use vary significantly depending on the geographic location of a deployment. For example, alcohol possession and consumption have long been banned for military personnel throughout nearly all of the Middle East,[2] although small-quantity consumption (one or two drinks) is allowed in a few locations. In addition, a 2008 report by the Army's Mental Health Advisory Team indicated that 8 percent of service members used alcohol in theater, which is somewhat lower than what we found in the 2015 HRBS (Mental Health Advisory Team, 2008). However, comparing the 2015 HRBS estimates with the Mental Health Advisory Team estimates is made difficult by several factors, such as telescoping and other recall biases among HRBS respondents; "rest and recreation" policies in or near theater, where alcohol use is often permissible; and the difference in examining alcohol use during deployment in an online, anonymous survey versus a survey administered in theater by a military organization.

As described earlier, the HRBS measured deployment-related substance use based on one item that asked service members about substance use during deployment in various frequency increments. We also derived estimates from reported substance use and deployment recency.

---

[2]  See, for example, Cucolo, 2009.

### Substance Use During Most-Recent Deployment

We begin with a discussion of substance use during deployment. Tables 10.18 through 10.23 present these results. These analyses are restricted to service members with one or more previous combat or noncombat deployments, and they focus on service member reports of substance use during their most-recent deployment. Key findings include the following:

- Overall, roughly two-thirds (67.6 percent) of all previously deployed service members reported using any substance during their most-recent deployment. Alcohol (36.2 percent) and cigarettes (28.0 percent) were among the most frequently used substances. Across all services, reported marijuana and opiate use was uncommon (0.1 percent for each) (Table 10.18).

- Previously deployed service members in the Marine Corps were the most likely to report substance use (including prescription drugs) during their most-recent deployment (77.2 percent), followed by those in the Navy (72.9 percent) and Coast Guard (71.5 percent); personnel in the Air Force were the least likely to report such use (62.0 percent) (Table 10.18).

- Consistent with prior HRBS reports, alcohol use during deployment varied widely by service branch: Reported use was highest among members of the Coast Guard (62.3 percent), followed by the Navy (55.8 percent) and the Marine Corps (45.4 percent), and was lowest in the Army (18.7 percent) (Table 10.18).

- Use of cigarettes, smokeless tobacco, or cigars during deployment was more frequent among those in the Marine Corps (Table 10.18), which is consistent with general patterns of tobacco use presented in Chapter Five and in the 2011 HRBS (Barlas et al., 2013).

- Prescription drug use during deployment was more commonly reported by service members in the Army (25.8 percent) than in any of the other services (Table 10.18).

- Previously deployed junior and mid-grade enlisted personnel (E1–E4, E5–E6) tended to report more cigarette use and smokeless tobacco use during their most-recent deployment than service members of other pay grades (Table 10.19). Junior officers also frequently reported alcohol and cigar use. Although cigar use was most commonly reported by mid-grade and senior officers, these pay grades reported the least cigarette use during their most-recent deployment. Prescription drug use during the most-recent deployment was highest among senior enlisted and warrant officers and lowest among junior enlisted and junior officers.

- More men (68.3 percent) than women (62.5 percent) reported using any substance during their most-recent deployment (Table 10.20). This was true also for cigarettes (28.6 percent compared with 23.8 percent), smokeless tobacco (21.0 percent compared with 4.2 percent), and cigars (25.1 percent compared with 10.8 percent). In contrast, significantly more women (28.5 percent) than men (17.5 percent) reported prescription drug use during their most-recent deployment.

- Significantly more younger service members (those aged 17–24) than older service members reported using alcohol, cigarettes, and smokeless tobacco during their most-recent deployment (Table 10.21). Service members in our oldest age group (those aged 45 or older) more commonly reported prescription drug use during their most-recent deployment than those in younger groups.

- Non-Hispanic white personnel were more likely than other racial or ethnic groups to report using any substance, alcohol, cigarettes, smokeless tobacco, and cigars during their most-recent deployment (Table 10.22). No significant differences by race/ethnicity were observed for prescription drug use.

- Significantly more service members with a high school degree or less reported using any substance, alcohol, cigarettes, and smokeless tobacco during their most-recent deployment (Table 10.23).

**Table 10.18**
**Substance Use During Most-Recent Deployment, by Service Branch**

| | Total (1) | Air Force (2) | Army (3) | Marine Corps (4) | Navy (5) | Coast Guard (6) |
|---|---|---|---|---|---|---|
| Any substance | 67.6% (65.8–69.5) | 62.0%[c,d,e] (59.0–65.0) | 63.7%[c,d,e] (59.9–67.4) | 77.2%[a,b] (73.3–81.2) | 72.9%[a,b] (69.6–76.3) | 71.5%[a,b] (69.4–73.6) |
| Alcohol | 36.2% (34.3–38.0) | 36.1%[b,c,d,e] (33.1–39.1) | 18.7%[a,c,d,e] (15.5–21.8) | 45.4%[a,b,d,e] (40.3–50.5) | 55.8%[a,b,c,e] (52.1–59.5) | 62.3%[a,b,c,d] (60.1–64.6) |
| Cigarettes | 28.0% (26.1–29.8) | 19.0%[b,c,d] (17.2–22.3) | 28.4%[a,c,e] (24.7–32.0) | 42.7%[a,b,d,e] (37.6–47.8) | 27.3%[a,c,e] (23.9–30.8) | 20.9%[b,c,d] (19.0–22.8) |
| Smokeless tobacco | 18.9% (17.2–20.5) | 13.7%[b,c] (11.4–16.1) | 19.6%[a,c] (16.4–22.9) | 33.7%[a,b,d,e] (28.7–38.7) | 14.8%[c] (12.0–17.7) | 15.0%[c] (13.3–16.6) |
| Cigars | 23.3% (21.6–25.0) | 15.6%[b,c,d] (13.4–17.8) | 26.5%[a,e] (23.1–29.9) | 29.6%[a,d,e] (25.0–34.1) | 21.8%[a,c] (18.7–24.8) | 18.7%[b,c] (16.9–20.5) |
| Prescription drugs | 18.9% (17.4–20.4) | 15.8%[b,e] (13.7–17.8) | 25.8%[a,c,d,e] (22.7–29.0) | 12.5%[b] (9.4–15.6) | 15.0%[b,e] (12.6–17.4) | 9.3%[a,b,d] (8.0–10.6) |
| Marijuana | 0.1% (0.0–0.2) | NA | 0.1% (0.0–0.2) | 0.3% (0.0–0.7) | 0.0% (0.0–0.1) | 0.1% (0.0–0.2) |
| Opiates | 0.1% (0.0–0.2) | 0.1% (0.0–0.2) | 0.1% (0.0–0.2) | 0.3% (0.0–0.7) | 0.0% (0.0–0.1) | NA |

NOTE: All data are weighted. 95-percent confidence intervals are presented in parentheses. Table includes only respondents who reported one or more previous combat or noncombat deployments.

[a] Estimate is significantly different from the estimate in column 2 (Air Force).

[b] Estimate is significantly different from the estimate in column 3 (Army).

[c] Estimate is significantly different from the estimate in column 4 (Marine Corps).

[d] Estimate is significantly different from the estimate in column 5 (Navy).

[e] Estimate is significantly different from the estimate in column 6 (Coast Guard).

NA = not applicable (zero individuals in the cell).

**Table 10.19**
**Substance Use During Most-Recent Deployment, by Pay Grade**

| | E1–E4 (1) | E5–E6 (2) | E7–E9 (3) | W1–W5 (4) | O1–O3 (5) | O4–O10 (6) |
|---|---|---|---|---|---|---|
| Any substance[g] | 64.5% (58.4–70.6) | 70.3% (67.4–73.3) | 67.6% (64.8–70.5) | 62.6% (58.4–66.7) | 65.6% (62.7–68.5) | 66.9% (64.5–69.3) |
| Alcohol | 39.8%[d] (34.0–45.6) | 36.5%[d] (33.5–39.4) | 32.2%[d,e] (29.8–34.7) | 24.1%[a,b,c,e,f] (21.0–27.3) | 38.7%[c,d,f] (36.1–41.4) | 33.3%[d,e] (31.1–35.5) |
| Cigarettes | 35.1%[c,d,e,f] (29.1–41.1) | 34.5%[c,d,e,f] (31.4–37.6) | 25.5%[a,b,d,e,f] (22.8–28.3) | 19.0%[a,b,c,f] (15.7–22.3) | 14.2%[a,b,c,f] (12.0–16.4) | 8.0%[a,b,c,d,e] (6.6–9.4) |
| Smokeless tobacco | 22.0%[f] (16.6–27.3) | 21.9%[c,e,f] (19.1–24.6) | 14.9%[b] (12.7–17.2) | 16.6%[f] (13.4–19.8) | 14.9%[b] (12.6–17.1) | 11.4%[a,b,d] (9.7–13.1) |
| Cigars | 20.5%[f] (15.2–25.9) | 22.4%[e,f] (19.6–25.2) | 19.7%[e,f] (17.2–22.2) | 23.1%[f] (19.5–26.7) | 29.8%[b,c] (27.0–32.7) | 30.8%[a,b,c,d] (28.3–33.2) |
| Prescription drugs | 12.8%[c,d,f] (8.5–17.1) | 19.1%[c,d] (16.5–21.7) | 25.7%[a,b,e] (23.0–28.5) | 26.8%[a,b,e] (23.0–30.5) | 15.9%[c,d,f] (13.6–18.2) | 22.1%[a,e] (19.9–24.3) |
| Marijuana | 0.1% (0.0–0.3) | 0.1% (0.0–0.2) | 0.0% (0.0–0.1) | NA | 0.1% (0.0–0.3) | 0.1% (0.0–0.2) |
| Opiates[g] | 0.1% (0.0–0.3) | 0.1% (0.0–0.3) | 0.0% (0.0–0.1) | 0.5% (0.0–1.2) | 0.1% (0.0–0.2) | 0.1% (0.0–0.2) |

NOTE: All data are weighted. 95-percent confidence intervals are presented in parentheses. Table includes only respondents who reported one or more previous combat or noncombat deployments.

[a] Estimate is significantly different from the estimate in column 1 (E1–E4).

[b] Estimate is significantly different from the estimate in column 2 (E5–E6).

[c] Estimate is significantly different from the estimate in column 3 (E7–E9).

[d] Estimate is significantly different from the estimate in column 4 (W1–W5).

[e] Estimate is significantly different from the estimate in column 5 (O1–O3).

[f] Estimate is significantly different from the estimate in column 6 (O4–O10).

[g] The omnibus chi-square test was not statistically significant ($p > 0.05$).

NA = not applicable (zero individuals in the cell).

**Table 10.20**
**Substance Use During Most-Recent Deployment, by Gender**

|  | Men (1) | Women (2) |
|---|---|---|
| Any substance | 68.3%[a] (66.3–70.4) | 62.5% (60.1–64.9) |
| Alcohol[b] | 36.5% (34.4–38.5) | 34.1% (31.8–36.3) |
| Cigarettes | 28.6%[a] (26.5–30.7) | 23.8% (21.5–26.1) |
| Smokeless tobacco | 21.0%[a] (19.1–22.9) | 4.2% (3.0–5.4) |
| Cigars | 25.1%[a] (23.1–27.0) | 10.8% (9.2–12.4) |
| Prescription drugs | 17.5%[a] (15.9–19.2) | 28.5% (26.2–30.7) |
| Marijuana | 0.1%[a] (0.0–0.1) | 0.3% (0.0–0.7) |
| Opiates | 0.1%[a] (0.0–0.1) | 0.4% (0.0–0.8) |

NOTE: All data are weighted. 95-percent confidence intervals are presented in parentheses. Table includes only respondents who reported one or more previous combat or noncombat deployments.

[a] Estimate is significantly different from the estimate in column 2 (women).

[b] The omnibus chi-square test was not statistically significant ($p > 0.05$).

**Table 10.21**
**Substance Use During Most-Recent Deployment, by Age Group**

|  | Ages 17–24 (1) | Ages 25–34 (2) | Ages 35–44 (3) | Ages 45+ (4) |
|---|---|---|---|---|
| Any substance[e] | 73.3% (67.0–79.6) | 67.2% (64.1–70.3) | 67.3% (64.6–70.0) | 63.3% (59.0–67.5) |
| Alcohol | 48.0%[c,d] (40.9–55.1) | 39.0%[c,d] (36.0–42.0) | 32.3%[a,b,d] (29.8–34.8) | 22.6%[a,b,c] (19.6–25.6) |
| Cigarettes | 41.6%[b,c,d] (34.6–48.6) | 28.8%[a,d] (25.9–31.7) | 26.8%[a,d] (24.0–29.7) | 11.0%[a,b,c] (8.4–13.6) |
| Smokeless tobacco | 27.7%[c,d] (21.0–34.3) | 20.2%[d] (17.5–22.8) | 15.8%[a] (13.6–18.1) | 12.2%[a,b] (9.1–15.3) |
| Cigars[e] | 22.6% (16.3–28.8) | 25.0% (22.2–27.8) | 22.2% (19.8–24.6) | 20.4% (17.6–23.3) |
| Prescription drugs | 15.0%[d] (9.4–20.6) | 14.2%[c,d] (12.0–16.5) | 21.9%[b,d] (19.7–24.2) | 32.7%[a,b,c] (28.6–36.9) |
| Marijuana | 0.0%[b] (0.0–0.0) | 0.2%[a] (0.0–0.3) | 0.0% (0.0–0.1) | 0.0% (0.0–0.1) |
| Opiates | NA | 0.2% (0.0–0.4) | 0.1% (0.0–0.1) | 0.1% (0.0–0.2) |

NOTE: All data are weighted. 95-percent confidence intervals are presented in parentheses. Table includes only respondents who reported one or more previous combat or noncombat deployments.

[a] Estimate is significantly different from the estimate in column 1 (ages 17–24).

[b] Estimate is significantly different from the estimate in column 2 (ages 25–34).

[c] Estimate is significantly different from the estimate in column 3 (ages 35–44).

[d] Estimate is significantly different from the estimate in column 4 (ages 45+).

[e] The omnibus chi-square test was not statistically significant ($p > 0.05$).

NA = not applicable (zero individuals in the cell).

**Table 10.22**
**Substance Use During Most-Recent Deployment, by Race/Ethnicity**

| | Non-Hispanic White (1) | Non-Hispanic Black (2) | Hispanic (3) | Non-Hispanic Asian (4) | Other (5) |
|---|---|---|---|---|---|
| Any substance | 72.9%[b,c] (70.8–75.1) | 52.1%[a,e] (45.9–58.2) | 60.4%[a] (54.6–66.2) | 61.6% (50.9–72.3) | 66.5%[b] (60.3–72.8) |
| Alcohol | 39.7%[b] (37.4–42.0) | 23.7%[a,e] (18.6–28.7) | 32.1% (27.0–37.1) | 37.4% (27.4–47.5) | 35.2%[b] (28.9–41.5) |
| Cigarettes | 30.8%[b] (28.4–33.2) | 18.8%[a] (13.8–23.7) | 23.4% (18.5–28.4) | 27.0% (17.6–36.3) | 29.2% (22.7–35.8) |
| Smokeless tobacco | 24.1%[b,c,d] (21.8–26.3) | 5.8%[a,e] (2.6–9.0) | 13.0%[a] (8.8–17.1) | 7.0%[a] (2.0–12.0) | 15.7%[b] (10.0–21.3) |
| Cigars | 26.4%[b,d] (24.2–28.6) | 17.0%[a] (12.5–21.5) | 19.2% (14.7–23.7) | 13.0%[a] (7.3–18.8) | 21.1% (16.2–26.0) |
| Prescription drugs[f] | 19.5% (17.5–21.5) | 19.0% (15.1–23.0) | 17.1% (13.2–21.1) | 16.8% (9.9–23.8) | 18.3% (13.8–22.9) |
| Marijuana | 0.0% (0.0–0.1) | 0.3% (0.0–0.8) | 0.0% (0.0–0.0) | NA | 0.3% (0.0–0.8) |
| Opiates | 0.1% (0.0–0.1) | 0.3% (0.0–0.8) | NA | NA | 0.4% (0.0–0.9) |

NOTE: All data are weighted. 95-percent confidence intervals are presented in parentheses. Table includes only respondents who reported one or more previous combat or noncombat deployments.

[a] Estimate is significantly different from the estimate in column 1 (non-Hispanic white).

[b] Estimate is significantly different from the estimate in column 2 (non-Hispanic black).

[c] Estimate is significantly different from the estimate in column 3 (Hispanic).

[d] Estimate is significantly different from the estimate in column 4 (non-Hispanic Asian).

[e] Estimate is significantly different from the estimate in column 5 (other).

[f] The omnibus chi-square test was not statistically significant ($p > 0.05$).

NA = not applicable (zero individuals in the cell).

**Table 10.23**
**Substance Use During Most-Recent Deployment, by Education Level**

| | High School or Less (1) | Some College (2) | Bachelor's Degree or More (3) |
|---|---|---|---|
| Any substance | 76.8%[b,c] (71.4–82.2) | 68.1%[a,c] (65.2–70.9) | 63.0%[a,b] (60.5–65.6) |
| Alcohol | 43.5%[c] (37.4–49.7) | 37.1%[c] (34.3–39.8) | 31.8%[a,b] (29.6–33.9) |
| Cigarettes | 45.2%[b,c] (39.0–51.5) | 31.1%[a,c] (28.3–33.9) | 16.3%[a,b] (14.2–18.4) |
| Smokeless tobacco | 31.1%[b,c] (25.1–37.0) | 19.4%[a,c] (17.0–21.8) | 12.9%[a,b] (10.9–14.9) |
| Cigars | 26.7% (20.9–32.5) | 20.2%[c] (17.7–22.6) | 25.9%[b] (23.8–28.1) |
| Prescription drugs[d] | 15.3% (10.6–20.1) | 19.3% (16.9–21.6) | 19.9% (18.1–21.8) |
| Marijuana[d] | 0.0% (0.0–0.1) | 0.1% (0.0–0.3) | 0.1% (0.0–0.1) |
| Opiates[d] | 0.0% (0.0–0.1) | 0.2% (0.0–0.3) | 0.1% (0.0–0.1) |

NOTE: All data are weighted. 95-percent confidence intervals are presented in parentheses. Table includes only respondents who reported one or more previous combat or noncombat deployments.

[a] Estimate is significantly different from the estimate in column 1 (high school or less).

[b] Estimate is significantly different from the estimate in column 2 (some college).

[c] Estimate is significantly different from the estimate in column 3 (bachelor's degree or more).

[d] The omnibus chi-square test was not statistically significant ($p > 0.05$).

## Substance Use and Combat Exposure

Tables 10.24 and 10.25 consider the effects of combat exposure on substance use. The results show service members who reported using each substance during their most-recent combat deployment (Table 10.24) and those who reported current (usually past-year) use of various substances (Table 10.25), by level of combat exposure. We limited these analyses to those deployed in the past three years (to better reflect substance use during recent rather than remote deployments). As discussed earlier in this chapter, we considered service members to have high combat exposure if they scored a five or more on our combat trauma exposure index, and we considered service members to have low to moderate combat exposure if they scored less than five on the index. Note that our measure of combat exposure is over a service member's lifetime and is thus not necessarily applicable to the person's most-recent deployment.

Overall, use of any substance was not significantly different between service members with high combat exposure (71.7 percent) and those with low to moderate exposure (67.6 percent) (Table 10.24).

Key findings related to tobacco use include the following:

- Among service members deployed in the past three years, those with high combat exposure were more likely than those with low to moderate exposure to use smokeless tobacco (22.4 percent compared with 16.9 percent) and cigars (28.1 percent compared with 19.5 percent) during their most-recent deployment (Table 10.24).
- Current cigarette use did not significantly differ by level of combat exposure (Table 10.25).

Key findings related to alcohol use include the following:

- Alcohol use during the most-recent deployment was reported more frequently among those with low to moderate combat exposure (48.6 percent) than among those with high combat exposure (28.9 percent) (Table 10.24).
- Current binge drinking (during the past month) was higher among those with low to moderate combat exposure (34.6 percent) than among those with high combat exposure (28.2 percent) (Table 10.25).

Key findings related to prescription drug use include the following:

- When compared with recently deployed service members with low to moderate combat exposure, those with high combat exposure more often reported using prescription drugs (regardless of prescription status) both during their most-recent deployment (26.5 percent compared with 13.8 percent) and in the past year (36.2 percent compared with 23.6 percent) (Tables 10.24 and 10.25, respectively). Specifically, they were more likely to report past-year use of stimulants (4.4 percent compared with 2.0 percent), sedatives (16.4 percent compared with 7.3 percent), pain relievers (25.8 percent compared with 17.1 percent), and antidepressants (14.0 percent compared with 4.9 percent).
- No significant differences by level of combat exposure were observed for current use of prescription anabolic steroids or for current prescription drug misuse (Table 10.25).

**Table 10.24**
**Substance Use During Most-Recent Deployment, by Level of Combat Exposure**

| | Total (1) | High Combat Exposure (2) | Low to Moderate Combat Exposure (3) |
|---|---|---|---|
| Any substance[b] | 69.3% (66.8–71.7) | 71.7% (68.1–75.3) | 67.6% (64.3–70.9) |
| Alcohol | 40.6% (38.2–43.0) | 28.9%[a] (25.5–32.3) | 48.6% (45.2–52.0) |
| Cigarettes[b] | 27.5% (25.0–29.9) | 27.6% (23.9–31.3) | 27.4% (24.2–30.6) |
| Smokeless tobacco | 19.2% (17.0–21.3) | 22.4%[a] (19.0–25.7) | 16.9% (14.2–19.7) |
| Cigars | 23.0% (20.9–25.2) | 28.1%[a] (24.6–31.7) | 19.5% (16.8–22.3) |
| Prescription drugs | 19.0% (17.1–20.8) | 26.5%[a] (23.3–29.7) | 13.8% (11.5–16.1) |
| Marijuana[b] | 0.1% (0.0–0.2) | 0.1% (0.0–0.3) | 0.1% (0.0–0.2) |
| Opiates[b] | 0.1% (0.0–0.3) | 0.2% (0.0–0.4) | 0.1% (0.0–0.2) |

NOTE: All data are weighted. 95-percent confidence intervals are presented in parentheses. Table includes only respondents who reported one or more combat or noncombat deployments in the past three years.

[a] Estimate is significantly different from the estimate in column 3 (low to moderate combat exposure).

[b] The omnibus chi-square test was not statistically significant ($p > 0.05$).

**Table 10.25**
**Current Substance Use, by Level of Combat Exposure**

| | Total (1) | High Combat Exposure (2) | Low to Moderate Combat Exposure (3) |
|---|---|---|---|
| Current smoker[b] | 13.8% (11.8–15.7) | 11.7% (9.1–14.3) | 15.1% (12.5–17.8) |
| Binge drinking in the past month | 32.0% (29.5–34.4) | 28.2%[a] (24.7–31.7) | 34.6% (31.3–37.9) |
| Any prescription drug use in the past year | 28.8% (26.4–31.1) | 36.2%[a] (32.4–39.9) | 23.6% (20.7–26.6) |
| Stimulants | 3.0% (2.0–3.9) | 4.4%[a] (2.6–6.1) | 2.0% (0.9–3.1) |
| Sedatives | 11.0% (9.6–12.5) | 16.4%[a] (13.6–19.2) | 7.3% (5.9–8.8) |
| Pain relievers | 20.7% (18.6–22.7) | 25.8%[a] (22.4–29.2) | 17.1% (14.4–19.8) |
| Anabolic steroids[b] | 1.7% (1.0–2.4) | 1.6% (0.7–2.4) | 1.8% (0.7–2.9) |
| Antidepressants | 8.6% (7.2–10.1) | 14.0%[a] (11.1–17.0) | 4.9% (3.5–6.3) |
| Any prescription drug misuse in the past year[b] | 4.4% (3.3–5.5) | 4.7% (3.1–6.3) | 4.2% (2.7–5.7) |

NOTE: All data are weighted. 95-percent confidence intervals are presented in parentheses. Table includes only respondents who reported one or more combat or noncombat deployments in the past three years.

[a] Estimate is significantly different from the estimate in column 3 (low to moderate combat exposure).

[b] The omnibus chi-square test was not statistically significant ($p > 0.05$).

## Substance Use and Traumatic Brain Injury

Tables 10.26 and 10.27 consider the effects of TBI on substance use. Studies have found that between 15 and 20 percent of Army soldiers returning from deployments to Afghanistan or Iraq meet screening criteria for mTBI and that mTBI after deployment is related to PTSD, depression, chronic pain, and lost work (Tanielian and Jaycox, 2008; Hoge, McGurk, et al., 2008; Wilk, Herrell, et al., 2012; Terrio et al., 2009). The results show service members who reported using each substance during their most-recent deployment (Table 10.26) and those who reported current (usually past-year) use of various substances (Table 10.27), by TBI status (probable mTBI or no TBI). Here again, we limited these analyses to those deployed in the past three years (to better reflect substance use during recent rather than remote deployments). Note that our measure of TBI is over a service member's lifetime and is thus not necessarily applicable to the person's most-recent deployment.

Overall, use of any substance was not significantly different between service members who indicated probable mTBI (74.0 percent) and those who did not (68.8 percent) (Table 10.26).

Key findings related to tobacco use include the following:

- Cigarette use during the most-recent deployment was reported by significantly more service members with probable mTBI (34.4 percent) than those without TBI (26.8 percent) (Table 10.26). Significant differences by TBI status also emerged for smokeless tobacco use during deployment (26.8 percent among those with probable mTBI compared with 18.2 percent without TBI).
- No significant differences were observed for current cigarette smokers between those with probable mTBI and those without TBI (Table 10.27).

Key findings related to alcohol use include the following:

- Reported alcohol use during the most-recent deployment was lower among service members who screened positive for mTBI (29.2 percent) than among those who did not screen positive for TBI (41.6 percent) (Table 10.26).
- No significant differences between those with probable mTBI and without TBI were observed for current binge drinking in the past 30 days (Table 10.27).

Key findings related to illicit and prescription drug use include the following:

- Use of marijuana and opiates during deployment was very rare; the sample did not meet the minimum number of reportable cases for such users, so estimates are not available by TBI status (Table 10.26).
- Service members with probable mTBI (32.1 percent) were more likely than those with no TBI (17.6 percent) to report using prescription drugs (regardless of prescription status) during their most-recent deployment (Table 10.26). Similarly, when compared with recently deployed service members with no TBI, those with probable mTBI reported greater use of any prescription drug in the past year (45.7 percent compared with 26.7 percent), prescription stimulants (6.5 percent compared with 2.5 percent), prescription sedatives (23.9 percent compared with 9.5 percent), pain relievers (32.3 percent compared with 19.2 percent), anabolic steroids (5.6 percent compared with 1.3 percent), and antidepressants (18.4 percent compared with 7.5 percent) (Table 10.27).
- No significant differences for current prescription drug misuse were observed between those with probable mTBI and those with no TBI (Table 10.27).

**Table 10.26**
**Substance Use During Most-Recent Deployment, by TBI Status**

| | Total (1) | Probable mTBI (2) | No TBI (3) |
|---|---|---|---|
| Any substance[b] | 69.3% (66.8–71.8) | 74.0% (67.1–80.9) | 68.8% (66.1–71.4) |
| Alcohol | 40.2% (37.7–42.7) | 29.2%[a] (23.0–35.3) | 41.6% (38.9–44.3) |
| Cigarettes | 27.6% (25.2–30.1) | 34.4%[a] (27.4–41.3) | 26.8% (24.2–29.4) |
| Smokeless tobacco | 19.1% (17.0–21.3) | 26.8%[a] (20.2–33.4) | 18.2% (16.0–20.5) |
| Cigars[b] | 23.0% (20.8–25.1) | 28.5% (22.1–34.9) | 22.3% (20.0–24.6) |
| Prescription drugs | 19.2% (17.2–21.1) | 32.1%[a] (25.6–38.6) | 17.6% (15.6–19.7) |
| Marijuana | 0.1% (0.0–0.2) | NA | 0.1% (0.0–0.2) |
| Opiates[b] | 0.1% (0.0–0.2) | 0.1% (0.0–0.2) | 0.1% (0.0–0.3) |

NOTE: All data are weighted. 95-percent confidence intervals are presented in parentheses. Table includes only respondents who reported one or more combat or noncombat deployments in the past three years.

[a] Estimate is significantly different from the estimate in column 3 (No TBI).

[b] The omnibus chi-square test was not statistically significant ($p < 0.05$).

NA = not applicable (zero individuals in the cell).

**Table 10.27**
**Current Substance Use, by TBI Status**

| | Total (1) | Probable mTBI (2) | No TBI (3) |
|---|---|---|---|
| Current cigarette smoker[b] | 13.9% (12.0–15.9) | 16.4% (10.8–22.0) | 13.7% (11.6–15.7) |
| Binge drinking in the past month[b] | 31.9% (29.5–34.4) | 34.1% (27.2–41.0) | 31.7% (29.0–34.3) |
| Any prescription drug use in the past year | 28.8% (26.5–31.1) | 45.7%[a] (38.6–52.9) | 26.7% (24.3–29.2) |
| Stimulants | 2.9% (2.0–3.9) | 6.5%[a] (2.9–10.0) | 2.5% (1.5–3.5) |
| Sedatives | 11.0% (9.6–12.5) | 23.9%[a] (18.1–29.7) | 9.5% (8.0–10.9) |
| Pain relievers | 20.6% (18.6–22.7) | 32.3%[a] (25.9–38.8) | 19.2% (17.0–21.4) |
| Anabolic steroids | 1.8% (1.0–2.5) | 5.6%[a] (1.8–9.4) | 1.3% (0.6–2.0) |
| Antidepressants | 8.7% (7.2–10.2) | 18.4%[a] (13.2–23.6) | 7.5% (6.0–9.0) |
| Any prescription drug misuse in the past year[b] | 4.4% (3.3–5.5) | 4.6% (2.4–6.8) | 4.3% (3.1–5.5) |

NOTE: All data are weighted. 95-percent confidence intervals are presented in parentheses. Table includes only respondents who reported one or more combat or noncombat deployments in the past three years.

[a] Estimate is significantly different from the estimate in column 3 (no TBI).

[b] The omnibus chi-square test was not statistically significant ($p > 0.05$).

## Deployment and Mental Health

Nearly one-fourth of service members returning from deployment may have mental health disorders, the most common of which are major depression, GAD, and PTSD (Tanielian and Jaycox, 2008; Ramchand, Schell, Jaycox, and Tanielian, 2011). Many service members who have been previously deployed experience other mental health conditions or cognitive impairments, such as TBI and related psychiatric comorbidities (Carlson et al., 2010). Additionally, other factors that may also be associated with deployment—such as high propensities of risk-taking, impulsivity, and anger (MacManus et al., 2015)—can be indicators of other mental health problems and adverse health-related behaviors, such as suicide ideation and attempts (Hawton et al., 2003; Novaco et al., 2012). Serious mental illnesses often trigger long-term negative health and social outcomes, such as marital instability and even homelessness, and understanding the long-term effects of deployment and combat exposure on mental health is vital to reducing such negative outcomes.

As described in Chapter Six, we measured depression in the HRBS using the PHQ-9, where scores of 15 or more indicated probable depression (Kroenke, Spitzer, and Williams, 2001). We measured anxiety using the GAD-7, where scores of 10 or more indicated probable GAD (Spitzer et al., 2006). PTSD was measured using the PCL-C, where scores of 50 or more indicated probable PTSD (Weathers et al., 1993).

### Current Mental Health and Combat Exposure

In this section, we present results for mental health indicators and social and emotional factors associated with mental health (Table 10.28), as well as indicators of self-harm, suicide ideation, and suicide attempts (Table 10.29), by combat exposure. We limited these analyses to service members with one or more combat or noncombat deployments in the past three years.

Key findings related to depression, GAD, and PTSD include the following:

- Significantly more recently deployed service members with high combat exposure met the criteria for probable GAD (18.8 percent) and probable PTSD (12.8 percent) compared with those exposed to low to moderate levels of combat (12.3 percent and 7.9 percent, respectively) (Table 10.28). Differences in probable depression were observed but did not reach statistical significance.
- The percentage of recent deployers with probable depression, GAD, and PTSD was similar to, but somewhat higher than, the rate for the overall 2015 HRBS population presented in Chapter Six (depression: 9.4 percent; GAD: 14.2 percent; and PTSD: 8.5 percent).

Key findings related to aggression and impulsivity include the following:

- Significantly more recently deployed service members who experienced high combat exposure reported any aggressive behavior in the past month (56.7 percent) compared with those who experienced low to moderate combat exposure (46.4 percent) (Table 10.28). The same was true for sustained aggressive behavior (10.4 percent compared with 7.1 percent). No significant differences were observed for high impulsivity.

Key findings related to self-harm, suicide ideation, and suicide attempts include the following:

- Significantly more service members with high combat exposure reported suicide ideation since joining the military (15.7 percent compared with 9.8 percent for those with low to moderate combat exposure) and during a deployment (6.8 percent compared with 3.7 percent) (Table 10.29).
- Service members with high combat exposure were less likely than those with low to moderate exposure to report suicide attempts prior to joining the military (1.0 percent compared with 3.8 percent) (Table 10.29).
- No statistically significant differences between high and low to moderate combat exposure were observed for the following indicators of self-harm and suicide ideation or attempts: lifetime NSSI, lifetime suicide ideation, recent (past 12 months) suicide ideation, suicide ideation before joining the military, recent (past 12 months) suicide attempts, attempts since joining the military, or attempts during deployment (Table 10.29).

**Table 10.28**
**Mental Health Indicators and Social and Emotional Factors Associated with Mental Health, by Level of Combat Exposure**

|  | Total (1) | High Combat Exposure (2) | Low to Moderate Combat Exposure (3) |
|---|---|---|---|
| Probable depression[b] | 10.4% (8.5–12.2) | 12.4% (9.4–15.3) | 9.0% (6.6–11.4) |
| Probable GAD | 15.0% (12.9–17.0) | 18.8%[a] (15.6–22.1) | 12.3% (9.7–14.9) |
| Probable PTSD | 9.9% (8.2–11.6) | 12.8%[a] (10.1–15.5) | 7.9% (5.6–10.1) |
| Any aggressive behavior in the past month | 50.6% (48.0–53.2) | 56.7%[a] (52.9–60.5) | 46.4% (42.9–49.9) |
| Aggressive behavior 5+ times in the past month | 8.4% (6.9–10.0) | 10.4%[a] (7.9–13.0) | 7.1% (5.1–9.1) |
| High impulsivity[b] | 12.2% (10.3–14.0) | 12.9% (9.9–16.0) | 11.6% (9.3–14.0) |

NOTE: All data are weighted. 95-percent confidence intervals are presented in parentheses. Table includes only respondents who reported one or more combat or noncombat deployments in the past three years.

[a] Estimate is significantly different from the estimate in column 3 (low to moderate combat exposure).

[b] The omnibus chi-square test was not statistically significant ($p > 0.05$).

**Table 10.29**
**Non-Suicidal Self-Injury, Suicide Ideation, and Suicide Attempts, by Level of Combat Exposure**

| | Total (1) | High Combat Exposure (2) | Low to Moderate Combat Exposure (3) |
|---|---|---|---|
| Lifetime NSSI[b] | 11.7% (9.9–13.6) | 11.2% (8.4–13.9) | 12.1% (9.7–14.6) |
| **Suicide ideation** | | | |
| Lifetime[b] | 17.7% (15.7–19.7) | 19.6% (16.4–22.8) | 16.4% (13.7–19.0) |
| Past 12 months[b] | 5.7% (4.3–7.1) | 6.3% (4.2–8.4) | 5.3% (3.5–7.1) |
| Since joining the military | 12.2% (10.5–14.0) | 15.7%[a] (12.8–18.6) | 9.8% (7.7–11.9) |
| Before joining the military[b] | 9.6% (8.0–11.3) | 8.2% (6.1–10.4) | 10.6% (8.3–12.9) |
| During deployment | 5.0% (3.7–6.2) | 6.8%[a] (4.6–9.0) | 3.7% (2.3–5.1) |
| **Suicide attempt** | | | |
| Lifetime | 4.6% (3.4–5.8) | 2.9%[a] (1.9–4.0) | 5.8% (3.8–7.7) |
| Past 12 months[b] | 1.3% (0.7–2.0) | 0.8% (0.2–1.4) | 1.7% (0.6–2.7) |
| Since joining the military[b] | 2.4% (1.6–3.3) | 2.0% (1.1–3.0) | 2.7% (1.5–4.0) |
| Before joining the military | 2.6% (1.6–3.6) | 1.0%[a] (0.5–1.4) | 3.8% (2.1–5.5) |
| During deployment[b] | 0.6% (0.2–1.0) | 0.5% (0.1–0.9) | 0.7% (0.0–1.4) |

NOTE: All data are weighted. 95-percent confidence intervals are presented in parentheses. Table includes only respondents who reported one or more combat or noncombat deployments in the past three years.

[a] Estimate is significantly different from the estimate in column 3 (low to moderate combat exposure).

[b] The omnibus chi-square test was not statistically significant ($p > 0.05$).

## Current Mental Health and Traumatic Brain Injury

In this section, we present results for mental health indicators and social and emotional factors associated with mental health (Table 10.30), as well as indicators of self-harm, suicide ideation, and suicide attempts (Table 10.31), by TBI status (probable mTBI or no TBI). We limited these analyses to service members with one or more combat or noncombat deployments in the past three years.

Key findings related to depression, GAD, and PTSD include the following:

- Almost three times as many recently deployed service members with probable mTBI screened positive for probable depression (24.5 percent) compared with those with no TBI (8.8 percent) (Table 10.30). Similarly, almost three times as many service members with probable mTBI screened positive for probable GAD (35.3 percent) compared with those with no TBI (12.6 percent).
- Nearly three in ten service members with probable mTBI had probable PTSD (29.5 percent) compared with less than one in ten for those with no TBI (7.6 percent) (Table 10.30).

Key findings related to aggression and impulsivity include the following:

- Among recently deployed service members, those with probable mTBI reported significantly more instances of any aggressive behavior in the past month (71.7 percent) than those with no TBI (48.2 percent), and those with probable mTBI reported frequent aggressive behavior almost three times as often (20.1 percent) as those with no TBI (7.1 percent) (Table 10.30).
- More than twice as many recently deployed service members with probable mTBI scored positively for high impulsivity (25.1 percent) as those with no TBI (10.7 percent) (Table 10.30).

Key findings related to self-harm, suicide ideation, and suicide attempts include the following:

- Significantly more recently deployed service members with probable mTBI reported any lifetime suicide ideation (28.6 percent) compared with personnel with no TBI (16.1 percent) (Table 10.31). Lifetime NSSI rates did not vary by TBI status.
- Suicidal thoughts at any time in the past 12 months, since joining the military, or during a deployment were reported more than twice as often among those with probable mTBI than among those with no TBI (in the past 12 months: 11.6 percent compared with 4.9 percent; since joining the military: 24.8 percent compared with 10.5 percent; during a deployment: 10.6 percent compared with 4.3 percent) (Table 10.31).
- Results from the survey suggest that significantly more recently deployed service members with probable mTBI reported a suicide attempt since joining the military (5.8 percent) compared with those with no TBI (2.0 percent) (Table 10.31).
- Suicide attempts prior to joining the military did not significantly vary by TBI status.

**Table 10.30**
**Mental Health Indicators and Social and Emotional Factors Associated with Mental Health, by TBI Status**

|  | Total (1) | Probable mTBI (2) | No TBI (3) |
|---|---|---|---|
| Probable depression | 10.5% (8.6–12.3) | 24.5%[a] (17.6–31.4) | 8.8% (6.9–10.6) |
| Probable GAD | 15.0% (13.0–17.1) | 35.3%[a] (28.0–42.6) | 12.6% (10.5–14.6) |
| Probable PTSD | 9.9% (8.2–11.7) | 29.5%[a] (22.5–36.6) | 7.6% (5.9–9.2) |
| Any aggressive behavior in the past month | 50.7% (48.1–53.3) | 71.7%[a] (65.7–77.7) | 48.2% (45.4–51.0) |
| Aggressive behavior 5+ times in the past month | 8.5% (6.9–10.0) | 20.1%[a] (14.1–26.1) | 7.1% (5.5–8.6) |
| High impulsivity | 12.2% (10.4–14.1) | 25.1%[a] (18.0–32.1) | 10.7% (8.8–12.6) |

NOTE: All data are weighted. 95-percent confidence intervals are presented in parentheses. Table includes only respondents who reported one or more combat or noncombat deployments in the past three years.

[a] Estimate is significantly different from the estimate in column 3 (no TBI).

Table 10.31
**Non-Suicidal Self-Injury, Suicide Ideation, and Suicide Attempts, by TBI Status**

| | Total (1) | Probable mTBI (2) | No TBI (3) |
|---|---|---|---|
| Lifetime NSSI[b] | 11.7% (9.9–13.5) | 16.4% (10.7–22.1) | 11.2% (9.2–13.1) |
| Suicide ideation | | | |
| Lifetime | 17.5% (15.5–19.5) | 28.6%[a] (22.1–35.2) | 16.1% (14.0–18.2) |
| Past 12 months | 5.7% (4.3–7.0) | 11.6%[a] (6.8–16.4) | 4.9% (3.6–6.3) |
| Since joining the military | 12.0% (10.3–13.7) | 24.8%[a] (18.3–31.2) | 10.5% (8.8–12.2) |
| Before joining the military[b] | 9.5% (7.9–11.1) | 9.7% (6.0–13.5) | 9.4% (7.7–11.2) |
| During deployment | 5.0% (3.7–6.2) | 10.6%[a] (6.0–15.2) | 4.3% (3.0–5.5) |
| Suicide attempt | | | |
| Lifetime | 4.5% (3.3–5.8) | 7.7%[a] (3.9–11.5) | 4.2% (2.9–5.5) |
| Past 12 months[b] | 1.3% (0.7–2.0) | 2.7% (0.2–5.2) | 1.1% (0.5–1.8) |
| Since joining the military | 2.4% (1.6–3.2) | 5.8%[a] (2.2–9.3) | 2.0% (1.2–2.8) |
| Before joining the military[b] | 2.6% (1.6–3.6) | 2.7% (0.9–4.5) | 2.6% (1.5–3.7) |
| During deployment[b] | 0.6% (0.2–1.0) | 1.4% (0.0–2.7) | 0.5% (0.0–1.0) |

NOTE: All data are weighted. 95-percent confidence intervals are presented in parentheses. Table includes only respondents who reported one or more combat or noncombat deployments in the past three years.

[a] Estimate is significantly different from the estimate in column 3 (no TBI).

[b] The omnibus chi-square test was not statistically significant ($p > 0.05$).

## Deployment and Physical Health

Many studies have explored the impacts of deployment and combat exposure on physical health. Hoge, Terhakopian, and colleagues (2007) found that PTSD was significantly associated with lower ratings of general health, lost productivity, increased rates of physical symptoms, and high somatic symptom severity among Army personnel. Other studies have found that between 15 and 20 percent of Army soldiers returning from deployments to Afghanistan or Iraq meet screening criteria for mTBI and that mTBI after deployment is related to PTSD, depression, chronic pain, and lost work (Tanielian and Jaycox, 2008; Hoge, McGurk, et al., 2008; Wilk, Herrell, et al., 2012; Terrio et al., 2009). Physical health decline associated with deployment and combat exposure has broad implications for military leaders and service members and directly affects overall military readiness. Understanding the prevalence of physical health issues across the services can inform early detection processes and treatment strategies to improve the general health and readiness of the armed forces.

As described in Chapter Seven, the 2015 HRBS measured physical symptoms using the Somatic Symptom Scale-8 (Gierk et al., 2014), and we created a measure of high physical symptom severity, defined as a summary score of eight or higher. Physical symptoms were also measured using the Somatic Symptom Scale-8; service members reported being not bothered at all, bothered a little, or bothered a lot by stomach or bowel problems; back pain; pain in the arms, legs, or joints; headaches; chest pain or shortness of breath; dizziness; feeling tired or having low energy; and trouble sleeping. In this section, we report estimates of service members with high physical symptom severity and those bothered a lot by at least one symptom (including headaches) in the past month, by combat exposure level (Table 10.32) and TBI status (Table 10.33). We limited these analyses to service members with one or more combat or noncombat deployments in the past three years.

Key findings related to physical symptoms and combat exposure include the following:

- Significantly more service members with high combat exposure reported high physical symptom severity (28.6 percent) compared with those with low to moderate combat exposure (18.8 percent) (Table 10.32).
- Significantly more service members who reported high combat exposure reported being bothered a lot by at least one symptom (including headaches) (46.5 percent) compared with those with low to moderate levels of combat exposure (31.8 percent) (Table 10.32).

Key findings related to physical symptoms and TBI status include the following:

- Nearly half of all recently deployed service members with probable mTBI had high physical symptom severity (47.3 percent) compared with one-fifth of those without TBI (19.6 percent) (Table 10.33).
- Among recently deployed personnel with probable mTBI, 62.2 percent reported being bothered a lot by at least one symptom (including headaches) in the past month, nearly twice that of those without TBI (35.0 percent) (Table 10.33).

**Table 10.32**
**Physical Symptoms in the Past 30 Days, by Level of Combat Exposure**

|  | Total (1) | High Combat Exposure (2) | Low to Moderate Combat Exposure (3) |
|---|---|---|---|
| High physical symptom severity | 22.8% (20.5–25.0) | 28.6%[a] (25.0–32.2) | 18.8% (15.9–21.6) |
| Bothered a lot by at least one symptom (including headaches) | 37.8% (35.3–40.3) | 46.5%[a] (42.6–50.4) | 31.8% (28.6–35.1) |

NOTE: All data are weighted. 95-percent confidence intervals are presented in parentheses. Table includes only respondents who reported one or more combat or noncombat deployments in the past three years.

[a] Estimate is significantly different from the estimate in column 3 (low to moderate combat exposure).

**Table 10.33**
**Physical Symptoms in the Past 30 Days, by TBI Status**

|  | Total (1) | Probable mTBI (2) | No TBI (3) |
|---|---|---|---|
| High physical symptom severity | 22.6% (20.4–24.9) | 47.3%[a] (40.1–54.5) | 19.6% (17.4–21.9) |
| Bothered a lot by at least one symptom (including headaches) | 37.9% (35.4–40.5) | 62.2%[a] (55.3–69.1) | 35.0% (32.3–37.6) |

NOTE: All data are weighted. 95-percent confidence intervals are presented in parentheses. Table includes only respondents who reported one or more combat or noncombat deployments in the past three years.

[a] Estimate is significantly different from the estimate in column 3 (no TBI).

## Summary

The analyses in this chapter provide insight into how deployment characteristics, including combat trauma exposure, are associated with active-duty service members' mental health outcomes and propensity for risk behaviors. In addition, the analyses focus on deployment-related injuries, substance use, and mental and physical health, given their potential impact on the health, well-being, and readiness of the overall force.

A majority of the 2015 HRBS sample had experienced at least one deployment since joining the military, and a majority of those deployments were to a combat zone. Just more than one-third of service members experienced a deployment within the past three years. Combat exposure was also common: Almost two-thirds of service members with one or more deployments reported previous exposure to at least one combat-related event, and 45.8 percent reported exposure to at least five such events. The most frequently reported events included receiving incoming fire from small arms, artillery, rockets, or mortars; being sent outside the wire on patrols; seeing dead bodies or remains; firing on the enemy; and being in a unit that suffered casualties. Men reported more combat experiences than women, although it will be important to track this statistic over time now that all combat positions are open to women.

Given the frequency of combat exposure, we also observed a significant number of previously deployed service members who reported current mental or physical health problems. Of those deploying recently (that is, in the past three years), 10.4 percent met the criteria for probable depression, 15.0 percent met the criteria for probable GAD, and 9.9 percent met the criteria for probable PTSD. About half of recently deployed service members reported aggressive behavior in the past month, and 8.4 percent reported such behavior at least five times in the past month. Of previously deployed service members, 27.7 percent suffered a combat injury, 11.9 percent screened positive for probable mTBI, and 8.6 percent experienced or reported postconcussive symptoms following a deployment-related injury. The percentage of service members suffering from high physical symptom severity and being bothered a lot by at least one physical symptom (including headaches) was also higher among recent deployers than nondeployers.

Use of alcohol, tobacco (including cigarettes, smokeless tobacco, and cigars), and prescription drugs during deployment was common. Service members with higher levels of combat exposure were also more likely to currently use alcohol, smokeless tobacco, and cigars during their most-recent deployment. Current use of prescription drugs (including stimulants, sedatives, pain relievers, and antidepressants) was also higher among the more-exposed group.

Among recently deployed service members, those with high combat exposure were more likely than those with low to moderate exposure to report suicide ideation both since joining the military and during a deployment.

TBI has become a signature physical injury among recent deployers, and results from this analysis indicate that service members currently suffering from probable mTBI were also more likely to report current cigarette use and use of prescription sedatives, pain relievers, and antidepressants than their peers without TBI. Further, probable mTBI was positively associated with probable depression, GAD, and PTSD, as well as aggressive behavior. Rates of high physical symptom severity and being bothered a lot by at least one physical symptom were also higher among those with probable mTBI. Furthermore, suicidal thoughts in the past 12 months, since joining the military, and during a deployment were reported more than twice as often among service members with probable mTBI compared with those without TBI.

Taken together, these results paint a picture of a force that has been exposed to combat and associated trauma in recent years. Perhaps as a result, service members with greater exposure showed elevated rates of mental (e.g., anxiety, PTSD) and physical (e.g. postconcussive symptoms, mTBI, somatic symptoms) health problems, as well as negative health-related behaviors (e.g., substance use) compared with their less-exposed peers. TBI remains a risk factor for other negative health outcomes. Future iterations of the HRBS should continue to monitor these trends in order to assess the associations between deployment and the health and well-being of service members.

# CHAPTER ELEVEN

# Summary and Policy Implications

The HRBS is DoD's flagship survey for understanding the health, health-related behaviors, and well-being of service members. At the request of the Defense Health Agency, RAND revised, administered, and analyzed the 2015 version of the survey. This report has detailed the methodology, sample demographics, and results across the following domains: health promotion and disease prevention; substance use; mental and emotional health; physical health and functional limitations; sexual behavior and health; sexual orientation, transgender identity, and health; and deployment experiences and health. We examined differences across several subgroups, including service branch, pay grade, gender, age group, race/ethnicity, and education level.

Between November 2015 and April 2016, 16,999 usable surveys were collected via the Internet. All surveys were anonymous, and the overall response rate was 8.6 percent. Although low response rates do not necessarily translate into biased data, they do reduce the precision with which estimates can be made and are associated with an increased probability of response bias. So, caution should be taken when reviewing results.

In this chapter, we provide a high-level overview of each of the domains covered in the survey. We then offer policy implications based on the survey's results of active-duty service members.

## Health Promotion and Disease Prevention

Within this domain, we examined physical activity, weight status, routine medical care, CAM use, sleep health, supplement and energy drink use, and texting while driving. Key findings include the following:

- Active-duty service members met or exceeded HP2020 targets for physical activity, and the majority (80.5 percent) reported playing electronic games outside of work or school for less than two hours per day.
- Overall, 32.5 percent of service members aged 20 or older were a normal weight, which is slightly below the HP2020 target (33.9 percent). In addition, 14.7 percent of service members were obese, which is well within the HP2020 obesity target of 30.5 percent.
- However, when looking at individual weight categories—underweight, normal weight, overweight, and obese—the majority of active-duty service members (65.7 percent) were overweight or obese. It is important to note that BMI, which was used to categorize individuals as overweight or obese, is an indirect measure of body fat, and muscular service members may have been misclassified into the overweight or obese categories.

- A majority of service members (93.2 percent) reported having a routine doctor checkup within the past two years, which may help to identify the early onset of chronic disease and ensure appropriate preventive care.
- CAM was common among respondents (47.6 percent); massage therapy, relaxation techniques, exercise or movement therapy (e.g., Tai Chi, yoga), and creative outlets (e.g., art, music, writing therapy) were the most frequently used.
- More than half (56.3 percent) of service members reported getting less sleep than they need, and 29.9 percent were moderately or severely bothered by lack of energy due to poor sleep. In addition, 8.6 percent reported using sleep medications every day or almost every day.
- Daily supplement use was not prevalent among service members; estimates ranged from 5.9 percent for herbal supplements to 16.9 percent for protein powder. More than half (51.0 percent) of service members reported using caffeinated energy drinks in the past month, and 7.2 percent reported daily energy drink use.
- Self-reported texting or emailing while driving was also not commonly reported. Approximately 12.8 percent of service members reported frequently or regularly texting or emailing while driving.

## Substance Use

Within this domain, we examined use of alcohol; tobacco; illicit drugs; and prescription drugs, including use as prescribed, misuse, and overuse. Key findings include the following:

- Nearly one in three service members (30.0 percent) was a current binge drinker. Rates of hazardous drinking, as measured by the AUDIT-C, were also high (35.3 percent).
- One in 12 service members (8.2 percent) experienced one or more serious consequences from drinking in the past year.
- Overall, 68.2 percent of service members perceived the military culture as supportive of drinking, and 42.4 percent indicated that their supervisor does not discourage alcohol use. These perceptions were even more common among younger and junior enlisted personnel, who were the most likely to binge drink.
- According to the survey, 13.9 percent of service members currently smoked cigarettes, and 7.4 percent smoked daily. Smokeless tobacco use was relatively high in the military, and e-cigarette use is a growing problem: 35.7 percent of service members had tried e-cigarettes, and 11.1 percent were daily e-cigarette smokers.
- Less than one-fifth of service members (16.9 percent) reported past-week exposure to secondhand smoke at work, which is less than among civilians (20.4 percent) but about the same as civilians working in smoke-free workplaces.
- Rates of illicit drug use were substantially lower among service members than among the general U.S. population. In the 2015 HRBS, use of any illicit drug, including marijuana or synthetic cannabis, was reported by 0.7 percent of service members.
- Use of prescription opioid pain relievers and sedatives have both decreased among service members by about 50 percent since the 2011 HRBS. Both drug types remained the most likely to be misused among the prescription drugs studied, and pain relievers were substantially more likely to be overused than any other prescription drug type.

## Mental and Emotional Health

We examined mental health indicators (i.e., probable depression, GAD, and PTSD); social and emotional factors associated with mental health (i.e., aggression, high impulsivity) history of unwanted sexual contact and physical abuse; self-harm, including suicide ideation and suicide attempts; mental health service utilization; and stigma. Key findings include the following:

- Overall, 17.9 percent of service members experienced at least one of three mental health problems—probable depression (9.4 percent), probable GAD (14.2 percent), or probable PTSD (8.5 percent)—and 9.7 percent suffered from two or more disorders.
- Almost half of service members (47.0 percent) reported any aggressive behavior in the past month, and 8.4 percent reported five or more episodes of such behavior; 12.7 percent met the criteria for high impulsivity.
- Lifetime unwanted sexual contact was reported by almost 16.9 percent of service members and was reported far more often by women (46.1 percent) than men (11.7 percent). The majority of service members (72.2 percent) reported that these events occurred while not on active duty; 38.2 percent reported an event that occurred while on active duty; and 10.4 percent reported that an event occurred both when on and when not on duty.
- Lifetime physical abuse was reported by 13.0 percent of service members. The data indicate that although relatively few military personnel have experienced physical abuse while on active duty (23.2 percent), a larger percentage of personnel have experienced physical abuse while not on active duty (79.3 percent).
- Lifetime NSSI was reported by 11.3 percent of service members, and 5.1 percent reported that this behavior occurred since joining the military. Almost one-fifth of service members (18.1 percent) reported thinking about trying to kill themselves at some point in their lives (12.3 percent since joining the military and 6.3 percent in the past 12 months). Overall, 5.1 percent of service members reported attempting to kill themselves at some point in their lives (2.6 percent since joining the military and 1.4 percent in the past 12 months).
- Among active-duty service members, 29.7 percent reported a self-perceived need for mental health services in the past 12 months, while 17.4 percent reported that others perceived that they should seek treatment.
- About one in four service members (26.2 percent) reported using mental health services. The percentage of service members reporting receipt of mental health services from a specialist (e.g., psychiatrist, psychologist, social worker) was about twice as high (18.8 percent) as the percentage reporting receipt of mental health services from a general medical doctor (9.9 percent) or from a civilian clergyperson or military chaplain (8.0 percent).
- The average active-duty service member reported using 4.5 mental health visits in the past year. Of these, 0.8 visits (18 percent) were to a civilian provider (e.g., paid out of pocket, by TRICARE, or by other private insurance), 2.5 visits (57 percent) were to a military provider, and 1.1 visits (25 percent) were to a self-help group or other provider. Similarly, of the 4.5 average annual visits, only half were to a mental health specialist, while 0.7 visits (16 percent) were to a general medical doctor, and 0.4 visits (9 percent) were to a civilian clergyperson or military chaplain.
- Among service members who said they needed care in the past year but did not receive it (36.1 percent), the most frequently endorsed reasons for not receiving mental health treat-

ment were a desire to handle my own problem (61.5 percent), belief it would harm my career (34.5 percent), belief that treatment would not help (33.5 percent), fear supervisor would have a negative opinion of me (31.5 percent), and concerns about confidentiality (30.1 percent).

- Across the services, 35.0 percent of service members indicated that seeking mental health treatment is damaging to one's military career. Although a downward trend was observed in the early 2000s, since the 2008 HRBS, the decline in perceived stigma has stalled (2002: 48.1 percent; 2005: 44.1 percent; 2008: 36.1 percent; 2011: 37.7 percent).

## Physical Health and Functional Limitations

We examined chronic conditions, physical symptoms, and health-related functional limitations. Key findings include the following:

- About two in five service members (38.6 percent) reported at least one diagnosed chronic physical health condition in their lifetime, and 6.2 percent reported three or more conditions. The most common provider-diagnosed conditions were high blood pressure (17.7 percent), high cholesterol (13.3 percent), and arthritis (12.3 percent).
- Among service members with a diagnosed condition, approximately one-third were taking related medications. The percentage of service members taking medications for their condition ranged from 3.9 percent among service members with skin cancer to 38.5 percent among those with physician-diagnosed ulcers.
- Among active-duty service members, 35.7 percent reported being bothered a lot by at least one physical symptom (including headaches) in the past 30 days. One in five (21.1 percent) had high physical symptom severity based on a survey of eight common physical symptoms. About one-third of service members reported that a health problem led to at least moderate impairment at work or school, in their social life, and in their family life or home responsibilities.

## Sexual Behavior and Health

Within this domain, we examined high-risk sexual behavior in the past year, including sex with more than one partner, sex with a new partner without using a condom, experience of STI, use of birth control during most-recent vaginal sex, and unintended pregnancy. Key findings include the following:

- Among active-duty service members, 19.4 percent had more than one sex partner in the past year.
- More than one-third (36.7 percent) of service members had sex with a new partner in the past year without using a condom.
- STI was reported by 1.7 percent of service members.
- About one in five service members (20.9 percent) were at high risk for HIV infection, defined as having sex with more than one partner in the past year, having a past-year STI other than HIV, or being a man who had sex with one or more men in the past year.

Overall, 73.5 percent of service members reported having been tested for HIV in the past year. Among service members at high risk for HIV infection, 79.4 percent were tested in the past year.

- Multiplying the 20.6 percent of untested high-risk individuals by the 20.9 percent of personnel at high risk for HIV infection means that 4.3 percent of service members overall were both at high risk for HIV infection and untested in the past year.

- Across all services, 22.2 percent of personnel used a condom the most-recent time they had vaginal sex. This percentage was significantly higher among unmarried and non-cohabiting service members (34.8 percent) than among married or cohabiting service members (14.2 percent).

- Among service members not already expecting a child or trying to conceive, 19.4 percent did not use birth control the most-recent time they had vaginal sex (within the past year). Significant differences were found by marital status: Among unmarried (including noncohabiting) service members, this percentage was 12.2 percent; among married and cohabiting service members, it was 24.0 percent.

- Unintended pregnancy was experienced or caused by 2.4 percent of military personnel. Two short-acting methods of contraception—birth control pills and condoms—were by far the most commonly used methods.

## Sexual Orientation, Transgender Identity, and Health

The 2015 HRBS provides the first direct estimate of the percentage of service personnel who identify as LGBT; to date, no prior examination of the health-related behavior or health status of LGBT service members exists.[1] Key findings include the following:

- In the 2015 HRBS, LGBT personnel made up 6.1 percent of service members. LGB (excluding transgender) personnel constituted 5.8 percent of service members. Key findings related to sexual orientation and transgender identity include the following:
  - Sexual attraction: 2.2 percent of men and 7.6 percent of women reported themselves as mostly or only attracted to members of the same sex.
  - Sexual activity: 3.3 percent of men and 9.4 percent of women had had sex with one or more members of the same sex in the past 12 months.
  - Sexual identity: 5.8 percent of active-duty service members identified as LGB (with 0.3 percent not responding to the sexual identity question). If nonresponders identified as LGB, the LGB percentage would be 6.0 percent.
  - Transgender identity: 0.6 percent of service members described themselves as transgender. Less than 1 percent of respondents (0.4 percent) declined to answer the transgender question. If all nonresponders were in fact transgender, the overall transgender percentage would be 1.1 percent.

---

[1]   As this report was in the final stages of production, findings from the 2016 Workplace and Gender Relations Survey of Active Duty Members were released, indicating that 12 percent of female service members and 3 percent of male service members identify as LGBT (Davis et al., 2017).

- LGBT personnel received routine medical care in percentages similar to non-LGBT personnel, with 81.7 percent reporting a routine checkup in the past 12 months. LGBT personnel were also less likely to be overweight than non-LGBT service members.
- The Navy had a higher percentage of self-identified LGBT service members (9.1 percent) than other service branches. LGBT identity was highest among junior enlisted and younger (below age 35) service members. The Navy also had the highest percentage of gay men serving (4.5 percent), while the Marine Corps had the largest percentage of bisexual women serving (18.5 percent).
- Compared with non-LGBT personnel, LGBT personnel reported more smoking, binge drinking, sexual behavior risky to their health, and adverse sexual health outcomes. LGBT personnel's rates were higher than the rates of non-LGBT personnel for binge drinking (37.6 percent compared with 29.3 percent), current cigarette smoking (24.8 percent compared with 16.0 percent), unprotected sex with a new partner (42.4 percent compared with 35.6 percent), more than one sexual partner in the past year (40.2 percent compared with 17.7 percent), STI in the past year (7.4 percent compared with 1.4 percent), and vaginal sex without birth control in the past year (31.5 percent compared with 21.6 percent).
- The percentages of LGBT personnel experiencing mental health issues and those with a history of unwanted sexual contact and physical abuse were particularly high compared with non-LGBT personnel. Specifically, rates were higher than non-LGBT peers for moderate depression (13.2 percent compared with 8.5 percent), severe depression (13.7 percent compared with 8.8 percent), lifetime history of NSSI (26.5 percent compared with 10.3 percent), lifetime suicide ideation (32.7 percent compared with 17.1 percent), lifetime suicide attempt (13.0 percent compared with 4.6 percent), suicide attempt in the past 12 months (4.8 percent compared with 1.2 percent), lifetime history of unwanted sexual contact (39.9 percent compared with 15.4 percent), and lifetime history of physical abuse (21.4 percent compared with 12.4 percent).

## Deployment Experiences and Health

Within this domain, we examined deployment frequency and duration; combat exposure; deployment-related injuries or TBIs, deployment-related substance use; and deployment-related mental and physical health. Key findings include the following:

- Among active-duty service members, 61.3 percent reported at least one deployment since joining the military. The majority of those with a previous deployment reported one or more combat deployments (80.9 percent), and 60.1 percent had spent more than 12 months deployed in their military career.
- A significant portion (64.9 percent) of previously deployed service members reported exposure to at least one combat-related event, and 45.8 percent reported at least five such exposures. The most commonly reported lifetime combat exposures included taking fire from small arms, artillery, rockets, or mortars (49.8 percent); being sent outside the wire on patrols (42.1 percent); seeing dead bodies or remains (38.6 percent); firing on the enemy (35.6 percent); and suffering unit casualties (35.6 percent).
- Of those reporting at least one previous deployment, 27.7 percent reported a combat injury, 11.9 percent screened positive for deployment-related mTBI, and 8.6 percent

experienced postconcussive symptoms following a deployment-related injury or reported they were currently experiencing postconcussive symptoms that could be related to a concussion-related event or head injury.

- Two-thirds of service members who had ever deployed (67.6 percent) reported some substance use during their most-recent deployment, and use of alcohol (36.2 percent), cigarettes (28.0 percent), cigars (23.3 percent), smokeless tobacco (18.9 percent), and prescription drugs (18.9 percent) were far more common than marijuana (0.1 percent) or opiates (0.1 percent).

- Among service members deployed in the past three years, those with high levels of combat exposure were more likely than those with low to moderate exposure to report using prescription drugs in the past year (specifically, stimulants, sedatives, pain relievers, and antidepressants). Service members with probable mTBI more often reported using prescription drugs during a deployment than those with no TBI. Current use of prescription stimulants, sedatives, pain relievers, anabolic steroids, and antidepressants was also higher among recently deployed service members with probable mTBI than among those with no TBI.

- Among service members deployed in the past three years, 10.4 percent met the criteria for probable depression, 15.0 percent met the criteria for probable GAD, and 9.9 percent met the criteria for probable PTSD. Half (50.6 percent) reported any aggressive behavior in the past month, and 8.4 percent reported such behavior at least five times in the past month. In addition, 12.2 percent met the criteria for high impulsivity.

- High combat exposure was associated with increased rates of probable GAD and PTSD (but not depression) among service members deployed in the past three years. Probable mTBI was associated with increased rates of probable depression, GAD, and PTSD, as well as a higher frequency of aggressive behavior and impulsivity.

- Among service members deployed in the past three years, 11.7 percent reported lifetime NSSI. Almost one-fifth (17.5 percent) of service members reported lifetime suicide ideation, including 5.7 percent reporting having such thoughts in the past 12 months, 12.0 percent since joining the military, and 5.0 percent during a deployment (although we cannot determine if ideation occurred during the most-recent deployment).

- Among service members deployed in the past three years, 4.5 percent reported a lifetime suicide attempt, including 1.3 percent reporting having made an attempt in the past 12 months, 2.4 percent since joining the military, 2.6 percent before joining the military, and 0.6 percent during a deployment (although, again, we cannot determine if the attempt occurred during the most-recent deployment).

- Among those deployed in the past three years, significantly more service members with high combat exposure than those with low to moderate exposure reported suicide ideation since joining the military (15.7 percent compared with 9.8 percent) and during a deployment (6.8 percent compared with 3.7 percent). Suicide ideation in the past 12 months, since joining the military, and during a deployment were reported more than twice as often among those with probable mTBI than among those with no TBI.

- Just more than one-fifth (22.8 percent) of service members deployed in the past three years had high physical symptom severity, and 37.8 percent reported being bothered a lot by at least one physical symptom (including headaches) in the past 30 days. High combat exposure and probable mTBI were both associated with worse somatic symptoms and pain.

## Policy Implications and Recommendations

We offer two sets of policy implications. The first addresses ways in which DoD and the Coast Guard can improve both the readiness and the health and well-being of the force. The second offers suggestions for future iterations of the HRBS.

### Force Readiness, Health, and Well-Being

At the beginning of the report, we noted that, because DoD has been downsizing and may continue to do so, it is more important than ever to understand how to strategically maximize force health and readiness. The results from the 2015 HRBS can be used to identify areas and subgroups where readiness may be at risk now or in the future. Therefore, we offer several observations to help DoD and the Coast Guard identify immediate and future threats to the readiness, health, and well-being of the force, and we outline relevant policy implications derived from those observations. We discuss these threats in order of magnitude, as determined by the research team.

**Although DoD and the Coast Guard are doing well in several areas, a few health outcomes and health-related behaviors warrant immediate attention given their clinical importance**. These outcomes and behaviors include the following:

- *Binge and hazardous drinking.* Roughly one-third of service personnel met criteria indicative of hazardous drinking and possible alcohol use disorder. Nearly one-third of service members reported binge drinking in the past month. Problematic drinking could be addressed by shifting the culture and climate surrounding alcohol use (e.g., communicating disapproval of heavy drinking and changing on-base prices and sales policies).
- *Smoking and e-cigarette use.* Cigarette smoking is a major health hazard. The health consequences of e-cigarette use are not yet established, but current research suggests that it may have a negative effect on health (Callahan-Lyon, 2014; Grana, Benowtiz, and Glanz, 2014). The dramatic increase in e-cigarette use, especially among younger service members, is consistent with other evidence from civilians and warrants continued tracking in the future.
- *Overweight or obesity.* DoD is already aware of high percentages of overweight and obesity among service members and currently has some policies in place (e.g., the Healthy Base Initiative; see also Defense Health Board, 2013). Nonetheless, the large percentage of the population that continues to meet the criteria for being overweight or obese is cause for concern. More-systematic tracking (such as during routine physical examinations) that account for muscle mass would provide more-precise estimates of overweight and obesity among members of the armed forces. If the large percentage of overweight service members is indeed correlated with physical fitness (i.e., BMI may be higher among those with more muscle mass), then this may be less of a concern. Unfortunately, the 2015 HRBS data do not allow us to determine if this is the case.
- *Inconsistent use of contraception.* Inconsistent use of contraception increases the risk for unintended pregnancy and presents a possible threat to readiness (because pregnancies reduce personnel availability). Across all services, one-fifth of service members did not use birth control during their most-recent vaginal sex (within the past year). Continued monitoring of use, as well as efforts to increase use of long-acting methods of contraception (e.g., IUDs), are warranted.

- *High risk for HIV infection.* High risk for HIV infection was defined as having sex with more than one partner in the past year, having a past-year STI other than HIV, or being a man who had sex with one or more men in the past year. Efforts to address this risk should focus on unmarried (noncohabiting) service members, of whom more than 40 percent were in the high-risk category. Revisions to policy could mandate increased HIV testing frequency for all those at high risk for HIV infection and could implement interventions to increase use of condoms with new partners. High-risk behaviors should also be monitored into the future.

- *Sleep.* More than half of service members reported getting less sleep than needed, and one-third were bothered by lack of energy due to poor sleep. Insufficient sleep is associated with adverse health outcomes and has the potential to impair military readiness (Troxel et al., 2015).

- *Energy drinks.* More than half of service members reported using energy drinks in the past month. CCEDs are associated with emergency room visits and other adverse health-related behaviors (e.g., alcohol use) (see Arria et al., 2010; Nordt et al., 2012).

- *High absenteeism and presenteeism due to health conditions.* Absenteeism refers to lost work days because of a health condition, and presenteeism refers to days present on duty but the usual level of performance is compromised because of a health condition. Overall, 13 percent of service members reported reduced productivity because of health conditions for at least two weeks in the past month. This has significant implications for productivity and suggests that there is a need to address this issue immediately through policy or programs that target the underlying health conditions (e.g., chronic disease, physical symptoms, functional impairment) that lead to reduced or limited productivity.

**DoD and the Coast Guard should consider heightened scrutiny and continued monitoring of several health outcomes and health-related behaviors, especially those related to mental health treatment and suicide.** Our findings include the following:

- While the percentage of service members seeking mental health services has gradually risen across HRBSs since 2002, so, too, has the percentage of service members reporting perceived mental health needs. In the 2015 HRBS, more than one-third of respondents who stated they had a need for mental health counseling reported not receiving counseling from any source. *To addresses this, efforts should be made to characterize the population reach of existing mental health services and to identify when certain types of individuals (based on demographic or military factors) are not receiving needed care.* Programs with the greatest reach should be identified, evaluated, and monitored for quality and effectiveness. Existing mechanisms, such as the Periodic Health Assessment, may be one way to identify service members in need of treatment. The key, however, is to do so in a nonstigmatizing, nonthreatening way.

- Despite the increase in service members seeking help, just more than one-third of respondents indicated that receipt of mental health care in the military system would result in damage to one's military career. Among those who indicated a need for treatment but who did not receive any, a similar percentage cited concern about harming their careers as a reason for not seeking treatment. Thus, stigma associated with mental health treatment remains a concern. HRBS indicators suggest that modest decreases in perceived stigma occurred from 2002 to 2008. Since then, however, stigma levels have remained largely unchanged, even as DoD has experienced persistent pressure to better define, operationalize, track, and reduce it. *Efforts are needed to develop, test, and implement consistent, military-relevant surveillance indices of mental health stigma, and research is needed to understand how and why stigma remains a barrier to care for many service members, despite DoD mitigation efforts.*

- Further, the results presented here found that roughly half of mental health services were delivered by nonspecialists. *Efforts should be made to better identify, improve, and evaluate the sources, quality, and outcomes of those nonspecialty mental health services in the military.*

- We also found that a significant minority of service members received mental health care in a civilian setting; *future research should better determine the reasons that service members seek mental health care services outside the military health system and the impact of these services on continuity of military mental health care.* Insufficient access to high-quality services and lack of continuity of care across the military and civilian systems may pose a real risk to service member well-being and to force health and readiness.

- Findings from the 2015 HRBS indicate that suicide ideation, which may be a marker of distress and mental anguish, is a major concern among service members. *The military is already devoting large amounts of funding to understand suicide in the military, but more information is needed on early precursors to suicide and how different strategies may be needed for different populations, depending on their level of risk.* Such prevention strategies also need to be evaluated to better understand their effectiveness, accessibility, and acceptability. The military continues to rely heavily on peer models (e.g., gatekeeper trainings) to prevent suicide, in which peers are instructed on how to intervene with service members in crisis. Little is known about whether service members have been witness to or concerned about such situations in the past; whether they have intervened; and if they did intervene, what they did, and if they did not intervene, why not. Understanding these nuances would allow the military to better tailor their prevention efforts and target their resources more effectively and efficiently.

**Results from the 2015 HRBS suggest that, based on demographics (e.g., age group), certain groups of service members warrant targeted intervention to prevent multiple negative health outcomes and to improve current health-related behaviors.** Cultural tailoring of prevention messages is a recommended public health strategy (Kreuter et al., 2003). For example, messages that resonate with service members who are 20 years old and single may not be as salient with those who are 40 years old and married. Similarly, messages that appeal to the Army or Marine Corps ethos may not work as well in the context of Air Force culture. Researchers are performing related work using data from the Army Study to Assess Risk and Resilience in Servicemembers, and a recently published article suggests that preventive interventions for high-risk individuals might reduce the risk of sexual violence victimization among Army women (Street et al., 2016). This could be a promising method for further targeting high-risk groups, such as those identified in the HRBS.

It is also worth noting that although targeted interventions may be designed with a specific subgroup of the population in mind, those interventions could typically benefit all active-duty service members. For example, health disparities between LGBT and non-LGBT service members warrant closer DoD and Coast Guard attention. Policies that enhance, for example, efforts to prevent substance use and sexual risk behaviors might address these disparities. Although one option is to target the LGBT population with clinical and population efforts, such an approach may stigmatize the target population. Therefore, it may be best to apply these efforts equally across the military, which could lead to broader population benefits. With regard to subgroups that might benefit from targeted interventions, our findings include the following:

- Consistently, the *Army, Navy, and Marine Corps* reported higher levels of mental health problems, suggesting a particular focus on these branches. Service members in the Army and Marine Corps also reported the highest use of CCEDs and the lowest levels of sleep quality. Rates of binge and hazardous drinking were concerning across all service branches, particularly in the Marine Corps. Understanding the reasons for inter-service variation may lead to service-specific programs that more directly address service-specific needs.

- *Women and service members with lower education levels* reported higher rates of mental health problems, including suicide ideation and attempts. Women also reported higher rates of impairment and presenteeism and lower levels of sleep quality. Binge drinking, loss of productivity related to drinking, sexual risk behaviors (e.g., multiple sex partners, sex with a new partner without a condom), and all forms of tobacco use were also greater among less-educated service members. Thus, these are high-risk groups, and efforts may need to be targeted directly to them.

- *Younger service members*, particularly those aged 17–24, were more likely than older service members to use energy drinks regularly and engage in binge, heavy, and hazardous drinking and sexual risk behaviors (except condom during the most-recent vaginal sex). In addition, a higher percentage of younger service members reported recent suicide ideation than older service members. Furthermore, high impulsivity was also more common among this group than among older service members, which suggests that there is an opportunity for military leaders to target prevention efforts by age group.

- *LGBT service members* reported higher rates of mental health problems (e.g., depression, suicide ideation) and possible precursors to subsequent problems (e.g., history of unwanted sexual contact, history of physical abuse) than their non-LGBT peers. They also reported higher rates of some health-related risk behaviors, including smoking, binge drinking, and STI, sex with more than one partner in the past year, and vaginal sex without use of birth control. These differences are not unlike those observed for LGBT people in the civilian population (Institute of Medicine, 2011). These findings suggest that policy and programmatic efforts are needed to target this population and that trends in the health and well-being of this population should continue to be monitored. This may be especially important in the Navy, which has the highest percentage of gay men serving and of LGBT service members overall, and in the Marine Corps, which has the highest percentage of lesbian and bisexual women serving.

**Finally, DoD and the Coast Guard should establish population benchmarks of health and health-related behaviors for the military.** Some benchmarks currently exist, primarily in the form of requirements to do (or, in some cases, not to do) certain behaviors (e.g., receive an annual health exam, abstain from using illicit drugs). However, in other cases, like overweight and obese status or leader attitudes toward smoking or alcohol use, no clear benchmarks for the military exist. General population benchmarks are available for many health outcomes and health-related behaviors (e.g., HP2020), but it is not clear whether they are truly applicable to the military—a characteristically unique population. Although the ultimate goal for many behaviors may be zero incidence of them, such a goal may not be realistic or attainable, especially in the short term. Thus, it could be very useful for DoD and the Coast Guard to develop population benchmarks designed to move the population averages in the desired direction. Periodic review and updating of these benchmarks would also be needed.

## Future Iterations of the HRBS

In this section, we offer suggestions for future iterations of the HRBS, based on several issues that we encountered during implementation of the survey. To provide some background for these recommendations, we offer a brief description of the environment in which we launched the survey. First, shortly before we sent invitation emails, we were alerted to a change in DoD information technology policy that meant that any hyperlinks included in emails sent from a non-DoD account would be identified as possibly hazardous and thus blocked. Further, some email servers were blocking invitation emails despite our attempts to "whitelist" the email address from which the invitations were sent and use the appropriate email certificates. Second, the 2014 HRBS had left the field a few months prior to the 2015 survey beginning, which increased the survey burden on an already highly surveyed population. Despite attempts to shorten the survey, survey length was a frequent complaint received via our email help desk.[2] Third, while the survey assured anonymity, it asked about very sensitive topics, including some that could result in a service member being dismissed from the military, which likely made some respondents reluctant to answer. Together, these events and conditions set the stage for an implementation of the HRBS that was less than optimal. To improve implementation, we offer the following recommendations.

*Dramatically shorten the survey and focus the content.* The HRBS is currently suffering from a bit of an identity crisis. Although originally designed to assess substance use, it has expanded well beyond that. In some cases, it duplicates, in self-report format, data that are already being collected or that can be culled from existing administrative data sets (e.g., service utilization). By focusing content on only that which cannot be obtained elsewhere, the survey could be dramatically shortened. Further, because the survey is already so long, it has lost some of its ability to be flexible and address new and emerging areas of concern. Added content areas require extra survey items, which result in a longer survey and ultimately may result in lower response rates (Fan and Yan, 2010) and lower quality of responses (Galesic and Bosnjak, 2009). With the help of an advisory committee, such as the one we used for the 2015 HRBS, survey content should be streamlined. DoD and the Coast Guard could also consider developing official policy about what should, and should not, be included in the survey content.

*Send survey invitations from a .mil account to address information technology issues.* Given our issues with blocked emails and blocked content within emails (e.g., the web link to the survey), future iterations of the HRBS should explore whether it is possible and advisable to send survey invitations from a .mil email address. Although this seems like an easy fix, it could have implications for how respondents view the security of their personal data. If respondents believe that a survey request for highly sensitive information coming from a military email account will lead to their responses not being anonymous (or confidential, as we discuss

---

[2]   The average length of completion for the survey was approximately 45 minutes. Several studies of college students suggest that 13 minutes or less is considered the ideal completion time to ensure a desirable response rate (see Fan and Yan, 2010).

below), data quality and response rates may deteriorate. A thoughtful analysis of the costs and benefits for using a military email address should be undertaken prior to the next iteration of the HRBS.

As an interesting aside, the information technology experiences we encountered may have introduced additional response bias into the survey. For example, if certain types of service members (e.g., junior enlisted or those in a particular service branch) are more (or less) likely to have access only to a DoD or Coast Guard computer, they may have been more (or less) likely to fill out the survey. One could imagine that a junior enlisted soldier with no laptop, tablet, or desktop computer may have had even more difficulty accessing the survey, given that he or she could not forward the invitation email to a personal device, where the links would not have been blocked. Future iterations of the HRBS should consider how technical issues may affect response rates.

*Explore options to contact nonresponders (confidential versus anonymous survey).* Switching from an anonymous survey to a confidential one would allow for targeted nonresponse messages. That is, it would be possible for the survey contractor, but *not* DoD or the Coast Guard, to know who has and has not completed the survey. The 2015 HRBS used up to nine generic email and four postcard reminders to all respondents because we could not discern who had and had not completed the survey. These were often viewed as annoying to participants, especially if they had already completed the survey. Sánchez-Fernández, Muñoz-Lieva, and Montros-Ríos (2012) have shown that personalized invitations to web-based surveys improve response rates, and this is true for both individuals who have not yet completed the survey and for those who have started but not completed a survey. Interestingly, the same study found that additional reminders after the second did not improve response rates. Fewer personalized reminders, compared with more impersonalized ones, resulted in the best response rates. In an experimental study, Sauermann and Roach (2013) found that use of both first and last names in survey contacts resulted in a 24-percent increase in response rates, and use of only first names resulted in a 48-percent increase in response rates. A confidential survey could also offer DoD and the Coast Guard information on what types of individuals are more or less likely to complete surveys (e.g., junior enlisted) and allow for survey weights to better account for nonresponse among certain subgroups. The 2014 RAND Military Workplace Study, using a confidential rather than anonymous approach, had a response rate of just more than 30 percent among active-duty service members (Morral, Gore, and Schell, 2016). Future iterations of the HRBS could use both an anonymous and a confidential approach in order to asses which may lead to the best response rates and the highest-quality data.

*Consider offering incentives.* Another consideration for future HRBSs is to offer an incentive, either as an enticement before completion or as payment after completion. Assuming any regulatory issues can be addressed, offering incentives for survey completion has the possibility of improving response rates. In a review of the literature, Singer and Ye (2013) found that incentives improve response rates across survey modes, including web-based, cross-sectional, and panels. Further, monetary incentives increase response rates more than gifts, and pre-paid incentives improve response rates more than promised ones (i.e., a gift card after completion). Another incentive option would be a lottery, based on completion of the survey, although Singer and Ye note that lotteries are generally not as effective as direct financial incentives at improving response rates. In the lottery scenario, active-duty service members who legitimately complete the survey would be automatically entered into a lottery. There is no clear consensus on how much an incentive should be, but larger incentives do result in higher response rates, albeit at a declining rate (Singer and Ye, 2013). Incentives could also be combined with a confidential survey in order to target nonresponders or demographic groups for which response rates are low.

*Investigate the feasibility of a service member panel.* Survey response rates continue to decline over time, both in civilian and military samples, and although it is not completely understood why this is happening, the trend suggests that alternative means of collecting information from individuals should be explored. One option is a panel, where individuals agree to remain available for interview for a period of time. After that time, the sample is replenished with new members, creating a mix of old and new members. Incentives can be used to encourage members to remain in the panel or to complete specific surveys. A panel design helps alleviate response burden, which could be a very beneficial for an already highly-surveyed population. Further, the panel would be available for all sorts of real-time data collection, and surveys need not be limited to health and health-related behaviors. However, it is important to note that the sampling design used to create a panel and the actual composition of panel members may limit the usefulness of the panel for addressing some issues. For example, low base rate behaviors (e.g., illicit substance use) may be very difficult to accurately assess via a panel without the size of the panel becoming unwieldy. Thus, a service member panel may be an option for some, but not all, of the topics in the HRBS. Nonetheless, the efficiency and reduced burden of a survey panel may represent an option for the HRBS in the future.

## Conclusion

The 2015 HRBS was designed to help DoD and the Coast Guard evaluate the current health and well-being of the force and address possible threats to readiness. This report provided an overview of health outcomes and health-related behaviors across seven domains. Going forward, this survey can be used to supplement data already collected by DoD and the Coast Guard to track key trends, as well as to inform policy initiatives and make programmatic decisions aimed at helping the force meet its mission today and into the future.

# 2015 DoD Health Related Behaviors Survey

This appendix presents the survey as it was programmed for respondents to view on the Internet. Text in parentheses and italics refers to instructions for the survey programmers and was not seen by respondents.

*(Programming instructions: Include date and time stamps for start and end.)*

*(Include both RAND and ICF logos on web survey.)*

*(INTRO SCREEN 1)*

## Welcome to the 2015 DoD Health Related Behaviors Survey

## WEB SURVEY HOME PAGE

Dear Service Member:

Before you begin this web survey, please read the privacy advisory and informed consent statement that follows. Click the Frequently Asked Questions (FAQs) button at the bottom of this page if you want to read more details about the study.

### PRIVACY ADVISORY

This survey is anonymous. The Defense Manpower Data Center has provided certain information about you to allow the RAND Corporation and ICF International to conduct this survey. Your name and contact information have been used to send you email and mail notifications about the survey. However, this information will not be linked to survey participation. RAND and ICF will not know who participated in the study or who did not, and will not give DoD or the Services information about this. RAND and ICF will not attempt to link your individual survey responses with your name, personal identifiers, or military records. The data that RAND and ICF will provide to DoD will be a reduced set of responses, treated in such a way as to make it difficult for DoD to identify any participant from his or her responses. Study staff have been trained to protect your individual survey responses and are subject to civil penalties for violating your confidentiality. DoD has agreed to these conditions to protect your privacy.

### INFORMED CONSENT STATEMENT

**Introduction:** You are being asked to complete an anonymous voluntary DoD-approved survey.

**Survey Contractors:** DoD has contracted with the RAND Corporation and ICF International to conduct the 2015 Health Related Behaviors Survey. RAND is a private, nonprofit organization that conducts research and analysis to help improve public policy and decision-making. RAND's data collection contractor is ICF International, a leading consulting services and technology solutions firm.

**Purpose:** The purpose of this survey is to provide an assessment of the health-related behaviors and lifestyles of military personnel that have the potential to impact readiness. The information will be used in scientific research to inform DoD of potential health problems in the military and help suggest ways to solve or prevent them. DoD and the Services use the results from this survey to inform policies and programs to optimize individual and overall health status and fitness.

**Selection:** You were selected at random from a computer-generated list of all Active Duty and Coast Guard personnel worldwide to represent your Service branch and component in this important research.

**Length:** This web survey will take approximately 40 minutes to complete.

**Voluntary Participation:** Your participation in this survey is voluntary. We hope that you will choose to participate; however, no negative action will be taken against you should you choose not to take part in the survey. Your decision to participate will not affect assignments, promotions, or benefits to which you are entitled, nor will there be any negative consequences from your chain of Command. If you choose to participate, you may skip questions you do not wish to answer and can stop participating in the survey at any point.

**Confidentiality:** Because of the sensitive nature of the information in the survey, RAND has taken several steps to allow your frank and honest responses. First, the survey is anonymous. Your name will not be associated with the responses you give and there are no identifying codes on the survey. We will not know who did and did not complete the survey. Second, the information you provide will be combined with that from other military personnel to prepare statistical reports. At no time will your individual survey data be given to anyone outside of DoD and the study team.

**Risks of Participation:** Some of the questions asked are sensitive in nature. The survey asks about a range of health issues, such as physical and mental health, substance use, sexual practices, stress, deployment related health and combat exposure. You may feel discomfort or distress in answering one or more of these items. Therefore, we encourage you to take the survey in private, where others will not see your computer screen.

It is okay to forward the survey link to a personal email address and you may complete the survey from a non-government, non-CAC enabled computer.

**(FREQUENTLY ASKED QUESTIONS)** *(hyperlink)*

*(INTRO SCREEN 2)*

In the event that any of the questions in the survey may cause you discomfort, please remember that the following resources are available to you.

**Military OneSource** (http://www.militaryonesource.com) is a free, 24-hour service that is available 7 days a week to provide a full range of services, across the deployment cycle, to military personnel and their families, at no cost. They can be reached at:

Stateside: CONUS: 1-800-342-9647
Overseas: OCONUS Universal Free Phone: 800-342-9647
Collect from Overseas: OCONUS Collect: 703-253-7599
En Español llame al: 877-888-0727
TTY/TDD: 866-607-6794

The **DoD Safe Helpline** (https://www.safehelpline.org/) provides worldwide live, confidential support, 24/7. You can initiate a report and search for your nearest Sexual Assault Response Coordinator (SARC). You can find links to Service-specific reporting resources and access information about the prevention of and response to sexual assault on their website or by calling the hotline at 1-877-995-5247.

The **Military Crisis Line** (http://veteranscrisisline.net/ActiveDuty.aspx) can also provide confidential support and consultation if you feel distressed. They can be reached at 1-800-273-8255 (then press 1).

*(INTRO SCREEN 3)*

**Who do you contact if you have questions or concerns about the survey?**

- **Questions about computer, technical, or survey problems:** Contact the ICF Survey Helpdesk's toll free number at 1-844-430-9640 or by email at DOD2015HealthSurvey@ icfsurveysupport.com.

- **Questions about the overall study or RAND:** Contact the RAND team by email at HRBS2015@rand.org.

- **Questions about your rights as a participant in this study:** Contact the RAND Human Subjects Protection Committee at 310-393-0411, ext. 6369 in Santa Monica, California.

- **Questions about the licensing of the survey:** Information about DoD surveys can be found at http://www.dtic.mil/whs/directives/collections/index.html; this survey's RCS # is DD-HA(BE)2189 and the expiration date is 02/09/2019.

You can print a copy of this Informed Consent Statement by clicking the following button:

**INFORMED CONSENT** *(hyperlink)*

Click the Next button if you agree to participate in the survey.

**NEXT** *(hyperlink)*

*(SURVEY START SCREEN)*

Please answer each question thoughtfully and truthfully. This will allow us to provide an accurate picture of the health behaviors and health needs of today's military members. If you prefer not to answer a specific question for any reason, just leave it blank. Use the navigation button (Next) to move to the next question. Please do NOT use your browser's forward and back buttons.

**Remember, the survey is anonymous. No one in the military will see your individual survey responses or be able to match your answers back to your name or other identifying information.**

If you do not have time to complete the survey now, please close your browser. If you can complete the survey now, please click below.

**START SURVEY NOW**

*(General skip programming instructions:*

*If a respondent skips an item, show screen with "You did not provide a response to this question. Please select a response below. Note that skipped items may result in you being asked questions later in the survey that do not apply to you."*

*If respondent again selects the forward option, skip the item.*

*General Rule: Show all items that require a fill if the fill item is skipped.)*

**Q0. How did you hear about this survey? Please check all that apply.**
1. Email from the study team (RAND or ICF)
2. Postcard from the study team (RAND or ICF)
3. Letter from the study team (RAND or ICF)
4. A website
5. Friend or colleague
6. Commander
7. Other

*(If 1 nor 2 nor 3 is selected, then the person is skipped out of the survey via a "thank you" screen. Respondents who skip the question are allowed to proceed with the survey.)*

*(THANK YOU SCREEN)*

Thank you for your interest in the 2015 HRBS. The survey relies on a randomly selected sample of service members who are asked to participate through an approved letter, email, or postcard from the RAND Corporation and their subcontractor ICF International. Unfortunately, because you indicated that you did not receive an invitation through one of those sources, you are not eligible to participate. We thank you for your time.

**Q1. In what Branch and Component are you serving? Select one response.**

1. Army (Active Component) *(Skip to Q6.)*
2. Army National Guard
3. Army Reserve
4. Navy (Active Component) *(Skip to Q6.)*
5. Navy Reserve
6. Marine Corps (Active Component) *(Skip to Q6.)*
7. Marine Corps Reserve
8. Air Force (Active Component) *(Skip to Q6.)*
9. Air National Guard
10. Air Force Reserve
11. Coast Guard (Active Component) *(Skip to Q6.)*
12. Coast Guard Reserve

*(If Q1 = blank, skip to Q3.)*

**Q2. What is your current National Guard or Reserve status? Select one response.**

1. Drilling unit Reservist/Traditional Guardsman
2. Individual Mobilization Augmentee (IMA)
3. Active Guard/Reserve Program (AGR/FTS/AR), in fulltime National Guard Duty
4. I don't know

**Q3. How many years or months have you served in the National Guard or Reserve? Please type in your response. If less than one year, enter number of months.**

Years _____ *(0 to 50)*          Months _____ *(0 to 11)*

*(Do not show warning if year is filled but month is blank or if year is blank but month is filled; respondent should not be able to enter 0 years and 0 months.)*

**Q4. Have you EVER served in the Active Component (e.g., USAF, USN, USMC, USA, USCG)? Please exclude any active military service that occurred while you were in the National Guard or Reserves (e.g., training, drill weekends, activations/mobilizations). Select one response.**

1. Yes
2. No

**Q5. In the PAST FIVE YEARS (since *(DATE FILL Month Year)*), have you been called to active military duty? Do NOT include days spent in reserve duty training, drill weekends, or active military service prior to five years ago. Select one response.**

1. Yes
2. No

**Q6. What is your current rank/rating (e.g., Captain or Sergeant)? Please type in your response.**

Rank (_____)

**Q7. What is your current pay grade? Select one response.**

1. E1–E4
2. E5–E6
3. E7–E9
4. W1–W5
5. O1–O3
6. O4–O10

**Q8. Are you male or female? Select one response.**

1. Male
2. Female

*(If Q1 = 1, 4, 6, 8, 11 (Active Army, Air Force, Coast Guard, Marine Corps, Navy), skip to Q11.)*

**Q9. Now we would like to ask about your employment situation outside the military. What is your current civilian work status? Please select the ONE most appropriate answer. Select one response.** *(Ask only if Q1 = 2, 3, 5, 7, 9, 10, 12 (Reserve Component or National Guard).)*

1. Working full-time; that is, 35 or more hours per week in one or more jobs; including self-employment
2. Working part-time (less than 35 hours per week)
3. Have a job, but out because I have been activated
4. Have a job, but out due to illness, leave, furlough, or strike (not because I was activated)
5. Have seasonal work, but currently not working
6. I do not currently have a civilian job

**Q10. What is the reason why you do not currently have a civilian job? Please select the ONE most appropriate answer. Select one response.** *(Ask only if Q1 = 2, 3, 5, 7, 9, 10, 12 (Reserve Component or National Guard) and Q9 = 6 (I do not currently have a civilian job).)*

1. Full-time homemaker/parent
2. Full-time student
3. Retired
4. Disabled
5. Looking for work, but unemployed
6. Not looking for work in a civilian job
7. Other

**Q11. What is the ZIP code or APO or FPO number for your CURRENT post, base, ship, or other duty station where you spend most of your duty time? Please type in your response.**

1. Zip Code _____ *(5 digits)*
2. APO _____ *(Text Box)*
3. FPO _____ *(Text Box)*

*(Do not show skip warning message if respondent completes 1 or 2 of the 3 fields.)*

**Q12. Which of the following best describes where you currently live? Select one response.**

1. Dorms/Barracks
2. Military housing (including privatized), on main base/installation
3. Military housing (including privatized), off main base/installation
4. Civilian housing that you own or pay mortgage on
5. Civilian housing that you rent, off base
6. Some other living situation (e.g., living with parents, temporary housing)

**Q13. Sometimes people have trouble paying their bills or getting by month to month. Which of the following best describes your financial condition over the past 12 months? Would you say you were… Select one response.**

1. Very comfortable and secure
2. Able to make ends meet without much difficulty
3. Occasionally have some difficulty making ends meet
4. Tough to make ends meet but keeping my head above water
5. In over my head

**Q14. What is the highest degree or level of school that you have completed? Select one response.**

1. 12 years or less of schooling (no diploma)
2. High school graduate—traditional diploma
3. High school graduate—alternative diploma (e.g., home school, GED)
4. Some college credit, but less than 1 year
5. 1 or more years of college, no degree
6. Associate's degree (e.g., AA, AS)
7. Bachelor's degree (e.g., BA, AB, BS)
8. Graduate or professional degree (e.g., MA, MS, Med, MEng, MBA, MSW, PhD, MD, JD, DVM, EdM)

**Q15. Are you Spanish/Hispanic/Latino? Select one response.**

1. Yes, Mexican, Mexican-American, Chicano, Puerto Rican, Cuban, or other Spanish/Hispanic/Latino
2. No, not Spanish/Hispanic/Latino

**Q16. What is your race? Please select ONE OR MORE responses that best characterize you.**

1. White
2. Black or African American
3. American Indian or Alaska Native
4. Asian (e.g., Asian Indian, Chinese, Filipino, Japanese, Korean, Vietnamese)
5. Native Hawaiian or other Pacific Islander (e.g., Samoan, Guamanian, Chamorro)
6. Other

**Q17. How old are you? Please type in your response.**

_____ *(2 digits; 17–70)*

**Q18. How tall are you without shoes on? Please type in your height in feet and inches.**

     Q18A: Feet: _____ *(1 digit; 4–7)*
     Q18B: Inches: _____ *(2 digits; 0–11)*

*(Soft check: Q18A < 5 and Q18B <= 0 and Q8 = Male; Q18A <= 4 and Q18B < 6 and Q8 = Female; Q18A <= 4 and Q18B < 6 and Q8 = missing.)* Q18-Height: **You entered __ feet __ inches. If this is correct, please hit NEXT below to continue. If this is not correct, please change your answer below.**

**Q19. How much do you weigh without shoes on?** (*IF FEMALE SHOW: If you are currently pregnant, what was your typical weight before pregnancy?*) **Please type in your weight in pounds.**

     Pounds: _____ *(3 digits; 0–500)*

*(Soft check: Q19 < 95 AND Q19 > 275 and Q8 = Male; Q19 < 95 and Q19 > 200 and Q8 = Female; Q19 < 95 or > 275 and Q8 = missing.)* Q19-Weight: **You entered __ pounds. If this is correct, please hit NEXT below to continue. If this is not correct, please change your answer below.**

**Q20. What is your current marital status? Select one response.**

1. Married
2. Single, never married
3. Cohabitating (living with fiancé(e), boyfriend, or girlfriend but not married)
4. Separated
5. Divorced
6. Widowed

*(If Q20 = 2, 4, 5, or 6, skip to Q23.)*

**Q21. Is your spouse or live-in fiancé(e), boyfriend, or girlfriend now living with you at your current duty location? Select one response.** *(Ask only if Q20 = 1 (married) or 3 (cohabitating) and Q1 = 1, 4, 6, 8, 11 (Active Component).)*

1. Yes
2. No

**Q22. Is your spouse or live-in fiancé(e), boyfriend, or girlfriend part of the military? Select one response.** *(Ask only if Q20 = 1 (married) or 3 (cohabitating).)*

1. Yes, Active Component
2. Yes, Reserve or Guard NOT on active military duty
3. Yes, Reserve or Guard on active military duty
4. No

**Q23. How many children under the age of 18 currently live with you? Please only include those children for whom you are legally responsible.**

_____ *(2 digits; 0–20)*

*(Change text of error message: "Response to this question must be between 0 and 20.")*

**Q24. Are you currently covered by any of the following health insurance plans? Check all that apply.**

*(If respondent checks box Q24j, do not allow answers in Q24a–i.)*

|  | **Check Box** |
|---|---|
| a. TRICARE or other military health care | |
| b. Enrolled in VA health care system (e.g., CHAMPVA) | |
| c. Federal Employees Health Benefit (FEHB) Program | |
| d. Insurance through a current or former employer, union, or school/college (for you or another family member) | |
| e. Insurance purchased directly from an insurance company or through a health insurance exchange or marketplace (for you or another family member) | |
| f. Medicare, for people age 65 and over, or people with certain disabilities | |
| g. Medicaid, Medical Assistance, or any kind of government-assistance plan for those with low incomes or disability | |
| h. Indian Health Service | |
| i. Any other type of health insurance or health coverage plan | |
| j. I do not currently have health insurance. | |

**Q25. During the past 12 months, did you use any of the following health approaches? Please select ONE response PER ROW.**

|  | 1. Yes | 2. No |
|---|---|---|
| a. Acupuncture |  |  |
| b. Relaxation techniques |  |  |
| c. Massage therapy |  |  |
| d. Energy healing (such as reiki, polarity therapy) |  |  |
| e. Exercise/movement therapy (such as Tai Chi, yoga) |  |  |
| f. Hypnosis or hypnotherapy (self or led by practitioner) |  |  |
| g. Guided imagery therapy (such as meditation or aromatherapy) |  |  |
| h. Creative outlets (such as art, music, or writing therapy) |  |  |
| i. Chiropractic |  |  |
| j. Biofeedback |  |  |
| k. Other |  |  |

**Q26. During the PAST 30 DAYS, how often did you do the following kinds of physical activity? Please select ONE response PER ROW.**

|  | 1. About every day | 2. 5–6 days a week | 3. 3–4 days a week | 4. 1–2 days a week | 5. Less than 1 day a week | 6. Not at all in the past 30 days |
|---|---|---|---|---|---|---|
| a. Moderate Physical Activity—exertion that raises heart rate and breathing, but you should be able to carry on a conversation comfortably during the activity |  |  |  |  |  |  |
| b. Vigorous Physical Activity—exertion that is high enough that you would find it difficult to carry on a conversation during the activity |  |  |  |  |  |  |
| c. Strength Training—including using weights or resistance training to increase muscle strength |  |  |  |  |  |  |

**Q27. During the PAST 30 DAYS, on the days you did the following, how long PER DAY did you typically do each? Please select ONE response PER ROW.**

*(Items in Q27 should show only if the parallel item in Q26 = 1, 2, 3, 4, or 5 (any response other than not at all in the past 30 days).)*

|  | 1. 60 or more minutes | 2. 30 to 59 minutes | 3. 20 to 29 minutes | 4. Less than 20 minutes |
|---|---|---|---|---|
| a. Moderate Physical Activity—exertion that raises heart rate and breathing, but you should be able to carry on a conversation comfortably during the activity |  |  |  |  |
| b. Vigorous Physical Activity—exertion that is high enough that you would find it difficult to carry on a conversation during the activity |  |  |  |  |
| c. Strength Training—including using weights or resistance training to increase muscle strength |  |  |  |  |

**Q28. Sometimes people have trouble getting as much exercise as they would like. Which of the following is the MAIN reason you have exercised less than you would like in the PAST 30 DAYS? Select one response.** *(Randomize.)*

1. I have exercised as much as I would like.
2. No access to facilities
3. Disabilities or injuries
4. Work commitments
5. Family commitments
6. Cost
7. Other

**Q29. Over the past 30 days, on average, how many hours per day did you play electronic games OUTSIDE OF WORK OR SCHOOL? Include games played on a computer, laptop, phone, tablet (e.g., iPad), or other handheld device (e.g., Nintendo DS), or gaming system (e.g., PlayStation). Select one response.**

1. None; I did not play electronic games outside of work or school
2. Less than 1 hour
3. 1–2 hours
4. 3–4 hours
5. 5–10 hours
6. 11 hours or more

**Q30. During the past 30 days, on how many days did you text or e-mail while driving a car or other vehicle? Select one response.**

1. I did not drive a car or other vehicle during the past 30 days
2. 0 days
3. 1 or 2 days
4. 3 to 5 days
5. 6 to 9 days
6. 10 to 19 days
7. 20 to 29 days
8. All 30 days

**Q31. Now you will be asked about certain medical conditions. Have you EVER been told by a doctor or other health professional that you had . . . ? Please select ONE response PER ROW.**

| | 1. Yes, within the past 2 years | 2. Yes, more than 2 years ago | 3. No |
|---|---|---|---|
| a. High blood pressure | | | |
| b. High blood sugar or diabetes | | | |
| c. High cholesterol | | | |
| d. Respiratory problems (including asthma, sinusitis, or chronic bronchitis) | | | |
| e. Arthritis | | | |
| f. Heart disease or other heart condition | | | |
| g. Ulcer (digestive system) | | | |
| h. Skin cancer | | | |
| i. Other cancer | | | |

**Q32. Are you currently taking medication for…? Please select ONE response PER ROW.**

*(Items in Q32 should show only if the parallel item in Q31 = 1 or 2 (yes).)*

|  | 1. Yes | 2. No |
|---|---|---|
| a. High blood pressure | | |
| b. High blood sugar or diabetes | | |
| c. High cholesterol | | |
| d. Respiratory problems (including asthma, sinusitis, or chronic bronchitis) | | |
| e. Arthritis | | |
| f. Heart disease or other heart condition | | |
| g. Ulcer (digestive system) | | |
| h. Skin cancer | | |
| i. Other cancer | | |

**Q33. During the PAST 30 DAYS, how much have you been bothered by any of the following problems? Please select ONE response PER ROW.** *(Randomize.)*

|  | 1. Not bothered at all | 2. Bothered a little bit | 3. Bothered a lot |
|---|---|---|---|
| a. Stomach or bowel problems | | | |
| b. Back pain | | | |
| c. Pain in your arms, legs, or joints | | | |
| d. Headaches | | | |
| e. Chest pain or shortness of breath | | | |
| f. Dizziness | | | |
| g. Feeling tired or having low energy | | | |
| h. Trouble sleeping | | | |
| i. Memory problems (or lapses) | | | |
| j. Balance problems | | | |
| k. Ringing in the ears | | | |
| l. Irritability | | | |
| m. Sensitivity to light | | | |
| n. Other problem not listed | | | |

**Q34. Thinking about any mental or physical symptoms you may have, how much do those symptoms impair your functioning in the following areas? Please select ONE response PER ROW.**

|  | Not at all | Mildly | | | Moderately | | | Markedly | | | Extremely |
|---|---|---|---|---|---|---|---|---|---|---|---|
|  | 0 | 1 | 2 | 3 | 4 | 5 | 6 | 7 | 8 | 9 | 10 |
| a. Work or school work |  |  |  |  |  |  |  |  |  |  |  |
| b. Social life |  |  |  |  |  |  |  |  |  |  |  |
| c. Family life/home responsibilities |  |  |  |  |  |  |  |  |  |  |  |

**Q35. Again, thinking about any mental or physical symptoms you may have, on how many days in the past 30 DAYS...**

|  | Number of days (0–30) |
|---|---|
| a. Did your symptoms cause you to miss school or work or leave you unable to carry out your normal daily responsibilities? |  |
| b. Did you feel so impaired by your symptoms that, even though you went to school or work, your productivity was reduced? |  |

**Q36. About how long has it been since you last visited a doctor for a routine check-up? A routine check-up is a general physical exam, not an exam for a specific injury, illness, or condition. Select one response.**

1. Within the past 12 months
2. More than 12 months ago but within the past 2 years
3. More than 2 years ago
4. I have never had a routine check-up

**Q37. In the PAST 30 DAYS, how often did you drink energy drinks/shots (e.g., Red Bull, Monster, 5-Hour Energy, Power Shots, etc.)? Select one response.**

1. Never
2. 1 to 3 times in the past month
3. 1 to 2 times per week
4. 3 to 6 times per week
5. Once per day
6. 2 to 4 times per day
7. 5 or more times per day

**Q38. In the PAST 12 MONTHS, how often did you take any of the following supplements? Please select ONE response PER ROW.** *(Randomize.)*

| | 1. Two or more times a day | 2. Once a day | 3. Every other day | 4. Once a week | 5. Once a month | 6. Never in the past year |
|---|---|---|---|---|---|---|
| a. Supplements for joint health and function (such as glucosamine, chondroitin, MSM) | | | | | | |
| b. Fish oil (such as omega-3 fatty acid) | | | | | | |
| c. Protein powder | | | | | | |
| d. Other body-building supplements that are legal (such as amino acids, Creatine, "Andro," Nitric oxide boosters) | | | | | | |
| e. Herbal supplements (such as Ginkgo biloba, Echinacea, Ginseng) | | | | | | |
| f. Weight loss products (such as Ripped Fuel, caffeine, Dexatrim, Lipo 6, Metabolife, QuickTrim, Xenadrine, Guarana/Mate, Green Coffee, Zi Xiu Tang Bee Pollen) | | | | | | |

**Q39. Thinking about your immediate supervisor(s) at the installation where you are currently stationed/assigned, how strongly does he/she DISCOURAGE the use of the following? Please select ONE response PER ROW.** *(Randomize.)*

| | 1. Not at all | 2. Somewhat discourages | 3. Strongly discourages |
|---|---|---|---|
| a. Cigarettes | | | |
| b. Chewing/smokeless tobacco | | | |
| c. Alcohol | | | |
| d. Marijuana | | | |
| e. Prescription drug misuse | | | |

**Q40.** These next questions are about drinks of alcoholic beverages. Throughout these questions, by a "drink," we mean a can or bottle of beer, a glass of wine or a wine cooler, a shot of liquor, or a mixed drink with liquor in it. We are not asking about times when you only had a sip or two from a drink.

Have you EVER, even once, had a drink of any type of alcoholic beverage? Please do not include times when you only had a sip or two from a drink. Select one response.

1.  Yes
2.  No *(Skip to Q53.)*

**Q41.** Think about the FIRST TIME you had a drink of an alcoholic beverage. How old were you the first time you had a drink of an alcoholic beverage? Please do not include any time when you only had a sip or two from a drink. *(Ask only if Q40 = 1 (yes drink ever).)*

Age: _____ *(2 digits; 1–99)*

**Q42.** In the PAST 12 MONTHS (365 days), on how many different DAYS would you estimate that you drank any type of alcoholic beverage? Your best guess is fine.

_____ *(3 digits; 0–365)*

*(If 0 (no drinking in the past 12 months), skip to Q53.)*

**Q43. Here are some things that might happen to people while or after drinking, or because of using alcohol. In the PAST 12 MONTHS did any of the following happen to you? Please select ONE response PER ROW. Remember, the survey is completely confidential.** *(Randomize.)*

| | 1. Yes | 2. No |
|---|---|---|
| a. I found it harder to handle my problems because of drinking. | | |
| b. I received UCMJ punishment (e.g., Court Martial, Article 15, Captain's Mast, Office Hours, Letter of Reprimand, etc.) because of my drinking. | | |
| c. I was arrested for a drinking incident not related to driving. | | |
| d. I had trouble on the job because of my drinking. | | |
| e. I didn't get promoted because of my drinking. | | |
| f. I got a lower score on my efficiency report or performance rating because of my drinking. | | |
| g. I hit my spouse/significant other after having too much to drink. | | |
| h. I got into a fight where I hit someone other than a member of my family when I was drinking. | | |
| i. My spouse or live-in fiancé(e)/boyfriend/girlfriend threatened to leave me or left me because of my drinking. | | |
| j. My spouse or live-in fiancé(e)/boyfriend/girlfriend asked me to leave because of my drinking. | | |
| k. I did something sexually that I regretted. | | |
| l. I had trouble with the police (civilian or military) because of my drinking. | | |
| m. I spent time in jail, stockade, or brig because of my drinking. | | |

**Q44. In the PAST 12 MONTHS did any of the following happen to you? Please select ONE response PER ROW.** *(Randomize.)*

|  | 1. Yes | 2. No |
|---|---|---|
| a. I operated power tools or machinery when I had too much to drink. | | |
| b. I drove a car or other vehicle when I had too much to drink. | | |
| c. I was arrested for driving under the influence of alcohol. | | |
| d. I rode in a car or other vehicle driven by someone who had too much to drink. | | |
| e. I drove or rode in a boat, canoe, or other watercraft when I had too much to drink. | | |
| f. I was hurt in an accident because of my drinking (e.g., vehicle, work, other). | | |
| g. My drinking caused an accident where someone else was hurt or property was damaged. | | |
| h. I received detoxification treatment in a hospital or residential center because of my drinking. | | |
| i. I had an illness connected with my drinking that kept me from duty for a week or longer. | | |
| j. I had to have emergency medical help because of my drinking. | | |
| k. I was hospitalized because of my drinking. | | |

**Q45. In the PAST 12 MONTHS, did any of the following things happen to you? Please select ONE response PER ROW.** *(Randomize.)*

|  | 1. Yes | 2. No |
|---|---|---|
| a. I was hurt in an on-the-job accident because of my drinking. | | |
| b. I was late for work or left work early because of drinking, a hangover, or an illness caused by drinking. | | |
| c. I did not come to work at all because of a hangover, an illness, or a personal accident caused by drinking. | | |
| d. I worked below my normal level of performance because of drinking, a hangover, or an illness caused by drinking. | | |
| e. I was drunk while working. | | |
| f. I was called in during off-duty hours and reported to work feeling drunk. | | |

**Q46. How often do you have a drink containing alcohol? Select one response.**

1. Never *(Skip to Q53.)*
2. Monthly or less
3. Two to four times a month
4. Two to three times a week
5. Four or more times a week

**Q47. How many drinks containing alcohol do you have on a TYPICAL DAY when you are drinking? Select one response.**

1.  1 or 2 drinks
2.  3 or 4 drinks
3.  5 or 6 drinks
4.  7 to 9 drinks
5.  10 or more drinks

**Q48. How often do you have SIX OR MORE ALCOHOLIC DRINKS on one occasion? Select one response.**

1.  Never
2.  Less than monthly
3.  Monthly
4.  Weekly
5.  Daily or almost daily

**Q49. Think specifically about the PAST 30 DAYS, up to and including today. In the past 30 days, on how many days did you drink one or more drinks of an alcoholic beverage?**

_____ *(2 digits; 0–30)*

*(If 0 (no drinking in the past 30 days), skip to Q53.)*

**Q50. On the day or days that you drank in the PAST 30 DAYS, how many drinks did you usually have each day? Count as a drink a can or bottle of beer; a wine cooler or a glass of wine, champagne, or sherry; a shot of liquor; or a mixed drink or cocktail.**

_____ *(2 digits; 1–90)*

**Q51. During the PAST 30 DAYS, on how many days did you have (If Q8 = 1 (male), insert "5"; if Q8 = 2 (female), insert "4") or more drinks of beer, wine, or liquor on the same occasion? Select one response.**

1.  About every day
2.  5 to 6 days a week
3.  3 to 4 days a week
4.  1 to 2 days a week
5.  2 to 3 days in the past 30 days
6.  1 day in the past 30 days
7.  Not at all in the past 30 days

**Q52. On those days when you worked during the PAST 30 DAYS, how often did you have a drink while you were working—either on the job, during your lunch break, or during a work break? Select one response.**

1. Every work day
2. Most work days
3. About half of my work days
4. Several work days
5. 1 or 2 work days
6. I didn't drink while working in the past 30 days

**Q53. Please indicate how much you agree or disagree with each of the following statements. Please select ONE response PER ROW.** *(Randomize.)*

|  | 1. Strongly Agree | 2. Agree | 3. Disagree | 4. Strongly disagree |
|---|---|---|---|---|
| a. It's hard to "fit in" in my command if you don't drink. |  |  |  |  |
| b. Drinking is part of being in my unit. |  |  |  |  |
| c. Drinking is part of being in the military. |  |  |  |  |
| d. Drinking is just about the only recreation available at my installation. |  |  |  |  |
| e. At parties or social functions at this installation, everyone is encouraged to drink. |  |  |  |  |
| f. At parties or social functions at this installation, nonalcoholic beverages are always available. |  |  |  |  |
| g. Leadership is tolerant of off-duty alcohol intoxication or drunkenness. |  |  |  |  |
| h. Drinking to the point of losing control is acceptable. |  |  |  |  |
| i. Others in my pay grade at this installation believe drinking to the point of losing control is acceptable. |  |  |  |  |

**Q54. In the past 12 months, where did you most often purchase alcohol? Select one response.**

1. Mainly on base/post
2. Mainly off base/post
3. Equally on and off base/post
4. I have not bought alcohol in the past 12 months

**Q55. Now we are going to ask you about smoke you might have breathed at work because someone else was smoking indoors. During the PAST 7 DAYS, on how many days did you breathe smoke at your workplace from someone other than you who was smoking tobacco?**

_____ *(2 digits; 0–7)*

**Q56. Next we would like to ask you some questions about your own use of cigarettes and other tobacco products. Please DO NOT INCLUDE electronic cigarettes or e-cigarettes in your answers, unless we specifically ask you about them. Have you smoked at least 100 cigarettes (approximately 5 packs) in your ENTIRE LIFE? Select one response.**

1. Yes
2. No *(Skip to Q64.)*

**Q57. How old were you the FIRST TIME you smoked part or all of a cigarette? If you have never smoked, please enter 0 (zero).**

Age: _____ *(2 digits; 0–99)*

**Q58. On how many of the PAST 30 DAYS did you smoke a cigarette?**

Number of Days: _____ *(2 digits; 0–30)*

*(If Q58 = 0 (no cigarettes in the past 30 days), skip to Q61.)*

**Q59. On average, on the days that you smoked in the past 30 days, how many cigarettes did you smoke a day?**

_____ *(2 digits; 0–99)*

**Q60. Do you NOW smoke cigarettes every day, some days, or not at all? Select one response.**

1. Every day
2. Some days
3. Not at all

**Q61. During the PAST 12 MONTHS, have you stopped smoking for more than one day BECAUSE YOU WERE TRYING TO QUIT SMOKING? Select one response.**

1. Yes, 1 time
2. Yes, 2 or more times
3. No

**Q62. In the PAST 12 MONTHS, has a medical doctor or other health care professional advised you to quit smoking or using other kinds of tobacco? Select one response.**

1. Yes
2. No
3. I don't smoke

**Q63. In the past 12 months, where did you most often purchase cigarettes? Select one response.**

1. Mainly on base/post
2. Mainly off base/post
3. Equally on and off base/post
4. I have not bought cigarettes in the past 12 months

**Q64. Have you EVER used chewing tobacco or snuff? Select one response.**

1. Yes
2. No *(Skip to Q67.)*

**Q65. During the PAST 12 MONTHS, how often on average have you used chewing tobacco or snuff? Select one response.**

1. About every day
2. 5–6 days a week
3. 3–4 days a week
4. 1–2 days a week
5. 2–3 days a month
6. About once a month
7. Less than once a month
8. I have not used chewing tobacco or snuff in the past 12 months *(Skip to Q67.)*

**Q66. When was the last time you used chewing tobacco or snuff? Select one response.**

1. Today
2. During the past 30 days
3. More than 1 month ago but within the past 6 months
4. More than 6 months ago but within the past year

**Q67. Have you EVER tried smoking cigars, cigarillos, or little cigars, even one or two puffs? Select one response.**

1. Yes
2. No *(Skip to Q69.)*

**Q68. During the PAST 30 DAYS, on how many days did you smoke cigars, cigarillos, or little cigars? Select one response.**

1. 0 days
2. 1 or 2 days
3. 3 to 5 days
4. 6 to 9 days
5. 10 to 19 days
6. 20 to 29 days
7. All 30 days

**Q69. Have you EVER tried smoking tobacco in a pipe or hookah, even one or two puffs? Select one response.**

1. Yes
2. No *(Skip to Q71.)*

**Q70. During the PAST 30 DAYS, on how many days did you smoke tobacco in a pipe or hookah? Select one response.**

1. 0 days
2. 1 or 2 days
3. 3 to 5 days
4. 6 to 9 days
5. 10 to 19 days
6. 20 to 29 days
7. All 30 days

**Q71. Have you EVER tried electronic cigarettes, e-cigarettes, or "vaping," even just one time? Select one response.**

1. Yes
2. No *(Skip to Q73.)*

**Q72. During the PAST 30 DAYS, on how many days did you use electronic cigarettes, e-cigarettes, or "vaping"? Select one response.**

1. 0 days
2. 1 or 2 days
3. 3 to 5 days
4. 6 to 9 days
5. 10 to 19 days
6. 20 to 29 days
7. All 30 days

**Q73. Next, we have some questions about your experience with a number of different substances. Have you EVER used the following? Please select ONE response PER ROW. Remember, your responses are confidential.** *(Randomize.)*

| | 1. Used in the past 30 days | 2. Used at least once in the past 12 months, but not in the past 30 days | 3. Used at least once in my life, but not in the past 12 months | 4. Never used in my life |
|---|---|---|---|---|
| a. Marijuana or hashish (such as "pot," THC, "weed") | | | | |
| b. Synthetic cannabis (such as "spice", K2, herbal smoking blend) | | | | |
| c. Cocaine (including crack) | | | | |
| d. LSD (such as "acid") | | | | |
| e. PCP (such as "angel dust" or marijuana laced with PCP) | | | | |
| f. MDMA (such as "Ecstasy" or "molly") | | | | |
| g. Other hallucinogens (such as peyote, mescaline, psilocybin-"shrooms") | | | | |
| h. Methamphetamine (such as "ice," "crystal meth," "speed," "crank") | | | | |
| i. Heroin (such as "smack") | | | | |
| j. GHB/GBL (such as "Liquid X," "Gamma 10") | | | | |
| k. Inhalants (such as aerosol sprays, gasoline, poppers, "whippets") | | | | |
| l. Synthetic stimulants (such as "bath salts") | | | | |

**Q74. Have you EVER used the following? Please select ONE response PER ROW.** *(Randomize. Within respondent, keep same order for Q74 through Q80.)*

| | 1. Used in the past 30 days | 2. Used at least once in the past 12 months, but not in the past 30 days | 3. Used at least once in my life, but not in the past 12 months | 4. Never used in my life |
|---|---|---|---|---|
| a. Prescription stimulants or attention enhancers ("go drugs," such as Adderall, amphetamines, Ritalin, prescription diet pills, etc.) | | | | |
| b. Prescription sedatives, tranquilizers, muscle relaxers, or barbiturates ("no go drugs," such as Ambien, Quaalude, Valium, Xanax, Rohypnol, Phenobarbital, Ketamine, etc.) | | | | |
| c. Prescription pain relievers (Oxcycontin/Oxycodone, Percocet, cough syrups with codeine, Methadone, hydrocodone, Vicodin, etc.) | | | | |
| d. Prescription anabolic steroids (such as Deca Durbolin, Testosterone, etc.) | | | | |
| e. Prescription anti-depressants (such as Cymbalta, Strattera, Prozac, Paxil, Zoloft, etc.) | | | | |

**Q75. How many days in the PAST 30 DAYS did you use the following? Please select ONE response PER ROW.**

*(Items for Q75 should show only if the parallel item in Q74 = 1 (used in the past 30 days).)*

| | 1. 11 or more days | 2. 4 to 10 days | 3. 1 to 3 days |
|---|---|---|---|
| a. Prescription stimulants or attention enhancers ("go drugs," such as Adderall, amphetamines, Ritalin, prescription diet pills, etc.) | | | |
| b. Prescription sedatives, tranquilizers, muscle relaxers, or barbiturates ("no go drugs," such as Ambien, Quaalude, Valium, Xanax, Rohypnol, Phenobarbital, Ketamine, etc.) | | | |
| c. Prescription pain relievers (Oxcycontin/Oxycodone, Percocet, cough syrups with codeine, Methadone, hydrocodone, Vicodin, etc.) | | | |
| d. Prescription anabolic steroids (such as Deca Durbolin, Testosterone, etc.) | | | |
| e. Prescription anti-depressants (such as Cymbalta, Strattera, Prozac, Paxil, Zoloft, etc.) | | | |

**Q76. Have you EVER been prescribed the following? Please select ONE response PER ROW.**

| | 1. Yes | 2. No |
|---|---|---|
| a. Prescription stimulants or attention enhancers ("go drugs," such as Adderall, amphetamines, Ritalin, prescription diet pills, etc.) | | |
| b. Prescription sedatives, tranquilizers, muscle relaxers, or barbiturates ("no go drugs," such as Ambien, Quaalude, Valium, Xanax, Rohypnol, Phenobarbital, Ketamine, etc.) | | |
| c. Prescription pain relievers (Oxcycontin/Oxycodone, Percocet, cough syrups with codeine, Methadone, hydrocodone, Vicodin, etc.) | | |
| d. Prescription anabolic steroids (such as Deca Durbolin, Testosterone, etc.) | | |
| e. Prescription anti-depressants (such as Cymbalta, Strattera, Prozac, Paxil, Zoloft, etc.) | | |

**Q77. Do you have a CURRENT prescription for this drug? Please select ONE response PER ROW.**

*(Items in Q77 should show only if the parallel item in Q76 = 1 (yes).)*

| | 1. Yes | 2. No, but I have had a prescription in the past 12 months | 3. No, I have NOT had a prescription in the past 12 months |
|---|---|---|---|
| a. Prescription stimulants or attention enhancers ("go drugs," such as Adderall, amphetamines, Ritalin, prescription diet pills, etc.) | | | |
| b. Prescription sedatives, tranquilizers, muscle relaxers, or barbiturates ("no go drugs," such as Ambien, Quaalude, Valium, Xanax, Rohypnol, Phenobarbital, Ketamine, etc.) | | | |
| c. Prescription pain relievers (Oxcycontin/Oxycodone, Percocet, cough syrups with codeine, Methadone, hydrocodone, Vicodin, etc.) | | | |
| d. Prescription anabolic steroids (such as Deca Durbolin, Testosterone, etc.) | | | |
| e. Prescription anti-depressants (such as Cymbalta, Strattera, Prozac, Paxil, Zoloft, etc.) | | | |

**Q78. When you used the drug in the PAST 12 MONTHS, how often did you use it? Please select ONE response PER ROW.**

*(Items in Q78 should show only if the parallel item in Q74 = 1 (used in the past 30 days) or 2 (used at least once in the past 12 months, but not in the past 30 days).)*

|  | 1. Used lower amount than prescribed | 2. Used as prescribed | 3. Used greater amount than prescribed |
|---|---|---|---|
| a. Prescription stimulants or attention enhancers ("go drugs," such as Adderall, amphetamines, Ritalin, prescription diet pills, etc.) |  |  |  |
| b. Prescription sedatives, tranquilizers, muscle relaxers, or barbiturates ("no go drugs," such as Ambien, Quaalude, Valium, Xanax, Rohypnol, Phenobarbital, Ketamine, etc.) |  |  |  |
| c. Prescription pain relievers (Oxycontin/Oxycodone, Percocet, cough syrups with codeine, Methadone, hydrocodone, Vicodin, etc.) |  |  |  |
| d. Prescription anabolic steroids (such as Deca Durbolin, Testosterone, etc.) |  |  |  |
| e. Prescription anti-depressants (such as Cymbalta, Strattera, Prozac, Paxil, Zoloft, etc.) |  |  |  |

**Q79. How did you obtain the following in the PAST 12 MONTHS? If you obtained it from more than one source, please select ONE OR MORE responses PER ROW.**

*(Items in Q79 should show only if the parallel item in Q74 = 1 (used in the past 30 days) or 2 (used at least once in the past 12 months, but not in the past 30 days).)*

| | 1. Health care provider at an MTF | 2. Health care provider at a VA Medical Facility | 3. Non-military doctor or health care worker | 4. Emergency room | 5. Internet/ mail order | 6. Family member or friend | 7. Dealer/ street pharmacist | 8. Other |
|---|---|---|---|---|---|---|---|---|
| a. Prescription stimulants or attention enhancers ("go drugs," such as Adderall, amphetamines, Ritalin, prescription diet pills, etc.) | | | | | | | | |
| b. Prescription sedatives, tranquilizers, muscle relaxers, or barbiturates ("no go drugs," such as Ambien, Quaalude, Valium, Xanax, Rohypnol, Phenobarbital, Ketamine, etc.) | | | | | | | | |
| c. Prescription pain relievers (Oxycontin/Oxycodone, Percocet, cough syrups with codeine, Methadone, hydrocodone, Vicodin, etc.) | | | | | | | | |
| d. Prescription anabolic steroids (such as Deca Durbolin, Testosterone, etc.) | | | | | | | | |
| e. Prescription anti-depressants (such as Cymbalta, Strattera, Prozac, Paxil, Zoloft, etc.) | | | | | | | | |

**Q80. What was the reason you took the following in the PAST 12 MONTHS? If there was more than one reason, please select ONE OR MORE responses PER ROW.**

*(Items in Q80 should show only if the parallel item in Q74 = 1 (used in the past 30 days) or 2 (used at least once in the past 12 months, but not in the past 30 days).)*

|  | 1. To control pain | 2. To feel good (get high or buzzed, etc.) | 3. To reduce depression or anxiety, or control stress | 4. To help me sleep | 5. To help me stay awake |
|---|---|---|---|---|---|
| a. Prescription stimulants or attention enhancers ("go drugs," such as Adderall, amphetamines, Ritalin, prescription diet pills, etc.) |  |  |  |  |  |
| b. Prescription sedatives, tranquilizers, muscle relaxers, or barbiturates ("no go drugs," such as Ambien, Quaalude, Valium, Xanax, Rohypnol, Phenobarbital, Ketamine, etc.) |  |  |  |  |  |
| c. Prescription pain relievers (Oxycontin/Oxycodone, Percocet, cough syrups with codeine, Methadone, hydrocodone, Vicodin, etc.) |  |  |  |  |  |
| d. Prescription anabolic steroids (such as Deca Durbolin, Testosterone, etc.) |  |  |  |  |  |
| e. Prescription anti-depressants (such as Cymbalta, Strattera, Prozac, Paxil, Zoloft, etc.) |  |  |  |  |  |

**Q81. During the PAST 12 MONTHS, on how many occasions (if any) have you taken a NON-PRESCRIPTION cough or cold medicine (robos, DXM, etc.) to get high? Select one response.**

1. Never
2. 1 to 2 times
3. 3 to 5 times
4. 6 to 9 times
5. 10 to 19 times
6. 20 or more times

**Q82. In the PAST 12 MONTHS, have you had to give a urine sample for a military-administered random unannounced drug test? Select one response.**

1. Yes
2. No

**Q83. How many times have you ever altered or tampered with a urine sample that you had to provide to the military? Select one response.**

1. 0 times
2. 1 time
3. 2 to 3 times
4. 4 or more times

**Q84. This next set of questions asks about sexual behavior. Please remember that your answers are strictly confidential. In the PAST 12 MONTHS, with how many different people did you have sexual intercourse, either vaginal or anal? Select one response.**

1. 20 or more people
2. 10–19 people
3. 5–9 people
4. 2–4 people
5. 1 person
6. I did not have vaginal or anal sex in the past 12 months.

**Q85. In the PAST 12 MONTHS, how often did you use a condom when having sexual intercourse (vaginal or anal) with a NEW sex partner? A new sex partner is someone you had sex with for the first time in the past 12 months. Select one response.**

1. Always
2. Often
3. Sometimes
4. Seldom
5. Never
6. I did not have a new vaginal or anal sex partner in the past 12 months.

**Q86. How many of your partners for ORAL, ANAL, or VAGINAL sex were male? (Include only partners in the PAST 12 MONTHS.) Select one response.**

1. 20 or more male partners
2. 10–19 male partners
3. 5–9 male partners
4. 2–4 male partners
5. 1 male partner
6. No male partners in the past 12 months

**Q87. How many of your partners for ORAL, ANAL, or VAGINAL sex were female? (Include only partners in the PAST 12 MONTHS.) Select one response.**

1. 20 or more female partners
2. 10–19 female partners
3. 5–9 female partners
4. 2–4 female partners
5. 1 female partner
6. No female partners in the past 12 months

**Q88. The last time you had vaginal sex, did you or your partner use any form of birth control? (Include only vaginal sex you had in the PAST 12 MONTHS.) Please select ALL THAT APPLY.** *(If 1–4 are selected, 5–12 cannot be selected.)*

1. I have not had vaginal sex in the past 12 months *(Skip to Q90.)*
2. No, we didn't use any form of birth control
3. No, I/my partner was already pregnant
4. No, I/my partner was trying to get pregnant
5. Yes, female sterilization (e.g. tubal ligation, hysterectomy)
6. Yes, male sterilization (vasectomy)
7. Yes, an IUD
8. Yes, a contraceptive implant (e.g. Implanon, Nexplanon)
9. Yes, birth control pills
10. Yes, birth control shots, birth control patch, contraceptive ring, or a diaphragm
11. Yes, condoms
12. Yes, some other method

**Q89. In the PAST 12 MONTHS, did you cause or did you have an unintended pregnancy? Select one response.**

1. Yes
2. No
3. Unsure *(Show only if Q8 = 1 (male).)*

**Q90. When was your last HIV test? Select one response.**

1. Within the past 12 months
2. More than 12 months ago but within the past 2 years
3. More than 2 years ago
4. I have never had an HIV test

**Q91. Have you ever had a sexually transmitted infection—such as gonorrhea, syphilis, chlamydia, HPV, or genital herpes? Select one response.**

1. Yes, contracted something within the past 12 months
2. Yes, contracted something more than 1 year ago
3. No
4. Have not been tested

**Q92. The next set of questions asks about how you have been feeling recently. Over the past 2 weeks, how often have you been bothered by any of the following? Please select ONE response PER ROW.**

|  | 1. Not at all | 2. Several days | 3. More than half the days | 4. Nearly every day |
|---|---|---|---|---|
| a. Little interest in doing things |  |  |  |  |
| b. Feeling down, depressed, or hopeless |  |  |  |  |
| c. Trouble falling or staying asleep, or sleeping too much |  |  |  |  |
| d. Feeling tired or having little energy |  |  |  |  |
| e. Poor appetite or overeating |  |  |  |  |
| f. Feeling bad about yourself—or that you are a failure or have let yourself or your family down |  |  |  |  |
| g. Trouble concentrating on things, such as reading the newspaper or watching television |  |  |  |  |
| h. Moving or speaking so slowly that other people could have noticed? Or the opposite—being so fidgety or restless that you have been moving around a lot more than usual |  |  |  |  |
| i. Thoughts that you would be better off dead, or of hurting yourself in some way |  |  |  |  |

**Q93. Over the past 2 weeks, how often have you been bothered by the following problems? Please select ONE response PER ROW.**

|  | 1. Not at all | 2. Several days | 3. More than half the days | 4. Nearly every day |
|---|---|---|---|---|
| a. Feeling nervous, anxious, or on edge |  |  |  |  |
| b. Not being able to stop or control worrying |  |  |  |  |
| c. Worrying too much about different things |  |  |  |  |
| d. Trouble relaxing |  |  |  |  |
| e. Being so restless that it's hard to sit still |  |  |  |  |
| f. Becoming easily annoyed or irritable |  |  |  |  |
| g. Feeling afraid as if something awful might happen |  |  |  |  |

**Q94. How many times in the PAST 30 DAYS did you . . . ? Please select ONE response PER ROW.**

|  | 1. Never | 2. One time | 3. Two times | 4. Three or four times | 5. Five or more times |
|---|---|---|---|---|---|
| a. Get angry at someone and yell or shout at them |  |  |  |  |  |
| b. Get angry with someone and kick or smash something, slam the door, punch the wall, etc. |  |  |  |  |  |
| c. Threaten someone with physical violence |  |  |  |  |  |
| d. Get into a fight with someone and hit the person |  |  |  |  |  |

**Q95. Please respond to each item by selecting ONE response PER ROW.**

|  | 1. Never | 2. Rarely | 3. Sometimes | 4. Usually | 5. Always |
|---|---|---|---|---|---|
| a. I have someone who will listen to me when I need to talk |  |  |  |  |  |
| b. I have someone to confide in or talk to about myself or my problems |  |  |  |  |  |
| c. I have someone who makes me feel appreciated |  |  |  |  |  |
| d. I have someone to talk with when I have a bad day |  |  |  |  |  |

**Q96. In your lifetime, have you EVER experienced any sexual contact that was unwanted, against your will, or occurred when you did not or could not consent (for example, unwanted sexual touching or oral, anal, or vaginal penetration)? Select one response.**

1. Yes
2. No *(Skip to Q98.)*

**Q97. When did the event(s) in the previous question occur? (That is, the unwanted sexual contact—for example, unwanted sexual touching or oral, anal, or vaginal penetration.) Select all that apply.**

1. While I was on Active military duty
2. While I was NOT on Active military duty
3. I never experienced unwanted sexual contact

**Q98. Have you EVER been physically abused, punished, or beaten by a person in authority or having some power over you such that you received bruises, cuts, welts, lumps, or other injuries? Select all that apply.**

1. Yes, while I was on Active military duty
2. Yes, while I was NOT on Active military duty
3. No, this has never happened to me

**Q99. Here is a list of problems and complaints that people sometimes have in response to stressful life experiences. How much have you been bothered by each of them in the PAST 30 DAYS? Please select ONE response PER ROW.**

| | 1. Not at all | 2. A little bit | 3. Moderately | 4. Quite a bit | 5. Extremely |
|---|---|---|---|---|---|
| a. Repeated, disturbing memories, thoughts, or images of a stressful experience from the past | | | | | |
| b. Repeated, disturbing dreams of a stressful experience from the past | | | | | |
| c. Suddenly acting or feeling as if a stressful experience were happening again (as if you were reliving it) | | | | | |
| d. Feeling very upset when something reminded you of a stressful experience from the past | | | | | |
| e. Having physical reactions (e.g., heart pounding, trouble breathing, sweating) when something reminded you of a stressful experience from the past | | | | | |
| f. Avoiding thinking about or talking about a stressful experience from the past or avoiding having feelings related to it | | | | | |
| g. Avoiding activities or situations because they reminded you of a stressful experience from the past | | | | | |
| h. Trouble remembering important parts of a stressful experience from the past | | | | | |
| i. Loss of interest in activities that you used to enjoy | | | | | |
| j. Feeling distant or cut off from other people | | | | | |
| k. Feeling emotionally numb or being unable to have loving feelings for those close to you | | | | | |
| l. Feeling as if your future will somehow be cut short | | | | | |
| m. Trouble falling or staying asleep | | | | | |
| n. Feeling irritable or having angry outbursts | | | | | |
| o. Having difficulty concentrating | | | | | |
| p. Being "super-alert" or watchful or on guard | | | | | |
| q. Feeling jumpy or easily startled | | | | | |

**Q100.** At any time in the PAST 12 MONTHS, did you feel that you needed counseling, therapy, or treatment from either a military or civilian mental health professional? Mental health professionals include psychologists, psychiatrists, clinical social workers, or other mental health counselors. Select one response.

1. Yes
2. No

**Q101.** At any time in the PAST 12 MONTHS, did SOMEONE ELSE tell you that you need counseling, therapy, or treatment from either a military or civilian mental health professional? Mental health professionals include psychologists, psychiatrists, clinical social workers, or other mental health counselors. Select one response.

1. Yes
2. No

**Q102.** In the PAST 12 MONTHS, did you receive counseling or mental health therapy/ treatment from the following? Please select ONE response PER ROW.

|  | 1. Yes | 2. No |
|---|---|---|
| a. Mental health professional at a military facility | | |
| b. Mental health professional at a civilian facility | | |
| c. General medical doctor at a military facility | | |
| d. General medical doctor at a civilian facility | | |
| e. Military chaplain | | |
| f. Civilian pastor, rabbi, or other pastoral counselor | | |
| g. Self-help group (AA, NA) | | |
| h. Other source of counseling, therapy, or treatment | | |

*(If Q102 a–h all = 2 (no), skip to Q105.)*

**Q103. In the PAST 12 MONTHS, how many visits did you make to the following for counseling or mental health therapy/treatment? Please type in the number of visits.**

*(Items in Q103 should show only if the parallel item in Q102 = 1 (yes).)*

|  | Number of visits (3 digits; 0–365) |
|---|---|
| a. Mental health professional at a military facility | |
| b. Mental health professional at a civilian facility | |
| c. General medical doctor at a military facility | |
| d. General medical doctor at a civilian facility | |
| e. Military chaplain | |
| f. Civilian pastor, rabbi, or other pastoral counselor | |
| g. Self-help group (AA, NA) | |
| h. Other source of counseling, therapy, or treatment | |

**Q104. During the past 12 months, did you take any medication that was prescribed for you to treat a mental or emotional condition? Select one response.**

1. Yes
2. No

**Q105. You said you needed counseling, therapy, or treatment in the PAST 12 MONTHS but that you did not receive it from any source on our list. Why didn't you receive counseling, therapy, or treatment? Please select ALL THAT APPLY.** *(Ask only if Q100 or Q101 = 1 (yes) and all responses to Q102 (a–h) = 2 (no). Randomize.)*

1. It was too difficult to arrange transportation.
2. It was too difficult to schedule an appointment.
3. It was too difficult to get time off work for treatment.
4. It was too difficult to get childcare.
5. It would have harmed my career.
6. I could have been denied security clearance in the future.
7. I could not afford the cost.
8. I was afraid my supervisor/unit leadership would have a negative opinion of me.
9. My commander or supervisor asked me/us not to get treatment.
10. My coworkers would have had less confidence in me if they found out.
11. I was concerned that the information I gave the counselor might not be kept confidential.
12. I wanted to handle the problem on my own.
13. I did not think treatment would help.
14. Other

**Q106.** In general, do you think it would damage a person's military career if the person were to seek counseling or mental health therapy/treatment through the military, regardless of the reason for seeking counseling? Select one response.

1. Yes
2. No

**Q107.** In your LIFETIME, how often have you intentionally hurt yourself—for example, by scratching, cutting, or burning—even though you were not trying to kill yourself? Select one response.

1. Never *(Skip to Q109.)*
2. 1 time
3. 2 or 3 times
4. 4 or 5 times
5. 6 or more times

**Q108.** SINCE JOINING THE MILITARY, how often have you intentionally hurt yourself—for example, by scratching, cutting, or burning—even though you were not trying to kill yourself? Select one response.

1. Never
2. 1 time
3. 2 or 3 times
4. 4 or 5 times
5. 6 or more times

**Q109.** In your LIFETIME, did you EVER seriously think about trying to kill yourself? Select one response.

1. Yes
2. No *(Skip to Q111.)*

**Q110.** Did you seriously think about trying to kill yourself during any of the following periods? Please select ONE response PER ROW.

|  | 1. Yes | 2. No |
|---|---|---|
| a. At any time in the past 12 months |  |  |
| b. Since joining the military |  |  |
| c. Before joining the military |  |  |
| d. During a deployment |  |  |

**Q111.** In your LIFETIME, have you EVER tried to kill yourself? Select one response.

1. Yes
2. No *(Skip to Q113.)*

**Q112a. Did you attempt to kill yourself during any of the following periods? Please select ONE response PER ROW.**

|  | 1. Yes | 2. No |
|---|---|---|
| a1. During the past 12 months, have you tried to kill yourself? |  |  |
| a2. Since joining the military, have you tried to kill yourself? |  |  |
| a3. Before joining the military, did you try to kill yourself? |  |  |
| a4. During a deployment, did you try to kill yourself? |  |  |

**Q112b. Did you get medical attention from a doctor or other health professional as a result of an attempt to kill yourself? Please select ONE response PER ROW.**

*(Items in Q112b should show only if the parallel item in Q112a = 1 (yes).)*

|  | 1. Yes | 2. No |
|---|---|---|
| b1. During the past 12 months, did you get medical attention from a doctor or other health professional as a result of an attempt to kill yourself? |  |  |
| b2. Since joining the military, did you get medical attention from a doctor or other health professional as a result of an attempt to kill yourself? |  |  |
| b3. Before joining the military, did you get medical attention from a doctor or other health professional as a result of an attempt to kill yourself? |  |  |
| b4. During a deployment, did you get medical attention from a doctor or other health professional as a result of an attempt to kill yourself? |  |  |

**Q113. How much do the following statements describe you? Please select ONE response PER ROW.** *(Randomize.)*

|  | 1. A great deal | 2. A lot | 3. Somewhat | 4. A little | 5. Not at all |
|---|---|---|---|---|---|
| a. You might say I act impulsively. |  |  |  |  |  |
| b. I like to test myself every now and then by doing something a little chancy or risky. |  |  |  |  |  |
| c. I often act in the spur of the moment without stopping to think. |  |  |  |  |  |
| d. Many of my actions seem to be hasty. |  |  |  |  |  |

**Q114.** Now we have some questions about your MOST RECENT deployment. Please think about both combat AND non-combat deployments. A combat zone deployment typically receives imminent danger pay (IDP), hazardous duty pay, and/or combat zone tax exclusion benefits. A non-combat deployment typically does not receive such benefits. When did your most recent combat or non-combat deployment BEGIN? Select one response.

1. Less than one year ago (12 months)
2. 1 to 3 years ago
3. 4 to 5 years ago
4. More than 5 years ago
5. I have never been deployed *(Skip to Q126.)*

*(If Q114 = 5 (I have never been deployed), skip to Q126.)*

**Q115.** When did that MOST RECENT combat or non-combat deployment END? Select one response.

1. Less than one year ago (12 months)
2. 1 to 3 years ago
3. 4 to 5 years ago
4. More than 5 years ago

**Q116.** Was your MOST RECENT deployment a combat zone or non-combat zone deployment? (A combat zone deployment typically receives imminent danger pay (IDP), hazardous duty pay, and/or combat zone tax exclusion benefits. A non-combat deployment typically does not receive such benefits.) Select one response.

1. Combat zone
2. Non-combat zone

**Q117.** During your MOST RECENT combat or non-combat deployment, how often did you use the following substances? Please select ONE response PER ROW. *(Randomize.)*

| | 1. Regularly or daily | 2. Once or twice a week | 3. Once or twice a month | 4. Once or twice a year | 5. Never |
|---|---|---|---|---|---|
| a. Alcohol | | | | | |
| b. Cigarettes | | | | | |
| c. Chewing/smokeless tobacco | | | | | |
| d. Cigars | | | | | |
| e. Prescription medications | | | | | |
| f. Marijuana | | | | | |
| g. Opium, heroin, morphine, etc. | | | | | |

**Q118. Next, we have some questions concerning ALL of your deployments while serving in the military. How many times have you been deployed? Include both combat and non-combat zone deployments. Select one response.**

1. 1 time
2. 2 times
3. 3 or more times

**Q119. Adding up ALL of your deployments while serving in the military, how long in TOTAL have you been deployed? Include both combat and non-combat zone deployments. Select one response.**

1. 1 to 6 months
2. 7 to 12 months
3. 13 to 24 months
4. 25 to 48 months
5. 49 months or more

**Q120. Thinking about ALL of your deployments while serving in the military, how many were COMBAT zone deployments? (The term "combat zone deployment," as used in this questionnaire, refers to a deployment where you received imminent danger pay (IDP), hazardous duty pay, and/or combat zone tax exclusion benefits.) Select one response.**

1. I have not had any combat zone deployments
2. 1 deployment
3. 2 deployments
4. 3 or more deployments

**Q121. During ANY deployment while serving in the military (COMBAT OR NON-COMBAT), did you EVER have any injury(ies) from any of the following events? Please select ALL THAT APPLY.**

1. Fragment
2. Bullet
3. Vehicular accident/crash (any vehicle, including aircraft)
4. Fall
5. Blast or explosion (IED, RPG, land mine, grenade, etc.)
6. I had an injury from another event
7. I did not have an injury during a deployment *(Skip to Q124.)*

**Q122. As a result of events in the previous question, did you receive a jolt or blow to your head that IMMEDIATELY resulted in the following? (This refers to injuries you had while serving on combat or non-combat deployments.) Please select ONE response PER ROW.**

|  | 1. Yes | 2. No |
|---|---|---|
| a. Lost consciousness or got "knocked out" for less than a minute |  |  |
| b. Lost consciousness or got "knocked out" for 1 to 20 minutes |  |  |
| c. Lost consciousness or got "knocked out" for more than 20 minutes |  |  |
| d. Felt dazed, confused, or "saw stars" |  |  |
| e. Didn't remember the event |  |  |
| f. Concussion or symptoms of a concussion (such as headache, dizziness, irritability, etc.) |  |  |
| g. Head injury |  |  |

**Q123. Are you currently experiencing any of the following problems that you think might be related to a possible head injury or concussion suffered while on a deployment? Please select ONE response PER ROW.** *(Randomize.)*

|  | 1. Yes | 2. No |
|---|---|---|
| a. Headaches |  |  |
| b. Dizziness |  |  |
| c. Memory problems (or lapses) |  |  |
| d. Balance problems |  |  |
| e. Ringing in the ears |  |  |
| f. Irritability |  |  |
| g. Sleep problems |  |  |
| h. Sensitivity to light |  |  |
| i. Other problem not listed |  |  |

**Q124. During ALL of your deployments while in the military, (COMBAT OR NON-COMBAT), how many times did each of the following EVER happen to you? Please select ONE response PER ROW.** *(Randomize.)*

| | 1. Never | 2. 1 to 5 times | 3. 6 to 19 times | 4. 20 to 50 times | 5. More than 50 times |
|---|---|---|---|---|---|
| a. I was sent outside the wire on combat patrols, convoys, or sorties. | | | | | |
| b. I, or members of my unit, received incoming fire from small arms, artillery, rockets, or mortars. | | | | | |
| c. I, or members of my unit, encountered mines, booby traps, or IEDs (improvised explosive devices). | | | | | |
| d. I worked with landmines or other unexploded ordnance. | | | | | |
| e. My unit fired on the enemy. | | | | | |
| f. I personally fired my weapon at the enemy. | | | | | |
| g. I was engaged in hand-to-hand combat. | | | | | |
| h. I was responsible for the death or serious injury of an enemy. | | | | | |
| i. I witnessed members of my unit or an ally unit being seriously wounded or killed. | | | | | |
| j. My unit suffered casualties. | | | | | |
| k. I saw dead bodies or human remains. | | | | | |
| l. I handled, uncovered, or removed dead bodies or human remains. | | | | | |
| m. Someone I knew well was killed in combat. | | | | | |
| n. I took care of injured or dying people. | | | | | |
| o. I interacted with enemy prisoners of war. | | | | | |
| p. I witnessed or engaged in acts of cruelty, excessive force, or acts violating rules of engagement. | | | | | |
| q. I was wounded in combat. | | | | | |
| r. I witnessed civilians being seriously wounded or killed. | | | | | |

**Q125. In the PAST 12 MONTHS, approximately how many months were you away in total for ALL deployments (both combat and non-combat zone deployments)? Select one response.**

1. I did not deploy in the past 12 months.
2. Less than 1 month
3. 1 to 3 months
4. 4 to 6 months
5. 7 to 9 months
6. 10 to 12 months

**Q126. People are different in their sexual attraction to other people. Which best describes your feelings? Select one response.**

1. Only attracted to males
2. Mostly attracted to males
3. Equally attracted to males and females
4. Mostly attracted to females
5. Only attracted to females
6. Not attracted to either males or females
7. Not sure

**Q127. Do you consider yourself to be…? Select one response.**

1. Heterosexual or straight
2. Gay or lesbian
3. Bisexual

**Q128. Some people describe themselves as transgender when they experience a different gender identity from their sex at birth. For example, a person born into a male body, but who feels female or lives as a woman. Do you consider yourself to be transgender?**

1. Yes
2. No

**Q129. On average, how many hours of sleep do you get in a 24-hour period? Please type in the number of hours for each row.**

| | |
|---|---|
| During the work/duty week? | _____ Hours *(2 digits; 0–24)* |
| During weekends/days off? | _____ Hours *(2 digits; 0–24)* |

**Q130. How much sleep do you need (per 24 hours) to feel fully refreshed and perform well? Select one response.**

1. 4 hours or less
2. 5 hours
3. 6 hours
4. 7 hours
5. 8 hours or more

**Q131. In the past week, how much were you bothered by lack of energy because of poor sleep? Select one response.**

1. Not bothered at all
2. Slightly bothered
3. Moderately bothered
4. Severely bothered

**Q132. Over the past week, how would you rate your satisfaction with your sleep? Select one response.**

1. Excellent
2. Good
3. Fair
4. Poor

**Q133. How often do you take prescription or over-the-counter (OTC) medications to help you sleep? Select one response.**

1. Every day
2. Almost every day
3. Seldom/rarely
4. Never

*(CLOSING SCREEN)*

**You have finished the 2015 DoD Health Related Behaviors Survey (HRBS)!** Thank you for taking the time to complete this important survey. Your participation, and your service to our country, is greatly appreciated.

In the event that any of the questions in the survey may have caused discomfort, we would like to remind you of several resources that are available.

**Military OneSource** (http://www.militaryonesource.com) is a free, 24-hour service that is available 7 days a week to provide a full range of services, across the deployment cycle, to military personnel and their families, at no cost. They can be reached at:

> Stateside: CONUS: 1-800-342-9647
> Overseas: OCONUS Universal Free Phone: 800-342-9647
> Collect from Overseas: OCONUS Collect: 703-253-7599
> En Español llame al: 877-888-0727
> TTY/TDD: 866-607-6794

The **DoD Safe Helpline** (https://www.safehelpline.org/) provides worldwide live, confidential support, 24/7. You can initiate a report and search for your nearest Sexual Assault Response Coordinator (SARC). You can find links to Service-specific reporting resources and access information about the prevention of and response to sexual assault on their website or by calling the hotline at 1-877-995-5247.

The **Military Crisis Line** (http://veteranscrisisline.net/ActiveDuty.aspx) can also provide confidential support and consultation if you feel distressed. They can be reached at 1-800-273-8255 (then press 1).

You may also contact the **National Suicide Hotline** at 1-800-273-TALK (8255).

# Invitation Letters and Letters of Support

This appendix reproduces recruitment materials, including the invitation letter from RAND and ICF International, as well as the letters of support from the DoD services and the Coast Guard.

1776 MAIN STREET  TEL 310.393.0411
P.O. BOX 2138  FAX 310.393.4818
SANTA MONICA, CA
90407-2138

September 29, 2015

John Smith |||||||||||||||||||||||||||||||||||||||||||  12345678A
980 Beaver Creek Drive
Martinsville, VA 24112
|||||||||||||||||||||||||||||||||||||||||||||||||||||||||||    1    1

**Subject: Invitation to Participate in the 2015 DoD Health Related Behaviors Survey (HRBS)**
**RCS # DD-HA(BE)2189 Expiration Date: 02/09/2019**

Dear Service Member:

You have been randomly selected to participate in the 2015 DoD Health Related Behaviors Survey (HRBS). We would like to invite you to fill out this **anonymous** survey on the Internet. The survey results will be used by the Department of Defense (DoD) to improve health behavior programs and policies that maintain a ready Total Force. Results from previous rounds of the HRBS have resulted in changes to tobacco policy, screening for alcohol use, and interventions to reduce prescription drug abuse. Results from prior surveys have been presented to the White House as well as Congress. In order to make the results of the 2015 HRBS as valid and reliable as possible, we need your support!

Please note that:

- This is a legitimate, **DoD-approved research study**, endorsed by the Services. Links to the letters of support from each Service can be found on the survey website.
- We will **not link** your individual survey responses to your name, personal identity, or military records.
- You can complete the **web survey** on a computer at home or at work. It takes about 40 minutes to fill out the survey.
- Our job at RAND is to make sure your survey responses are kept **anonymous** and are reported accurately. Your participation will make a difference.

RESEARCH AREAS
Children and Families
Education and the Arts
Energy and Environment
Health and Health Care
Infrastructure and
Transportation
International Affairs
Law and Business
National Security
Population and Aging
Public Safety
Science and Technology
Terrorism and
Homeland Security

OFFICES
Santa Monica, CA
Washington, DC
Pittsburgh, PA
New Orleans, LA
Jackson, MS
Boston, MA
Cambridge, UK
Brussels, BE

Please don't miss this opportunity to help DoD develop and enhance health promotion programs that will help Service members improve their health, well-being, and overall fitness. The survey results will have a direct impact on policies of interest to you, the Services, and the Department of Defense.

For more information, please read the enclosed **FREQUENTLY ASKED QUESTIONS** handout about the 2015 HRBS and why your participation is so important to the success of this study.

**You can complete the survey now by going to the following secure website maintained by ICF, our data collection contractor.**

**Survey website:**  www.DoD2015HealthSurvey.com

**Computer or technical questions about the website?**  Please contact the ICF Survey Helpdesk's toll free number at 1-844-430-9640 or email DoD2015HealthSurvey@icfsurveysupport.com

We greatly appreciate your time and cooperation in this important effort.

Sincerely,

Charles C. Engel, MD, MPH, RAND Project Co-Leader

Sarah Meadows, Ph.D., RAND Project Co-Leader

OBJECTIVE ANALYSIS.  EFFECTIVE SOLUTIONS.

**THE ASSISTANT SECRETARY OF DEFENSE**

**1200 DEFENSE PENTAGON**
**WASHINGTON, DC  20301-1200**

**HEALTH AFFAIRS**

AUG 2 0 2015

Dear Service Member:

You are invited to participate in the 2015 Department of Defense (DoD) Survey of Health Related Behaviors, which we have asked the independent, non-profit RAND Corporation to design, implement, and analyze.  This health survey is important to the DoD and the Services, and I would like to strongly encourage you to participate in this web-based survey.

The purpose of this survey is to assess the health related behaviors and lifestyles of military personnel that have the potential to impact readiness.  We use data from this survey to improve education, training, treatment, and counseling to support the Services and optimize individual and overall health status and fitness.

To protect Service members' privacy, the 2015 health survey is anonymous.  This means we do not ask military members for their name or other personal identifiers on the survey.  No one, including DoD, the Services, or our contractors, will link your individual survey responses with your name, other personal identifiers, or military records.  We have instructed our contractors to implement procedures to keep the survey anonymous.  No one will know who actually filled out the web survey.  DoD and the Services have agreed to this condition to protect your privacy to the extent allowed by law, so you can feel comfortable answering the survey questions truthfully and honestly.

Although your participation in the survey is entirely voluntary, I hope you will recognize its importance and find time to sit down and answer these questions about your health.  This survey can be completed using a government computer during duty hours or on a home computer with Internet access.

For further information about the survey and instructions for accessing and completing the survey on the Internet, please read the attached RAND Corporation letter and Frequently Asked Questions.  Thank you for your continued service to our Country and thank you in advance for your time and assistance in this important effort.

Sincerely,

Jonathan Woodson, M.D.

Attachments:
As stated

# DEPARTMENT OF THE AIR FORCE
## WASHINGTON DC

0 6 OCT 2015

OFFICE OF THE ASSISTANT SECRETARY

MEMORANDUM FOR U.S. AIR FORCE SURVEY PARTICIPANT

FROM: Deputy Assistant Secretary (Reserve Affairs and Airman Readiness)

SUBJECT:   2015 Department of Defense Survey of Health Related Behaviors among Active
Personnel

The Department of Defense has asked the RAND Corporation and ICF International,
independent research organizations, to conduct the 2015 DoD Health Related Behaviors Survey
(HRBS). This survey is being conducted with randomly selected military members from all
Service branches and all components.

The 2015 HRBS asks about health-related behaviors such as diet, exercise, stress,
substance use and other health issues related to readiness. Some of the questions are personal. To
protect your privacy, the survey is anonymous. This means you do not provide your name or
other personal identifiers on the survey. Neither DoD, the Air Force, RAND, nor ICF will link
your individual survey responses with your name, other personal identifiers, or your military
records. No one will know who did and did not complete the survey.

The RAND Corporation and ICF will send you instructions via mail and email for
accessing and completing the 2015 HRBS if you are randomly selected to participate. The survey
will take about 40 minutes to finish. It can be completed on the web using a government
computer during duty hours or a home computer with Internet access.

Your participation in the 2015 HRBS is critical to assessing health-related readiness and
for making program and policy decisions that sustain a healthy and ready force. Although your
participation in the survey is entirely voluntary, I hope you will choose to support this vital effort
by responding promptly if you are asked.

Thank you in advance for your time and assistance in this important effort.

JOHN A. FEDRIGO
Deputy Assistant Secretary
(Reserve Affairs and Airman Readiness)

**DEPARTMENT OF THE ARMY**
HEADQUARTERS, UNITED STATES ARMY MEDICAL COMMAND
2748 WORTH ROAD
JBSA FORT SAM HOUSTON, TEXAS  78234-6000

MCHB-IP-H

0 6 OCT 2015

MEMORANDUM FOR Service Member Participants of 2015 Department of Defense Health Related Behaviors Survey

SUBJECT:  2015 Department of Defense Health Related Behaviors Survey

1.  The Department of Defense (DoD) has asked the RAND Corporation and ICF International, independent research organizations, to conduct the **2015 DoD Health Related Behaviors Survey (HRBS).**  This survey is being conducted with randomly selected military members from all Service branches and components.

2.  The 2015 HRBS asks about health-related behaviors such as diet, exercise, stress, substance use and other health issues related to readiness; some of the questions are personal.  **To protect your privacy, the survey is anonymous.**  This means you do not provide your name or other personal identifiers on the survey.  Neither the DoD, Army, RAND Corporation, nor ICF International will link your individual survey responses with your name, other personal identifiers or your military records.  No one will know who did and did not complete the survey.

3.  The RAND Corporation and ICF International will send you instructions via mail and email for accessing and completing the 2015 HRBS if you are randomly selected to participate.  The survey will take about 40 minutes to finish.  It can be completed on the web using a government computer during duty hours or a home computer with internet access.

4.  **Your Participation in the 2015 HRBS is critical to assessing health-related readiness and for making program and policy decisions that sustain a healthy and ready Force.**  Although your participation in the survey is entirely voluntary, I hope you will choose to support this vital effort by responding promptly if you are asked.  Thank you in advance for your time.

5.  Our point of contact is Ms. Laura Mitvalsky, Army Public Health Center (Provisional), (410) 436-2303, or email laura.a.mitvalsky.civ@mail.mil.

Serving to Heal…Honored to Serve!

Encl

GERALD C. ECKER
Command Sergeant Major
US Army Medical Command

PATRICIA D. HOROHO
Lieutenant General
The Surgeon General and
    Commanding General, USAMEDCOM

**DEPARTMENT OF THE NAVY**
HEADQUARTERS UNITED STATES MARINE CORPS
3280 RUSSELL ROAD
QUANTICO, VIRGINIA 22134-5103

IN REPLY REFER TO
6260
MF
1 9 OCT 2015

From:   Commandant of the Marine Corps

Subj:   2015 Department of Defense Survey of Health Related Behaviors

1.  The Department of Defense (DoD) has asked the RAND Corporation and ICF International, independent research organizations, to conduct the 2015 DoD Health Related Behaviors Survey (HRBS).  This survey is being conducted with randomly selected military members from all Service branches and all components.

2.  The 2015 HRBS asks about health-related behaviors such as diet, exercise, stress, substance use and other health issues related to readiness.  Some of the questions are personal.  To protect your privacy, the survey is anonymous.  This means you do not provide your name or other personal identifiers on the survey.  Neither DoD, the Marine Corps, RAND, nor ICF will link your individual survey responses with your name, other personal identifiers, or your military records.  No one will know who did and did not complete the survey.

3.  The RAND Corporation and ICF will send you instructions via mail and email for accessing and completing the 2015 HRBS if you are randomly selected to participate.  The survey will take about 40 minutes to finish.  It can be completed on the web using a government computer during duty hours or a home computer with Internet access.

4.  Your participation in the 2015 HRBS is critical to assessing health-related readiness and for making program and policy decisions that sustain a healthy and ready force.  Although your participation in the survey is entirely voluntary, I hope you will choose to support this vital effort by responding promptly if you are asked.

5.  Call the ICF Survey Helpdesk for computer, technical, or survey questions: by phone toll free at (844) 430-9640 or by email at DoD2015HealthSurvey@icfsurveysupport.com.  Your Headquarters Marine Corps point of contact for this survey is LCDR Sam Stephens at (703) 784-9568 and sam.stephens@usmc.mil.

6.  Thank you in advance for your time and assistance in this important effort.


W. S. HARVEY
Sergeant Major
Marine and Family
Programs Division


B. W. WHITMAN
Director
Marine and Family
Programs Division

**DEPARTMENT OF THE NAVY**
OFFICE OF THE CHIEF OF NAVAL OPERATIONS
2000 NAVY PENTAGON
WASHINGTON, DC 20350-2000

4730
Ser N17/Ü070
1 Sep 15

From:  Director, Twenty-First Century Sailor Office (N17)
To:    U.S. Navy Survey Participant

Subj:  2015 DEPARTMENT OF DEFENSE SURVEY OF HEALTH RELATED BEHAVIORS AMONG
       ACTIVE DUTY PERSONNEL

1.  If you have been randomly selected to participate in the 2015
Department of Defense (DoD) Health Related Behaviors Survey (HRBS) for
Active Duty personnel, I strongly encourage you to support this vital
effort by responding promptly when asked to complete the survey.

2.  The RAND Corporation and ICF International, independent research
organizations are conducting the HRBS on behalf of DoD.  This survey is
being conducted with randomly selected military members from all service
branches.

3.  The 2015 HRBS asks about health-related behaviors such as diet,
exercise, stress, substance use, and other health issues related to
readiness.  Some of the questions are personal.  To protect your privacy,
the survey is anonymous.  This means you do not provide your name or other
personal identifiers on the survey.  Neither DoD, the Navy, RAND, nor ICF
will be able to link your individual survey responses with your name,
other personal identifiers, or your military records.

4.  The RAND Corporation and ICF will send you instructions via mail and
email for accessing and completing the 2015 HRBS if you are randomly
selected to participate.  The survey will take about 40 minutes to
complete.  It can be completed on the web using a government computer
during duty hours or a home computer with internet access.

5.  Your participation in the 2015 HRBS is critical to assessing health-
related readiness and for making program and policy decisions that sustain
a healthy and ready force.  Although your participation in the survey is
entirely voluntary, I hope you will choose to support this vital effort by
responding promptly if you are asked.

6.  I want to thank you in advance for your time and participation in this
important study effort.

Sincerely,

A. M. BURKHARDT
Rear Admiral, U.S. Navy

**U.S. Department of Homeland Security**

**United States Coast Guard**

Commandant
United States Coast Guard

2703 Martin Luther King Jr. Ave. S.E.
Washington, DC 20593-7581
Staff Symbol: CG-11
Phone: (202) 475-5130

6500

# MEMORANDUM

OCT – 1 2015

From:    Erica G. Schwartz, RADM
         CG-11

Reply to    Mark Mattiko
Attn of:    202.475.5148

To:      Active Duty Members of the Coast Guard

Subj:    PARTICIPATION IN THE 2015 HEALTH RELATED BEHAVIORS SURVEY

1. The Department of Defense (DoD) has asked the RAND Corporation and ICF International, independent research organizations, to conduct the 2015 Health Related Behaviors Survey (HRBS). This survey is being conducted with randomly selected military members from all Service branches and all components.

2. The 2015 HRBS asks about health-related behaviors such as diet, exercise, stress, substance use and other health issues related to readiness. Some of the questions are personal. To protect your privacy, the survey is anonymous. This means you do not provide your name or other personal identifiers on the survey. Neither DoD, the Coast Guard, RAND Corporation, nor ICF International will link your individual survey responses with your name, other personal identifiers, or your military records. No one will know who did and did not complete the survey.

3. The RAND Corporation and ICF International will send you instructions via mail and email for accessing and completing the 2015 HRBS if you are randomly selected to participate. The survey will take about 40 minutes to finish. It can be completed on the web using a government computer during duty hours or a home computer with Internet access.

4. Your participation in the 2015 HRBS is critical to assessing health-related readiness and for making program and policy decisions that sustain a healthy and ready force. Although your participation in the survey is entirely voluntary, I hope you will choose to support this vital effort by responding promptly if you are asked.

5. Thank you in advance for your time and assistance in this important effort.

#

# 2015 DoD Health Related Behaviors Survey Frequently Asked Questions

**What is the purpose of the 2015 DoD Health Related Behaviors Survey (HRBS)?** This survey assesses the health-related behaviors and lifestyles of military personnel that have the potential to impact readiness. The survey results will be used to monitor Service members' needs, develop policies, and improve health programs and services for military members and their families.

**How long is the survey?** This survey takes about 40 minutes.

**Who is doing this study?** The Department of Defense (DoD) asked the RAND Corporation and its data collection contractor, ICF International, to conduct an independent, objective assessment of Service members' health status and health-related behaviors.

**Who is the RAND Corporation?** RAND is a private, nonprofit organization that conducts research and analysis to help improve public policy and decisionmaking.

**Who is ICF International?** ICF is a leading consulting services and technology solutions firm. ICF manages the technical aspects of the web survey operations and can help you with any computer or technical problems.

**Why did you pick me?** You were randomly selected from all Active Component and Coast Guard personnel to represent your Service branch in this important research.

**How did you get my name?** We obtained your name from the Defense Manpower Data Center (DMDC), which maintains DoD personnel records. Because we are doing an official, approved DoD survey, DMDC was authorized to give us military members' names and contact information for research purposes only. We are just using your name to send you information about the survey via email and mail. Study staff will NOT link your survey responses to your name or a survey ID code. The survey is anonymous.

**How will the survey findings be used?** RAND will report survey findings in a way that does not identify individuals to the Services, DoD, or the public. The information you provide will be combined with that from other military personnel to prepare statistical reports. At no time will your individual data be reported.

**Why should I participate?** This is your chance to be heard on issues that directly affect the health, well-being, and readiness of military members and their families. The survey results will help inform DoD of potential health problems in the military and help suggest ways to solve or prevent them.

**Will my answers be kept private?** Yes. As noted earlier, this survey is anonymous. This means that RAND and ICF will not give DoD information about who participated in the study, or match your individual responses on this survey with your name, identity, military records, or a survey identification code. DoD has agreed to this condition to protect your privacy.

**Can I complete the survey during duty hours/on a government computer?** Yes. The Service Chief endorsement letters posted on the survey website indicate that you can use a computer at work to do the survey.

**What do I do if I experience any discomfort or distress from filling out the survey?** Some questions on the survey are sensitive in nature and it is possible that you may feel discomfort in answering one or more of these items. If you are having any suicidal thoughts, please seek help immediately. We encourage you to contact your unit's chaplain or a mental health professional. Other resources can be found below:

**Military OneSource** (http://www.militaryonesource.com) is a free, 24-hour service that is available 7 days a week to provide a full range of services, across the deployment cycle, to military personnel and their families, at no cost. They can be reached at:

> Stateside: CONUS: 1-800-342-9647
> Overseas: OCONUS Universal Free Phone: 800-3429-6477 or 703-253-7500
> Collect from Overseas: OCONUS Collect: 703-253-7599
> En Español llame al: 877-888-0727 / TTY/TDD: 866-607-6794.

**DoD Safe Helpline** (https://www.safehelpline.org/) provides worldwide live, confidential support, 24/7. You can initiate a report and search for your nearest Sexual Assault Response Coordinator (SARC). You can find links to Service-specific reporting resources and access information about the prevention of and response to sexual assault on their website or by calling the hotline at 1-877-995-5247.

**Military Crisis Line** (http://veteranscrisisline.net/ActiveDuty.aspx) can also provide confidential support and consultation if you feel distressed. They can be reached at 1-800-273-8255 (then press 1).

**Do I have to take the survey?** The survey is entirely voluntary, though we hope you will recognize its importance and make time to complete it. If you choose to take the survey, you may stop at any time.

**Did I already answer these questions in earlier DoD surveys?** Some Service members may have completed surveys like this one in the past. This survey is conducted approximately every three years to get a comprehensive update about the health behaviors of military members. Since DoD wants to understand trends in members' experiences in the Services, it is important that you take the 2015 survey to tell us about your current health.

**Who do I contact if I have questions or concerns about the survey?**

- **Contact the ICF Survey Helpdesk for computer, technical, or survey questions:** by phone toll free at 1-844-430-9640 or by email at DoD2015HealthSurvey@icfsurveysupport.com.
- **Contact RAND for questions about the overall study:** Email: HRBS2015@rand.org.
- **Questions about your rights as a participant in this study:** Contact the RAND Human Subjects Protection Committee at 310-393-0411, ext. 6369 in Santa Monica, California.

**What do I need to do to fill out the web survey?** You should go to the following website link www.DoD2015HealthSurvey.com. If you have problems accessing the website, contact the ICF survey helpdesk listed above.

**Do I have to complete the web survey in one sitting?** Yes. Please try to complete the survey in one session. To protect your privacy, if you stop before you are finished with the survey, you will need to start the survey over from the beginning when you come back to the website.

**Will I ever see the results of the survey?** Yes. When the survey results are available, an executive summary will be available.

# Description of Measures Used in the 2015 DoD Health Related Behaviors Survey

This appendix provides details for key measures used in each chapter. Only measures that required significant recoding or that are combinations of multiple survey items are shown. When applicable, we provide references for existing scales or indices.

## Chapter 3: Demographics

*Housing status (Q12).* Housing status included the following four categories:

- living in dorms or barracks on an installation: dorms/barracks (Q12 = 1)
- other housing on an installation: military housing (including privatized) on main base (Q12 = 2)
- housing off an installation: military housing (including privatized) off main base (Q12 = 3), civilian housing that you own or pay mortgage on (Q12 = 4), and civilian housing that you rent, off base (Q12 = 5)
- other living situations: some other living situation (e.g., living with parents, temporary housing) (Q12 = 6).

*Education level (Q14).* Education level included the following three categories:

- high school or less: 12 years or less of schooling (no diploma) (Q14 = 1), high school graduate—traditional diploma (Q14 = 2), and high school graduate—alternative diploma (Q14 = 3)
- some college: some college credit, but less than 1 year (Q14 = 4); 1 or more years of college, no degree (Q14 = 5); and associate's degree (Q14 = 6)
- bachelor's degree or more: bachelor's degree (Q14 = 7) and graduate or professional degree (Q14 = 8).

*Race/ethnicity (Q15, Q16).* Race/ethnicity included the following categories:

- Hispanic: Mexican, Mexican-American, Chicano, Puerto Rican, Cuban, or other Spanish/Hispanic/Latino (Q15 = 1)
- non-Hispanic white: not Spanish/Hispanic/Latino (Q15 = 2) and white (Q16 = 1)
- non-Hispanic black: not Spanish/Hispanic/Latino (Q15 = 2) and black or African American (Q16 = 2)

- non-Hispanic Asian: not Spanish/Hispanic/Latino (Q15 = 2) and Asian (e.g., Asian Indian, Chinese, Filipino, Japanese, Korean, Vietnamese) (Q16 = 4)
- other: not Spanish/Hispanic/Latino (Q15 = 2) and American Indian or Alaska Native (Q16 = 3), Native Hawaiian or other Pacific Islander (e.g., Samoan, Guamanian, Chamorro) (Q16 = 5), other (Q16 = 6), or more than one race in Q16.

*Parental status (Q23).* Parental status is one if Q23 = 1 or more.

## Chapter 4: Health Promotion and Disease Prevention

*Weight status (Q18, Q19).* Two standard items asked respondents to report their height (Q18) and weight (Q19). Weight status was based on BMI, which was calculated as

$$\frac{\text{weight (lb)} * 703}{\text{height (in.)}^2}.$$

For service members aged 20 or older, we categorized BMI using CDC criteria (CDC, 2015a), and for service members younger than age 20, we used age- and sex-specific definitions established by the CDC (CDC, 2015b).

- Weight was categorized as follows for service members aged 20 or older:
  - underweight: BMI < 18.5 kg/m2
  - normal: BMI 18.5–24.99 kg/m2
  - overweight: BMI 25.00–29.99 kg/m2
  - obese: BMI ≥ 30.0 kg/m2.
- Weight was categorized as follows for service members younger than age 20:
  - underweight: BMI < 5th percentile for age or gender
  - normal: BMI 5th – < 85th percentile for age or gender
  - overweight: BMI 85th – < 95th percentile for age or gender
  - obese: BMI ≥ 95th percentile for age or gender.

*Physical activity (Q26, Q27).* Respondents were asked about the frequency (Q26) and duration (Q27) of moderate and vigorous physical activity in the past 30 days. These two questions were combined into two categorical measures of moderate and vigorous physical activity.

- MPA was categorized as
  - < 150 minutes per week
  - 150–299 minutes per week
  - 300+ minutes per week.
- VPA was categorized as
  - < 75 minutes per week
  - 75–149 minutes per week
  - 150+ minutes per week.

*Sleep (Q129, Q130).* Respondents were asked to enter their average number of sleep hours (Q129). They were allowed to enter different response options for "during the work/duty week" and "during the weekends/days off." Respondents were next asked how many hours of sleep per night they need to feel fully refreshed and perform well (Q130). We generated a categorical measure comparing the average hours of sleep per 24 hours compared with the average number of hours needed to feel fully refreshed and perform well.

The agreement between sleep received compared with sleep needed to feel fully refreshed was categorized as follows:

- enough sleep: sleep received = sleep needed
- less sleep that needed: sleep received < sleep needed
- more sleep than needed: sleep received > sleep needed.

## Chapter 5: Substance Use

### Alcohol

*Serious consequences from drinking (Q43, Q44c, Q44f–k).* Based on endorsement of any of Q43a–m, Q44c, or Q44f–k, individuals were classified as experiencing serious drinking consequences in the past year. The items and scoring were similar to those used to derive a serious consequences indicator in the 2008 HRBS, but adding items Q43g ("I hit my spouse/significant other after having too much to drink") and Q43k ("I did something sexually that I regretted").

*Risk behaviors from drinking (Q44a,b,d,e).* Respondents who endorsed any of Q44a, b, d, or e were categorized as engaging in risk behaviors from drinking in the past year. This measure was identical to one included in the 2011 HRBS.

*Productivity loss from drinking (Q45a–f).* Respondents who endorsed any item in Q45(a–f) were considered to have experienced past-year job-related productivity loss from drinking. The measure was identical to one from the 2008 HRBS.

*Hazardous drinking/possible disorder (Q46, Q47, Q48).* This classification was based on the AUDIT-C, where scores of three or more for women and four or more for men were used as cut-offs indicating probable hazardous drinking or a probable alcohol use disorder (Bradley et al., 2007; Bush et al., 1998).

*Heavy drinking (Q49, Q50).* Respondents who reported drinking five or more drinks on a typical day in the past 30 days (Q50 ≥ 5) and who also drank on five or more days in the past 30 days (Q49 ≥ 5) were classified as heavy drinkers. This definition is consistent with that used in the NSDUH (CBHSQ, 2015a).

*Binge drinking (Q51).* Respondents who binge drank at least once in the past 30 days (Q51 ≤ 6)—that is, men who drank five or more drinks and women who drank four or more drinks on the same occasion at least once in the past 30 days—were classified as current binge drinkers. This definition is identical to that used by the CDC in the Behavioral Risk Factor Surveillance System (CDC, 2012).

*Military drinking culture (Q53).* Respondents who agreed or strongly agreed with any of Q53a–d or Q53g–i or who disagreed or strongly disagreed with Q53f were classified as perceiving the military culture as supportive of drinking. This item was drawn from the 2005 HRBS.

**Tobacco**

*Secondhand smoke exposure (Q55).* Respondents who indicated they had breathed smoke at work at least once in the past seven days (Q55 ≥ 1) were classified as exposed to secondhand smoke in the workplace. Q55 was drawn from the National Adult Tobacco Survey (King et al., 2014) and was new to the HRBS in 2015.

*Current cigarette smoking (Q56, Q58, Q60).* Those responding to Q60 with every day (Q60 = 1) or some days (Q60 = 2), who were lifetime smokers (Q56 = 1), and who smoked in the past 30 days (Q58 ≥ 1) were classified as current cigarette smokers. This definition is consistent with the definition from the National Health Interview Survey (CDC, 2015d) and the 2011 HRBS.

*Daily smoking (Q56, Q58, Q60).* Those who responded to Q60 with "every day" (Q60 = 1) and who were lifetime (Q56 = 1) and past-month (Q58 ≥ 1) smokers were classified as daily smokers. This measure was based on the National Health Interview Survey (CDC, 2015d).

*Average number of cigarettes smoked per day (Q59).* This measure was defined only for those who were categorized as daily smokers (see above).

*Smoking cessation attempt (Q61).* Respondents who indicated that they had tried to stop smoking for at least one day at least one time (Q61 = 1 or 2) were classified as making a quit attempt in the past year. Q61 was drawn from the National Health Interview Survey (CDC, 2015f).

*Ever used smokeless tobacco (Q64).* Respondents who said yes to Q64 (Q64 = 1) were classified as ever using smokeless tobacco. A comparable item was included in the 2011 HRBS but was revised for 2015 to remove reference to "other smokeless tobacco."

*Current smokeless tobacco use (Q64, Q66).* Respondents who reported ever using smokeless tobacco (Q64 = 1) and who said they used it in the past 30 days (Q66 = 1 or 2) were classified as current users. This measure is comparable to the measure used in the 2011 HRBS.

*Current cigar smoking (Q67, Q68).* Respondents who indicated that they had ever tried cigars or cigarillos (Q67 = 1) and who said they smoked them at least once in the past 30 days (Q68 ≥ 2) were classified as current cigar smokers. Q67 and Q68 were drawn from the National Youth Tobacco Survey (Office on Smoking and Health, 2015), but brand examples included in that survey were omitted from the 2015 HRBS.

*Ever used e-cigarettes (Q71).* Q71 is similar to an item in the National Youth Tobacco Survey (Office on Smoking and Health, 2015). RAND added the phrase "even just one time" to the end of the item and omitted brand examples.

*Current e-cigarette use (Q71, Q72).* Respondents who had ever tried e-cigarettes (Q71 = 1) and indicated that they used e-cigarettes at least once in the past 30 days (Q72 ≥ 2) were classified as current e-cigarette users. Q72 is similar to a question in the National Youth Tobacco Survey

(Office on Smoking and Health, 2015), but brand examples included in that survey were omitted from the 2015 HRBS version. The 2011 HRBS measured past-year e-cigarette use only.

*Daily e-cigarette use (Q72).* Respondents who had ever tried e-cigarettes (Q71 = 1) and who indicated that they used e-cigarettes 30 of the past 30 days (Q72 = 7) were classified as daily e-cigarette users.

### Illicit Drug Use and Prescription Drug Use, Misuse, and Overuse

*Past-year use of marijuana, hashish, or synthetic cannabis (Q73a,b).* Respondents who said they had used marijuana, hashish, or synthetic cannabis in the past 30 days (Q73a or Q73b = 1) or at least once in the past 12 months, but not in the past 30 days (Q73a or Q73b = 2) were classified as using one or more of these substances in the past year. Q73 is very similar to an item in the 2011 HRBS. RAND made minor clarifying changes in wording for some items and response options and added an additional substance (synthetic stimulants, Q73l) for the 2015 HRBS.

*Current use of marijuana, hashish, or synthetic cannabis (Q73a,b).* Respondents who said they had used marijuana, hashish, or synthetic cannabis in the past 30 days (Q73a or Q73b = 1) were classified as current users of one or more of these substances.

*Past-year use of any illicit drug other than marijuana, hashish, or synthetic cannabis (Q73e–l).* Respondents who said they had used any of the substances in Q73e–l in the past 30 days (Q73e–l = 1) or at least once in the past 12 months, but not in the past 30 days (Q73e–l = 2) were classified as past-year users of an illicit drug other than marijuana, hashish, or synthetic cannabis.

*Current use of any illicit drug other than marijuana, hashish, or synthetic cannabis (Q73e–l).* Respondents who said they had used any of the substances in Q73e–l in the past 30 days (Q73e–l = 1) were classified as current users of one or more of these substances.

*Past-year use of any illicit drug (Q73a–l).* Respondents who said they had used any of the substances in Q73 in the past 30 days (Q73a–l = 1) or at least once in the past 12 months, but not in the past 30 days (Q73a–l = 2) were classified as using one or more of these substances in the past year.

*Current use of any illicit drug (Q73a–l).* Respondents who said they had used any of the substances in Q73 in the past 30 days (Q73a–l = 1) were classified as current users of any illicit drug.

*Lifetime use of any prescription drug (Q74).* Respondents who said they had used any of the prescription drugs in Q74 in the past 30 days (Q74a–e = 1); at least once in the past year, but not in the past 30 days (Q74a–e = 2); or at least once in their life, but not in the past 12 months (Q74a–e = 3) were categorized as lifetime prescription drug users. A comparable item was included in the 2011 HRBS. For the 2015 version, RAND modified the item to reduce respondent burden and added a drug (antidepressants, Q74e).

*Past-year use of any prescription drug (Q74).* Respondents who said they had used any of the prescription drugs in Q74 in the past 30 days (Q74a–e = 1) or at least once in the past 12 months, but not in the past 30 days (Q74a–e = 2) were categorized as using prescription drugs in the past year.

*Current use of any prescription drug (Q74).* Respondents who said they had used any of the prescription drugs in Q74 in the past 30 days (Q74a–e = 1) were categorized as current prescription drug users.

*Any past-year prescription drug misuse (Q74, Q77).* Respondents who said they had used any of the prescription drugs in Q74 in the past 30 days (Q74a–e = 1) or at least once in the past 12 months, but not in the past 30 days (Q74a–e = 2) and who indicated they did not have a prescription in the past 12 months (Q77a–e = 3) for that same type of prescription drug were classified as misusing prescription drugs in the past year.

*Any past-year prescription drug overuse (Q74, Q77, Q78).* Respondents who said they had used any of the prescription drugs in Q74 in the past 30 days (Q74a–e = 1) or at least once in the past 12 months, but not in the past 30 days (Q74a–e = 2), who also had a valid prescription for that same drug (Q77 = 1 [current prescription] or 2 [prescription in the past 12 months]), and who reported that they used a greater amount than prescribed (Q78 = 3) were categorized as overusing prescription drugs. Q78 was drawn from the 2011 HRBS, and for the 2015 item, RAND slightly reworded the question and added a drug (antidepressants, Q78e).

## Chapter 6: Mental Health

*Probable depression (Q92).* Respondents completed the PHQ-9 (Kroenke, Spitzer, and Williams, 2001), a standard brief measure of depression, that ascertained how many days in the past two weeks service members had experienced common depressive symptoms, such as feeling down, depressed, or hopeless; having trouble falling or staying asleep, or sleeping too much; and having little interest in doing things (Q92a–i). The PHQ-9 is a self-administered version of the PRIME-MD (Primary Care Evaluation of Mental Disorders) diagnostic instrument for common mental disorders. The PHQ-9 is the depression module, which scores each of the nine criteria from the *Diagnostic and Statistical Manual of Mental Disorders* (DSM)-IV on a scale between 0 (not at all) and 3 (nearly every day). Respondents with sum scores greater than or equal to 15 were categorized as having probable depression.

*Probable generalized anxiety disorder (Q93).* As part of the survey, respondents completed the GAD-7, a self-reported questionnaire for screening and severity measuring of GAD (Löwe et al., 2008; Spitzer et al., 2006). Respondents were asked how often, during the past two weeks, they have been bothered by each of the seven core symptoms of GAD, such as having trouble relaxing or feeling afraid, as if something awful might happen (Q93a–g). The GAD-7 items describe the most-prominent features of the DSM-IV diagnostic criteria A, B, and C for GAD (Löwe et al., 2008). Respondents with sum scores greater than or equal to 10 were categorized as having probable GAD.

*Aggressive behavior (Q94).* To assess levels of aggressive behavior, respondents were asked to report how often in the past 30 days they had expressed anger in explosive or aggressive ways, as illustrated in four scenarios (e.g., threaten someone with physical violence, get angry at someone and yell or shout at them) (Q94a–d). Responses for each item ranged from never to five or more times in the past 30 days. This four-item measure has been used extensively in the Army's Land Combat Study to characterize aggressive behavior among service members (see, for example, Killgore et al., 2008; Thomas et al., 2010; Wilk, Bliese, Thomas, et al., 2013). Two categories of aggressive behavior were calculated based on responses. If personnel responded that they expressed any of the behaviors one or more times in the past 30 days, they were categorized as showing any aggressive behavior in the past month. If personnel responded that they expressed any of the behaviors five or more times, they were categorized as showing aggressive behavior 5+ times in the past month.

*Unwanted sexual contact (Q96, Q97).* To assess lifetime experience of unwanted sexual contact among service members, respondents were asked if they have ever in their lifetime experienced any sexual contact (such as sexual touching or oral, anal, or vaginal penetration) that was unwanted, against their will, or occurred when they did not or could not consent. If respondents answered yes (Q96 = 1), a follow-up question asked whether the unwanted sexual contact occurred while on active military duty or while not on active military duty, and respondents could select both.

*Physical abuse (Q98, Q99).* We refined the six yes-or-no items used in the 2011 HRBS to distinguish lifetime physical abuse while on active military duty and not on active military duty. Specifically, respondents were asked whether they had ever been "physically abused, punished, or beaten by a person in authority or having some power over you such that you received bruises, cuts, welts, lumps, or other injuries?" If respondents answered yes (Q98 = 1), a follow-up question asked if the physical abuse had occurred while on active military duty or while not on active military duty, and respondents could select both.

*Probable posttraumatic stress disorder (Q99).* To assess probable PTSD, respondents were asked to complete the PCL. The PCL is a standardized self-report rating scale for PTSD and comprises 17 items that correspond to the key symptoms of PTSD. A research team from the National Center of Posttraumatic Stress Disorder developed the scale in 1993 (Weathers et al., 1993). The PCL has a variety of purposes, including screening individuals for PTSD, diagnosing PTSD, and monitoring symptom change during and after treatment. A validation study conducted with a sample of 352 service members showed that both the Primary Care PTSD Screen and the PCL had good diagnostic efficiency (Bliese et al., 2008). The PCL-C (civilian version) is useful because it can be used with any population. The symptoms endorsed may not be specific to just one event, which can be helpful when assessing survivors who have symptoms resulting from multiple events. Respondents in the 2015 HRBS were shown a list of 19 problems and asked how much they have been bothered by these symptoms in the past 30 days (Q99a–q). Respondents indicated how much they had been bothered by a symptom over the past month using a five-point scale ranging from 1 (not at all) to 5 (extremely). Respondents with sum scores greater than or equal to 50 were categorized as having probable PTSD.

*Non-suicidal self-injury (Q107, Q108).* Respondents were asked, "In your lifetime, how often have you intentionally hurt yourself—for example, by scratching, cutting, or burning—even though you were not trying to kill yourself?" For those who indicated an affirmative answer (Q107 = 2–5), respondents were asked how often such self-harm had occurred since joining the military (Q108). For both questions, response options ranged from never to six or more times. These questions were taken from the 2011 HRBS; the 2015 item was adapted to state "not trying to kill yourself" instead of "not trying to commit suicide" (see Beaton, Forster, and Maple, 2013, for an explanation about why the latter wording should be avoided).

*Suicide ideation (Q109, Q110).* Respondents were asked, "In your lifetime, did you ever seriously think about trying to kill yourself?" This item was adapted from the 2011 HRBS, which asked, "Have you ever seriously considered suicide?" The 2015 question is less ambiguous and maps directly to questions asked in the NSDUH (CBHSQ, undated). Respondents who indicated that they had seriously thought about trying to kill themselves (Q109 = 1) were then asked whether they had had those thoughts at any time in the past 12 months, since joining the military, before joining the military, and during a deployment.

*Suicide attempts (Q111, Q112a, Q112b).* Respondents were asked, "In your lifetime, have you ever tried to kill yourself?" This item was adapted from the 2011 HRBS, which asked, "Have you ever attempted suicide?" The 2015 question is less ambiguous and maps directly to questions asked in the NSDUH (CBHSQ, undated). Respondents who indicated that they had tried to kill themselves were then asked whether they had done so during the past 12 months, since joining the military, before joining the military, and during a deployment. Respondents who answered yes (Q112a1–a4 = 1) to any of these four periods were then asked, specific to the referent period, whether they received medical attention from a doctor or other health professional as a result of an attempt to kill themselves (Q112b). This question was also derived from the NSDUH.

*High impulsivity (Q113).* The impulsivity item in the 2015 HRBS was adapted from the 2011 HRBS. This measure was specific to impulsivity, whereas the 2008 measure included items on risk-taking behaviors. Individuals responded to four items that assessed the frequency of impulsive behavior. The impulsivity scale was constructed from items that were combined and factor-analyzed using principal axis factor analysis in the 1990 HRBS survey. A single factor was suggested (with a Cronbach's alpha of 0.80) using the following items:

1. I often act on the spur of the moment without stopping to think.
2. I get a real kick out of doing things that are a little dangerous.
3. You might say I act impulsively.
4. I like to test myself every now and then by doing something a little chancy.
5. Many of my actions seem to be hasty.

Item 1 was adapted from Eysenk and Eysenk (1978), and items 3 and 5 were adapted from Jackson (1974). We excluded item 2 from the list for the 2015 HRBS. Response options for how much the statements describe the respondent ranged from "a great deal" to "not at all." We reverse-coded the items and created mean scores for each respondent. In line with the 2011 HRBS scoring, survey respondents with a mean score between 3 and 5 ("somewhat" to "a great deal") were categorized as having high impulsivity.

## Chapter 7: Physical Health and Functional Limitations

*Physical symptoms (Q33).* Respondents completed a symptom checklist comprised of eight common physical symptoms (stomach or bowel problems; back pain; pain in arms, legs, or joints; headaches; chest pain or shortness of breath; dizziness; fatigue; sleep troubles) (Gierk et al., 2014). Response options included not bothered at all, bothered a little bit, and bothered a lot in the past 30 days. We generated two measures of pain based on the following items: back pain; pain in the arms, legs, or joints; and headaches.

- We categorized a respondent as having pain if they indicated that they were bothered a little bit or a lot by back pain or pain in the arms, legs, or joints (Q33b or c = 2 or 3). We categorized respondents as having pain (including headaches) if they indicated that they were bothered a little bit or a lot by back pain; pain in the arms, legs, or joints; or headaches (Q33b, c, or d = 2 or 3).

We also developed a summary score by assigning each symptom a score of 0 (not bothered at all), 1 (bothered a little bit), or 2 (bothered a lot) and adding the values across all eight measures (score range = 0–16). Respondents whose summary score was 8 or more were categorized as having high physical symptom severity.

*Functional limitations (Q34).* Functional limitations were assessed using a modified version of the Sheehan Disability Scale (Sheehan, Harnett-Sheehan, and Raj, 1996). Respondents completed five items assessing the extent that health problems impair functioning in three domains: work or school, social life, and family life or home responsibilities. Respondents who indicated that a domain was diminished moderately, markedly, or extremely (Q34a–c ≥ 4) were categorized as having a functional impairment.

## Chapter 8: Sexual and Reproductive Health

*More than one sex partner in the past 12 months (Q84).* The item was adapted from the 2010 National HIV Behavioral Surveillance System Questionnaire. Those providing a response of at least two people (Q84 ≤ 4) were categorized as having more than one sex partner in the past 12 months.

*Past-year sex with a new sex partner without using a condom (Q85).* The item was adapted from the 2011 HRBS. RAND added "(vaginal or anal)" after "intercourse" to more clearly define the behavior being measured. Those who gave responses of never, seldom, sometimes, or often (Q85 = 2, 3, 4, or 5) were categorized as having sex with a new partner without using a condom.

*Used a condom during most-recent vaginal sex (Q88).* Respondents were asked whether they used any form of birth control the most-recent time they had vaginal sex. Those who responded "yes, condoms" (Q88 = 11) were categorized as using a condom during their most-recent vaginal sex.

*Did not use birth control during most-recent vaginal sex (Q88).* Respondents were asked whether they used any form of birth control the most-recent time they had vaginal sex. Those who responded "no, we didn't use any form of birth control" (Q88 = 2) were categorized as not using birth control during their most-recent vaginal sex.

*Used sterilization or long-acting contraception during most-recent vaginal sex (Q88).* Respondents were asked whether they used any form of birth control the most-recent time they had vaginal sex. Those responding "yes, female sterilization" (Q88 = 5); "yes, male sterilization" (Q88 = 6); "yes, an IUD" (Q88 = 7); or "yes, a contraceptive implant" (Q88 = 8) were classified as using sterilization or long-acting contraception. Those responding with "yes, birth control pills" (Q88 = 9); "yes, birth control shots, birth control patch, contraceptive ring, or a diaphragm" (Q88 = 10); "yes, condoms" (Q88 = 11); or " yes, some other method" (Q88 = 12) were classified as using short-acting contraception, and those responding "no, we didn't use any form of birth control" (Q88 = 2) were categorized as not using any method of contraception during their most-recent vaginal sex. Individuals using both short- and long-acting contraception were categorized as using long-acting contraception.

*Past-year unintended pregnancy (Q89).* Respondents were asked whether they caused or had an unintended pregnancy in the past 12 months. Those responding yes (Q89 = 1) were categorized as causing or experiencing an unintended pregnancy in the past year.

*Past-year HIV test (Q90).* Respondents were asked when their last HIV test occurred. Those responding "within the past 12 months (Q90 = 1) were categorized as having an HIV test in the past year.

*Past-year sexually transmitted infection (Q91).* Respondents were asked whether they had ever had an STI. Those responding "yes, contracted something within the past 12 months" (Q91 = 1) were categorized as having a past-year STI.

*High risk for HIV infection (Q8, Q84, Q86, Q87, Q91).* The 2015 HRBS defined those at high risk for HIV infection as men who had sex with one or more men in the past year, those who had vaginal or anal sex with more than one partner in the past year, and those who had a past-year STI (CDC, 2011; CDC, 2016c). Men who had sex with one or more men were determined based on the measures for same-sex activity (described below; Q86, Q87) and gender (Q8). The derivations of vaginal or anal sex with more than one partner in the past year (Q84) and past-year STI (Q91) are described above.

## Chapter 9: Sexual Orientation, Transgender Identity, and Health

*Same-sex activity (Q8, Q86, Q87).* This measure was determined based on responses to Q8 (gender), Q86, and Q87. Men providing any response to Q86 other than "no male partners in the past 12 months" (Q86 = 6) were categorized as having one or more same-sex partners. All other men responding to Q86 were categorized as not having such a partner. Women providing any response to Q87 other than "no female partners in the past 12 months" (Q87 = 6) were categorized as having one or more same-sex partners. All other women responding to Q87 were categorized as not having such a partner.

*Same-sex attraction (Q126).* The item was asked of Coast Guard respondents to the 2011 HRBS. A comparable item that excludes the response option "not attracted to either males or females" (Q126 = 6) has been included in prior national surveys (Chandra, Mosher, and Copen, 2011) and is recommended by the Sexual Minority Assessment Research Team expert panel on measurement of sexual orientation (Sexual Minority Assessment Research Team, 2009).

*Sexual identity (Q127).* This item was chosen based on recommendations by the Sexual Minority Assessment Research Team expert panel (Sexual Minority Assessment Research Team, 2009). Service members giving a response of "gay or lesbian" (Q127 = 2) or "bisexual" (Q127 = 3) were categorized as LGB.

*Transgender identity (Q128).* The item was chosen based on recommendations by the Gender Identity in U.S. Surveillance Group expert panel (Herman, 2014). Service members giving a response of yes (Q128 = 1) to Q128 or a response of "gay or lesbian" (Q127 = 2) or "bisexual" (Q127 = 3) to Q127 were categorized as LGBT.

## Chapter 10: Deployment Experiences and Health

*Previous deployment history (Q114).* Respondents were asked to report when their most-recent deployment (combat or noncombat) started. Any reported start time other than "I have never been deployed" (Q114 = 5) indicated the respondent had at least one previous deployment. Those who reported that they have never been deployed were skipped past all remaining questions pertaining to deployment. Respondents who indicated they had deployed (Q114 ≤ 4) were included in each of the following questions related to deployment and were categorized as having at least one previous deployment.

*Recent deployment (Q115).* To assess the recency of military service members' deployments, respondents were asked to report when their most-recent deployment started and ended. Respondents who indicated that they had a deployment that ended within three years of the 2015 HRBS survey (Q115 = 1 or 2) were categorized as recently deployed (or deployed within the past three years).

*Type of most-recent deployment (Q116).* To examine the effect of recent deployments by deployment type on various health-related behaviors, respondents were asked whether their most-recent deployment was to a combat or noncombat zone. Although respondents could report being exposed to combat scenarios on noncombat deployments, the survey defined a combat-zone deployment as one that typically receives imminent danger pay, hazardous duty pay, or combat-zone tax exclusion benefits.

*Deployment-related alcohol, tobacco, and substance use (Q117).* Respondents were asked how often they used the following substances during their most-recent deployment: alcohol, cigarettes, chewing/smokeless tobacco, cigars, prescription medications, marijuana, and opiates (opium, morphine, heroin, etc.). Response options were provided on a five-point scale, ranging from never (Q117 = 5) to regularly or daily (Q117 = 1). Respondents who indicated they had used one of the substances with any frequency while deployed were categorized as having used that substance during their most-recent deployment.

*Number of previous deployments in a lifetime (Q118).* To measure total deployments to combat and noncombat zones across all years of service, respondents were asked how many times they had deployed while serving in the military. Response options included 1 time (Q118 = 1), 2 times (Q118 = 2), and 3 or more times (Q118 = 3).

*Duration of previous deployments (Q119).* An item asked about the total duration of time spent deployed in combat and noncombat zones across all years of military service. Response options included 1 to 6 months (Q119 = 1), 7 to 12 months (Q119 = 2), 13 to 24 months (Q119 = 3), 25 to 48 months (Q119 = 4), and 49 months or more (Q119 = 5).

*Number of combat deployments (Q120).* To measure total deployments to combat zones, respondents were asked how many of all their deployments were combat-zone deployments. Response options were provided on a 4-point scale, ranging from "I have not had any combat deployments" to "3 or more combat-zone deployments."

*Deployment-related injury and possible traumatic brain injury (Q121, Q122).* Probable TBI was assessed using the Brief Traumatic Brain Injury Screen (Schwab et al., 2006). The first of a set of items (Q121) asked about six events experienced during deployment, including any injury that may have resulted from a fragment (Q121 = 1), bullet (Q121 = 2), vehicular accident/crash (Q121 = 3), fall (Q121 = 4), blast or explosion (Q121 = 5), or injury from other event (Q121 = 6). Respondents who indicated that they had experienced an injury from any of these events were categorized as having a deployment-related injury.

The second item (Q122) asked whether an injury received during any deployment resulted in any of the following outcomes:

- lost consciousness or got "knocked out" for less than a minute (Q122a = 1)
- lost consciousness or got "knocked out" for 1 to 20 minutes (Q122b = 1)
- lost consciousness or got "knocked out" for more than 20 minutes (Q122c = 1)
- felt dazed, confused, or saw stars (Q122d = 1)
- didn't remember the event (Q122e = 1)
- concussion or symptoms of a concussion (such as headache, dizziness, irritability, etc.) (Q122f = 1)
- head injury (Q122g = 1).

Respondents who answered that they had experienced an injury in Q121 and indicated that, as a result of the event, they lost consciousness or got "knocked out" for less than a minute (Q122a = 1), lost consciousness or got "knocked out" for 1 to 20 minutes (Q122b = 1), felt dazed, confused, or "saw stars" (Q122d = 1), or didn't remember the event (Q122e = 1) were categorized as screening positive for probable mTBI. Respondents who answered that they had an injury in Q121 and indicated that they lost consciousness or got "knocked out" for more than 20 minutes (Q122c = 1) were categorized as screening positive for probable moderate to severe TBI.

*Postconcussive symptoms (Q121, Q122, Q123).* A positive screen for postconcussive symptoms required a positive screen for mTBI or moderate to severe TBI (Q121 and Q122; see above) and either (1) endorsement of four or more of the symptoms in Q123 (headaches, dizziness, memory problems or lapses, balance problems, ringing in the ears, irritability, sleep problems, sensitivity to light, other) or (2) a positive response for "concussion or symptoms of a concussion (such as headache, dizziness, irritability, etc.)" in Q122.

*Military experiences during deployment (Q124).* To measure combat-related traumatic experiences, the 2015 HRBS used an 18-item inventory that asked about exposure to various combat situations during deployment. The item is a composite of several existing combat exposure scales, including a seven-item scale used by the VA (National Center for PTSD, 2016a; Hoge, Castro, et al., 2004; Keane et al., 1989) and the 17-item Deployment Risk and Resilience Inventory (National Center for PTSD, 2016b; Vogt et al., 2013). Respondents were asked to indicate the number of times, across all previous deployments, they had experienced each combat-related event, such as, "I personally fired my weapon at the enemy," "my unit suffered casualties," and "I was wounded in combat" (Q124a–r). Response options were provided on a five-point scale, ranging from never (Q124 = 1) to more than 50 times (Q124 = 5). We created a summary score using each item: more than 50 times = 4, 20 to 50 times = 3, 6 to 19 times = 2, 1 to 5 times = 1, and never = 0. We then examined the distribution of these responses in our data and determined that a score of 5 or more would serve as a cutoff. Respondents with a score of 5 or more were categorized as having high combat exposure, and those with scores of less than 5 were categorized as having low to moderate exposure. This question represents cumulative exposure across all previous deployments. It also reflects different patterns of exposure; for example, a service member who experienced five different events once each and a service member who experienced one event 50 or more times would both receive a score of 5 on the measure and be categorized as having high combat exposure.

*Duration of deployments in the past 12 months (Q125).* Respondents were asked about total duration of time spent deployed in combat and noncombat zones in the past 12 months. Response options included "I did not deploy in the past 12 months" (Q125 = 1), "less than 1 month" (Q125 = 2), "1 to 3 months" (Q125 = 3), "4 to 6 months" (Q125 = 4), "7 to 9 months" (Q125 = 5), and "10 to 12 months" (Q125 = 6).

# References

Acosta, J., A. Becker, J. L. Cerully, M. P. Fisher, L. T. Martin, R. Vardavas, M. E. Slaughter, and T. L. Schell, *Mental Health Stigma in the Military*, Santa Monica, Calif.: RAND Corporation, RR-426-OSD, 2014. As of January 9, 2017:
http://www.rand.org/pubs/research_reports/RR426.html

Adler, A. B., T. W. Britt, L. A. Riviere, P. K. Kim, and J. L. Thomas, "Longitudinal Determinants of Mental Health Treatment-Seeking by U.S. Soldiers," *British Journal of Psychiatry*, Vol. 38, 2015, pp.142–149.

Armed Forces Health Surveillance Center, "Associations Between Repeated Deployments to Iraq (OIF/OND) and Afghanistan (OEF) and Post-Deployment Illnesses and Injuries, Active Component, U.S. Armed Forces, 2003–2010: Part II. Mental Disorders, by Gender, Age Group, Military Occupation, and 'Dwell Times' Prior to Repeat (Second Through Fifth) Deployments," *Medical Surveillance Monthly Report*, Vol. 18, No. 9, September 2011. As of July 16, 2016:
https://www.afhsc.mil/documents/pubs/msmrs/2011/v18_n09.pdf

Arria, A. M., K. M. Caldeira, S. J. Kasperski, K. E. O'Grady, K. B., Vincent, R. R. Griffths, and E. D. Wish, "Increased Alcohol Consumption, Nonmedical Prescription Drug Use, and Illicit Drug Use Are Associated with Energy Drink Consumption Among College Students," *Journal of Addiction Medicine*, Vol. 4, 2010, pp. 74–80.

Assistant Secretary of Defense for Health Affairs, *Periodic Health Assessment Policy for Active Duty and Selected Reserve Members*, Memorandum 06-006, February 16, 2006.

Babor, T., *Alcohol: No Ordinary Commodity: Research and Public Policy*, Oxford, UK: Oxford University Press, 2010.

Barlas, F. M., W. B. Higgins, J. C. Pflieger, and K. Dieckler, *2011 Department of Defense Health Related Behaviors Survey of Active Duty Military Personnel*, ICF International, 2013.

Barsky, A. J., H. M. Peekna, and J. F. Borus, "Somatic Symptom Reporting in Women and Men," *Journal of General Internal Medicine*, Vol. 16, No. 4, 2001, pp. 266–275.

Beaton, S., P. Forster, and M. Maple, "Suicide and Language: Why We Shouldn't Use the 'C' Word," *InPsych*, Vol. 35, No. 1, 2013. As of July 20, 2016:
https://www.psychology.org.au/Content.aspx?ID=5048

Belsher, B. E., J. Curry, P. McCutchan, T. Oxman, K. A. Corso, K. Williams, and C. C. Engel, "Implementation of a Collaborative Care Initiative for PTSD and Depression in the Army Primary Care System," *Social Work in Mental Health*, Vol. 12, No. 5–6, 2014, pp. 500–522.

Bliese, P. D., K. M. Wright, A. B. Adler, O. Cabrera, C. A. Castro, and C. W. Hoge, "Validating the Primary Care Posttraumatic Stress Disorder Screen and the Posttraumatic Stress Disorder Checklist with Soldiers Returning from Combat," *Journal of Consulting and Clinical Psychology*, Vol. 76, No. 2, 2008, pp. 272–281.

Bradley, K. A., A. F. DeBenedetti, R. J. Volk, E. C. Williams, D. Frank, and D. R. Kivlahan, "AUDIT-C as a Brief Screen for Alcohol Misuse in Primary Care," *Alcoholism: Clinical and Experimental Research*, Vol. 31, No. 7, 2007, pp. 1208–1217.

Bramoweth, A. D., and A. Germain, "Deployment-Related Insomnia in Military Personnel and Veterans," *Current Psychiatry Reports*, Vol. 15, No. 10, 2013, pp. 401–404.

Bray, R. M., L. L. Hourani, K. L. R. Olmstead, M. Witt, J. Brown, M. R. Pemberton, M. E. Marsden, B. Marriott, S. Scheffler, and R. Vandermaas-Peeler, *2005 Department of Defense Survey of Health Related Behaviors Among Active Duty Military Personnel*, RTI International, 2006.

Bray, R. M., L. L. Hourani, K. L. Rae, Jill A. Dever, J. M. Brown, A. A. Vincus, M. R. Pemberton, M. E. Marsden, D. L. Faulkner, and R. Vandermaas-Peeler, *2002 Department of Defense Survey of Health Related Behaviors Among Military Personnel*, RTI International, 2003.

Bray, R. M., M. R. Pemberton, L. L. Hourani, M. Witt, K. L. R. Olmstead, J. M. Brown, B. Weimer, M. E. Lane, M. E. Marsden, S. Scheffler, R. Vandermaas-Peeler, K. R. Aspinwall, E. Anderson, K. Spagnola, K. Close, J. L. Gratton, S. Calvin, and M. Bradshaw, *2008 Department of Defense Survey of Health Related Behaviors Among Active Duty Military Personnel*, ICF International, 2009.

Brick, J. Michael, and Douglas Williams, "Explaining Rising Nonresponse Rates in Cross-Sectional Surveys," *Annals of the American Academy of Political and Social Science*, Vol. 645, No. 1, 2013, pp. 36–59.

Brown, G. K., T. T. Have, G. R. Henriques, S. X. Xie, J. E. Hollander, and A. T. Beck, "Cognitive Therapy for the Prevention of Suicide Attempts: A Randomized Controlled Trial," *Journal of the American Medical Association*, Vol. 294, No. 5, 2005, pp. 563–570.

Bryan, C. J., and A. O. Bryan, "Nonsuicidal Self-Injury Among a Sample of United States Military Personnel and Veterans Enrolled in College Classes," *Journal of Clinical Psychology*, Vol. 70, No. 9, 2014, pp. 874–885.

Bryan, C. J., A. O. Bryan, A. M. May, and E. D. Klonsky, "Trajectories of Suicide Ideation, Nonsuicidal Self-Injury, and Suicide Attempts in a Nonclinical Sample of Military Personnel and Veterans," *Suicide and Life-Threatening Behavior,* Vol. 45, No. 3, 2015, pp. 315–325.

Bryan, C. J., M. D. Rudd, E. Wertenberger, S. Young-McCaughon, and A. Peterson, "Nonsuicidal Self-Injury as a Prospective Predictor of Suicide Attempts in a Clinical Sample of Military Personnel," *Comprehensive Psychiatry*, Vol. 59, 2015, pp. 1–7.

Bush, K., D. R. Kivlahan, M. B. McDonell, S. D. Fihn, and K. A. Bradley, "The AUDIT Alcohol Consumption Questions (AUDIT-C): An Effective Brief Screening Test for Problem Drinking, Ambulatory Care Quality Improvement Project (ACQUIP)—Alcohol Use Disorders Identification Test," *Archives of Internal Medicine*, Vol. 158, No. 16, 1998, pp. 1789–1795.

Caird, J. K., K. A. Johnston, C. R. Willness, M. Asbridge, and P. Steel, "A Meta-Analysis of the Effects of Texting on Driving," *Accident Analysis and Prevention*, Vol. 71, 2014, pp. 311–318.

Callahan-Lyon, Priscilla, "Electronic Cigarettes: Human Health Effects," *Tobacco Control*, Vol. 23, Supp. 2, 2014, pp. ii36–ii40.

Capaldi, V. F. II, M. L. Guerrero, and W. D. Killgore, "Sleep Disruptions Among Returning Combat Veterans from Iraq and Afghanistan," *Military Medicine,* Vol. 175, No. 8, 2011, pp. 879–888.

Carlson, K. F., D. Nelson, R. J. Orazem, S. Nugent, D. X. Cifu, and N. A. Sayer, "Psychiatric Diagnoses Among Iraq and Afghanistan War Veterans Screened for Deployment-Related Traumatic Brain Injury," *Journal of Traumatic Stress,* Vol. 23, No. 1, 2010, pp. 17–24.

CBHSQ—*See* Center for Behavioral Health Statistics and Quality.

CDC—*See* Centers for Disease Control and Prevention.

Center for Behavioral Health Statistics and Quality, "National Survey on Drug Use and Health," web page, undated. As of January 9, 2017:
https://nsduhwebesn.rti.org/respweb/homepage.cfm

———, *Behavioral Health Trends in the United States: Results from the 2014 National Survey on Drug Use and Health*, Rockville, Md.: Substance Abuse and Mental Health Services Administration, SMA 15-4927, 2015a. As of July 19, 2016:
https://www.samhsa.gov/data/sites/default/files/NSDUH-FRR1-2014/NSDUH-FRR1-2014.pdf

———, *Results from the 2014 National Survey on Drug Use and Health: Detailed Tables*, Rockville, Md.: Substance Abuse and Mental Health Services Administration, 2015b. As of January 9, 2017:
http://www.samhsa.gov/data/sites/default/files/NSDUH-DetTabs2014/NSDUH-DetTabs2014.htm#tab2-46b

Centers for Disease Control and Prevention, "Sleep and Sleep Disorders: Data and Statistics," web page, 2009. As of July 19, 2016:
http://www.cdc.gov/sleep/data_statistics.html

———, "HIV Testing Among Men Who Have Sex with Men—21 Cities, United States, 2008," *Morbidity and Mortality Weekly Report*, Vol. 60, No. 21, 2011, pp. 694–699.

———, "Energy Drink Consumption and Its Association with Sleep Problems Among U.S. Service Members on a Combat Deployment—Afghanistan," *Morbidity and Mortality Weekly Report*, Vol. 61, No. 44, 2012, pp. 895–898.

———, *Best Practices for Comprehensive Tobacco Control Programs*, Atlanta, Ga.: U.S. Department of Health and Human Services, 2014. As of July 19, 2016:
https://www.cdc.gov/tobacco/stateandcommunity/best_practices/pdfs/2014/comprehensive.pdf

———, "About Adult BMI," web page, 2015a. As of July 19, 2016:
https://www.cdc.gov/healthyweight/assessing/bmi/adult_bmi/

———, "About Child & Teen BMI," web page, 2015b. As of July 19, 2016:
https://www.cdc.gov/healthyweight/assessing/bmi/childrens_bmi/about_childrens_bmi.html

———, "Crude and Age-Adjusted Rates of Diagnosed Diabetes per 100 Civilian, Non-Institutionalized Population, United States, 1980–2014," Diabetes Public Health Resource web page, 2015c. As of July 26, 2016:
http://www.cdc.gov/diabetes/statistics/prev/national/figage.htm

———, "Current Cigarette Smoking Among Adults—United States, 2005–2014," *Morbidity and Mortality Weekly Report*, Vol. 64, No. 44, 2015d, pp. 1233–1240.

———, "High Cholesterol Facts," web page, 2015e. As of July 26, 2016:
http://www.cdc.gov/cholesterol/facts.htm

———, *2014 National Health Interview Survey: Public Use Data Release*, National Center for Health Statistics, June 2015f. As of January 9, 2017:
ftp://ftp.cdc.gov/pub/Health_Statistics/NCHS/Dataset_Documentation/NHIS/2014/srvydesc.pdf

———, "Chronic Diseases: The Leading Causes of Death and Disability in the United States," Chronic Disease Prevention and Health Promotion web page, 2016a. As of July 26, 2016:
http://www.cdc.gov/chronicdisease/overview/index.htm

———, "High Blood Pressure Fact Sheet," Division for Heart Disease and Stroke Prevention web page, 2016b. As of July 26, 2016:
http://www.cdc.gov/dhdsp/data_statistics/fact_sheets/fs_bloodpressure.htm

———, "HIV/AIDS: Testing," web page, 2016c. As of July 19, 2016:
http://www.cdc.gov/hiv/basics/testing.html

———, "Lifetime Risk of Symptomatic Osteoarthritis (OA)," web page, 2016d. As of July 26, 2016:
http://www.cdc.gov/arthritis/data_statistics/arthritis-related-stats.htm

Chandra, A., W. D. Mosher, and C. Copen, *Sexual Behavior, Sexual Attraction, and Sexual Identity in the United States: Data from the 2006-2008 National Survey of Family Growth*, National Health Statistics Report, No. 36, March 2011.

Cherpitel, C. J., "Alcohol, Injury, and Risk-Taking Behavior: Data from a National Sample," *Alcoholism: Clinical and Experimental Research*, Vol. 17, No. 4, 1993, pp. 762–766.

———, "Substance Use, Injury, and Risk-Taking Dispositions in the General Population," *Alcoholism: Clinical and Experimental Research*, Vol. 23, No. 1, 1999, pp. 121–126.

Ciccone, D. S., D. K. Elliott, H. K. Chandler, S. Nayak, and K. G. Raphael, "Sexual and Physical Abuse in Women with Fibromyalgia Syndrome: A Test of the Trauma Hypothesis," *Clinical Journal of Pain*, Vol. 21, No. 5, September/October 2005, pp. 378–386.

Clement, S., O. Schauman, T. Graham, F. Maggioni, S. Evans-Lacko, N. Bezborodovs, C. Morgan, N. Rusch, J. S. Brown, and G. Thornicroft, "What Is the Impact of Mental Health-Related Stigma on Help-Seeking? A Systematic Review of Quantitative and Qualitative Studies," *Psychologic Medicine*, Vol. 45, No. 1, 2015, pp. 11–27.

Cohen, D. A., R. A. Scribner, and T. A. Farley, "A Structural Model of Health Behavior: A Pragmatic Approach to Explain and Influence Health Behaviors at the Population Level," *Preventive Medicine*, Vol. 30, No. 2, 2000, pp. 146–154.

Contractor, A. A., J. D. Elhai, T. H. Fine, M. B. Tamburrino, G. Cohen, E. Shirley, P. K. Chan, I. Liberzon, S. Galea, and J. R. Calabrese, "Latent Profile Analyses of Posttraumatic Stress Disorder, Depression and Generalized Anxiety Disorder Symptoms in Trauma-Exposed Soldiers," *Journal of Psychiatric Research*, Vol. 68, September 2015, pp. 19–26.

Coulter, I. D., S. Newberry, and L. Hilton, *Regulation of Dietary Supplements in the Military: Report of an Expert Panel*, Santa Monica, Calif.: RAND Corporation, CF-288-SAMUELI, 2011. As of July 19, 2016: http://www.rand.org/pubs/conf_proceedings/CF288.html

Creed, F. H., I. Davies, J. Jackson, A. Littlewood, C. Chew-Graham, B. Tomenson, G. Macfarlane, A. Barsky, W. Katon, and J. McBeth, "The Epidemiology of Multiple Somatic Symptoms," *Journal of Psychosomatic Research*, Vol. 72, No. 4, 2012, pp. 311–317.

Crosby, A. E., L. Ortega, and C. Melanson, *Self-Directed Violence Surveillance: Uniform Definitions and Recommended Data Elements*, Atlanta, Ga.: Centers for Disease Control and Prevention, 2011.

Crum-Cianflone, N. F., and I. Jacobson, "Gender Differences of Postdeployment Post-Traumatic Stress Disorder Among Service Members and Veterans of the Iraq and Afghanistan Conflicts," *Epidemiology Review*, Vol. 36, 2014, pp. 5–18.

Cucolo, A. A. III, "Prohibited Activities for Multi-National Division-North," General Order Number 1, Iraq: Department of the Army, November 4, 2009. As of January 9, 2017: https://www.nytimes.com/interactive/projects/documents/general-order-no-1-prohibited-activities-for-soldiers

Dall, T. M., Y. Zhang, Y. J. Chen, R. C. Askarinam Wagner, P. F. Hogan, N. K. Fagan, S. T. Olaiya, and D. N. Tornberg, "Cost Associated with Being Overweight and with Obesity, High Alcohol Consumption, and Tobacco Use Within the Military Health System's TRICARE Prime-Enrolled Population," *American Journal of Health Promotion*, Vol. 22, No. 2, 2007, pp. 120–139.

Davern, M., "Nonresponse Rates Are a Problematic Indicator of Nonresponse Bias in Survey Research," *Health Services Research*, Vol. 48, No. 3, 2013, pp. 905–912.

Davis, Lisa, Amanda Grifka, Kristin Williams, and Margaret Coffey, eds., *2016 Workplace and Gender Relations Survey of Active Duty Members*, Alexandria, Va.: U.S. Department of Defense, Office of People Analytics, May 2017. As of July 26, 2017: http://www.sapr.mil/public/docs/reports/FY16_Annual/Annex_1_2016_WGRA_Report.pdf

Defense Health Board, *Implications of Trends in Obesity and Overweight for the Department of Defense*, Falls Church, Va., November 22, 2013.

Defense Manpower Data Center, "Active Duty Military Personnel Master File," provided to RAND, September 2014.

Department of the Navy, *Periodic Health Assessment for Individual Medical Readiness*, Secretary of the Navy Instruction 6120.3, September 14, 2007.

Diamond, Jeremy, "Trump to Reinstate U.S. Military Ban on Transgender People," CNN, July 26, 2017. As of July 27, 2017: http://www.cnn.com/2017/07/26/politics/trump-military-transgender/index.html

Dillman, D. A., J. D. Smyth, and L. M. Christian, *Internet, Mail, and Mixed-Mode Surveys: The Tailored Design Method*, 3rd ed., Hoboken, N.J.: Wiley and Sons, 2009.

DoD—*See* U.S. Department of Defense.

Douglas, J. M., Jr., and K. A. Fenton, "Understanding Sexual Health and Its Role in More Effective Prevention Programs," *Public Health Reports*, Vol. 128, Supp. 1, 2013.

Escobar, J. I., J. M. Golding, R. L. Hough, M. Karno, M. A. Burnam, and K. B. Wells, "Somatization in the Community: Relationship to Disability and Use of Services," *American Journal of Public Health*, Vol. 77, No. 7, 1987, pp. 837–840.

Eysenck, S. B. G., and H. J. Eysenck, "Impulsiveness and Venturesomeness: Their Position in a Dimensional System of Personality Description," *Psychological Reports*, Vol. 43, December 1978, pp. 1247–1255.

Fan, W., and Z. Yan, "Factors Affecting Response Rates of the Web Survey: A Systematic Review," *Computers in Human Behavior*, Vol. 26, No. 2, March 2010, pp. 132–139.

Fanslow, J., and E. Robinson, "Violence Against Women in New Zealand: Prevalence and Health Consequences," *New Zealand Medical Journal*, Vol. 117, No. 1206, November 2004, pp. 1–12.

Finer, L. B., and M. R. Zolna, "Declines in Unintended Pregnancy in the United States, 2008–2011," *New England Journal of Medicine*, Vol. 374, No. 9, 2016, pp. 843–852.

Flores, A. R., J. L. Herman, G. J. Gates, and T. N. T. Brown, *How Many Adults Identify as Transgender in the United States?* Los Angeles: The Williams Institute, 2016.

Frayne, S. M., K. M. Skinner, L. M. Sullivan, T. J. Tripp, C. S. Hankin, N. R. Kressin, and D. R. Miller, "Medical Profile of Women Veterans Administration Outpatients Who Report a History of Sexual Assault Occurring While in the Military," *Journal of Women's Health and Gender-Based Medicine*, Vol. 8, 1999, pp. 835–845.

Fukuda, K., R. Nisenbaum, G. Stewart, W. W. Thompson, L. Robin, R. M. Washko, D. L. Noah, D. H. Barrett, B. Randall, B. L. Herwaldt, A. C. Mawle, and W. C. Reeves, "Chronic Multisymptom Illness Affecting Air Force Veterans of the Gulf War," *Journal of the American Medical Association*, Vol. 280, No. 11, 1998, pp. 981–988.

Gadermann, A. M., C. C. Engel, J. A. Naifeh, M. K. Nock, M. Petukhova, P. N. Santiago, B. Wu, A. M. Zaslavsky, and R. C. Kessler, "Prevalence of DSM-IV Major Depression Among U.S. Military Personnel: Meta-Analysis and Simulation," *Military Medicine*, Vol. 177, No. 8, Supp., 2012, pp. 47–59.

Gahche, J., R. Bailey, V. Burt, J. Hughes, E. Yetley, J. Dwyer, M. F. Picciano, M. McDowell, and C. Sempos, "Dietary Supplement Use Among U.S. Adults Has Increased Since NHANES III (1988–1994)," NCHS Data Brief No. 61, 2011.

Galesic, M., and M. Bosnjak, "Effects of Questionnaire Length on Participation and Indicators of Response Quality in a Web Survey," *Public Opinion Quarterly*, Vol. 73, No. 2, 2009, pp. 349–360.

Gates, G. J., *Lesbian, Gay, and Bisexual Men and Women in the U.S. Military: Updated Estimates*, Los Angeles: The Williams Institute, 2010. As of June 1, 2016:
https://escholarship.org/uc/item/0gn4t6t3

Gates, G. J., and F. Newport, "Special Report: 3.4% of U.S. Adults Identify as LGBT," Gallup, 2012. As of June 1, 2016:
http://www.gallup.com/poll/158066/
special-report-adults-identify-lgbt.aspx?utm_source=LGBT&utm_medium=search&utm_campaign=tiles

Gerteis, J., D. Izrael, D. Deitz, L. LeRoy, R. Ricciardi, T. Miller, and J. Basu, *Multiple Chronic Conditions Chartbook*, Rockville, Md.: Agency for Healthcare Research and Quality, AHRQ Publication No. Q14-0038, 2014.

Gierk, B., S. Kohlmann, K. Kroenke, L. Spangenberg, M. Zenger, E. Brahler, and B. Löwe, "The Somatic Symptom Scale-8 (SSS-8): A Brief Measure of Somatic Symptom Burden," *JAMA Internal Medicine*, Vol. 174, No. 3, 2014, pp. 399–407.

Goertz, C., B. P. Marriott, M. D. Finch, R. M. Bray, T. V. Williams, L. L. Hourani, L. S. Hadden, H. L. Colleran, and W. B. Jonas, "Military Report More Complementary and Alternative Medicine Use Than Civilians," *Journal of Alternative Complementary Medicine*, Vol. 19, No. 6, 2013, pp. 509–517.

Golding, J. M., "Sexual Assault History and Physical Health in Randomly Selected Los Angeles Women," *Health Psychology*, Vol. 13, No. 2, March 1994, pp. 130–138.

Grana, R., N. Benowitz, and S. A. Glantz, "E-Cigarettes: A Scientific Review," *Circulation*, Vol. 129, May 2014, pp. 1972–1986.

Groves, R. M., "Nonresponse Rates and Nonresponse Bias in Household Surveys," *Public Opinion Quarterly*, Vol. 70, No. 5, 2006, pp. 646–675.

Halbesleben, J. R. B., and M. V. Whitman, "Evaluating Survey Quality in Health Services Research: A Decision Framework for Assessing Nonresponse Bias," *Health Services Research*, Vol. 48, No. 3, 2013, pp. 913–930.

Harris, E. C., and B. Barraclough, "Suicide as an Outcome for Mental Disorders: A Meta-Analysis," *British Journal of Psychiatry*, Vol. 170, 1997, pp. 205–228.

Harwood, H. J., Y. Zhang, T. M. Dall, S. T. Olaiya, and N. K. Fagan, "Economic Implications of Reduced Binge Drinking Among the Military Health System's TRICARE Prime Plan Beneficiaries," *Military Medicine*, Vol. 174, No. 7, 2009, pp. 728–736.

Hawton, K., K. Houston, C. Haw, E. Townsend, and L. Harriss, "Comorbidity of Axis I and Axis II Disorders in Patients Who Attempted Suicide," *American Journal of Psychiatry*, Vol. 160, No. 8, 2003, pp. 1494–1500.

Headquarters, Department of the Army, *Standards of Medical Fitness*, Army Regulation 40-501, Washington, D.C., 2007. As of July 19, 2016:
http://www.au.af.mil/au/awc/awcgate/army/r40_501.pdf

Herman, J. L., ed., *Best Practices for Asking Questions to Identify Transgender and Other Gender Minority Respondents on Population-Based Surveys*, Gender Identity in U.S. Surveillance Group, Los Angeles: Williams Institute, 2014.

HHS—*See* U.S. Department of Health and Human Services.

Hoedeman R., A. H. Blankenstein, B. Krol, P. C. Koopmans, and J. W. Groothoff, "The Contribution of High Levels of Somatic Symptom Severity to Sickness Absence Duration, Disability and Discharge," *Journal of Occupational Rehabilitation*, Vol. 20, No. 2, 2010, pp. 264–273.

Hoffman, D. L., E. M. Dukes, and H. U. Wittchen, "Human and Economic Burden of Generalized Anxiety Disorder," *Depression and Anxiety*, Vol. 25, No. 1, 2008, pp. 72–90.

Hoge, C. W., J. L. Auchterlonie, and C. S. Milliken, "Mental Health Problems, Use of Mental Health Services, and Attrition from Military Service After Returning from Deployment to Iraq or Afghanistan," *Journal of the American Medical Association*, Vol. 295, No. 9, 2006, pp. 1023–1032.

Hoge, C. W., C. A. Castro, S. C. Messer, D. McGurk, D. I. Cotting, and R. L. Koffman, "Combat Duty in Iraq and Afghanistan, Mental Health Problems, and Barriers to Care," *New England Journal of Medicine*, Vol. 351, No. 1, 2004, pp. 13–22.

Hoge, C. W., S. H. Grossman, J. L. Auchterlonie, L. A. Riviere, C. S. Milliken, and J. E. Wilk, "PTSD Treatment for Soldiers After Combat Deployment: Low Utilization of Mental Health Care and Reasons for Dropout," *Psychiatric Services*, Vol. 65, No. 8, 2014, pp. 997–1004.

Hoge, C. W., D. McGurk, J. L. Thomas, A. L. Cox, C. C. Engel, and C. A. Castro, "Mild Traumatic Brain Injury in U.S. Soldiers Returning from Iraq," *New England Journal of Medicine*, Vol. 358, No. 5, 2008, pp. 453–463.

Hoge, C. W., A. Terhakopian, C. A. Castro, S. C. Messer, and C. C. Engel, "Association of Posttraumatic Stress Disorder with Somatic Symptoms, Health Care Visits, and Absenteeism Among Iraq War Veterans," *American Journal of Psychiatry*, Vol. 164, No. 1, 2007, pp. 150–153.

Hubacher, D., H. Spector, C. Monteith, P.-L. Chen, and C. Hart, "Long-Acting Reversible Contraceptive Acceptability and Unintended Pregnancy Among Women Presenting for Short-Acting Methods: A Randomized Patient Preference Trial," *American Journal of Obstetrics and Gynecology*, online first, 2016, pp. 1–9.

Hyams, K. C., F. S. Wignall, and R. Roswell, "War Syndromes and Their Evaluation: From the U.S. Civil War to the Persian Gulf War," *Annals of Internal Medicine*, Vol. 125, No. 5, 1996, pp. 398–405.

Institute of Medicine, *Use of Dietary Supplements by Military Personnel*, Committee on Dietary Supplement Use by Military, Food, and Nutrition Board, Washington, D.C.: National Academy of Sciences, 2008.

———, *The Health of Lesbian, Gay, Bisexual, and Transgender People: Building a Foundation for Better Understanding*, Washington, D.C.: National Academies Press, 2011.

Jackson, D. N., *Personality Research Form Manual*, Goshen, N.Y.: Research Psychologists Press, 1974.

Jacobson, I. G., M. A. K. Ryan, T. I. Hooper, T. C. Smith, P. J. Amoroso, E. J. Boyko, and N. S. Bell, "Alcohol Use and Alcohol-Related Problems Before and After Military Combat Deployment," *Journal of the American Medical Association*, Vol. 300, No. 6, 2008, pp. 663–675.

Jacobson, I. G., M. R. White, T. C. Smith, B. Smith, T. S. Wells, G. D. Gackstetter, and E. J. Boyko, "Self-Reported Health Symptoms and Conditions Among Complementary and Alternative Medicine Users in a Large Military Cohort," *Annals of Epidemiology*, Vol. 19, No. 9, 2009, pp. 613–622.

Jakupcak, M., D. Conybeare, L. Phelps, S. Hunt, H. A. Holmes, B. Felker, M. Klevens, and M. E. McFall, "Anger, Hostility, and Aggression Among Iraq and Afghanistan War Veterans Reporting PTSD and Subthreshold PTSD," *Journal of Traumatic Stress*, Vol. 20, No. 6, 2007, pp. 945–954.

Jeffery, D. D., and M. Mattiko, "Alcohol Use Among Active Duty Women: Analysis AUDIT Scores from the 2011 Health-Related Behavior Survey of Active Duty Military Personnel," *Military Medicine*, Vol. 181, Supp. 1, 2016, pp. 99–108.

Jitnarin, N., W. S. C. Poston, C. K. Haddock, S. A. Jahnke, and R. S. Day, "Accuracy of Body Mass Index–Defined Obesity Status in U.S. Firefighters," *Safety and Health at Work*, Vol. 5, No. 3, 2014, pp. 161–164.

Kahn, J. A., R. A. Kaplowitz, E. Goodman, and S. J. Emans, "The Association Between Impulsiveness and Sexual Risk Behaviors in Adolescent and Young Adult Women," *Journal of Adolescent Health*, Vol. 30, 2002, pp. 229–332.

Kann, L., E. O. Olsen, T. McManus, W. A. Harris, S. L. Shanklin, K. H. Flint, B. Queen, R. Lowry, D. Chyen, L. Whittle, J. Thornton, C. Lim, Y. Yamakawa, N. Brener, and S. Zaza, "Sexual Identity, Sex of Sexual Contacts, and Health-Related Behaviors Among Students in Grades 9–12: United States and Selected Sites, 2015," Centers for Disease Control and Prevention, *Morbidity and Mortality Weekly Report*, Vol. 65, No. 9, 2016. As of August 12, 2016:
http://www.cdc.gov/mmwr/volumes/65/ss/ss6509a1.htm?s_cid=ss6509a1_x

Keane, T. M., J. A. Fairbank, J. M. Caddell, R. T. Zimering, K. L. Taylor, and C. Mora, "Clinical Evaluation of a Measure to Assess Combat Exposure," *Psychological Assessment*, Vol. 1, No. 1, 1989, pp. 53–55.

Kessler, R. C., "Posttraumatic Stress Disorder: The Burden to the Individual and to Society," *Journal of Clinical Psychiatry*, Vol. 61, Supp. 5, 2000, pp. 4–12.

———, "The Costs of Depression," *Psychiatric Clinics of North America*, Vol. 35, No. 1, 2012, pp. 1–14.

Kessler, R. C., P. Berglund, O. Demler, R. Jin, K. R. Merikangas, and E. E. Walters, "Lifetime Prevalence and Age-of-Onset Distributions of DSM-IV Disorders in the National Comorbidity Survey Replication," *Archives of General Psychiatry*, Vol. 62, No. 6, 2005, pp. 593–602.

Kessler, R. C., W. T. Chiu, O. Demler, and E. E. Walters, "Prevalence, Severity, and Comorbidity of Twelve-Month DSM-IV Disorders in the National Comorbidity Survey Replication (NCS-R)," *Archives of General Psychiatry*, Vol. 62, No. 6, 2005, pp. 617–627.

Kessler, R. C., S. Zhao, S. J. Katz, A. C. Kouzis, R. G. Frank, M. Edlund, and P. Leaf, "Past-Year Use of Outpatient Services for Psychiatric Problems in the National Comorbidity Survey," *American Journal of Psychiatry*, Vol. 156, No. 1, 1999, pp. 115–123.

Killgore, W. D., D. I. Cotting, J. L. Thomas, A. L. Cox, D. McGurk, A. H. Vo, C. A. Castro, and C. W. Hoge, "Post-Combat Invincibility: Violent Combat Experiences Are Associated with Increased Risk-Taking Propensity Following Deployment," *Journal of Psychiatric Research*, Vol. 43, No. 13, 2008, pp. 1112–1121.

Kilpatrick, D. G., R. Acierno, H. S. Resnick, B. E. Saunders, and C. L. Best, "A 2-Year Longitudinal Analysis of the Relationships Between Violent Assault and Substance Use in Women," *Journal of Consulting and Clinical Psychology*, Vol. 65, No. 5, October 1997, pp. 834–847.

Kilpatrick, D. G., C. N. Edmunds, and A. Seymour, *Rape in America: A Report to the Nation*, Arlington, Va.: National Victim Center and Medical University of South Carolina, 1992.

Kim, P. Y., T. W. Britt, R. P. Klocko, L. A. Riviere, and A. B. Adler, "Stigma, Negative Attitudes About Treatment, and Utilization of Mental Health Care Among Soldiers," *Military Psychology*, Vol. 23, No. 1, 2011, pp. 65–81.

Kimbrel, N. A., K. L. Gratz, M. T. Tull, S. B. Morissette, E. C. Meyer, B. B. DeBeer, P. J. Silvia, P. C. Calhoun, and J. C. Beckam, "Non-Suicidal Self-Injury as a Predictor of Active and Passive Suicidal Ideation Among Iraq/Afghanistan War Veterans," *Psychiatry Research*, Vol. 227, No. 2–3, 2015, pp. 360–362.

King, Brian A., D. M. Homa, S. R. Dube, and S. D. Babb, "Exposure to Secondhand Smoke and Attitudes Toward Smoke-Free Workplaces Among Employed U.S. Adults: Findings from the National Adult Tobacco Survey," *Nicotine & Tobacco Research*, Vol. 16, No. 10, 2014, pp. 1307–1318.

Kish, L., *Survey Sampling*, New York: John Wiley & Sons, 1965.

Knapik, J. J., R. A. Steelman, S. S. Hoedebecke, E. K. Farina, K. G. Austin, and H. R. Lieberman, "A Systematic Review and Meta-Analysis on the Prevalence of Dietary Supplement Use by Military Personnel," *BMC Complementary and Alternative Medicine*, Vol. 14, May 2014, p. 143.

Korn, E. L., and B. I. Graubard, "Confidence Intervals for Proportions with Small Expected Number of Positive Counts Estimated from Survey Data," *Survey Methodology*, Vol. 24, No. 2, 1998, pp. 193–201.

Koss, M. P., "The Negative Impact of Crime Victimization on Women's Health and Medical Use," in Alice J. Dan, ed., *Reframing Women's Health: Multidisciplinary Research and Practice*, Thousand Oaks, Calif.: Sage Publications, 1994.

Kreuter, M. W., S. N. Lukwago, R. D. Bucholtz, E. M. Clark, and V. Sanders-Thompson, "Achieving Cultural Appropriateness in Health Promotion Programs: Targeted and Tailored Approaches," *Health Education and Behavior*, Vol. 30, No. 2, 2003, pp. 133–146.

Kroenke, K. A., "Patients Presenting with Somatic Complaints: Epidemiology, Psychiatric Co-Morbidity and Management," *International Journal of Methods in Psychiatric Research*, Vol. 12, No. 1, 2003, pp. 34–43.

———, "Practice and Evidence-Based Approach to Common Symptoms: A Narrative Review," *Annals of Internal Medicine*, Vol. 161, No. 8, 2014, pp. 579–586.

Kroenke, K. A., J. L. Jackson, and J. Chamberlin, "Depressive and Anxiety Disorders in Patients Presenting with Physical Complaints: Clinical Predictors and Outcome," *American Journal of Medicine*, Vol. 103, No. 5, 1997, pp. 339–347.

Kroenke, K. A. and R. L. Spitzer, "Gender Differences in the Reporting of Physical and Somatoform Symptoms," *Psychosomatic Medicine*, Vol. 60, No. 2, 1998, pp. 150–155.

Kroenke, K. A., R. L. Spitzer, and J. B. Williams, "The PHQ-9: Validity of a Brief Depression Severity Measure," *Journal of General Internal Medicine*, Vol. 16, No. 9, 2001, pp. 606–613.

Kroenke, K. A., R. L. Spitzer, J. B. Williams, M. Linzer, S. R. Hahn, F. V. deGruy III, and D. Brody, "Physical Symptoms in Primary Care: Predictors of Psychiatric Disorders and Functional Impairment," *Archives of Family Medicine*, Vol. 3, No. 9, 1994, pp. 774–779.

Krosnick, J. A., "Survey Research," *Annual Review of Psychology*, Vol. 50, 1999, pp. 537–567.

Larson, M. J., B. A. Mohr, D. D. Jeffery, R. S. Adams, and T. V. Williams, "Predictors of Positive Illicit Drug Tests After OEF/OIF Deployment Among Army Enlisted Service Members," *Military Medicine*, Vol. 181, No. 4, 2016, pp. 334–342.

Leon, A. C., M. Olfson, L. Portera, L. Farber, and D. V. Sheehan, "Assessing Psychiatric Impairment in Primary Care with the Sheehan Disability Scale," *International Journal of Psychiatry in Medicine*, Vol. 27, No. 2, 1997, pp. 93–105.

Link, B., and J. C. Phelan, "Conceptualizing Stigma," *American Review of Sociology*, Vol. 27, 2001, pp. 363–385.

Lipari, R., K. Piscopo, L. A. Kroutil, and G. K. Miller, "Suicidal Thoughts and Behavior Among Adults: Results from the 2014 National Survey on Drug Use and Health," 2015. As of August 2, 2016: http://www.samhsa.gov/data/sites/default/files/NSDUH-FRR2-2014/NSDUH-FRR2-2014.pdf

Löwe, B., O. Decker, S. Müller, E. Brähler, D. Schelberg, W. Herzog, and P. Y. Herzberg, "Validation and Standardization of the Generalized Anxiety Disorder Screener (GAD-7) in the General Population," *Medical Care*, Vol. 46, No. 3, 2008, pp. 266–274.

MacGregor, A. J., K. J. Heltemes, M. C. Clouser, P. P. Han, and M. R. Galarneau, "Dwell Time and Psychological Screening Outcomes Among Military Service Members with Multiple Combat Deployments," *Military Medicine,* Vol. 179, No. 4, 2014, pp. 381–387.

MacManus, D., R. Rona, J. Dickson, G. Somaini, N. Fear, and S. Wessely, "Aggressive and Violent Behavior Among Military Personnel Deployed to Iraq and Afghanistan: Prevalence and Link with Deployment and Combat Exposure," *Epidemiologic Reviews*, Vol. 37, January 2015, pp. 196–212.

McLay, R. N., W. P. Klam, and S. L. Volkert, "Insomnia Is the Most Commonly Reported Symptom and Predicts Other Symptoms of Post-Traumatic Stress Disorder in U.S. Service Members Returning from Military Deployments," *Military Medicine*, Vol. 175, No. 10, 2010, pp. 759–762.

Meadows, S. O., L. L. Miller, and S. Robson, *Airman and Family Resilience: Lessons from the Scientific Literature*, Santa Monica, Calif.: RAND Corporation, RR-106-AF, 2015. As of January 9, 2017: http://www.rand.org/pubs/research_reports/RR106.html

Mental Health Advisory Team, *Mental Health Advisory Team (MHAT) V—Operation Iraqi Freedom 06–08: Iraq; Operation Enduring Freedom 8: Afghanistan*, Office of the Surgeon, Multi-National Force–Iraq; Office of the Command Surgeon; and Office of the Surgeon General, U.S. Army Medical Command, February 14, 2008.

Miller, K. E., "Energy Drinks, Race, and Problem Behaviors Among College Students," *Journal of Adolescent Health*, Vol. 43, No. 5, 2008, pp. 490–497.

Miller, L. L., and E. Aharoni, *Understanding Low Survey Response Rates Among Young U.S. Military Personnel*, Santa Monica, Calif.: RAND Corporation, RR-881-AF, 2015. As of January 9, 2017: http://www.rand.org/pubs/research_reports/RR881.html

Morral, A. R., K. L. Gore, and T. L. Schell, eds. *Sexual Assault and Sexual Harassment in the U.S. Military*, Vol. 2: *Estimates for Department of Defense Service Members from the 2014 RAND Military Workplace Study*, Santa Monica, Calif.: RAND Corporation, RR-870/2-1-OSD, 2016. As of August 11, 2016: http://www.rand.org/pubs/research_reports/RR870z2-1.html

Mullen, M., "On Total Force Fitness in War and Peace," *Military Medicine*, Vol. 175, No. 8, Supp. 1, 2010, pp. 1–2.

Mysliwiec, V., J. Gill, H. Lee, T. Baxter, R. Pierce, T. L. Barr, B. Krakow, and B. J. Roth, "Sleep Disorders in U.S. Military Personnel: A High Rate of Comorbid Insomnia and Obstructive Sleep Apnea," *Chest*, Vol. 144, No. 2, 2013, pp. 549–557.

Mysliwiec, V., L. McGraw, R. Pierce, P. Smith, B. Trapp, and B. J. Roth, "Sleep Disorders and Associated Medical Comorbidities in Active Duty Military Personnel," *Sleep,* Vol. 36, No. 2, 2013, pp. 167–174.

National Center for Complementary and Integrative Health, *The Use of Complementary and Alternative Medicine in the United States*, Bethesda, Md., 2007. As of July 19, 2016: https://nccih.nih.gov/research/statistics/2007/camsurvey_fs1.htm

National Center for PTSD, "Combat Exposure Scale (CES)," web page, U.S. Department of Veterans Affairs, February 23, 2016a. As of July 30, 2016: http://www.ptsd.va.gov/professional/assessment/te-measures/ces.asp

———, "Deployment Risk and Resilience Inventory-2 (DRRI-2)," web page, U.S. Department of Veterans Affairs, February 23, 2016b. As of July 30, 2016: http://www.ptsd.va.gov/professional/assessment/deployment/index.asp

National Defense Research Institute, *Sexual Orientation and U.S. Military Personnel Policy: An Update of RAND's 1993 Study*, Santa Monica, Calif.: RAND Corporation, MG-1056-OSD, 2010. As of May 2, 2016: http://www.rand.org/pubs/monographs/MG1056.html

————, *Sexual Assault and Sexual Harassment in the U.S. Military: Top-Line Estimates for Active-Duty Service Members from the 2014 RAND Military Workplace Study*, Santa Monica, Calif.: RAND Corporation, RR-870-OSD, 2014. As of August 11, 2016:
http://www.rand.org/pubs/research_reports/RR870.html

National Institutes of Health, *Clinical Guidelines on the Identification, Evaluation, and Treatment of Overweight and Obesity in Adults: The Evidence Report*, Bethesda, Md., National Heart, Lung, and Blood Institute and National Institute of Diabetes and Digestive and Kidney Diseases, NIH Publication No. 98-4083, September 1998.

Nock, M. K., G. Borges, E. J. Bromet, J. Alonso, M. Angermeyer, A. Beautrais, R. Bruffaerts, W. T. Chiu, G. de Girolamo, S. Gluzman, R. de Graaf, O. Gureje, J. M. Haro, Y. Huang, E. Karam, R. C. Kessler, J. P. Lepine, D. Levinson, M. E. Medina-Mora, Y. Ono, J. Posada-Villa, and D. Williams, "Cross-National Prevalence and Risk Factors for Suicidal Ideation, Plans and Attempts," *British Journal of Psychiatry*, Vol. 192, No. 2, 2008, pp. 98–105.

Nock, M. K., R. J. Ursano, S. G. Heeringa, M. B. Stein, S. Jain, R. Raman, X. Sun, W. T. Chiu, L. J. Colpe, C. S. Fullerton, S. E. Gilman, I. Hwang, J. A. Naifeh, A. J. Rosellini, N. A. Sampson, M. Schoenbaum, A. M. Zaslavsky, and R. C. Kessler, "Mental Disorders, Comorbidity, and Pre-Enlistment Suicidal Behavior Among New Soldiers in the U.S. Army: Results from the Army Study to Assess Risk and Resilience in Servicemembers (Army STARRS)," *Suicide and Life-Threatening Behavior*, Vol. 45, No. 5, 2015, pp. 588–599.

Nordt, S. P., G. M. Vilke, R. F. Clark, L. Cantrell, T. C. Chan, M. Galinato, V. Nguyen, and E. M. Castillo, "Energy Drink Use and Adverse Effects Among Emergency Department Patients," *Journal of Community Health*, Vol. 37, No. 5, 2012, pp. 976–981.

Novaco, R. W., R. D. Swanson, O. I. Gonzaelez, G. A. Gahm, and M. D. Reger, "Anger and Postcombat Mental Health: Validation of a Brief Anger Measure with U.S. Soldiers Postdeployed from Iraq and Afghanistan," *Psychological Assessment*, Vol. 24, 2012, pp. 661–675.

Novins, D. G., J. Beals, C. Croy, and S. M. Manson, "Methods for Measuring Utilization of Mental Health Services in Two Epidemiologic Studies," *International Journal of Methods in Psychiatric Research*, Vol. 17, No. 3, 2008, pp. 159–173.

Office of the Deputy Assistant Secretary of Defense for Military Community and Family Policy, *2014 Demographics: Profile of the Military Community*, Washington, D.C.: U.S. Department of Defense, 2014. As of July 26, 2016:
http://download.militaryonesource.mil/12038/MOS/Reports/2014-Demographics-Report.pdf

Office of the Under Secretary of Defense for Personnel and Readiness, *Population Representation in the Military Services: Fiscal Year 2014 Summary Report*, Washington, D.C.: U.S. Department of Defense, 2015. As of August 8, 2016:
https://www.cna.org/pop-rep/2014/

Office on Smoking and Health, *2014 National Youth Tobacco Survey: Methodology Report*, Atlanta, Ga.: Centers for Disease Control and Prevention, 2015.

Owen, N., P. B. Sparling, G. N. Healy, D. W. Dunstan, and C. E. Matthews, "Sedentary Behavior: Emerging Evidence for a New Health Risk," *Mayo Clinic Proceedings*, Vol. 85, No. 12, 2010, pp. 1138–1141.

Peterson, Alan L., H. H. Severson, J. A. Andrews, S. P. Gott, J. A. Cigrang, J. S. Gordon, C. M. Hunter, and G. C. Martin, "Smokeless Tobacco Use in Military Personnel," *Military Medicine*, Vol. 172, No. 12, 2007, pp. 1300–1305.

Pietrzak, E., S. Pullman, C. Cotea, and P. Nasveld, "Effects of Deployment on Mental Health in Modern Military Forces: A Review of Longitudinal Studies," *Journal of Military and Veterans' Health*, Vol. 20, No. 3, 2012, pp. 24–36.

Pietrzak, R. H., C. A. Morgan III, and S. M. Southwick, "Sleep Quality in Treatment-Seeking Veterans of Operations Enduring Freedom and Iraqi Freedom: The Role of Cognitive Coping Strategies and Unit Cohesion," *Journal of Psychosomatic Research*, Vol. 69, No. 5, 2010, pp. 441–448.

Plumb, T. R., J. T. Peachey, and D. C. Zelman, "Sleep Disturbance Is Common Among Servicemembers and Veterans of Operations Enduring Freedom and Iraqi Freedom," *Psychological Services*, Vol. 11, No. 2, 2014, pp. 209–219.

Ramchand, R., J. Acosta, R. M. Burns, L. H. Jaycox, and C. G. Pernin, *The War Within: Preventing Suicide in the U.S. Military*, Santa Monica, Calif.: RAND Corporation, MG-953-OSD, 2011. As of January 9, 2017: http://www.rand.org/pubs/monographs/MG953.html

Ramchand, R., N. K. Eberhart, C. Guo, E. Pederseen, T. D. Savitsky, T. Tanielian, and P. Voorhies, *Developing a Research Strategy for Suicide Prevention in the Department of Defense: Status of Current Research, Prioritizing Areas of Need, and Recommendations for Moving Forward*, Santa Monica, Calif.: RAND Corporation, RR-559-OSD, 2014. As of January 9, 2017: http://www.rand.org/pubs/research_reports/RR559.html

Ramchand, R., R. Rudavsky, S. Grant, T. Tanielian, and L. Jaycox, "Prevalence of, Risk Factors for, and Consequences of Posttraumatic Stress Disorder and Other Mental Health Problems in Military Populations Deployed to Iraq and Afghanistan," *Current Psychiatric Reports*, Vol. 17, No. 5, 2015, pp. 17–28.

Ramchand, R., T. L. Schell, L. H. Jaycox, and T. Tanielian, "Epidemiology of Trauma Events and Mental Health Outcomes Among Service Members Deployed to Iraq and Afghanistan," in J. I. Rusek, P. P. Schnurr, J. J. Vasterling, and M. J. Friedman, eds., *Caring for Veterans with Deployment-Related Stress Disorders; Iraq, Afghanistan, and Beyond*, Washington, D.C.: American Psychological Association, 2011.

Ramchand, R., T. L. Schell, B. R. Karney, K. C. Osilla, R. M. Burns, and L. B. Caldarone, "Disparate Prevalence Estimates of PTSD Among Service Members Who Served in Iraq and Afghanistan: Possible Explanations," *Journal of Trauma Stress*, Vol. 23, No. 1, 2010, pp. 59–68.

Ramchand, R., T. L. Schell, T. Tanielian, B. A. Griffin, E. M. Friedman, R. Beckman, and C. Vaughan, "Psychological and Behavioral Health of Service Members and Their Spouses," in S. O. Meadows, T. Tanielian, and B. R. Karney, eds., *The Deployment Life Study: Longitudinal Analysis of Military Families Across the Deployment Cycle*, Santa Monica, Calif.: RAND Corporation, RR-1388-A/OSD, 2016, pp. 155–194. As of January 9, 2017: http://www.rand.org/pubs/research_reports/RR1388.html

Regier, D. A., W. E. Narrow, D. S. Rae, R. W. Manderscheid, B. Z. Locke, and F. K. Goodwin, "The De Facto U.S. Mental and Addictive Disorders Service Syndrome: Epidemiologic Catchment Area Prospective 1-Year Prevalence Rates of Disorders and Services," *Archives of General Psychiatry*, Vol. 50, No. 2, 1993, pp. 85–94.

Resnick, H., R. Acierno, A. E. Waldrop, L. King, D. King, C. Danielson, K. J. Ruggiero, and D. G. Kilpatrick, "Randomized Controlled Evaluation of an Early Intervention to Prevent Post-Rape Psychopathology," *Behavioral Research and Therapy*, Vol. 45, No. 10, October 2007, pp. 2432–2447.

Rock, C., "Multivitamin-Multimineral Supplements: Who Uses Them?" *American Journal of Clinical Nutrition*, Vol. 85, No. 1, Supp., 2007, pp. 277S–279S.

Rona, R. J., N. T. Fear, L. Hull, N. Greenberg, M. Earnshaw, M. Hotopf, and S. Wessely, "Mental Health Consequences of Overstretch in the UK Armed Forces: First Phase of a Cohort Study," *British Medical Journal*, Vol. 335, No. 7620, 2007, pp. 603–607.

Rush, T., C. A. LeardMann, and N. F. Crum-Cianflone, "Obesity and Associated Adverse Health Outcomes Among U.S. Military Members and Veterans: Findings from the Millennium Cohort Study," *Obesity*, Vol. 24, No. 7, 2016, pp. 1582–1589.

Sánchez-Fernández, J., F. Muñoz-Lieva, and F. J. Montros-Ríos, "Improving Retention Rate and Response Quality in Web-Based Surveys," *Computers in Human Behavior*, Vol. 28, No. 2, 2012, pp. 507–514.

Santiago, P. N., J. E. Wilk, C. S. Milliken, C. A. Castro, C. C. Engel, and C. W. Hoge, "Screening for Alcohol Misuse and Alcohol-Related Behaviors Among Combat Veterans," *Psychiatric Services*, Vol. 61, No. 6, 2010, pp. 575–581.

Sareen, J., B. J. Cox, T. O. Afifi, M. B. Stein, S. L. Belik, G. Meadows, and G. J. G. Asmundson, "Combat and Peacekeeping Operations in Relation to Prevalence of Mental Disorders and Perceived Need for Mental Health Care: Findings from a Large Representative Sample of Military Personnel," *Archives of General Psychiatry*, Vol. 64, No. 7, 2007, pp. 843–852.

Sauermann, H., and M. Roach, "Increasing Web Survey Response Rates in Innovation Research: An Experimental Study of Static and Dynamic Contact Design Features," *Research Policy*, Vol. 42, 2013, pp. 273–286.

Savin-Williams, R. C., "How Many Gays Are There? It Depends," in D. A. Hope, ed., *Contemporary Perspectives on Lesbian, Gay, and Bisexual Identities*, New York: Springer, 2009, pp. 5–41.

Sax, L. J., S. K. Gilmartin, and A. N. Bryant, "Assessing Response Rates and Nonresponse Bias in Web and Paper Surveys," *Research in Higher Education*, Vol. 44, No. 4, 2003, pp. 409–432.

Schnurr, P. P., "Understanding Pathways from Traumatic Exposure to Physical Health," in U. Schnyder and M. Cloitre, eds., *Evidence Based Treatments for Trauma-Related Psychological Disorders: A Practical Guide for Clinicians*, Switzerland: Springer, 2015, pp. 87–103.

Schoenborn, C. A., and R. M. Gindi, "Electronic Cigarette Use Among Adults: United States, 2014," *NCHS Data Brief*, No. 217, October 2015, pp. 1–8.

Schwab, K. A., G. Baker, B. J. Ivins, M. Sluss-Tiller, W. Lux, and D. Warden, "The Brief Traumatic Brain Injury Screen (BTBIS): Investigating the Validity of a Self-Report Instrument for Detecting Traumatic Brain Injury (TBI) in Troops Returning from Deployment in Afghanistan and Iraq," *Neurology*, Vol. 66, No. 5, 2006, p. A235.

Seal, K. H., Ying Shi, Gregory Cohen, Beth E. Cohen, Shira Maguen, Erin E. Krebs, and Thomas C. Neylan, "Association of Mental Health Disorders with Prescription Opioids and High-Risk Opioid Use in U.S. Veterans of Iraq and Afghanistan," *Journal of the American Medical Association*, Vol. 307, No. 23, 2012, pp. 2489–2489.

Seelig, A. D., I. G. Jacobson, B. Smith, T. I. Hooper, E. J. Boyko, G. D. Gackstetter, P. Gehrman, C. A. Macera, T. C. Smith, and Millennium Cohort Study Team, "Sleep Patterns Before, During, and After Deployment to Iraq and Afghanistan," *Sleep*, Vol. 33, No. 12, 2010, pp. 1615–1622.

Sexual Minority Assessment Research Team, *Best Practices for Asking Sexual Orientation on Surveys*, Williams Institute, Los Angeles: UCLA School of Law, November 2009.

Sharp, M. L., N. T. Fear, R. J. Rona, S. Wessely, N. Greenberg, N. Jones, and L. Goodwin, "Stigma as a Barrier to Seeking Health Care Among Military Personnel with Mental Health Problems," *Epidemiologic Review*, Vol. 37, January 2015, pp. 144–162.

Sheehan, D. V., K. Harnett-Sheehan, and B. A. Raj, "The Measurement of Disability," *International Clinical Psychopharmacology*, Vol. 11, Supp. 3, June 1996, pp. 89–95.

Sheffler, J. L., N. C. Rushing, I. H. Stanley, and N. J. Sachs-Ericsson, "The Long-Term Impact of Combat Exposure on Health, Interpersonal, and Economic Domains of Functioning," *Aging and Mental Health*, Vol. 20, No. 11, 2016, pp. 1202–1212.

Singer, E., and C. Ye, "The Use and Effects of Incentives in Surveys," *Annals of the American Academy of Political and Social Science*, Vol. 645, No. 1, 2013, pp. 112–141.

Skipper, L. D., R. D. Forsten, E. H. Kim, J. D. Wilk, and C. W. Hoge, "Relationship of Combat Experiences and Alcohol Misuse Among U.S. Special Operations Soldiers," *Military Medicine*, Vol. 179, No. 3, 2014, pp. 301–308.

Spitzer, R. L., K. Kroenke, J. B. W. Williams, and B. Löwe, "A Brief Measure for Assessing Generalized Anxiety Disorder: The GAD-7," *Archives of Internal Medicine*, Vol. 166, No. 10, 2006, pp. 1092–1097.

Stamatakis, E., M. Hamer, and D. W. Dunstan, "Screen-Based Entertainment Time, All-Cause Mortality, and Cardiovascular Events: Population-Based Study with Ongoing Mortality and Hospital Events Follow-Up," *Journal of the American College of Cardiology*, Vol. 57, No. 3, 2011, pp. 292–299.

Steinberg, L., "A Social Neuroscience Perspective on Adolescent Risk-Taking," *Developmental Review*, Vol. 28, No. 1, 2008, pp. 78–106.

Street, A. E., A. J. Rosellini, R. J. Ursano, S. G. Heeringa, E. D. Hill, J. Monahan, J. A. Naifeh, M. V. Petukhova, B. Y. Reis, N. A. Sampson, P. D. Bliese, M. R. Stein, A. M. Zaslavsky, and R. C. Kessler, "Developing a Risk Model to Target High-Risk Preventive Interventions for Sexual Assault Victimization Among Female U.S. Army Soldiers," *Clinical Psychological Science*, Vol. 4, No. 6, 2016, pp. 939–956.

Substance Abuse and Mental Health Services Administration, "Update on Emergency Department Visits Involving Energy Drinks: A Continuing Public Health Concern," *The DAWN Report*, Rockville, Md., January 10, 2013. As of January 9, 2017:
http://www.samhsa.gov/data/2k13/DAWN126/sr126-energy-drinks-use.pdf

———, "Population Data/NSDUH," web page, August 30, 2016. As of January 9, 2017:
https://www.samhsa.gov/data/population-data-nsduh

Sundin, J., N. T. Fear, A. C. Iversen, R. J. Rona, and S. C. Wessely, "PTSD After Deployment to Iraq: Conflicting Rates, Conflicting Claims," *Psychological Medicine*, Vol. 40, No. 3, 2010, pp. 367–382.

Swinkels, C. M., C. S. Ulmer, J. C. Beckham, N. Buse, and P. S. Calhoun, "The Association of Sleep Duration, Mental Health, and Health Risk Behaviors Among U.S. Afghanistan/Iraq Era Veterans," *Sleep*, Vol. 36, No. 7, 2013, pp. 1019–1025.

Tanielian, T., and L. Jaycox, eds., *Invisible Wounds of War: Psychological and Cognitive Injuries, Their Consequences, and Services to Assist Recovery*, Santa Monica, Calif.: RAND Corporation, MG-720-CCF, 2008. As of July 26, 2016:
http://www.rand.org/pubs/monographs/MG720.html

Terhakopian, A., N. Sinaii, C. C. Engel, P. P. Schnurr, and C. W. Hoge, "Estimating Population Prevalence of Posttraumatic Stress Disorder: An Example Using the PTSD Checklist," *Journal of Traumatic Stress*, Vol. 21, No. 3, 2008, pp. 290–300.

Terrio, H., L. A. Brenner, B. J. Ivins, J. M. Cho, K. Schwab, K. Scally, R. Bretthauer, and D. Warden, "Traumatic Brain Injury Screening: Preliminary Findings in a U.S Army Brigade Combat Team," *Journal of Head Trauma Rehabilitation*, Vol. 24, 2009, pp. 14–23.

Thomas, J. L., J. E. Wilk, L. A. Riviere, D. McGurk, C. A. Castro, and C. W. Hoge, "Prevalence of Mental Health Problems and Functional Impairment Among Active Component and National Guard Soldiers 3 and 12 Months Following Combat in Iraq," *Archives of General Psychiatry*, Vol. 67, No. 6, 2010, pp. 614–623.

Thombs, D. L., R. J. O'Mara, M. Tsukamoto, M. E. Rossheim, R. M. Weiler, M. L. Merves, and B. A. Goldberger, "Event-Level Analyses of Energy Drink Consumption and Alcohol Intoxication in Bar Patrons," *Addictive Behaviors*, Vol. 35, No. 4, 2010, pp. 325–330.

Thota, A. B., T. A. Sipe, G. J. Byard, C. S. Zometa, R. A. Hahn, L. R. McKnight-Eily, D. P. Chapman, A. F. Abraido-Lanza, J. L. Pearson, C. W. Anderson, A. J. Gelenberg, K. D. Hennessy, F. F. Duffy, M. E. Vernon-Smiley, D. E. Nease, Jr., and S. P. Williams, "Collaborative Care to Improve the Management of Depressive Disorders: A Community Guide Systematic Review and Meta-Analysis," *American Journal of Preventive Medicine*, Vol. 42, No. 5, 2012, pp. 525–538.

Toblin, R. L., P. J. Quartana, L. A. Riviere, K. C. Walper, and C. W. Hoge, "Chronic Pain and Opioid Use in U.S. Soldiers After Combat Deployment," *JAMA Internal Medicine*, Vol. 174, No. 8, 2014, pp. 1400–1401.

Troxel, W. M., R. A. Shih, E. R. Pedersen, L. Geyer, M. P. Fisher, B. A. Griffin, A. C. Haas, J. R. Kurz, and P. S. Steinberg, *Sleep in the Military: Promoting Healthy Sleep Among U.S. Servicemembers*, Santa Monica, Calif.: RAND Corporation, RR-739-OSD, 2015. As of January 9, 2017:
http://www.rand.org/pubs/research_reports/RR739.html

Tsan, J. Y., J. E. Zeber, E. M. Stock, F. Sun, and L. A. Copeland, "Primary Care–Mental Health Integration and Treatment Retention Among Iraq and Afghanistan War Veterans," *Psychological Services*, Vol. 9, No. 4, 2012, pp. 336–348.

Turchik, J. A., and S. M. Wilson, "Sexual Assault in the U.S. Military: A Review of the Literature and Recommendations for the Future," *Aggression and Violent Behavior*, Vol. 15, No. 4, July–August 2010, pp. 267–277.

U.S. Air Force, *Preventive Health Assessment*, Air Force Instruction 44-170, 2014.

U.S. Department of Defense, *DoD Physical Fitness and Body Fat Programs Procedures*, DoD Instruction 1308.3, Washington, D.C., November 5, 2002. As of July 19, 2016:
http://www.dtic.mil/whs/directives/corres/pdf/130803p.pdf

————, *Deployment Health*, DoD Instruction 6490.03, Washington, D.C., August 11, 2006. As of January 9, 2017:
http://www.dtic.mil/whs/directives/corres/pdf/649003p.pdf

————, *Human Immunodeficiency Virus (HIV) in Military Service Members*, DoD Instruction 6485.01, Washington, D.C., June 7, 2013a. As of January 9, 2017:
http://www.dtic.mil/whs/directives/corres/pdf/648501p.pdf

————, *DoD Nutrition Committee*, DoD Instruction 6130.05, Washington, D.C., October 3, 2013b. As of July 19, 2016:
http://www.dtic.mil/whs/directives/corres/pdf/613005p.pdf

————, *Individual Medical Readiness (IMR)*, DoD Instruction 6025.19, Washington, D.C., June 9, 2014. As of July 19, 2016:
http://www.dtic.mil/whs/directives/corres/pdf/602519p.pdf

U.S. Department of Health and Human Services, "Healthy People 2020," web page, 2010a. As of July 19, 2016:
https://www.healthypeople.gov/

————, "Healthy People 2020: Heart Disease and Stroke," web page, 2010b. As of September 13, 2016:
https://www.healthypeople.gov/2020/topics-objectives/topic/heart-disease-and-stroke/objectives

————, "Healthy People 2020: Mental Health and Mental Disorders," web page, 2010c. As of July 19, 2016:
https://www.healthypeople.gov/2020/topics-objectives/topic/mental-health-and-mental-disorders/objectives

————, "Healthy People 2020: Nutrition and Weight Status," web page, 2010d. As of July 19, 2016:
https://www.healthypeople.gov/2020/topics-objectives/topic/nutrition-and-weight-status/objectives

————, "Healthy People 2020: Physical Activity," web page, 2010e. As of July 19, 2016:
https://www.healthypeople.gov/2020/topics-objectives/topic/physical-activity/objectives

————, "Healthy People 2020: Sleep Health," web page, 2010f. As of September 13, 2016:
https://www.healthypeople.gov/2020/topics-objectives/topic/sleep-health/objectives

————, *The Health Consequences of Smoking—50 Years of Progress: A Report of the Surgeon General*, Atlanta, Ga.: U.S. Department of Health and Human Services, Centers for Disease Control and Prevention, National Center for Chronic Disease Prevention and Health Promotion, and Office on Smoking and Health, 2014. As of June 17, 2016:
http://www.surgeongeneral.gov/library/reports/50-years-of-progress/full-report.pdf

Vogt, D., B. N. Smith, L. A. King, D. W. King, J. Knight, and J. J. Vasterling, "Deployment Risk and Resilience Inventory-2 (DRRI-2): An Updated Tool for Assessing Psychosocial Risk and Resilience Factors Among Service Members and Veterans," *Journal of Traumatic Stress*, Vol. 26, No. 6, 2013, pp. 710–717.

Vojvoda, D., E. Stefanovics, and R. A. Rosenheck, "Treatment of Veterans with PTSD at a VA Medical Center: Primary Care Versus Mental Health Specialty Care," *Psychiatric Services*, Vol. 65, No. 10, 2014, pp. 1238–1243.

Wang, P. S., M. Lane, M. Olfson, H. A. Pincus, K. B. Wells, and R. C. Kessler, "Twelve-Month Use of Mental Health Services in the United States: Results from the National Comorbidity Survey Replication," *Archives of General Psychiatry*, Vol. 62, No. 6, 2005, pp. 629–640.

Ward, B. W., J. M. Dahlhamer, A. M. Galinsky, and S. S. Joestl, "Sexual Orientation and Health Among U.S. Adults: National Health Interview Survey, 2013," *National Health Statistics Reports*, No. 77, Hyattsville, Md.: National Center for Health Statistics, July 15, 2014. As of August 12, 2016:
http://www.cdc.gov/nchs/data/nhsr/nhsr077.pdf

Weathers, F. W., B. T. Litz, D. S. Herman, J. A. Huska, and T. M. Keane, *The PTSD Checklist (PCL): Reliability, Validity, and Diagnostic Utility*, paper presented at the 9th Annual Conference of the International Society for Traumatic Stress Studies, San Antonio, Tex., 1993.

Weaver, T. L., and G. A. Clum, "Psychological Distress Associated with Interpersonal Violence: A Meta-Analysis," *Clinical Psychology Review*, Vol. 15, No. 2, 1995, pp. 115–140.

Wesensten, N. J., and T. J. Balkin, "The Challenge of Sleep Management in Military Operations," *U.S. Army Medical Department Journal*, October–December 2013, pp. 109–118.

Wilk, J. E., P. D. Bliese, P. Y. Kim, J. L. Thomas, D. McGurk, and C. W. Hoge, "Relationship of Combat Experiences to Alcohol Misuse Among U.S. Soldiers Returning from the Iraq War," *Drug and Alcohol Dependence*, Vol. 108, No. 1–2, 2010, pp. 115–121.

Wilk, J. E., P. D. Bliese, J. L. Thomas, M. D. Wood, D. McGurk, C. A. Castro, and C. W. Hoge, "Unethical Battlefield Conduct Reported by Soldiers Serving in the Iraq War," *Journal of Nervous and Mental Disease*, Vol. 201, No. 4, 2013, pp. 259–265.

Wilk, J. E., R. K. Herrell, G. H. Wynn, L. A. Riviere, and C. W. Hoge, "Mild Traumatic Brain Injury (Concussion), Posttraumatic Stress Disorder, and Depression in U.S. Soldiers Involved in Combat Deployments: Association with Postdeployment Symptoms," *Psychosomatic Medicine*, Vol. 74, No. 3, 2012, pp. 249–257.

Williams, E. C., M. A. Frasco, I. G. Jacobson, C. Maynard, A. J. Littman, A. D. Seelig, and E. J. Boyko, "Risk Factors for Relapse to Problem Drinking Among Current and Former U.S. Military Personnel: A Prospective Study of the Millennium Cohort," *Drug and Alcohol Dependence*, Vol. 148, 2015, pp. 93–101.

Winner, B., J. F. Peipert, Q. Zhao, C. Buckel, T. Madden, J. E. Allsworth, and G. M. Secura, "Effectiveness of Long-Acting Reversible Contraception," *The New England Journal of Medicine*, Vol. 366, No. 21, 2012, pp. 1998–2007.

Wolkowitz, O. M., A. Roy, and A. R. Doran, "Pathological Gambling and Other Risk-Taking Pursuits," *Psychiatric Clinics of North America*, Vol. 8, No. 2, 1985, pp. 311–322.

Wright, K. M., O. A. Cabrera, P. D. Bliese, A. B. Adler, C. W. Hoge, and C. A. Castro, "Stigma and Barriers to Care in Soldiers Postcombat," *Psychological Services*, Vol. 6, No. 2, 2009, pp. 108–116.

# Index